AGL 2515

SO-BIW-484

BCC WITHDRAWN/COCOA

AT ISSUE

Politics
in the
World Arena

FIFTH EDITION

AT ISSUE

Politics in the World Arena

FIFTH EDITION

Steven L. Spiegel

University of California, Los Angeles

ST. MARTIN'S PRESS
New York

Library of Congress Catalog Number: 87-060557
Copyright © 1988 by St. Martin's Press, Inc.
All rights reserved.
Manufactured in the United States of America.
21098
fedcba
For information, write St. Martin's Press, Inc.,
175 Fifth Avenue, New York, NY 10010
cover design: Ben Santora
ISBN: 0-312-00325-0

Acknowledgments

"The U.S. and Third-World Dictatorships," by Ted Galen Carpenter. Reprinted from *USA Magazine*, May, 1986. Copyright, 1986, by the Society for the Advancement of Education.

"In Defense of Interventionism," by Charles Krauthammer. Reprinted by permission of *The New Republic*, © 1986, The New Republic, Inc.

"Gorbachev and the Third World," by Francis Fukuyama. Reprinted by permission of *Foreign Affairs*, (Spring, 1986). Copyright, 1986, by the Council of Foreign Relations, Inc.

"Eastern Europe and the Future of the Soviet Empire," by Vojtech Mastny. Reprinted by permission of *SAIS Review*, Volume 5:1, Winter/Spring 1985.

"Misunderstanding Africa," by Xan Smiley. *The Atlantic Monthly*, September 1982. Copyright © 1982 by author. Reprinted by permission.

"Fundamentalist Muslims Between America and Russia," by Daniel Pipes. Reprinted by permission of *Foreign Affairs*, (Summer, 1986). Copyright, 1986, by the Council of Foreign Relations, Inc.

"North-South Interdependence," by Ivan L. Head. Reprinted by permission of the *Bulletin of the Atomic Scientists*, a magazine of science and world affairs. Copyright © 1983 by the Educational Foundation for Nuclear Science, Chicago, Il. 60637.

"The Perversion of Foreign Aid," by Nick Eberstadt. Mr. Eberstadt is a Visiting Fellow at the Harvard University Center for Population Studies and a Visiting Scholar at the American Enterprise Institute. Reprinted from *Commentary*, 1986 by permission; all rights reserved.

"International Framework and South-South Cooperation," by K. P. Saksena. Reprinted, with the permission of Sage Publications India Pvt., Ltd., from *International Studies*, Vol.22 No.3 (1985), pp. 199–214; © School of International Studies, Jawaharlal Nehru University, New Delhi.

"Nicaragua: A Speech to My Former Comrades on the Left," by David Horowitz. Copyright © 1986 by author. Reprinted from *Commentary*, June, 1986, by permission; all rights reserved.

"The U.S. and the Contras," by Aryeh Neier. Reprinted with permission from *The New York Review of Books*. Copyright © 1980 Nyrev, Inc.

"Iran and the Americans," by Shaul Bakhash. Reprinted with permission from *The New York Review of Books*. Copyright © 1987 Nyrev, Inc.

"Reflections on Terrorism," by Walter Laqueur. Reprinted by permission of *Foreign Affairs*, (Fall 1986). Copyright, 1986 by the Council of Foreign Relations, Inc.

"Managing the U.S.-Soviet Relationship," by Jerry F. Hough. Reprinted from *World Policy Journal*, Vol. III, #1 (Winter 1985–1985) World Policy, 777 UN Plaza, NY NY 10017. Copyright © World Policy Journal, 1986.

Acknowledgments and copyrights continue at the back of the book on pages 535–536, which constitute an extension of the copyright page.

To the memory of my father

Preface

The fifth edition of *At Issue*, like the previous four, seeks to provide a selection of the most useful and interesting articles on the major political, economic, and social issues in current international affairs— among them, racial and ethnic conflict, the balance of power, alternative superpower intervention strategies, the possibility of world order, and the crisis of foreign policy-making institutions. My aim is to give students a general sense of the complexities and dynamics of present-day world politics while providing background information on specific issues. Though my concern is not focused exclusively on the problems encountered by Americans in formulating and conducting foreign policy, this volume is generally oriented toward the world problems which affect the United States. The book is designed for use in American foreign policy courses, as well as courses in world politics.

As books on politics in the world arena become dated very quickly, each new edition of *At Issue* has retained fewer than a half dozen readings from the previous edition. The new articles presented here have been chosen from more than 500 essays examined in an extensive investigation of the major journals and periodicals which cover international affairs. The preferences and reactions of my students were seriously considered and affected the final selection. Among the criteria examined were readability, the variety and range of both the problems addressed and the ideological and national views represented, and the likelihood of continuing relevance in the face of probable changes in events.

I am grateful to many people who have given me advice and assistance in the preparation of this fifth edition. I am especially indebted to dozens of colleagues around the country who have used the first four editions and have generously taken the time to make suggestions for improving the book. From its beginning, this volume has been a collaborative effort with my students in world politics and American foreign policy courses at UCLA. Their encouragement and vigorous participation have made the project an exciting one.

Jennifer Morrison coordinated the review of materials and their synthesis with exceptional enthusiasm and devotion. She somehow managed the complex tasks of administrative supervision and intellectual exploration, while always remaining undaunted by crisis and equal to new problems that were constantly arising.

Many critics claim that today's undergraduate and graduate students are only interested in career and personal gain. On this project, however, I was fortunate indeed to be assisted by an extraordinary group, many of whom spent hours and even days searching and re-examining libraries' shelves to fill gaps in a partially completed manuscript. Sylvia Torres spent a summer home from Harvard during the initial perusals when the possibilities seemed unlimited. Bimal I. Ghandi combined definite views with tolerant understanding in seeking articles he favored. Henry J. Kerner could always be counted on to accomplish the tasks assigned and to read his articles incisively and carefully. Through the turmoil, Tracy E. Loomis was quietly ready to engage in a wide variety of clerical and research tasks as the deadline rapidly approached. Julia Storberg read tons of articles until late at night as we weighed alternatives and confronted difficult decisions. Jay K. Footlik contributed to the reading, devoted countless hours, prepared the final copy, and remained stoically committed as we sent him off to distant libraries to find missing pieces. Jill Anne Peasley was always prepared to assist with helpful tasks when needed. Robin Lofton, April de Lauren, and Katja Weber were conscientious and extremely helpful at various stages of manuscript development. Jim Rapath and Sue White also contributed their time and effort. I am deeply grateful for their willingness to weather the frustrations of a task made more difficult by the growing fluidity of international affairs.

As always, my wife Fredi provided invaluable consultation and inspiration. When the multitude of articles seemed beyond comprehension, she offered the encouragement that made it possible to conclude the task in an expeditious and orderly manner. I again wish to thank Mira, Nina, and Avi for keeping out of the piles of papers and heaps of magazines that cluttered the house while this edition was being prepared.

The subjects discussed in this volume represent some of the most important questions now facing the world's leaders, and many of the articles present grim alternatives and disturbing analyses. In my opinion, humor, or at least an appreciation of irony, sometimes seems to be the only possible response to the vicissitudes of world politics, and I trust that the occasional touch of humor in this volume will not be mistaken for levity. Above all, I hope that the reader's experience with this book will help create a study of international politics which is both enjoyable and intellectually rewarding.

Steven L. Spiegel

Contents

Preface vii

Prologue 1

Part One **THE CONFLICT OF PEOPLES** 5

Imperialism and Intervention: Dynamism
of the Strong 9

1 The U.S. and Third-World Dictatorships: A Case
   for Benign Detachment   *Ted Galen Carpenter*   9
2 In Defense of Interventionism
   Charles Krauthammer   23
3 Gorbachev and the Third World
   Francis Fukuyama   40
4 Eastern Europe and the Future of the Soviet Empire
   Vojtech Mastny   54

Religious and Ethnic Nationalism 67

5 Misunderstanding Africa
   Xan Smiley   67
6 Fundamentalist Muslims Between America and Russia
   Daniel Pipes   83

Haves vs. Have-Nots: Upheaval Between North and
South 102

7 North-South Interdependence
   Ivan L. Head   102

[xi]

8   The Perversion of Foreign Aid
    Nick Eberstadt   107
9   International Framework and South-South Cooperation:
    Constraints and Opportunities   *K. P. Saksena*   125

    Revolution: The Weak Respond   **140**

10 Nicaragua: A Speech to My Former Comrades
    on the Left   *David Horowitz*   140
11 The U.S. and the Contras
    Aryeh Neier   149
12 Iran and the Americans
    Shaul Bakhash   158
13 Reflections on Terrorism
    Walter Laqueur   168

Part Two   THE BURDEN OF THE STRONG   **181**

    Competitors and Allies: Pas de Deux   **187**

14 Managing the U.S.-Soviet Relationship
    Jerry F. Hough   187
15 How Vulnerable is the West?
    Richard Pipes   213
16 Do We Still Need Europe?
    Eliot A. Cohen   239
17 The Evolution of the U. S.-Japan Alliance
    William C. Sherman   253
18 International Bargaining and Domestic Politics:
    U. S.-China Relations Since 1972   *Robert S. Ross*   262

    The Global Balance of Power: Can the Great Powers
    Rule the World?   **292**

19 Dateline Middle East: The Dangers of Disengagement
    Charles McC. Mathias, Jr.   292
20 Paying Less Attention to the Middle East
    Richard N. Haass   302
21 The Race for South Africa
    Paul Johnson   311
22 Sanctions and South Africa
    Cosmas Desmond   323

    Arms: The Crisis Imposed by Technology   **342**

23 The Present Danger
    Noam Chomsky   342
24 The Case Against Arms Control
    Seymour Weiss   351
25 The War for Star Wars
    George W. Ball   360
26 The Return of Strategic Defense
    Leon Sloss   383
27 Reykjavik: An Icelandic Saga
    Stanley Hoffmann   394
28 Nuclear Proliferation: A Cause for Optimism?
    D. W. Hiester   401

Part Three   THE CRISIS OF INSTITUTIONS   413

    The Crisis of International Institutions   416

29 The U.N.: A Dream of Peace
    Christoph Mühlemann   416
30 After the Fall: The Politics of Oil
    Edward L. Morse   426

    The Crisis of National Institutions   444

31 Uniqueness and Pendulum Swings in U. S. Foreign Policy
    Geir Lundestad   444
32 United States Foreign Policy-Making: Chaos or Design?
    Nicholas Wheeler and Phil Williams   464
33 Logic, Bribes, and Threats
    Charles William Maynes   481

Part Four   THE PROBLEMS OF A CHANGING WORLD ECONOMY:
WILL THE WORLD AS WE KNOW IT SURVIVE?   495

34 The Changed World Economy
    Peter F. Drucker   497
35 Redefining National Security
    Lester R. Brown   517

List of Contributors   531

AT ISSUE

Politics
in the
World Arena

FIFTH EDITION

PROLOGUE

The purpose of this volume is threefold: to gain an improved understanding of the dynamics of current world politics; to identify the crucial
developments in international politics with which American foreign
policy must deal; and to explore the major issues that will require careful
and painful decisions on the part of policy makers in the years ahead.
The readings in *At Issue* are designed to provide material for discussion
and debate in the hope that they might contribute to a new American
approach toward the rest of the world. Such an approach should be
devoted less to ideological abstractions and simple contrasts between
weakness and strength or internationalism and isolationism, and inclined more toward a recognition and respect of the distinct cultures in
which the peoples of the world exist.

The book is divided into four parts. The first, "The Conflict of
Peoples," examines the nature and causes of current conflicts between
great and small nations, between the satisfied and dissatisfied. Current
Soviet and American intervention policies are examined. The role of
religious and ethnic differences in conflict is stressed, but the effects of
economic gaps between the rich and poor nations and of conflicting
great-power aims are considered as well. We also examine the turmoil in
the Third World, which has led to a growing crisis between North and
South and to a diverse set of responses to the affluent West on the part
of parties that feel disadvantaged—responses that range from revolution
to the strategy of terrorism, to economic challenges raised by countries
that are dependent on the export of a single commodity.

The second part, "The Burden of the Strong," concentrates on the
relations between the major powers. We assess the relations between
the United States and the Soviet Union; the effect of China and its
domestic politics on the global balance of power; the role of both the
Western European states and Japan as allies of the United States, and
their potentially increased importance in the world power balance; and
the future of great-power relations within Europe and Asia. We also

consider the role of armaments—especially nuclear weapons—in the balance of power between the United States and the Soviet Union and between less powerful nations that are members of the international system.

The third part, "The Crisis of Institutions," deals with the problems that plague political institutions on all levels of global society. The role of the United Nations and the future of the Organization of Petroleum Exporting Countries (OPEC) are considered. Will the United Nations wither, or will it revive and play an effective role in an increasingly complex international environment? Has OPEC passed its prime? Is there a future for the type of resource-oriented international institution that OPEC represents? Will the revolution that OPEC seemed to create in international politics in the 1970's turn out to be ephemeral? The third part also focuses on the nation-state, paying special attention to the United States. We explore conflicting philosophies about the content of foreign policy and about organizational constraints and bureaucratic procedures that, some claim, cause governments to act in seemingly irrational ways.

Finally, in the fourth part, "The Problems of a Changing World Economy," we pay special attention to developments in world economic patterns, population growth, the food supply, and new areas of high technology, and to their possible effects on rich and poor nations alike. As new technologies developed, enabling people of different cultures to come into closer contact through faster means of travel and communication, many observers hoped for a comparable increase in international understanding and cooperation. Reality, however, has moved in another direction as various groups have used improved communications for destructive ends. The transistor radio has become a means of whipping the masses into frenzied hatred, the jet airplane an instrument of destruction and a tool of terrorists, the oil well a symbol of exploitation and blackmail, and the computer a source of international competition and conflict.

Placing all of these subjects in perspective, it is ironic indeed that at a time when the superpowers have reached a virtual nuclear standoff, the number of people killed in local upheavals has increased at an accelerating rate. The atomic bombs dropped on Hiroshima and Nagasaki killed or wounded approximately 220,000 Japanese; but as many as 3 million people were killed in the 1971 war for independence in Bangladesh, more than 2 million died in the unsuccessful effort to establish an independent state of Biafra, 4 to 5 million people perished in Indochina during the prolonged and continuing civil strife in that area, and the Iran-Iraq war in the 1980's has thus far produced over a million casualties. On the one hand, the nuclear balance of terror has made the great powers cautious; on the other, however, weaker states and groups have improved their capacity to engage in traditional but nonetheless enormously destructive types of conflict.

It is evident that future challenges to American foreign policy will be severe, and debates over how to deal with the problems raised by recent crises are growing. There are pronounced differences between those who see relations between the industrial and Third World states as critical to world politics and those who still believe that the confrontation between communist and capitalist states is central. There are debates in the United States about how to handle producer-consumer relations of the type epitomized by OPEC and the oil-importing nations. There are divergent perspectives about the future role of high technology and about whether America should lean toward protectionism or toward free trade policies. There are disputes about the proper approach to the Soviet Union on such issues as arms control and human rights, uncertainty over the appropriate role of strategic defense in nuclear deterrence, disagreements about the significance of the Soviet invasion of Afghanistan in December 1979, conflicts over the meaning of Soviet actions in Eastern Europe, arguments about future policy directions in Western Europe, deep and bitter conflicts over the strategic and moral factors at the heart of alternatives in Central America and South Africa, and debates about proper directions toward the Middle East on such issues as the Iran-Iraq war and the Palestinian question. There are those who would redefine the needs of national security and transfer expenditures from defense to the domestic arena, while at the same time others believe that defense spending must be increased if the Soviet threat is to be thwarted. There are those who believe that a viable future can emerge only through increasing interdependence, while others assert that only military deterrence can provide the basic structure for a balance of world power. As international politics becomes increasingly complex and frustrating, the diversity of methods for dealing with specific problems increases. The observer is often perplexed by the resulting multitude of analyses and prescribed solutions.

In this edition we focus on these debates in an effort to comprehend both the dilemmas raised by current international conditions and the range of solutions that has been offered to deal with them. No one explanation or answer can be all-encompassing. Yet an examination of particular points of view can begin to lead us toward unraveling the political complexities of the modern world and provide a guide for judging the successes and failures of any government that may be in power.

PART ONE

The Conflict of Peoples

The first part of this volume concentrates on conflicts between peoples: disputes between nations or groups in close proximity who are thrust into conflict by economic, ideological, social, or ethnic divergence; and disputes between strong and weak powers over differences in military strength and wealth. Each article focuses on deeply held attitudes that people have toward other people and, at the same time, each offers a different perspective on the origins of international conflicts.

The opening section addresses the problem of great-power intervention in the affairs of weaker states. The discussion focuses on the United States and the Soviet Union. In the first two articles Ted Galen Carpenter and Charles Krauthammer provide diametrically contrasting views of the appropriate role of the United States in the Third World. Carpenter favors a restrained, "conciliatory non-interventionist posture toward the Third World," a policy of "benign detachment," as the best means of protecting America's interests and reputation. Krauthammer attacks this "realist" perspective maintained by Carpenter and several other authors. He identifies instead with the Reagan Doctrine, which claims a higher moral ground by supporting anti-communist and even anti-radical revolution in a variety of countries around the world, from Afghanistan to Nicaragua. These two articles provide the essence of the 1980's foreign policy debate in the United States over the appropriate approach Washington should take toward intervention and relations with the Third World.

The debate in the Kremlin over the proper course of Soviet policy is obviously more obtuse to outsiders. Francis Fukuyama analyzes the reassessment that he believes has been undertaken by the Soviet elite toward its policy with the Third World. Fukuyama argues that Soviet policy is in a period of consolidation—reinforcement of positions in countries that already have client regimes, but a reluctance to assume new commitments and the expenditure of new resources.

Any discussion of Soviet intervention policy also necessarily includes a consideration of Eastern Europe. Vojtech Mastny addresses the dynamics and vicissitudes of Soviet control in the light of the region's growing instability and heterogeneity. He believes the Soviet Union has been "increasingly ill-equipped and reluctant to act effectively" in the area. For example, he shows how the Soviet invasion of Czechoslovakia in 1968 to crush a reformist communist movement has resulted in ideological, political and economic stagnation in that country. He also deals with the continuing consequences of the Polish crisis. On December 13, 1981, the Polish military, at the behest of the Polish Communist party and the Soviet Union, suddenly moved to suppress the Solidarity labor movement led by Lech Walesa. These dramatic events and many quieter developments have gradually led to the ferment Mastny identifies.

In the second section we examine one of the major reasons why both the United States and the Soviet Union have had such great difficulty controlling states that are weaker than themselves: the rise of indigenous ethnic and religious nationalism. In the modern world these forces have generated important political forces both within and between states. Despite the seeming popularity of Marxist doctrine throughout the world, ethnicity and religious identification have, in fact, become stronger bases for loyalty than has class. Thus, we are faced with a paradoxical situation in which recent technological improvements in communication and transportation—changes that should lead to "unification"—coincide with a period of "fragmentation" in which people tend to identify with entities that are different from and often smaller than their nation-state. Instead of causing cooperative impulses, the new world "disorder" has frequently led to intensified conflict.

The two articles in this section highlight the difficulty of trying to fit developing states into European models of political activity and organization. Both essays challenge established explanations for the political instability occurring in the Middle East and Africa. Xan Smiley, in "Misunderstanding Africa," explains the pervasive impact of tribalism on the politics of an area in which nation-states were superimposed on colonial frontiers that had cut across actual tribal divisions. Smiley challenges both liberal and Marxist preconceptions about what is required to end black Africa's cycle of dependence and inferiority.

From the impact of ethnic differences on political practice, we turn to the effect of religious belief. Daniel Pipes examines the impact of Islamic fundamentalism on the politics of the Muslim world. He distinguishes between conservative and radical fundamentalists, and proceeds to explain the political implications of their contrasting attitudes toward both the East and the West. Pipes stresses that although fundamentalists have as great or even greater differences with the Soviet Union as with the United States, America's greater attractiveness leads them to treat it as the primary adversary.

The Pipes and Smiley articles should lead the reader to an understanding of the need to take account of two dimensions in international politics that are often ignored. In the third section we turn to more traditional and better-known issues: the gap between "have" and "have-not" countries and the more familiar problems of exploitation, inequality, economic development, and perceived ethnic discrimination. The complaint of most Third World countries was voiced by the late President Houari Boumedienne of Algeria in a speech delivered to the United Nations General Assembly in April 1974: "The will to gain and cling to their position of dominance over world resources has been the guiding principle in the behavior of the major imperialist powers of the world."

In this section the accuracy of Boumedienne's statement is examined from a number of conflicting perspectives. First, Ivan L. Head offers a point of view sympathetic to the Boumedienne position, arguing that the Northern nations have consistently refused to accept their dependence on the South "in economic, environmental, military and political terms" and therefore to rectify the structural inequities that exist between them. He discusses Southern contributions to the North (for example, as critical markets for exports and the sale of arms, or as sources of a favorable balance of trade) and calls upon the North to share power more equitably in the making of international decisions affecting important economic and financial issues.

Foreign aid is one means of transferring resources to the less developed world. Nick Eberstadt traces the specific evolution of American foreign aid policy, though there are implications inherent in his analysis for the Western world as a whole. Eberstadt believes that American policy as it has come to be practiced often affects "the poor and the unprotected" adversely. He argues that American foreign aid has progressively become a matter of direct budgetary assistance to weaker governments. Because of this misplaced objective, many recipients may well be worse off after receiving American aid.

K. P. Saksena confronts precisely the problems raised by Head and Eberstadt. Because the industralized countries are not transferring wealth on a large scale to developing countries and because aid may be ineffective, he advocates greater cooperation among the weaker states themselves. He admits that this action may be a second-best alternative to the restructuring of the international economic order and to North-South cooperation. Yet, he believes that collective self-reliance is the only way that the less developed countries will begin to stem the continued deterioration of their global economic position. This article, like the two preceding it, should establish a framework of analysis that goes beyond the usual characterizations of North-South relations as being ruled by guns, greed, or guilt.

From an analysis of the relations between "haves" and "have-nots," which understandably focuses on economic questions, we move to an examination of the actual turmoil occurring in the Third World. In this section we concentrate particularly on the question of revolution.

The first two articles assume diametrically opposite positions toward the Sandinista revolution in Nicaragua and the counterrevolution led by the *contras*. To David Horowitz, the Sandinistas are the students of Fidel Castro, oppressors who are closely tied to the Soviet Union and international communism. He believes that both in Cuba and in Nicaragua revolutions with democratic potential were stolen by communist oppressors. On the other hand, Aryeh Neier weighs the impact of the Sandinista's revolution on the country and compares the human rights record of both the Sandinistas and the *contras*. In 1986 the Administration persuaded the Congress to fund an additional $100 million in military assistance to the *contras*. Even beforehand Neier was convinced that it had still not produced an "intellectually and morally persuasive argument" for sponsoring the war.

The United States, like many other countries, has also been directly affected by the consequences of another major revolution, the events in Iran since 1978. Shaul Bakhash attempts to explain developments in the Islamic Republic created by the Ayatollah Khomeini. His article is actually an extensive review of a book on the Iranian revolution by R. K. Ramazani, *Revolutionary Iran: Challenge and Response in the Middle East.* Through this vehicle Bakhash is able to assess the misconceptions of the revolution by the Reagan administration. These failings contributed to the disastrous sale of arms in 1985 and 1986. The President or his aides hoped to gain freedom for the hostages, establish the basis for dealing with so-called Iranian moderates, and allow for the circuitous transfer of funds to the *contras* around the stipulations of Congress.

A focus on actions by the revolutionary Iranian government leads to another question. Is the use of terrorism another instrument employed by revolutionaries or is it a criminal act? In the 1980's this question has become a critical theme in the conduct of international politics. Walter Laqueur, in his comprehensive discourse on the subject, attempts to place the issue in perspective: its relative practical and political importance, its historical significance, the most effective means of combating the threat. Thus, by the end of the section, the role of revolutions in contemporary international politics can be viewed from a variety of dimensions.

IMPERIALISM AND INTERVENTION: DYNAMISM OF THE STRONG

1

The U.S. and Third-World Dictatorships: A Case for Benign Detachment

TED GALEN CARPENTER

It is a central dilemma of contemporary American foreign policy that the world's leading capitalist democracy must confront an environment in which a majority of nations are neither capitalist nor democratic. U.S. leaders have rarely exhibited ingenuity or grace in handling this delicate and often frustrating situation.

The current turmoil in Central America is illustrative of a larger problem. American officials assert that this vital region is under assault from doctrinaire communist revolutionaries trained, funded, and controlled by the Soviet Union. Danger to the well-being of the U.S. is immediate and serious, Administration spokesmen argue, and it is imperative that the Marxist-Leninist tide be prevented from engulfing Central America. Accomplishing this objective requires a confrontational posture toward the communist beachhead (Nicaragua) combined with massive support for all "friendly" regimes, ranging from democratic Costa Rica to autocratic Guatemala. Washington's Central American policy displays in microcosm most of the faulty assumptions underlying America's approach to the entire Third World.

The current strategy of the U.S. betrays a virtual siege mentality. It was not always thus. Throughout the 19th century, U.S. policymakers exuded confidence that the rest of the world would emulate America's political and economic system, seeing the U.S. as a "beacon on the hill" guiding humanity to a better future. As late as the 1940's, most Americans and their political representatives still believed that democracy would triumph as a universal system. The prospective breakup of the European colonial empires throughout Asia and Africa was generally viewed as an opportunity, not a calamity. Scores of new nations would emerge from that process, and Americans were confident that most would choose the path of democracy and free enterprise, thus isolating the Soviet Union and its coterie of Marxist-Leninist dictatorships in Eastern Europe.

The actual results were acutely disappointing. No wave of new democracies occurred in this "Third World"; instead, decolonization produced a plethora of dictatorships, some of which appeared distressingly friendly to Moscow. This development was especially disturbing to Washington since it took place at a time when America's Cold War confrontation with the U.S.S.R. was at its most virulent. The nature and magnitude of that struggle caused American leaders to view the Third World primarily as another arena in the conflict. Consequently, the proliferation of left-wing revolutionary movements and governments seemed to undermine America's own security and well-being.

Washington's response to this adversity has been a particularly simplistic and unfortunate one. American leaders increasingly regarded any anti-communist regime, however repressive and undemocratic it might be at home, as an "ally," a "force for stability," and even a "friend." At the same time, they viewed leftist govenments—even those under democratic procedures—as little more than Soviet surrogates, or at least targets of opportunity for communist machinations.

A portent of this mind-set among the U.S. policymakers surfaced during the earliest stages of the Cold War. Pres. Harry Truman's enunciation of the so-called Truman Doctrine in 1947 proclaimed the willingness of the U.S. to assist friendly governments resisting not only external aggression, but also "armed minorities" in their own midst. It was an ominous passage, for the U.S. was arrogating the right to intervene in the internal affairs of other nations to help preserve regimes deemed friendly to American interests. Although Washington had engaged in such conduct throughout Central America and the Caribbean for several decades, those incidents were a geographical aberration in what was otherwise a noninterventionist foreign policy. The Truman Doctrine raised the specter that America's meddlesome paternalism in one region might now be applied on a global basis.

Although Truman stressed that the *status quo* was not "sacred," his doctrine soon made the U.S. a patron of repressive, reactionary regimes around the world. It was a measure of how far that trend had developed by 1961 that Pres. John F. Kennedy could proclaim in his inaugural address America's determination to "support any friend, oppose any foe" in the battle against world communism. Today, leading foreign policy spokesmen such as Henry Kissinger, Alexander Haig, and Jeane Kirkpatrick express a fondness for "friendly" authoritarian regimes that would have seemed incomprehensible to most Americans only a few decades ago.

A false realism as well as moral insensitivity characterize American policy toward Third World dictatorships. There is a disturbing tendency to view such regimes in caricature, regarding right-wing governments as valuable friends whose repressive excesses must be ignored or excused, while perceiving leftist insurgent movements and governments as mortal threats to America's national interest, justifying a posture of unrelenting hostility. For example, the Reagan Administration pursues a confrontational policy toward the Marxist government of Nicaragua, terminating all aid programs, imposing a trade embargo, and supporting rebel guerrillas. At the same time, Washington lavishes economic and military aid upon equally repressive "allies" in South Korea, Taiwan, Zaire, and elsewhere.

The consequences of this simplistic and morally inconsistent strategy are highly unfortunate. America finds itself involved far too often in futile or mutually destructive confrontations with left-wing regimes. Even worse is the evolution of a cozy relationship between Washington and a host of right-wing authoritarian governments. A pervasive perception of the U.S. as the sponsor and protector of such dictatorships has undermined America's credibility as a spokesman for democracy, caused Third World peoples to equate both capitalism and democracy with U.S. hegemony, and established a milieu for rabidly anti-American revolutions. It is an approach that creates a massive reservoir of ill will and, in the long run, weakens rather than strengthens America's national security.

A FLAWED POLICY

Washington's policy toward Third World dictatorships is seriously flawed in several respects. One fundamental defect is the tendency to view largely internal struggles exclusively through the prism of America's ongoing cold war with the Soviet Union. Secretary of State John Foster Dulles was an early practitioner of this parochial viewpoint during the 1950's, when he insisted that the emerging nations of Asia and Africa "choose sides" in that conflict. Nonalignment or neutralism Dulles viewed as moral cowardice or tacit support for the U.S.S.R. Such an attitude only antagonized nonaligned leaders who were concerned primarily with charting a postcolonial political and economic course for their new nations and cared little about an acrimonious competition between two alien superpowers. The chilly relationship between India, the Third World's leading democracy, and the U.S. throughout this period was due in large part to Washington's hostility toward Prime Minister Jawaharlal Nehru's policy of nonalignment.

American policymakers have learned few lessons from Dulles' errors in the subsequent quarter-century. During the 1960's, Washington still saw internal political conflicts in nations as diverse as Vietnam and the Dominican Republic exclusively as skirmishes in the larger Cold War. A decade after the victory of one faction in the complex tribal, linguistic, and economic struggle in Angola, former Secretary of State Henry Kissinger describes that war as part of "an unprecedented Soviet geopolitical offensive" on a global scale. Kissinger's former boss, Gerald Ford, likewise interprets the episode purely as a struggle between "pro-Communist" and "pro-West" forces. Former UN Ambassador Jeane Kirkpatrick views such countries as Mozambique and Nicaragua not as nations in their own right, but as components of the Soviet empire. Similarly, Pres. Reagan's bipartisan commission on Central America describes the multifaceted conflicts of that troubled region as part of a Soviet-Cuban "geo-strategic challenge" to the U.S.

This failure to understand the complexities and ambiguities of Third World power rivalries has impelled the U.S. to adopt misguided and counterproductive strategies. One manifestation is an uncritical willingness to embrace repressive regimes if they possess sufficient anticommunist credentials.

At times, this tendency has proven more than a trifle embarrassing. During a toast to the Shah of Iran on New Year's Eve, 1977, Pres. Jimmy Carter lavished praise on that autocratic monarch: "Iran, because of the great leadership of the Shah, is an island of stability in one of the more troubled areas of the world. This is a great tribute to you, Your Majesty, and to your leadership, and to the respect and admiration and love which your people give to you." Apparently concluding that America's vocal enthusiasm for the Shah and his policies during the previous quarter-century did not link the U.S. sufficiently to his fate, the President emphasized: "We have no other nation on earth who [sic] is closer to us in planning for our mutual military security."

Barely a year later, the Shah's regime lay in ruins, soon to be replaced by a virulently anti-American government. Carter's assumption that the Shah was loved by the Iranian people was a classic case of wishful thinking. CIA operatives in the field warned their superiors that the American perception was a delusion, but those reports were ignored because they did not reflect established policy. Blind to reality, the Carter Administration identified itself and American security interests with a regime that was already careening toward oblivion.

One might think that American leaders would have gained some humility from the wreckage of Iranian policy and at least learned to curb vocal expressions of support for right-wing autocrats. Unfortunately, that has not been the case. Less than four years after Carter's gaffe, Vice Pres. George Bush fawned over Philippine dictator Ferdinand Marcos: "We stand with you sir. . . . We love your adherence to democratic principle [sic] and to the democratic processes. And we will not leave you in isolation."

It is a considerable understatement to suggest that the burgeoning Philippine opposition (which contained many legitimate democrats, such as Salvador Laurel and Butz Aquino) did not appreciate effusive praise for the man who suspended the national constitution, declared martial law, governed by decree, and imprisoned political opponents to perpetuate his own power. From the standpoint of long-term American interests (not to mention common decency and historical accuracy), Bush should have considered how a successor Philippine government might perceive his enthusiasm for Marcos. During his second presidential campaign debate with Walter Mondale, Reagan not only defended this nation's intimate relationship with the Marcos regime, but also implied that the only alternative to Marcos was a communist takeover— which proved to be a gross distortion of reality.

Ill-considered hyperbole with respect to right-wing autocratic governments places the U.S. in an awkward, even hypocritical posture. Equally unfortunate is the extensive and at times highly visible material assistance that Washington gives such regimes. For more than three decades, the U.S. helped train and equip the military force that the Somoza family used to dominate Nicaragua and systematically loot that nation. Similarly, the American government provided lavish military hardware to the Shah of Iran as well as "security" and "counterinsurgency" training to SAVAK, the Shah's infamous secret police. Throughout the same period, Washington gave similar assistance to a succession of Brazilian military governments, a parade of Guatemalan dictatorships, the junta that ruled from 1967 to 1974, and several other repressive governments. Most recently, the U.S. gave the Marcos regime economic and military aid totaling more then $227,000,000, plus millions more in payments for the military installations at Clark Field and Subic Bay. Despite ample signs of that government's increasingly shaky tenure, the Reagan Administration asked Congress to increase aid by nearly 20%. Congress exhibited little enthusiasm for that approach, approving instead a significantly smaller sum and attaching various "human rights" restrictions.

Warm public endorsements of autocratic regimes combined with substantial (at times lavish) material support produce an explosive mixture that repeatedly damages American prestige and credibility. Many of those governments retain only the most precarious hold on power, lacking significant popular support and depending heavily upon the use of terror to intimidate opponents. When repressive tactics no longer prove sufficient, the dictatorships can collapse with dramatic suddenness—as in Iran. American patronage thus causes the U.S. to become closely identified with hated governments and their policies. The domestic populations see those regimes as little more than American clients—extensions of U.S. power. Consequently, they do not view the ouster of a repressive autocrat as merely an internal political change, but as the eradication of American domination.

Moreover, there is a virtual reflex action to repudiate everything American—including capitalist economics and Western-style democracy. The U.S. unwittingly contributes to that process. By portraying corrupt, autocratic rulers as symbols of the "free world," we risk having long-suffering populations take us at our word. They do not see capitalism and democracy as those systems operate in the West, enabling people to achieve prosperity and individual freedom. Instead, Third World people identify free enterprise and democratic values with the corruption and repression they have endured. Historian Walter LaFeber, in *Inevitable Revolutions*, describes how that reasoning has worked in Central America: "U.S. citizens see [capitalist democracy] as having given them the highest standard of living and the most open society in the world. Many Central Americans have increasingly associated capitalism with a brutal oligarchy-military complex that has been supported by U.S. policies—and armies."

HOSTILITY TO THE LEFT

The flip side of Washington's promiscuous enthusiasm for right-wing autocrats is an equally pervasive hostility toward leftist Third World regimes and insurgent movements. There have been occasional exceptions to this rule throughout the Cold War era. For example, the U.S. developed a cordial relationship with communist Yugoslavia after Premier Josef Tito broke with the Soviet Union in 1948. A similar process occurred during the 1970's, when the Nixon Administration engineered a rapprochement with China, ending more than two decades of frigid hostility. These achievements are instructive and should have demonstrated to American policymakers that it is possible for the U.S. to coexist with Marxist regimes. However, that lesson has not been learned, and such incidents of enlightenment stand as graphic exceptions to an otherwise dreary record.

More typical of America's posture is the ongoing feud with the Cuban government of Fidel Castro. The campaign to oust or, failing that, to make him a hemispheric pariah, was shortsighted, futile, and counterproductive from the outset. It served only to give him a largely undeserved status as a principled, courageous revolutionary and to drive his government into Moscow's willing embrace. Soviet defector Arkady Shevchenko recalls a 1960 conversation with Nikita Khrushchev in which the latter viewed America's hostility toward Cuba with undisguised glee. Describing U.S. efforts to "drive Castro to the wall" instead of establishing normal relations as "stupid," Khrushchev accurately predicted that "Castro will have to gravitate to us like an iron filing to a magnet."

Apparently having learned little from the Cuban experience, the Reagan Administration seems determined to make the same errors with the Sandinista government of Nicaragua. Washington's attempts to isolate the Managua regime diplomatically, the imposition of economic sanctions, the "covert" funding of the contra guerrillas, and the use of apocalyptic rhetoric to describe the internal struggle for power in that country all seem like an eerie case of *deja vu*. Reagan's depiction of the contras as "the moral equal" of America's own Founding Fathers constitutes ample evidence that U.S. policymakers have not learned to view Third World power struggles with even modest sophistication. One need not romanticize the Sandinista regime, excuse its suppression of political dissent, or rationalize its acts of brutality (*e.g.*, the treatment of the Miskito Indians), as the American political left is prone to do, to advocate a more restrained and detached policy. Administration leaders fear that Nicaragua will become a Soviet satellite in Central America; Washington's current belligerent course virtually guarantees that outcome. As in the case of Cuba nearly three decades ago, the U.S. is creating a self-fulfilling prophecy.

The American government's hostility toward left-wing regimes in the Third World has even extended to *democratic* governments with a leftist slant. An early victim of this antipathy was Iranian Prime Minister Mohammed Mossadegh. Evidence now clearly shows extensive CIA involvement (including planning and funding) in the 1953 royalist coup that enabled the Shah to establish himself as an absolute monarch. Mossadegh's "crime" was not that he was communist, but that he advocated policies inimical to powerful Anglo-American economic interests. A year later, the left-leaning reformist government of Jacobo Arbenz in Guatemala suffered the same fate. This time, American complicity in the overthrow of a democratically elected government was even more blatant. The U.S. Ambassador to Guatemala reportedly boasted that he had brought the counterrevolution to a successful conclusion barely "forty-five minutes behind schedule." Even Reagan's bipartisan commission on Central America concedes U.S. assistance in the coup, and Washington's role has been amply documented elsewhere.

Buoyed by such successes, the U.S. helped oust Patrice Lumumba, the first elected Prime Minister of the Congo (now Zaire), in 1960. Like

Mossadegh and Arbenz, Lumumba had committed the unpardonable sin of soliciting communist support. There is also some evidence of American complicity in the 1973 military coup that toppled the government of Chilean Pres. Salvador Allende. We do know that the Nixon Administration sought to thwart Allende's election in 1970, discussed a coup with disgruntled elements of the military immediately following that election, and ordered steps to isolate and destabilize the new government economically. No less a figure than Henry Kissinger, then serving as National Security Advisor, concedes that the U.S. authorized covert payments of more than $8,800,000 to opponents of the Allende government during the three years preceding the coup. Given the relatively modest size of the Chilean economy and population, an infusion of such an amount of money certainly created a considerable political impact, but Kissinger and Nixon both blame Allende's downfall entirely on internal factors. The Marxist president's pursuit of disastrous economic programs together with his systematic attempts to undercut the conservative middle class and harass political opponents undoubtedly galvanized the opposition, weakening his already precarious political position. Nevertheless, it would be naive to accept at face value the Nixon Administration's protestations of innocence regarding the coup, especially in light of Kissinger's ominous assertion that Allende was "not merely an economic nuisance or a political critic but a geopolitical challenge."

It is reprehensible for a government that preaches the virtues of noninterference in the internal affairs of other nations to have amassed such a record of interference. The level of shame mounts when American meddling undermines a sister democracy and helps to install a repressive autocracy. Yet, in Iran, Guatemala, Zaire, and Chile, that was precisely what happened. Post-Mossadegh Iran endured the Shah's corrupt authoritarianism for 25 years before desperately embracing the fanaticism of the Ayatollah Khomeini. Guatemala after Arbenz has witnessed a dreary succession of military dictatorships, each one rivaling its predecessor in brutality. The ouster of Patrice Lumumba facilitated the rise to power of Mobuto Sese Seko in Zaire. His regime is regarded as one of the most corrupt and repressive on any continent.

Perhaps Chile is the saddest case of all. Although deified by Western liberals, Allende has his unsavory qualities. His enthusiasm for Marxist economic bromides pushed his nation to the brink of disaster. He also exhibited a nasty authoritarian streak of his own, including an intolerance of political critics. Nevertheless, his actions remained (although sometimes just barely) within constitutional bounds. Moreover, he was the last in an unbroken series of democratically elected rulers stretching back more than four decades—an impressive record in Latin America. The Pinochet dictatorship that replaced Allende is conspicuous for its brutal and systematic violation of individual liberties. Yet, Kissinger can assert that the "change in government in Chile was on balance favorable—even from the point of view of human rights." Such a view reflects either willful blindness or an astounding cynicism.

STRATEGIC, ECONOMIC, AND IDEOLOGICAL JUSTIFICATIONS

Those individuals who justify America's existing policy toward the Third World cite strategic, economic, and ideological considerations. On the strategic level, they argue that the U.S. must prevent geographically important regions from falling under the sway of regimes subservient to the Soviet Union. Otherwise, a shift in the balance of global military power could jeopardize American security interests, perhaps even imperil the nation's continued existence. Economically, the U.S. must maintain access to vital supplies of raw materials and keep markets open for American products and investments. It is not possible, this argument holds, for an economy based upon free enterprise to endure if the world is dominated by state-run Marxist systems. Finally, beyond questions of strategic and economic self-interest, the U.S. must thwart communist expansionism in the Third World to ensure that America and its democratic allies do not become islands in a global sea of hostile, totalitarian dictatorships.

All these arguments possess a certain facile appeal, but they hold up only if one accepts some very dubious conceptions of America's strategic, economic, and ideological interests. Moreover, proponents have often employed these arguments as transparent rationalizations for questionable foreign policy initiatives.

The notion that the United States must assist and defend right-wing regimes while opposing leftist insurgencies or governments for its own strategic self-interest depends on several important subsidiary assumptions. Those who justify America's Third World policy on this basis generally define "strategic interests" in a most expansive manner. In its crudest form, this approach regards Third World states as little more than bases or forward staging areas for American military power. Such a rationale is convincing only if one assumes that the United States truly possesses "vital" strategic interests in regions as diverse as Southeast Asia, the Persian Gulf, Central Africa, and South America, and that successor regimes in regional "keystone" nations would be hostile to those interests.

One can and should question whether the U.S. actually has strategic interests, vital or otherwise, in areas thousands of miles removed from its own shores. How a plethora of small, often militarily insignificant nations, governed by unpopular and unstable regimes, could augment U.S. strength in a showdown with the Soviet Union is a mystery. One could make a more plausible argument that attempts to prop up tottering allies weaken America's security. These efforts drain U.S. financial resources and stretch defense forces dangerously thin. Worst of all is the risk that a crumbling Third World ally could become an arena for ill-advised American military adventures. As we saw in Vietnam, the entrance to such quagmires is easier to find than the exit.

The inordinate fear of successor governments is equally dubious, for it assumes that such regimes would inevitably be left-wing and subservient to Moscow. Neither assumption is necessarily warranted. The ouster of a right-wing autocracy does not lead ineluctably to a radical leftist government. Vigorous democracies succeeded rightist dictatorships in Portugal and Greece. Moreover, even in cases where a staunchly leftist government does emerge, subservience to Moscow can not be assumed. Such pessimism may have had some validity in the bipolar ideological environment of the late 1940's and early 1950's, but, given the diffusion of power away from both Moscow and Washington in the past 30 years, it is now dangerously obsolete. When China and the U.S.S.R. are mortal adversaries, Yugoslavia charts a consistently independent course, and such a country as Rumania—in Moscow's own geopolitical "backyard"—dares exhibit maverick tendencies on selected foreign policy issues, the assumption that a Marxist Third World state will be merely a Soviet stooge is clearly unwarranted.

ECONOMIC FACTORS

The economic thesis for current U.S. foreign policy is no more persuasive than the strategic rationale. Assumptions that rightist governments serve as pliant instruments of American economic objectives or that left-wing regimes become commercial adversaries can not be sustained as a general rule. It is true that countries ruled by right-wing autocrats tend to be friendlier arenas for U.S. investment, but the price in bureaucratic restrictions and "commissions" (*i.e.*, bribes) to key officials is often very high. Moreover, governments of whatever ideological stripe usually operate according to principles of economic self-interest, which may or may not correspond to American desires.

Washington received a rude awakening on that score in the 1970's, when its closest Middle East allies—Iran and Saudi Arabia—helped engineer OPEC's massive oil price hikes. Neither U.S. client was willing to forgo financial gain out of any sense of gratitude for political and military support. Much the same situation occurred in 1980, when the Carter Administration invoked a grain embargo against the Soviet Union for the latter's invasion of Afghanistan. The U.S. encouraged, even pressured, its allies to cooperate in that boycott. Nevertheless, the Argentine military junta, a regime that the U.S. had routinely counted upon to stem the tide of leftist insurgency in Latin America, promptly seized the opportunity to boost its grain sales to the U.S.S.R.

Just as right-wing regimes exhibit a stubborn independence on economic matters, revolutionary leftist governments are not inherent commercial enemies. When the U.S. has allowed trade with leftist countries to occur, that trade has usually flourished. The lucrative oil and mineral commerce with the Marxist government of Angola is a case in point. Similarly, once the emotional feud with mainland China ceased in the 1970's, commercial and investment opportunities for the United States also began to emerge. Although a Marxist state dominating the global market in some vital commodity might conceivably attempt to blackmail the U.S., that danger is both remote and theoretical.

Economic realities exert a powerful influence that often transcends purely political considerations. Most Third World governments, whether right-wing or left-wing, benefit from extensive commercial ties with the industrialized West, particularly the U.S. America is often the principal market for their exports and is a vital source of developmental capital. Revolutionary rhetoric, even when sincerely believed, can not change that fundamental equation. It is no coincidence that Third World governments have rarely instituted economic boycotts; most embargoes originate as a deliberate U.S. policy to punish perceived political misdeeds.

Rather than adopting economic sanctions as a device for political intimidation, the U.S. should relish the prospect of promoting commercial connections to the greatest extent possible. Nothing would more readily provide evidence to left-wing leaders that a system based on private property and incentives is vastly superior to the lumbering inefficiencies of Marxist central planning. On those rare occasions when the U.S. has pursued a conciliatory, rather than a truculent and confrontational, approach, the results have been gratifying. The Marxist regime in Mozambique, for instance, first looked to the Soviet bloc for economic as well as ideological guidance, only to confront arrogant Russian imperialism and a recipe for economic disaster. The disillusioned leadership now has begun to turn away from the U.S.S.R. and open its country to Western trade and investment, a process that is likely to accelerate in the coming years.

The most misguided justification for America's attachment to right-wing Third World states lies in the realm of politics and ideology. Proponents assume an underlying ideological affinity between authoritarian systems and Western democracies. They insist that, while rightist regimes may be repressive, such governments are natural U.S. allies in the struggle against world communism. Conversely, revolutionary leftist movements are "totalitarian" in origin and constitute accretions to the power of that global menace.

No one has advanced this thesis more passionately and at greater length than former U.S. Ambassador to the United Nations Jeane Kirkpatrick. While conceding that "traditional" autocracies sometimes engage in practices that offend American "sensibilities," Kirkpatrick clearly finds those regimes more palatable than their leftist adversaries. She asserts that "traditional authoritarian governments are less repressive than revolutionary autocracies," are "more susceptible to liberalization," and are "more compatible with U.S. interests." That being the case, American aid to keep such friendly regimes in power is not only justified, but becomes something akin to a moral imperative.

Even if one concedes that the repression practiced by leftist dictatorships is more pervasive and severe than that of right-wing dictatorships, a more fundamental issue still exists—American complicity. The U.S. has neither the power nor the requisite moral mandate to eradicate injustice and oppression in the world. At the same time, as the most powerful and visible symbol of democracy, America does have an obligation not to become a participant in acts of repression and brutality. Our sponsorship of right-wing autocracies violates that crucial responsibility. Assisting dictatorial regimes makes the U.S. government (and by extension the public that elects it) an accomplice in the suppression of other people's liberty. In a profound way, such complicity constitutes a stain on our democratic heritage.

Kirkpatrick's contention that traditional autocracies are more susceptible to liberalization likewise misses a fundamental point. She asserts that autocratic regimes sometimes "evolve" into more democratic forms, whereas no analogous case exists with respect to revolutionary socialist governments. Yet, her own examples—Spain, Greece, and Brazil—do not involve evolutionary transformations, but, rather, the *restoration* of democratic systems that right-wing elements had destroyed. History demonstrates that, while communist revolutionaries oust competing repressive systems, rightist insurgents habitually overthrow democratically elected governments. There is only one instance of a successful communist uprising against an established democracy—the takeover of Czechoslovakia in March, 1948. Conversely, right-wing coups and revolutions have erased numerous democratic regimes. Spain (1936), Guatemala (1954), Brazil (1964), Greece (1967), the Philippines (1972), Chile (1973), and Argentina (1976) represent only the most prominent examples. It may be more difficult to eradicate leftist (especially totalitarian) systems than it is to replace rightist regimes, but right-wing autocratic movements pose the more lethal threat to functioning democracies. No fact more effectively demolishes the naive notion of an underlying affinity between democracies and rightist dictatorships. The two systems are not allies; they are inherent adversaries.

AN ALTERNATIVE

A new foreign policy must eschew inconsistent moral posturing as well as amoral geopolitics. The most constructive alternative would stress "benign detachment" toward *all* Third World dictatorships, whatever their ideological orientation.

The concept of benign detachment is grounded in the indisputable reality that, for the foreseeable future, the U.S. will confront a Third World environment in which a majority of nations are undemocratic. It would unquestionably prove easier to function in a community of capitalist democracies, but we do not have that luxury. Democracy and capitalism may emerge as powerful doctrines throughout the Third World, but such a transformation would be long-term, reflecting indigenous historical experiences. We certainly can not hasten that process by abandoning our own ideals and embracing reactionary autocrats. In the interim, the U.S. must learn to coexist with a variety of dictatorships. Benign detachment represents the most productive and least intrusive method of achieving that objective.

This approach would reject the simplistic categorization of right-wing regimes as friends and Marxist governments as enemies. It would require redefining America's national interests in a more circumspect manner. No longer should Washington conclude that the survival of a reactionary dictatorship, no matter how repressive, corrupt, and unstable it might be, somehow enhances the security of the U.S. A policy of benign detachment would likewise repudiate the notion that there is an underlying kinship between rightist autocracies and Western democracies. Right-wing dictatorships are just as alien to our values as their left-wing counterparts.

America's primary objective should be a more restrained and even-handed policy toward repressive Third World regimes. Cordial diplomatic and economic relations should be encouraged with *all* governments that are willing to reciprocate, be they democratic, authoritarian, royalist, or Marxist. This would require normalizing diplomatic and commercial relations with such countries as Cuba, Nicaragua, and Vietnam while curtailing aid to so-called allies.

Conservatives invariably protest that this position is a manifestation of a liberal double standard. It is not. In fact, conservatives ignore the actual effects such policies have had in the past. Take the case of mainland China. Throughout the 1950's and 1960's, Washington's attempts to isolate the People's Republic of China only caused that nation to turn inward and fester, producing a particularly oppressive and regimented system. Since the U.S. abandoned its misguided strategy in the early 1970's, China has become a far more open and progressive nation. Deng Xiaoping and his followers now eagerly welcome Western trade and investment, particularly in the field of high technology. Equally important are the changes sweeping the domestic economy. Chinese officials are dismantling crucial elements of Marxist central planning, decentralizing production, creating incentives, and even legalizing certain forms of private property. All those developments should be gratifying to Americans who believe in the virtues of a market economy. Moreover, the first, albeit hesitant, signs of political liberalization in China are beginning to emerge. Prominent Chinese spokesmen even assert publicly that Karl Marx was not infallible and that many of his ideas are irrelevant in the modern era—sentiments that would have merited the death sentence only a few years ago.

While the U.S. initiative in establishing cordial political and economic relations with China can not account entirely for this movement toward liberalization, there is no question that it helps facilitate progressive trends. Conservatives who advocate isolating Cuba, Vietnam, Nicaragua, and other Marxist nations would do well to ponder that point. Liberals who endorse economic sanctions against South Africa should consider whether their suggested strategy is not counterproductive as well.

A policy of benign detachment is not isolationist—at least insofar as that term is used to describe a xenophobic, "storm shelter" approach to world affairs. Quite the contrary, it adopts a tolerant and optimistic outlook, seeing Third World states not merely as pawns in America's cold war with the Soviet Union, but as unique and diverse entities. Extensive economic relations are not merely acceptable, they are essential to enhancing the ultimate appeal of capitalism and democracy. There is even room for American mediation efforts to help resolve internecine or regional conflicts, provided that all parties to a dispute desire such assistance and our role harbors no danger of political or military entanglements. The U.S. need not practice a surly isolation. America can be an active participant in Third World affairs, but the nature of such interaction must be limited, consistent, and nonintrusive.

A policy of benign detachment would bring numerous benefits to the U.S. No longer would America be perceived as the patron of repressive, decaying dictatorships, or as the principal obstacle to indigenous change in the Third World. Our current foreign policy tragically identifies the U.S. and—even worse—its capitalist democratic system with the most reactionary elements around the globe. This foolish posture enables the Soviet Union to pose as the champion of both democracy and Third World nationalism. It is time that America recaptured that moral high ground. If the U.S. allowed the people of Third World nations to work out their own destinies instead of trying to enlist them as unwilling combatants in the Cold War, Russia's hypocritical, grasping imperialism would soon stand exposed. Moscow, not Washington, might well become the principal target of nationalistic wrath throughout Asia, Africa, and Latin America. Moreover, the inherent inequities and inefficiencies of Marxist economics would soon become evident to all but the most rabid ideologues.

Equally important, a conciliatory noninterventionist posture toward the Third World would reduce the risk of U.S. military involvement in complex quarrels generally not relevant to American security. Savings in terms of both dollars and lives could be enormous. Our current policy threatens to format a plethora of "brush fire" conflicts with all the attendant expense, bitterness, and divisiveness that characterized the Vietnam War.

Finally, and not the least important, reducing our Third World commitments would put an end to the hypocrisy that has pervaded U.S. relations with countries in the Third World. It is debilitating for a society that honors democracy and fundamental human rights to embrace regimes that scorn both values. A nation that believes in human liberty has no need for, and should not want, "friends" who routinely practice the worst forms of repression. A policy of detachment would restore a badly needed sense of honor and consistency to American foreign policy.

2

In Defense of Interventionism

CHARLES KRAUTHAMMER

Realism is back. The realpolitik school of foreign policy is enjoying something of a revival. As might be expected from a foreign policy outlook that disdains ideology, the phenomenon crosses ideological lines. A scan of the latest issues of the three major foreign policy quarterlies shows how many lines are crossed. Reading from right to left, we find Robert Tucker in *National Interest*, George Kennan in *Foreign Affairs*, and a pair of articles in *Foreign Policy* by Alan Tonelson and Christopher Layne, each offering a version of realism. And for historical weight, the revenge of the realists coincides with the publication of a new edition of the realist classic, Hans Morgenthau's *Politics Among Nations*.

In the 38 years since the book's first edition, the fortunes of the realist school have fluctuated, but judging from Morgenthau's disciples, the central themes remain remarkably unchanged: that idealism in foreign policy is moralism misplaced and dangerous. That such idealism—a mix of universalism, sentimentalism, and ideological utopianism—has characterized American foreign policy since its emergence from 19th-century and, later, interwar isolationism. That it must be replaced with a literally disillusioned foreign policy centered on its proper object, national interest, variously defined, but classically by Morgenthau: "interest defined as power."

What accounts for the return of realism, a political philosophy never very congenial to American sensibilities?

Historically, the nemesis of Morgenthauian realism was liberal internationalism, which, from Franklin Roosevelt through Lyndon Johnson, dominated American foreign policy thinking. Its vision was that of an activist, interventionist America; its aim was the promotion abroad of both freedom and world order; and its preferred means were to be international institutions (such as the U.N.), the rule of law, and collective security.

As Thomas Hughes, president of the Carnegie Endowment, points out, the liberal internationalist consensus encompassed, in fact, two internationalisms: the U.N. system and the anticommunist alliance. The U.N. system appealed particularly to the postwar left emerging from the antifascist alliance. Anticommunism appealed to the right and cemented the Truman-Vandenberg alliance, which ended conservative isolationism. The first was "soft inclusionist internationalism stressing universality"; the other, "a harder exclusionist internationalism" pledged to the defense of the West.

The marriage was uneasy and did not last. With Vietnam came divorce. Liberal internationalism split into its two original tendencies. On the left, the fracture produced a foreign policy school that gave rhetorical allegiance to universalist ends (now renamed "human rights") and urged continued reliance on traditional internationalist means, such as the U.N., to achieve them.

The insistence on the means (justified now by a doctrine of interdependence) makes the allegiance to the ends suspect. In 1946 we did not know quite how powerless international institutions would prove to be. (To be sure, the realist had no illusions.) By 1986 we do know. Whatever else may be said of the U.N., the Organization of American States, the World Court, etc., they are not particularly effective instruments of American foreign policy. They are often (as was, for example, UNESCO) a positive hindrance to American aims and action. To insist, therefore, that they be relied upon is effectively to betray indifference to those aims and actions. It is to choose a foreign policy of passivity and quiescence. And to insist on these means as a *substitute* for American action, as is the dominant view of the Democratic Party (the 1984 party platform is an ode to multilateralism), is, in fact, to choose a new and ill-disguised form of isolationism.

The other heir of liberal internationalism has been variously called the new globalism, global unilateralism, interventionism, or simply a return to containment. In my view, it is best called neo-internationalism because it adheres most faithfully to the ends—and thus the internationalist spirit—of the old liberal internationalism.

Neo-internationalism insists that the end of American foreign policy is not just the security of the United States, but what John Kennedy called "the success of liberty." That means, first, defending the community of democratic nations (the repository of the liberal idea), and second, encouraging the establishment of new liberal polities at the frontier, most especially in the Third World. Both missions require for their success an assertive, activist, interventionist American foreign policy.

Neo-internationalism retains the vision of its predecessor, but has given up on the means, on the grounds that faith in them was based on utopian assumptions. The international arena is not a community, but a state of nature. The mere existence of international institutions and conventions does not prove the contrary. A post office in the state of nature is not evidence that conflict has given way to community. At most, it is evidence of the hope for such a transition. The refusal of the warring parties to agree to social contract or any other means of monopolizing power is more telling evidence. It shows that the hope remains only a hope.

For the U.N. to serve as an instrument of peace it needed to be a committee of the Great Powers acting in concert. As the postwar world rapidly evolved into two warring camps, the chances for that disappeared. The neo-internationalist response to that development is best characterized by Stanley Hoffmann: "the old ideals of collective security, international law, and resistance to aggression [were] now interpreted as the cause of the free world against the Soviet Union." Or, as Hughes would have it, a "harder exclusionist internationalism" displaced the "soft inclusionist internationalism stressing universality." U.N. gave way to Cold War.

Neo-internationalism gave up the old means and replaced them with unilateral Western, and if necessary, unilateral American action. But its aims (like those of its East bloc counterpart and parallel, proletarian internationalism) remained supranational in scope and ideological in spirit.

THE THREE-CORNERED DEBATE

The conflict between neo-isolationism and neo-internationalism has, since Vietnam, dominated the foreign policy debate in the United States. It still characterizes the parliamentary debate in Congress, where liberals and Democrats tend to gravitate to the former position, conservatives and Republicans to the latter.

But there is a third side and it does not lie in the middle. Realism challenges the premises of both. On the question of means, the realists side with the neo-internationalists. Realists have few illusions about international law or the U.N. or other such means for securing American interests. As to ends, realists reject all internationalist pretensions, whether rhetorical (neo-isolationist) or real (neo-internationalist). The realist concern is precisely, and exclusively, with American interests, and not with freedom, human rights, or any other woolly and expansive ideological ends inherited from liberal internationalism.

The fracturing of the liberal internationalist consensus into its component and warring schools, and the rise of the realists in opposition to both, thus have produced a three-cornered debate. Neo-isolationists fault the others for giving up on international institutions and world order. Neo-internationalists fault the others for giving up on the promotion of freedom. And realists fault the others for abandoning the notion of the national interest.

In theory the realist critique should be directed equally at both descendants of liberal internationalism. In practice it is not. Its fire today is reserved for neo-internationalism. Why? The answer has to do with the correlation of forces: the progressive weakness of the neo-isolationist school and the rising strength of neo-internationalism.

Neo-isolationism hardly requires concentrated attack, since it collapses so easily of its own weight: the contradiction between its ends and means. It embraces traditional American values abroad but forswears the means to realize them. Such a view still has emotional, and thus political, appeal—it offers grand visions with minimal exertion—and therefore regularly flowers in election years. But it is intellectually spent.

One small example. Senator Paul Simon, Democrat of Illinois, writing in the *New York Times*, urges that the United States submit to compulsory jurisdiction of the World Court for reasons of "not just idealism but also realism." (Everyone wants to be known as a realist.) How so? "It behooves us to support an international forum where we can redress grievances against nations that refuse to abide by the norms of civilized states." But what possible effect can World Court rulings have on nations that Simon himself defines as outlaw nations? No matter. Simon then cites his one example to show how the court can be useful: its assistance to the U.S. position in the Iranian hostage crisis. How sad that the hostage crisis, a supreme demonstration of the impotence and irrelevance of the mechanisms of international law, is all that Simon can find to buttress his case.

The realists, therefore, see a real threat coming from a newly ascendant neo-internationalism. What particularly concerns them is the rapid rise of the centerpiece of contemporary neo-internationalism, the idea around which the (nonnuclear) foreign policy debate now revolves: the Reagan Doctrine.

THE REAGAN DOCTRINE

A year ago the phrase "Reagan Doctrine" did not even have a meaning. Today its meaning is clear, and its promise, for the realists, a present danger.

To be sure, before 1985 the Reagan Doctrine was a term used often, but indiscriminately. It meant any part of the Reagan foreign policy that critics found offensive. It was most popular with Soviet bloc spokesmen. For a time in the East European countries it was to mean "the possibility of waging and winning a limited nuclear war using preemptive offensive strike weapons such as cruise and Pershing missiles" (Prague radio, February 1984). According to Nicaraguan foreign minister Miguel D'Escoto (April 9, 1984), it was "the right of a country when it believes its interests are best served to practice covert activities." Moscow even stretched it once to mean establishing "axes and triangles and other military political organizations" using Middle Eastern countries from Saudi Arabia to Turkey as part of "an experimental strategy of setting up broad fronts against the Socialist world."

It no longer means whatever the user wants it to mean. Since President Reagan's 1985 State of the Union address, it has come to mean something very specific: American support for anticommunist revolution as the centerpiece of a revived and revised policy of containment. In effect, ten years after Vietnam, a coherent policy reasserting the return of active American intervention in the world has been formulated.

The president himself has yet to use the term, and it can be argued that he has yet to implement fully the policy. But he certainly did enunciate the theory: "We must not break faith with those who are risking their lives on every continent from Afghanistan to Nicaragua to defy Soviet-supported aggression." The legitimacy of support for "freedom fighters," subsequently promoted by the president and amplified by Secretary of State George Shultz, has become the pillar of the Reagan policy of containment.

This policy deserves the honorific "doctrine" because it is a successor to the Truman, Nixon, and Carter doctrines, which variously attempted forms of containment. These previous formulations had sought to limit the expansion of the Soviet empire by means of direct American assistance for counterinsurgency, suppport for regional powers, or the threat of unilateral American intervention. The Reagan Doctrine faces a new historical situation—the overextension of the Soviet empire during the 1970s—and proposes a new approach: supporting and thus legitimizing challenges by indigenous insurgencies to vulnerable new Soviet acquisitions. The Reagan Doctrine is thus both an ironic parallel to Khrushchev's doctrine of "national liberation," long a preferred instrument of Soviet expansionism, and a direct challenge to the Brezhnev doctrine, which proclaims that the Soviet bloc does not contract.

Rolling back Soviet acquisitions (albeit only at the periphery, where there is no threat of general war) is the innovation of the Reagan Doctrine. But it is part of a larger, neo-internationalist vision of America's role in the world. The elements are simple: Anticommunist revolution as a tactic. Containment as the strategy. And freedom as the rationale.

One of the realist critics describes this revived internationalism well. Christopher Layne calls it "global containment—recast as the Reagan Doctrine," which "commits the United States to resisting Soviet and Soviet-supported aggression wherever it arises; to building American-style democracies in Third World countries; and to rolling back communism by aiding anticommunist insurgencies." Precisely.

THE REALIST CRITIQUE

For the realists, this return to "crusading ideological internationalism," as Layne puts it, is a disaster. The point of foreign policy, they argue, is not the promotion of ideology but the protection of national interest. As Morgenthau wrote 40 years ago, statesmen must distinguish "between their 'official duty,' which is to think and act in terms of the national interest, and their *personal* wish,' which is to see their own moral values and political principles realized throughout the world." (His italics.)

The realist critique of the Reagan Doctrine and, more generally, of neo-internationalism revolves around national interest. There is a problem, however, with national interest as a guiding foreign policy idea: at some point it must be endowed with meaning. When that is done, one of three things results: (1) if it is defined strictly, the definition must be so narrow as to lead directly to (often acknowledged) isolationism; (2) if it is defined crudely and arbitrarily as a kind of synonym for ad hoc pragmatism, it is no foreign policy guide at all; (3) if it is defined expansively, it leads to a foreign policy little different in practice from the neo-internationalism it purports to critique.

Start with the narrow definition. For a small country, national interest means national security and very little else. A small country does not have the luxury of other interests. Its interest is survival. Milan Kundera once defined a small nation as "one whose very existence may be put in question at any moment. A small nation can disappear and knows it." Czechoslovakia, for example, is a small nation. Lithuania was. The United States is not.

A great power is practically defined by its having interests beyond the security of its borders. Therefore, if it decides nonetheless to take national interest to mean only national security, it essentially renounces its position as a great power. All the more so for a superpower. For a superpower, national security is a given. The idea of anyone making an assault on American national territory or even threatening it in a meaningful way is, at best, farfetched. If the security of the United States is the only goal of American foreign policy, all that is needed is a minimal deterrent arsenal, a small navy, a border patrol, and hardly any foreign policy at all.

In his attempt in *Foreign Affairs* to rescue us from our current follies by means of "the sterner requirements of political realism," George Kennan bears out this proposition rather cheerfully. He starts by defining a country's national interest narrowly: "military security, the integrity of its political life and the well-being of its people." He ends by declaring the need for a foreign policy whose essential virtue lies "in our own minding of our own business wherever there is not some over-whelming reason for minding the business of others." A superpower concerned only with safety faces no such overwhelming reasons. Which is why Kennan sees no reason not to call himself a "neo-isolationist."

Christopher Layne's realist attack on the Reagan Doctrine shows just where this narrow definition of national interest can lead. "There is no Third World region or country whose loss would decisively tip the superpower balance against America." As for the loss of raw materials, we could get around that by "diversifying sources of supply, by stockpiling, by developing synthetic replacements, and by using natural substitutes." In other words, autarky, economic isolationism. And, finally, the cornerstone of his new foreign policy based on national interest: Marshall Plan II, a firm timetable for a phased American withdrawal from Europe and Japan.

General Marshall might not be amused. Nor Morgenthau. Nor some modern realists. This isolationism of the right is even more extreme than that of the left, few of whose adherents are ready to pull out of Europe and Japan. (Neither is Kennan. He writes off only the Third World.) Most realists say they don't mean an autarkical Fortress America when they invoke national interest as the sole criterion for American intervention.

What, then, do they mean?

Some mean pragmatism: be concrete, don't be bound by ideological rules, don't make foreign policy decisions abstractly. Tonelson offers this "concrete idea of national interest—a finite set of intrinsically important goals either essential or beneficial to the country's survival, its prosperity, the psychological well-being of its population, or any combination of these." He believes that foreign policy decisions should be made on a case-by-case, region-by-region basis, each on its own merits. Overarching ideas—ideology—become traps.

His nemesis is abstractness. His solution is arbitrariness. "Psychological well-being" can mean nearly anything. And what is an "intrinsically important goal"? It doesn't solve anything to argue for a case-by-case choice of goals, unless one has some firm idea of what the guiding national interest criterion means. Without a strict and applicable definition, the pursuit of "goals" becomes an excuse for ad hoc policy made in response to the pressures and prejudices of the moment.

The fallacy here is the idea that national interest is some objective thing waiting only to be discovered. A great power does not find its interests. It chooses them. Which is why realists disagree wildly about what is, in fact, an American interest. They disagree not just about border issues, like Korea, but about core issues, like Europe. Tucker claims that Europe and Japan constitute the core of American national interest abroad. Layne calls for an American pullout. Both are certain that their position is dictated by considerations of national interest.

But beyond physical security, national interest dictates nothing. A superpower *claims* an interest. It is not given. Once a great power defines national interest beyond the terms of its own safety, it necessarily enters the realm of values. There are no objective criteria for deciding whether the Persian Gulf, Southeast Asia, Grenada, or even Europe are vital American interests. It depends on what you think we are to do in the world. To have any interest beyond one's boundaries and one's immediate security is, in other words, to talk about oughts.

Realists, of course, resist the word. The result is tautology. Robert Tucker writes of Soviet vital interests: "Where a policy of [Reagan Doctrine, anticommunist] liberation is materially injurious to Soviet vital interests, it entails a risk of confrontation with Moscow; where it entails no risk of dangerous confrontation, it is not materially injurious to Soviet vital interests and position." Apply this to, say, Nicaragua. How are we to know whether the Soviets will risk conflict over it? If it is a vital Soviet interest. How are we to know if it is a vital Soviet interest? By observing whether they are prepared to risk conflict over it.

The "pragmatic" variant of the "national interest" school, so appealing in principle is useless in practice. It provides no answer to the question of how to act. It forces a change only in the terms of the discussion. Instead of asking, "Shall we do X?" a policymaker is required to ask, "Is X a national interest?" But without a strict definition of national interest, he still does not know what to do.

There is a third way, originally conceived by Morgenthau, to define national interest, and it solves this problem. Morgenthau did not mean national interest to be a synonym for isolationism, nor did he mean it to be the semantic dodge offered by pragmatism. He meant something quite specific: interest defined as power. The pursuit of the national interest meant the pursuit of national power and the practice of balance-of-power politics in the classical 19th-century mode.

Realism as realpolitik. Finally, a definition that means something. But what are its implications? What is so striking about the realpolitik version of the national interest criterion is how little the foreign policy it produces differs, in practice, from that of the "ideological" foreign policy it attacks. The reason is, of course, simple: unlike the 19th century, the 20th century (and particularly the postwar world) has seen the superimposition of ideological conflict on traditional great power conflicts. Ideology and power overlap.

The overlap shows up dramatically even in Morgenthau's writing in the later 1940s. He criticizes Wilson for the way he took us into World War I: it was not to make the world safe for democracy, but to preserve the balance of power in Europe. But Wilson's decision was right, says Morgenthau. He says the same about FDR taking us into World War II. "For Roosevelt, as for Wilson before him, the war was being fought for universal humanitarian ideals," whereas, in fact, it was another balance-of-power exercise, not an ideological crusade. Most important, Morgenthau argues the same for the cornerstone of postwar internationalism, the Truman Doctrine. Another good policy, says Morgenthau, again justified for the wrong reasons. It was necessary to retain the traditional balance of power in the Eastern Mediterranean, rather than to launch an ideological war against totalitarianism.

Today the overlap is equally striking, and the reason obvious. The Soviet Union is not just an ideological opponent, but it is also the great rival to American power in the world. Take away communist ideology, and leave only an expansionist and dynamic Soviet Empire—which is the realist analysis of the world—and one might still choose American policies similar to those arrived at by way of ideological, Reagan Doctrine neo-internationalism. Containment, building alliances, even supporting anti-Soviet insurgencies can all be justified as balance-of-power instruments.

REALPOLITIK VS. NEO-INTERNATIONALISM

Neo-internationalists would not deny it. What, then, separates them from realpolitik realists? Two things. (1) Rationale: why we should intervene abroad, and (2) analysis: why others intervene abroad.

Rationale For the Morgenthauian, power is an end in itself. For the neo-internationalist, this is insufficient reason, particularly in a democracy, for intervention. Power must be in the service of some higher value. And that value is freedom, or more generally the spread of Western political norms: pluralism, (human) rights, and democracy.

The neo-internationalist does not deny that the spread of these values supports American power, nor that American power is needed to support the spread of these values. He does deny the central realist premise: that the purpose of such foreign exertions is the increase of America's power for its own sake.

He denies it because he does not believe it. He believes that the American conflict with the Soviet Union is not simply the blind struggle of two imperialisms, but a struggle with a moral meaning and a moral purpose; that, the emergence of political liberty being an episodic and unusual historical phenomenon, we live in a rare historical moment; that because of historical accident (the exhaustion of Europe in two world wars) the United States is the one nation on whom the success of liberty most depends; and that such a fragile commodity, which provides the philosophical basis of the American polity itself, is a good worth defending in and of itself.

Furthermore, the neo-internationalist denies that power is an end in itself because the American people do not believe it. Why have American leaders so consistently appealed to ideology? The reason is that America has no stomach for balance-of-power politics. Henry Kissinger, often considered the quintessential realist, knew that well. He always made sure to subordinate his realism to the requirements of ideology. There is a very strong—and, given America's geographic isolation, a very logical—native American instinct against intervention for any reason. If Americans are going to intervene in the world, it has to be for something more than just interest defined as power. It is interest defined as values.

Analysis And finally, the neo-internationalist denies that power is an end in itself because it is not clear that even our adversaries believe it. Here is where realpolitik realists and neo-internationalists part ways on analysis. Realism factors ideology out of international affairs. The axiom of realism, that nations naturally pursue interest defined as power, blinds one to the crucial connection between belief, however irrational, and foreign policy. (It also produces a paradox: If the pursuit of power for its own sake is the natural activity of states, why are realists always needed to teach it to them?)

Take away the ideological perspective, and one simply misses a crucial determinant of international action. It is perhaps imprudent—unrealistic—for the Sandinistas to pursue an internationalist foreign policy (proletarian variety), allying themselves with Cuba and the Soviet Union, and attempting to turn their neighbors into like-minded states by means of subversion. But that does not prove they are not doing so. It certainly does not prove that they do not want to do so. That requires empirical evidence.

Of course ideology alone does not dictate foreign policy. Not all countries ruled by Marxist-Leninists are pro-Soviet and anti-American. Yugoslavia and China are the outstanding counterexamples. Neo-internationalism does not deny that Nicaragua could, in principle, turn into a Yugoslavia or a China. It simply suggests that one judge the chances of that happening by examining the words, actions, and history of the Ortega brothers or Tomas Borges rather than by deciding what a "realist" Nicaraguan foreign policy would look like. After all, Nicaragua's intrinsic "national interests" could not have changed terribly much between 1978 and today. Its foreign policy has.

Ironically, it is the realist analysis that is trapped in dogmatism. It simply assumes that nations are driven by the quest for power, not by ideology. Realists are forever insisting, for example, that the Soviet Union is not messianic but simply imperialist. What is the basis for assuming that Gorbachev is driven in no part by a belief in the superiority of his social system? That is a proposition for which the evidence lies overwhelmingly on the other side.

THE CARDINAL SINS: UNIVERSALISM

Realists insist that their quarrel with neo-internationalism is about more than just rationale and analysis. The heart of their concern is consequences, the consequences of the great cardinal sins of internationalism: universalism and moralism.

Once ideology rather than national interest becomes the lodestar of American foreign policy, the United States becomes universally committed. This theme appears in every realist critique. JFK's ramparts of freedom are too vast. A commitment to freedom necessarily implies that it must be defended everywhere at all times, perhaps even at all cost. It becomes impossible to set priorities, impossible to practice prudence. Neo-internationalists will put an American under every tree. The consequences are clear: at home, ruinous cost and bankruptcy; abroad, overextension and disaster.

Morgenthau defined prudence as "the adaptation of morality to circumstances." Precisely. Why, then, the assumption that the moralist or ideologist cannot accomplish the same feat of adaptation? Neo-internationalism insists on the legitimacy of intervention, both on strategic and moral grounds. But legitimacy is a necessary, not a sufficient, condition for intervention. An ideologically founded neo-internationalism does not imply that no prudential judgment is required. After the question "Should it be done?" is answered, the question "Can it be done at reasonable cost?" must immediately follow. This holds true whether the answer to "Should it be done?" derives from considerations of power politics or ideology.

Take, for example, the East bloc version of internationalism. It is universal in hopes and goals, but prudent in practice. It ceded Grenada to overwhelming force without making threatening gestures elsewhere where it had a predominance of power. Nor has it committed itself to Nicaragua, where it is also in a position of relative weakness. There is no reason why a Western foreign policy, also universal in aspiration, need be any less prudent in application. Does anyone believe that if the Afghan guerrillas falter, Reagan Doctrine advocates would push for American troops to carry the fight?

A prudent neo-internationalism requires only that one keep in mind that a foreign policy based on the idea of freedom has two objectives: (A) assuring the security of the existing democratic world, and (B) attempting to promote democracy in places where it does not yet exist. The principal threat to these objectives is the Soviet Union. Therefore containing its power must be a primary obligation of an ideologically based foreign policy. (Hence the overlap with a foreign policy of pure realpolitik.) But it is not the sole obligation. (Hence the departures from a foreign policy of pure realpolitik.)

How does this play out in practice? Objectives A and B are usually compatible, as in, for example, U.S. support for revolution in Third World countries ruled by pro-Soviet, Leninist regimes, and U.S. support for democratic "third forces" in countries, like Chile or the Philippines, ruled by pro-American despotisms. In both cases, the imperatives to contain Soviet power and to promote freedom on the ground are in harmony.

But occasionally they are not, in which case prudence must adjudicate between them. Consider three examples.

China Should the United States enter into some alignment with China against the Soviet Union? First of all, any American foreign policy will have a negligible effect on internal Chinese developments. And there is no plausible democratic alternative to the regime in Peking. Thus objective B is not a consideration. And since a vigorous anti-Soviet China does weaken the Soviets' geostrategic position, and thus contributes to objective A, support for China is both prudent and wholly consistent with neo-internationalist ideals.

Taiwan Should the United States abandon Taiwan to strengthen ties with China? Since doing so would have a marginal effect on China's Soviet policy, but a major effect on the degree of freedom in Taiwan, the neo-internationalist answer must be no. (Note that if realpolitik is the only consideration, the second point should be considered irrelevant and sentimental.)

Cambodia Should the United States support the anti-Vietnamese insurgents? From the point of view of objective A, yes: the insurgency bleeds Vietnam and prevents it from consolidating control over all of Indochina. However, the leading guerrilla force is the Khmer Rouge, support for which must be incompatible with a foreign policy that proclaims the promotion of freedom as its objective. The Reagan Doctrine must exclude support for genocidists, or betray its ideological justification. (I have even come to the view that military aid—as opposed to rehabilitative and resettlement aid—to the non-Communist Cambodian insurgents is unjustified, so long as their contribution to the war is marginal and so long as it appears certain, as it now does appear, that any insurgent victory would mean the return to power of the Khmer Rouge.) Here is a case where consideration B overrides consideration A. Note, first, that if this were a life-and-death struggle, as was the war against Hitler, prudence would dictate the contrary conclusion: in such a case, alliance with Stalin, forerunner to Pol Pot, is permissible. Note, further, that in the Cambodian case ideology exerts a *restraining* influence on American foreign policy. Pure realpolitik would permit a more interventionist "universalist" policy of support for the Khmer Rouge.

The realists' claim that prudence is their exclusive property is so mystifying that it must be explained as deriving from the Vietnam experience. "If we had not been so ideologically committed, we would have gotten out earlier." But Kissinger and Nixon, who went to China in the midst of the war and who kept us in, in the hope of withdrawing on better terms, were hardly starry-eyed ideologists. They were perhaps the most realpolitik-oriented foreign policy leaders of the postwar era.

"What about, in the first place, getting into a war we couldn't win?" But we did not know we couldn't win. And as soon as we did, that was reason enough for both realist and neo-internationalist to get out.

"But the realist would have known that Vietnam was not a vital interest." What does that mean? In any calculation of realpolitik, control of Indochina and the acquisition of naval bases on the South China Sea must be considered strategic assets, for the United States and all the more so for the Soviet Union, which had no alternative bases in the region.

The point is not that Cam Ranh Bay was worth ten years of war. Only that invoking the realist phrase "national interest" does not tell you what cost Cam Ranh Bay would have justified. Was Grenada a vital American interest? American security was hardly vitally compromised while Grenada was in pro-Soviet hands. Does that mean the invasion was a mistake?

Realists are right that cost-benefit calculations need to be applied to intervention. But their application of this standard to interventions they don't like makes one suspect that they may be guided less by objective criteria than they claim. Consider the current warning that the Reagan Doctrine is economically ruinous and militarily dangerous. It is, in fact, in purely economic terms astonishingly cheap. Aid to the *contras* is now $27 million, and the administration wants $100 million. Even at that level it amounts to three-hundredths of one percent of the defense budget. Nor is the threat of "overextension" any greater. Reagan Doctrine intervention in Afghanistan and Nicaragua (and Angola, if aid is now "covertly" to go to UNITA) confronts Soviet expansionism without the expenditure of American lives and without any direct threat to the Soviet Union. If these are the consequences of universalism, then it ranks as one of the most cost-effective tools of American foreign policy.

THE CARDINAL SINS: MORALISM

Realism is left with one last charge against neo-internationalism, a charge that brings out what little passion realism permits itself. The charge is moralism. Morgenthau inveighed against "the moral disease of the crusading spirit in politics." Forty years later George Kennan ("Morality and Foreign Policy," *Foreign Affairs*, Winter 1985–86) has devoted 6,000 words to updating the argument.

"Government is an agent, not a principal," he writes. "Its primary obligation is to the *interests* [his emphasis] of the national society it represents, not to the moral impulses that individual elements of that society may experience." Note the false opposition. The opposition should be to "the moral impulses *of the national society*." If government is an agency, of course it should not bow to the impulses of individuals. But if government is an agency, why should it not be an agent for the moral impulses *of the society*? This Kennan does not say, though by linguistic device he pretends to have proved it should not.

Assume, for the sake of argument, that government should respond only to the interests and not the moral impulses of the national society. (Think, by the way, of how absurd this principle is if applied to domestic affairs.) Does it then follow that there is to be morality in the conduct of foreign policy? Is it all cynicism?

No, says Kennan. We should observe certain moral rules. First, avoid "the histrionics of moralism." This means act correctly "without self-consciousness or self-admiration, as a matter of duty or common decency." These are, however, matters of style. Kennan confuses etiquette with morality. Miss Manners for statesmen is not yet morality.

Kennan's second exception does require him to engage in real moral discourse. Notice what happens to the realist when he approaches this forbidden zone. Kennan opposes clandestine operations. He admits that Stalinist secret operations presented a great apparent danger to post-war Europe. For our part, however, we should not reciprocate. Why this exception to the anti-moralist rule? Because "excessive secrecy, duplicity and clandestine skulduggery are simply not our dish." (More manners.) And because we should prevent too many repetitions of operations like the capture of the *Achille Lauro* hijackers. He does say the American diversion of the plane bearing the hijackers was correct. "But such operations should not be allowed to become a regular and routine feature of the governmental process." (If the capture is justified, by what logic should operations like it not be?)

The anti-moralism of the stern realist comes to this: (1) Political morality should not be part of our foreign policy. (2) An exception is carrying out clandestine operations: they are not our dish. (3) An exception to this exception is the capture of the *Achille Lauro* hijackers. (4) Similar exceptions to the exception are not permitted.

A moral philosopher Kennan is not. However, the incoherence of his position results not just from tortured logic, but from the anti-moralist pose Kennan adopts. It must be so. No realist can possibly believe his own anti-moralist hard line. Therefore, when he tries to entertain moral considerations or acknowledge fundamental moral constraints, language fails him. Having forfeited a moral vocabulary, he is led to absurdities.

Consider. Kennan asks himself the obvious: Are not these restrictions on secret operations "a serious limitation on our ability to contend with forces now directed against us? Perhaps; but if so, it is a limitation with which we shall have to live. The success of our diplomacy has always depended, and will continue to depend, on its inherent honesty and openness of purpose. . . . "

Kennan wants to come out for honesty and openness—good idea—but he cannot use "moralist" language. So he must claim that they are the key to success in foreign policy. Really? The Soviets have achieved in 70 years perhaps the greatest foreign policy successes since the British empire; their diplomacy is hardly a monument to honesty and open-ness. Perhaps the most open and honest American diplomacy since World War II was conducted by Jimmy Carter. It was hardly crowned with success.

Anti-moralism leads to worse than absurdity. Consider Kennan again. He anticipates the charge that his anti-moralism might be taken as "an apology" for awful regimes. How could that be, protests Kennan, coming from "one who regards the action in Afghanistan as a grievous and reprehensible mistake of Soviet policy, a mistake that could and certainly should have been avoided?"

Now, this is taking moral neutrality to the extreme. Again, it is a direct result of the poverty of the moral language that the realist permits himself. The most Kennan can say about a Soviet "action" that lies somewhere between brutal tyranny and outright genocide is that it is a mistake, as in "Stalin's mistakes" or "Mao's deviations." Kennan adds that "certain of the procedures of the South African police have been no less odious to me than to many others." Certain procedures. This is moral mendacity of a high order.

That such speech should be a consequence of "the sterner require-ments of political realism" should give pause to realists, particularly since they are forever warning about consequences. The realist case against moralism is an argument about manners. It is opposed to moral preening. Fine, but that amounts to a case against moralizing, hardly a difficult one to make. The case against moral content in foreign policy simply turns on itself.

THE FUTURE OF REALISM

Realism finds itself at a historically awkward moment. It was born in opposition to Wilsonian utopianism. It flourished as a critique of liberal internationalism and its excessive faith in parchment barriers. When liberal internationalism split in two, it was the left isolationist heir that retained the utopianism and disdain for power that realism had always found so distasteful. And yet realism today does not direct much ammunition at this corner of the three-cornered debate. It concentrates its fire instead on neo-internationalism.

The principal reason is that neo-isolationism is in decline, and neo-internationalism, now centered around the Reagan Doctrine, in power. But there is irony here, since the great lesson of realism was its insistence on the centrality of power in international relations, and neo-internationalism fully absorbed that lesson.

Something else is needed to explain the vehemence of the realist attack on neo-internationalism and its relative neglect of neo-isolation-ism. There *is* another reason, and it provides a hint of where realism may be headed: many realists like where the neo-isolationists come out, even if they prefer a different route for getting there. Realism is not isolationism, but can be and seems increasingly drawn to it.

Realism and isolationism have no necessary affinity. Morgenthau's realism is, in principle, very expansive, and Morgenthau himself was a resolute opponent of isolationism. The pursuit of power is hardly a prescription for a passive foreign policy. But many of the new realists seem less inclined toward the notion of "interest defined as power" or to the practice of balance-of-power politics. They prefer to define interest as security, or define interest not at all, and retire.

We may, therefore, see a fracturing of the realist school paralleling the fracture of the liberal internationalism. One wing adopts a constricted view of American national interest, producing a minimalist form of realism. It finds common cause with left neo-isolationism, providing it, in effect, with a right wing. (The first stirrings: Anthony Lewis championed Layne's realism in the *New York Times*.)

The other realist wing, defining interest as power, finds common cause, on many issues, with neo-internationalism. (Morgenthau himself later adopted the view that the central fact of the U.S.-Soviet conflict was ideological and that power politics had to take that into account.) This school will still disagree with neo-internationalism on doctrinal foundation, on analysis, and on a range of issues. But its outlook would remain activist and interventionist.

The three-cornered debate may thus soon collapse into two. As debate about the Reagan Doctrine intensifies, alliances will form. Some realists, of the realpolitik school, will suppress their disdain for the ideological language of Reagan Doctrine neo-internationalism and take up its cause. But judging from the recent outpouring of realist writing, I suspect that most who call themselves realists will suppress instead their disdain for the ideological language of the left and take up the neo-isolationist cause. Some of these realists, like Kennan, will have no difficulty calling themselves neo-isolationists. Others will simply put forward more Marshall Plans II—and III and IV—and do neo-isolationist work, for which they will modestly decline to ask acknowledgment.

3

Gorbachev and the Third World

FRANCIS FUKUYAMA

Over the past five or six years, and particularly since the death of
Leonid Brezhnev in November 1982, a wide-ranging reassessment has
been taking place in elite Soviet policy circles concerning the Third
World.

This reassessment has led to a distinct shift in the way the Soviets
perceive and discuss developing countries, reflected in such documents
as the new party program published in October 1985, and the report of
General Secretary Mikhail Gorbachev to the recently concluded 27th
Party Congress.[1] Gone are the ringing offers of military and economic
support for the "liberated countries." Instead the program says only
that the Soviet party "has *profound sympathy* for the aspirations of
peoples who have experienced the heavy and demeaning yoke of
colonial servitude"—a tepid phrase used repeatedly by both Gorbachev
and his patron and predecessor, Yuri Andropov, to signal the limits of
Soviet support for Third World clients.[2] The radical "socialist-oriented"
states—regimes like Angola, Ethiopia, Nicaragua and Afghanistan that
came to power with the help of the Soviet Union and its allies in the
1970s—must, according to the party program, develop their economics
"mainly through their own efforts." The Soviet Union will provide
economic aid, training and defense assistance (in that order), but only
"to the extent of its abilities." The document then leaves the subject of
Moscow's Marxist-Leninist allies altogether and suggests that "real
grounds exist for cooperation [between the Soviet Union and] young
states which are traveling the capitalist road," that is, countries like
Argentina, Brazil, and the oil-producing nations of the Persian Gulf with
market-oriented economies and strong political ties with the West.

The significance of these unremarkable phrases is perfectly clear to
anyone who has followed past Soviet pronouncements on the Third
World. No more is heard the optimism of the previous party program
(adopted in 1961) that "a mighty wave of national liberation revolutions
is sweeping away the colonial system and undermining the foundations
of imperialism," or that socialism is capable of transforming "a backward country into an industrial country within the lifetime of a single
generation."[3]

Gorbachev's Party Congress address de-emphasizes the Third World.
Gone is the assertive self-congratulation found in Brezhnev's addresses
to the 25th and 26th Party Congresses in 1976 and 1981, in which he

celebrated advances of Soviet clients in Southeast Asia and Africa, noted the trend toward increasingly radical socialist solutions to economic development questions, and praised Moscow's military role in preventing the "export of counterrevolution." Gorbachev's speech omitted separate discussion of the Third World altogether, mentions not a single Soviet client by name, and accords no special status to "Socialist-oriented" countries.

The rhetorical turnabout implies a sharply diminished Soviet interest in the Third World—indeed, a profound disillusionment with the activism of the second half of the 1970s and its accompanying support for marginal Marxist-Leninist states.

But anyone expecting these shifts in Soviet pronouncements to signal a retreat from established positions will be disappointed. Soviet foreign policy in the early 1980s has stressed consolidation; the changing Kremlin leadership is disinclined to take on costly new commitments and hopes to limit the expense of existing ones. Such consolidation, however, has not led Moscow to contemplate seriously negotiating its way out of places like Afghanistan or Cambodia. Indeed, under Gorbachev the Soviets have demonstrated a renewed willingness to expend resources and to take tough measures to back up important clients like Angola, Afghanistan, Ethiopia and Libya.

II

Moscow's reassessment of the Third World is directed against the foreign policy legacy of the late Brezhnev years, that is, the period of extraordinary Soviet activism that began with the joint Soviet-Cuban intervention in Angola in 1975, continued through the second joint Soviet-Cuban involvement on behalf of Ethiopia in 1977–78 and Moscow's support for Vietnam's invasion of Cambodia in 1978, and culminated in the Soviet invasion of Afghanistan in December 1979.

The activism of this period resulted in an increase in the number of Moscow's Third World clients as well as a shift in the political character of its client base. The number of self-professed Marxist-Leninist clients rose from three (in addition to Moscow's traditional "bourgeois nationalist" allies like India, Syria or Algeria) in the mid-1960s to almost twenty a decade and a half later.

The new clients of the 1970s tended to be small, weak states, more susceptible to Soviet influence and control. They lent each other mutual support when threatened with "counterrevolution" and voted consistently with the Soviet Union in international forums. Angola, Mozambique, South Yemen, Afghanistan and Ethiopia established formal vanguard parties; these elite, centralized organizations modeled on the Soviet Communist Party provided an institutional basis for continued Soviet influence that would not be dependent on the fate or whims of individual leaders. With East German assistance these states set up internal security apparatuses to keep themselves in power.

The Soviets realized concrete military advantages, gaining access to new facilities in Vietnam, Angola, Ethiopia and South Yemen. The evident success of Soviet and Cuban intervention in bringing their friends to power gave Soviet foreign policy a dynamism and credibility that it had lacked. Soviet prestige also profited from the espousal of Marxism-Leninism by young radicals in the Third World—the latter being virtually the only people in the world who still seemed to believe in this moribund ideology.

Despite these evident successes, there was a dark side to the Soviet position in the Third World bequeathed by Brezhnev to his successors. The problematic character of this legacy was first discussed by officials responsible for Soviet Third World policy in the Central Committee's International Department before being taken up by the party's top leadership.[4] In this as in other areas of policy, Brezhnev's death in November 1982 seems to have broken a logjam, and it permitted a more thorough airing of three broad issues: the economic cost of the Third World empire, the impact on U.S.-Soviet relations of Soviet activism, and the poor economic and political performance of Moscow's recently acquired Marxist-Leninist allies.[5]

With regard to economic cost, it was clear that a number of political leaders resented the growing burden of military and economic assistance to Third World clients. In addition to the steadily increasing subsidy to Cuba (currently estimated at $5 billion a year), Soviet activism in the late 1970s saddled Moscow with costly new multibillion-dollar obligations to countries like Vietnam, Ethiopia, Afghanistan and Angola. The total cost of the Soviet empire rose, according to one recent calculation, from an estimated range of $13.6 billion to $21.8 billion in 1971, to between $35.9 billion and $46.5 billion in 1980.[6] At the same time, the growth rate of the Soviet GNP fell precipitously, due to a declining rate of growth in labor productivity. According to the CIA, the Soviet leadership decided to cut back the rate of growth in both investment and defense spending.

The most prominent critic of open-ended assistance to Third World clients was Brezhnev's immediate successor, Yuri Andropov. His statements reveal a consistent skepticism concerning heavy Soviet involvement in the Third World.[7] In June 1983 he delivered a lengthy statement setting forth his views on relations with the developing world in which he emphasized important qualifications on Soviet support:

> We contribute also, *to the extent of our ability*, to [the socialist-oriented states'] economic development. But on the whole their economic development, just as the entire social progress of those countries, can be, of course, only the result of the work of their peoples and of a correct policy of their leadership.[8]

These phrases would be repeated in the party program almost verbatim more than two years later, as would several others from that speech. Andropov was the first senior political leader to revive the dictum of Lenin and Khrushchev that the Soviet Union's chief influence on the world revolutionary movement comes about less through direct economic assistance than as a result of the force of its example as a developed socialist society. Put another way, the Soviet Union helps its friends best by helping itself first.[9]

The second point of criticism of the Brezhnev legacy concerned the impact of Soviet activities in the Third World on relations with the United States. Throughout the period of détente in the 1970s, Soviet spokesmen consistently asserted Moscow's "right" to support national liberation movements and simultaneously pursue normalized relations and strategic arms control with the United States. They resisted American attempts to link behavior in the Third World to overall East-West relations. Whatever the theoretical merits of this argument, by the end of the decade it was clear that the United States would not accept this Soviet interpretation of détente: the Soviet invasion of Afghanistan led directly to the Carter Administration's withdrawal of the second Strategic Arms Limitation Talks treaty from Senate consideration, just as the whole sequence of earlier Soviet interventions had poisoned the well of U.S.-Soviet understanding.

Since the early 1980s there has been evidence of a recognition in some Soviet circles of the deleterious consequences of Third World activism for the larger East-West relationship. Not surprisingly, this was most apparent among those Soviet commentators concerned primarily with relations with the United States. For example, both Fedor Burlatskiy, head of the philosophy department of the Institute of Social Sciences, and Aleksander Bovin, political commentator and occasional mouthpiece for Brezhnev and Andropov, suggested that measures be taken to insulate the central relationship from developments in the Third World, either through new superpower "rules" or through regional negotiations. During the "imminence of war" campaign to block Euromissile deployment, Andropov stated quite frankly that the worsening of relations between the United States and the Soviet Union under the Reagan Administration made Soviet support for Third World allies vastly more risky and less feasible.

The final criticism of the Brezhnev legacy concerned the emphasis placed on Marxist-Leninist regimes and vanguard parties. Moscow's favored clients of the 1970s did not, as a whole, prosper in the decade following their arrival in power. They tended to be economically backward even by Third World standards, states whose developmental problems were compounded by overzealous efforts to transform their economies along socialist lines. In Mozambique and South Yemen, agricultural production dropped sharply for several years in a row, and

Addis Ababa's (and Moscow's) inability to feed the Ethiopian population became an international scandal. In many parts of Africa, socialism
had increasingly come to be associated with poverty.

Perhaps more serious were political difficulties: precisely because
these regimes proclaimed adherence to Marxism-Leninism, they tended
to be narrowly based, lacking the broad nationalist legitimacy enjoyed
by the previous generation of leaders like Nasser, Sukarno and Nehru.
The fact that many of them had come to power with the help of the
Soviet Union, Cuba and other socialist states, or depended on them for
continuing support, made them suspect in the eyes of their own
populations.

It is by now a commonplace observation that for the first time a large
number of pro-Soviet Marxist-Leninist regimes—including Afghanistan,
Angola, Mozambique, Nicaragua, Cambodia and Ethiopia—have come
under attack by indigenous guerrillas, forcing Cuba, Vietnam and the
Soviet Union itself to deploy large numbers of combat troops in a
counterinsurgency role. In an ironic turnabout, Moscow now faces the
possibility of a Marxist-Leninist regime being overthrown by an anti-
communist national liberation movement, a prospect heightened by the
Reagan Administration's policy of supporting the guerrillas.

The Soviets, of course, nowhere openly admitted that their clients
were unpopular or faced domestic insurgencies. Nor was there unhappiness with the Marxist-Leninist vanguard party as the *theoretical* solution to the problem of influence in the Third World. What many Soviet
commentators did, rather, was to distance themselves from their
erstwhile allies and raise serious doubts as to whether the Marxism-
Leninism of countries like Angola, Ethiopia or Afghanistan was anything more than declaratory. By the early 1980s, the Soviet theoretical
literature was replete with remarkably frank criticims of self-proclaimed
Marxist-Leninist clients for such mistakes as "leftism," "voluntarism"
and making a "premature transition into socialism," admitting that
these errors had in many cases alienated the leaderships from the
"broad mass of the population."

The emerging consensus that most self-proclaimed Marxist-Leninist
clients were simply not sufficiently developed to permit their conversion
into genuine socialist societies was neatly summed up by Andropov: "It
is one thing to proclaim socialism as one's aim and quite another to build
it. For this, a certain level of productive forces, culture, and social
consciousness are needed."[10] The current party program continues this
downgrading of vanguard parties.[11] The civil war that broke out
between two Marxist factions in South Yemen in January 1986 could
only have confirmed Soviet skepticism, since it broke out within the
"vanguard" Yemen Socialist Party. The conflict demonstrated the tribal
mentality underlying the party's thin veneer of socialist ideology and

the weakness of Soviet control despite penetration by various socialist bloc states of South Yemen's party and internal security organs.

Indeed, the performance of the Third World Marxist-Leninist clients has been so poor that at least one influential Soviet official responsible for Third World affairs has suggested shifting emphasis away from them to large, geopolitically important countries with relatively well-developed economies like Mexico, Brazil and India.[12] This approach, endorsed in the 1985 party program, would seek to exploit the "contradictions" (i.e., conflicts of interest) between capitalist-oriented Third World states and the United States and other developed Western countries. It represents a return to a Khrushchevite catholicism toward the developing world without Khrushchev's illusions that countries courted by the Soviet Union would one day become communist.

The bottom line of the broad-ranging Soviet reassessment of the early 1980s is clear: the Soviet leadership would like to reduce the costs of its Third World empire in favor of the development of its own economy; within its empire, it would like to shift emphasis away from weak, narrowly based regimes to larger, more influential ones, even if this means cultivating capitalist-oriented states in place of Marxist-Leninist regimes. These conclusions are not those of some obscure academic specialist, but have been endorsed at the highest levels of the party.

But, to paraphrase Andropov, it is one thing to proclaim a new policy, and another to implement it. How has the critique of the Brezhnev legacy translated into current behavior, and how might it be manifested in the future?

III

Soviet interest in the Third World can be measured in two ways: by the risks Moscow is willing to take on behalf of clients, established or prospective; and in the military and economic resources it allocates to them.[13]

As evidence of a lower risk-taking propensity in the early 1980s, one can point to the fact that the Soviets have not intervened in the Third World on a scale comparable to their initiatives of the later 1970s, including their invasion of Afghanistan. While the absence of large interventions clearly reflects an absence of easy opportunities, it is not difficult to imagine certain instances in which the Soviet leadership could have exhibited less restraint. For example, Moscow did not move beyond routine airspace violations to attacks on Afghan mujahedeen bases and camps across the border in Pakistan in the face of steadily increasing U.S. support for the insurgency. Nor did it make serious efforts to sponsor Baluchi separatism and otherwise destabilize Pakistan, as some observers had feared at the beginning of the decade. The

Soviets have up to now been fairly cautious in marketing weapons to Iran or excessively adding to Persian Gulf instability by encouraging ethnic or religious separatism. The Soviets have been cautious in avoiding political contacts with the New People's Army in the Philippines, and even indulged in the misplaced opportunism of cultivating President and Mrs. Marcos as they were falling from power.

In Mozambique, Moscow's unwillingness to expend more resources has had a very damaging effect on its political position. The ruling Mozambique Liberation Front (FRELIMO) was a charter member of Moscow's "second generation" of clients and converted itself into a formal vanguard party in 1977. Since 1980 Moscow has merely stood by as Maputo gradually slipped further into the South African orbit, under the relentless pressure of a guerrilla war waged by the Pretoria-backed Mozambique National Resistance (RENAMO), and the regime's own economic mismanagement. While the Soviet Union increased its military and economic assistance for Maputo incrementally during the early 1980s and made symbolic gestures like the dispatch of naval combatants to Mozambican ports, it did not undertake a major intervention to rescue FRELIMO through, for example, the deployment of Cuban or Soviet combat forces. As a result, FRELIMO was forced to turn first to the West (including its former colonial masters, the Portuguese) and eventually to South Africa itself, a process that culminated in the March 1984 Nkomati ceasefire agreement.

Moscow's failure to provide Mozambique with economic assistance appears to have been much more critical in causing this turn than its failure to provide military security. In 1979, FRELIMO security chief Sergio Vieira warned his Soviet hosts that "economics is the key to a revolution's viability. We would not like to be a model of 'poor socialism'."[14] Between 1978 and 1982, Mozambique received an estimated $175 million in economic support from Moscow, less than one-tenth of the aid and credits received from Western countries during the same period. Moscow and its East European allies denied Mozambique membership in the Council for Mutual Economic Assistance when the latter applied in 1980, since this would have required a costly "leveling up" of its economy.

In spite of these examples, it is very clear that the reassessment has not implied an across-the-board slackening of commitment to important clients around the world. Even as Mozambique was slipping away from Moscow, the latter took considerable pains to protect its investment in Angola, where Soviet-Cuban prestige was much more heavily engaged.[15]

The Soviets concluded a multibillion-dollar military and economic aid package with the Popular Liberation Movement of Angola (MPLA) regime in Luanda in 1983. They also directed a major military offensive against Jonas Savimbi's National Union for the Total Independence of

Angola (UNITA) late in the summer of 1985 (in which Soviet advisers participated in the fighting down to the battalion level) and are currently preparing for another offensive in 1986. In these measures the Soviets again collaborated with the Cubans, who raised their troop presence from a low of perhaps 17,000 men at the beginning of the decade to the current level of approximately 35,000.

Indeed, if one surveys Soviet behavior in other parts of the Third World during the early 1980s, it is clear that Mozambique is an isolated case. Where necessary, the Soviets have been willing to take active military measures to support existing clients, even when involving risks comparable to those of the previous decade. The most significant of these was when Moscow deployed its own combat forces to man air defense sites in Syria in the aftermath of the 1982 Lebanon war. When the decision to deploy SA-5 missiles was taken in August or September 1982, Ariel Sharon was still Israel's defense minister; Moscow could not have known that it could remain aloof from a renewal of fighting between Israel and Syria.

The Soviets have been mounting offensives of steadily increasing intensity against Afghan mujahedeen positions in places like the Panjshir Valley each summer for the past five years, even as they conduct desultory talks on withdrawal with Pakistan. The Soviets supported not only the MPLA offensive against UNITA in 1985, but also Vietnam's dry-season offensive against the Cambodian resistance in November 1984. The Soviet presence in Southeast Asia has been growing steadily, with the stationing of Badger long-range bombers at their base in Cam Ranh Bay in late 1983. The Soviets have traditionally been very wary of providing Kim Il Sung with modern weapons for fear that he would go to war; but as a result of the North Korean leader's visit to Moscow in 1984, Moscow agreed to transfer to North Korea MiG-23 fighter aircraft.

By and large, Moscow has shown a similar willingness to pay whatever necessary to maintain its political position with established clients. The growth rate of its large subsidy to Cuba has tapered off somewhat since 1980 with the ending of the period of intense Cuban combat activity in Africa, but remains substantial, as does that of the subsidy to Vietnam. The Soviets concluded three multibillion-dollar arms deals with India in the early 1980s, which included rights to manufacture under license advanced MiG-27, -29, and -31 aircraft.[16] Soviet assistance to Nicaragua has mounted steadily, including a commitment for $200 million obtained by President Daniel Ortega during his visit to Moscow in April 1985. Deliveries to Moscow's major Arab clients—Syria, Iraq and Libya—have all increased during the 1980s, though economic considerations compete with political ones in explaining Soviet motivations. While military assistance to certain clients like Ethiopia and the two Yemens may have fallen slightly, this probably reflects the clients' lower immediate needs rather than an across-the-board decision to cut back.

Kremlinological evidence notwithstanding, early indications suggest that Gorbachev is, if anything, trying to stake out a more combative position in the Third World. Already during his tenure in office the Soviet Union has supported major offensives against the guerrillas in Angola and Afghanistan, and concluded a highly visible arms deal with Nicaragua in the immediate aftermath of Congress' voting down military aid to the "contras." In December 1985, Moscow provided Libya with SA-5 antiaircraft missiles just as a crisis between Washington and Tripoli over a terrorist incident was breaking.

Thus, whatever the practical policy consequences of the recent Soviet reassessment of the Third World, it is clear that they do not include a diminution of Soviet support for *existing* clients. This should not surprise us: retrenchment need not imply withdrawal and a sharply reduced willingness to live up to commitments, as it did for the United States during and after Vietnam. Soviet policy in the early 1980s is best described as a kind of "muscular consolidation," that is, greater caution in taking on new commitments, and concentration on the problem of protecting established Soviet positions. In the short run this has implied *increasing* levels of political and material assistance where it is already entrenched, despite a desire to reduce costs over the long term.

IV

This characterization of Soviet policies of the past few years does not seem to provide fully satisfactory answers to the issues raised by the internal reassessment. The period of consolidation has neither brought about substantial monetary savings—just the contrary—nor an appreciable change in the character of Moscow's client base. It is possible that this has been due to the prolonged succession process, which has brought three general secretaries to power in as many years and has weakened top-level direction of Soviet foreign policy. Can we expect a much sharper change in direction once Gorbachev consolidates his own domestic power base?

In the political sphere, Gorbachev's line of march is toward cultivation of key capitalist-oriented Third World countries—by implication at the expense of radical but weak Marxist-Leninist clients. Early evidence of this orientation may be Moscow's establishment of diplomatic relations with Oman and the United Arab Emirates in 1985. Such a shift fits in nicely with the multilateralist thrust of Gorbachev's overall foreign policy, which has sought to improve the atmospherics of Soviet relations with influential American allies in Western Europe and Japan. The Soviets, of course, have always kept open their lines of communication with the capitalist Third World; in the late 1970s, for example, Moscow assiduously cultivated the right-wing junta in Buenos Aires in order to protect its rapidly growing economic ties with Argentina.

But it is far from clear how a shift in emphasis to the capitalist Third World could be implemented much beyond the current state of affairs. Given the enormous amount of prestige invested in acquiring and keeping its Marxist-Leninist clients from the 1970s, the Soviet Union cannot abandon them now that the project of transplanting Leninism to the Third World has gone sour, any more than it could abandon bourgeois nationalist allies like India in the 1970s.

An example of Moscow's dilemma is Angola: however disappointing its performance, the Soviets are stuck with the MPLA, both in view of the efforts of the socialist bloc in 1975 to put it into place, and because of the special ideological status it was accorded in the past. A significant lessening of Soviet-Cuban support could very possibly lead to its overthrow by UNITA, and this in turn would have adverse consequences for the Soviet Union's status as a great power. The same is true of Afghanistan. Despite Moscow's encouraging noises about interest in withdrawal at the time of the November 1985 summit meeting between Gorbachev and President Reagan, the Soviets will have to consider carefully the implications for their worldwide position—including the situation in Soviet Central Asia itself—if they appear to be retreating under pressure from a Western-supported Islamic insurgency, an act that will inevitably look more like weakness than statesmanship.

Renewed emphasis on the capitalist Third World poses another problem as well: it is not clear what the Soviet Union has to offer large, geopolitically important states like Mexico and Brazil. Obviously, Moscow's package of internal and external security measures, so important to the survival of a small Marxist-Leninist regime like Angola, is of limited value to larger and more self-confident states. While the Soviets have had profitable economic dealings with Argentina in the past, their economic competitiveness in the Third World is dwarfed by that of the Western industrial countries, both as a market and as a source of technology or finished goods. Soviet relations with Brazil, which is itself a major exporter of arms, will never resemble those with South Yemen, let alone Cuba. The Soviet Union can at most hope to establish diplomatic relations with a few capitalist countries and play a marginally more important role in the politics of some regions.

In the economic sphere, the message of the recent reassessment is straightforward: concentrate on building the Soviet economy at home and discontinue pouring resources into dubious new Third World adventures. But it is difficult to see what opportunities Gorbachev will have for saving substantial amounts of money.

The lion's share of the Soviet "foreign assistance" budget for the Third World (including both military and economic aid) goes to Cuba and Vietnam, which occupy positions much like Israel and Egypt for the United States. If the Soviets are to conserve resources on a scale that will have any considerable effect on the domestic Soviet economy, they will have to start economizing here. In the Soviet view, however, Cuba and Vietnam are not even part of the Third World, but full-fledged "socialist" countries on a par with the East European allies; the Cuban and Vietnamese portfolios are not even handled by the Central Committee's International Department, but by the Liaison with Socialist Countries Department within the Central Committee. Like Israel and Egypt in the U.S. foreign assistance budget, their share of the pie may be virtually sacrosanct.

This means that budget cuts will have to be made in the tier of clients below Cuba and Vietnam—states like Angola, Ethiopia, Syria and India. But not only will the savings available from these clients be considerably smaller, any cuts will have much more damaging political consequences. The Soviet Union already has a poor reputation among its clients as a source of support for economic development, a factor that played an important role in the turn of countries like Mozambique away from the Soviet Union. Should Moscow decide nonetheless to cut current aid levels, the United States and other Western countries would obviously be presented with opportunities to encourage the defection of further clients from the Soviet camp.

The one area where Gorbachev has a much greater degree of flexibility is in deciding whether to take on new clients and commitments when opportunities arise. We can expect the present Soviet leadership to be more selective in responding to appeals for help from revolutionary movements or regimes than the Kremlin leadership of the 1970s, particularly if these appeals come from small radical Marxist-Leninist groups in weak, economically backward countries. But this conclusion can be stretched too far: the Soviets' postulated lower propensity to exploit new opportunities applies only to situations whose risks and benefits are comparable to those of the previous decade. It by no means implies that the Soviets would avoid cultivating relations with a communist Philippines, should the New People's Army ever take power after Marcos, or that Moscow would not intervene in a chaotic post-Khomeini Iran. In both cases, but particularly the latter, the risks and benefits are larger by an order of magnitude than adventures like Angola or the Horn of Africa; Moscow may find the potential gains so great as to overwhelm the restraining considerations.

Gorbachev's future choices are constrained in many ways. He does not have attractive alternatives either to exchange his current clients for ones of a higher quality, or to save substantial amounts of money. Indeed, it is likely that he will have to pay an incrementally increasing bill simply to stay where he is. As a new leader with little foreign policy experience, he has a strong incentive to demonstrate to both internal and external audiences a certain toughness in support of Third World allies that have come under open pressure from the United States. This may account for his initial stance in support of Angola, Afghanistan, Nicaragua and Libya. In the longer run, there is no reason why Gorbachev could not constrain Third World expenditures if he were willing to take some political risks. To date, Gorbachev has spoken a great deal about major reorientations in both domestic and foreign policy without making the fundamental structural reforms or concessions necessary to bring them about. If this also comes to characterize his policy toward the Third World, then the inconclusive pattern of behavior of the past five years is likely to persist for the remainder of the decade.

V

A crucial variable affecting the level of Soviet activism and commitment in the Third World is the policy of the United States. The Soviet reassessment was brought about in no small measure by America's somewhat belated reaction to Soviet activism in the late 1970s. As we have seen, the Soviets have taken some account of the subversive effect that their behavior had on the broader U.S.-Soviet relationship, and of how the arrival of a more belligerent Reagan Administration raised the dangers of superpower confrontation and therefore restricted Soviet options for supporting clients. In this respect the unraveling of détente that began in the late 1970s has had a salutary effect. American support for Afghan mujahedeen and the contras in Nicaragua (together with Chinese backing of the Khmer resistance and South African patronage of UNITA and RENAMO) have accentuated the problems of Moscow's clients by damaging Soviet prestige, costing the socialist bloc economic resources and effort, and forcing the Soviet political leadership to reconsider the wisdom of taking on such shaky commitments.

To the extent that the Soviets have been forced to reconsider the costs and consequences of Third World expansionism, the reassessment has been all to the good. But Moscow's unwillingness to discuss seriously negotiated solutions to regional conflicts—reflected in its unbending positions on Afghanistan and Cambodia—raises the question of whether the reassessment has gone far enough. Whatever second thoughts Soviet specialists and political leaders may be having, the Soviet Union cannot be compared to the United States at the close of the Vietnam War, with that conflict's massive impact on American elite opinions and social fabric. This suggests that the present would be an inopportune time to ease the pressure on exposed Soviet positions, which might relieve the Soviet leadership of the responsibility for making difficult decisions in the future.

At the same time, the admission of vulnerability implicit in the Soviet reassessment suggests that the moment might be right for a somewhat different emphasis in American policy. The United States can make use of a number of different instruments in dealing with the Soviets and their clients in the Third World, including outright military pressure, economic incentives of aid, trade and investment, or political and diplomatic means. The "Reagan Doctrine" thus far has primarily emphasized the first of these. Military pressure plays an extremely important role in driving up the costs of the Soviet empire. But since not one anti-communist insurgency is likely to defeat outright the regime it is fighting, military pressure alone is not likely to achieve a reduction of Soviet influence.

Nor will economic inducements work in isolation from other means. Much of the Soviet reassessment has centered around the costs of the empire, and many Western observers have pointed out that Moscow's inability to provide its clients with sufficient economic assistance is a major vulnerability that the West can exploit. But the Soviets have been aware of this problem too.

For some time they have been counseling their clients *not* to cut their economic ties with the global capitalist economic order and to accept Western assistance, while leaving their political/military security apparatus in the hands of the socialist bloc. The Soviets thereby maintain their political influence while allowing the West to pick up the economic bill. A good example of this was Ethiopia, where the Marxist-Leninist government received massive Western humanitarian assistance without changing its relationship to Moscow or having to alter the disastrous policies that were in large measure responsible for having brought on the famine in the first place. Showering Soviet clients with economic aid and investment without tying that aid to certain clear standards of political performance risks playing directly into Moscow's hands.

The United States needs to combine military pressure and economic inducements in a political framework reflecting the real possibilities of each Third World region. In a case like Afghanistan, this involves direct negotiations with Moscow to secure the eventual withdrawal of Soviet forces, while in most others it requires efforts to wean vulnerable clients away from their Soviet mentors. Earlier successful efforts to break clients out of the Soviet orbit, such as the U.S. courtship of Egypt in the 1970s and South Africa's handling of Mozambique, invariably involved a careful combination of military sticks with economic and political carrots. The Administration appears to be moving in this direction with President Reagan's proposal for regional negotiations in his speech to the U.N. General Assembly in October 1985. The choice of format for such talks requires careful consideration, however, since few countries can be expected to retreat from established positions or change sides altogether under the scrutiny of open negotiations.

Moscow will not be happy about attempts to break clients out of its orbit, and at some point will be forced to respond. It is important not to overestimate Soviet weaknesses, particularly in the military sphere, which traditionally has been an area of comparative advantage for Moscow. While the Soviets were embarrassed by UNITA's successes in the early 1980s, they eventually responded with massive aid to Luanda and a major offensive that seriously weakened Savimbi's organization, to the point where earlier Western hopes for the MPLA's overthrow have been replaced by fears for UNITA's survival. A similar scenario may unfold should the United States dramatically increase the quality of weapons going into Afghanistan.

But if the United States is willing to live with these risks in the short run, compelling the Soviets to escalate their economic and military investment in existing clients is not necessarily a bad thing. It will only underline their weaknesses and exacerbate existing Soviet resource allocation dilemmas. Through such policies the United States can hope that Moscow's reassessment of the Third World will not be a closed book, but will continue and deepen through the remainder of the decade.

NOTES

1. The party program is reproduced in *Pravda*, Oct. 26, 1985. An English translation has been published by the Novosti Press Agency Publishing House, *The Programme of the Communist Party of the Soviet Union*, 1985. The text of Gorbachev's speech appears in the 2nd edition of *Pravda*, Feb. 26, 1986.

2. Italics added. Gorbachev first used the word "sympathies" in his "inaugural" address following the death of Konstantin Chernenko. See *Pravda*, March 11, 1985.

3. The previous party program, adopted by the 22nd Party Congress, was published in *Pravda*, Nov. 2, 1961.

4. I am indebted to Stephen Sestanovich for many insights on this issue. See his article, "Do the Soviets Feel Pinched by Third World Adventures?" *The Washington Post*, May 20, 1984.

5. A fuller discussion of the Soviet debate is contained in the author's study, *Moscow's Post-Brezhnev Reassessment of the Third World*, Santa Monica, Calif.: The Rand Corporation, No. R-3337-USDP, February 1986.

6. Charles Wolf *et al.*, *The Costs of the Soviet Empire*, Santa Monica, Calif.: The Rand Corporation, No. R-3073/1-NA, September 1983, p. 19. Figures are in 1981 dollars and include Eastern Europe.

7. See in particular Andropov's speeches, "Leninism: Science and Art of Revolutionary Creative Effort," *FBIS Daily Report, Soviet Union*, April 23, 1976, and "Under the Banner of Lenin, Under the Party's Leadership," *Izvestia*, Feb. 23, 1979.

8. "Speech of the General Secretary of the Central Committee of the CPSU Comrade Yu. V. Andropov," *Kommunist*, No. 9, June 1983 (italics added.)

9. Naturally, following Andropov, a number of senior Soviet leaders repeated this formula, including Ivan Kapitonov, then Central Committee secretary for light industry, Geidar Aliyev, a full Politburo member and first deputy premier, and Boris Ponomarev, chief of the International Department of the Central Committee, now retired.

10. *Kommunist, loc. cit.*

11. This downgrading (already visible in Brezhnev's 1981 report to the 26th Party Congress) is evident in the program's reference only to "revolutionary democratic parties" rather than communist or Marxist-Leninist ones, and its call for ties with "all national progressive parties."

12. This official is Karen Brutents, currently a deputy of the Central Committee's International Department, who is likely to inherit overall responsibility for Third World policy in this critical bureau. See his articles in *Pravda*, Feb. 2, 1982, and Jan. 10, 1986, and in *Kommunist*, No. 3, February 1984.

13. "Risks," in this context, include the possibility of damaging the overall atmosphere of U.S.-Soviet relations, getting involved in a protracted local conflict, and losing face through overcommitment to an unreliable client. The risks of direct military conflict with the United States have arisen on occasion in Third World conflicts, but the Soviets have generally been eager to avoid them. Their unwillingness to assume such risks now is therefore not a particularly meaningful indicator of their intentions.

14. Quoted in Seth Singleton, "The Natural Ally: Soviet Policy in Southern Africa," in Michael Clough, ed., *Changing Realities in Southern Africa*, Berkeley: Institute of International Studies, University of California, Berkeley, 1982, p. 213.

15. Even in Mozambique, military restraint was probably due to simple prudence rather than the broad considerations raised in the reassessment. Soviet options for military intervention were very limited there, given Mozambique's proximity to South Africa and its distance from the Soviet Union, and the strength of Pretoria's stake relative to Moscow's. In any case, there is no evidence that FRELIMO ever requested a Soviet-Cuban intervention.

16. The net wealth transferred by the Soviets is of course less than military and economic aid disbursements since Moscow recoups a certain amount in hard currency sales, trade, debt repayment and guest-worker labor.

4

Eastern Europe and the Future of the Soviet Empire

VOJTECH MASTNY

For Moscow, whatever happens in Eastern Europe has an air of fatality. No other part of the world, apart from the Soviet Union itself, is as decisive in determining the future of the whole Soviet system of power. Not even relations with the United States bear so directly on the very existence of that system, except in the unlikely event of a war between the superpowers. Neither do relations with China, which Moscow can easily prevent from taking a dangerous turn. Eastern Europe is different because the six Warsaw Pact countries, though formally foreign, are, in effect, part of the extended Soviet homeland. As such, they are particularly vulnerable.

This peculiar relationship is the ambivalent legacy of Stalin, who considered the acquisition of an empire the main safeguard of Soviet security as he understood it. Yet, forty years later the empire has become a major source of Soviet insecurity. Only in Eastern Europe (except for the special case of Afghanistan), has Moscow felt repeatedly compelled to intervene by force in order to safeguard its interests.

As the empire was being formed in 1945, George Kennan anticipated with remarkable accuracy what might happen:

> Russian government now has a heavy responsibility to itself: namely, to hold the conquered provinces in submission. For there can be little doubt that many of the peoples concerned will be impatient and resentful of Russian rule. And successful revolts on their part against Moscow authority might shake the entire structure of Soviet power.
>
> The great question of Russia's new world position, as seen from Moscow, is whether the Soviet state will be able to carry successfully these new responsibilities, to consolidate its hold over the new peoples, to reconcile this with the traditional political structure of the Russian people, to make of its conquests a source of strength rather than weakness. This is the real question of Russia's future.[1]

Kennan derived his prescience from a keen sense of history—a quality more commonly attributed to East European, including Russian, than to Western political culture. For better or for worse, East Europeans have traditionally been inclined to look to experiences and antecedents for clues to their present predicaments. And in that longer-term perspective, the Soviet empire, like its predecessors, can only be regarded as a transitory one. Another American statesman with a historical bent, Henry Kissinger, remarked upon this elementary truth concerning the rise and fall of empires as he began his government career (although he did not find an appreciative audience when he applied his reasoning to the United States). As secretary of state under Ford, Kissinger also ventured to predict that there just might not be a Soviet problem to worry about in a generation or two.

However, the flaw inherent in such a long-term perspective is that predicting the inevitable is easier than estimating when and how it will happen. Nevertheless, it is possible and indeed necessary to pause and view the present as a stage in the process begun in 1945 (or, rather, in 1939 when Stalin, then in collusion with Hitler, first embarked on his quest for security through imperial expansion), and whose end cannot yet be foreseen. The historical vantage point can then help to account for what has changed over those years rather than to merely record what has remained the same.

What has remained the same is self-evident and not very enlightening: namely, the Soviet desire and determination to preserve control over Eastern Europe. However, the desire and the determination were not enough to prevent one country, Yugoslavia, from evading the Soviet grip even as the empire was being formed, or to prevent yet another, Albania, from following suit later on. The others that became part of the Soviet orbit in 1945 are still subject to Moscow's will, but that, too, has changed.

The differences in the internal conditions of the individual countries and in their relations with Moscow provide the true measure of the change that has taken place. There was once a time—from 1948 until shortly after Stalin's death—when the Soviet Union attempted systematically to turn all these countries into replicas of itself. Today, however, little is left of that quixotic attempt to make uniformity out of diversity in this notoriously heterogeneous part of Europe. So much have the historic differences reasserted themselves while new ones have been added that one is tempted to predict the region's relapse into nineteenth-century "Balkanization."

At that time, Eastern Europe was reputed to be the powder keg of the continent, and not without reason. Certainly the uncontrollable dynamism of the local nationalisms partly explains the origins of World War I. It has been argued more recently—significantly, though, not by any professionals whose area of expertise is Eastern Europe or the Soviet Union—that the region could again explode and even bring the superpowers into the fray.[2] Soviet spokesmen, to be sure, have not been averse to promoting the self-serving image of their country as the supposedly indispensable *Ordnungsmacht* which alone is capable of keeping the lid on this caldron of nationalist passions. After Moscow's 1968 intervention in Czechoslovakia, for example, President of the Supreme Soviet Nikolai Podgornyi insinuated in a conversation with United States Ambassador Jacob Beam that this action prevented "the beginning of another World War."[3]

The argument evokes the preposterous image of the Soviet Union as something of an updated nineteenth-century Britain, which preferred to keep the unruly peoples of the disintegrating Ottoman Empire under its tutelage for the sake of international stability. But if there exists a resemblance with a great power of that era, it is more with Austria-Hungary. And the similarities are not encouraging for Moscow—despite the definite nostalgia among today's East Europeans who, in view of their subsequent experience with the alternatives, have been quite inclined to regret the disappearance of the empire that their forefathers had so readily helped to dismantle.

A sense of the diminishing vitality of the ruling nationality, increasingly outnumbered by other ethnic groups that are resentful of its claim to predominance, is as alarming for Moscow as the growing political impasse in Eastern Europe, reminiscent of Austria-Hungary's declining years. But in Austria-Hungary at least intellectual creativity flourished, resulting in much imaginative thinking about how the empire could be revitalized by accommodating the diverse interests of its components—before the accident of World War I rendered all of this obsolete. The sterility of mind that is the hallmark of today's Soviet polity provides a striking contrast.

How much of a powder keg is Eastern Europe today in comparison with the years before 1914? The changes that have taken place in the area tend to accentuate the differences rather than the similarities between the crisis that provoked World War I and the present condition of the world. Admittedly, following the 1919 peace settlement, which was widely resented throughout Eastern Europe, the region remained full of international problems; on balance, however, these began to diminish until outside powers, namely Germany and Italy, chose to exacerbate them for their own purposes during the 1930s. Thus, if World War II also came from Eastern Europe, this was not the consequence of any of its persisting problems, but rather the quite avoidable result of the ambitions entertained by the Fascist powers eager to manipulate some of its frustrated peoples as their pawns.

World War II, to be sure, rekindled nationalist excesses in Eastern Europe—as it did in other parts of the world. But it also generated new efforts to overcome divisive nationalism by creating some structure of regional cooperation—witness, for example, the Polish-Czechoslovak or Yugoslav-Bulgarian confederation projects. These efforts never came to fruition not because they were imperfect, but because the Soviet Union was bent on a very different kind of international settlement. Soviet-made order was imposed arbitrarily upon unwilling populations that, even after a change of generations, have merely acquiesced to it without ever accepting it as the normal state of affairs. For the first time in history, Eastern Europe became integrated under the auspices of a single imperial power rather than several of them. Moreover, this new hegemonial power, regarded by its foreign subjects as inferior in almost every respect except sheer size and brute force, proceeded to mold them more thoroughly in its own image than any of its predecessors had ever attempted.

The common experience of the East Europeans under Moscow's domination has produced a unifying effect by generating a resentment that has tended to overshadow persistent national animosities. Moreover, the nature of these animosities has changed. Boundaries are no longer being seriously contested—a tribute to the accomplishment of the peacemakers of 1919 who drew most of them. (A notable exception is the altered boundaries that the Soviets arbitrarily imposed during World War II on the Baltic peoples and the Poles. Significantly, these created the deepest and most lasting resentments.) Also, little is left of that parochial nationalism that breeds hatred out of ignorance and physical isolation. Even if they are not deeply in love with each other, East Europeans today at least know each other better. Their movement across national boundaries, if restricted by Western standards, is more extensive than it has ever been. And thanks to the revolution in mass communications, which gives them access to Western media, they are among the best-informed people in the world.

The process of political maturation in Eastern Europe makes a renewed outburst of nationalistic passion unlikely. Certainly such an outcome is less likely there than in many other parts of the world, including parts of Western Europe—witness the examples of Northern Ireland or the Basque country. The crisis that shook Poland to its foundations has been a model of moderation by comparison. It demonstrated political subtlety and a sense of responsibility all the more remarkable for a people not previously reputed to possess an abundance of such qualities. Hardly anyone in Eastern Europe today seriously argues that it is possible or even desirable to attempt to break out of the Soviet bloc in the foreseeable future—even those who find Moscow's domination intolerable. The memory of the failed Hungarian uprising of 1956 reinforces such doubts.

But the history of Eastern Europe since that landmark year has been replete with other challenges to the Soviet-imposed order. Mounted with great resourcefulness, these challenges have never ceased to amaze outsiders. Their conspicuous inability to anticipate events in the region has accentuated the precariousness of the so-called Yalta order of a divided Europe, which not only the Soviets but many Westerners—albeit for different reasons—would rather see as permanent.[4] And the challenges, each more subtle and complex than its predecessor, have found the Soviet Union increasingly ill-equipped and reluctant to act effectively.

In 1968 the Czechoslovak reformers' attempt to revitalize Marxism by giving it a "human face" challenged the very essence of Soviet communism. In his article of May 1945, Kennan anticipated that Moscow's newly acquired western lands could become the same hotbed of ideological contagion for the Soviet empire as they had been for the tsars.[5] And although the Czechs professed the same ideology as the Soviets themselves, their challenge to the Kremlin rulers was no less revolutionary than that posed by the radical Socialists from the western lands to the tsar's autocracy before World War I. It mattered little that the Prague reformers wanted to change the system from within in an evolutionary way; if brought to the logical conclusion, their efforts would eventually have led to something very similar to democracy.

But by 1968 Marxism was no longer the foundation of Soviet rule in Eastern Europe, if it ever had been. During their stormy meetings with the Czechoslovak Politburo at the height of the crisis, Brezhnev and his associates left no doubt about their contempt for any Communist idealism.[6] Their attitude marked the distance traveled since the time when the spread of Soviet power was identified with the spread of communism, emphasizing the futility of any attempt to reform the system by revitalizing its ideology. Communism with a human face has been discredited not because the Soviet intervention did not give it a chance to succeed, but because even its erstwhile proponents concluded that such a notion was a contradiction in terms.

In any case, never again would Soviet power in Eastern Europe be challenged by introducing an alternative version of Marxism. Not only has the doctrine lost the necessary appeal, but the putative alternative has also lost relevance in view of the fact that Soviet rule rests simply upon power. As Kennan wrote in 1945, Soviet policy "has behind it no great idea which could inspire the various peoples of the area and bind them together into a single political entity with a single purpose. Pure Marxism is dated."[7] Hence, the restabilization of the empire that followed the intervention in Czechoslovakia did not involve a reimposition of uniformity on the basis of a common ideology. Instead, the Soviet Union has been tolerating considerable diversity while trying to reinforce the relationships of political and economic dependence to circumscribe the freedom of action of the different countries. Ideological incentives to maintain the cohesion of the bloc have thus been replaced by material ones, and military compulsion always looms in the background as a last resort.

But Moscow has also been trying to reduce its subsidization of Eastern Europe in order to turn the economic liability into an economic asset. On the one hand, in the mid-1970s it hardened the favorable terms of trade that the East Europeans had so far been enjoying with the Soviet Union, particularly in regard to fuel and raw materials. On the other hand, it let them seek access to Western credits, advanced technology, and even consumer goods. Whether Moscow allowed this politically risky development by design or by default, Eastern Europe's growing economic interdependence with the West—far more extensive than what the Soviet Union itself ever risked in regard to its own, more robust economy—proved profoundly destabilizing by the end of the decade.

The Polish crisis, which ended a decade of the region's temporary stability, was of a different kind altogether. Although the economic breakdown which discredited the Polish regime served as the catalyst of the crisis, the challenge to Soviet rule was more subtle and ran deeper. Having learned from both the Hungarian and the Czechoslovak experiences, the Poles tried neither to break out of the Soviet bloc nor to reform it from within. Instead, the Polish opposition applied pressure on a weakened regime from without in an effort to compel it to specific concessions that would eventually change it. At issue was not assuming the responsibility for government but rather influencing the manner in which it governs. The challenge was embodied in a spontaneous yet highly disciplined mass movement that was neither violent nor ideological, but rather profoundly political and, as such, particularly difficult to grapple with.

Apart from the special difficulty of dealing with Eastern Europe's most populous and most anti-Soviet nation at a time of unprecedented economic distress, the elusive political character of the Polish crisis sufficiently explains the extreme Soviet reluctance to intervene directly or militarily. It took Moscow more time than it had taken in Czechoslovakia or in Hungary (or in East Germany in 1953) to meet the challenge, and, arguably, it was never really met. Perhaps because the Russians abstained from assuming full responsibility for a solution, there has been no solution. Ultimately, the problem was one of political participation, and the martial-law regime that denied such participation has been unable to make much progress toward even its stated goals—other than the restoration of order in a very narrow sense of the word.

While one may easily understand the Soviets' decision not to intervene militarily, it is much harder to understand the manner in which they ultimately did intervene—which is, incidentally, far more suggestive of future trends than a military invasion. Although Moscow undoubtedly approved of the coup by the Polish military in December 1981 (though perhaps only after its successful execution), conclusive proof that General Jaruzelski and associates acted as simple Soviet agents is still not (and may never be) available. What the Polish events did prove was the existence in Eastern Europe of power groups that have vested interests in the status quo and are willing and able to act to preserve their prerogatives—motives not necessarily inspired by Moscow.

The particular interests of such groups may or may not coincide with those of the Soviets. In the Polish case, there apparently has been a broad coincidence. The Romanian situation, however, offers no such converging views. Similarly, the interests of the ruling groups may or may not coincide with the preferences of their subjects. Such a coincidence exists to a large degree in Hungary and, perhaps, in a different sense, in Bulgaria, but not in Czechoslovakia or East Germany.

At a time of protracted leadership weakness in Moscow, dating from the last years of Brezhnev, the ascendancy of the East European elites as political actors in their own right is a portentous development. Under such circumstances, the presence of a relatively new and untried leadership in Moscow can provide some of its more established and experienced counterparts in Eastern Europe with opportunities for enhancing their freedom of action if they wish—not against Soviet interests but rather in areas where the Soviet Union has been unwilling or unable to define its interests. And considering the magnitude of both domestic and international problems at hand, such areas are likely to be expanding rather than contracting.

How have the East European regimes availed themselves of the opportunities inherent in this extraordinary situation? In very different ways, and in accordance with their respective political cultures. Again, similar challenges tend to accentuate the historic differences among the six countries which their different experiences under Communist rule have further magnified.

Bulgaria has the distinction of having been ruled by the longest continuously functioning leadership in Soviet Eastern Europe—that of Todor Zhivkov. The record of this leadership indicates a most pervasive pro-Soviet conformism, sustained among the populace by the region's last relatively intact tradition of Russophilism. It is true that, to some extent, appearances have been deceptive; the historic stereotype of Bulgaria's willing acceptance of all things Russian has been belied, for example, by the attempted military coup in 1965 which, though not anti-Soviet, aimed at securing for Bulgaria something more than a semblance of partnership.[8] Since the conspicuously lenient suppression of the plot, the regime has accentuated the nation's historic identity while dwelling on the allegedly total harmony of its interests with those of the Soviet Union, but it has also been seeking Moscow's recognition as a particularly valuable partner in common ventures abroad.

In the pursuit of these frequently shady ventures—witness Bulgarian involvement in the attempt to assassinate Pope John Paul II—the Bulgarians have displayed much greater sensitivity to their reputation than has the Soviet Union. But the desire to maintain a good reputation in the West is hardly enough of an incentive to justify a substantial departure from the present course. Nor does the relatively good condition of the Bulgarian economy—always favored by Moscow as a showcase of Soviet-style central planning and therefore unencumbered by excessive indebtedness to Western creditors—provide such an incentive. Even after Zhivkov departs from the scene, which can happen momentarily, his successors are less likely to feel an urge to expand their freedom of action than are their counterparts elsewhere in the Soviet bloc.

Among them, the Romanians have gone the farthest in securing such a freedom for themselves. They have demonstrated impressive skill in ascertaining, and quite possibly stretching the limits of, Soviet tolerance. They have also managed to exploit it to a degree hardly imaginable at the time when Stalin insisted on subjugating their country with exemplary thoroughness. Nor could he, having ranked it near the top of his strategic priorities in Eastern Europe, have suspected that Romania would, for his successors, rank near the bottom.

But what has been the value of the Romanian accomplishment—other than providing a sense of satisfaction to the family of Nicolae Ceausescu and his sycophants, possibly the most corrupt ruling group anywhere in Europe? A victim of economic mismanagement second only to Poland, Romania's standard of living is the lowest in the Soviet bloc while its record of domestic repression, including suppression of ethnic minorities, is among the worst. Its relatively independent foreign policy, never more than an irritant to Moscow, has been yielding diminishing returns. Not surprisingly, therefore, the quest for autonomy Romanian-style, with its special brand of autocracy and nepotism, has not been emulated nor is it likely to be.

The present Polish regime resembles the Romanian one in its narrow social base of support, managerial incompetence, and proclivity for repression. But while Ceausescu started out as a recognized champion of nationalism and has still retained that aura among many of his compatriots, Jaruzelski and his cohorts have never ceased to be viewed as traitors by theirs. Moreover, they have faced more pressing problems both in keeping the Soviet Union reassured and in managing at least a modicum of domestic consensus.

It is ironic that the regime which theoretically should enjoy the greatest freedom of action because of its indispensability to Moscow (it prevented further erosion of the Soviet position in Poland after all other alternatives had failed) is probably incapable of realizing the potential. In contrast to the Byzantine subtlety of the Romanians, the Polish rulers have thus far manifested disproportionate rigidity and arrogance. Such attitudes are perhaps to be expected whenever the military has traditionally been accorded too much social prestige. (Significantly, strongmen in uniform with successful political records are usually those who had been politicians first; for example, Pilsudski in prewar Poland, to whom Jaruzelski bears so little resemblance.) In any case, what distinguishes the present Polish leadership from the Bulgarian one is not so much its unwillingness to formulate and pursue its own interests as its inability to do so.

In this respect, Poland may be trailing even behind Czechoslovakia, though in a rather curious way. On the one hand, Prague has done something Warsaw has not: It has publicized its people's unhappiness about a crucial Soviet foreign policy decision—the deployment of Soviet missiles on its territory. Admittedly, this has been done gingerly and indirectly—by reporting about "stacks" of critical letters received by the party newspaper—but it has been done all the same.[9] On the other hand, this most profoundly reactionary government in all Eastern Europe has preserved its familar propensity for outdoing even Moscow as a vociferous defender of orthodoxy. Not only has it been overzealous in publicly condemning any deviations occurring in other "fraternal" countries; it has also excelled in abusive words and actions with regard to the West.

In Czechoslovakia, the advent of more imaginative and less crude policies has been made difficult not because its problems are not sufficiently grave, as may be the case in Bulgaria, but because they are creeping rather than acute, and thus harder to address. In Chapter 77, for example, the Prague regime has had as an adversary the most long-lived organized dissident group in Eastern Europe; yet the group is minuscule and, for the most part, isolated amidst a politically passive population. Nor has the religious revival among Czech youths—a novelty in this country's pervasively profane society—been a challenge whose significance can be easily ascertained. There are other creeping challenges—from the obsolescent industrial plant to an alarming environmental deterioration—that may call for decisive action, yet they are unlikely to rouse a regime that has survived by immobility.

As in Czechoslovakia, the Soviet missile deployments have become an issue in East Germany, only more conspicuously. Opposition from Protestant churches has been publicized there sympathetically by a regime otherwise reputed to be Moscow's most reliable satellite.[10] But the reputation can be misleading; it has never implied the same degree of obsequiousness that has been the hallmark of offical Czechoslovak political culture. The most insecure of all Eastern European states because of its artifical origins and persistent uncertainty about its very *raison d'être* in view of higher Soviet interests, the regime in the German Democratic Republic (GDR) has had to try harder than others to impress upon Moscow its indispensability. Its systematic effort in that direction has amounted to a coherent policy of national interest as determined by the ruling group—more coherent than anywhere else in the Soviet bloc with the possible exception of Romania. However, unlike in Romania, there are implications for the future.

The pursuit of this peculiar "national" interest by the astute men in power in East Berlin has occasionally collided with Soviet wishes—as in 1971 when Walter Ulbricht went too far in trying to obstruct Moscow's incipient normalization of relations with Bonn, and thus was removed. But unlike then, when the Soviet Union had to teach the East Germans a lesson about how such relations ought to be handled, now a different sort of lesson seems to be driven home. By their rapprochement with Bonn at a time when Soviet relations with the West are all but frozen, the East Germans are implicitly demonstrating that more trade and fewer missiles may not be only in their own but also in Soviet interest.[11] And the Russians, who in 1968 had been so outraged at the Czechs' particular attempt to define the common interest, have proved this time more willing to listen—or at least more willing to tolerate the experiment, their veto of Party Secretary Erich Honecker's planned visit to West Germany notwithstanding. In effect, a strong government of a client state has been seizing the initiative from a weak government of the dominant power in a bid for more partnership rather than mere subordination. Such a trend, if it persists, would amount to a novelty deserving close attention.

A bid for more partnership with Moscow does not necessarily make a regime more popular with its own people. Yet the East German one has taken steps in that direction as well, and in doing so has assumed risks. The easing of restrictions on emigration, which enabled thousands of disgruntled GDR citizens to leave the country, has seriously compromised its purported claim of absolute loyalty to a Communist regime. That the concession has been largely purchased by West German money does not detract from its significance, for it shows that matters of principle previously regarded as sacrosanct are now for sale. Thus, East

Germany has emerged rather unexpectedly at the forefront of developments in a part of the world where other countries used to be harbingers of the unexpected.

Among these, Hungary continues to figure prominently for its efforts to expand its autonomy—with, rather than against, the Soviet Union. Like his East German counterparts, János Kádár has long succeeded in persuading Moscow of his indispensability, having started out as the rare party figure of any stature in his own country who had not been discredited before the 1956 revolution. Not only has he proved his personal indispensability, but, unlike his Polish counterparts today, he has also been able to overcome the consequences of the 1956 upheaval by measured repression and conciliation, presiding eventually over a government that boasts both a measure of popular acceptance for its moderation unmatched in Eastern Europe and Soviet respect for its effectiveness.

The secret of the Hungarians' success has been in adapting the Soviet form and giving it another substance without advertising the transformation. Their collectivization of agriculture has been exceptionally productive while maintaining a "human face," which it does by providing extensive concessions to private enterprise. And the Soviets, well aware that the experiment is not applicable to their own problems, have been contemplating it with fascination and perhaps envy instead of alarm. In effect, they have acknowledged that the Eastern European way can be better than the Soviet way—a proposition the Hungarians have now tried to elevate to a principle. As Central Committee member Mátyás Szürös wrote in the January 1984 issue of *Társadalmi Szemle*, the problems of individual states of the Soviet bloc "do not call for uniform solutions, but much more for methods that make optimum allowances for [national] characteristics," adding that "national interests can be subordinated to common interests only in an extraordinary situation."[12]

Assuming the avoidance of situations liable to be defined as extraordinary, what are the prospects for Eastern Europe as part of the Soviet empire? A decade ago, in December 1975, the same question was raised at a discussion during the meeting of American diplomats in London, where Helmut Sonnenfeldt coined the phrase "organic relationship"— a term that later caused much outrage by its apparent legitimation of the Soviet domination of the area.[13] Whatever the consequences of the London discussion, it began a much-needed effort to view current trends in a long-term perspective, thus giving policy a better sense of purpose.

The concept of an organic relationship as originally formulated in 1975 presumed that the kind of relationship with the Soviet Union imposed upon the East Europeans as part of the "Yalta order" was unnatural and therefore dangerous. According to Sonnenfeldt, it had to be replaced by a system which, while recognizing the geopolitical realities of predominant Soviet interest in the region, would be based on more solid foundations than sheer power. Otherwise, in his opinion, Eastern Europe's centrifugal forces might "sooner or later explode, causing World War III."[14]

Since these words were uttered, Eastern Europe has grown even more unstable and heterogeneous. Many developments, particularly those in Poland, have demonstrated the diminishing viability of the system that prescribes to different peoples the domestic political structures of Moscow's choice. But these developments have also demonstrated that this unnatural state of affairs need not explode into a World War III; formidable inhibitions are in effect on all sides.

The more organic relationship between Moscow and its dependencies was first advocated against the background of a dramatically rising Soviet power, and as a response to it. Today Soviet power, huge though it is, is no longer as dynamic as it used to be, and many Soviet triumphs have been jeopardized by internal weakness or offset by Western gains. For several years now there has been a weak leadership in Moscow but not in Washington. In Soviet terms, the "world correlation of forces" can hardly be regarded nearly as favorable for Moscow as it was in the heyday of détente.

However, during the last decade, the Soviet Union has made little, if any, progress in making its rule in Eastern Europe more palatable and less dependent on power alone. It has not managed, or even tried, to revitalize the ideological foundations of its hegemonial claim. It has relied increasingly on economic compulsion, not on economic incentives. In fact, the economic benefits of the Soviet system have declined both for the ruling nation and its subjects. Moscow has to subsidize much of Eastern Europe, while its inhabitants continue to believe—rightly or wrongly—that the Soviet connection is the reason for their material backwardness. And the economic gap between East and West is meanwhile growing, not diminishing.

This continued inability of the Soviet Union to base its rule in Eastern Europe on anything else but sheer power—whether military, political, or economic—may be unfortunate, but seems unlikely to change. The future of the troubled empire seems rather to depend on whether the Soviets will feel compelled to modify the only relationship they are able to have by reducing its power content—out of necessity, to be sure, rather than of any conviction about the merits of retreating from power. There are few signs of change in the possible Soviet conduct that the West can less afford to miss.

In August 1983 the *Observer* referred to Hungarian sources in reporting a recent Kádár-Andropov meeting. On the agenda was supposedly the possibility of a reunited Germany in a neutralized Europe free from both Soviet and American troops.[15] The feasibility of the proposition or the accuracy of the report are open to question, but the subject is significant. Regardless of Andropov's demise, discussions involving a radical redefinition of Soviet security interests are bound to be taking place in the Kremlin—probably with inconclusive results.

In this novel setting, the East European leaders can, if they so choose, impress upon their Soviet counterparts the notion that partnership rather than mere subordination is an idea whose time has come. If, as a result, the Soviet empire subsequently evolves in the direction of a looser commonwealth, this may or may not benefit the peoples involved. Nor, for that matter, would the evolution necessarily be welcome to the West which, after all, has flourished while the Soviet Union has maintained its oppressive rule in Eastern Europe. But in the new situation, the answers to both of these questions would be found less in Moscow and increasingly in the different national capitals in the region. The United States and other Western countries would then have much greater opportunity to influence the outcomes. And if those outcomes fail to meet their expectations, it would no longer be easy to simply blame the Russians.

NOTES

1. George F. Kennan, *Memoirs, 1925–1950*, (Boston: Little, Brown, 1967), 533.

2. For an example of the argument by a specialist in American foreign policy, see Roy E. Licklider, "Soviet Control of Eastern Europe: Morality versus American National Interest," *Political Science Quarterly* 91 (Winter 1976–77): 619–28.

3. Quoted in Adam B. Ulam, "Why the Status Quo in Eastern Europe Is a Threat to Soviet Security," in *Détente*, George Urban, ed. (New York: Universe Books, 1976), 213.

4. The case for a partitioned Europe is argued in A. W. DePorte, *Europe between the Superpowers: The Enduring Balance* (New Haven, Conn.: Yale University Press, 1979).

5. Kennan, *Memoirs*, 534.

6. Zdeněk Mlynář, *Nightfrost in Prague: The End of Humane Socialism* (New York: Karz, 1980), 237–41.

7. Kennan, *Memoirs*, 537.

8. James F. Brown, *Bulgaria under Communist Rule* (New York: Praeger, 1970), 173–87.

9. "Adverse Reaction to Soviet Missiles Seems to Be Growing in Czechoslovakia," *Soviet East/European Report* (Radio Free Europe/Radio Liberty) 1 (1 January 1984), 1.

10. "East German Party Daily Prints Church Letter Urging Bloc Nations to Begin Disarming." *Soviet/East European Report* 1 (15 November 1983), 1.

11. James Markham in the *New York Times*, 2 June 1984.

12. "National Interests Given Higher Priority than Internationalism by Hungarian Official," *Soviet/East European Report* 1 (14 February 1984), 1. For the follow-up, see "Soviet Union Joins Warsaw Pact Debate on National Interests vs. Internationalism," *Soviet/East European Report* 1 (1 June 1984), 1.

13. "State Department Summary of Remarks by Sonnenfeldt," *United States National Security Policy vis-à-vis Eastern Europe (The "Sonnenfeldt Doctrine")*, 94th Cong., Committee on International Relations, House of Representatives, Hearings before the Subcommittee on International Security and Scientific Affairs, 12 April 1976, 41–44.

14. Ibid., 43.

15. Lajos Lederer, *Observer* (London), referred to in *The German Tribune*, 14 April 1983.

RELIGIOUS AND ETHNIC NATIONALISM

5

Misunderstanding Africa

XAN SMILEY

Heavy self-censorship is a standard feature of reporting by Western journalists everywhere in the Third World, but nowhere is it more rigorously in force than in black Africa. For one thing, a reporter has to be as kind to the country he's writing about as possible, if he is to have any hope of returning. (Exercising such caution is known in the journalist's trade as "being a good operator"—one of the highest terms of praise.) A more subtle goad to mind what one says than any visa restriction is a reporter's own guilt. If he wants to show—as most Western whites do—that he sympathizes with the blacks whom his ancestors have oppressed, then he may fudge so much that be becomes a liar. For example, examining the "underlying causes" of the continent's malaise, a reporter will assign them to anything or anybody except the Africans themselves, and he will blame the West for having "warped the African mind"—that is, for having destroyed Africa's traditional cultures without offering anything tangible in return. Or he will look the other way, and write admiringly about literacy schemes, health projects, and dams rather than about "rehabilitation camps," abandoned hospitals, and schools decaying from neglect. Above all, if he is to survive in respectable journalistic circles, he must paint over the rank incompetence, cruelty, and corruption of the new elites—be they right-wing or left-wing—and ignore the amorality and inertia among the ordinary people.

The distortions go unchallenged, because Africa, vast as it is, no longer seems of great importance to the rest of the world. Journalists know that its tale of woe has become repetitive; that the great global power game will not be played out there; that the grand social and economic experiments of post-independence Africa have lost their charm; in short, that Africa is a fad that has passed. "Not on the front burner now," say hard-nosed news editors. "Well, South Africa." Long breath. "That's a bit different, of course."

In the heady days just after independence, Africa beckoned. The natural wealth and beauty, then as now, were enormous. How easy to tap them! A few crash programs to combat illiteracy and disease; the transformation of the cream of the new generation into black white men at universities in the U.S., Britain, and France; the education of the masses; and presto! Strategically, foreigners argued, the continent was ripe for investment. Outsiders wanted to use African ports, build airfields, and make friends. Chou En-lai said that Africa was ready for revolution, while Che Guevara put his own theories into practice in the forests of eastern Zaire (then still the Congo). Kwame Nkrumah, Léopold Senghor, Kenneth Kaunda, and Julius Nyerere all came up with smart new names for ideas that had been around for centuries; they talked glowingly of—respectively—Pan-Africanism, Negritude, Humanism, and Ujamaa (or Familyhood). In Kenya, Jomo Kenyatta cried "Harambee"—roughly speaking, "Pull together." And in Zaire, President Mobutu was taken seriously by both Africans and Europeans for a while, when he coined "Mobutisme," which means (as any chuckling taxi driver in Kinshasa will tell you) "the marriage between Mobutu and the people." The essence of the new ideal—at the most fashionable and therefore fuzziest end of the spectrum—was to hark back to an indigenous, specifically African, state of grace. Because socialism and capitalism sounded somewhat European, other names were found: "communalism," and "African socialism," for example. An ideal of sharing, without the connotations of regimentation or repression, was conjured up. The good will of the West was unstinting: the jungle and the bush did seem a fine laboratory for new ideas, and the guilt of former colonizers could undergo a bit of expiation in the African sun.

Almost nowhere has it worked. The guilt is still there, and the guilty ones—or rather we, their descendants—are soured rather than satisfied. The Africans are a little less innocent and much less agreeable. The good will trickles away. Today, two of the most prosperous countries in Africa are still colonies, as far as their economies are concerned. The Ivory Coast, for one, is officially independent, but its wealth is managed by 60,000 Frenchmen, who have put the country's economy at the top of the African league, judged by every possible yardstick of productivity and development. Similarly, Zimbabwe enjoys the legacy of Ian Smith's white Rhodesia. Although the prime minister, Robert Mugabe, is a professed Marxist, he is reluctant to dismantle the white machine in view of 1980's 13 percent increase in gross national product, the highest in Africa. (It was still a most respectable 8 percent in 1981). The handful of other economies in Africa that tick over (like Nigeria's, which is fueled by the fluke of oil finds) have some expensive natural resource to exploit. Kenya, only meagerly blessed in resources, and politically and economically again under strain, has made some brave strides from a thin base. Botswana has been aided by diamonds more or less controlled by a South African firm; Cameroon, by oil and a shrewd but repressive dictatorship. Gabon, a harshly ruled former French colony, is another oil producer, which has successfully followed an International Monetary Fund program. But most countries have experienced a steady slide toward penury, and the slide has been most spectacular among those, such as Ghana and Tanzania, whose futures once seemed most exciting.

A crude and probably flattering guess is that since independence, perhaps a dozen of the fifty members of the Organization of African Unity (OAU) have marginally progressed: that is to say, the average citizen of these countries enjoys a better all-round living now than before the colonial shackles were shed; more people are educated; health services have expanded. Maybe a third of the OAU countries are marking time. The remainder have actually gone backward. The pattern of political misery has usually conformed to the economy. Barely a dozen states allow their citizens any real measure of individual freedom or dissent. The political prisons are fuller than at any time during the colonial era. Dawn has been followed by night.

When I first went out to Kenya from England fifteen years ago (my maternal grandparents had settled there in 1919, but I was brought up entirely in Europe, and so had never known them), I was eager to rebut the evil-minded prejudices and contemptuous prophecies of the hairy-kneed relics of settlerdom. Nothing irritated me more than the smug assertion that Africa would "revert to bush," or that the "ordinary decent bloody Af will soon be sorry that we've gone." Well, most of the Africans still are not sorry. But lately, old men, and even the not-so-old, throughout Africa, have been bearding me with requests for "the Queen to come back." And in many places I have seen once-neat houses falling into ruin, roads breaking up, farms reverting to patches of subsistence, and the bush physically reclaiming slices of Africa that had briefly been tamed by men—white men, one recollects with embarrassment, or rather, to be more precise, white men bossing black men about.

One of the great Western myths is that it is primarily the lack of aid and sympathy from the West (or North, as we must now learn to call ourselves, thanks to the strictures of Willy Brandt's cogent report) that has caused the rot. Up to a point, Brandt's book, *North–South: A Program for Survival*, was right. Money, aid, training, and more equitable marketing systems to correct the imbalance between rich countries and poor countries—all these are needed. Yet it is mainly the fault of the Africans themselves that African economies have collapsed, just as it is the triumph of the Japanese that their economy has flourished, even though the country is totally lacking in mineral resources and was bankrupted by World War II.

Look at Zaire, once the Belgian Congo, a country more handsomely endowed than most in the world. Formerly you could drive from any point in that vast state to any other within a couple of days, river crossings included. Now only three out of nine regions are accessible to the capital, Kinshasa, by ordinary vehicle. Bridges have collapsed, and it is unlikely that they will be repaired. Roads have been washed away, overtaken by rain and jungle. The pothole, one of the symbols of modern Africa, decorates every road, uncontested. The national airline, Air Zaire, known to jocular locals as Air Jamais or Air ZigZag, is barely functional. President Mobutu periodically "borrows" one of the airline's Boeings to drop in on his home village of Gbadolite, which is in the heart of nowhere but is replete with an international-class jet runway and a mausoleum built for his late wife out of marble transported from France at several million dollars' cost.

The most reliable mode of transport into the interior is, as in Conrad's day, the river steamer, now frequently raided by pirates (often unpaid soldiers). To go from the capital to the provincial center of Kisangani (once Stanleyville), for instance, takes six days upstream, five days down. Regional commissioners—in colonial terminology, governors—are like semi-independent chieftains or warlords, exacting taxes, sometimes in the shape of ivory tusks or smuggled diamonds; dispensing patronage and rough justice according to their own inclinations; and thereafter paying mild allegiance to the shrewd paramount chief, the gangster figure of Mobutu, far away in Kinshasa or in even more remote Gbadolite. An eccentric Frenchman traveling downstream by raft from the distant headwaters of the Zaire River was recently greeted by joyful villagers as the harbinger of a returning Belgian administration.

Zaire, it is true, is a far-gone case. But it is by no means alone. When Ghana gained its independence, in 1957, it had the second highest per capita income in Africa, and the best-educated black middle class. But by the time the maverick cult figure Kwame Nkrumah was toppled, nine years later, the opposition leadership had been jailed and the country bankrupted. Five coups and three executed heads of state later, a frail democracy was resuscitated in 1980, but on New Year's Eve, 1981, Flight Lieutenant Jerry Rawlings, another cult figure, patriotic in a naive way, again took power by the barrel of a gun. Whatever he does, the economy and moral well-being of Ghana will take a generation to recover. Today the minimum urban hourly wage barely suffices to buy half a loaf of bread or a bottle of beer.

The list of African catastrophes is long, and the most compelling cases are those where the future once seemed most brilliantly assured. Guinea, for instance, under Sékou Touré, proudly severed the French link and forged instead a Russian one (and gave honorary citizenship to Stokely Carmichael). In the years since, it has reduced itself almost irretrievably to bankruptcy. The Russians have been flung out now and the French asked back, and the repression has relaxed a little, but since independence seventy cabinet ministers have been murdered or thrown into jail. When a body politic is thus strangled, the economy invariably languishes. Recovery becomes a distant mirage.

Why has Africa, on its own, failed? Julius Nyerere and other charismatic African leaders have a host of explanations, and they are all valid, as far as they go. Drought, disease, illiteracy, and the brutal heritage of years of neglect and underdevelopment under colonialism do encumber many countries. More aid would help, to be sure, though sometimes aid makes matters worse, by inhibiting the people's resourcefulness. The fluctuations of international markets cruelly hit many countries that are dependent on the prices of raw materials for export: for example, when the world copper price drops by half, as it did in 1975, a country like Zambia, which is almost entirely dependent on copper production, is left in acute distress. The oil price eats huge holes in many African budgets before anything much can be disbursed for real development. But, all this granted, the overwhelming reason for Africa's grim failure is that the continent is very badly governed by the Africans.

The first large obstacle to African progress is the gross artificiality of the states, whose borders were crudely decided by colonial map-makers and hurriedly confirmed after independence by tiny black elites. There is hardly a country in Africa whose population is homogeneous. Totally disparate people, tribes with less in common than, say, Poles and Spaniards, have been thrown together in arbitrary political entities and told to choose governments. The lack of cultural and linguistic affinity within the new countries has prevented any real national consensus from emerging in most of them. In other words, tribalism is incorrigibly stronger than a spurious nationalism based on recently drawn colonial boundaries, and remains by far the most important power in politics throughout the continent.

There have been quite a number of instances where, in the first anti-colonial glow of independence, a leader has been so attractive that nationals across the tribal spectrum have supported him; Nkrumah, of Ghana, to give him his due, was one such. Or where there is a plethora of tribes, as in Tanzania, a single outstanding figure has been able to gain wide acceptance. But in practically every African country tribal loyalties have predominated and, to the chagrin of the Marxists, they have proved far more resilient than class loyalties. In Nigeria, with an enormous, growing, and often ill-treated urban proletariat, there is no left-wing workers' party of any substance: the odds are that a poor Yoruba will still vote for a rich Yoruba; a poor Hausa for a rich one; a poor Ibo for a rich one.

Again and again, I have been told by authorities in African countries that such-and-such an ancient tribal leader is a "busted flush," that "only the old still follow him," and so on. But they bob back time and again: the Yoruba vote for the aging Awolowo; the Kenyan Luo will not abandon Oginga Odinga; the Luanda secessionists in Shaba (formerly Katanga), Zaire's copper province, will back any strong leader who follows in the footsteps of Moise Tshombe, even though in the mythology of modern Africa he was a traitor. (However the ideology may be dressed up, whether the guns come from Angola via the Soviet Union or, as occurred twenty years ago, through Belgian mining interests and from white South Africa and Rhodesia, Shaba treasures the memory of Tshombe.)

Furthermore, it can be comfortably promised that where one ethnic group is the largest and most sophisticated in the land, the country will be ungovernable without that group's consent. In Kenya, President Daniel arap Moi, himself from a tiny group, has to have the backing of the Kikuyu if he is to rule with any efficiency. Similarly, Uganda will never attain stability until the Baganda—the key tribal group—are at the heart of government, an utter impossibility so long as their adversary Milton Obote rules. Kaunda cannot now govern Zambia effectively because he has alienated the main Zambian tribe, the Bemba. In Angola, Dr. Jonas Savimbi's group, the Ovimbundu, is the largest in the country at 35 to 40 percent of the population, and I assume there will never be peace and prosperity there until they are accommodated.

Tribal politics means that high positions are meted out largely on the basis of tribal balance. This undermines the people's faith in being able to succeed on merit alone. The prevailing expectation is that the tribal representatives will amass fortunes in government, out of which they will reward their clansmen's loyalty. In a continent where the gap between the rich and the poor is a mighty abyss, this system does have the advantage of encouraging a trickle-down—circuitous, perhaps—of wealth. For instance, when Tom Mboya, the Kenyan trade-unionist statesman, was assassinated (probably by members of a rival tribe who feared his popularity), he was paying for the education of 300 children.

It can be argued that patronage by individuals (in an ungenerous mood, one might add bribery, nepotism, and corruption) is less deadening than patronage by the state. Often, in the face of white South African accusations that "all of Africa north of the Zambesi is corrupt," I have felt obliged to defend the need for patronage, as a mechanism for spreading wealth while serving also to mediate among competing tribes and power factions. One can go on to draw analogies between an arguably "creative patronage" in Africa and the patronage that prevailed in corrupt but progressive Georgian England. Many African struggles mirror European history: the growth of the larger nation-states, dynastic wars, tribal schisms presented as religious ones (in Africa, for "religion" read "ideology"). There are many leading African figures who, while forced to engage in patronage in order to survive, are serving the common good at the same time that they are enriching themselves.

That has been so in many societies. And yet, in the end, good can never prevail where corruption is institutionalized, even though a majority of the people may appear to accept it. A professional middle class can never operate efficiently when decisions are made according to graft. Parallels again: it was only in the early part of the last century that corruption ceased to be a way of life in Britain (not that it has ceased altogether now, but it has ceased to be accepted as normal). The reason, it seems, is that the middle class—the technocrats, the professional civil servants—was no longer willing to let the old landed interests rule and become prosperous at the expense of the rest, and the middle class had become economically and thence politically important enough to make itself felt. Finally, enough politicians of the "new" and often more middle-class kind decided that peculation was a sin and that they should lead by example: Sir Robert Peel, for instance, a rather grimly sober figure, refused to take bribes, and his colleagues were shamed into following suit. Likewise in Africa, it is only this mixture of example and middle-class muscle that can curb the politicians' excesses: the muscle is growing, but there is no sign whatever of the political example. Nigeria's President Shagari has promised to set a new, austere standard of conduct, but it has become clear that the old, northern Nigerian elite upon whom he must rely is unwilling to imitate him.

The one-party system has been adopted throughout Africa to counter the divisive tendencies exacerbated by tribalism. Indeed, there is a very good case for a single-party system. Multi-party politics in Africa has invariably deteriorated into a competition between tribal blocs or alliances; in Nigeria this is still the case, despite the constitution's dexterous checks and balances, designed to prevent tribal voting patterns entirely. In addition, the concept of a loyal opposition, presupposing some basic national consensus usually absent in Africa, is considered by most ordinary Africans to be crazy: neither that consensus nor any form of liberal individualist tradition exists. People's attitudes are fiercely determined by ties of family and clan. At its gentlest, politics means that a nascent opposition will be absorbed by traditional African palaver into the single party; if not, it is silenced, perhaps violently. The secret ballot thus becomes unnecessary. When, last year, I discussed with a group of Zimbabwean secondary-school teachers the danger that people who hold minority views would be afraid to vote, the teachers proved to be unanimously hostile to the secret ballot, for the simple reason that it is "un-African."

So rigid control—which easily slides into repression and authoritarianism—is the order of the day, and the leadership, lacking any stimulating competition from within, inevitably becomes fossilized. This process has occurred in almost every single-party state in Africa. There is a small, brave band of sub-Saharan countries—Senegal, Gambia, Zimbabwe, Nigeria, Botswana, Mauritius—that have allowed their people a measure of pluralist political choice. Uganda still allows an opposition party but the fear and chaos there are such that oppositionists are afraid to take advantage of the law. Leaders such as Kenneth Kaunda, of Zambia, and Julius Nyerere, of Tanzania, men whose basic ideals are laudable and whose grandiose prospectuses for the African future have been taken in earnest by the West, have destroyed all vigorous, constructive political discussion, because they feared it.

A change that may gradually soften the grimness of the one-party system is the greater willingness of some African leaders—President Shagari, of Nigeria, for example—to allow national power to be devolved from the central executive to the periphery, especially to give a longer leash to tribal impulses. The problem is how to give regional interests freedom to speak for themselves without letting them demand wholesale secession. Federalism, as countless old British administrators will tell you, "never works." All the same, the OAU has been unduly inflexible for fear that a flood of secessionist feeling would be released if one secessionist movement—the one in Eritrea, for example, where the majority of the people undoubtedly desire secession from Ethiopia—were given official Pan-African blessings.

In general, nonetheless, I strongly believe that the greater the redrawing of the artificial colonial boundaries of Africa, the better. Yes, a thousand disturbing new nationalisms could be provoked across the continent. But why not, when most of the fifty OAU nations show no sign of emerging into real entities? Somalis will never wish to be part of Kenya or Ethiopia; why should they? Redraw the map instead. Let Chad break up into separate parts. Set Shaba free from Zaire. Let the Western Sahara have its patch of desert and phosphate. I never met a Biafran, even today, after all the suffering of the Nigerian civil war, who does not look back on the Biafran adventure with pride. At a dinner in Lagos some months ago, where the guests were mainly Ibo (i.e., Biafran), not one person was willing to say that the secessionist idea had been a mistake, despite the loss of a million lives.

When opposition views or discontent can find no outlet, the temptation is for soldiers, often up-jumped, thuggish sergeant-majors from the colonial era, to intervene: nearly half of the OAU's member states are led by men whose experience and power arose from the army. The general moribundity of African political systems is starkly illustrated by the fact that until recently, Africa was the only continent where not a single political leader had ever been peacefully voted out of office. (In June, the government of Mauritius, an OAU member although it is an island far out in the Indian Ocean with a population of predominantly Indian descent, was dismissed in a free general election.) A few military regimes—in Nigeria in 1979, in Ghana until the first of this year, and briefly in the Upper Volta, whose experiment ended abruptly in a coup this year—have been generous enough to give power back to civilians. One great leader, the poet-president Léopold Senghor, of Senegal, stepped down voluntarily to make way for his own protégé—an astonishing action in black African history. But this handful is all, which is a wretched record.

The stifling of dissent in black Africa militates against effective government: the leader, all too often sheltered within a circle of sycophants, loses touch with his people. There is virtually no domestic press in Africa worthy of the name. Some exceptions can be made: Hilary Ngweno's *Weekly Review* in Kenya and in Senegal an array of polemical but legal broadsheets—one pro-Soviet, one Maoist, one pro-Albanian (yes), one Islamic-fundamentalist. Also in Senegal there is the boisterously irreverent *Politicien*, which is modeled on the *Canard Enchaîné*, of Paris, and is the only legal satirical paper in Africa. Nigeria has a dynamic free press, but lacks a single paper with even a modicum of objectivity. Despite harassment and the steady erosion of its liberties, South Africa's press is still, along with Nigeria's, the freest in Africa. Elsewhere on the continent, politicians can expect their activities to be glorified rather than interpreted by native journalists, and most begin to believe the publicity, though most of them are also sensible enough to have numbered bank accounts in Zurich, just in case the unthinkable should happen.

But fantasy is better than reality. The ascent into deification, the endless harping on the rhetoric of liberation, the show of symbols of power, the ceaseless renaming of streets and towns in order to "reflect the new reality"—they become the very substance of the ruler's new world. The motorcade of Mercedes-Benz, the wailing sirens, the glossy, glass-encased airports, the posters extolling the virtues of the leader, the honorific titles: by these means, the president becomes the "guide," or "the savior." Even the puritanical Nyerere has become "Mwalimu" (the Teacher); one less modest, such as Amin, becomes Conqueror of the British Empire, or Emperor, like Sergeant Bokassa, the now-exiled Central African ruler who ordered the murder of a hundred schoolchildren who had been demonstrating against him. And somehow, as the dream of national or pan-African glory evaporates, these tinselly trappings of independence become a substitute for material advance. The speeches grow even longer, as though it were the length rather than the content that now matters to the masses.

Mobutu's ornate stick, with carved bird's head at the top, woven in ebony with snakes and images of women with blank faces and meaningfully distended bellies, becomes a kind of wand of potency. The late Jomo Kenyatta's omnipresent fly whisk had the same effect. In the absence of tangible European-style wealth, in the form of (for example) a healthy balance of payments, the game of "authenticity"—the search for a primal, idealized African condition that is supposed to have prevailed before the rape of the black mother by the white man—has overtaken the half-baked expectations that were ritually mouthed at independence. Instead, the glory of the leader, the sanctity of the "committees of national salvation," and so forth, have become all. The people, often in the absence of mundane benefits for themselves, are expected to bask in the reflected glory of their new king-leaders. No one officially minded when young Kenyans wore T-shirts with Kenyatta's portrait emblazoned across the chest; but when button-up shirts with the same picture began to be sold, they were banned, because when one unbuttoned the shirt, one was "splitting *mzee*'s head open." The image, the word, is paramount. Thus the Congo improves by becoming Zaire.

There is a strange duality in African thinking. The fruits of the West are desirable and must be acquired, but the ways of the West—"the colonization of the mind"—and in particular the Western methods of acquisition, must be rejected. Material glitter is cherished, but the boring methodical rigor with which nations are built, and the dreary civic obligations that give cement to political decisions, are somehow to be dispensed with. In theory, rural health programs are to be embarked upon, but in practice, you hardly ever find a young black doctor willing to tolerate a stint in the bush, away from the bright lights of the big town: the point of the long grind of training is to get *out* of the bush. Similarly, the urge to own land is powerful throughout Africa, but most educated Africans consider it beneath them to undertake commercial farming. The population of the continent is rising at a furious rate: an increase of almost 4 percent of the population per year in some countries. Ministers make rousing speeches in favor of UNESCO and other agencies in their attempts to encourage family planning, but when it comes to limiting their own families, the new elites reject birth control as un-African—an imperialist plot to keep black numbers down. Technocrats want industrialization and higher productivity, but punctuality, it still seems, is regarded as a bit of a white man's joke. A visiting IMF dignitary or Western diplomat would never arrange a sit-down dinner in Africa: no guest can be relied upon to turn up.

Training? Money from outside? A large-scale redistribution of wealth from North to South? Yes, of course that would help. But nothing fundamental in Africa will change until there is a revolution in the attitude of the middle class and then, by optimistic extension, in the attitude of the apathetic masses. Nigeria, awash with oil, will never function as an equitable or stable society so long as the civil servants are "not on seat" when you go round to visit them (telephones usually are not worth trying) because they are running private businesses on the side. Most senior Nigerian soldiers are likewise engaged in private business a good deal of the time.

It is not that there is a lack of talent. Many able technocrats despise the old-style, tub-thumping politicians who lay down the law. Yet few civil services are apolitical. So why bother to stand apart as a professional, when you benefit yourself and your family by swimming along with the flotsam and jetsam of corruption and patronage?

Angry revolutions have from time to time spoiled the fun, but by and large the rural and urban masses are amazingly stoical in the face of the flaunted privilege and fortunes of the new elites. It is simply the prerogative of the big man to be fat, to throw weight around. So long as the big man is generous and provides beer for the boys—(and many of them are remarkably profligate)—the *wananchi*—the people of the soil, the small fry—seem to accept their lot. Above all, they seem to acknowledge that if the roles were reversed, they would behave no differently.

A well-known Kenyan politician sold off thousands of dollars of food aid during a year of famine. The people knew it. But he had suffered during the liberation struggle and he was—still is—a mesmerizing demagogue. Though they know he is a crook, the people still elect him by an overwhelming majority. Style counts for much. The masses loved the promises of land and riches that the Kenyan populist parliamentarian J. M. Kariuki liked to make them—so much so that the Kenyatta elite were obliged to assassinate him. But in earlier days, when "JM" was assistant minister for tourism in charge of the anti-poaching drive and Mrs. Kariuki's car was found to contain a pile of illicit elephant tusks, no one turned a hair. There is no conflict between campaigning for the underprivileged on the one hand and stealing a bit of state property on the other. The only people you truly trust are your family, your clan, and maybe your tribal leaders, but nobody else. In Nigeria you "play politics": to an outsider, the rhetoric of idealism is embarrassing in its effusion. People seem to mean it as it flows off the tongue, but no one really believes it. Politics is generally a game of power and wealth, but in Africa the play is more brazen.

Demoralization breeds self-hatred. The years of freedom have mounted up, mocking the plausibility of the excuses for failure. You can be poor and proud if your oppression is self-evident and your situation not of your own making. But a generation has now passed since independence. Although the mechanisms for controlling international markets and for lending cash remain firmly in the hands of the West,

Africans know deep down that they themselves must break the cycle of dependence and inferiority. The Japanese did it. So, in theory, must they. That is what Nyerere said, and he was right, and for a while he brilliantly inspired people with the promise of self-reliance. If all his cabinet had been of his own quality, perhaps he could have succeeded. Instead, in Tanzania and even more acutely in the rest of Africa, post-colonial freedom has brought an increase in self-doubt.

One of the saddest, most self-demeaning developments in black Africa is that the ordinary African, seeing the poor results of a generation of independence, is more convinced than ever of an imaginary superiority of the white man. The wheel has turned so far that I know of many black Africans who prefer to hire whites, even if their qualifications are poor, as managers of farms, hotels, and all sorts of enterprises requiring administrative skill, simply because they are white. Ask an African which airline he would rather travel on if he values his safety: the odds are, he would prefer not to travel on an African line. If they can pay the price, people will go to a white doctor; schoolchildren will trudge miles every day to study under a white teacher. And as the rhetoric of black power blows more clamorous, it seems that the Africans are stuck more firmly than ever in the prison of low self-esteem.

I frequently wonder at the lack of bitterness Africans show toward their recent European masters. In Zimbabwe, for example, it seems extraordinary that so little nationalist venom is vented upon Ian Smith. But his old adversaries appear to think: "He's a tribal chieftain. Of course we don't much like his white tribe, and they don't like us. But he did only what seemed to be best for his bunch." Indeed, Smith's style and nerve are admired more than the piety of many white friends of black Africa. Conversely, again and again I sense that liberal well-wishers are despised: What, it is asked, is their *real* game; and why, by the way, are liberal South Africans—the Oppenheimers, for instance—often the richest of the lot? Few Africans seem to believe that such people can cherish disinterested humanitarian motives alongside the wish for their own survival, that self-interest can be coupled with a genuine, enlightened liberalism. Given this perspective, Tiny Rowland, head of the vast, Africa-wide Lonrho conglomerate, with his business verve, and Ian Smith, cunning as a rat, strike an African as at least understandable, real men. He can get on with them.

It may be argued that this amoral, undisciplined fatalism is common to all the demoralized, exploited people of the Third World. But comparisons do not fully bear this out. There are no African guerrillas with the unflinching discipline of the Vietcong. The Polisario fighters trying to win the Western Sahara from the king of Morocco come closest. They are hardly in the mainstream of sub-Saharan Africa, though; it was only in 1975 that the Polisario freed their own black slaves. There is no

Communist Party leader who rivals the charismatic brilliance of Fidel Castro. These days, Lt. Col. Mengistu Haile Mariam, the bloodstained Ethiopian leader, is nearest.

Yet lessons are being learned. With a generation passed, the collectivist ideals of the early days have been wholeheartedly discredited across the continent. The Soviet Union is less of a force in Africa than ever before. Of the OAU's fifty members, only three—Angola, Mozambique and Ethiopia—voted for the Soviet Union during a key Afghan debate in the United Nations. Perhaps another half-dozen countries would normally tend to take the Soviet line against the American one. A dozen countries have a token presence of Cuban doctors or East German telephone-tappers. But most OAU members are to a greater extent than before conscious that friendship with the West is likely to yield the most material benefit. Even the Angolans are coming to this point of view, because the Russians do not have the best technology to offer. And Africans now know that in personal relations the Chinese and Russians are no less racist than the West Europeans and Americans.

Moreover, the benefits of a liberal, free-enterprise economy are increasingly recognized. Africa is still overwhelmingly rural, and the peasants universally expect governments to encourage them in their drive for betterment. The *kulak* remains a cant term in Marxist discussions of the African malaise: he must be destroyed. But it is in countries such as Kenya and the Ivory Coast, where the *kulak* has been given succor from state or private sources to help raise capital, borrow fertilizer, and so forth, that overall agriculture advancement has been most visible. It is interesting to note that the countries with the most liberal economies tend to be the ones that give their citizens the most political freedom. Kenya, for instance, has one of the best presses in Africa (though now, in a time of sharpening economic and internal political differences, it is coming under pressure from politicians who wish to manipulate it). By contrast rigidly socialist Tanzania, across the border, is also politically less liberal.

Amid all this confusion (and I appear, with my secessionist sentiment, to be encouraging it) the Western journalist, equipped with political sympathies that are wholly incompatible with the ruthlessness of Africa, tries to push his pen—a losing battle. In African eyes, a journalist is a messenger-boy: you write the big man's speeches, or justify his zanier whims. There is no such thing as objectivity, although that is a much-favored word among those who pursue it least. Africans ridicule Westerners who believe that journalists can be objective. If you broadly support the cause of the Zimbabwean guerrillas, it is inconceivable that you might report a massacre carried out by Zimbabwean guerrillas. All that people want to know is whose side you are on.

It is probably true that the run-of-the-mill mass-circulation papers in the United States and Europe are not as interested as they might be in the building of dams, the eradication of illiteracy, and the glories of anti-malaria schemes. Their readers prefer to have their racist prejudices confirmed by gory tales of Emperor Bokassa's cannibalism or the threats, jocular if macabre, of the Liberian ruler, Samuel Doe, to shoot his national football team if it loses its match. This is unfair to Africa.

The serious Western press, on the other hand, bends over backward to see the black point of view, and this, paradoxically, is also unfair to Africa. In 1981 there were massacres in Nigeria; 7,000 people, by conservative estimates, died when police suppressed religious riots in Kano. In another instance, fifty prisoners suffocated in a prison van in Lagos; in another, sixty suspected smugglers perished in a cell in the Ivory Coast. To my knowledge, not a single British or American television crew covered any of these events, nor would there have been the slightest chance that they would have been given permission to do so if they had cared to ask. The incidents rated an obscure paragraph for a day or two. Imagine the weeks' worth of stories and editorials in the world press that would have attended such events in South Africa. Then try to recall the minimal coverage of the genocide in Burundi in 1972, where as many as a quarter of a million Hutu—the lowest figure I have seen is 80,000—were systematically slaughtered by the Tutsi elite. The caste system in Burundi has notable parallels with that of South Africa, yet to this day there has not been a whimper of protest from the OAU. But we apply different standards to different situations, black-on-black (to use Andy Young's phrase) is not as bad as white-on-black oppression.

In fact, I happen to agree that South Africa should suffer as much adverse publicity as possible, to help make it change its beastly ways. I do not swallow Reagan's argument of "constructive engagement." But the double standard we, as Africanist reporters, are expected to apply is—or should be—a little troublesome to the conscience. In fact, we encourage illiberal and authoritarian regimes to get away with it handsomely: Angola and Mozambique, for example, allow no freedom whatsoever to journalists inside their countries. Journalists cannot leave the capitals unaccompanied; visas are hard to come by and no writer who reports adversely can expect another one. Angola is naturally determined to portray Dr. Jonas Savimbi, the anti-goverment guerrilla leader, as a burnt-out gangster of no real account, but no journalist has been allowed to wander freely in the central highlands, where Savimbi claims to be popular. Likewise Savimbi seems reluctant to take journalists up into the central plateau himself. (He takes them instead around the sparsely populated southeastern corner of Angola, which is more or less uncontested by the government in Luanda.) All one can honestly assert is that each side has far less freedom of movement in the center of the country than it publicly insists. It is disgraceful, however, that experienced journalists, in order to be better placed to "go farther in next time," have to pull their punches in describing what they see or (often more significantly) what they cannot see.

In contrast to Angola and Mozambique, one can only ruefully reflect upon journalism in Rhodesia during the war there. In the end, more and more probing reporters, myself included, fell afoul of the authorities and were prevented from returning, but before that, never once was I prevented from traveling exactly where I wanted, fear permitting. One hopped into a car on one's own, hoped there were no land mines planted ahead, and drove. At the height of the war, there was no town that was inaccessible by ordinary unaccompanied vehicle. And one wrote about it. Not once did I have to hold back critical observations for fear of expulsion (I may, I think, have been the first journalist inside Rhodesia to describe the Rhodesian use of napalm). In Angola or Mozambique, however, it is a battle to get out of the capital, even with a state-appointed interpreter and guide to go along.

But then Smith, in his pitiful and deceitful way, was half bound by the rules, which he recognized but flouted, of the liberal West. He liked the illusion (he may even have believed it) that his press was "free." In Angola and Mozambique, there is no such illusion: as a journalist you are allowed to write if it helps the government. And this applies to a great extent throughout Africa. Until four years ago, no English-language newspaper was allowed to have a permanent representative in Lagos, the capital of the largest state in Africa. So when we were occasionally let in, we pandered to the authorities and kept off sensitive subjects. It emasculated reporting but allowed another trip.

"Excuses, excuses, excuses," heckled a colleague on the London *Observer* whose métier is to harass Western politicians—mainly British ones—in a way that would be quite unheard of for the political writer in Africa. He's right. In the end, through a remorseless determination to wear the fixed, understanding smile, to see the "underlying causes" of the African malaise, one becomes unintentionally racist. We Western reporters have allowed Africans to play by different rules when it suits them while heaping moral anger and ridicule upon white supremacists for their scarcely unusual desire to assert their own tribal dominance. By trying too hard to be fair to the blacks, the *Observer* and countless other benign voices further insult Africa. Positive discrimination is, after all, discrimination. If we want Africans to be treated as equals, it is time we judged and damned them as equals.

The confusion is noticeably worse for American journalists, whose consciences are constantly pricked by the seeming parallels of black America and black Africa. White Americans all too often come to black Africa determined to "help the black man," on the assumption that all he needs is money, education, and freedom from prejudice. But in fact there are no similarities between the state of the black American and that of the black African. The former, whether he or she likes it or not, is wholly and irredeemably American in aspirations and culture, and needs simply to be treated as well as or as badly as white Americans are. In Africa, the white liberal confuses sameness with equality. The black Africans are equal, yes: but through centuries of different customs they are by no means the same in their aspirations and attitudes as Americans, white or black. To treat them on a basis of sameness is to impose values that another people may not wish to share.

So the liberal guilt is not, in the end, assuaged. Marxists can deftly circumvent the awkward questions: the amorality of Africa and its leadership is deliberately fostered by the conspiring international capitalists, who forge an alliance of avarice and evil between the multinational boss class and a handpicked caucus of neo-colonial black puppets. The masses are ready for Lenin. Even tribalism, the Marxists argue, is deliberately whipped up by international capitalism to keep the Africans divided and to allow the puppets to manipulate their own sectors of the people for their own base (capitalist) motives.

But the Western liberal is further adrift than the Marxist. The liberal explanations and excuses are simply not enough. The brutal fact is that the white liberal, intent on giving Africa the benefit of his own ideals, is the friend of the soon-to-be-liberated African only until the latter is in power. Once African power is achieved, it is plain that for most Africans, leaders and led, liberalism is a West European absurdity. They would rather deal with Castro and Tiny Rowland, and they do.

The final humiliation for the serious Western reporter is that, in general, Africa is recognized to be back where it was fifty years ago: a continent of little international importance, sparsely populated though growing too fast to feed itself, inherently unstable politically, with little hope of realizing its economic (especially agricultural) potential for at least a generation or two. The numerous and much-touted future "breadbaskets" and "granaries" are still empty: the green hills and savanna of southern Sudan, for instance. The food just will not grow, so long as the political instability remains and attitudes are utterly at odds with the demands of Western technology or organizational methods. Long-term investors are probably less willing now than they were ten years ago to take risks in Africa: ideologists are less willing to practice their social experiments there. Even the strategic arguments weigh less heavily. If Togo is pro-Western, Benin is likely to be pro-Soviet, and so on. Burundi, ideologically probably more "right-wing" than its mini-rival Rwanda, had a small Russian and Cuban presence; so, in return, Rwanda, though marginally more leftist, has more Belgians. And in most cases, it matters not a jot to the rest of the world. Africa's weakness, indeed, may prove to be its eventual strength. No one is going to drop a neutron bomb on it.

One French correspondent begins almost every piece as follows: "In potentially mineral-rich and strategically crucial X. . . ." It could be Chad, Mauritania, Sudan, Malawi, Gabon, you name it. Most countries in Africa have three or four adjacent territories, can offer airbase facilities, have "untapped wealth." Most OAU members have a potential seaport. But the artificiality of the states, their tribal confusion, the weakness of ideology, and the waywardness of leaders all make Africa too complicated by far for any superpower to wade into with assurance. There is potential for plunder at high risk by adventurers, and there is the prospect of febrile escapism for reporters like myself, bored with the gray monotony of the West. But sensible people these days—foreign governments, businesses, and journalists—are learning to keep out.

6

Fundamentalist Muslims between America and Russia

DANIEL PIPES

America is worse than Britain; Britain is worse than America. The Soviet Union is worse than both of them. They are all worse and more unclean than each other! But today it is America that we are concerned with.
—*Ayatollah Khomeini, October 1964*[1]

When President Reagan and General Secretary Mikhail Gorbachev met in Geneva last November, the fundamentalist Muslim rulers of Iran devised their own interpretation of the summit conference. "The biggest worry of the two superpowers," Radio Teheran announced, "is neither the 'star wars' nor the speedy buildup of nuclear weapons, but the revolutionary uprising of the world's Muslims and the oppressed." Iran's President Sayed Ali Khamenei asserted that the two leaders, fearful of revolutionary Islamic ideology and the distrubing effect it has across the Third World, met to figure out "how to confront Islam."[2]

The rulers of Iran are convinced that the United States and the Soviet Union conspire together to keep Third World peoples in line. President Khamenei believes that the superpowers have already divided the world between them and disagree only on the exact disposition of territories.

The summit, in this view, provided a convenient occasion for them to negotiate their small differences.

Muslim fundamentalists offer a most peculiar interpretation of super-power relationships, derived from an awareness of what many in the West overlook: cultural similarities between the United States and the Soviet Union far outweigh the differences between them. By looking beyond political disagreements, fundamentalist Muslims see how much the two share. If American and Soviet citizens alike have difficulty recognizing themselves—or, for that matter, each other—as they are portrayed by fundamentalist Muslims, this eccentric assessment moti-vates a significant body of opinion through the Muslim world.

One might expect the fundamentalists' views to imply equal antipa-thy to the two superpowers. But this is not the case: even a cursory review of their news reports, commentaries, speeches and sermons reveals a preoccupation with America that borders on the obsessive. Although a good word is rarely said about the Soviet Union, neither is much said that is negative; it receives but a small fraction of the hatred and venom directed at the United States.

If the two superpowers hatch joint conspiracies and work together to oppress the Third World, why this imbalance? If the two states are so similar, why does America attract so much more abuse? Is there anything the United States can do to direct more of the fundamentalist hostility toward the Soviet Union?

II

From the point of view of culture, the differences between the United States and the Soviet Union have only secondary importance in the eyes of fundamentalists. (For simplicity, "the United States" here includes America and its allies; "the Soviet Union" includes the entire Soviet bloc.) Knowledgeable Muslims note that both cultures inherited the legacies of Greece, Rome, Christianity, Humanism, the Enlightenment and nineteenth-century rationalism. They recognize the common Euro-pean origins of American liberalism and Soviet Marxism.

The two Western cultures are alike—and different from Islam—in many ways. Men wear pants, women wear skirts, and everyone sits on chairs. The intelligentsia in both countries listen to the same classical music, attend the same plays and admire the same oil paintings. Of special importance is the similarity in customs relating to the sexes—all of them rejected by fundamentalist Muslims: female athletics, coeduca-tion, female employment, mixed social life, mixed swimming, dancing, dating, nightclubs, and so on.

Both powers are perceived as having similar plans for imperial expansion, continuing the scramble for colonies among the European states a century ago. "Before, it was the British that brought us misfortune," says Ayatollah Ruhollah Khomeini; "now it is the Soviets on the one hand, and the Americans on the other."[3] American and Soviet forces exist for the same purposes; their tanks, ships, planes and missiles look the same. Thus, the multinational peacekeeping force maintained in Lebanon from 1982 to 1984 was seen as an army of occupation no less than the Soviet troops in Afghanistan. The United States Central Command, established in 1983 to deter Soviet attacks in the Persian Gulf, looks to Muslim fundamentalists like mere camouflage for putting the instruments of American military expansion in place.

Arguments between the two powers over freedom, equality, democracy and so on have little relevance to fundamentalist Muslims. As an Egyptian member of the Muslim Brethren commented to me in 1971, "Capitalism and Communism are not our concern; let the Christians fight these matters out on their own." The superpowers appear to share the belief that Western civilization is superior to all others, and fundamentalists sense strong elements of anti-Muslim sentiment among Americans and Russians alike. It hardly matters, therefore, who wins the superpower contest, for both sides aim to destroy Islamic culture and end Muslim independence. Ideally, the two giants will turn against each other and mutually exhaust themselves, thereby posing less of a threat to other peoples.

Fundamentalists rejoice in being the objects of superpower hostility, regarding this as proof of their independence. They argue that Muslims should avoid close cooperation with either power: no economic concessions, political deals or intelligence agents, much less foreign soldiers or bases, should be permitted to compromise the Islamic identity. Umar at-Talmasani, an Egyptian fundamentalist, advises Muslims to "give up the United States and Russia and gird your loins. . . . We condemn the U.S. and Russian attitudes to us and we will reject, resist, and use every means to preserve our rights."[4] Iran's negative neutrality is summed up by the oft-repeated slogan, "Neither East nor West."

As Talmasani implies, violence is a legitimate tactic for preventing close relations with either superpower. Fundamentalist Muslims overthrew the shah's pro-Western government in Iran, then held American diplomats hostage for over a year. They assassinated Anwar al-Sadat in Egypt for his close ties to the United States. The Soviet Union also feels fundamentalist opposition. Many of the mujahadeen troops battling the Soviet forces in Afghanistan are fundamentalist inspired. Former President Jafar al-Numeiri of the Sudan applied the Islamic law while persecuting Sudanese communists, sparring with Soviet friends such as Ethiopia and Libya, and reducing relations with Moscow to a minimum. Syrian fundamentalists mounted a campaign of assassinations against Soviet personnel in Syria during 1979–80. Fundamentalists in Lebanon took four Soviet diplomats hostage in 1985, killing one of them.

Fundamentalists monitor closely the relative strengths of the Soviet Union and the United States in any given time and place, and respond accordingly. The greater its military, economic and cultural presence, the more the superpower attracts the brunt of fundamentalist hostility. The fundamentalists' approach appears evenhanded: they opposed the Soviet presence in Egypt before 1973 as they opposed the American presence thereafter. Saudi relations with the United States are condemned just as those between Libya and the Soviet Union. Even when a superpower helps Muslims in wars against non-Muslims, fundamentalists suspect its motives. Soviet aid to the Arab struggle against Israel and American aid to the Afghan rebels are seen with suspicion: the two powers, pursuing their own struggle, are only exploiting Muslims.

III

Fundamentalist Muslims base their views on public and private life, indeed their entire existence, on the sacred law of Islam, the Shari'a. This massive body of regulations, drawn from precepts found in the Koran and other Islamic writings, covers everything from the most public aspects of life—a penal code based on corporal punishment, taxes in accordance with Koranic levies, second-class citizenship for non-Muslims living under Muslim rule—to the most intimate, such as personal hygiene and sexual relations.

Full implementation of this law has always eluded Muslims, and the disparity between its norms and the realities of public life has brought schism. Traditionalists accepted this disparity; their flexibility does much to make Islam an immensely appealing religion to peoples of many backgrounds. Then, over the past century or so, secularists have come to believe that success in the modern world requires discarding anything that stands in the way of emulating the West. Reformist Muslims have tried to interpret the Shari'a in such a way that its precepts could be made compatible with Western ways.

Fundamentalists, however, became convinced that the law of Islam can and must be implemented in its every detail. For them, the exact fulfillment of God's commands in the Shari'a is a duty incumbent on all believers, as well as the Muslims' principal source of strength. The law is as valid today, they insist, as in past centuries. Fundamentalist Muslims contrast the splendor of medieval Islamic civilization with the backwardness and poverty of twentieth-century Muslims, and blame this degeneration on the influences from Europe.

Although the fundamentalist outlook has existed in Islam since the seventh century, and even gained some early political successes, it became a powerful force only in the 1920s. While modern Muslim elites typically respond to encounters with Europe by experimenting with secularism and reformism, the masses prefer fundamentalism. Fundamentalism offers them an instrument with which to fend off frightening European influences and preserve accustomed ways. Hashemi Rafsanjani, speaker of the Iranian parliament, has stated what every fundamentalist believes: "Islam is important because it is capable of defeating Western culture."[5]

Although fundamentalists think they are returning to well established ways and recreating an ancient way of life, in fact they espouse a radical program that has little precedent. While a fundamentalist like Ayatollah Khomeini is often seen as "medieval," he is actually unlike anyone who lived in past centuries. He responds to the specific challenges of the twentieth century with modern solutions, such as placing theologians in positions of political power and imposing an Islamic economy. To view Khomeini as medieval is to misunderstand how profoundly he is a creature of his time.

If secular and reformist Muslims, experimenting with a diversity of political viewpoints, may feel attracted to one or another of the superpowers, fundamentalists are fervent in their hostility to both, as well as to all Western ideologies.

As increasing numbers of Muslims are attracted to European ways, winning them back to the Shari'a and keeping others from straying becomes the fundamentalists' preoccupation. They portray Western civilization as aesthetically loathsome, ethically corrupt and morally obtuse. They whisper dark rumors of conspiracy, claiming that the West spreads its culture to weaken the Muslims and steal their resources. They ignore the West's economic and cultural achievements, harping on its unemployment and pornography. To discredit secularist and reformist Muslims, fundamentalists call them lackeys of the Western powers.

But denigrating the West is not enough. To attract lapsed Muslims, fundamentalists must imbue Islam with some of the same features that Western civilization offers. Specifically, they transform the theology and law of traditional Islam into a modern ideology, a set of economic, political and social theories. They contend that Islam contains a systematic political program comparable to, but better than, those originating in Europe. For them, liberalism leads to anarchy, Marxism to brutality, capitalism to heartlessness, socialism to poverty. In the succinct words of the Malaysian leader Anwar Ibrahim: "We are not socialist, we are not capitalist, we are Islamic."[6] Making Islam into an ideology endows the religion with unprecedented bulk and authority. In the famous declaration by Hasan al-Banna, founder of the Muslim Brethren organization, "Islam is a faith and a ritual, a nation and a nationality, a religion and a state, spirit and deed, holy text and sword."[7]

Differences in sect and location hardly affect the fundamentalist viewpoint. Communal disagreements aside, Shi'ite and Sunni fundamentalists hardly differ in goals or methods. Though resident in different parts of the Muslim world—West Africa, the Middle East, Central Asia and Southeast Asia—fundamentalists everywhere resemble each other. When in opposition, they all pressure governments to reject Western influences; when in power they attempt to extirpate Western ways directly.

Differences that do exist reflect varying levels of commitment. The conservative fundamentalists promote their ideals in peaceable ways, through missionary work, education and personal virtue. They believe in evolutionary change. Though inclined to blame current problems— poverty, military defeat, injustice, moral laxness—on the state's divergence from the sacred law, they do not rebel against the authorities. To enhance their popularity, shaky rulers sometimes appeal to conservative fundamentalists by applying the Shari'a where it can be done conveniently.

If conservative fundamentalists fear that the enormous appeal of Western culture erodes Islamic customs and laws, radical fundamentalists worry about the very survival of Islam. A key radical thinker, Sayyid Qutb, wrote in 1964 that the modern age presents "the most dangerous *jahiliyya* [anti-Islamic barbarity] which has ever menaced our faith." For Qutb, "everything around is *jahiliyya*; perceptions and beliefs, manners and morals, culture, art and literature, laws and regulations, including a good part of what we consider Islamic culture.[8]

Radicals attack their governments for ignoring the Shari'a, and claim power for themselves on the grounds that they alone aspire to implement the whole body of Islamic precepts. Extreme danger justifies extreme action; radicals pursue revolutionary change through violence.

Although far less numerous than the conservatives, radical fundamentalists have a greater political impact. Their well-articulated program sets the agenda and their extensive infrastructure of mosques and Sufi brotherhoods poses the most acute challenge to governments. A proven willingness to use violence and a determination to succeed frequently make them invulnerable to conventional security measures. Like communists, radical fundamentalists form fronts to use others; they themselves, however, are hardly ever used or co-opted. Radicals succeeded in overthrowing the government in Iran; they present significant challenges to the authorities in Morocco, Tunisia, Nigeria, Egypt, Syria, Saudi Arabia, Malaysia and Indonesia.

Numerically, fundamentalists constitute a small minority in most Muslim societies and they are embattled. Implementing the Shari'a arouses strong opposition among non-Muslims and secularist and reformist Muslims. It also alienates those other fundamentalists who would apply the law differently or want power for themselves. Meeting as they do with massive resistance, fundamentalists who achieve power suspect their opponents of the worst motives and respond with repression. This has been the pattern in the Sudan, Iran and Pakistan.

Because they are primarily concerned with a matter internal to Muslim society—the application of Islamic law—fundamentalists have limited interest in non-Muslims. Notwithstanding their long-term plans to convert infidels and spread the rule of Islam, fundamentalists are, in the short term, defensive. Christians, Hindus and other non-Muslims are of concern only to the extent that they obstruct efforts to live by the Shari'a: culturally, by enticing individual Muslims from the law; politically, by depriving Muslim states of their independence. Fear is the key to fundamentalist attitudes toward non-Muslims; the greater they perceive a threat, the more intense their hostility.

While the threats of culture and power come from many quarters, the superpowers present them most acutely. If, in fundamentalist eyes, the United States and the Soviet Union "aim to destroy the Islamic culture"[9] and jeopardize the independence of Muslim countries, fundamentalist Muslims direct special hostility toward these two countries.

IV

The United States is a far bigger worry for fundamentalist Muslims than the Soviet Union; its cultural and economic influence far exceed the Soviets', its ideology is more threatening, and its intentions are seen as more hostile. In short, America presents the greater set of obstacles to life under the Islamic law.

In cultural matters, the world largely ignores the Soviet Union. Who uses the Cyrillic alphabet, learns Russian, listens to Radio Moscow, watches Soviet films or vacations in the Crimea? The dreary state culture of the U.S.S.R. has virtually no impact on the Muslim world and its vibrant dissident culture does not reach there. Only pre-revolutionary culture has a presence outside the Soviet Union.

America and its allies, however, have an immense cultural impact. The Latin alphabet, English language, the BBC, Hollywood and the Riviera have a near-universal attraction. Whatever Americans and their government do exercises a deep fascination. American television programs and films are regularly discussed and decried. U.S. domestic issues, especially racial, criminal and economic problems, are known in detail. America's popular music, video games, comics, textbooks, literature and art reach throughout the Muslim world. Its clothing, foods, household items and machines are found in towns and villages. Most Western sexual customs, such as mixed dancing, exist in the Soviet Union as well as the United States, but they are known to Muslims around the world from the latter; some abhorred practices, say pornography or beauty pageants, exist only in the United States.

American influence also touches Muslims in more profound ways. In the delicate area of religion, America exports both Christianity (the traditional rival of Islam) and secularism (its modern rival). Christian missionaries—all but forgotten in the United States and Western Europe—loom large for the fundamentalists, who see them as leaders of a systematic assault on Islam. Fundamentalists discern a strong crusading component to U.S. foreign policy. "The U.S. attitude is motivated by several factors, but the most important, in my view," writes Umar at-Talmasani, the Egyptian fundamentalist leader, "is religious fanaticism. . . . This attitude is a continuation of the crusader invasion of a thousand years ago."[10]

Ironically, anti-religious ideas also come from the United States. Although Moscow, not Washington, aggressively sponsors atheism, its heavy-handed, doctrinaire approach carries little weight beyond the confines of the Soviet bloc. Freethinkers, anti-clerics and atheists the world over get their inspiration from America.

This points to a yet greater irony: Marxism itself comes to Islam mostly from the free world. Marxist thought in America and Western Europe is dynamic and in tune with new intellectual developments, whereas the version purveyed by the Soviet government is hidebound and dull. Worse, because the Soviet authorities constantly bend their ideals to meet the practical needs of being a superpower, these lack intellectual honesty or even consistency. The prison writings of Antonio Gramsci have infinitely more appeal than the speeches of Brezhnev. Students sent to study in Paris, not Moscow, become the fervent Marxists. Even on the Soviet Union's own ideological turf, then, America poses the greater challenge.

Fundamentalist Muslims are convinced that journalists from both the Soviet Union and the United States try to weaken Islam by spreading misinformation about their religion. A Reuters correspondent was expelled from Iran for filing "biased and at times false reports" in May 1985.[11] Again, while the suspicion is addressed to both camps, it is the American journalists who matter, not their Soviet counterparts. News judgments are made in New York City; the international prominence of an event depends on the emphasis given it by the editors of the major wire services, newspapers, magazines and television networks. Accordingly, Muslims know the news as it is generated in New York; they are almost oblivious of how the Soviet media cover the news.

Foreign schools are perhaps the greatest threat of all, taking impressionable young Muslims, teaching them Western languages and infecting them with alien ideas. The prominent role Christian missionaries have played historically in education makes this issue all the more alarming. Again, it is Khomeini who best expresses the fundamentalists' concern: "We are not afraid of economic sanctions or military intervention. What we are afraid of is Western universities."[12] That which Americans see with special pride—the spread of advanced education—fundamentalist Muslims see as exceptionally dangerous.

In sum, the more attractive an alien culture, the more fundamentalist Muslims fear it and fight it. A leading Iranian mullah declared that the main objective of the Islamic revolution is to "root out" American culture from Muslim countries.[13] He probably never thought of Soviet culture as a comparable threat.

In the realm of economics, should fundamentalist Muslims wish to seek a scapegoat for their poverty, the vast financial, industrial and commercial influence of the United States provides the obvious target. America's economic institutions cast a long shadow. Its oil producers, multinational enterprises, transportation networks and banking institutions dominate their fields. American corporations beckon ambitious Muslims with lucrative jobs. The dollar is the international currency, U.S. government paper is the single greatest instrument for short-term investments, and Wall Street offers the largest capital market. The International Monetary Fund and the World Bank are widely perceived as American-dominated.

Consistent with their fear of the West, fundamentalists regard foreign economic activity in their countries as exploitative. They make quasi-Marxist arguments, claiming that the United States owes much of its prosperity to cheap labor and resources (especially oil) from the Muslim world. Foreign investments and multinational corporations are accused of skimming off the most valuable assets of Muslim countries with the help of local governments and elites. Fundamentalists even see U.S. aid to Muslim countries as proof of a sellout by their own governments; this became especially clear in post-1979 Egypt.

In contrast, the Soviet Union has negligible economic influence. A moribund Soviet economy inspires no one to adopt its version of state capitalism as a model. The ruble has no international role. The U.S.S.R. hardly participates in the oil trade with Muslim countries and its other trade is marginal. It has almost no money to invest outside its satellites. Conversely, foreigners cannot invest in Latvian industry or Siberian mines. That the Soviet Union has so little presence in the world economy insulates it from blame; fundamentalists cannot make it the cause of their tribulations.

The presence of large numbers of Americans and West Europeans in Muslim countries exacerbates fundamentalist sensitivities. Tourists gawk, trample through sacred sites and behave immodestly. Foreign residents infect the local population with non-Islamic practices. Except for hippies, anthropologists and volunteers—each objectionable in its own way—Americans live in the best parts of town, enjoying facilities beyond the reach of most Muslims, indulging in activities forbidden by Islamic law. Soviet tourists are virtually non-existent outside the Soviet bloc, while Soviet residents in Muslim countries are few in number, are rarely seen, and travel in tightly supervised groups.

America is ubiquitous. As he walks through the modern section of almost any town, a fundamentalist Muslim would encounter—and object to—most of what he sees: signs in English and French, glossy advertisements promoting Marlboro cigarettes, Coca Cola and electronic imports; theaters showing American feature films; kiosks carrying *Time* and *Newsweek*; luxury hotels housing American tourists; radios blaring rock music. By contrast, Russian influence derives almost exclusively from its military prowess; take that away and the Soviet international presence is very small indeed.

V

The U.S. government represents liberal values, the Soviet government stands for Marxism as interpreted by Lenin. From the fundamentalist Muslim's point of view, these American and Soviet ideologies are about equally irreconcilable with Islamic tenets and about equally obnoxious. But, like the everyday cultures, the two ideologies are not equally threatening.

At first glance, liberalism appears preferable. Like Islam, it respects religious faith, the family unit and private property. Marxism, of course, abolishes these and replaces them with dialectical materialism, the state and communal ownership. A closer look, however, reveals the shallowness of this reading. Marxist attacks on the family belong to the distant past and no longer have real force. And while the Marxist rejection of private property goes much further than any views of fundamentalist Muslims, many of the latter believe in severely restricting the right of private property as a means to achieve social justice. Muhammad Baqir as-Sadr, the Iraqi thinker whose book on economics has greatly influenced the Iranian government, argues that ownership of property in Islam should be neither wholly private nor entirely public but a mix of the two.[14]

In one key area—religion—most fundamentalists reject Marxism, but even here the difference can be reduced. Marxist theory requires atheism, but socialism as such need not. Believers can redistribute wealth as well as atheists. Some Muslims inject God into Marxism, others produce hybrid theories of "Arab socialism" or "Islamic socialism." Fundamentalists are hopeful that Marxists will see the error of their doctrine on this point. For example, Hashemi Rafsanjani noted recently that "as a result of the achievements of the Islamic revolution in Iran, Marxist theorists and among them Cuba's Fidel Castro, have been gradually reviewing their academic outlooks on religion and abandoning their judgment of religion as an 'opium of the masses'." Rafsanjani quoted Castro as saying that religion could serve as a revolutionary drive for the masses.[15]

If fundamentalist Islam has few conflicts with Marxism, the areas of agreement between these two ideologies are numerous, especially when they are contrasted to liberalism.

Authoritative founding scriptures The Koran and the works of Marx and Engels constitute bodies of unalterable but highly malleable doctrine. Comprehensive written theories take precedence over experience and common sense. The assumption that truth is knowable permeates fundamentalist Islam and Marxism. Liberalism has no writ, no dogma, no authoritative interpreters.

Highly specified patterns of behavior All-embracing systems provide guidance on a wide variety of matters, great and small. Fundamentalist Islam begins with the private sphere and then extends to control the public, while Marxism moves in the other direction, but in the end both regulate private and public affairs alike. Specific regulations in the two systems differ profoundly, of course, but details matter less than the fact that each of them aspires to regulate the whole of life. Liberalism leaves its citizens alone as much as possible.

Pervasive government involvement In the ideal Islamic or Marxist society, no activity takes place without reference to the guiding philosophy: education, art, literature, economics, law, warfare, sexuality and religion all have political significance. And if theory has something to say about every aspect of life, the government cannot be far behind. Because fundamentalist Muslims and Marxists have specific goals which require that the government shape its citizens, government becomes an instrument for molding society. Their codes incline them toward authoritarianism (government control of politics only) and even totalitarianism (government control of all aspects of life.) Only a minority of fundamentalist Muslims and not all Marxists go in this direction, but the totalitarian temptation exists in both ideologies.

Anti-individualism Fundamentalist Muslims and Marxists share a distaste for what they view as the decadence and crass materialism of Western life. The self-indulgent and individualistic features of contemporary American life are especially worrisome. Dismissing the philosophical and political rationales behind the freedom of expression, both condemn its manifestations and, to a surprising degree, find the same manifestations most loathsome. Fundamentalist Muslim and Marxist visions of a structured society contrast with the free-wheeling, undisciplined, open way of life in America and Western Europe. Individualism threatens the stability of the fundamentalist and Marxist orders in equal measure and is anathema to both. Both emphasize community needs over those of the individual and place a higher priority on equality than on freedom.

Ambitious programs Fundamentalist Muslims and Marxists have noble-sounding visions of society that they seek to impose on their citizens. The brotherhoods of Muslims and workers should transcend geographic, linguistic, ethnic and other differences. Islam prohibits war among Muslims; Marxism demands total allegiance to the class. Islam outlaws the charging of interest on money and Marxism prohibits private profit. Islam prescribes very low taxation rates; Marxism calls for massive income redistribution. Islam calls for a society in harmony with God's laws; Marxism envisages a society in accord with "scientific" principles. Both scorn the modest, realistic expectations of liberalism, choosing to pursue higher standards.

Inability to fulfill goals Each system requires an impossible transformation in behavior; humans cannot live up to divine or scientific standards. Muslims and socialists alike have long clashed among themselves, starting with the Battle of the Camel in A.D. 656 (for Muslims) and the First World War (for socialists). The current division of the world into national states frustrates fundamentalists as much as Marxists.

Discouragement of dissent Anyone living in a fundamentalist or Marxist order who proceeds his own way can expect to meet severe punishment. Why should those who know total truth tolerate dissent? Freedom of expression makes no sense to fundamentalists and Marxists, who discourage divergent ideas. In contrast, the liberal governments of the United States and Western Europe allow each citizen to live as he wishes (within obvious limitations) and to attempt to convince others of the truth of his ideas.

For these many reasons Muslim fundamentalists, when they think about it, find the Soviet ideological program less alien than the American. Finally is the fact that Muslims and Marxists alike see themselves as successors to Western civilization and have mounted its only sustained challenges. Islam claims that Muhammad's revelation replaces Christianity as the final religion; Marxism claims that socialism succeeds capitalism as the final stage of economic evolution. In the face of these ambitions, the continued prosperity and power of America riles both fundamentalist Muslims and Marxists and stimulates bonds between them, for all their differences.

VI

In political and military terms, one might expect fundamentalist Muslims to see the Soviet Union as their greatest threat. After all, Muscovy was already conquering Muslim Lands in the fourteenth century; the Russian territorial push at the expense of Muslims continued under the tsars until the 1880s, with the conquest of Muslim territories in the Caucasus and Central Asia. Although the Bolsheviks before 1917 promised independence to these regions, once in power the communist government devoted enormous resources to securing its hold on the tsarist colonial territories. The Soviet Union today includes within its state frontiers nearly 50 million Muslims, the only large body of Muslims still governed by a European power. The long-term conquest of Muslim lands resumed in late 1979 with the invasion of Afghanistan.

As the following commentary on Iranian radio makes clear, fundamentalist Muslims know the Soviet record:

> Tsarist aspirations concerning the [Persian] Gulf region did not change in the era of the socialist October Revolution. Soviet policy adhered to the same aspirations concerning the Gulf region, its warm waters, and its strategic oil resources and the hugh reserve that the region has in this respect. When the Red Army invaded Afghan territory in 1979, Moscow covered another section of the way to the region with the hope of extending it in the future.[16]

The American record could not differ more. While Moscow assembled an empire stretching from Germany to Mongolia, the United States encouraged the disbanding of European empires. From Woodrow Wilson's Fourteen Points in 1918 to Dwight Eisenhower's handling of the Suez crisis in 1956, American leaders pressured the British, French and other West European states to withdraw from Muslim lands.

Yet American anti-imperialism seems to be forgotten when the fundamentalists examine the world around them. America's close relations with Great Britain and France make it, in the eyes of many Muslims, heir to their imperial mantle. Close relations with Israel anger them. And the United States is held responsible even for Soviet activities: when the Soviet Union established diplomatic relations with several Persian Gulf states in 1985, Iranian officials interpreted this as an American ploy. "Washington is doubtlessly in the picture and background of these developments, since the U.S. monopoly of influence, in any case, leaves no room for Soviet infiltration. . . . [Perhaps] there is a tacit agreement between Washington and Moscow to defend the region vis-à-vis a third party [i.e. Iran] that threatens the interests of both sides."[17] Iranian fundamentalists blame Washington for the expansion of Moscow's influence! However dangerous the Soviet Union, the United States always looks worse.

Khomeini's pungent anti-Americanism sets the tone for the Iranian government and affects the views of fundamentalist Muslims world wide. Khomeini believes that the United States wishes to take economic control of Iran: "Everything in our treasury has to be emptied into the pockets of America."[18] He interprets Iraq's attack on Iran in September 1980 as an American plot and ascribes Iraq's continued resistance to American assistance. Iranian commentaries accuse the United States of deploying its finest "resources in the fields of politics, military and culture" against Iran.[19] For all these reasons, Khomeini concludes, "Iran is a country effectively at war with America."[20]

He sees the U.S. aggression toward Iran as part of a larger pattern: America "has appointed its agents in both the Muslim and non-Muslim countries to deprive everyone who lives under their domination of his freedom." Make a single mistake and the Americans will pounce: "The danger that America poses is so great that if you commit the smallest oversight, you will be destroyed." In short, "America plans to destroy us, all of us."[21] The United States is largely successful, too, at least in regard to the places Khomeini cares most about: as he stated in September 1979, "Today, the world of Islam is captive in the hands of America."[22]

The Soviet danger is not unimportant: "We are at war with international communism no less than we are struggling against the global plunderers of the West . . . the danger represented by the communist powers is no less than that of America."[23] Khomeini hates the Soviet Union (a "concentration camp") as much as the United States ("a brothel on a universal scale").[24] But Iran maintains better relations with the Soviet Union.

Fundamentalist Muslims believe they see eye-to-eye with the Soviet Union on the question of colonialism, as well as its alleged successor, neoimperialism. More important, after World War II, the Soviet Union provided a useful balance to America's preponderant power. As Sayyid Qutb of Egypt wrote in 1951, the Muslims "are in temporary need of the communist power."[25] For similar reasons, the Iranian foreign minister today calls for improved political, trade and scientific relations with the U.S.S.R.

Russia's empire is as obscure as the films it produces: continuing efforts at the absorption of tens of millions of Muslims into Soviet society are virtually invisible. The invasion of Afghanistan attracted some attention, but only a small fraction of what a comparable American military effort would. Moscow's colonial-style control of South Yemen goes almost unnoticed. The global influence of American news media has the effect of exaggerating Washington's role and diminishing Moscow's. In Khomeini's eyes, the Russian record of expansion against Iran over the past 250 years pales in comparison with the U.S. role during the 25 years before the Islamic revolution. As he sees it, the

United States put the shah in power in 1953 and kept him there through 1978. Khomeini believes that Iran in that period had become "an official colony of the U.S."[26] The Soviets may loom across a long border, but the Americans have already ruled the country, as the fundamentalist leadership sees it, and are planning to do so again.

Less challenged by or aware of the Soviet Union, radical fundamentalists fear it less. In more positive terms, they slightly but consistently favor the Soviet Union over the United States. So long as America and its way of life attract traditionalist, secularist and reformist Muslims, fundamentalists will direct most of their hostility toward the United States.

VII

This analysis has several major implications. Of the four main reasons why fundamentalist Muslims are more anti-American than anti-Soviet, three are fixed. The cultural influence, economic dynamism and alien ideology of the United States will remain as they are, no matter who the American leaders are or what course their policy takes. No specific action will make the country less objectionable to fundamentalists. Conversely, nothing the Soviet Union can do will win it a cultural, economic or ideological role comparable to America's.

In other words, what America is, not what it does, constitutes its greatest challenge to fundamentalist Muslims. Little can be done to avert collisions between America and the fundamentalists. Were the U.S. government willing to take every step to appease the fundamentalists, most problems would remain. Disclaiming the Carter Doctrine, disbanding the Central Command, renouncing Israel and supporting fundamentalist forces in Lebanon and Afghanistan would still leave the advertisements, ideologies, schools and multinational corporations that attract Muslims. Ultimately, Washington can do very little to reduce the fears of fundamentalists.

There remains one positive step open to the United States: to attempt to convince fundamentalists that with regard to the fourth factor, the political-military threat, the Soviet Union threatens them more. The fundamentalist view that the United States presents the main threat to Muslim independence is simply wrong: in fact, the Soviet Union does. Reminding the fundamentalists of basic facts—who rules 50 million Muslims in the Caucasus and Central Asia, who controls South Yemen, who has troops in Afghanistan—might increase their attention to Soviet behavior. The goals of such an effort would be modest; the point of directing attention to the Soviet empire is not to make friends for the United States, but to impress upon the fundamentalists the real nature of the dangers they face.

The American government has many means for making fundamentalist Muslims (and others) more aware of the Soviet threat: speeches by leading politicians, Voice of America programs, statements at the United Nations and other international forums, and so forth. Making the Soviet threat to Muslims a major theme would almost certainly provoke international discussion and would be much to America's benefit.

For American policymakers, the problem of dealing with fundamentalist Muslims arises in three situations: when they oppose pro-American governments, when they oppose pro-Soviet governments and when they control governments.

Tempting as it is to rush in and assist a friendly Muslim ruler facing powerful fundamentalist opposition, this often proves counterproductive. When embattled rulers accept American aid they become more vulnerable to accusations of selling their independence to Washington. The fundamentalist Muslims' extreme sensitivity to even the slightest hints of dependence on a superpower renders the dilemma of helping one's friends without arousing more opposition especially acute.

To make matters worse, Muslim rulers sometimes refuse to acknowledge the full danger of arousing fundamentalist anger. The shah of Iran associated too closely with the United States; the same was true of Sadat. As secularist or reformist Muslims, these leaders were so oriented to the West that they consistently underestimated the problem of foreign contamination and the power of fundamentalists. Sadat became so absorbed by his reputation in the West—the Nobel Peace Prize, ovations from the U.S. Congress—that he lost touch with his own power base, the Egyptian military. (This problem plagues the Soviet Union and its Muslim clients as well. In Afghanistan, Nur Muhammad Taraki and Hafizullah Amin underestimated their Islamic opposition as badly as any American allies; likewise, the Soviet Union misunderstood the depths of resistance to their invasion.) Friendly Muslim leaders cannot be allowed unilaterally to expand their relationship with the United States: Americans must take part in this decision.

In assessing ties to friendly Muslim countries, caution must be exercised not to make the United States unnecessarily the focus of fundamentalist anger. Fundamentalists attack what they see with their own eyes. Importing wheat prompts less animosity than the import of films and clothes. American soldiers isolated from indigenous populations pose less of a problem than soldiers stationed in cities. Quiet cooperation with a friendly government provokes less opposition than open declarations of support at public meetings. Strong relations need not have a high profile: ideally, they are almost invisible.

When communist or pro-Soviet forces threaten, pro-American regimes are tempted to promote fundamentalists as a counterweight, or even to bring them into the government. But this tactic involves great danger. The Tunisian and Egyptian governments encouraged fundamentalists in the early 1970s, only to lose control of those movements by the end of the decade. Secularist politicians in Turkey and the Sudan formed coalitions with fundamentalists in the mid-1970s, then had to accede to fundamentalists efforts to impose the Shari'a. And, when a non-fundamentalist like the late Zulfikar Ali Bhutto of Pakistan tries to win fundamentalist support by imposing Islamic law, distrust remains.

Imposition of the Shari'a creates three sources of tension with the United States. First, Americans have difficulty supporting a government that flogs alcohol-drinkers, cuts off the hands of thieves and stones adulterers. Abhorrent to Western morals, these practices create American ill will. Second, widespread opposition to the fundamentalists' version of the law leads to an upsurge of repression and instability, and this in turn leads to anti-Americanism. Third, the strengthening of some of America's most profound antagonists inevitably sours relations with the United States.

In one way, conservative fundamentalists threaten American interests more than the radicals, for they can make their influence felt within regimes friendly to the United States, while radicals oppose the authorities too much to be tempted into a coalition. Ultimately, however, radical fundamentalists are the real danger. As even more profound enemies of the United States than Marxists, their ascension to power almost always harms the United States and its allies.

Should the United States be invited to counsel Muslim allies on the question of cooperating with the fundamentalist opposition, its advice should be straightforward. Unless special circumstances dictate otherwise, it opposes application of the Shari'a and discourages enhancing the power of fundamentalists. The United States should neither assist fundamentalist movements that oppose friendly governments nor encourage its friends to appease them. Contact with radical fundamentalists is necessary, of course, to understand their views and to monitor their influence, but no assistance should be provided.

In the case of fundamentalist Muslims opposing governments allied with the Soviet Union, the United States is naturally tempted to provide aid to the fundamentalists. But this should only be done with extreme caution, if at all, and with full awareness of the perils involved. Even short-term aid can have dangerous consequences. Support for fundamentalists might make them the only alternative to communists; the United States can inadvertently strengthen the two extremes against the middle, squeezing out its natural allies between Soviet clients and fundamentalist Muslims. The moderates, whose views more closely correspond to America's, might be destroyed in the process.

Noting these dangers, fundamentalist Muslim groups should receive U.S. aid only when two conditions are met: the government they oppose creates very major problems for the United States; and the fundamentalists make up the only non-communist opposition.

Libya, Syria and Afghanistan all meet the first criterion. But fundamentalists are only a minor element in the opposition to Muammar al-Qaddafi's regime; American aid should therefore go only to the non-fundamentalist opposition. In Afghanistan too the second condition is not met, for non-fundamentalist mujahadeen groups are active both in the fighting in Afghanistan and in refugee politics in Pakistan; these deserve military, political and financial support from the United States. In Syria, however, the second condition is met. The Muslim Brethren constitute the only serious opposition to the regime of Hafiz al-Assad, and they have shown determination and resourcefulness. There being no moderate force to support, Syrian fundamentalists could properly receive U.S. aid.

As for fundamentalists in power, they divide into two types, conservatives and radicals. The former usually seek good relations with the United States and, keeping the profound differences between their goals and those of the United States in mind, ties should be cultivated. Disagreement on long-range goals means that cooperation with a superpower is limited to tactics. Pakistan resembles China in the way it works with the United States against the Soviet Union: both countries take money and aid without giving friendship. The application of Islamic law creates human rights problems, so the United States cannot become too closely associated with fundamentalist leaders, as it did with Jafer al-Numeiri in the Sudan.

Radicals have terrible relations with the United States, and for obvious cultural, economic and ideological reasons. Notwithstanding their fears of Western civilization, the United States should do its best to make the Soviet danger to Muslim independence better known. Even so adamant an opponent as Khomeini is likely to dwell less on America as he becomes more aware of Soviet expansionism.

NOTES

1. Immam Khomeini, *Islam and Revolution*, trans. Hamid Algar, Berkeley, Calif.: Mizan Press, 1981, p. 185.
2. Radio Teheran, Nov. 17, 1985; Islamic Republic News Agency, Nov. 17, 1985.
3. Khomeini, *op. cit.*, p. 221.
4. Umar at-Talmasani, *Ash-Shab* (Cairo), July 9, 1985.
5. Islamic Republic News Agency, Aug. 10, 1985.
6. *The New York Times*, March 28, 1980.
7. Hasan al-Banna, *al-Mutamar al-khamis*, p. 10, quoted in Richard P. Mitchell, *The Society of the Muslim Brothers*, London: Oxford University Press, 1969, p. 233.
8. Sayyid Qutb, *Maalim fil-Tariq*, quoted in Emmanuel Sivan, *Radical Islam*, New Haven and London: Yale University Press, 1985, p. 25.
9. Sheikh Muhammad Mahdi Shams ad-Din, vice chairman of the Supreme Shi'ite Assembly of Lebanon, Islamic Republic News Agency, Nov. 16, 1985.
10. Umar at-Talmasani, *loc. cit.*
11. Islamic Republic News Agency, May 23, 1985.
12. Quoted in Shaul Bakhash, *The Reign of the Ayatollahs*, New York: Basic Books, 1984, p. 122.

13. *The New York Times*, Jan. 29, 1984.

14. Muhammad Baqir as-Sadr, *Iqtisaduna*, 3d ed., Beirut: Dar al-Fikr, 1969, pp. 257–268.

15. Islamic Republic News Agency, Nov. 15, 1985.

16. Teheran International Service, Nov. 16, 1985.

17. *Ibid.*

18. Khomeini, *op. cit.*, p. 221.

19. Radio Teheran, Oct. 30, 1985.

20. Khomeini, *op. cit.*, p. 305.

21. Khomeini, *op. cit.*, pp. 214, 286, 306.

22. Radio Teheran, July 31, 1985.

23. Khomeini, *op. cit.*, p. 286.

24. Quoted in Amir Taheri, *The Spirit of Allah: Khomeini and the Islamic Revolution*, Chevy Chase, Md.: Adler & Adler, 1986, p. 298.

25. Sayyid Qutb, *al-Salam al-Alami wal-Islam*, Cairo, 1951, cited in Richard P. Mitchell, *op. cit.*, p. 271.

26. Khomeini, *op. cit.*, p. 215.

HAVES VS. HAVE-NOTS: UPHEAVAL BETWEEN NORTH AND SOUTH

7

North-South Interdependence

IVAN L. HEAD

Facts are elusive, whether they be pursued in a scientific laboratory, a court of justice or the columns of a newspaper. Still more are they elusive in the political arena.

In each of these environments, for every hypothesis there is, and should be, one or more counter-propositions. It is a reflection of the human condition, however, that neither hypothesis nor proposition always springs forth from wholesome circumstance. Suspicion, greed, intolerance and prejudice combine insidiously to make the search for truth and identification of fact constantly difficult and on occasion perilous. In the result, the truth remains hidden—sometimes for unconscionable periods of time, sometimes with incalculable costs.

To scientists, the most infamous example is that of Galileo. In the worlds of politics and journalism, historians may in future determine that one of the most glaring incidents is that of the present refusal to accept as factual the relationship between countries developed and developing. Can this refusal be likened to the treatment of Galileo? The inclination of some political leaders to weigh international relationships in simple terms, arrayed most often on an East-West axis and measured constantly on a scale of friendship and ideology, makes the analogy a tempting one. What was the climate in which Galileo found himself? In *The Ascent of Man*, Jacob Bronowski wrote:

> In 1622 Rome created the institution for the propagation of the faith from which we still derive the word propaganda. Catholics and Protestants were embattled in what we should now call a cold war, in which, if Galileo had only known it, no quarter was given to a great man or small. The judgment was very simple on both sides: who is not for us is—a heretic.

The denial by the Catholic Church for 200 years of the true nature of the solar system did not cause the Earth or the other planets to pause for one second in their revolutions about the sun. The denial did, however, suffocate scientific enquiry in the vast realm of Catholicism for two centuries, and gave an opportunity to the Protestant nations to gain a predominant position in scientific endeavors.

The hypothesis now being denied by all too many leaders of the industrialized countries has nothing to do with Copernican theory. It pertains very much, however, to another form of revolution, one without astronomical meaning but one which is as potentially capable of causing fundamental and far-reaching change as was the scholarship of Copernicus and its defense by Galileo. It is the dependence of the nations of the North—in economic, environmental, military and political terms—on the nations of the South. The extent of dependency varies from country to country and from sector to sector, yet dependency there is.

In the industrialized countries there is understandable resistance to the concept of dependence on others, unwillingness to accept that a nation's fate or health or freedom of movement is held hostage beyond its shores. Yet when last did the nations of the North, individually or in unison, undertake successfully a major foreign policy initiative that was not a reaction to events elsewhere, most often in the South, sometimes in the East?

Notwithstanding this pattern of reaction, the Northern nations appear incapable of proposing changes in global relationships which would at once acknowledge that dependence—or, better, interdependence—and move toward easing the structural inequities which, unattended, guarantee an ever worsening sequence of events.

What is the evidence of dependence that Northern leaders choose to reject? The Brandt Commission, reporting on North-South relations, as was its mandate, concluded: "At the beginnings of the 1980s the world community faces much greater dangers than at any time since the Second World War." The Global 2000 Report warned that unless steps are taken to reduce worldwide pressures on cropland, pastures, forests, mineral and water resources, the world will become even "more crowded, more polluted, less ecologically stable and more vulnerable to disruption than the world we live in now."

Of dependence, the evidence is clear. World Bank figures reveal that in 1979, 43 percent of Japanese merchandise exports were sold in the non-oil-exporting developing countries; 36 percent of U.S. merchandise exports that year went to the same markets, as did 32 percent of Australian merchandise exports. What this means for the United States is that one U.S. worker out of 20 is producing exports for the Third World.

These imports by the less developed countries in the 1970s grew at a pace more than 50 percent faster than merchandise trade among the industrialized countries. Thus, the European Economic Community and the United States send more than one-third of all their exports to the developing countries. In comparative terms this means that the United States exports twice as much to the developing countries as to the nations of the European Economic Community, and the community exports three times as much to the developing countries as to the United States.

Even these figures do not reveal the comparative trade advantage enjoyed by the Organization for European Cooperation and Development. A recent report to the Trilateral Commission shows that in 1979 Japan's export-import ratio in trade of manufactured goods with the South was seven-to-one; that of Europe four-to-one; that of North America two-to-one. This overwhelming advantage in value-added goods explains why, between 1973 and 1977, exports to the South created five million new jobs in Organization countries.

Agricultural products are part of this export trade as well, and in immense quantities. U.N. Food and Agricultural Organization statistics reveal that developing countries imported food in 1979 to the value of $38 billion, most of it from the industrialized North.

To sustain or to improve this purchasing pattern, the developing countries must have the means to pay. It is to insure such means that they seek reforms in the international financial institutions. Such reforms are blocked by the industrialized countries on the grounds that their own stagnant economies must first be put in order. Yet such blockage refuses to accept that economies North and South are trapped inexorably in the turbulence of the post-Keynesian period. If either is to emerge, it must be in cooperation with the other.

And so emerge the self-contradictory communiqués from summits and from capitals: admission of inability to deal effectively with domestic economic crisis; exasperation at continued political instability in so many regions; yet refusal to acknowledge the need for multilateral solutions.

At a time when international cooperation has never been more necessary, the preferred instrument of foreign policy seems to be the unilateral threat. And the more obvious the failures, the more ominous become the threats. Without acceptance of responsibility, circumstances become ever more somber.

- Of the slightly more than 150 countries in the international community, some 100 are in food deficit positions.
- At present rates of destruction, the world's forest cover will be halved by the year 2000.
- By that same year, the population of this planet will have increased by two billion—the equivalent of one new Bangladesh every year for the next 20 years.

These three categories of human activity intersect again and again. The global carrying capacity is sorely tested by excessive population increases with unsustainable demands upon forests for fuelwood and upon arable land for agricultural production. The rapid depletion of forest cover threatens incalculable future effects on the carbon dioxide balance in the atmosphere and likely wide-ranging changes in weather patterns. The disappearance of forest cover leads to soil drifting and erosion, to unwanted silting of rivers, of soil buildup behind power dams and the blockage of harbors.

But for the most part, Northern leaders and communicators refuse to look beyond domestic-economic or Eastern-based security issues. These governments encourage Southern countries to believe that their main problem is communism, and invite them to mortgage their futures to purchase arms. The United States is now by far the largest exporter of arms to the Third World, responsible for 45 percent of all sales. The second largest exporter, the Soviet Union, trails with 27.5 percent of the total. What contribution does this activity make to the goal of stability? Premier George Price of Belize replies:

> The only issue that counts in Central America is the North-South Dialogue. If you don't bring stability and justice to the markets in sugar and coffee, you will never have stability and justice in the countries that produce them.

Accumulating evidence demonstrates that the situation is not one in which the South is absorbing infinite Northern largesse, distributed on generous concessional terms; rather, it is the North that is the net beneficiary of North-South money flows. In 1976, the industrialized countries enjoyed the advantage of a $70 billion favorable balance of trade with the developing countries—a sum 3.5 times the total flow of development assistance in the reverse direction. This immense flow of funds from South to North has been made possible only by credits from international financial institutions and private banks, by dexterously recycling petro-dollars. This pattern cannot continue indefinitely; indeed is not continuing. The exposure of Northern banks to massive Southern debt is a matter of grave concern.

Some observers have remarked that international relations between North and South today are not unlike owner-worker relations a century or so ago. In the pre-trade-union period, prior to the Reform bills in the

British Parliament, workers played no part in either the economic or political structures. If there was work, they were hired; if none, they were laid off and became dependent upon charity. It was unthinkable, said the privileged, that the franchise could be extended to irresponsible, uneducated persons who owned no land. Workers cannot dictate the terms of their employment, said entrepreneurs; if they are not satisfied with their wages, they need not work.

Now, many decades later, the privileged North looks upon the South in a way that we would find appalling were we to apply it to our own domestic situations. Suggestions that the developing countries be given some responsibility for the direction of the World Bank or the International Monetary Fund, that an energy affiliate be created at the Bank, that terms of trade be altered so as to remove the built-in Northern advantage—all are rejected by the North. The advocates of change are paid no heed, as if they were dissident agents of a competing religion.

In February 1983 the Brandt Commission published a second report, surveying the international scene over the three years between reports. Developments in that period, writes Willy Brandt in his introduction,

> served to confirm some of the worst fears expressed. . . . The world's prospects have deteriorated rapidly. . . . Further decline is likely to cause the disintegration of societies and create conditions of anarchy in many parts of the world.

Sober second thoughts, indeed.

The North-South dialogue is very much more than a simple matter of transfer of resources. What it comes down to is a sharing of power and of responsibility among the countries of the world. When the South speaks in terms of a new international economic order, it asks that the international system be one that is not tilted permanently against it in terms of commodity prices, access to credit, flows of technology and the control of markets and decisions, most of which are determined in the North. When we tell the South to raise itself by its own bootstraps, we must be very sure that we are not standing on those bootstraps.

The world around us is changing at a breathtaking pace. We in the North may participate in and influence those changes, or we can default and pretend we can get along without the world, as if a North American or European ghetto were either possible or desirable. The first option leads to survival; the second guarantees disaster.

Development in the South is imperative for a future that works: an economic imperative because of the interdependence of our economies; an ecological imperative because of the singleness of our biosphere; a political imperative because of the tinderbox nature of international disputes. But it is more. Pope John Paul II stated, in a speech in Tokyo, that "the building of a more just humanity or a more united international community is not just a dream or a vain ideal. It is a moral imperative."

It is the obligation of all of us who make some claim to scientific method and to orderly thought processes to insure that our futures are molded by the Galileos and not by their opponents.

8

The Perversion of Foreign Aid

NICK EBERSTADT

The attitude of the American people toward the world's poor, and toward our government's effort to attend to their distress, is seldom examined by those who frame our policies toward the international economy and the less developed regions of the earth. It is instructive, however, to listen to what the American people have to say.

Surveys of public opinion consistently show a deep concern about the plight of needy people in other countries—a concern higher among the public at large than among those groups pollsters designate as "public-opinion leaders." While attitudes about most other aspects of foreign policy tend to vary with the times, the public's interest in aiding the desperately poor has remained remarkably constant. In 1982, as in previous years, nearly 60 percent of the respondents polled by the Chicago Council on Foreign Relations said they viewed "combating world hunger" as a "very important" objective for the United States; only 5 percent felt it to be "not important." As in previous surveys, combating world hunger ranked far ahead of "protecting American business abroad," and even ahead of "defending our allies' security" or "matching Soviet military strength," as an international concern. Though these results may surprise some who consider themselves experts on foreign policy, they are not a fluke; to the contrary, they are in keeping with a wide range of findings from other polls.

Paradoxically, while the public's commitment to aiding the wretched of the earth gives all the signs of an unwavering consensus, its attitude toward foreign-aid *programs* appears to be thoroughly hostile. Since 1974 the Chicago Council on Foreign Relations has asked respondents to volunteer their views of "the 2 or 3 biggest foreign-policy problems facing the nation today." "Reducing foreign aid" is always one of the two top concerns. In these surveys neither the arms race, nor the threat of nuclear war, nor even relations with the Soviet Union has yet evoked the sort of response elicited by the idea of cutting foreign aid, which is by far the most unpopular program in the federal budget. In 1978— foreign aid's "best" year in the Chicago Council surveys—over four times as many interviewees favored cutbacks as approved of increases, leaving the program with a net rating of minus 39 percent. Even at the height of the disillusionment with the Vietnam war or on the eve of the "Reagan revolution," neither defense nor domestic welfare was held in such low esteem.

What can explain these strong—and yet apparently contradictory— feelings about helping the world's poor? One possibility is that they are only a specific example of a more general proposition: that the public's opinions about international problems are ill-considered, volatile, and vaguely irrational. But there is also a perfectly logical explanation for this ostensible paradox. The American public may think its government's programs for aiding the world's poor defective, or positively injurious. On this view, the stronger the public's commitment to the world's poor, the more forcefully it would reject programs that seem untrue to that commitment.

Interestingly enough, America's elites do not appear to share the deep misgivings of the public about U.S. foreign-aid programs. According to a number of surveys, the overseas-relief, development, and security policies which our people find so objectionable are considered utterly unexceptionable by our "public-opinion leaders." Such surveys typically indicate that leaders view foreign aid as a "non-issue."

This cleavage between the public and the opinion-makers is highly significant. At different times in American history the general public has come to an understanding about the world before its leaders. We are now at such a point. The American people seem to recognize an important fact about world affairs that continues to elude their leaders— namely, that the American government's efforts to bring relief, prosperity, and security to impoverished peoples in other countries have gone seriously wrong.

II

The descent of our foreign-aid policies from their original purposes is a poignant story. Its outlines must be recounted, if only to recall how far we have strayed from our initial objectives and principles. . . .

"Development assistance" to low-income countries began in 1949, on the heels of the Marshall Plan. It was a new and radical idea in international relations. Unlike emergency relief, it was not framed in response to disaster. Unlike reparations, it was a state-to-state resource transfer prompted by volition, not indemnity. Unlike military aid or security assistance, it was not meant, in any immediate sense, to apply American will to distant regions of the earth.

Development assistance, as outlined in President Truman's Point Four program in his 1949 State of the Union address, reflected the American preference that other peoples avail themselves of the good things the 20th century had to offer, including the skills and knowledge which made mass affluence possible. It was consistent with our vision of the postwar world. The United States had already created an international monetary and financial system which could contribute to a nation's economic advancement. We were now stating our willingness to help interested governments move their countries into the international economic updraft that the new order had made possible.

The idea of such assistance—of fostering the competence of new governments to deal with their nations' economic problems—received an enthusiastic reception from the world community. By the end of 1949 the United Nations had unanimously endorsed an international plan of action modelled directly on America's Point Four programs, though more modest in resources and scope.

The leitmotif of development assistance in its first few years was the connection between the policies and actions of governments in poor nations and their economic consequences. This connection was taken to be inescapable and obvious. Alluding to the "shortage" of Western capital in the less developed countries—a problem that agitated many leaders in Latin America, Asia, and Africa at the time—Truman's Assistant Secretary of State for Economic Affairs observed that "the real decision must be made by these countries themselves, since only they can decide whether they want our capital to participate in their development. If they want it, they must, in turn, create the 'climate' to attract it."

Nor was this perspective a matter of partisan dispute. Early in 1953, President Eisenhower's Assistant Secretary of State for Economic Affairs warned Congress that the limits on the effectiveness of our technical-assistance programs came from the attitude of recipient governments: "There is a strong tendency to build steel mills when the best economic interest of that particular country would be served by growing a little more food. . . . But the attraction of being self-sufficient, of having these monuments of industry . . . seems to be so great that we have difficulties in getting them to understand wherein their own economic salvation lies."

Development assistance as America envisioned it, unfortunately, was not quite what the new, nationalist elites in less developed countries were looking for. Regardless of their professed political ideologies, these new regimes were almost uniformly preoccupied with augmenting the power of the state apparatus under their control. To many stewards of new states in the 1950's, the goal of building state power seemed, indeed, to be threatened by the liberal international economic order the

United States was promoting. An orientation toward international markets and free flows of foreign capital might remove vital decisions about national destiny from their hands. What seemed more in keeping with their desire to focus the national will through the medium of government was some system of central economic planning.

This approach to "nation building," later dignified by the title "development planning," was in fact an application and perfection of the techniques the combatant powers had used to marshall and apply resources against one another in World War II. Around the globe, poor societies in the 1950's were, in effect, putting themselves on a wartime footing. They were going long on steel and short on food; relying on trade where they must, but on autarky where they might.

The extent to which this emphasis on command planning clashed with the American conception of the function of development assistance was not immediately appreciated in the United States—where, after all, the popular preoccupation was with demilitarizing the economy as quickly as possible, and with disassembling wartime economic controls so that the tempo of civilian life might resume. If this conflict in time helped bring about a very large shift in American ideas, in the early 1950's such changes were still far off. The United States had not only firm principles, but clear operational rules by which to guide its foreign-aid policies. It attempted to separate overseas humanitarian aid from the economic interests of lobby groups at home. It made scrupulous distinctions between grants (which were charitable) and loans (which were to be commercial). Perhaps most importantly, it let it be known that there was a difference between military aid and development assistance, and that the demarcation was essential to the purposes and prospects of both programs.

III

One by one, these precepts about foreign aid were to fall.

The first abrupt departure occurred in 1954, when Congress authorized the Food For Peace program. On the East coast, Food For Peace was justified as a humanitarian gesture by which American bounty could be put to the service of a hungry world; in the Midwest its workings were perhaps more honestly discussed. The champion of Food For Peace, Senator Hubert Humphrey, represented Minnesota, a state then beset by agricultural "overproduction." So long as the farmers' ability to produce outstripped the market's demand for their produce, competitive restructuring of the farming industry would be inevitable, and, just as inevitably, it would be small farmers who would be "restructured" off the land. These were Senator Humphrey's constituents, and the Food For Peace program, PL 480, addressed their problems. PL 480 would authorize the purchase of massive quantities of grain and other foodstuffs, subsidizing their sale in the markets of poor nations or giving food outright to governments.

For American farmers, the immediate impact of PL 480 legislation was incontestably beneficial. For the poor nations, the consequences were more ambiguous. Heavily subsidized American imports very often drove down local food prices; while this might not have raised qualms in capitals intent upon forced-pace industrialization, it nevertheless caused problems in rural hinterlands, where standards of living were, typically, significantly lower than in the cities.

What is more, recipient governments often resold the food America gave them for cash, so that they could pursue projects that foreign lenders had denied them as economically unwise. A concessionary device permitting recipient governments to repay "food loans" in their own local currencies relieved them of the pressure to value their foreign exchange realistically, with predictable consequences for both budget discipline and export incentives. (This also paved the way for several international economic panics, as when the Indian government suddenly discovered it owed the United States more rupees than it had in central reserves—and nationalized the entire private banking system to compensate.)

Perhaps most tellingly, only a tiny fraction of PL 480's allocations was earmarked for regions hit by famine or disaster. This fact was not lost on overseas observers, who had been warned by Marxists and other anti-Americans that the U.S. would export its own domestic economy problems and call the result charity.

The next radical deviation from principle came over the issue of "soft," or subsidized, loans. In 1946, American authorities had resolved that concessionary loans to foreign governments would have no place among the techniques of American statecraft; such loans, it was felt, would create a dangerous and needless confusion between charity and commerce. After our first soft loan, a large one to the United Kingdom to stabilize the sterling-based currencies, our National Advisory Council on Monetary and Financial Problems, which had sanctioned the offering, stated: "It is the view of the Council that the British case is unique, and will not be a precedent for loans to any other country."

Within ten years, soft loans were becoming a preferred vehicle for U.S. foreign aid. Soft loans seemed to vitiate the need for hard choices. Skeptical inquiries from taxpayers over specific projects could be deflected by assurances that the U.S. expected in time to be fully repaid on its principal. Foreign governments would hear that soft loans gave them great financial leverage, since along with the concessionary bequest the arrangement provided a large pool of working capital. Soft loans thus seemed to offer protection to those aid initiatives whose usefulness was most open to question; yet this naturally made the loans a magnet for precisely those proposals which were least justifiable and most likely to waste resources. If soft loans at this time seemed like a "cheap" way of paying for foreign aid, it was only because one of their major costs had been forgotten: their impact on beneficiary governments' conception of, and attitude toward, capital transfer from abroad.

In 1948 the president of the World Bank had urged member nations not to fall into the trap of soft lending; by 1959, the idea of a soft-loan facility *at the Bank* was gaining acceptance; by 1961, this facility, the International Development Authority (IDA), was established under World Bank auspices, and with American blessings. Two decades earlier, a principal American proponent of a World Bank, Secretary of the Treasury Henry Morgenthau, had said that the institution he was proposing would "scrupulously avoid undertaking loans that private investors are willing to make on reasonable terms." IDA was true to the late Secretary's wish only in the sense that the sorts of projects it encouraged, and the terms that it financed, were generally unlikely to be attractive to private investors.

IV

The most fateful departure from previously enunciated principles of foreign aid, however, concerned the separation of military and development assistance. The Eisenhower years saw a profound shift in American foreign-aid patterns. Between 1949 and 1953, military grants and political aid for beleaguered but friendly regimes had accounted for scarcely a sixth of our foreign aid; between 1953 and 1961 they made up over half our bequests.

Security assistance was a calculated response to a pressing problem. Shortly after the victory of the Communist armies on the Chinese mainland, Communist forces from North Korea attacked our allies in the South, and drew us into war. Strengthening the defensive capability of the states in our alliance system seemed the surest way to deter further outside attacks. There was also a widespread threat, in relatively open societies, of internal subversion by armed, and generally anti-democratic, domestic groups. Security assistance was to address this problem as well: it included not only military aid but police training, political advice, covert activities, and unrestricted financial bequests just to buy time (and thereby, with luck, political stability).

Military/security assistance proved to be a highly effective program. With American aid, South Korea and Taiwan were able to secure themselves against potential enemies. Greece and Turkey were stabilized and strengthened, both militarily and politically. Insurgencies were suppressed in, among other places, the Philippines and Thailand. In Iran, a demagogue who was deemed anti-American was turned out of office, and the Shah (who we took to be pro-American) was returned to the throne from which he had been deposed. There were many other, less heralded, achievements as well.

In the late 1950's and early 1960's, security assistance had widespread public support, while development aid was not nearly so well regarded. Hence, to win acceptance for their overall foreign-aid programs, American statesmen began to draw on the legitimacy of security assistance to protect, and even conceal, development aid.

The process began with a change in legislation: the 1953 Mutual Security Act, which for the purposes of congressional appropriations linked development aid to security assistance. Even so, the two programs were kept operationally—and conceptually—distinct. Eric Johnston, at the time Eisenhower's Point Four adviser, spoke for the administration when he said, "I think the Point Four program . . . should not in any way be confused with military aid to countries."

That distinction was lost during the Kennedy administration. President Kennedy went so far as to argue that development aid *was* security assistance, and therefore that advocates of a strong American security posture should support development bequests. As he put it: "I urge those who want to do something for the United States, for this cause, to channel their energies behind the new foreign-aid program to help prevent the social injustice and economic chaos upon which subversion and revolt feeds." The "new foreign-aid program" to which he referred was the Agency for International Development (USAID), the organization which supervises and administers America's development programs in less developed countries to this very day.

In attempting to broaden and strengthen the domestic constituency behind development spending, President Kennedy had, perhaps accidentally, fundamentally altered the understanding of what development assistance was supposed to be. No longer was it a transfer of skills and a building of basic infrastructure so that governments of poor societies might better take advantage of the economic opportunities afforded them by growing international markets. It was now a program to quell domestic discontent in low-income regions—linking aid to stability through a series of complex syllogisms which ultimately equated rising living standards with diminishing political opposition. This attitude, at once cynical and naive, suggested that counterinsurgency and the diffusion of agricultural research were part and parcel of a single process, differing only in degree.

V

The efforts to paralyze AID were symptoms of a broader problem of the Vietnam and post-Vietnam era: American foreign policies had come to lack legitimacy in the eyes of a substantial portion of Congress and the public. A period of groping and confusion had begun, during which America's foreign economic policies in general, and foreign-aid policies in particular, broke away from the bipartisan principles which had been established in the early postwar years, and at a speed which sometimes suggested free fall. The events which derailed our foreign-aid policies were specific and discrete, yet in retrospect they seem to form a single, continuing chain of practical and moral errors.

In 1971 and 1972 President Nixon's foreign-aid proposals were defeated in Congress; funding for them was arranged only through a catch-all "continuing resolution" at the end of each session. To restore congressional confidence in the foreign-aid program, and in the presidential purposes behind it, a new code for American development programs was worked out. These were written into law in the Foreign Assistance Act of 1973 and the Mutual Development and Cooperation Act of the same year. At the time, these acts were described as a compromise. They read today as something very different.

The Foreign Assistance Act of 1973 states as directly as such legislation can that our postwar policies toward poorer nations had been a failure: "The conditions which shaped the United States foreign-assistance program in the past have changed. . . . [O]ur relations with the less developed countries must be revised to reflect these realities." The problem, it was suggested, was that the strategy of export-oriented, self-sustaining growth which we had advocated since the 1940's did not actually benefit the common people of the countries it transformed: in the words of the Mutual Development and Cooperation Act, "economic growth does not necessarily lead to social advancement by the poor."

The Foreign Assistance Act implied that American power abroad had been secured through alliances with local leaders who had little interest in the welfare of their own public. Hence, the new American approach to foreign aid "should be . . . targeted on the basics"—meaning that it should be judged by its direct and immediate impact on the living standards of the poorest strata of the recipient nations. "Through the restructured program the United States would be telling the developing countries . . . 'Do not forget the immediate needs of your poorest people.' . . ."

The "reforms of 1973" had sweeping consequences for American development efforts. In establishing "basic human needs" as the ultimate arbiter by which development would be judged, they shifted the purpose of AID from assisting self-sustaining growth to affecting living standards through emergency-style distribution of outside food, medicine, clothing, and materials for shelter. These "basic human needs" stipulations came on top of the operational restrictions which had already been imposed on AID, with their implicit bias against development proposals with deferred benefits or with consequences principally measured in efficiency or productivity.

Thus, American bequests increasingly came to be seen as a means of facilitating a steady flow of funds to the governments of less developed countries for use in whatever purposes they might choose. Though AID administrators could argue that their grants were "tied" to various purposes or conditions, local leaders generally understood the simple truth that, once received, government revenues were fungible—transferable from one objective to the next—and that aid bequests would become all the more fungible when meant to be applied to an operating budget.

There was a final notable aspect of the legislation of 1973: the explicit purpose of development-assistance programs was rewritten in a seemingly slight but nonetheless significant way. Provision 102(a) of the Foreign Assistance Act of 1967 had read: "Development is primarily the responsibility of the people of the less developed countries themselves." In the 1973 legislation, the equivalent passage read, "Development planning must be the responsibility of each sovereign nation." With this semantic change, America was retreating from the concepts of economic health and self-sustaining growth and implicitly repudiating the notion that international markets and free flows of private capital should serve as the instruments by which people might raise themselves to mass affluence. Instead, we had come to endorse, and seemingly to require of recipients of our aid, adherence to the very system of comprehensive planning which our leaders had decried as inimical to the interests of poor peoples scarcely twenty years earlier.

The "reforms of 1973" (also known as the "New Directions" legislation) may yet be hard fully to evaluate, but it is clear that they have had at least one effect. Before Vietnam, the United States could point to a number of self-reliant and prospering economies—Greece, Taiwan, and South Korea among them—which had "graduated" out of American development aid. Since the "reforms of 1973," there have been no new graduates.

VI

The decoupling of American development assistance from the policies which had previously been regarded as the best means for improving the economic health of poor nations also bespoke a loss of faith in the United States. It was no longer naturally assumed that American interests and preferences, pursued in practical fashion, would benefit the peoples of the world. To serve the weak and helpless of the earth, Americans were now advised to restrain themselves and their impulse to international action. The United States was urged instead to assist with the one thing it had which poor governments manifestly lacked: money.

As American-administered development programs took on the trappings of relief work, and as the terms "development aid" and "reparations" came to be used interchangeably (in 1973 Nixon administration officials had secretly discussed post-war "development aid" proposals with Hanoi), there arose simultaneously a tendency to give aid through international institutions rather than channeling it directly from our government to the beneficiary capital. Through "multilateralization," it was argued, donor "pressure" on recipient governments might be made to diminish, even as aid outlays were made to rise.

The multilateralization of aid was made easier by the impressive growth of the World Bank under Robert McNamara, the former U. S. Secretary of Defense who had left the Defense Department around the time of the Tet offensive to assume the Bank's presidency. As admirers testified at his retirement in 1981, he oversaw a tenfold increase in the Bank's annual commitments. McNamara accomplished this remarkable feat by reinterpreting the Bank's mission, and its operating rules.

The Bank's Articles of Agreement specify that bank funds must be used for "productive investment"; they neglect, however, to qualify the sorts of spending which may be labeled productive investment. McNamara took command of the definition of the term. A growing body of economic research was detailing the connection among education, productive knowledge, and economic growth: the results suggested that augmenting "human capital" was as integral to economic development as was deepening the base of "physical capital." McNamara used this research to argue that health, nutrition, education, family planning, and other social services were in fact investments, and thus legitimate avenues for the application of Bank funds.

While the prerogative for lending was being expanded, the standards for evaluating loans were simultaneously being relaxed. McNamara outlined the Bank's new view of lending in 1970: "What contributes the most to the development of the borrowing country should be the decisive factor in both Bank and IDA operations. . . . Any policy which can be justified for IDA as consistent with its development function can, I believe, be equally justified for the Bank, and the Bank itself should adopt it." Since IDA was in the business of dispensing "soft" loans—"of doubtful validity," as David Baldwin pointed out nearly twenty years ago, "by any measured banking standard"—a large pool of capital was being declared exempt from the scrutiny which private loans must customarily withstand.

McNamara's efforts to expand the Bank's financial involvement in less developed countries, while relinquishing some of the rights (and obligations) traditionally assumed to be incumbent on portfolio managers, was consistent, in some ways, with his view of the problems facing the poor nations, and the world. Like many of his contemporaries in Congress, McNamara felt that international development efforts had largely failed the poor. As he told the delegates of UNCTAD III in Santiago, Chile in 1972: "Development programs have been directed largely at gross economic goals, and have failed to insure that all nations and all groups within nations, have shared equitably in economic advance." The Bank's new "basic human needs" (or "social investment") programs were informed by that opinion.

McNamara had decided that an ongoing "global transfer" of public funds would be necessary to meet the problem of world poverty. In his words, "the rich countries have a responsibility to assist the less developed nations. It is not a sentimental question of philanthropy. It is a straightforward issue of social justice." The idea of unconditional concessionary transfers from Western people to low-income governments was echoed and amplified by a number of officials who rose to prominence in the Bank during the McNamara years; they gave form to McNamara's more vaguely stated notion through their support of "global negotiations" for the expanded and unrestricted transfer of money from the governments of the "North" to the governments of the "South."

Like many other large institutions, the World Bank has never spoken with a single voice or acted as if by a single hand. Nevertheless, the change in direction during the McNamara years was unmistakable: the felt obligation to provide money to poor nations was growing: the right to monitor its disbursement was more and more open to question. The World Bank had come a long way from the Bretton Woods conference, when Secretary Morgenthau introduced it to the world with these words: "The chief purpose of the International Bank for Reconstruction and Development is to guarantee private loans through normal investment channels."

Some observers have seen in McNamara's initiatives at the World Bank a sort of expiation for presumed pangs of conscience over his prosecution of the war in Vietnam as Secretary of Defense. A less sentimental and more straightforward interpretation might be that the McNamara initiatives simply formalized, and globalized, the new development policies that the United States had experimented with in Vietnam. In any event, the two were characterized by the same effort at divorcing the living standards of national populations from the productive base which would ordinarily be expected to sustain them.

VII

The period of drift and decline in American policies toward the world's poor continued under President Jimmy Carter. Elected in 1976 on a campaign promise to restore moral purpose to American politics, Carter seemed to find it extremely difficult in practice to determine whether any use at all of American power overseas was in fact moral. The administration's sensitivity to criticism on this score, and its ambivalence about American purpose, were highlighted in its foreign-aid policies.

The administration enthusiastically embraced the 1973 "reforms," with their seeming evidence that America was interested in directly aiding the world's poor. It created the International Development Cooperation Agency (IDCA)—an umbrella organization above USAID—to remove development-assistance programs from the direct chain of command within the State Department, and thus to shield the United States from charges that it was using foreign aid to further America's purposes of state. It agreed to a continuing cutback in military and security assistance, since (it was argued) these monies might be used for questionable or even inhumane purposes by our chosen allies.

The Carter administration also commissioned two major studies of world poverty. The first, the Presidential Commission on World Hunger, warned of "the continuing deterioration of the world food situation." It stated that "corporations sometimes badly undercut efforts to alleviate hunger and malnutrition," and equivocated about the extent to which international trade might help reduce hunger. Rather, the report explained, "redirecting income from the rich to the poor" would be a principal vehicle for reducing hunger in poor nations, and foreign aid could figure importantly in this process. Among the recommendations of the commission were a "total" debt forgiveness for the "poorest" developing countries; an easing of IMF lending conditions; an immediate doubling of U. S. development outlays; an increase in "Food For Peace" authorizations and a relaxation of the conditions for disbursing such produce; the promotion of a United Nations code to regulate international businesses operating in less developed countries; and the establishment of a public organization in the United States to lobby for these goals.

The second study, the "Global 2000" report, warned of an impending and generalized series of environmental problems born of overly rapid population growth in the less developed countries and excessive economic growth in the affluent nations. One implication of this computer-model study was that the sort of sustained economic advancement which would be necessary to draw the world's poor countries out of mass poverty might seriously destabilize the fragile global eco-system, possibly causing ruin for all. By seeming to question the feasibility of continuing economic growth, "Global 2000" led some observers to conclude that the only viable way to assist poor nations was through the transfer of existing wealth from the Western states.

Without fully realizing it, the Carter administration had thus ended up accepting as counsel in dealing with the less developed countries many of the basic tenets of the United Nation's proposed New International Economic Order. What did not seem to be entirely understood was that the New International Economic Order was a call for the liquidation of the liberal international economic order which America had helped to create, and continued to lead.

VIII

Ronald Reagan's decisive victory over President Carter in 1980 seemed to presage more than just a shift in attitudes toward the use of American power on the international scene. The Reagan administration came into office with an articulated, and internally consistent, vision of America's political and economic role in the world. This vision had implications not only for the international political struggle between the United States and the Soviet Union, but also for American policies toward the world economy and toward development.

President Reagan's critics were quick to brand him a reactionary; there was some accuracy in this characterization, albeit inadvertent. More than any President in a generation, Ronald Reagan explicitly embraced the precepts which had guided the foreign economic policies of Presidents Roosevelt and Truman. He emphasized this return to earlier principles in a major speech on international economic development in Philadelphia in October 1981.

"Economic health" was the theme underlying the President's prescriptions for promoting international advancement. There was, he said, a "need to revitalize the U. S. and the world economy as a basis for the social and economic progress of our own and other nations." At the same time, there was "a need for a clearer focus on the real meaning of development and our development record." "The postwar economic system," he asserted, "was created on the belief that the key to national development and human progress is individual freedom—both political and economic."

President Reagan identified five principles by which development might be encouraged:

First, stimulating international trade by opening up markets, both within and between countries; . . .

Second, tailoring particular development strategies to the specific needs and potential of individual countries. . . .

Third, guiding assistance toward the development of self-sustaining productive capacities. . . .

Fourth, improving in many countries the climate for private investment. . . .

Fifth, creating a political atmosphere in which practical solutions can be moved forward—rather than founder on a reef of misguided policies that restrain and interfere with the international marketplace or foster inflation.

Development assistance, in the President's vision, was to be put to the service of these principles. He promised to "work to strengthen the World Bank and other international institutions," and pledged to make available American technical know-how, food, and money "toward the development of self-sustaining productive activities" in poor nations. The President's words suggested that a dramatic change—or more properly, a historic restoration—of American policies was under way.

The Reagan administration's actions, however, suggested something quite different. Instead of bringing America's foreign-aid policies back into alignment with the goals and ideals that had originally animated them under Roosevelt and Truman, the Reagan administration allowed American programs to continue down the path which had been charted in the 1970's. So smooth, in fact, was the trajectory that it would be difficult to tell which administration was in power from the statements and actions of its development apparatus. No less than during the Carter years, American development programs under Reagan seemed to be at systematic variance with the objectives of the international order we nominally supported. The administrators of these programs, more-over, appeared increasingly intent upon concealing the discrepancy from the American public.

IX

The principal spokesman for the Reagan administration's development programs has been its acting director of IDCA and administrator of AID, M. Peter McPherson. Mr. McPherson made clear his perspective in his first presentation before the House Foreign Affairs Committee in 1981. "We have learned," he said, "that continued progress in Third World development is of growing importance to our own domestic and international well-being. In the past year, public awareness of our interdependence has been highlighted by the Presidential Commission on World Hunger, the Brandt Commission [a panel of inquiry, created by Robert McNamara and headed by former Chancellor Willy Brandt of West Germany, that advocated "massive" and "automatic" transfers of revenue from Western governments to "Southern" states] and the 'Global 2000' study." Embracing the findings of these reports, he instructed the congressional committee on their significance: "Failure to make acceptable progress in ameliorating conditions of poverty can only lead to domestic instability and increasing frustration on the part of Third World governments over the workings of the international system and the distribution of economic and institutional power in that system as it is now constituted." To observers of the North-South "dialogue," the device of wrapping a request for aid in a veiled threat may have been familiar, but in the deliberations between appointed representatives of the executive branch and elected representatives of the American people this procedure was something quite new. It had not been seen under President Carter.

To move American development programs back to the stimulation of "self-sustaining productive capacities," as the President had pledged, it would have been necessary to challenge the "New Directions" legislation of the 1970's. AID made no effort to do so. Two years into his appointment, and again before the House Foreign Affairs Committee, McPherson may have suggested why. Reflecting on the early 1970's, he remarked:

> The political, social, and economic structure which had evolved in many less developed countries had produced little improvement in economic well-being for the poor of those countries. To help correct this situation, a new concern with the effects of our assistance on the poor majority emerged a decade ago, in the form of the current New Directions legislation [of 1973].

This was an implicit endorsement, not only of the legislation but of the analysis which had prompted it. That analysis, of course, held that the postwar order America had created could not be relied upon to advance the interests of the world's poor.

In 1983, in an aid request, McPherson told Congress that "trade and debt pressure is particularly serious for stability and longer-run economic progress in the low-income countries. . . . Our foreign-assistance program can play an important role in their recovery." It was a revealing analysis. The problems to which he referred were both financial (relating to balance-of-payments shortfalls) and short-term (being exacerbated by a presumably cyclical drop in international economic activity). But development programs, as generally imagined, involve technical transfers and long-term horizons. A "development program" could play an important role in a short-term economic recovery only if it were intended to infuse monies directly into a pool of current spending.

AID's presentations left little doubt about the Agency's view of the propriety of direct budgetary transfers. An AID policy paper on health assistance, for example, noted that "by 1982, one half of the Agency's development assistance budget for health supported the delivery of basic health services in LDCs." Such "development-assistance" is, necessarily, a direct bequest from the U. S. Treasury, applied to the operating revenues of recipient states. Whatever may be said of such charitable donations, they are in no sense "self-sustaining."

Confusion over the distinction between recurrent expense and productive investment likewise marked AID's agricultural program. The agency's Fiscal Year 1983 presentation to Congress proposed to increase agricultural productivity in the less developed countries through the following activities:

supporting land tenure arrangements and agrarian reform policies; encouraging small farmer organizations and local participation; disseminating and developing new technologies; protecting the environmental and natural resource base through better land management; halting and reversing deforestation by developing renewable energy alternatives to firewood, testing fast-growing tree species, and supporting woodlots for fuel; increasing the availability of water, improved seed, credit, and other agricultural inputs at reasonable prices; reducing post-harvest food losses; and facilitating small-farmer access to markets.

In this conspectus of agricultural productivity, only one item seemed to be missing: any mention of the prices paid to producers. Yet it is prices, unfortunately, which often prove decisive in the success or failure of agricultural development, determining as they do the returns which may be derived from increasing production or adopting innovations.

The President had suggested that misguided policies played an important role in perpetuating poverty in the less developed regions; his AID administrator expressed a very different view. In 1983, McPherson told Congress that "the critical problem of excessive population growth in the Third World . . . constitutes the primary obstacle to increasing per-capita food production, reducing malnutrition and chronic disease, and conserving dwindling non-renewable resources." This formulation, with its implication that parents in less developed nations irrationally choose "excessive" numbers of children, could be understood as excusing governments in those nations from responsibility for agricultural difficulties, hunger problems, or the management of natural resources. It also appeared to lend legitimacy to governmental efforts to control population growth.

AID had maintained that it would only condone voluntary family planning. But even as a position paper to this effect was being circulated publicly, the agency was participating in a $50-million grant to China from the UN Fund for Population Activities. China was pursuing a population campaign known as the "one child norm," requiring parents to agree to have only a single off-spring. The campaign appears to have been horribly unpopular with the overwhelming majority of the Chinese people, and the Chinese government found it necessary to use pressure, threats, and far-reaching punishments against married couples to enforce the decree. (Many infant girls and ablebodied women are thought to have died as a result of this program.) Since most of the funding in which AID participated was earmarked for Chinese "population education activities" and for health clinics (at which quotas of sterilizations and abortions were being fulfilled in accordance with the population plan), it would have required extreme mental agility to dissociate the

Reagan administration's development money from the practice of involuntary population control.

Still another area in which AID seemed to disagree with received American policy was on the issue of private enterprise. AID is committed by law to refrain from using its funds to displace private investment or private commercial activity. Despite this, AID's 1983 budget presentation before Congress stated that, since energy "has become a field of major concern to AID," the agency had "increasingly broadened its assistance to encompass technical assistance to expand indigenous supplies of coal, oil, and gas. . . ." The projects involved were not described, but it would seem difficult to reconcile these activities with AID's legal mandate.

The question of private enterprise, and its legitimate scope within development, seems to have troubled AID administrators deeply during the Reagan years. One attempt to resolve the issue was the creation of a Bureau of Private Enterprise. In a sense, however, this only compounded the problem: for the first time in its history, AID was formally and explicitly separating the job of encouraging private commerce from its overall responsibilities in promoting "development." Moreover, the private-enterprise initiative did not have enthusiastic AID backing. In its heyday it was allocated $27 million; since then, its funding has declined. Although no other program receives such extensive coverage in AID's annual budget presentation before Congress, the private-enterprise initiative now accounts for something less than one-half of one percent of AID's expenditures.

Recently, it is true, AID statements and publications have begun to express formal support for the liberal international economic order. But if the tone has changed, AID's priorities have not. In 1984, a top-level internal document on strategy and objectives for a second Reagan term proposed that AID's mission be redefined to include the following goals: the raising of life expectancy in all developing countries to over 60 years; the reduction of infant-mortality rates in all developing countries to 75 per thousand, or below; and the increase to 70 percent of literacy rates in all developing countries. As the draft noted, this change in mandate would require a "renewal" in America's commitment to development funding: indeed, to follow through on such a program in a world where recipient governments maintain sovereign authority over their economic and social policies, this renewed commitment would have to be not only major but virtually open-ended.

This internal AID document contained a number of formal concessions to the notions of "self-sustaining growth" and "policy reform." Yet as it was outlined, AID's plan for promoting development would not emphasize policies to create self-sustaining growth or to encourage conditions by which living standards might undergo an internally generated transformation; it would, rather, concentrate on the direct and restitutive redress of poverty through social spending. If the rhetoric of the Carter commissions and the Brandt commission had been carefully airbrushed out of AID's public statements in the 1984 election year, such thinking was still clearly acceptable in the inner recesses of the Reagan administration's development apparatus.

X

The record of the last decades shows, in sum, that America's foreign-aid policies are in trouble—not because the American people lack compassion for the suffering of others overseas, and not because Americans are unwilling to devote their nation's resources to helping other peoples, but because the policies themselves are formulated and implemented in such a way as to suggest that the United States no longer understands the nature of the problems facing poor people and poor countries. Far from contributing to the goal of self-sustaining economic progress in the low-income regions, our funds are instead being directed to a tragic extent into the construction of barriers against such progress and in some cases may actually be paying for the creation of poverty, albeit in new and pernicious variants. This state of affairs can continue only at great human cost to those whom we mean to help—and at great moral cost to our nation.

The cost, indeed, may be more consequential than is commonly appreciated by cool-headed advocates of a "pragmatic" American foreign policy. The experience of the United States in the world arena since the end of World War I suggests that, for our nation more than any other, power and principle are inseparable. When the legitimacy and moral purpose of American initiatives overseas have been commonly understood and accepted, our government has proved able to mobilize awesome resources in the pursuit of its objectives. When, by contrast, the legitimacy and moral purpose of American efforts have become open to question, the domestic base of support has dramatically diminished, and with it the possibility of pursuing those efforts with any hope of success.

The premises of the liberal international economic order the United States labored to create from the wreckage of World War II remain valid, and the instruments of this order remain capable of creating extraordinary opportunities for general material advance throughout all regions of the world. The failures of American aid policies in recent decades are a reflection not on the soundness of the conceptions that originally brought these policies to life but rather on the degree to which current practice has become divorced from original purpose. America's foreign-aid policies today stand in contradistinction to the thrust and purpose of

America's overall foreign policy, and to the values and ideals of the American people. How we deal with this contradiction will affect not only the poor and the unprotected of the earth, whose champions we should rightly be, but our own conception of ourselves and our ability to function in the world of nations.

9

International Framework and South-South Cooperation: Constraints and Opportunities

K.P. SAKSENA

The failure to implement the Programme of Action of the New International Economic Order (NIEO) and the stalemate over the launching of Global Negotiations have led to increasing emphasis on regional[1] and inter-regional cooperation among the developing countries, generally referred to as South-South cooperation. This approach of 'collective self-reliance' is viewed, not as an alternative to the need to restructure the existing economic order, or as a substitute for North-South cooperation, but as the second best option open to the developing countries in their effort to stem the deterioration of their global economic position and the consequences of the failure of the global system to accommodate their interests.

Whatever the rhetoric and the exhortations which characterize the various declarations of the Group of 77 and the non-aligned summits on the subject, the question that we still need to ask is: How far can South-South cooperation help mitigate the present plight of the developing countries? Is the existing global system friendly or hostile to such cooperation? What are the constraints holding up South-South cooperation within the existing international framework? And what are the opportunities available? These and other related questions are the subject of analysis in this article.

It should be noted, however, that the regional approach as a way of organizing functional cooperation among a group of states is not a new one.

Indeed the period immediately following the Second World War witnessed a proliferation of regional organizations. The emergence of such organizations was due, however, to the exigencies of the Cold War, and such functional cooperation as was sought was generally confined to political and security matters. It is significant to note that several of these organizations—for instance, the South-East Asia Treaty Organization (SEATO) and the Central Treaty Organization (CENTO)— were not so much a product of the common or shared interests of the countries of the regions concerned as of 'sponsorship' by *outside* powers.

In Europe the two rival groups of states have gone a step further and instituted organizations for economic cooperation as well. However, the rationale behind these organizations, that is, the factors that contributed to their inception and which have since sustained their growth, are very different from those characterizing the efforts of the newly emerging nations of Asia, Africa, and Latin America (the so-called Third World). This is so because these 'new' nations, though politically independent and legally sovereign, took shape in a world still dominated, both militarily and economically, by the 'old', industrially advanced countries with a European or European-derived political culture. In other words, the new states were at the time of their birth, as the title of a book succinctly suggests, *the weak in the world of the strong*.[2] The coming together of some of the developing countries, therefore, to institute regional organizations for economic cooperation and to make them viable called for a different kind of effort and planning. An attempt to 'imitate' the European 'success story' could lead to serious difficulties, as the Latin Americans,[3] who were the first among the developing countries to initiate schemes for regional economic integration, learnt to their cost. The factors that the countries of the Third World must deal with today are very different from those which prompted and promoted regional cooperation among the industrialized countries of Europe. The countries of the Third World have to take into account the constraints which the contemporary international economic system imposes on them. Here is a system, a legacy of historical development, which operates to the advantage of the industrialized countries of the North and in which the countries of the Third World have little or no say even when matters affecting their vital interests come up.

While, therefore, discussing the problems and prospects of regional economic cooperation among the countries of the Third World, we need to take into account the international economic framework within which a regional cooperation enterprise has to operate.

THE GREAT DIVIDE

To begin with, let us consider the reality of the existing international framework. While demonstrating the growing interdependence of the world, it also reflects, *inter alia*, a sharp division between the industrialized countries of the 'European' world which constitute the North[4] and the developing countries of the Third World which constitute the South. Trade and commerce, science and technology, banks and insurance companies, airlines and shipping companies—all tie the world together, but the strings are held by the rich, industrialized countries, which constitute the centre of economic power. The rest of the world is merely the periphery. It is true that the industrialized countries are themselves divided into two groups—the market economy countries of the West and the Socialist or centrally planned economy countries of the East.[5] But both had their 'take-off' from the same background, and both gained an advantage, with considerable range of variation for economic development, from the colonial, imperialistic era, which was largely responsible for what is now the well established ascendancy of the North over the South.

The industrialized North represents 26 per cent of the world population but controls 80 per cent of world resources. On the other hand the countries of the non-European world, which now number more than 125, represent three-fourths of the world population, but their share of the world resources is just 20 per cent. Nearly half of the people of the countries of the non-European world live below the poverty line (see Table 1).

What is particularly relevant in the context of the present study is that both sides of the European world are well organized in terms of institutional arrangements for coordinating their economic policies and actions for the safeguard and promotion of their common interests and external economic relations. There are the Organization for Economic Cooperation and Development (OECD) and a network of other institutions on the one side and the Council of Mutual Economic Assistance (COMECON) on the other. The newly emerging countries of Asia and Africa and the not-so-new states of Latin America represent a motley crowd, and they have not yet acquired, notwithstanding the Group of 77 and the non-aligned movement, any institutional arrangements worth the name to coordinate their policies and actions and safeguard their collective interests.

QUEST FOR A NEW INTERNATIONAL ECONOMIC ORDER

The lopsidedness of the existing international framework of economic relations has led to the demand for an equitable sharing of the world resources. The various demands made over the decades have been concretized in the form of a declaration for a New International Economic Order and a Programme of Action.[6] Since then there has been a lot of activity, but the result has been commensurate neither with the

Table 1
North–South: Basic Indicators

(1)	North (All Members of the OECD and the European Members of the COMECON) (2)	South (the Rest of the World) (3)
Population	1.16 billion	3.70 billion
Population: average annual growth rate	Less than 1.0 per cent to less than 2.0 per cent	2.0 per cent to 3.0 per cent and over
GNP	$7,286 billion	$1,517 billion
GNP per capita	$5,000 to $17,440	$80 to $4,220[a]
Shares in fuel energy exports	24.3 per cent; (15.6 per cent–OECD) (8.1 per cent–COMECON)	75.7 per cent[b]
Shares in primary products (other than fuel)	41.7 per cent; (33.6 per cent–OECD) (8.1 per cent–COMECON)	58.3 per cent
Shares in manufactures and industrial products	90.4 per cent; (80.9 per cent–OECD) (9.5 per cent–COMECON)	9.6 per cent
Share in total merchandise exports (excluding gold)	72.6 per cent; (63.4 per cent–OECD) (9.2 per cent–COMECON)	27.4 per cent[c]
Adult literacy percentage of population	99 per cent	51 per cent[d]
Population per physician	553; (630–OECD) (497–COMECON)	6,250[e]
Percentage of population with access to safe waters	100 per cent	42 per cent[f]
Life expectancy at birth	73 years	54 years

[a] These figures exclude Singapore ($5,240); Trinidad and Tobago ($5,670); Capital Surplus Oil Exporters (CSOE); Libya ($8,450); Kuwait ($20,900); Saudi Arabia ($12,600); and the United Arab Emirates ($24,660).

[b] Shares in the fuel energy exports among the countries of the South are: 34.4 per cent, Capital Surplus Oil Exporters; and 41.3 per cent, other developing countries, including member countries of the Organization of Petroleum Exporting Countries (OPEC) but excluding the Capital Surplus Oil Exporters.

[c] The shares in total merchandise export of the South are 10.2 per cent; and the four Capital Surplus Oil Exporters and others including OPEC (other than CSOE), 21.4 per cent.

[d] Adult literacy in some countries of the South is as low as 8 per cent.

[e] Population per physician in the South ranges from 8,450 (in Ethiopia) to 480 (in Mongolia).

[f] In some countries of the South like Afghanistan and Ethiopia, the percentage of the population with access to safe water is as low as 6 percent.

Sources: *World Development Report, 1983; United Nations Yearbook of International Trade Statistics*, various issues.

amount of activity nor with the gravity of the situation. The crisis in the world economy is there for anyone to see, but a new order is still not in sight.

In this context, the Cancun Summit (October 1981) was perhaps, as many in the South thought, the most significant event. For the first time twenty-two heads of State/Government, representing both the rich North and the poor South, met to discuss problems of the world economy. What actually happened was that the North looked at the face of poverty of millions in the South and stared it down. Although the leaders of the North agreed that the world economy was in a shambles, they believed that they would themselves try to find ways and means of resurrecting it by planning and coordination of their policies through the 'summitry of seven' and through the institutions they controlled. They were not prepared to grant the poor of the South any share in the decision-making process as far as the world economy was concerned, although the decisions they made affected the vital interests of the countries of the South as well. They were guardedly prepared to have another set of dialogue with the South some time later, but reserved the right to claim that they never promised anything especially in terms of money or an equitable sharing of the world resources.

The Cancun Summit did have a 'final' message for the poor countries, one that could not have been shouted out more clearly: the only way out of the bind they found themselves in was 'collective self-reliance'.

COLLECTIVE SELF-RELIANCE AS AN ALTERNATIVE?

From the beginning 'self-reliance' through bargaining has been the *raison d'être* of the Group of 77. In fact the desire to strengthen the 'joint negotiation capacity' of the developing countries *vis-à-vis* the developed countries of both East and West was the motivating force behind the formation of the Group of 77. However, over the years, the objective of self-reliance through bargaining, in the North-South context, has been supplemented by the concept of collective self-reliance through economic cooperation among the developing countries themselves. The various conferences held and the numerous permanent working groups set up within the Group of 77 reflect this change. The full integration of this new approach was initiated by the Arusha Programme for Collective Self-Reliance and Framework for Negotiations (1979).[7]

The programme for South-South cooperation was further elaborated at the Caracas Conference held in April 1981.[8] Its report identified seven sectors. While no specific priority was assigned to any of these sectors, parts of the programme dealing with such issues as finance, transfer of technology, and trade, were considerably more detailed and specific than those dealing with other sectors such as food and agriculture, energy, raw materials, and industrialization.

The Arusha Programme, supplemented by the one drawn up at Caracas, had two objectives—to bring about changes in the existing international framework by promoting economic cooperation (ECDC) and technical cooperation (TCDC), and at the same time to restructure the world economy. It recognized that although South-South cooperation had great potentialities, it could not be a substitute for North-South negotiations. In other words, although the regional approach among the developing countries held great promise, it was no alternative for North-South negotiations. It was just a stepping-stone to a peaceful and equitable sharing in global economic management.

We know that as regards the objective of restructuring the world economy, no progress was made. There was no indication that North-South negotiations would be renewed in the foreseeable future. UNCTAD VI (Belgrade, June 1983) also failed to provide any push in that direction.

As regards the other objective, namely that of promoting South-South cooperation, it was regarded not only as a means of reshaping the division of labour between nations, but also as a part of the industrialization strategy. However, this too failed to yield any tangible results.

Is the grip of the North over the South so strong, or do the countries of the South lack the political will to generate the necessary cooperation?

ECONOMIC LIMITS: LACK OF INFRASTRUCTURE

Indeed there are limits to, and institutional obstacles in the way of, South-South cooperation. Let us examine the question of South-South trade. It is, of course, true that an expansion of trade would reduce the age-old dependence of the countries of the South upon the rich countries of the North and improve their bargaining power. It would also help overcome the limitations of size of the domestic market, exploit complementary resources through regional specialization, reduce exposure to risks or cyclical fluctuations, and, in the long run, foster indigenous technological development. There can be little doubt that all this lies within the realm of possibility. However, any plan to extend South-South cooperation is bound to come up in practice against enormous difficulties. Hence, at the regional or interregional level, the promotion of trade should be attempted after the necessary preparations have been made. An attempt should be made to seek a redeployment of industries so as to make them complementary. The necessary infrastructure, including transport and communications links, needs to be established, before any attempt to promote intra-regional trade is made.

Industrialization is a major goal of development planning in most developing countries. The emphasis, of course, varies from country to country. In the early stages, any strategy of industrialization generates a demand for raw materials, intermediate inputs, and capital goods. While most raw materials can be procured in the developing world, and this should be conducive to the South-South trade, the ability of the South to meet its own demand for intermediate goods and capital goods is limited. It is not as if production abilities or capacities are non-existent in the South. Many developing countries manufacture intermediate or capital goods. A few countries, such as Argentina, Brazil, and India, even export them. It is, however, important to place the magnitude of the problem in its proper perspective.

It is not just that the industrialized nations of the North are so much richer; there is more to it. Over 90 per cent of the world's manufacturing industries are in the North; most patents and new technology are the property of transnational corporations of the market-economy countries of the North. Again, the North controls a large share of the world investments and world trade in raw materials and manufactured goods. Because of its economic power, the North dominates the international economic system—its rules and regulations, its international institutions of trade, money and finance, shipping, insurance, etc. As the Latin Americans, for instance, have learnt it the hard way, it is cheaper to 'ship' their goods to the ports of North America and Western Europe than to the ports of a neighbouring country in Latin America.

THE COLONIAL HERITAGE

The existing pattern, as is well known, is neither an entirely natural development nor an accident. It is very much the outcome of two historical phenomena: the Industrial Revolution and colonialism. The two coincided in history. Their cause-effect relationship may be a matter for debate, but it is very clear that the development of industries in the European world (that includes all members of the OECD as well as the European component of COMECON) was helped, in great measure, by the massive infusion of wealth from the colonial territories in Africa, Asia, and Latin America. While industrialization increased the wealth of the European world, the development of the other continents was being retarded. In some areas, no doubt, the development of transport and communication, as also the educational system, was accelerated under colonial rule, but this was done primarily to ensure cheap supplies of raw materials for European factories and to create consumer markets for the products of these factories. The net result was a widening of the gap between the more affluent people of the industrialized countries and the increasingly deprived populations in Africa, Asia and Latin America. The situation remains essentially unchanged, although most of the countries which once formed part of the colonies are now politically independent and legally sovereign.

INSTITUTIONAL OBSTACLES

The point emphasized here is that, over a long period of time, the infrastructure of international trade and commerce was so developed as to constitute institutional obstacles in the way of expanding trade among the so-called developing countries. Take, for instance, the case of undivided India of the colonial period, which is now split into three or more different states. Even the development of the Indian railways was oriented to the requirements of the British-dominated export industries. The railways neglected the question of development of local industries along their lines. Nor did they take into account the question of integrating trade within the subcontinent. As Gunnar Myrdal aptly notes:

> Being constructed primarily from the point of view of the British economy, with the aim first of facilitating military-security and secondly getting the raw material out cheaply and British goods in, . . . the railways, instead of exerting spread effects as in Western Europe, served to strengthen the colonial relationship and further subordinate the Indian to British economy.[9]

Thus, by and large, the existing situation is that the facilities for transport, shipping, insurance, and banking, as well as the channels of communication and marketing, remain oriented to the trade between the North and the South and, of course, to the trade within the North. No comparable infrastructure exists for South-South trade. Thus, there are historical factors constituting institutional obstacles in the path of expanding trade among the developing countries. It is far easier for the countries of Africa, Asia, and Latin America to trade with Western Europe or North America than to trade with one another. It is easier, even today, for Colombo to communicate by telephone with New Delhi via London than to attempt a direct contact. Again, the countries of the Third World find it simpler to buy Zambian copper at the London Metal Exchange and Kenyan tea at the London Tea Auctions than to do so directly from the original source. Instances of this sort abound.

Again, although the so-called aid programmes which the developed countries of the North initiated during the post-colonial period met the minimum needs of the developing countries, they were largely a tied-up kind of aid. The purchase of technology by the developing countries, tied imports to the original source, and the terms of technology transfer from the North often restricted exports. Further, the import of manufactured goods depended on the availability of credit; and export credits were largely controlled by the North.

There is yet another institutional factor which also has historical origins. In many areas of international trade, the developing countries do not participate as completely 'independent' buyers and sellers. This is because transnational corporations (TNCs), which have their base in the developed world of the North, are responsible for a significant proportion of their trade. These TNCs play a dominant role in the export of primary commodities, particularly those originating from mines, plantations, or cash-crop agriculture. This, broadly, is the result of historical forces and very much a legacy of the colonial era. In the 1970s, for example, five companies accounted for 75 per cent of the world tea market; six companies controlled 50 per cent of the manganese-ore capacity; three companies controlled 60 per cent of the banana imports (90 per cent in the United States alone); and six companies controlled 76 per cent of the world aluminia production capacity.

The various studies conducted by the UNCTAD Secretariat indicate that the role of the TNCs has tended to increase and that, at the same time, the primary commodities market has shifted from single commodity traders to the multi-commodity trading firms which largely emerged in the wake of the liquidation of small and medium-size trading companies. By the end of 1970s, well over two-thirds of the global trade in commodities was being dominated by these traders. In the year 1980, about 70 to 80 per cent of global primary commodity trade, worth roughly $890 billion, was being controlled by multi-commodity traders. In most cases, some three to six transnational traders accounted for the bulk of the market: about 85 to 90 per cent cotton; 70 to 75 per cent of natural rubber; 80 to 85 per cent of tobacco; 85 per cent of copper; 80 per cent of tin; and 80 to 85 per cent of bauxite.[10]

MONETARY AND FISCAL PROBLEMS

As in the case of international trade, the international monetary system too is controlled by the industrialized countries of the North. The developing countries have little or no say; their role, as Pierre-Paul Schweitzer aptly notes, has been that of 'innocent bystanders and victims'.[11]

The currencies of the industrialized countries are, by virtue of their share in the world trade and for other reasons, 'acceptable' throughout the world. They are known as 'hard' currencies. Conversely, the currencies of the developing countries, which are weak agricultural economies and which have only small shares in the world trade, have 'soft' currencies which they cannot use beyond their national borders. To buy vitally important manufactured goods as well as science and technology from others and to pay for such essential services as shipping and insurance, they need 'hard' currencies which they can earn only by means of their exports to the industrialized countries.

Till 1971, the monetary affairs of the world were governed by the Bretton Woods system, which centred on fixed currency values as expressed in terms of US dollars and gold; and naturally the United States had a dominant role in that system. When the system broke down in 1971, a new system of floating exchange rates was introduced. This floating rate system is based on the exchange rate relationship between the currencies of the major industrialized countries of the West, which are determined daily in the markets by the law of supply and demand, often mitigated in its impact by limited intervention by the governments of the Western countries. The central rule thus became one of more or less 'managed floating'. It now governs all major currencies although, within the European Economic Community (EEC), a limited zone of more fixed currency relationships has been created. Currencies of most of the developing countries are pegged—by maintaining a fixed, if adjustable, relationship—to one of the major currencies or a basket of these 'hard' currencies. Sharp variations in the major currencies thus send shock waves throughout the world.

How does this situation affect the ability of the countries of the Third World in regard to financing their economic and social development projects?

It should be noted that the developing countries themselves (barring a few hard cases—as, for instance, Nepal) supply most of the money for their development projects; funds come from trade and domestic savings primarily. Until the early 1970s, most of the non-oil exporting developing countries obtained over 80 per cent of their funds from domestic resources. The remaining part was obtained from foreign sources, including aid from the developed market-economy countries, centrally planned countries, and oil-exporting developing countries. This inflow of foreign money has, of late, declined sharply. Likewise, the prices of the primary commodities, their major items of export, which alone can get them 'hard' currencies continue to show a declining trend. As such, funds urgently needed to buy technological know-how and machinery from the industrialized countries and to pay the heavily rising bills relating to oil imports have to be obtained by raising loans in 'hard' currencies. Such loans could again be obtained only from the industrialized countries of the West either in terms of foreign aid which is tied to specific purchases or in terms of loans from commercial banks. During the last five years, thanks to the fiscal policy of the United States, the bank rates of interest have risen steeply. The result is that the debt burden of all developing countries, which, in 1971, amounted to US $64.1 billion went up to US $300 billion in 1978. By the end of 1982, it is estimated to have reached as high a level as US $600 billion. The 'servicing' charges on the loans alone went up from US $11 billion in 1971 to US $90 billion in 1981.

One way the developing countries can earn some hard currency is by exporting raw material to the industrialized countries. Export of raw material accounts for about 85 per cent of their foreign-exchange earnings every year (63 per cent, if petroleum is excluded). Here again they are facing serious difficulties: the prices of raw materials have been going down and the prices of manufactured goods imported by them have risen steadily in the post-war period. This means that the developing countries have had to export more and more of their own commodities to import the same amount of manufactured goods from the developing countries. In the jargon of the economists, their 'terms of trade' have deteriorated quite fast.

Yet another problem is that a large number of raw materials in the world market (excluding the centrally planned economies) are controlled, as noted earlier, by a few giant TNCs based in the developed countries. The developing countries which face this concentration of 'buying power' of the multitrading firms in respect of raw materials are unorganized and subject to exploitation by TNCs.

Let us consider another aspect of the situation. For a large number of developing countries there is scope for export of textiles and other semimanufactured goods which, because of the availability of comparatively little labour cost in the developing countries, could have a good market in the industrialized countries of the North. But then, the latter have resorted to the quota system and 'protectionism'.[12]

Thus, it is clear that the countries of the Third World are largely the 'done' and not the 'doers' in the world economy. They have little or no say in matters which vitally affect their economic interests and are hence subject to all kinds of exploitation.

It is not just the question of economic exploitation alone. The rich industrialized North often decides to arm the poor 'rulers' of the various countries in the South with highly sophisticated weapons, partly to enable them to control their angry people and partly to give them an edge over their neighbours. This obliges the neighbours to go in for similar military hardware and, in the process, destroy their own economies. And thus the game goes on. This is what is happening, for instance, on the Indo-Pakistan subcontinent.

Although the debt burden of the countries of the Third World has reached the phenomenal figure of US $600 billion, arms purchases continue unabated. A research study carried out at the instance of the US Congress indicates that in 1982 alone, the United States signed new arms contracts with the countries of the Third World for $15 billion. The Soviet Union signed new contracts during the same year worth $10 billion. West European suppliers—Britain, France, Italy, and West Germany—signed new arms agreements with the developing world worth $11 billion during the same year.[13]

NO ALTERNATIVE TO RESTRUCTURING

From the analysis presented in the preceding pages, one conclusion, *inter alia*, is inevitable. This conclusion is that the problem of regional economic cooperation among the developing countries cannot be viewed in isolation from other factors having global dimensions. All-round concerted efforts are needed to secure emancipation from the present plight. What is most essential is that the existing framework of the global economy should be restructured to bring about an equitable sharing of the world resources. In other words, South-South cooperation in the interest of economic development cannot be a substitute for a New International Economic Order. It is, therefore, necessary that the global negotiations covering the entire gamut of economic issues, including trade, transport, energy, food, and money, have to be reactivated. These negotiations, as noted earlier, are at present stalemated. No doubt one cause of this stalemate is the sheer complexity of the issues involved. Another, and more important, cause is that a rational approach based on equity and fair play seems impossible in a situation when these issues are discussed among unequals; and one side not only holds the trumps but also has a network of institutions for acting and reacting in a concerted, well coordinated manner, while the other side having only the number cards is largely 'disorganized'. However, the existing lopsidedness of the system cannot continue for long. Change in the international structure, as predicted by the well-known economist, Mahbub-ul Haq, is 'inevitable', whether there is a dialogue or not. The question is whether the pace of change can be accelerated through common consent and whether the pains of transition can be eased through a negotiated peaceful process. The failure of the dialogue so far implies that the change will continue to be disorderly and disruptive. The case for resumption of global negotiations is that it can lead to an orderly transition and that bargains can be struck by which all sides may gain, though not necessarily in equal measure.[14]

SOUTH-SOUTH COOPERATION: THE OPPORTUNITIES

The analysis presented in the preceding pages indicates the limits and constraints of regional cooperation among the developing countries in a world economy which is characterized by interdependence and where the strings are held by outside powers. But there is certainly a strong case why the developing countries should come together.

It is true that the existing international framework posits serious constraints, but these difficulties and obstacles are not insurmountable. Indeed, it is imperative to surmount them if the developing countries are to pull themselves out of the present plight of economic servitude, and the only way to make a beginning in that direction is through collective efforts for cooperation at the regional/inter-regional level.

There is more to the imperative of inter-governmental regional cooperation. As is well known, the territorial framework of most of the developing countries is not a product of historical development as such; it is largely the legacy of the colonial era. Boundaries were artificially drawn to suit the interests of the colonial powers and in utter disregard of geo-economic, ethnic, and cultural considerations. In many cases, natural resources are so located that without cooperation among the neighbouring states, they cannot be put even to adequate (much less optimum) utilization. Only a handful among the newly emerged nations are homogeneous. Some of these states are so small in size, population, and/or resources that they cannot at all benefit from the advances being made in science and technology. The only choice before them is to enter into cooperative efforts with other states which are linked to them geographically or otherwise.

Thus, it is clear that what may appear to be difficult for one developing country would be much less difficult if several of them combined their efforts. True, there is a lack of the necessary infrastructure for trade, but that deficiency can be met only by well-coordinated, action-oriented policies. The obstacles in the way of South-South trade imply that it is important to establish the necessary infrastructure before making an attempt to promote trade relations. Intra-regional transport and communication links have to be established; complementarities, credit, and market facilities have to be initiated before intra-regional trade could be a viable and mutually beneficial arrangement. Furthermore, besides trade, there are other areas where cooperation could help in promoting economic development and mutual interest. As a consequence of the development over the past two or three decades, the developing countries have now a larger potential for cooperation. Their productive capacities, infrastructures, and skilled manpower have grown. Differences in the level of development provide conditions for interchange of experience and transfer of technology, though in a limited way, such as did not exist earlier. However, conditions have to be created whereby countries which are in a position to provide given services can enter into cooperative arrangements with countries which require such services to mutual advantage. It is mainly at the regional level and among states lying in immediate proximity that collective self-reliance in the full meaning of the expression can be built up as a system having a comprehensive South-South relationship.

OPTIMUM UTILIZATION OF RESOURCES

Countries with geographical or other links could build up economic cooperation for the optimum utilization of industrial resources, agricultural land, and energy and mineral resources. Regional cooperation and coordination in the development, processing, and marketing of such resources can assure the optimum scale of production, avoid wasteful duplication in investment and infrastructure, and improve the application of the appropriate technology and know-how. In some instances the nature of the resources is such that regional development offers the best solution. This is particularly the case with energy resources; with the exception of oil, energy is not readily transportable. Hydro-electric power, natural gas, geo-thermal energy and low-quality coal can be exploited best on a regional basis. Likewise, rivers, lakes, and inland seas call for regional cooperation for optimum development. Labour could also be considered a regional resource.

Migration can either be a disruptive or harmonizing factor. Regional regulation could share the optimum and harmonize the employment of valuable workforces. Human resources could further be developed on a regional basis, through joint programmes of learning and skilled training.

Likewise, financial cooperation on a regional basis can be an important instrument, particularly in the context of renegotiation of external debts, coordination of legislations concerning direct foreign investment, and channelling of aid to maximize the chances of achieving the development objectives of the participating countries. In some cases additional forms of monetary and financial integration may be feasible, such as agreement on relative exchange rates and payments.

Regional cooperation can thus yield long-term benefits in many areas. These include: (a) enlargement of the size of regional production through joint investment and preferential treatment; (b) greater concentration of foreign-exchange savings in the area of capital goods and technologies essential for autonomous industrial and agricultural development; (c) enlargement of the size of regional exports through more efficient utilization of the human, financial, and natural resources and infrastructures of the region; and (d) ability to attract more outside capital and transfer of technologies (including agreements with TNCs) through effective collective bargaining and more assured returns.

In addition to economic benefits, regional cooperation can generate healthy interactions in the social, political, and cultural spheres as well and thereby strengthen the stability of the participating states and promote solidarity among them.

There is another vital area where regional cooperation could yield fruitful results—the quest for a New International Economic Order. India's Minister for External Affairs, P.V. Narasimha Rao, while addressing a meeting of the Group of 77 in New York, succinctly observed:

> Unless we succeed in our efforts at collective self-reliance, we shall always be negotiating with the developed countries from a position of weakness and the North-South dialogue is likely to remain in the impasse we find it today.[15]

Once the developing countries establish their status in the world economy the global negotiations would acquire a new dimension. This could lead to a more equitable and mutually beneficial framework of global interdependence.

NOTES

1. The words 'region' and 'regional organization' have given rise to much confusion and difficulty in their application to inter-governmental organizations. The term 'region' in the abstract is politically meaningless. One might ask: 'In relation to what subject matter is the term used in any particular context?' It is clear that what is a region for one purpose may not be a region for another. Geographical Europe has, for example, proved in practice to be a 'region' for many purposes of a technical character, such as transport. And it may well be a region for environmental purposes too, which are perfectly capable of inter-governmental handling on an all-Europe basis. Geographical Europe, however, has not yet proved to be a 'region' for most economic or political purposes. Again, should we treat the whole of Asia as one region? If so, how should one define its geographical boundaries? Should South Asia be defined as a 'region' or as a 'subregion'? Then there are the so-called functional/regional organizations, such as the Organization for Economic Co-operation and Development (OECD), whose membership cuts across geographical continents. To avoid all this confusion, therefore, a region is treated as a convenient geographical area controlled by sovereign governments whose interests in any particular subject are sufficiently compatible for them to be able to enter into effective multilateral co-operation. The term 'subregion' has, for a similar reason, been avoided. Any set-up, whether covering all or most of the geographical continent concerned or just a part of it, is treated as a region. Likewise, we have used the term 'regional organization', in view of the prevailing political and economic circumstances, to include not only those instituted geographically, but also functionally and politically by more than two states.

2. Robert L. Rothstein, *The Weak in the World of the Strong: The Developing Countries in the International System* (New York, N.Y., 1977).

3. The reference here is to the Latin American Free Trade Association (LAFTA) and the Central American Common Market (CACM). After some initial success, the two failed to strike root on account of, *inter alia*, lack of transport and communications, links for regional trade, the role of transnational corporations, and other external factors.

4. The expression 'European' is used here in the civilizational sense. The term 'North' includes all the twenty-four members of the OECD (the countries of Western Europe, Canada, the United States, Australia, New Zealand, and Japan) and the European component of COMECON (East Europeans, including the Soviet Union). On this point, see the Brandt Commission Report, *Report of the Independent Commission on International Development Issues, North-South: A Program for Survival* (Cambridge, Mass., 1980), pp. 31–32.

5. Could we club together the Western World and the Socialist countries of Eastern Europe? It is true that what the developing countries are seeking to shake off is the dominance of the Western countries over the existing international economic system. They happen to be a part of this system willy-nilly, and it has hitherto functioned to their detriment. To that extent, the Socialist countries of Eastern Europe are not much to blame. However, both groups of countries have, historically, grown out of the soil of Europe. They have both had their initial 'take-off' in the banking houses of the sixteenth century, in the industrial development of the 17th and 18th centuries, and in imperialism and colonialism, which reached their climax in the nineteenth century and lasted till the second half of the present century. It is true that most of the countries of the Soviet group have not had the advantage of building a colonial empire. Nevertheless, the advancement of technology and the rapid industrialization obtained by other European Powers through colonialism also yielded 'spill over' benefits to their neighbouring countries in Eastern Europe, including Tsarist Russia, which became a Marxist-Socialist state in 1917. It should also be noted that while the other European Powers built up overseas empires, during the nineteenth century, the empire of Tsarist Russia embraced the whole of Central Asia and touched the Indo-Afghan borders in the south and the Pacific Ocean in the east.

Notwithstanding the differences in ideology, economic system, etc., the two have more in common than either of them has with the Third World. Their conflict is referred to as Cold War between the East and the West. But East and West of what? Europe, of course. Indeed, whatever the conflict of interests between the two, it largely derives from one common element, namely their competitive strategy to dominate the areas and peoples constituting the Third World. On this point, see in particular K.P. Saksena, "The United Nations and the North-South Conflict", in M.S. Rajan and S. Ganguly, eds., *Great Power Relations: World Order and the Third World* (New Delhi, 1981).

6. For a perceptive analysis of the Declaration and the Programme, see M. Dubey, "Problems of Establishing a New International Economic Order", *India Quarterly* (New Delhi), vol. 32, no. 3, July–September 1976, pp. 269–89. See also L.K. Jha, *North-South Debate* (Dehli, 1982); and K.B. Lall, *Struggle for Change: International Economic Relations* (New Delhi, 1983).

7. Group of 77, Arusha Programme for Collective Self-Reliance and Framework for Negotiations (UNCTAD V, Manila), Doc. TD/236/1979.

8. Group of 77, Final Report of the High-Level Conference on Economic Co-operation among the Developing Countries, Caracas (Caracas, G/77/FR).

9. Gunnar Myrdal, *Asian Drama: An Inquiry into the Poverty of Nations* (New York, N.Y., 1968), vol. 1, pp. 456–57.

10. See in particular Fredrick F. Clairmonte, "Reflections on Power: TNCs in the Global Economy", *CTC Report* (UN Centre on Transnational Corporations, United Nations, New York, N.Y.), no. 15, Spring 1983, pp. 37–39.

11. Cited in *UN Chronicle* (New York, N.Y.), October 1982, p. 43. The former Managing Director of the International Monetary Fund made this observation in 1971, when the Bretton Woods system broke down.

12. For a comprehensive study of the recent resort to trade restrictions, factors influencing trade policies, and the implications of the production of the developing countries, see S.J. Anjaria *et al.*, *Development in International Trade Policy* (Washington D.C., 1983).

13. Cited in the *Times of India* (New Delhi), 22 April 1983.

14. Mahbub-ul Haq, "Negotiating the Future", *Foreign Affairs* (New York, N.Y.), Winter 1980–81, pp. 398–417.

15. Cited in the *Times of India* (New Delhi), 5 October 1983.

REVOLUTION: THE WEAK RESPOND

10

Nicaragua: A Speech to My Former Comrades on the Left

DAVID HOROWITZ

Twenty-five years ago I was one of the founders of the New Left. I was one of the organizers of the first political demonstrations on the Berkeley campus—and indeed on any campus—to protest our government's anti-Communist policies in Cuba and Vietnam. Tonight I come before you as the kind of man I used to tell myself I would never be: a supporter of President Reagan, a committed opponent of Communist rule in Nicaragua.

I offer no apologies for my present position. It was what I thought was the humanity of the Marxist *idea* that made me what I was then; it is the inhumanity of what I have seen to be the Marxist *reality* that has made me what I am now. If my former comrades who support the Sandinistas were to pause for a moment and then plunge their busy political minds into the human legacies of their activist pasts, they would instantly drown in an ocean of blood.

The issue before us is not whether it is morally right for the United States to arm the *contras*, or whether there are unpleasant men among them. Nor is it whether the United States should defer to the wisdom of the Contradora powers—more than thirty years ago the United States tried to overthrow Somoza, and it was the Contradora powers of the time who bailed him out.

The issue before us and before all people who cherish freedom is how to oppose a Soviet imperialism so vicious and so vast as to dwarf any previously known. An "ocean of blood" is no metaphor. As we speak here tonight, this empire—whose axis runs through Havana and now Managua—is killing hundreds of thousands of Ethiopians to consolidate a dictatorship whose policies against its black citizens make the South African government look civilized and humane.

A second issue, especially important to me, is the credibility and commitment of the American Left.

In his speech on Nicaragua, President Reagan invoked the Truman Doctrine, the first attempt to oppose Soviet expansion through revolutionary surrogates. I marched against the Truman Doctrine in 1948, and defended, with the Left, the revolutions in Russia and China, in Eastern Europe and Cuba, in Cambodia and Vietnam—just as the Left defends the Sandinistas today.

And I remember the arguments and "facts" with which we made our case and what the other side said, too—the Presidents who came and went, and the anti-Communists on the Right, the William Buckleys and the Ronald Reagans. And in every case, without exception, time has proved the Left wrong. Wrong in its views of the revolutionaries' intentions, and wrong about the facts of their revolutionary rule. And just as consistently the anti-Communists were proved right.

Today the Left dismisses Reagan's warnings about Soviet expansion as anti-Communist paranoia, a threat to the peace, and a mask for American imperialism. We said the same things about Truman when he warned us then. Russia's control of Eastern Europe, we said, was only a defensive buffer, a temporary response to American power—first, because Russia had no nuclear weapons; and then, because it lacked the missiles to deliver them.

Today, the Soviet Union is a nuclear superpower, missiles and all, but it has not given up an inch of the empire which it gained during World War II—not Eastern Europe, not the Baltic states which Hitler delivered to Stalin and whose nationhood Stalin erased and which are now all but forgotten, not even the Kurile Islands which were once part of Japan.

Not only have the Soviets failed to relinquish their conquests in all these years—years of dramatic, total decolonization in the West—but their growing strength and the wounds of Vietnam have encouraged them to reach for more. South Vietnam, Cambodia, Laos, Ethiopia, Yemen, Mozambique, and Angola are among the dominoes which have recently fallen into the Soviet orbit.

To expand its territorial core—which apologists still refer to as a "defensive perimeter"—Moscow has already slaughtered a million peasants in Afghanistan, an atrocity warmly endorsed by the Sandinista government.

Minister of Defense Humberto Ortega describes the army of the conquerors—whose scorched-earth policy has driven half the Afghan population from its homes—as the "pillar of peace" in the world today. To any self-respecting socialist, praise for such barbarism would be an inconceivable outrage—as it was to the former Sandinista, now *contra*, Edén Pastora. But praise for the barbarians is sincere tribute coming from the Sandinista rulers, because they see themselves as an integral part of the Soviet empire itself.

"The struggle of man against power is the struggle of memory against forgetting." So writes the Czech novelist Milan Kundera, whose name and work no longer exist in his homeland.

In all the Americas, Fidel Castro was the only head of state to cheer the Soviet tanks as they rolled over the brave people of Prague. And cheering right along with Fidel were Carlos Fonseca, Tomas Borge, Humberto Ortega, and the other creators of the present Nicaraguan regime.

One way to assess what has happened in Nicaragua is to realize that wherever Soviet tanks crush freedom from now on, there will be two governments in the Americas supporting them all the way.

About its own crimes and for its own criminals, the Left has no memory at all.

To the Left I grew up in, along with the Sandinista founders, Stalin's Russia was a socialist paradise, the model of the liberated future. Literacy to the uneducated, power to the weak, justice to the forgotten— we praised the Soviet Union then, just as the Left praises the Sandinistas now.

And just as they ignore warnings like the one that has come from Violetta Chamorro, the publisher of *La Prensa*, the paper which led the fight against Somoza, and a member of the original Sandinista junta— "With all my heart, I tell you it is worse here now than it was in the times of the Somoza dictatorship"—so we dismissed the anti-Soviet "lies" about Stalinist repression.

In the society we hailed as a new human dawn, 100 million people were put in slave-labor camps, in conditions rivaling Auschwitz and

Buchenwald. Between 30 and 40 million people were killed—in peace-time, in the daily routine of socialist rule. While leftists applauded their progressive policies and guarded their frontiers, Soviet Marxists killed more peasants, more workers, and even more Communists than all the capitalist governments together since the beginning of time.

And for the entire duration of this nightmare, the William Buckleys and Ronald Reagans and the other anti-Communists went on telling the world exactly what was happening. And all that time the pro-Soviet Left and its fellow-travelers went on denouncing them as reactionaries and liars, using the same contemptuous terms with which the Left attacks the President and his supporters today.

The Left would *still* be denying the Soviet atrocities if the perpetrators themselves had not finally acknowledged their crimes. In 1956, in a secret speech to the party elite, Khrushchev made the crimes a Communist fact; but it was only the CIA that actually made the fact public, allowing radicals to come to terms with what they had done.

Khrushchev and his cohorts could not have cared less about the misplaced faith and misspent lives of their naive supporters on the Left. The Soviet rulers were concerned about themselves: Stalin's mania had spread the slaughter into his henchmen's ranks; they wanted to make totalitarianism safe for its rulers. In place of a dictator whose paranoia could not be controlled, they instituted a dictatorship by directorate—which (not coincidentally) is the form of rule in Nicaragua today. Repression would work one way only: from the privileged top of society to the powerless bottom.

The year of Khrushchev's speech—which is also the year Soviet tanks flattened the freedom fighters of Budapest—is the year that tells us who the Sandinistas really are.

Because the truth had to be admitted at last, the Left all over the world was forced to redefine itself in relation to the Soviet facts. China's Communist leader Mao liked Stalin's way better. Twenty-five million people died in the "great leaps" and "cultural revolutions" he then launched. In Europe and America, however, a new anti-Stalinist Left was born. This New Left was repelled by the evils it was now forced to see, and embarrassed by the tarnish the Soviet totalitarians had brought to the socialist cause. It turned its back on the Soviet model of Stalin and his heirs.

But the Sandinista vanguard was neither embarrassed nor repelled. In 1957, Carlos Fonseca, the founding father of the Sandinista Front, visited the Soviet Union with its newly efficient totalitarian state. To Fonseca, as to Borge and his other comrades, the Soviet monstrosity was their revolutionary dream come true. In his pamphlet, *A Nicaraguan in Moscow*, Fonseca proclaimed Soviet Communism his model for Latin America's revolutionary future.

This vision of a Soviet America is now being realized in Nicaragua. The *comandante* directorate, the army, and the secret police are already mirrors of the Soviet state—not only structurally but in their personnel, trained and often manned by agents of the Soviet axis.

But the most important figure in this transformation is not a Nicaraguan at all. For twenty years, from the time the Sandinistas first arrived in Havana, they were disciples of Fidel Castro. With his blessings they went on to Moscow, where Stalin's henchman completed their revolutionary course. Fidel is the image in which the Sandinista leadership has created itself and the author of its strategy. Its politburo, the *comandante* directorate, was personally created by Fidel in Havana on the eve of the final struggle, sealed with a pledge of millions in military aid. It was Fidel who supplied the arms with which the Sandinistas waged their battles, just as he supplied the Cuban general—Zenen Casals—who directed their victorious campaign (just as the Soviets supplied the general who directed Fidel's own victory at the Bay of Pigs). *Without Castro's intervention, Arturo Cruz and the other anti-Somoza and pro-democratic contras would be the government of Nicaragua today.*

And it was Fidel who showed the Sandinistas how to steal the revolution after the victory, and how to secure their theft by manipulating their most important allies: the American Left and its liberal sympathizers.

Twenty-five years ago Fidel was also a revolutionary hero to us on the New Left. Like today's campus radicals, we became "coffee-pickers" and passengers on the revolutionary tour, and we hailed the literacy campaigns, health clinics, and other wonders of the people's state.

When Fidel spoke, his words were revolutionary music to our ears: "Freedom with bread. Bread without terror." "A revolution neither red nor black, but Cuban olive-green." And so in Managua today: "Not [Soviet] Communism but Nicaraguan *Sandinismo*" is the formula Fidel's imitators proclaim.

Fidel's political poems put radicals all over the world under his spell. Jean-Paul Sartre wrote one of the first and most influential books of praise: "If this man asked me for the moon," he said, "I would give it to him. Because he would have a need for it."

When I listen to the enthusiasts for the Sandinista redeemers, the fate of a hero of the Cuban revolution comes to my mind. For in the year that Jean-Paul Satre came to Havana and fell in love with the humanitarian Fidel, Huber Matos embarked on a long windowless night of the soul.

The fate of Huber Matos begins with the second revolution that Fidel launched.

All the fine gestures and words with which Fidel seduced us and won our support—the open Marxism, the socialist humanism, the independent path—turned out to be calculated lies. Even as he proclaimed his color to be olive-green, he was planning to make his revolution Moscow red.

So cynical was Fidel's strategy that at the time it was difficult for many to comprehend. One by one Fidel began removing his own comrades from the revolutionary regime and replacing them with Cuban Communists.

Cuba's Communists were then a party in disgrace. They had opposed the revolution; they had even served in the cabinet of the tyrant Batista while the revolution was taking place!

But this was all incidental to Fidel. Fidel knew how to use people. And Fidel was planning a *new* revolution he could trust the Communists to support: he had decided to turn Cuba into a Soviet state. And Fidel also knew that he could no longer trust his own comrades, because they had made a revolution they thought was going to be Cuban olive-green.

Although Fidel removed socialists and the Sandinistas removed democrats, the pattern of betrayal has been the same.

To gain power the Sandinistas concealed their true intention (*a Soviet state*) behind a revolutionary lie (*a pluralist democracy*). To consolidate power they fashioned a second lie (*democracy, but only within the revolution*), and those who believed in the first lie were removed. At the end of the process there will be no democracy in Nicaragua at all, which is exactly what Fonseca and the Sandinistas intended when they began.

When Huber Matos saw Fidel's strategy unfolding in Cuba, he got on the telephone with other Fidelistas to discuss what they should do. This was a mistake. In the first year of Cuba's liberation, the phones of revolutionary legends like Huber Matos were already tapped by Fidel's secret police. Huber Matos was arrested.

In the bad old days of Batista oppression, Fidel had been arrested himself. His crime was not words on a telephone, but leading an attack on a military barracks to overthrow the Batista regime. Twelve people were killed. For this Fidel spent a total of eighteen months in the tyrant's jail before being released.

Huber Matos was not so lucky. Fidel was no Batista, and the revolution that had overthrown Batista was no two-bit dictatorship. For his phone call, Huber Matos was tried in such secrecy that not even members of the government were privy to the proceedings. When it was over, he was sentenced to solitary confinement, in a cell without sunlight, for *twenty-two years*. And even as Fidel buried his former friend and comrade alive, he went on singing his songs of revolutionary humanism and justice.

Milan Kundera reveals the meaning of this revolutionary parable of Huber Matos and Fidel. Recalling a French Communist who wrote poems for brotherhood while his friend was being murdered by the poet's comrades in Prague, Kundera says: "The hangman killed while the poet sang."

Kundera explains: "People like to say revolution is beautiful; it is only the terror arising from it which is evil. But this is not true. The evil is already present in the beautiful; hell is already contained in the dream of paradise. . . . To condemn Gulags is easy, but to reject the poetry which leads to the Gulag by way of paradise is as difficult as ever." Words to bear in mind today as we consider Nicaragua and its revolution of poets.

To believe in the revolutionary dream is the tragedy of its supporters; to exploit the dream is the talent of its dictators. Revolutionary cynicism, the source of this talent, is Fidel's most important teaching to his Sandinista disciples. This is the faculty that allows the *comandantes* to emulate Fidel himself: to be poets and hangmen at the same time. To promise democracy and organize repression, to attack imperialism and join an empire, to talk peace and plan war, to champion justice and deliver Nicaragua to a fraternity of inhumane, repressive, militarized, and economically crippled states.

"We used to have one main prison, now we have many," begins the lament of Carlos Franqui, a former Fidelista, for the paradise that Nicaragua has now gained. "We used to have a few barracks; now we have many. We used to have many plantations; now we have only one, and it belongs to Fidel. Who enjoys the fruits of the revolution, the houses of the rich, the luxuries of the rich? The *comandante* and his court."

To this grim accounting must be added the economic ruin that Fidel's Marxism has wrought. Among the proven failures of the Marxist promise, this is the most fateful of all. The failure of Marxist economies to satisfy basic needs, let alone compete with the productive capitalisms of the West, has produced the military-industrial police states which call themselves socialist today. Nicaragua, with its Sandinista-created economic crisis and its massive military build-up, is but the latest example of this pattern.

Twenty-five years ago we on the Left applauded when Fidel denounced Cuba's one-crop economy and claimed that U.S. imperialism was the cause of the nation's economic plight. It seemed so self-evident. Cuba was a fertile island with a favorable climate, but U.S. sugar plantations had monopolized its arable land, and the sugar produced was a product for export, not a food for Cubans. The poor of Cuba had been sacrificed on the altar of imperialist profit. Whenever we were confronted by the political costs Castro's revolution might entail, we were confident that this gain alone—Cuba's freedom to grow food for Cubans—would make any sacrifice worthwhile. The same illusion—that the revolution will mean better lives for Nicaragua's poor—underlies every defense of the Sandinistas today.

It is nearly three decades since Cuba's liberation, and Cuba is still a one-crop economy. But the primary market for its sugar is now the Soviet Union instead of the United States. Along with this have come other economic differences as well. Cuba's external debt is now *200 times* what it was when Fidel took power. And it would be far greater if the Communist *caudillo* had not mortgaged his country to his Soviet patron. So bankrupt is the economy Castro has created that it requires a Soviet subsidy of over $4 billion a year, one-quarter of the entire national income, to keep it afloat. Before the revolution, Cubans enjoyed the highest per-capita income in Latin America. Now they are economic prisoners of permanent rationing and chronic shortages in even the most basic necessities. The allotted rations tell a story in themselves: two pounds of meat per citizen per month; 20 percent less clothing than the allotment a decade earlier; and in rice, a basic staple of Cuba's poor, *half* the yearly consumption under the old Batista regime.

The idea that Marxist revolution will mean economic benefit for the poor has proved to be the most deadly illusion of all. It is *because* Marxist economies *cannot* satisfy economic needs—not even at the levels of the miserably corrupt capitalisms of Batista and Somoza—that Marxist states require permanent repression to stifle unrest and permanent enemies to saddle with the blame.

This is also why Castro has found a new national product to supply to the Soviet market (a product his Sandinista diciples are in the process of developing in their turn). The product is the Cuban nation itself, as a military base for Soviet expansion.

The event that sealed the contract for this development was the moment of America's defeat in Vietnam in April 1975. This defeat resulted in America's effective withdrawal from the crucial role it had played since 1945, as the guardian of the international status quo and the keeper of its peace.

To the Soviet imperialists, America's loss was an opportunity gained. In 1975 the Kremlin began what would soon be a tenfold increase in the aid it had been providing to Cuba. Most of the aid was of military intent. Toward the end of the year, 36,000 Cuban troops surfaced in Africa, as an interventionary force in Angola's civil war. Soviet aid to Cuba tripled and then quintupled as Castro sent another 12,000 Cuban troops to provide a palace guard for Ethiopia's new dictator, Mengistu Haile Mariam, who had thrown himself into the Soviet embrace with a campaign which he officially called his "Red Terror." A year after his henchmen had murdered virtually the entire graduating class of the high schools of Addis Ababa—just the most poignant of Mengistu's 100,000 victims—Fidel presented him with a Bay of Pigs medal, Cuban socialism's highest award.

Ethiopia's dictator is only one of the international heroes who regularly pass through the Cuban base to be celebrated, trained, and integrated into a network of subversion and terror that has come to span every continent of the globe. And in the Sandinista revolution Fidel's colonial plantation has produced its most profitable return: an opportunity for Moscow to expand its investment to the American land mass itself.

Nicaragua is now in the grip of utterly cynical and utterly ruthless men, exceeding even their sponsors in aggressive hostility to the United States. The Soviets may be the covert patrons of the world's terrorist plague, but not even they have had the temerity to embrace publicly the assassin Qaddafi as a "brother" the way the Sandinistas have. The aim of the Sandinista revolution is to crush its society from top to bottom, to institute totalitarian rule, and to use the country as a base to spread Communist terror and Communist regimes throughout the hemisphere.

The Sandinista anthem which proclaims the Yankee to be the "enemy of mankind" expresses precisely the revolutionaries' sentiment and goal. That goal is hardly to create a more just society—the sordid record would dissuade any reformer from choosing the Communist path—but to destroy the societies still outside the totalitarian perimeter, and their chief protector, the United States.

Support for the *contras* is a first line of defense. For Nicaraguans, a *contra* victory would mean the restoration of the democratic leadership from whom the Sandinistas stole the revolution in the first place, the government that Nicaragua would have had if Cuba had not intervened. For the countries of the Americas, it would mean a halt in the Communist march that threatens their freedoms and their peace.

In conclusion, I would like to say this to my former comrades and successors on the Left: you are self-righteous and blind in your belief that you are part of a movement to advance human progress and liberate mankind. You are in fact in league with the darkest and most reactionary forces of the modern world, whose legacies—as the record attests—are atrocities and oppressions on a scale unknown in the human past. It is no accident that radicals in power have slaughtered so many of their own people. Hatred of self, and by extension one's country, is the root of the radical cause.

As American radicals, the most egregious sin you commit is to betray the privileges and freedoms ordinary people from all over the world have created in this country—privileges and freedoms that ordinary people all over the world would feel blessed to have themselves. But the worst of it is this: you betray all this tangible good that you can see around you for a socialist pie-in-the-sky that has meant horrible deaths and miserable lives for the hundreds of millions who have so far fallen under its sway.

11

The US and the Contras

ARYEH NEIER

As far back as a quarter of a century ago, some American policy analysts and military strategists were discussing, in broad outline, plans for a war like the one the United States is sponsoring in Nicaragua. We should undertake "counter-revolutionary offensives in countries subverted to communism," according to a March 1961 article in *Military Review*, to give *them* a dose of the "political warfare" they wage against us. *Military Review*, a US Army journal, defined political warfare as

> a sustained effort by a government or political group to seize, preserve or extend power, against a defined ideological enemy. . . . It embraces diverse forms of coercion and violence including strikes and riots, economic sanctions, subsidies for guerrilla or proxy warfare and, where necessary, kidnappings or assassination of enemy elites.

"Counterrevolutionary offensives" were much on the minds of some US officials when that article was published. Fidel Castro had seized power in Cuba just two years previously. And John F. Kennedy, who was committed to developing America's capacity to fight unconventional wars to stop communism, had just become president.

Today, a quarter of a century later, the United States is mired in the most drawn-out "counterrevolutionary offensive" we have yet undertaken. The political warfare we launched to overthrow the Sandinista government in Nicaragua has dragged on for more than five years— longer than our participation in any war in US history for which we have had primary responsibility except the war in Vietnam. The end of our war in Nicaragua is nowhere in sight. Though the wars in Afghanistan, Angola, Cambodia, and El Salvador, in which we are also engaged in varying degrees, have lasted longer, they differ in that the forces we are aiding would have engaged in combat, or did engage in combat, without us. As Christopher Dickey makes clear in *With the Contras*, there would be no war in Nicaragua except for the United States. We organized, recruited, trained, guided, financed, and supplied the *contras*, and we speak to the world in their behalf. That does not mean that they would now disappear if we withdrew our support. Nor does it mean that we exercise control even though we provide essential support. Regardless of the limits on our ability to exercise control, however, the *contras* are our creature, much as Frankenstein's "miserable monster" was his creature after getting out of control. We are responsible for the *contras*.

That the *contras* murder civilians, and rape, torture, and execute prisoners, has been reported previously by others. Amnesty International discusses several cases of abuses by the *contras* in its new report, *Nicaragua: The Human Rights Record*, and concludes that "the number of captives tortured and put to death by FDN forces [the largest of the *contra* armies] since 1981 is impossible to determine, but is believed to total several hundred." Dickey's approach is different, however. Other accounts have focused on the victims. As Dickey's title suggests, he focuses on the killers. Reading Dickey makes it all the more plain that it is grotesque to refer to them, as President Reagan does, as "the democratic resistance," "freedom fighters," or, most extravagantly, as "the moral equal of the Founding Fathers."

Dickey discusses a number of the reasons why we launched this war. What most of these reasons, and others that could be mentioned, come down to is that we were intent, and remain intent, on showing that "we" can do to "them" whatever "they" do to "us." If they launch a war against us in El Salvador, we can launch a war against them in Nicaragua. If they assert control over their part of the world by invading Afghanistan or by crushing Solidarity in Poland, we will show that no one messes with us in our part of the world. If they practice a "Brezhnev doctrine"—what's mine is mine and what's yours is up for grabs—we'll show them that what they may think is theirs is also up for grabs. As President Reagan said recently, the way to prove America's resolve to Mikhail Gorbachev is to fund the *contras*.[1]

Christopher Dickey reported on Central America for nearly four years for *The Washington Post*. As he tells the story, the US began organizing the *contra* war in July 1979, at the moment that the Sandinistas were triumphing over the forces of President Anastasio Somoza, by rescuing key members of Somoza's National Guard so that they could resume the fight another day. At the outset it was a haphazard operation, undertaken by an informal network of active and retired CIA operatives. It is unclear from Dickey's account whether policy-making officials of the Carter administration knew what was going on; probably they were only dimly aware. To get around political constraints that might have been imposed by Carter, or by the Congress after Reagan took office, the military government in Argentina was enlisted to transform the remnants of Somoza's *guardias* into a fighting force. In the process, the Argentine military acquired the belief that the United States would repay the favor by siding with them, or by staying neutral, when they invaded the Falklands/Malvinas in 1982.

In December 1981, CIA director William Casey reported to the House and Senate Permanent Select Committees on Intelligence (known as "oversight committees," which Dickey calls "a curious locution that meant they oversaw intelligence activities but seemed to imply they overlooked them") that President Reagan had decided to undertake a covert war against Nicaragua. The Reagan administration, under the leadership of Assistant Secretary of State Thomas O. Enders, had been working on that war since it took office the previous January. "By the time it told Congress what was happening," Dickey writes, "all the actors were in place and it was just a matter of pulling the curtain aside for a glimpse of the set."

In the early days of the war, much of the action revolved around a daring *contra* commander, a former *guardia* sergeant known as Suicida. Dickey, along with James LeMoyne (then of *Newsweek*, now of *The New York Times*), accompanied Suicida's forces from their base in Honduras on a raid into Nicaragua. Suicida is Dickey's central character: an effective leader who accounted for much of the *contra* military punch during 1982 and 1983. Along with some of his ex-*guardia* associates, Suicida also helped to build the *contra* reputation for savagery. Initially directed against the Sandinistas, but then also against each other, that savagery eventually brought down Suicida. He was executed by the *contra* leadership in the fall of 1983.

To regulate savagery, but not to stop it, the CIA produced its own infamous manual, "Psychological Operations in Guerrilla Warfare." Though the current political leadership of the *contras*, the Nicaraguan Opposition Union (UNO), and their sponsors in the Reagan administration proclaim their democratic intentions, democracy was not on the CIA's agenda in 1983 when it published the manual. Instead, the manual speaks of the time when "a *comandante* of ours will literally be able to shake up the Sandinista structure, to replace it." The manual goes on to tell how to wage political warfare, including the "kidnappings and assassinations of enemy elites" specified by *Military Review* in 1961. It explicitly recommends kidnappings, advising the *contras* to "kidnap all officials of the Sandinista government and replace them"; in discussing assassinations, however, the manual uses CIA-speak, advising the *contras* to "neutralize carefully selected and planned targets" such as judges. This advice appears directly under the heading "Selective Use of Violence for Propagandistic Effects."

Public disclosure of the manual and of the CIA's role in mining the harbors of Nicaragua, combined with reports of the terror tactics employed by the *contras* to ruin the 1984–1985 coffee harvest (Dickey's narrative leaves off before this point), led to a vote by Congress in April 1985 denying continuing US financial support to the *contras*. In short order, however, the Reagan administration turned around the Congress, getting it to appropriate $27 million in "humanitarian" aid to them in June 1985. The quick change was made possible by the Sandinistas themselves (Daniel Ortega visited Moscow immediately following the April vote denying funding to the *contras*), by a rhetorical campaign of denunciations of the Sandinistas by President Reagan, and by an attempt to transform the image of the *contras*.

UNO was formed during this period and the most widely respected Nicaraguan opponent of the Sandinistas, Arturo Cruz, was persuaded to identify himself with it. Cruz, while exercising little influence, had provided the Sandinistas with an attractive public face during their first two years in power, including a stint as their ambassador to Washington. So far, at least, the *contras* appear to be using him in the same way. He has pursued an effort to get them to stop murdering civilians and prisoners, and to investigate and punish those engaged in past abuses. This effort has not yet had a discernible impact. Even so, his association with UNO has been all-important to the Reagan administration in persuading Congress to resume funding to the *contras*.

The association of Arturo Cruz with the effort to overthrow the Sandinistas raises the question of what kind of government might emerge if the *contras* triumph. If Cruz cannot succeed in curbing the way they conduct the war, what influence would he exert over the men with the guns after they prevail? The conventional wisdom about the war that "they" are waging against "us" in nearby El Salvador is that, if the left wins, the political leaders Guillermo Ungo and Ruben Zamóra would have little to say in its revolutionary government. Those who have been doing the fighting in the hills, it is said, would not share real power with social democrats in suits and ties who spent the war years on the lecture circuit. Would it be any different in Nicaragua after the *contras* have engaged in four, five, six, or seven years of combat? As to the United States, though it showed itself, like Frankenstein, "capable of bestowing animation upon lifeless matter," controlling what it created is another matter. A government formed by the *contras* would be economically and militarily dependent on the United States, but our experience previously in Nicaragua and elsewhere in Central America should teach us that this is no assurance that it would be a decent government. The best clue we have about how the *contras* would govern is how they fight the war. On Christopher Dickey's evidence, and on the evidence of their more recent conduct, it is difficult to be sanguine.

Even if we thought that we could go beyond "bestowing animation" on the *contras* and that we could control the way they fight and the way they would govern; and even if we trusted Ronald Reagan, William Casey, and the others who might exercise control, the larger question remains: Should we be doing this? In answering this question, assume the worst. Let's say that Nicaragua, in the words of *Military Review*, has been "subverted to communism," that it is another Cuba. Should we launch a war to overthrow its government?

In answering that question, it is worth thinking for a moment about the Soviet Union's war against Afghanistan. Suppose that Afghanistan had a terrible, oppressive government before the Soviet Union invaded (which it did). And suppose that the Soviet Union were intent on imposing a much better government (an unlikely supposition, but perhaps no more unlikely than that the ex-*guardias* among the *contras* would reveal themselves as democrats once they take power in Nicaragua). Would that justify the Soviet Union in launching a war against Afghanistan?

If the answer is no, then the only justification we have for launching a war against Nicaragua is that they do it to us. But are we like them, and should we behave like them?

In effect, the Reagan administration's response is that we may not be like them, but we should behave like them. If we don't behave like them and demonstrate the determination to carry the fight to them, they will take advantage of us everywhere. "The Soviet Union's perception of United States strength and resolve in the next year depends largely on Congressional moves involving aid to Nicaraguan rebels," President Reagan told a group of Republican senators on January 21, according to White House spokesman Larry Speakes.[2]

An alternate response could be that because we are not like them, we don't have to behave like them. *We* don't have to bully small countries that we consider obnoxious. Our side has more options. We dominate the world, not by flexing our muscles, but economically, technologically, ideologically, linguistically, and culturally. The only idea around for which *they* can rally support is anti-Americanism. What we do in Nicaragua may succeed in ridding us of the Sandinistas. The costs, however, will include a considerable enhancement of the power of that idea—in the United States itself, in Latin America, and everywhere else except, ironically, within the Soviet empire, where pro-Americanism is too powerful an idea to be challenged.

It does not follow, of course, from an argument against US sponsorship of the *contras* that we must never aid guerrilla forces struggling against oppressive governments. Support for the Afghan rebels, for example, could be readily endorsed by many antagonists of aid to the *contras*. President Reagan occasionally lumps the two groups together under the label "freedom fighters," and pairs the forces against which they are struggling as "totalitarian." Probably the President does this to advance the cause of the *contras*. Its actual effect, however, may be to stigmatize, or at least to trivialize, the cause of the *mujahedin*.

The differences between the two struggles should be obvious. The Soviet Union claims it sent troops in to aid an ally combating a rebellion sponsored by foreign powers. This is transparent nonsense. It invaded; it governs with the aid of a puppet government; it practices unspeakable cruelties; it has driven close to a third of the Afghans out of their homeland into the misery of refugee existence; and, whatever support the *mujahedin* get from the United States and other countries, they are a home-grown product fighting for their freedom against a foreign op-pressor. Much of the Afghan population has rallied to their cause.

In contrast, in Nicaragua, whatever numbers of Soviets, Bulgarian, East German, or Cuban technicians and military advisers may be present, it is wholly unconvincing to label the Sandinistas as anyone's puppets. Theirs was a home-grown revolution. They have aligned themselves with the Soviet Union; they are not democrats; they have shown no respect for freedom of expression; but as Amnesty International's report demonstrates, they have largely—though not entirely—avoided the worst cruelties practiced by the government that preceded them and by the governments in nearby El Salvador and Guatemala. The number of refugees who have fled Nicaragua since 1979 is between 3 and 4 percent of the population, roughly equivalent to the number who returned after the Sandinistas seized power. Few Nicaraguans are fleeing now, and as many are returning. The *contra* war would never have got started without the intervention of the United States. It would continue for a while if we abandoned it, but unless we enlist another sponsor in the way that we brought in the Argentines at the outset, most likely it would eventually fade away. Many Nicaraguans are antagonistic to the Sandinistas, but no sizable segment of the population has rallied to the *contra* cause.

Demonstrating to the Soviet Union our resolve and our determination to control our part of the world is, in my view, the dominant reason that we launched the *contras*. As time passes, this acquires greater urgency to the Reagan administration because, having sponsored a war to over-throw the Sandinistas for so long, it finds it increasingly humiliating not to succeed. This sense of urgency may propel us to go further and do the job ourselves if it becomes apparent that the *contras* have failed. Though I believe that such geopolitical considerations are primary, the Reagan administration has also advanced two important subsidiary rationales that warrant consideration: we aim to stop the Sandinistas from arming the Salvadoran guerrillas; and we aim to pressure them to transform their system to make it democratic. President Reagan concentrated on those arguments in this year's State of the Union address, telling the Congress that:

> This is a great moral challenge for the entire free world. Surely, no issue is more important for peace in our own hemisphere, for the security of our frontiers, for the protection of our vital interests—than to achieve democracy in Nicaragua and to protect Nicaragua's democratic neighbors.

As to protecting "Nicaragua's democratic neighbors," it is probably best to examine this proposition by accepting the premise that they are democratic. Protecting them could mean stopping the flow of arms and/or stopping the flow of ideas. We have a legitimate interest in the first, but not in the second. (After all, what is a democracy if not a place where ideas may flow?) It is a matter of considerable dispute whether Nicaragua has made significant shipments of arms to El Salvador or elsewhere in recent years. Christopher Dickey contends that Nicaragua was shipping arms at the beginning of 1981, but stopped. He reports:

> By January 14, US intelligence had picked up an avalanche of incriminating evidence, including a truck with a roof full of M-16s rolling through Honduras.[3] The game was over and the chits were being called in. "You people are just irresponsible," Ambassador Pezzullo told Borge and Daniel Ortega when he saw them at a cocktail party. "We've got you red-handed." And the Sandinistas knew it. They began taking measures to recoup. By March they had shut down the airfield at Pamplona that had been used to supply the Salvadorans. The airplanes were decommissioned, the pilots dispersed.

The Reagan administration claims that arms shipments have continued; others, such as former CIA analyst David MacMichael, whose assignment was to monitor such shipments, claim that they have been negligible since 1981. Whichever side is right, this hardly seems a good argument for sponsoring the *contra* war. Unquestionably, the Sandinistas would agree to forego shipping arms (indeed, it is an agreement they have already made) in exchange for an end to the war and, since Nicaragua does not share a border with El Salvador, policing such an agreement would not be difficult. Neither Costa Rica nor Honduras has so far been threatened by Sandinista forces; and the president-elect of Costa Rica, Oscar Arias Sanchez, recently said he opposes military aid to the *contras*. "If I were Mr. Reagan," he said, "I would give that money to Guatemala, El Salvador, Honduras, and Costa Rica for economic aid and not military aid to the contras."[4] The principal Latin American democracies, moreover, strongly oppose aid to the *contras*. In an interview published on March 10, President Belisario Betancur of Colombia told *The Washington Post*, "All of Latin America doesn't like the Reagan proposal. . . . I think an initiative such as the request for $100 million is wrong. I know we can get more through negotiation."

If we are sponsoring a war to promote democracy, the obvious question is: why go after Nicaragua? The world is full of undemocratic countries. In the Western hemisphere, we could have sponsored wars against Chile, Cuba, Paraguay, Suriname, and Haiti before the ouster of Duvalier—each of them even less democratic than Nicaragua. If we define our interest in democracy as going beyond installing elected civilian governments and determine that we want those governments to abide by the rule of law and to respect human rights, we could also launch wars against our allies in El Salvador and Guatemala. Indeed, if our concern is human rights, we might also make war on Colombia and Peru. Though these are democracies, like the Nicaraguan government they are challenged by guerrilla movements. Their armed forces have committed terrible abuses of human rights against suspected civilian sympathizers of the guerrillas.

Amnesty International's new report fairly assesses the human rights situation in Nicaragua. It begins:

> Amnesty International's concerns in Nicaragua include a pattern of frequent, although generally short-term, imprisonment of prisoners of conscience; prolonged pretrial incommunicado detention of political prisoners, and restrictions on their right to a fair trial; and poor prison conditions for political prisoners. Amnesty International has received some reports of torture, arbitrary killings and unacknowledged detention carried out by military personnel in remote areas undergoing armed conflict. However, the organization has also received information on the public trial and imprisonment of military personnel found responsible for such abuses.

There is little new information here. The abuses discussed by Amnesty have been reported previously by others (including by the organization with which I am associated, Americas Watch). Even so, the publication of Amnesty's report is an important event as it puts the imprimatur of the world's most prestigious group concerned with human rights on findings that are hotly disputed.

Denunciation of the Sandinistas for their abuses of human rights, Amnesty makes clear, is well warranted. The organization does this evenhandedly, measuring Nicaragua's performance according to the same standards that it applies elsewhere. It is neither an apologist for the abuses committed by the Sandinistas, nor does it exaggerate their abuses in order to further an ideological crusade.

Amnesty's findings will not please the sponsors of the military campaign to overthrow the Sandinistas. Its report shows that, subsequent to 1982, the *contras* committed most of the violent abuses of human rights in Nicaragua. Nineteen-eighty-two was the year in which the worst Sandinista abuses against the Miskito Indians took place. Including a massacre at Leimus in late December 1981, close to a hundred Miskitos were murdered or "disappeared" after detention by Nicaraguan government forces. Thereafter, Nicaragua's treatment of the Miskitos improved and thousands of Indians have now returned to the places from which they were forcibly relocated or fled, and they are now rebuilding their communities. Today the major form of human rights abuse in Nicaragua is severe harassment of dissenters, particularly those protesting the draft and those suspected of sympathizing with the *contras*.

Amnesty's findings on Nicaragua contrast with what the organization reported on Guatemala at about the same time:

> Under successive administrations the regular police and military forces, as well as paramilitary groups acting under government order or with official

complicity, have been responsible for massive instances of human rights violations, including torture, "disappearances" and extrajudicial executions directed at people from all sectors of Guatemalan society. Some victims have been seized or shot down in broad daylight in the presence of witnesses by uniformed military or security agents. Others have been abducted or murdered by heavily armed men in civilian clothes using weaponry and vehicles normally issued only to government agencies, while uniformed military or police force units stood by, making no effort to apprehend the assailants. The bodies of other victims have been thrown into ravines, dumped at roadsides or buried in unmarked mass graves.

Guatemala's is an extreme case. Almost any country's human rights record would not look so bad if it were evaluated according to that standard. Accordingly, it is probably more instructive to read Amnesty's report on Nicaragua alongside its most recent report on some other Latin American country, such as Peru. That democratic though troubled country, like Nicaragua, is beset by economic disaster as well as by warfare against especially brutal guerrilla forces (though those forces have less chance of overthrowing the government than the guerrillas combating the Sandinistas and they do not enjoy the advantage of backing from a major foreign power). Amnesty cited the names of more than a thousand persons who had disappeared, following detention by the Peruvian security forces, between January 1983 and the end of 1984. Also, Amnesty reported that Peru's security forces extrajudicially executed some 420 persons during that two-year period.

That other countries have dreadful human rights records does not excuse the abuses committed by the Sandinistas. On the other hand, it does suggest that it is difficult to justify on human rights grounds President Reagan's choice of Nicaragua as the country to improve by sponsoring a war against it.

Is it nevertheless true that the *contra* war promotes democracy and human rights in Nicaragua? This question seems to me to be unanswerable. We have no way of knowing whether the Sandinistas would be more repressive or less repressive if there were no war. Too many factors enter into the equation to make any calculation that can be defended. Ordinarily, of course, governments behave worse when their security is threatened. On the other hand, perhaps the Reagan administration is right in contending that Nicaragua is sui generis and that the war forces the Sandinistas to liberalize to try to maintain European and Latin American support. Maybe the Sandinistas will "cry uncle," in President Reagan's words, and permit the development of a more democratic system. This isn't usually the way to promote democracy, however, and the guess that it will work in this instance is hardly a basis on which to launch a war.

The most destructive aspect of the administration's claim that the US is sponsoring a war to promote human rights is that it debases the human rights cause. Amnesty International's method of carefully documenting a country's human rights record is to measure it against recognized international standards, to denounce abuses, and to enlist citizens worldwide to intercede on behalf of individual victims. This is not only a better way to promote human rights in particular circumstances; it also promotes respect for the human rights cause.

In the Reagan administration's efforts to justify its sponsorship of the *contra* war, it frequently shifts ground: sometimes it argues for demonstrating toughness to the Russians; sometimes for stopping the subversion of Nicaragua's neighbors; sometimes for promoting democracy in Nicaragua. If each argument is faulty by itself, do these rationales achieve a collective strength by reinforcing one another? In short-run domestic political terms, the answer is probably yes. The administration's strategy has worked in getting the Congress and a large segment of the American public to go along with our proxy war. It may even succeed in creating the political climate that would permit the administration to send in American troops or, perhaps, only American planes. In any other terms, the administration has failed. Its three poor rationales do not substitute for one intellectually and morally persuasive argument for sponsoring the *contra* war.

NOTES

1. See Bernard Weinraub, "Reagan Will Seek $100 Million in Aid for the Contras," *The New York Times* (January 22, 1986).
2. Bernard Weinraub, *The New York Times* (January 22, 1986).
3. When I visited Central America in 1981, US officials showed me such a truck—possibly the same one mentioned by Dickey. For some years thereafter, that truck was exhibited to visitors to the region.
4. *The Washington Post* (February 20, 1985), p. A5.

12

Iran and the Americans

SHAUL BAKHASH

In the fall of 1985, R.K. Ramazani, a historian at the University of Virginia, urged in an article in *Foreign Policy* that the United States "bury the hatchet" with Iran and seek a reconciliation with the Islamic Republic. He emphasized, of course, the strategic importance of improving relations with a country of over 45 million people that borders on the Soviet Union, Pakistan, Afghanistan, and Turkey. More important, he detected a new and more pragmatic direction in Iran's foreign policy. This moderating trend, he believed, provided the opening for an American initiative. He felt that exploiting this opening should be a matter of some urgency. "America's failure to temper its containment policy [toward Iran]," he wrote, "could destroy any chance for exploring any opportunity for reconciliation that may already exist."[1]

Ironically, at the very time Mr. Ramazani was making his plea, the Reagan administration was taking the first tentative steps to establish contact with Iranian officials. That initiative, we now know, turned out very badly. While there is much to be said in favor of talks between the US and Iran, the Reagan administration's approach to Iran was ineptly handled. Aside from the domestic effects of this much publicized affair, the bungled initiative suggests, at the very least, a misreading of the play of politics in Iran itself.

It is on the Iranian side of this equation that Mr. Ramazani's book, which elaborates the argument of his *Foreign Policy* article, is particularly useful. He provides an account of the ideology, practice, and evolution of Iran's foreign policy since the overthrow of the Shah in 1979. He believes this policy must be seen in its regional setting, and examines the reaction of the neighboring states and the countries of the Middle East to the Iranian revolution. Hence, the "challenge and response" of his book's subtitle.

The foreign policy of the Islamic Republic, from the beginning, displayed a mixture of revolutionary zeal and pragmatic calculation. It dramatically reversed some of the foreign policies pursued under the Shah and continued others. Iran broke off relations with Israel and South Africa. Relations with the United States grew strained and then cracked after American hostages were taken in November 1979. A mood of national and Islamic assertiveness and a strong reaction against foreign influence led most Western businessmen and technicians to leave the country.

Clerics associated with Iran's religious leaders toured the Persian Gulf states preaching revolution and Khomeini's message of Islamic militancy. To the consternation of the foreign ministry, one senior cleric, Ayatollah Sadeq Ruhani, revived the Iranian claim to Bahrain and warned its ruler he would have him overthrown if he did not treat his people with more consideration. Iran's first president, Abolhasan Bani-Sadr, predicted the conservative regimes of the Gulf would be "swept away like dust in the wind" once their peoples followed the Iranian example.

Iraq's invasion of Iran greatly exacerbated this radical temper. When he sent his divisions into Iran in September 1980, the Iraqi president, Saddam Hussein, believed he could stimulate the overthrow of the revolutionary government, seize Iranian territory, and establish Iraqi primacy in the Gulf region. This proved to be a colossal blunder. The invasion allowed Ayatollah Khomeini and his lieutenants to unite a deeply divided country against a foreign enemy, to rebuild the badly weakened armed forces, and to expand the Revolutionary Guards considerably. The Guards today constitute one of the pillars of the regime's authority.

The war also exacerbated Iran's relations with the Arab states of the Gulf, who felt called upon to extend material, financial, and diplomatic support to Iraq. It pushed Iran to cement ties with two radical Arab states, Libya and Syria. Syria remains Iran's most important Arab ally. The war also reinforced the inclination of some elements of the Iranian regime to attempt to subvert the Gulf states. Iran, in the first of what was to become a string of similar allegations, was accused of supporting a plot to overthrow the government of Bahrain in December 1981.

Following the Israeli invasion of Lebanon in the summer of 1982, Iran dispatched a contingent of several hundred Revolutionary Guards to Lebanon to help fight the Israelis. It used its presence in Lebanon and its connection with the Shi'ite community there in a number of ways. Circumstantial evidence linked Iran to the bombing of the American embassy and American and French military barracks in Beirut in 1982 and 1983. Iran used Islamic propaganda and a network of sympathetic clerics to extend the Iranian presence from the Bekáa Valley southward to areas up to now dominated by Nabih Berri's more moderate Amal Shi'ite movement.

Iran's new rulers gradually evolved an ideology that served as both the rationale and impetus for their ambitious foreign policy. A central feature of this ideology, which Mr. Ramazani describes in one of his many excellent chapters, is the concept of Iran as a "redeemer state," the champion of the world's *mustaz'afin*, or disinherited classes, in their struggle against the *mustakberin*, the powerful classes or the oppressor states. Iran, according to the prime minister, Mir-Hussein Musavi, is destined to spread justice throughout the world and make possible "the liberation of mankind." The Iranian nation must grow in power and resolution, Ayatollah Khomeini has said, "until it has vouchsafed Islam to the entire world."

This struggle of the disinherited against the powerful and the exploiters is aimed at the United States and the Soviet Union, and at great power domination of the Islamic world. The slogan "neither East nor West" implies not merely neutrality between the superpowers but the creation of an Islamic movement powerful enough to stand up to them both. Iran's revolution itself, Iran's leaders believe, will not be secure until Saudi Arabia and the other Gulf states throw off American protection and have regimes that, like Iran's, are nonmonarchical, populist, Islamic, and dominated by the clerical establishment.

This world view helps to explain Iran's commitment to exporting revolution. Against Iraq, in Khomeini's view, Iran is involved in a defensive war with an idolatrous regime that poses a threat to Islam itself. Elsewhere, the export of the revolution is to be achieved, Ramazani writes, not by the sword but by example, propaganda, and the creation of institutions that can promote Iran's Islamic vision.

Ayatollah Khomeini, for example, has energetically supported the idea that the hajj, the great annual pilgrimage that last year brought some two million pilgrims to Mecca, must serve a political rather than a primarily religious purpose. It is to be used, he has said, to forge Islamic unity, to oppose the great powers, and to permit Muslims "to express their grievances against their ruthless oppressors," that is, against their own leaders. In 1983 Iranian pilgrims in Mecca participated in demonstrations that appeared to be directed as much against the Saudi state as against the US and the Soviet Union. Ayatollah Khomeini responded to Saudi protests by advising Saudi leaders themselves to use the hajj for political purposes so that they "would have no need for America, AWACS planes, or other superpowers." Iran has also created institutions such as the World Congress of Friday Leaders, to promote Islamic unity. Ayatollah Khomeini told delegates to the 1984 congress to return to their countries and "call upon the people to rebel as Iran did."

Ramazani stresses, however, that all this reflects only one aspect of Iran's post-revolution foreign policy. First, behind the revolutionary rhetoric, one can discern the continuity of Iran's traditional security concerns, for example in the Persian Gulf. The government of the Ayatollah, like the government of the Shah, seeks to underwrite Iranian security in the Gulf by securing recognition for Iran's primacy in the region, by maintaining control of vital sea lanes, and by preserving a military edge. "The Shah used to insist on the preservation of Iran's expanding 'security perimeter,' " Ramazani writes, "and the Khomeini regime insists on spreading Iran's 'security umbrella.' " Between 70 and 80 percent of Iran's imports continue to come from Western Europe and Japan. Relations with the Soviet Union are "correct" but the clerics share the traditional Iranian suspicion of the USSR. In February 1985, presumably on the strength of information about Soviet agents working in Iran provided by Vladimir Kuzichkin, a Soviet agent who had defected to England, the government arrested the leaders and over one thousand members of the Tudeh (Communist) party, and later expelled eighteen Soviet diplomats from the country.

Second, Iran has shown a streak of pragmatism and good sense even in periods when the radical strain seemed strongest at Tehran. Thus both Iran and Saudi Arabia acted to prevent the expansion of the

Iran-Iraq war to neighboring states: "The mutual restraint between Saudi Arabia and Iran reflected the fact that the ideological conflict between the two countries was tempered significantly by a perceived mutuality of interest."

Third, external pressures and internal difficulties, especially during the last two and a half years, led officials to blunt the more radical features of Iran's foreign policy. Despite leaks in the arms embargo imposed by the US, Iran had considerable difficulty in obtaining the weapons it needed for its war with Iraq. The Gulf states, led by Saudi Arabia, adopted what Mr. Ramazani aptly describes as a policy of "containment . . . by conciliation, disapprobation, and deterrence" toward Iran.

At home, the war with Iraq, along with falling oil prices and general disorganization, greatly exacerbated economic problems and fed public dissatisfaction. Already in 1984, the government, facing a shortage of foreign exchange, sharply curtailed imports. Its problems grew more severe in 1986 when oil revenues probably amounted to ony $6 billion, or half the previous year's level. Food rations have been tightened, gasoline rationing has been introduced, and factories have been shut or put on short shifts for a lack of spare parts and raw materials.

Iranian air defenses have proved more vulnerable to Iraqi aerial bombing, which inflicted severe damage on refinery and oil export facilities in 1986. This development explains Iran's recent eagerness to obtain spare parts for its Hawk missiles, even if from the "Great Satan."

Signs of war weariness and public dissaffection have also been evident. Antigovernment demonstrations broke out in working-class districts of Tehran in April 1985, partly to protest the government's inability to protect civilian areas from Iraqi aerial bombing. This summer, representatives of the cabinet and of the influential Association of the Seminary Teachers of Qum separately urged Khomeini to seek a nonmilitary solution to the war. He turned both groups down. In August, the former prime minister, Mehdi Bazargan, now in the opposition but allowed a limited degree of freedom, issued an open letter to Khomeini. He described Khomeini's insistence on prosecuting the war against Iraq as a formula for the destruction of the country's youth and its economy.[2]

Such internal and external difficulties explain the government's attempt beginning some two years ago, and in the face of opposition from hard-line elements, to break out of its diplomatic isolation. In October 1984, Khomeini gave this attempt his blessing, and said failure to establish normal relations with foreign states could mean "defeat, annihilation, and burial." The West German minister was told in a visit to Tehran in 1984 that Iran desired expanded relations with the West. Iran sought to distance itself from terrorist acts in the Middle East. It refused to cooperate with the hijackers who in December 1984 flew a Kuwaiti aircraft to Tehran and demanded the release of political prisoners in Kuwaiti jails. It used its good offices to help secure the release of Americans taken hostage after the hijacking of a TWA flight to Beirut in June 1985. Earlier this year, Iran offered to resume shipments of natural gas to the Soviet Union, which were halted over a price dispute in 1979. The government resolved a longstanding financial claim with France; and in OPEC it has made common cause on oil policy with its old rival, Saudi Arabia.

Mr. Ramazani has such developments in mind when he speaks of an "emerging realism" in Iranian foreign policy. In a passage that succinctly expresses the central thesis of his book, he writes:

> With respect to every major issue, including the war with Iraq, Iranian policy has consistently contained elements of self-restraint, pragmatism, and even, occasionally, helpfulness. The revolutionary regime's bark has been worse than its bite, its rhetoric more strident than its actions, its declared policies more belligerent than its intentions.

This catches nicely the mixture of ideology and pragmatism, bravado and realism, that has characterized Iranian foreign policy over the last three years. Despite the easing of relations between Iran and some of the Western European states, Mr. Ramazani, I think, minimizes the difficulties, on the Iranian side, of opening a dialogue with the US; for the "Great Satan" remains a special case. Moreover, having so forcefully delineated the ideological underpinnings of Iranian foreign policy, Mr. Ramazani might have said more on the strains arising from the gap between Iranian ideology and practice. Khomeini remains highly suspicious of America. There are elements hostile to the US among the senior clerics and in the Revolutionary Guards and the Revolutionary Committees. However pressed by war and economic difficulties, the government cannot afford to alienate constituencies in these powerful organizations. For seven years the public has been fed a steady diet of anti-American rhetoric. Any sudden reversal of policy would sorely test the government's credibility.

Khomeini and his lieutenants believe the influence they have gained among Shi'ites in Lebanon and Muslims elsewhere derives from Iran's uncompromising stand against Israel and the US; and thus while the general drift of Iran's recent foreign policy is unmistakable—a point Ramazani argues with eloquence—the road to improved foreign relations, especially with the US, will be rocky and erratic. Nevertheless, he has written with sparkling clarity on a difficult subject, and with both passion and objectivity on an issue which, for both Iranians and Americans, is still laden with much emotional baggage. The book went to press before revelations of American arms transfers to Iran captured the headlines. But it provides the perspective from which one can make better sense of recent developments.

The Reagan administration has variously described its Iran initiative as an attempt to establish contact with "moderates" in the Khomeini regime; to put the US in a better position to deal with the post-Khomeini period; to counter Soviet influence in Tehran; to persuade Iran to refrain from supporting terrorism and to assist in regaining US hostages; and to help end the Iran-Iraq war. Several difficulties undermine these explanations. Saudi and Israeli arms dealers appear to have been central both in initiating contacts between the Iranians and Americans, and, along with an Iranian arms dealer, in acting as intermediaries between them— not promising auspices for serious negotiations on matters apart from arms sales. Most of these men, notwithstanding their claims to the contrary, were concerned primarily with personal profit, yet the US had to rely on them for insight into the politics of the Iranian leadership and its aims in entering discussions. It was these men who presumably led McFarlane to make his ill-judged trip to Tehran. If the US wanted a dialogue with the Iranians, it might more reasonably have worked through Pakistan or Turkey, or its European allies, some of whom maintain excellent relations with the Islamic Republic. The exchange of arms for hostages came to dominate the relationship and at some stage the arms sales took on the added and wholly extraneous purpose of funneling money to the *contras* in Nicaragua.

Administration officials have also displayed more confusion than clarity regarding the "moderates" with whom they claimed to be in contact on the Iranian side. Mr. McFarlane has sometimes spoken as if these "moderates" were dissidents within the regime, risking their lives to make contacts with Americans, and preparing themselves for the post-Khomeini power struggle.

If such dissidents did exist, it would be the height of irresponsibility to speak of them so often and so publicly. The landscape of the Iranian revolution is strewn (sometimes literally) with the bodies of men who were believed to be friends of the US. Nor does it make sense to talk as if the United States has the means to inject itself into domestic Iranian politics and to influence the shape of the power structure that would emerge after Khomeini.

Shipments of arms could not regularly come into Iran without the knowledge and concurrence of a number of senior officials, nor could large amounts of funds to pay for them go out. Thus, whether in arms sales or in talks about other matters, American officials were dealing with the Iranian government. Within this government, of course, there are men with a variety of political views. If the US is to deal with Iran, it must have a more informed idea of the nature of this government, the role and inclinations of the people within it, the manner in which it works and makes decisions, and its relations to Ayatollah Khomeini. This calls for close observation of Iranian politics. It requires probing discussions with Iranian officials, if not directly then through reliable intermediaries, rather than arms merchants of questionable motives and dependability. The vexed question of arms sales could then be examined with respect to America's broader goals, Iran's ultimate war aims, Iraq's continuing access to sophisticated weapons, and the increasing tendency of the Baghdad regime to use its arms to bomb civilian and economic targets in Iran.

When the arms transfer story first became known, it was apparent that not only the American press, and particularly television, but American officials themselves had not been paying much attention to Iran for a number of years. Now, with national attention concentrated on the domestic repercussions of the Iranian arms deal and the *contra* connection, Iran once again appears virtually forgotten. Yet developments in Iran bear watching, for there has been considerable if guarded discussion in Iran about the wisdom, or desirability, of contacts with the US. And the outcome of that debate is relevant to US interests.

In Iran, with its controlled press, the story of the arms shipments has not aroused much furor. Iranian officials have persistently denied that they sought official contact with the US, that they held any high level negotiations with American representatives, or even that they bought arms directly from the US. The denials are even more vehement with regard to Israel; for while the US is only the "Great Satan," Israel does not theoretically have the right to exist. Iran's leaders have simply sought to portray the entire affair as a victory for Iran. McFarlane's visit to Iran, and President Reagan's radio-TV address, in which he described the Iranian revolution as a fact of history, have been treated as a recognition of the importance of Iran and its revolution.

Ayatollah Khomeini described Mr. McFarlane as a kind of humble pleader at the Iranian court: "They want to ask forgiveness and our nation does not want to accept," he said in a speech on November 20. "All the big states are in a race to establish relations" with Iran. He described the White House as a "Black House" whose inhabitants are full of "humility" and "trembling" at the mess they have created.[3]

Yet conflicting voices are emerging from Tehran. The prime minister ruled out any negotiations with the "criminal" US, and senior officials roundly denounced Americans. But the powerful speaker of parliament, Ali-Akbar Hashemi-Rafsanjani, repeated late in November, and again in December, Iran's offer to use its influence with groups holding American hostages in Lebanon in exchange for access to some $480 million in Iranian funds blocked by the US and to arms purchased and paid for under the Shah but whose delivery was prohibited by presidential order. This suggests the Islamic Republic still wants US arms, although the government is having some difficulty explaining this to its own public. It also suggests Khomeini continues to trust Rafsanjani to negotiate for these arms through intermediaries. Whether he would also permit more extensive discussions remains to be seen.

There have also been signs of disaffection. Even before the McFarlane story broke, in early October, Ayatollah Khomeini created a sensation in Iran by allowing the arrest of Mehdi Hashemi, the head of the Revolutionary Guards unit responsible for supporting liberation movements abroad. Hashemi is also a relative of Khomeini's probable successor, Ayatollah Hussein-'Ali Montazeri, a long standing proponent of relatively restrained policies at home and aggressive ones abroad. (He has favored the private sector in Iran and has argued for less severe treatment of political prisoners.) Hashemi had been effective in helping spread Iranian influence in Lebanon. However, he and his armed groups had considerable autonomy in Lebanon and elsewhere. It seems clear that they did not always follow government policy, and Hashemi's arrest appears to reflect an attempt by the government to establish firmer control over its own foreign policy, and over ambitious political groups at home.

Hashemi's arrest may also have been connected with the discussions for exchanging hostages for arms. The story of McFarlane's visit to Iran was first leaked to *Al-Shira'a*, a magazine published in Lebanon and close to the radical Shi'ite groups there. While *Al-Shira'a* has now become famous, no one in the US seems to have noticed that it also published a long defense of Hashemi and described him as a revolutionary opposed by more conservative Iranian elements. "There are now two opposing logics in Iran," *Al-Shira'a* wrote, "the logic of the state and the logic of the revolution."[4] The editor later claimed that the report on McFarlane's mission had been deliberately leaked to him by Ayatollah Montazeri's office, because of his "personal links with the Montazeris," and that he ran the story "within the context of Iran's current power struggle."[5] *Al-Shira'a*'s account served the interests of the Hashemi faction in the Montazeri camp, although there is no evidence that Montazeri himself was involved in the leak. Hashemi's arrest and his "confession" to various crimes on television in December are clear indications that the Hashemi faction is out of favor. Care has been taken to dissociate Montazeri from Hashemi; and while Hashemi's humiliation hurt Montazeri, his position as Khomeini's deputy and successor has not been affected.

On the same day that Rafsanjani first discussed the details of McFarlane's trip to Iran, just after the revelations in *Al-Shira'a*, another cleric, Ayatollah Musavi Khoeniha, implicitly denounced the very idea of negotiations with the U.S. Khoeniha, now prosecutor-general, was the mentor to the "Students of the Imam's Line" who seized the hostages at the US embassy in Tehran in 1979. Describing the struggle against the US as "the foundation of the revolution," Khoeniha accused the US of wanting to weaken Iran's revolutionary will. "We should never surrender to America," he said, "never be deceived by America . . . [never] consider it our friend or forget our enmity for America."[6]

The "Students of the Imam's Line" themselves, who had not been heard from for some time, reappeared when they issued a declaration indirectly critical of contacts with the United States. Mehdi Bazargan, the perennial gadfly, made an open statement demanding that the full story of these contacts be told to the Iranian people. In mid-November, eight deputies of parliament submitted a question asking the minister of foreign affairs to provide details on any contacts with the United States. One of the signers, Jalal ad-Din Farsi, formerly had a reputation for pro-Soviet proclivities.

Ayatollah Khomeini moved quickly to crush this move by the deputies. On November 20 he sharply criticized them, saying they were encouraging division and schism. He clearly wished to avoid the divisive debates that would have occurred if the deputies' question had been discussed. However, if the opponents of any sort of dialogue with the United States have been silenced, they have not yet been reconciled. We may not have heard the last of such rumbles, and their real effects are yet to be understood.

The greatest mistake of all would be to interpret prematurely the different messages coming out of Tehran as reflecting a clear-cut contest between pro-US "moderates" and rabid anti-American revolutionaries. The situation is considerably more complex. Although individual clerics and officials around Khomeini have been identified, more or less, with consistent policies on domestic and foreign questions, there is much shifting and maneuvering among the top leaders. A group of pragmatists around Rafsanjani are on the ascendant, but these and other leaders must tailor their policies to powerful and conflicting domestic constituencies, to the exigencies of war and a faltering economy, to the rival claims of others in the leadership, and, in the person of Khomeini, to a demanding and unbending taskmaster. These conditions offer opportunities, as the Europeans have realized, for trade and other contacts with Iran. However, if anything has become clear, it is that exploration of future relations with Iran will require an approach that is subtle, cautious, and informed—as opposed to the ill-conceived secret arms traffic of the past year.

NOTES

1. "Iran: Burying the Hatchet," *Foreign Policy* (Fall 1985), p. 52.

2. For a detailed description of Bazargan's letter, see my "Trouble in Tehran," *New Republic* (December 1, 1986), p. 16.

3. *Kayhan* (November 22, 1986), p. 18.

4. *Iran Times* (November 21, 1986), p. 15. A full translation of the *Al Shira'a* article appeared in the *Iran Times* on November 14 and November 21.

5. AP report, *The New York Times* (December 7, 1986), p. 25.

6. *Kayhan* (November 10, 1986), p. 6.

13

Reflections on Terrorism

WALTER LAQUEUR

Fifty years hence, puzzled historians will try to make sense of the behavior of Western governments and the media in the 1980s regarding terrorism. They will note that presidents and other leaders frequently referred to terrorism as one of the greatest dangers facing mankind. For days and weeks on end, television networks devoted most of their prime-time news to covering terrorist operations. Publicists referred to terrorism as the cancer of the modern world, growing inexorably until it poisoned and engulfed the society on which it fed.

Naturally, our future historian will expect that a danger of such enormity must have figured very highly on the agenda of our period—equal, say, to the dangers of war, starvation, overpopulation, deadly disease, debts and so on. He will assume that determined action was taken and major resources allocated to fight against this threat. But he will be no little surprised to learn that when the Swedish prime minister was killed in 1986, the Swedish government promised a reward for information leading to the apprehension of his killer that amounted to less than ten percent of the annual income of an investment banker or a popular entertainer; that the French government offered even less for its terrorists; that West Germany was only willing to pay a maximum of $50,000 "for the most dangerous" ones. The United States offered up to $500,000,[1] again not an overwhelming sum considering the frequency of the speeches about terrorism and the intensity of the rhetoric.

Surely (our historian will expect) major investments were made in the research and development of technological means to preempt and combat the terrorists. Again, to his consternation, he will discover that the sum the United States devoted to this purpose—about $20–30 million—was considerably less than any second-rank pharmaceutical firm allocates for research and development.

His confusion will further deepen when he learns that the number of Americans killed inside the United States in 1985 as the result of terrorist attack was two, and that the total number of U.S. civilians killed abroad between 1973 and the end of 1985 was 169. In countless articles and books, our historian will read about the constantly rising number of terrorist attacks. Being a conscientious researcher he will analyze the statistics, which are bound to increase his confusion, for he will find that more American civilians were killed by terrorists in 1974 (22) than in 1984 (16).

On the basis of these and other facts, our historian will lean toward revisionism. He may well reach the conclusion that there was no terrorism, only a case of mass delusion—or that hysteria was deliberately fanned by certain vested interests such as producers of antiterrorist equipment, perhaps, or the television networks which had established a symbiotic relationship with the terrorists, who provided them with free (or almost free) entertainment for long periods.

These are, of course, the wrong conclusions. The impact of terrorism is measured not only in the number of its victims. Terrorism is an attempt to destabilize democratic societies and to show that their governments are impotent. If this can be attained with a minimum effort, if so much publicity can be achieved on the basis of a few attacks, no greater exertion is needed. Furthermore, in the 1980s there have been ominous new developments such as the emergence of narco-terrorism and the occurrence of state-sponsored terrorism on a broader level than before. If terrorism has never been a serious threat as far as America is concerned, let alone other major powers such as the Soviet Union, China or Japan, it is also true that in certain Latin American countries, and in places like Turkey and Italy, it was for a while a real danger.

In short, there has been (and is) a terrorist menace in our time. But the historian of the future will still be right in pointing to the wide discrepancy between the strong speeches and the weak actions of those who felt threatened. And he must be forgiven if he should draw the conclusion that those living in this "age of terrorism" perhaps never quite understood the exact nature of the threat.

II

What is terrorism? It would be highly desirable if all discussions of terrorism, of its motives and inspiration, its specific character, its modes of operation and long-term consequences, were based on a clear, exact and comprehensive definition. Ideally, there should be agreement as to whether terrorism is violence in general or some particular form of violence; whether the emphasis should be on its political aims or its methods of combat or the extra-normal character of its strategy; whether its purposive, systematic character should be singled out or, on the contrary, its unpredictability and its symbolic aspect or perhaps the fact that so many of its victims are innocents.

Agreement on a definition, alas, does not exist, and there is no reason to assume that it will in the foreseeable future. The author of an excellent research guide to terrorism, published a few years ago, listed 109 different definitions of terrorism provided between 1936 and 1981.[2] There have been more since; the U.S. government alone has provided half a dozen, which are by no means identical. Most experts agree that terrorism is the use or threat of violence, a method of combat or a strategy to achieve certain goals, that its aim is to induce a state of fear in the victim, that it is ruthless and does not conform to humanitarian norms, and that publicity is an essential factor in terrorist strategy.

Beyond this point definitions differ, often sharply, which is by no means surprising, be it only because the character of terrorist groups has been subject to change. There is little, if anything, in common between the Russian terrorists of the nineteenth century and Abu Nidal; a definition trying to cover both as well as others would be either very vague or very misleading. There is no such thing as terrorism pure and unadulterated, specific and unchanging, comparable to a chemical element; rather, there are a great many terrorisms. Historians and sociologists are not in full agreement on what socialism is or fascism was. It would be unrealistic to expect unanimity on a topic so close to us in time. But the absence of an exact definition does not mean that we do not know in a general way what terrorism is; it has been said that it resembles pornography, difficult to describe and define, but easy to recognize when one sees it.

According to one school of thought, "state terrorism" is the all-important issue. It is true that the number of victims and the amount of suffering caused by oppressive, tyrannical governments has been infinitely greater than that caused by small groups of rebels. A Hitler or a Stalin killed more people in one year than all terrorists throughout recorded history.

The concentration on the relatively insignificant acts of violence by small groups of people (known in professional language as "sub-state actors") is therefore denounced in the Third World and some radical circles as a political maneuver, intended to distract our attention from the truly important issues of our time. There is a view that the strategies and tactics of terrorism have recently become integral components in both the domestic and foreign political realms of the modern state. Why "recently" and why "modern state"? Has it not always been the case?

There are basic differences in motives, function and effect between oppression by the state (or society or religion) and political terrorism. To equate them, to obliterate the differences, is to spread confusion. The study of the Inquisition or the Gestapo or the Gulag is of undoubted importance, but it will shed no light whatsoever on contemporary terrorism.

If there has been a significant development during the last decade, it is not oppression by the state but state-sponsored terrorism. This latter is not, of course, a product of the 1970s; attempts to undermine the political or social order in other countries have been made by ambitious or revengeful rulers since time immemorial. The term destabilization may be new, but the use of proxies is as old as the hills. There are, however, certain new features to this old acquaintance that make it both more dangerous and more pervasive than in the past. It has become more frequent because resistance to it has been weak and uncoordinated. It has become more brazen: Mussolini, one of the chief practitioners of state-sponsored terrorism in the 1930s, would reject any imputation of responsibility with great indignation. In full uniform, shedding bitter tears, he attended the service in Rome in honor of Yugoslavia's King Alexander, who had been assassinated at his behest. Today's Qaddafis, on the other hand, do not stick to such proprieties, but claim the right to engage in acts of terror within the territory of other countries. Above all, there is the danger that state-sponsored terrorism will escalate into full military conflict, with the incalculable consequences of all-out war in this age.

Some of the obfuscation concerning terrorism stems from the belief in some circles that contemporary terrorism is basically revolutionary, a reaction against social and national injustice, and therefore worthy of support or at least understanding. But, in fact, terrorism is by no means the monopoly of the extreme left; quite frequently it is used by the extreme right and neo-fascists. Those trying to find mitigating circumstances for "revolutionary terrorism" find themselves sooner or later in the uncomfortable position of performing the same service for their political enemies. Terrorism is not an ideology but a strategy that can be used by people of different political convictions. Contemporary terrorism is certainly not the brainchild of Marxism-Leninism or Muslim fundamentalism, even though proponents of these creeds have made notable contributions to its spread.

Terrorism is neither identical to guerrilla warfare nor a subspecies of it. The term "urban guerrilla" is as common as it is mistaken. Terrorism is indeed urban, but not "guerrilla" in any meaningful sense; the difference is not one of semantics but of quality. A guerrilla leader aims at building up ever-growing military units and eventually an army, in order to establish liberated zones in which propaganda can be openly conducted, and eventually to set up an alternative government. All this is impossible in cities. In many instances, guerrilla movements and other insurrectional groups do have footholds in cities, but they are usually not of much consequence, because in the urban milieu there are no opportunities for guerrilla warfare. There is a world of difference between a temporary zone of control and the establishment of an alternative government.

Some Western experts, and especially the media, have great difficulty accepting the basic differences among various forms of violence. "Terrorists," "commandos," "partisans," "urban guerrillas," "gunmen," "freedom fighters," "insurgents" and half a dozen other terms are often used interchangeably, frequently as a result of genuine confusion, sometimes probably with political intent, because the guerrilla has, on the whole, a positive public relations image, which the terrorist clearly does not possess.

Soviet writers on this subject have fewer inhibitions about calling a spade by its rightful name. In a recent study, one of them noted that "urban guerrilla is a fraudulent concept, scheduled to mask ordinary terrorism."[3] Soviet ideologists are by no means opposed to the use of revolutionary violence. On the other hand, they know that terrorism carried out by marginal groups almost always causes more harm than good to the cause it sponsors. It is easy to think of guerrilla movements that defeated the forces opposing them, but it is very difficult to remember more than a few cases in which terrorism has had any lasting effect.

III

How to eradicate terrorism? Moralists believe that terrorism is the natural response to injustice, oppression and persecution. Hence their seemingly obvious conclusion: remove the underlying causes and terrorism will wither away! This sounds plausible enough, for happy and content people are unlikely to commit savage acts of violence. Although this may be true as an abstract general proposition, it seldom applies in the real world, which is never quite free of conflicts.

The historical record shows that, while in the nineteenth century terrorism frequently developed in response to repression, the correlation between grievance and terrorism in our day and age is far less obvious. The record also shows that in more recent times the more severe the repression, the less terrorism tends to occur. This is an uncomfortable, shocking fact that has therefore encountered much resistance. But it is still true that terrorism in Spain gathered strength only after General Franco died, that the terrorist upsurges in West Germany, France and Turkey took place under social democratic or left-of-center governments, that the same is true with regard to Peru and Colombia, and that more such examples could easily be adduced.

Terrorism has never had a chance in an effective dictatorship, but hardly a major democratic country has entirely escaped it. There is a limit to the perfection of political institutions, and, however just and humane the social order, there will always be a few people deeply convinced that it ought to be radically changed and that it can be changed only through violent action. The murder of Sweden's prime minister, Olof Palme, is just one illustration that shows that "objective factors" cannot account for the actions of a fringe group.

Nationalist-separatist terrorism has been doing better than that of the extreme left and right, and it is not difficult to understand why. National groups and minorities usually have grievances, and some of them may be quite justified. In some instances, they can be put right; in others assuaged, but frequently neither may be possible. In an ideal world, each group of people, however small, claiming the right of full independence and statehood, should receive it. But in some cases, given the lack of national homogeneity and the intermingling of ethnic and religious groups, no basic redress may be feasible.

Even at this late date, it may be possible for the Turks to accept responsibility for the Armenian massacres during World War I, to apologize to the descendants of the victims, and to show contrition. But an Armenian state on Turkish territory (as Asala, the Secret Army for the Liberation of Armenia, demands) would be an absurdity: Armenians no longer live in eastern Turkey, nor do they have any intention of settling there. Nor would a Sikh state in the Punjab be viable. The Sikhs, in any case, are not an oppressed minority in contemporary India: the president of India is a Sikh and so are most of India's military leaders. The majority of Sikhs do not even want a state of their own.

The Basque Homeland and Liberty group (ETA) and the Corsican militants are also fighting for independent statehood. But even if these ministates would be viable, which is uncertain, these groups' demands are by no means shared by most of their fellow countrymen, let alone by the majority populations in either the Basque region or Corsica, which are of different ethnic backgrounds (Spanish and French, respectively) from the terrorist groups.

Nor is it certain that the establishment of new, independent states would put an end to terrorism. On the contrary, there could well be an intensification of the struggle between various terrorist groups, between moderates who want to proceed with the business of statehood and radicals who claim that what has been achieved is only a beginning and that the borders of the new state should be expanded. The Tamils in Sri Lanka have been fighting with as much relish against each other as against their common enemy, and there is no reason to assume that this would stop if they were to get a state of their own.

The high tide of PLO activities both on the political and the terrorist level was in the mid-1970s. True, even then much of Middle Eastern terrorism had only a tenuous connection with Israel but was indigenous to the region. Since then this trend has become even more pronounced: some of the terrorist groups, such as Abu Nidal's or Abu Mussa's, serve the highest bidder among the Arab governments. They have killed considerably more Arabs than Israelis. As for Shi'ite terrorism, this never had much to do with Israel except at times when the Israelis happened to get in the Shi'ites' way.

No effort should be spared to pursue the peace process between Arabs and Israelis. But few serious students of this conflict argue that if a Palestinian state were to come into existence in the foreseeable future, terrorism would decrease. No settlement that recognizes Israel would be to the liking of Palestinian radicals. This does not make the search for a solution of the conflict undesirable or unnecessary, but there should be no illusions with regard to its likely consequences so far as the persistence of terrorism is concerned.

IV

wrong!!!

It is frequently argued that there is no defense against extremists willing to sacrifice their lives and that arresting or shooting terrorists cannot solve the problem because the "blood of the martyrs is the seed of the church." Historical experience does not confirm such wisdom.

The number of potential terrorists inside every country is limited. On the basis of a painstaking analysis, a recent study reaches the obvious conclusion that "the more terrorists in prison, the lower the violence level."[4] This does not, of course, apply to a mass insurrection supported by the overwhelming majority of the population, but it is true with regard to terrorist groups.

Shi'ite propensity to engage in terrorist suicide attacks has been very much exaggerated. True, there have been a few cases, but not more than four or five of such operations. Furthermore, this readiness to commit suicide can be found at all times and for many reasons. Ten members of the Irish Republican Army starved themselves to death—despite the express ban of the Catholic church against suicide; members of Baader-Meinhof also killed themselves, not to mention the mass suicide in Jonestown. When the Japanese authorities asked for kamikaze candidates during the last year of the war, many thousands volunteered and some 4,600 were killed. It is not so much a matter of a specific religion but of fanaticism, and a psychological predisposition. What Voltaire wrote about the subject seems still relevant today: the entire species (of fanatics) is divided into two classes—the first does nought but pray and die, the second wants to reign and massacre.

Terrorism has been stamped out with great ease not only by modern dictatorships; it has been defeated also by governments that are anything but modern. In 1981, Ayatollah Khomeini's former allies from the left, the mujahedeen and some other groups, turned against the new rulers of Iran. They were many and experienced; within three months they succeeded in killing the prime minister, many chiefs of police, half the government and the executive committee of the ruling party, not to mention dozens of members of parliament. Perhaps never before had a terrorist onslaught been so massive and so successful. Yet within another three months, the terrorists either were dead or had escaped abroad. The government acted with great brutality; it killed without discrimination; it extracted information by means of torture; it refused as a matter of principle to extend medical help to injured terrorists. And it broke the back of the terrorist movement.

The Turkish authorities liquidated terrorism with much less violence. During the year preceding the declaration of martial law in September 1980, some 3,000 Turks of both the left and the right, and not a few innocent bystanders, had been killed. Mass arrests and a few dozen executions of convicted murderers were sufficient to cause the collapse of terrorism within a matter of days. Argentina suppressed the Montoneros and the ERP (People's Revolutionary Army) with great inhumanity, whereas Uruguay succeeded vis-à-vis the Tupamaros with a minimum of violence.[5]

The power of the state is infinitely greater than that of terrorists, and it will always prevail, provided there is the determination or the ruthlessness to do so. But can a democratic society subdue terrorism without surrendering the values central to the system? Again, experience shows that it can be done without great difficulty. The Italian authorities defeated the Red Brigades, while acting strictly within the law, by a mixture of overdue political reform, penetration of the terrorist ranks, and the promise of substantial reduction in prison terms to the penitents. Terrorist movements do not have an unlimited life span. If terrorists realize after a few years that the murder of a few politicians (and many innocents) has not brought them any nearer their goals, their resolve weakens.

The nationalist-separatist terrorists hold out longer, for their basis of support is stronger and they may have assistance from foreign countries. But even in Northern Ireland and the Basque region of Spain, the level of violence is lower now than eight or ten years ago, and the Armenian Asala has all but disappeared.

A dialectical process seems to dictate the policy of democratic societies toward terrorists. As long as terrorism is no more than a nuisance, a democracy will rightly resist any attempt to curtail its traditional freedoms. Once terrorism becomes more than a nuisance, once the normal functioning of society is affected, there will be overwhelming pressure on the government to defeat the threat by all available means. Hence the paradoxical conclusion that the more successful the terrorists, the nearer their ultimate defeat. There are exceptions to every rule, but in this case they are few and far between.

V

State-sponsored terrorism is mainly the instrument of dictators with ambitions far in excess of their power base. The chief protagonist of this kind of terrorism between the two world wars was not Hitler but Mussolini, who used various groups of Balkan terrorists to destabilize neighboring countries such as Yugoslavia. The Soviet Union was also active in the field, but its operations were mainly limited to the assassination of emigré political leaders such as Trotsky. Today's mini-Mussolinis in the Middle East and in Central America rule small or relatively weak countries. Libya is an extreme example: but for its investment in terrorism, it would be not much more important than Mauritania or the Yemens. Libyan sponsorship of terrorism has been largely the initiative of one man, Muammar al-Qaddafi. But the balance sheet of a decade of such sponsorship is not impressive: publicity has not resulted in political clout. Qaddafi is still only a minor troublemaker, isolated among the Arabs, distrusted and kept at a distance even by those who support him at the United Nations or take his money. The Syrian and Iranian sponsors of terrorism have been more discriminating in their targets and therefore, within limits, more successful.

The attitude of the Soviet bloc has been ambiguous. It has used terrorism as a weapon to destabilize certain countries, but only as a minor instrument in its general arsenal of political warfare, and this for two reasons. The Soviets will never extend support openly; it has to be carefully laundered through a series of subcontractors and middlemen. But this also means that they cannot have full control over the terrorists; the gunmen may land them in situations that were not planned, and which may be politically harmful. To engage in international terrorism is to play with a fire that is difficult to control.

Mention has already been made of the other reason: Marxist-Leninists believe in mass action rather than individual terror, and past experience tends to show that they are by and large correct. Far from weakening a society, terrorism has quite frequently had the opposite, immunizing effect, bringing about greater internal cohesion. The effect of the murder of the Italian leader Aldo Moro is one example; the consequences of terrorism on the internal situation in Israel is another. Far from diverting resources from national defense, the terrorist threat strengthens the feeling that more ought to be done for national security, which plays into the hands of the forces of law and order. Seen in a wider perspective, systematic terrorism is a mixed blessing from the Soviet point of view. It may cause friction between the United States and its allies, many of which have been taking a softer line vis-à-vis international terrorism. But such a rift is not about matters of principle—no one in Europe actually likes international terrorism. Even Greek Prime Minister Andreas Papandreou wants it to go away—at least to a neighboring country. It is an embarrassment, bad for the image of the country affected; tourism suffers, and there are all kinds of other negative consequences.

For these consequences the governments of Western Europe to a large extent have to blame themselves. For years they have permitted themselves to be blackmailed, beginning with the establishment of Libyan people's bureaus, which replaced legations and embassies in open contravention of diplomatic practice. Yet the European governments more often than not preferred to close their eyes, as they did when Libyan emigrés and their own nationals were gunned down in broad daylight in their cities.

Appeasement is not reprehensible per se; at one stage or another all countries have made concessions to terrorists. If appeasement had worked, a good case could be made in its favor: why endanger the lives of European nationals in the Middle East; why sacrifice trade and goodwill just because of a few isolated incidents? But appeasement has had no beneficial results; the fact that former Austrian Chancellor Bruno Kreisky and Papandreou were nice to Qaddafi and that France and Italy had a special relationship with various Middle Eastern terrorist groups did not give them immunity from terrorist attack. The contrary happened, and the reasons seem obvious. Israel is a difficult target, and the terrorists rightly assume that Americans would react violently if they carried their operations to America's shores. Given the circumstances, it was only natural that terrorists would prefer soft targets in Europe. But there is a limit to the patience of European governments, which are willing to put up with isolated incidents but not with systematic campaigns. If the French, Spanish and other governments have adopted of late sterner measures against the sponsors of international terrorism, this was not so much for love of America but because their own interests were affected—and because domestic pressure was growing.

VI

As internal terrorism has declined in the Western world after the last decade and as international terrorism has become more frequent, the need for full international cooperation against terrorism has been invoked a great many times. It is a hopeless undertaking, however, as long as some states sponsor, finance, equip and train terrorists and provide sanctuaries for them. Spokesmen for democratic societies will continue to proclaim that terrorism is abhorred and condemned by the whole civilized world. But the civilized world does not extend that far these days, and proceedings in the United Nations have shown that it is very difficult to have terrorism condemned even on paper, unless some of the leading communist or Third World countries just happen to be on the receiving end of terrorist operations—which helps to clear their minds but, unfortunately, not for very long.

These debates will no doubt go on for many years; it may be wrong to pay too much attention to them. International terrorism is an extra-legal activity, and thus the contribution of our legal experts is bound to have a limited effect. Specific bilateral agreements or pacts among several countries may be of certain value; the exchange of information between NATO countries and others has improved during the last decade, and as a result some terrorist attacks have been prevented. Under certain conditions quiet diplomacy, such as issuing unpublicized warnings, has been of help; in other circumstances pre-emptive publicity has helped. Most sponsors of state terrorism do not want their involvement to become known. They will, at the very least, temporarily scale down their involvement once they realize that what was meant to be a high-value, low-risk undertaking might escalate into an armed conflict in which the risks are high and the value is at best uncertain.

But truly effective concerted action against terrorism is possible only on the basis of the strategy first advocated by the nineteenth-century Russian terrorists. This is "hitting the center," meaning those rulers of countries who are sponsors of international terrorism. But hitting the center may not be easy for a variety of reasons. The responsibility for a certain terrorist action or campaign cannot always be easily proved. The aggrieved party may find it difficult to provide sufficient hard evidence. Smoking guns are seldom left at the scene of the crime in this kind of business. Even if there is evidence, to reveal it would often mean giving away the identity of well-placed intelligence sources in the terrorist hierarchy, of which there are probably not many.

For a country or a group of countries subject to attacks by international terrorism, there are, broadly speaking, three ways to react. Given the natural inertia of democratic governments and the difficulties involved, the obvious reaction is to condemn the attack but to refrain from any physical act of retaliation. As long as these attacks occur relatively rarely and inasmuch as they do not result in many victims, this is a feasible policy. But lack of reaction is usually interpreted as a sign of weakness, in which case the attacks will become more frequent and murderous. The sponsors of international terrorism resemble in many respects children trying to find out by trial and error how far they can go in provoking the adults until punishment will be meted out to them.

If an escalation in international terrorist attacks does take place, the obvious way to retaliate is to pay back the sponsors in their own coins. As General George Grivas, head of the EOKA (the National Organization of Cypriot Combatants) in Cyprus and a man of great experience in the field, once put it: to catch a mouse, one uses a cat, not a tank (or an aircraft carrier). But democratic countries may not have cats, meaning a truly effective covert action capability, or "active measures," to use the well-known Soviet term. Even if they have a capability of this kind, they may find it difficult to use, be it because terrorist acts are much easier to carry out in open societies than in dictatorships or because those who engage in covert action on behalf of a democratic country are not normally permitted to kill enemy leaders. In the United States there is an absolute prohibition by presidential order.

What alternatives exist? In some cases diplomatic action may have some success; on other occasions economic sanctions may have a certain impact, but only if there is agreement between the major Western countries. Otherwise, in the absence of "cats," retaliation takes the form of military action. Such escalation involves risks: innocent people are likely to get killed, and those who retaliate will be blamed for creating a new dangerous situation. This has been the fate of the Israelis, who for a long time combined covert action with surgical air strikes (which, on occasion, hit the wrong target). It was also the fate of the United States after the strike against Libya in April 1986: those who retaliate become attackers, and there will be a great deal of handwringing and dire warnings. No government will lightly take such a course of action. It will only do so if it has good reason to believe that the alternative—refraining from counteraction—would have fateful consequences, and if public opinion at home is so strongly in favor of retaliation that it cannot safely be ignored. This is particularly true with regard to a superpower, whose freedom of action is by necessity more restrained than that of a small country. The more powerful a country, the stronger the constraints to act cautiously, for everything a major power does is important; it may turn a local incident into an international conflict.

VII

Thus the inclination will still be to wait and see. Terrorism may not outgrow the nuisance stage, but if it does, a one-time, limited application of military force may be sufficient to drive the lesson home. There is a tendency to magnify the importance of terrorism in modern society: society is vulnerable to attack, but it is also astonishingly resilient. Terrorism makes a great noise, but so far it has not been very destructive. Our media resemble the Bedouin warriors described by Lawrence of Arabia, who were sturdy fighters except for their mistaken belief that weapons were dangerous in proportion to the noise they created.

But what if terrorism does outgrow the nuisance stage, and what if the one-time lesson administered is not sufficient? In theory, the state sponsors of terrorism should never let this come to pass. For once they succeed in provoking the superpower, the political calculus changes, and they are bound to lose in a confrontation with a much more powerful nation. Only gross miscalculation can lead them into such a course of action. Unfortunately, it is not certain that rational behavior will always prevail on their part. In this case the victims of state-sponsored terrorism must act. They could bring back General Grivas' cats, which is difficult in a democratic society and perhaps undesirable. Or they can choose deliberate escalation, hitting back with military force against elusive terrorist targets. If there is at the present time a terrorist threat, it is not the one usually adduced, that of destroying societies from within. It is the danger of terrorist provocation leading well beyond the confines of mere terrorism and counterterrorism. This danger cannot be reduced without Soviet cooperation. The Qaddafis and Assads will act much more cautiously when they know that they cannot count on automatic Soviet help, once their transgressions lead to retribution. Terrorism, in other words, may not be very important, but like some minor diseases, it can have unpleasant and even dangerous consequences if neglected.

NOTES

1. According to the 1984 Act to Combat Terrorism. But it is not certain whether the U.S. government would in fact be in a position to pay, for the sum total allocated for this purpose was $2 million.
2. Alex Schmid, *Political Terrorism: A Research Guide*, New Brunswick, N.J.: Transaction, 1984.
3. Viktor Vladimirovich Vityuk, *Pod chuzhim znamenami. Litsemeria i samo-obman levovo terrorizma*, Moscow: Mysl, 1985, p. 22.
4. Christopher Hewitt, *The Effectiveness of Anti-Terrorist Policies*, Lanham, Md.: University Press of America, 1984, p. 47.
5. They reconstituted themselves as a legal political party in 1985 and are doing quite well.

PART TWO
The Burden of the Strong

We turn now from the tensions between strong and weak powers and between different ethnic and ideological groups to a discussion of relations among the great powers. During the Nixon-Ford-Kissinger era (1969–1977) American foreign policy was directed primarily toward the great powers: the Soviet Union in particular, but also China, Japan, and key Western European states. The foreign policy of this era stressed the belief that the creation of a balance of power among the major states would produce a more stable international order, at least on the higher levels of the international hierarchy. But the Middle Eastern war of 1973, the ensuing Arab oil embargo, the OPEC price rises, and the escalating Third World demands for greater economic equality were stark reminders of the need for another focus in American foreign policy.

The Carter administration came to power in 1977 convinced that a new era could be forged by concentrating more heavily on North-South relations and issues of economic interdependence rather than on competition with the Soviet Union. As President Carter stated in his Notre Dame commencement address in May 1977,

> The unifying threat of conflict with the Soviet Union has become less intensive even though the competition has become more extensive. . . . We can no longer separate the traditional issues of war and peace from the new global questions of justice, equity, and human rights.

In the context of this statement, the Soviet invasion of Afghanistan in December 1979 was both a disillusioning and disruptive experience for many people—particularly for a president who had attempted to establish a new direction in American foreign policy.

The Reagan administration, by contrast, believed that the Soviet Union had gained militarily on the United States and sought to re-orient American policy toward confronting this perceived threat and, particularly, Moscow's willingness to use this new advantage in the world arena. Many in Reagan's administration believed that the United States could not ignore the nature of the Soviet system and its oppression of its own people. In a 1983 speech to the National Association of Evangelicals in Orlando, Florida, President Reagan declared (clearly referring to the Soviet Union),

> Let us pray for the salvation of all those who live in that totalitarian darkness—pray they will discover the joy of knowing God. But until they do, let us be aware that while they preach the supremacy of the state, declare its omnipotence over individual man and predict its eventual domination of all peoples on the Earth—they are the focus of evil in the modern world.

Given the power of the United States in the international system, the attitudes and the commitments of the Reagan administration to a dramatically increased defense budget had immediate effects on relations between the Soviet Union, the United States, Europe, Japan, and China. The issues were intensified after the President met with Mikhail Gorbachev in Geneva in November 1985 and in Reykjavik in October 1986, and there continued to be much public discussion about the possibility of significantly reducing the nuclear arsenals of both superpowers. These issues are addressed in the first section of Part Two, entitled "Competitors and Allies: Pas de Deux."

We begin with two articles that present dramatically opposite positions toward the relationship between the United States and the Soviet Union. Jerry Hough's position is decidedly to the left of the Reagan administration. He calls upon "moderates" to declare a "fresh start" toward Soviet-American relations in which the key elements are possible cooperation, adjustment to the potential of the Gorbachev era, and arms control.

When the reader turns to the next article by Richard Pipes, he or she will encounter a totally different worldview. Pipes emphasizes that since 1917 the USSR has pursued a grand strategy designed to subvert capitalist countries. He believes that many businessmen, academics, and politicians in the West are misled by Moscow's use of Western political jargon, which avoids confrontational phrasing. According to Pipes, the Kremlin's conciliatory rhetoric feeds the special interests of each of these groups and therefore many in the West—even government officials—are insufficiently sensitive to the Soviet threat.

From this debate, we move to three articles on particular segments of the great power competition. Eliot Cohen addresses the changing role of Europe in world politics and questions whether it still carries the same weight in America's global strategic concerns by comparison with

Northeast Asia, the Middle East, and Central America. He also argues that Europe continues to be a military asset located on a strategically crucial continent, but here, too, Europe's position relative to other areas has declined since the early 1950's. Meanwhile, the proportion of American military power devoted to the European theater has increased. Therefore, he argues that alliance strategies should be adjusted with new programs that take account of the changing global equation.

Just as Cohen challenges "accepted wisdom" about Europe, William Sherman disputes the perception that the Japanese-American alliance is deteriorating. Using his personal experiences in the State Department as a guidepost, he traces the post-World War II evolution of the alliance, pointing out in the process the gradual improvement in relations between the two countries. Sherman is a supporter of closer ties, but he realistically sets out the alternatives which stand before Tokyo and Washington including improvement, deterioration, or a continuation of the status quo.

No discussion of relations among the great powers could be complete without a consideration of the critical triangular relationship between the United States, the Soviet Union, and China. Robert Ross sets out to explain the evolution of this unique three-way interaction since the United States and China began to deal directly and publicly with each other again in 1971. He traces the changes from the mid-1970's when the United States was in the "pivot position," sought after by both Moscow and Beijing, to the mid-1980's, when that enviable position fell to China. Ross argues that alterations in the pattern of relations among the three powers cause the changes in their contacts, but the timing of these changes is affected by domestic politics.

Having reviewed the competitions and alliances among the great powers, we move to the second section of Part Two, which examines the effect of great power policies on the concerns and interests of weaker countries. In this edition we have selected two issues in which the United States confronts agonizing alternatives: the Middle East and South Africa. In each of these cases there are difficult strategic, political, economic, and moral issues at stake. As unstable areas in transition, they are part of the Soviet-American global conflict. Their instability demands difficult decisions by leaders in both Washington and Moscow, as Francis Fukuyama reminded us in section one. Although the Soviet-American competition is not a zero-sum game, events in each of these areas are testimony to the difficulties the strongest powers have in controlling developments abroad. In the United States, each of these issues is also a source of deep and continuing internal division among individuals and groups of differing ideological, ethnic, religious, and political persuasions.

The first two articles, by former Senator Charles McC. Mathias, Jr. and Richard N. Haass, deal with the Palestinian question and the appropriate American approach to the Arab-Israeli dispute. They are precise mirror images of each other. Mathias warns against lessened American involvement and attention to the peace process lest Washington's influence and interests suffer. For these very reasons, Haass favors lessened attention. Thus, the two men agree on what the objective of American Middle East policy should be—namely, advancing the peace process. They differ only on the tactics the U.S. should pursue in terms of whether there is a need for an activist American approach and in their assessment of the regional situation. Haass is more confident that the time is available to permit patience and a more subtle policy. Both men wrote before Israel and Egypt agreed to arbitration of the Taba border dispute, a tiny strip on the Sinai frontier. They also wrote on the eve of the October 1986 switch in offices between Israel's Shimon Peres (who became Foreign Minister) and Yitzhak Shamir (who became Prime Minister). The disagreement between Haass and Mathias reflects continual divisions in the United States on the course America should pursue in this volatile region.

In our two South Africa pieces, even the objectives diverge. Both Paul Johnson and Cosmas Desmond are dealing with pressure for complete disinvestment from South Africa. There the similarity between them ends. Johnson sees the country as typical of the fragmented ethnic and social conditions that exist today throughout Africa. But he argues that South Africa is wealthier than other African states and is "in many respects a free country." He believes that disinvestment will only halt the dismantling of apartheid, a process propelled by capitalist necessities.

Writing even before the U.S. Congress overrode the President's veto on limited sanctions against South Africa in the summer of 1986, Desmond celebrates the growth of the disinvestment campaign. By comparison with Johnson, he argues in favor of "radical political change" and suggests that apartheid is a vehicle for the enrichment of whites, including whites in foreign countries. Whereas Johnson sees foreign investment as a vehicle for the breakdown of apartheid, Desmond believes it has the opposite effect. Both analysts agree that disinvestment would create political change in South Africa, but whereas to Johnson the consequences would be disastrous, to Desmond they would be beneficial. The reader is left to weigh these contrasting analyses for himself and to make his own judgement.

As these debates only begin to suggest, the competition between the two superpowers causes considerable difficulty in their ability to deal with weaker nations, for they must always balance great power policies against policies designed for allies, clients, and weaker foes. A central concern in relations between the superpowers is the nuclear balance between them. Several articles in our next section examine the arms race, including alternative approaches to nuclear strategy and arms control and the problem of nuclear proliferation.

The debate over defense policy in the West is suggestive of contrasting philosophies about the content of foreign policy and the manner in which each country should conduct itself in world affairs. This debate is reflected in the next two articles, each of which presents different approaches toward the world situation and builds on these basic assumptions in producing recommendations for a coherent defense policy. First, Noam Chomsky ties the threat of nuclear war to the activities of nuclear powers. As is clear in the following essays, most authors dealing with the nuclear threat stress the size and character of nuclear arsenals, but to Chomsky these are important yet secondary issues. Chomsky believes the disarmament movement must work to put forth a general program to constrain state violence. The effort to control and reverse the strategic arms race is viewed as only one aspect of disarmament.

Seymour Weiss, however, assumes the opposite position. He argues that such problems as the arms race, wasteful military expenditures, or the drift toward nuclear war cannot be "attenuated or corrected" by arms control. Rather, he sees a process of self-delusion, which has only aided the Soviets in their competition with the United States. The problem, as Weiss sees it, is that arms control is politically popular, but it is dangerous because it establishes false hopes when Soviet and American political objectives remain "in radical conflict".

The importance of the contrast between Chomsky and Weiss is that their basic assumptions diverge so drastically that they produce totally different attitudes toward the use of military power. Chomsky focuses on restraining the policies of Western states; Weiss distrusts the intentions and behavior of the Soviet Union. Each author believes that one aspect of the current reliance on the use of military force is illusory: whereas Chomsky is opposed to the reliance on the use of force itself, Weiss believes that attempts to control the nuclear arms race will make matters worse for the United States.

The next two authors, George Ball and Leon Sloss, both agree on the fundamentals of nuclear deterrence theory, but they have opposite positions toward the President's Strategic Defense Initiative, known popularly as "Star Wars." Ball stresses the technical, economic, and diplomatic difficulties of the proposed program. Even before the Reagan-Gorbachev summit in Geneva in November 1985 and the mini-summit in Reykjavik in October 1986, he was already predicting severe difficulties in negotiations with the Soviet Union over the President's commitment to the Star Wars proposal.

None of these arguments appeal to Leon Sloss. He believes that the United States and its allies—unlike the Soviet Union—have undervalued strategic defense for two decades. Therefore, Star Wars will play a significant role in reinforcing America's nuclear deterrent even if it is not "perfect, or even near-perfect" in protecting population centers or even the missiles themselves. Sloss advises that the West needs a better balance between offensive and defensive weapons.

With these arguments over SDI as background, Stanley Hoffmann assesses the events of the Reykjavik summit in the context of ongoing Soviet-American negotiations. Future developments in the superpower relationship will need to be understood in the light of the issues raised at one of the most mercurial occurrences in the history of the postwar competition between Moscow and Washington.

While more immediate matters that are at issue in international politics frequently gain the headlines, lurking just beneath the surface is the problem of nuclear proliferation. The outcome of this issue may be the most devastating of all. D.W. Hiester argues strongly that nuclear proliferation is profoundly destabilizing, but that the spread of these weapons is not inevitable. He maintains that an energetic effort is needed, which should be directed at leaders in countries that are most likely to "go nuclear". This program should emphasize the political, economic, and military costs of a decision to acquire nuclear weapons. He thus provides us with a possible route out of a world of many nuclear powers.

COMPETITORS AND ALLIES: PAS DE DEUX

14

Managing the U.S.-Soviet Relationship

JERRY F. HOUGH

For years, a substantial number of Americans have called for improved Soviet-American relations. Some have gone so far as to advocate a fundamental restructuring of international relations—a movement away from interstate conflict and nuclear deterrence—but the moderates have had more modest goals: a capping of military expenditures, arms control that would reduce the danger of nuclear war in case a crisis did occur, a lessening of international political tension and the domestic political strains it produces, and what is usually called a management of the Soviet-American relationship.

In fact, for the past 40 years, the United States and the Soviet Union have managed to avoid war with each other—no mean achievement in light of the history of the first part of the century. Especially since Nikita Khrushchev's removal, the most serious potential conflicts have been handled quite safely. The Vietnam War (even the bombing of Soviet ships in Haiphong harbor), the Israeli-Egyptian War of 1973, the various Lebanese crises, the Iran-Iraq War—none of these came even close to producing the disasters they might have. Even in the Reagan-era atmosphere of U.S.-Soviet confrontation, the Lebanon crisis and the Iran-Iraq War were dealt with quietly and well.

Yet avoiding catastrophes is in some ways all that the United States and the Soviet Union have succeeded at; otherwise, U.S.-Soviet relations have not followed the course the moderates have advocated. Even the SALT-II arms control agreement that was finally negotiated (but not ratified) had so little real meaning that the Reagan administration could abide by its provisions and still conduct an enormous militiary buildup. And mutual suspicion and bad feeling still seem to run high. President Reagan has described the Soviet Union as an evil empire whose people do not even have a word for freedom in their language and whose leaders consider lying and cheating to be moral behavior. The Soviet press has scarcely been more flattering, describing the Strategic Defense Initiative as part of an American strategy to launch a nuclear first strike against the Soviet Union.

The Reagan-Gorbachev 1985 summit changed the tone of the language somewhat, at least temporarily. But behind the surface rhetoric, some harsh things were being said. At his press conference, Gorbachev, referring to SDI, accused the United States of "just itching to get . . . world domination. It's an old, longstanding ambition." And Reagan, for his part, kept bringing up "regional issues," but by limiting these to Afghanistan, Angola, Cambodia, Ethiopia, and Nicaragua, he perpetuated the image of the Soviet Union as the focus of evil. (If he had included the Middle East, where there are common interests in keeping Lebanese factions or Iran and Iraq from dragging us into war, the effect would have been dramatically different.) Gorbachev's response was blunt: "On the world stage some people still do blame Moscow for everything . . . Enough of that sort of stupid remark has been made before . . . Can one be so irresponsible to give those kinds of opinions on these sorts of issues?"

In what remains basically a tense atmosphere, those who favor an improvement in Soviet-American relations must face several questions. First, in a relationship that is essentially nasty in character, can dangerous conflicts continue to be managed safely now that a major generational change is under way in both countries? To an extent that is seldom realized, international relations in the postwar era have been dominated by people whose views were shaped by the events leading to World War II. Soviet officials such as Andrei Gromyko and Dmitri Ustinov were already in high foreign policy and defense posts in 1939. All postwar U.S. presidents, with the exception of Jimmy Carter, were born in a very narrow period from 1908 to 1917. The interventionist-isolationist debate of the 1930s shaped their thinking on foreign policy. In 1939, Ronald Reagan was 28, while John F. Kennedy was 22 and had just finished an honors thesis on "Why England Slept."

The tendency of the Reagan-Gromyko generation to think unconsciously in terms of 1930s diplomacy has led to many counterproductive and unwise decisions on both sides. Since these men were in their mid-thirties when the atomic bomb was dropped and in their fifties when intercontinental ballistic missiles were deployed, it has been difficult for them to grasp the impact of nuclear weapons on war and international relations. On the other hand, this generation's memories have made it inclined to restraint, and in the West have created a strong collective security ethos. There are many unwritten, unspoken agreements and assumptions that have kept Soviet-American conflicts from approaching the brink. Reagan has been especially cautious because he came out of the isolationist tradition. Thus the challenge for the new generation now coming to power is to retain those assumptions and habits of thought that lead to restraint, while shedding those aspects of the old generation's thinking that have become anachronistic.

The second question that advocates of an improvement in U.S.-Soviet relations must face is a tactical one. Moderates have been appealing for more relaxed Soviet-American relations for years—even decades. Many of the statements in President Kennedy's speech at American University in 1963 remain worthy of reiteration nearly a quarter of a century later. Yet such appeals have not been successful; and it is no longer adequate simply to restate them—one must find ways to do so more effectively.

So far, there is little evidence that moderates are moving in this direction. Instead, in the debate about the Soviet Union they seem to be retreating rather than advancing new arguments. The peace movement has become relatively quiescent; Democratic politicians have essentially fallen silent. The general reluctance to criticize the President during the months before the summit may be attributable to temporary tactical considerations, but the 1984 campaign suggests that the problem goes much deeper.

In 1984, public opinion polls indicated that President Reagan was more vulnerable on foreign policy than on domestic questions. Yet the subject was almost completely ignored in the Democratic Party platform. The subsection on "United States-Soviet Relations" contained two sentences, one condemning Soviet persecution of dissidents and Andrei Sakharov, the other condemning the repression of Eastern Europe. Even indirect references to the Soviet-American relationship were limited to a single paragraph calling for arms control.

The leading speeches at the 1984 Democratic Convention had the same character. Mario Cuomo and Gary Hart each spent about 15 words discussing relations with the Soviet Union, basically limiting themselves to a criticism of the president's rhetoric. Cuomo did not mention arms control. Geraldine Ferraro did not refer once to U.S.-Soviet relations in her convention speech, and she uttered one sentence about arms control—an endorsement of the nuclear freeze. Walter Mondale did devote 15 percent of his speech to foreign policy, but this scarcely suggested that it would be the major theme of his campaign, and at any rate he did little more than call for negotiations.

Clearly, Democratic politicians have not found a politically effective way of dealing with Soviet-American relations. This is not to lambaste them out of hand, however—the task they face is tremendously difficult.

Nevertheless, in a democracy, it is not enough to speak to the specialists or to those who are already committed; one must also lead the broader public to a more sophisticated understanding of international relations. Thus as those of us who want improved relations look toward 1988, we must think about how to manage the U.S.-Soviet relationship domestically as well as abroad.

THE MODERATES' TACTICAL PROBLEMS

There are many reasons it has been difficult to manage the Soviet-American relationship in a calm manner—toward what the Soviets used to call a "normalization of relations" but now increasingly call "civilized" relations. One obstacle is that moderates always face a major political problem when they call for a more measured policy vis-à-vis the country's enemy. Normally, a moderate policy must be justified by downplaying the enemy threat—for example, by discussing the implications of the slowdown in the Soviet military buildup. Such statements will quickly be answered by a barrage of technical arguments and by accusations of naiveté or even pro-Soviet attitudes. A public that cannot master the technical details is likely to conclude that, for safety's sake, the more threatening assessment should be accepted. In the end, the party that advocates a more moderate policy may simply look gullible.

Similarly, criticizing a president's bargaining position and supporting a position close to the Soviet one can bring on accusations of disloyalty. After all, in any negotiation the initial bargaining position of each side is always unreasonable, if only to allow room for concessions and compromises. To call for a revision in the president's position makes it look as though Americans are "bargaining with themselves." To praise the Soviet position is to praise a position that still has room for compromise, even if the Soviets are sincerely eager for a fair settlement; to describe the Soviet bargaining position as preferable to the American one is to undercut European support for the American position.

Moderates have recognized this tactical difficulty, but unfortunately the steps they have taken to solve it have often been at least as damaging as the original problem. First, they have engaged in harsh Soviet-bashing. Every conciliatory statement they make is prefaced by fervent assertions about the repressiveness of the Soviet system, the aggressiveness of Soviet foreign policy, and so forth. They call for arms control yet say it should be coupled with a strong defense. Paradoxically, in the year before Ronald Reagan accepted zero growth in defense spending (allowing for inflation), all the Democratic presidential candidates except George McGovern and Jesse Jackson pledged 4- to 5-percent increases over inflation.

Second, moderates have spoken a great deal about the dangers of nuclear war and the paramount need to avoid it, emphasizing dialogue and arms control negotiations. Though they insist on the importance of cooperation where the two countries have common interests, they also stress the need to compete vigorously with the Soviet Union and to pressure the Soviet Union on domestic human rights issues. And they keep all these points about dialogue, arms control, and the combination of competition and cooperation at a very general level in order to avoid the charge of undercutting the president's bargaining position.

Moderates have assumed that such an approach is politically necessary, and perhaps they are right. Yet this approach has some disastrous political consequences. For one thing, if the moderates do not challenge the conservatives' definition of the situation, they are virtually certain to lose on specific issues. If, for instance, the Soviet military buildup is as relentless as the conservatives say, then the Reagan military program is a logical response. If Andropov's bargaining position on the SS-20s was as unreasonable as the president claimed, then one can hardly fault him for rejecting it, and one can hardly deny his contention that the Soviet Union is responsible for the breakdown of arms negotiations. But what if the Andropov proposal was in fact so forthcoming—as it was—that it was grossly advantageous to the West and could have been the first step in important negotiations?[1] One would have to make this case—that a good deal was available—in order to convincingly criticize the president.

Furthermore, the moderates' compromise—saying little, only speaking generally about the danger of war, and calling vaguely for moderation—has its own enormous political costs. When nuclear war seems a lively possibility, as it did after the Cuban missile crisis, the nuclear issue can gain substantial public support. But when nuclear war seems remote, politicians who emphasize the dangers of nuclear weapons may raise public doubts about their ability to conduct an effective foreign policy vis-à-vis the Soviet Union. Those who emphasize the danger of nuclear war to the exclusion of other considerations may even create the impression that they will be subject to nuclear blackmail on every issue. The American public might reason that a politician who treated the avoidance of nuclear war as an absolute would cave in any time the Soviet Union chose to use a nuclear threat, on any issue from the Middle East to Western Europe. Popular stereotypes make women who focus on the nuclear question particularly vulnerable to this type of suspicion.

There is another way in which the moderates' vague and general calls for arms control and negotiations, coupled with tough language, create the impression of weakness. The American population assumes that this type of criticism of the conservatives means that the moderates would like to follow a substantially different policy but are simply afraid to stand up to the conservatives in public debate, how can they be expected to stand up to the Soviet Union?

The U.S. public may worry even more that a moderate who is afraid to stand up to the conservatives in public debate will also be afraid to stand up to them once in power. Sophisticated analysts have argued that a right-wing leader can often take actions—such as Nixon's opening to China—that a liberal cannot. One should not assume that less sophisticated persons are not listening to these assessments.

For the general public knows that a president may need great courage to stick to a chosen policy or to abandon it when events warrant. The exact timing of America's recognition of China was not crucial, but sometimes the issues are much more pressing, involving war and peace. When the United States was bogged down in Lebanon in 1983, Henry Kissinger and Lawrence Eagleburger insisted that this was a crucial test of will in U.S.-Soviet relations and that the United States and Israel should take on Syria. President Reagan had the courage to disregard their advice and to retreat. He quickly "retired" Eagleburger. Would a President Mondale have felt able to do so? Would American defense spending have been cut to no real growth in 1985 if the Democrats had won the election, or would the final result have been some compromise between their 4-percent promise and the higher proposal of the Republicans? The likely answers to these questions may make the public feel that in 1984 the peace candidate was Ronald Reagan, not Walter Mondale. Americans want the sense that their president has the courage not only to stand up to the Russians when necessary, but also to retreat when necessary—and furthermore that he has the wisdom to know which issues warrant which response.

The final problem with a vague moderate position is that the conservatives can very easily coopt it. Think back to the moderate clichés. The United States should both compete with the Soviet Union and cooperate with it, especially in avoiding war. Well, President Reagan certainly competes vigorously, but he has informally cooperated with the Kremlin to avoid being dragged into serious conflict with it either in Lebanon or in the Iran-Iraq war. After getting his administration off to a hostilely anti-Soviet beginning, Reagan has pressed for dialogue and negotiations. It was he, not Mikhail Gorbachev, who pushed for a summit. Critics may say—rightly, in my opinion—that his arms control proposals have been singularly one-sided, but at least he has "ratified" the SALT-II agreement by observing its provisions (for the moment, anyway). He did accept no real growth in his defense budget. And even his utopian vision of a defensive shield against nuclear weapons is not much more unrealistic than a vague proposal for a total, negotiable, verifiable freeze on nuclear weapons—and it certainly has a much stronger emotional appeal. Perhaps it is understandable that the Democrats said so little about Soviet-American relations during the 1984 presidential campaign.

WHO'S SETTING THE TERMS?

Another reason why the moderates have failed to advance a convincing alternative to the conversatives' position is that the moderates have acquiesced to the conservatives' interpretation of Soviet behavior, especially their view of which Soviet actions are illegitimate relative to the norms of international relations.

The Soviet Union, the conservatives say, violated "the code of detente." It has followed an expansionist policy, been adventuristic in the Third World, invaded Afghanistan, stood behind the imposition of martial law in Poland, and threatened Europe with a huge conventional force. The Soviet Union is leading an ideological crusade against the United States—and who talks about normal, civilized relations with a country with whom one is at war? Who talks about "managing" relations with such a country? Instead, we should be talking about victory.

Implicitly, the moderates have in fact challenged the notion of all-out ideological war with the Soviet Union; that is the essential message of all the talk about "managing" the relationship. Yet the point needs to be made more explicit. Soviet leaders do *not* have an ideological sense of total war with capitalist states. That sense, which did exist under Lenin and Stalin, eroded enormously under Khrushchev and Brezhnev, and it almost certainly will erode even further with a new generation coming to power.

Events have drastically changed the assumptions of Soviet foreign policy. Nuclear weapons have vastly reduced Eastern Europe's military value as a buffer zone and Western Europe's attractiveness as a potential area of new conquests. The split with China demonstrated that communist revolutions need not lead to Soviet foreign policy gains. The absence of radical revolutions in industrializing Third World societies has convinced most Soviet specialists that Marx was right: that capitalism follows feudalism, and that the natural course of Third World development is along the West European path.

Yet even if Soviet leaders no longer have a sense of total war with the West, they have, of course, done things that by all standards of international relations are deeply illegitimate. What moderates must do—which has not yet been done in the American political discourse—is to distinguish between national actions that are legitimate and those that are not.

It is, for example, deeply illegitimate to invade a country either to take over its territory or to impose or maintain a particular political system in it. Soviet behavior in Eastern Europe and Afghanistan clearly has been of such character. Providing arms and support to rebel movements in a country is also very dubious behavior under international law, but covert activity by both sides has become so widespread—and so non-covert—that the actual norms of international behavior have become murky. The real story in Angola in the mid-1970s was that both the United States and the Soviet Union (and a number of other actors) were too deeply involved in the Angolan civil war and that each sincerely believed, with good reason, that the other had overstepped its bounds. A real code of detente is badly needed to cover these types of questions.

In other areas, Soviet foreign policy has been extraordinarily unwise and deserves severe criticism. The large-scale sale of arms to aggressive Somalia in the early 1970s, for example, was legal enough, but it was foolish in the extreme. Ironically, this step has seldom been criticized; the Soviet Union has been primarily condemned for the much more legitimate step of coming to Ethiopia's defense once Somalia invaded with the help of Soviet arms.

What needs to be understood, however, is that much of the Soviet behavior that both conservatives and moderates denounce as illegitimate is, in fact, completely in accord with the norms of international relations. Nicaragua's Sandinista revolution received little or no Soviet support before it was successful; the Ethiopian revolution resulted from a wholly indigenous military coup. Both revolutions produced political regimes that do not fit the American model, but this in no way lessens their sovereign rights.

Mikhail Gorbachev was quite right when he stated in his press conference:

> The desire of every people to realize its sovereign right in the political sphere, the economic sphere, and the social sphere is a natural desire. People may like or dislike this policy, but it reflects internal pressures in each particular country, the interests of a particular people, who have a sovereign right. The right to choose—to choose their path, system, methods, forms, to choose their friends—that is the right of every people. If we do not acknowledge that, I do not know how we can build international relations.

That includes the right to form alliances, to purchase arms from abroad, and to invite in foreign troops. Both the West European democracies and the South Korean dictatorship have—and exercise—the right to ally with the United States and to have American troops on their soil. Dictatorial Chad has the right to invite in French troops to protect it from Libya; in fact, France has intervened in a number of places in Africa, sometimes under American pressure.

There is nothing in international law that forbids Nicaragua, Ethiopia, and Angola to invite in Soviet and Cuban troops and advisors or to receive Soviet arms. Nothing in international law states that Nicaragua cannot receive Soviet MIG-21s—after all, Pakistan, near the Soviet border, purchases the American equivalent of the more advanced Soviet

MIG-29s (and Cuba already has MIG-23s). Under international law, the Soviet Union has as much right as the United States to supply arms and seek influence.

Alas, Hans Morgenthau was fundamentally right when he insisted that the essential characteristic of a nation-state's behavior is to seek to expand its power and influence and to defend its interests. This is true of the United States, and it is true of Denmark. To think that the Soviet Union should observe a code of detente in which it, as a superpower, abandons efforts to extend its influence—even in the Middle East, directly on its border!—is to think like an idealist such as Cordell Hull, not like a member of the realist school of international relations.

In short, the United States has had a tendency to lump together as illegitimate and immoral both those Soviet actions that truly violate the norms of international relations and those that do not. The U.S. sense that much of the latter type of competition is illegitimate stems from America's isolationist past and from its assumption that all conflictual international relations are a dirty, illegitimate business. Or, worse, it is the kind of assumption an infant makes—that anyone who opposes his interests is behaving inadmissibly. Washington has applied double standards, insisting on its right to take actions it calls illegitimate when Moscow takes them. At the United Nations, President Reagan condemned the use of military force to impose one's political system on another country; then after the summit he vigorously defended aid to Angolan "freedom-fighters." Unfortunately, this is reality rather than parody.

If the United States is to become a sophisticated participant in international relations, it must learn to distinguish between Soviet actions that are legitimate, even though they may conflict with U.S. interests, and those that are not. If America wants to expand the rules of the game that already exist, it must decide which constraints it is willing to accept for itself as well as for the Soviet Union, for international norms must be mutual. There is simply no basis in international law for covert U.S. aid to rebels in Angola and Ethiopia, as one cannot even make the case that those countries are exporting revolution.

Above all, the United States must come to accept conflict of interests as natural. If players in a poker game become morally outraged that others around the table are trying to win, they cannot concentrate on playing coolly and effectively themselves. The same is true of countries participating in international relations. Moderates who begin talking up this idea will find that they sound pragmatic and even tough-minded without reinforcing conservative clichés—and, therefore, without providing support for the conservatives. If moderates characterize the conservatives' attitudes as part of our old isolationist past, they can make the conservatives seem old-fashioned and out-of-date and can make themselves look modern and sophisticated.

WHO WROTE THE HISTORY?

Not only do moderates need to challenge the conservatives' images of Soviet behavior, they also need to reject the version of the history of the past 20 years that the conservatives have promulgated. The right wing has depicted Moscow as taking advantage of detente in the 1970s to activate its foreign policy and make major advances. (Only recently has the right begun emphasizing Soviet decline, misattributing it to Reagan's military actions and buildup.) The moderates have responded to the conservative view of history simply by saying that although certain Soviet actions may be deplorable the threat they pose at the moment is limited; moderates have not made the argument that the Soviets have been losing in the superpower competition. Serwyn Bialer's 1982 statement was typical: "the Soviet Union remains in an ascendant phase of great-power ambition . . . At the present juncture Soviet foreign policy can best be described as a holding operation [but] we face a long-term situation where Soviet external expansion will accompany internal decline."[2]

But in fact, the basic conservative view is fundamentally mistaken; accepting it has contributed to unnecessary anxiety in the United States and to a misunderstanding about how to handle the Soviet Union. It is not accurate to suggest that the Soviet Union took advantage of detente to activate its foreign policy. Soviet foreign policy was already extraordinarily active in the late 1960s and early 1970s, before detente. Moscow had given massive military aid to North Vietnam, which resulted in tens of thousands of American deaths—probably the single most important factor in shaping profoundly anti-Soviet attitudes in America over the past decade. The pre-1972 period also saw the invasion of Czechoslovakia, a large-scale military buildup between 1968 and 1972, irresponsibly large arms shipments to Somalia, strong support of India against Pakistan over Bangladesh, the shipping of missiles to Egypt, and the use of Soviet pilots there in 1970 in air wars with Israel.

Essentially, the United States tried detente as a way of moderating Soviet behavior. To some extent, this tactic worked, as evidenced by the muted Soviet reaction to the bombing of Haiphong, Soviet withdrawal of personnel from Egypt to signal the coming war, and the reduction in the rate of growth of Soviet military spending. But the effects of detente should always have been expected to remain limited. When the United States continued to use covert action against Salvador Allende in Chile and, with China, supported Zairian troops in Angola, the Kremlin got the sense that *America* was trying to take advantage of detente—and furthermore was reneging on the economic part of the bargain when it passed the Jackson-Vanik and Stevenson amendments. Whatever hopes

Washington had of greater Soviet restraint—and they never should have been too bright—faded.

An even more serious problem with the conservatives' image of the Soviet Union on the move in the 1970s is that, whatever Moscow intended and attempted, it was not doing well. America's unnecessary preoccupation with Vietnam through the first half of the 1970s masked the fact that the United States has been winning the Soviet-American competition for the past quarter-century.[3] This success has resulted from the attractiveness of the Western economic system in its various permutations—including East Asian—compared with the Soviet system, as well as the availability of Western capital at a time when the Soviet Union has had no excess of its own.

In the 1950s and early 1960s, this situation was by no means a foregone conclusion. Communist revolutions had occurred in China and North Vietnam, communists won an electoral victory in Kerala in India, Castro proclaimed himself a socialist, and a series of other nationalist leaders—Nasser, Sukarno, Nkrumah, Ne Win, and others—were moving to the left as well. Soviet theorists were convinced that capitalist development would never produce sustained, balanced growth and that nationalism would push Third World political development toward socialism. Many in the West feared that this might be true—that the Soviet model might be bad for the consumer but was good for growth and, therefore, quite attractive for economically backward countries. In 1959, CIA Director Allen Dulles testified before Congress that Sputnik symbolized the possibility that the Soviet Union might gain technological superiority; in the late 1960s, unrest among the young in Western Europe suggested the possibility of instability there.

But now it turns out that the Soviet economic system, as it has existed for 30 years, is bad for growth and industry in the electronics-computer age, while the state-capitalist variants of the Western model have proven much more effective. Some of the most economically successful Third World countries have deliberately integrated into the world economy and pursued an aggressive export-oriented strategy. The technology, capital, and markets the United States can offer have been the keys to its success with these Third World countries; in this connection, the multinational corporation has been far more important than foreign aid.

Radical revolutions are actually occurring only in pre-industrial countries—the Afghanistans, the Yemens, the Ethiopias, the Nicaraguas—while the politics of the industrializing Third World countries—even the Egypts, Indias, and Indonesias, let alone the Argentinas and Brazils—have been moving to the center and the right. Nationalism has proved a powerful force, but it has been a nationalism that follows independent goals rather than pro-Soviet ones, or often the divisive nationalism of dissatisfied ethnic groups within multinational societies.

The nationalism that created real difficulties for the United States was that of noncommunist countries such as Saudi Arabia and Iran during the oil crisis of 1973, and the right-wing Shiite movement in Iran, which precipitated the fall of the shah and the second oil crisis. Those were America's real foreign policy defeats during the 1970s, not such pinpricks as Angola, Mozambique, or Nicaragua.

In Europe, the political situation has become so nonthreatening for Americans that we simply take it for granted. The past decade has been a very difficult one for European economies, but communist parties have lost strength virtually everywhere, even in countries such as Spain and Portugal where a decade ago radical chances seemed bright. The only signficant communist party—Italy's—has become virtually indistinguishable from the social-democratic one, except that its strong anti-Americanism has been supplemented by an even stronger anti-Sovietism.

Beyond its economic difficulties, the Soviet Union has had problems in the military sphere: the Soviet technological lag has adversely affected weapons development and the slowdown in Soviet economic growth has halted the increase in military procurement. The level of these procurements is in dispute, but the CIA has estimated that no growth occurred from 1976 to 1982—and this was William Casey's CIA, whose analysts have been protecting themselves by deciding fifty-fifty questions on the high side. Since the Soviet Union has been using up a fair amount of its military procurements in the Afghan war, those available for augmentation of its European forces must have declined. And the arms of the East European components of the Warsaw Pact remain hopelessly outmoded.

In many categories, the Soviet armed forces and their equipment exceed those of the United States alone, but the non-U.S. members of the NATO alliance have two-and-a-half times the GNP and number of troops of the United States. The United States has Japan on its side, and Japan has a GNP equivalent to the Soviet Union's. For what little it is worth, China is also anti-Soviet.

Not only is the military balance much more equal or even tilted to the West when America's NATO allies' military forces are included, but only a person with a Pearl Harbor complex would think that war was likely to break out at present force levels. Indeed, only a person with a Pearl Harbor complex who also forgot the years of rising Japanese-American tension and the clear signs of impending war could think that way. If tension began to increase seriously and the Soviet Union began taking the steps necessary to modernize East European armies, the industrial might of the United States, Western Europe, and Japan could shift the military balance very rapidly.

Another reason America has been winning the Soviet-American competition is that developments inside the communist world have sharply reduced Moscow's interest in military aggression. Hence deterring such aggression has been a very easy task. Though Stalin could think that communizing the world would produce a system of Soviet satellites and reduce any military threat to the Soviet Union, that Eastern Europe would subsidize the Soviet economy, and that military conquests would rebound to Moscow's benefit, now the world situation has changed. India's and China's relations with Moscow have demonstrated that a capitalist country can be more friendly and less threatening than a socialist one. The situation in Eastern Europe showed that a communist regime needs to identify with nationalism in order to survive, and that deviating from the Soviet Union is the way to achieve that goal. Eastern Europe also made it clear that internal deviations in a socialist country can be extremely threatening to Moscow because they may spread to the Soviet Union. (In a real sense, Solidarity was far more of a threat to the Kremlin than the installation of American Pershing-2 missiles in Europe.)

Essentially, the Soviet Union no longer has an interest in conquering Western Europe. Detente has allowed Moscow to develop relatively stable and mutually beneficial relations with Europe, particularly in the economic sphere. At least some Soviet specialists have come to recognize that, as Georgi Arbatov, the Kremlin's top U.S. specialist, put it on Soviet television, "Everybody is dependent on the stability of the international economic system and international monetary system."

Consider what would happen if the Soviet Union did try to take over Western Europe. It would have to create a united communist Germany, which might be as big a problem as communist China. Communist regimes in countries like Italy would surely cause Moscow much more trouble than Solidarity did. Dismantling NATO would deprive the Kremlin of its major justification for stationing troops in Eastern Europe. Furthermore, the communist economies that would be established in Western Europe would not be able to produce the same quality of technology for the Soviet Union that the capitalist economies have been able to.

Promoting revolution in the Third World also has limited benefits, even when it is successful. A Third World radical regime will vote with the Soviet Union in the United Nations, and is more likely to buy Soviet arms and to give the Soviet Union access to its ports. Nevertheless, hypothetical communist regimes in, say, the Persian Gulf would not give the Soviet Union cut-rate prices on petroleum, but would simply sell it on the open market. If Moscow reoriented its policies and courted moderate regimes, it would find clients and customers among them and would not have to rely on radicals.

But the Soviet Union has not reoriented its policies to fit the changing world environment—a further reason the United States has been winning the superpower competition. Moscow has continued to focus on radical regimes in the Third World and has failed to implement the kind of economic reform that would enable it to export technology and that would make its economic model more attractive. It has maintained the secrecy that has fueled fears of a Soviet military threat, stimulating a Western military buildup just when the Soviet economic slowdown has restrained the growth of the Soviet military budget.

To some extent, these policy choices may have resulted from the inflexibility of an aging leadership. But we should consider the possibility that the policy was deliberate. The Brezhnev-Gromyko generation endured two wars with Germany, and retained an intense memory of Japan's military might in 1905 and during the 1930s. For these men, a bipolar policy focusing on the American relationship may have seemed the best way to ensure that the United States maintain control over Germany and Japan and keep them nonnuclear.

In addition, the Brezhnev generation of leaders may have considered secrecy a good means of hiding military weakness. As one thinks of the various American exaggerations of Soviet military strength—the bomber gap, the missile gap, the ABM, the relentless 5 percent buildup of the 1970s—one is struck by the number of cases in which the Soviet Union deliberately furthered these misperceptions by boasting and bluffing. The Brezhnev leaders wanted the Soviet people to believe that their country had reached the equality with America that the Communist Party had promised. The more the United States contended that the Soviet Union was militarily superior, the more the Soviet leaders were legitimated in the eyes of the Soviet people. And even though this secrecy contributed to the continued U.S. buildup, the Brezhnev Kremlin knew it would not be in power long enough to feel the consequences of America's military expansion. Its primary concern was short-term political stability.

THE GORBACHEV CHALLENGE

Given that the past decade has seen the Soviet Union sluggish and the United States basically winning the competition, there has been no pressure on Washington to break out of the basic pattern of its postwar policy. Even though that policy has been criticized, a majority of the American public will in the end not support significant change unless the existing policy is shown to be a losing one.

But if the Soviet Union begins to present a more serious challenge to the United States, the United States will need to respond, and the public will be more receptive to the possible need for new ideas. And, of course, if Soviet policy changes substantially, there may be a real opening for what President Reagan has called a "fresh start" in Soviet-American relations.

In fact, Gorbachev has been promising drastic change. His stated goal is to bring Soviet technology up to world standards; at Geneva he even spoke of "the desire for us . . . to gain some sort of superiority in computer sciences, in radio communication." He recognizes that this will require "revolutionary changes" in the economic system, a "historic transformation" of the Soviet economy. He deliberately closed his *Time* interview[4] by stating that "foreign policy is a continuation of domestic policy" and then by posing a question: "I ask you to ponder one thing. If we in the Soviet Union are setting ourselves such truly grandiose plans in the domestic sphere, then what are the external conditions that we need to be able to fulfill those domestic plans?" The next sentence, the last sentence in the entire interview—"I leave the answer to that question to you"—was enigmatic. But clearly a foreign policy that is a continuation of a grandiose change in domestic policy should change in a grandiose way itself. Gorbachev's selection of a foreign minister who had never worked in Moscow, let alone in the foreign policy establishment, certainly suggested that foreign policy experience was not necessary and might even be counterproductive. That, too, implied that Moscow might be taking a new direction.

Many Americans have tremendous difficulty taking Gorbachev's statements seriously. They assume that the Soviet Union can never change. They see Russian political culture as inherently conservative, Russian national character as too insecure and suspicious for open relations with foreigners, communist ideology as so hostile to Western institutions and values that it rejects any reform using market mechanisms, the Soviet economy as so backward that only imported technology keeps it from being nonfunctional, and the Soviet bureaucracy as all-powerful and dedicated to the status quo. These beliefs—in themselves half-truths—are usually expressed in horror and alarm; in fact, they represent the comfortable—even wishful—assumption that the United States will never be seriously challenged.

The coming years are likely to prove how wrong this assumption is. Mikhail Gorbachev came to power at a time when the population and the elite were fed up with 10 years of ill and inactive leaders. . . . The institutional power of the general secretary, the old ideological traditions on which he can call, and the ambivalence even among opponents of reform all weigh in Gorbachev's favor. The new general secretary's time horizon is very different from that of his predecessors. Brezhnev knew that he would not live past the mid-1980s and that he could get along by muddling through. Gorbachev, on the other hand, hopes to stand on the Lenin mausoleum in the year 2000 to usher in the new century—preferably in triumph. If this is to occur, he cannot ignore real problems for 15 years at a stretch.

Gorbachev has a powerful incentive to undertake fundamental reform because of the serious consequences that technological backwardness is having on Soviet foreign policy, military power, and ideological legitimacy—and hence in the long run on political stability. Unlike such communist countries as Poland, the Soviet Union has successfully identified the regime with the achievement of Russian national goals and aspirations—in World War II, for example, and in the Soviet Union's attainment of superpower status. This appeal to nationalistic sentiment has strengthened the stability of the Soviet regime. If Soviet technological backwardness weakens this link with patriotism, it will also weaken stability.

Furthermore, this backwardness has tremendous potential impact on future Soviet security. The Soviet Union has been able to solve narrow, top-priority military technical problems—for example, the guidance system for its intercontinental missiles—but it took 20 to 25 years longer than the United States to acquire the ability to produce solid-fuel intercontinental ballistic missiles, to catch film ejected from satellites, and to orbit satellites at 25,000 miles. So far this has posed no insuperable military problems. But as Moscow looks ahead to the impending computerization of Western armies, to the threat of a successful Strategic Defense Initiative (or at least important military spin-offs from it), and to modernization of Chinese forces, it must sense a potential window of military vulnerability in the early 21st century. It will be impossible to computerize Soviet armed forces, as is needed, unless all of Soviet society is computerized, including the Moslem borderlands that will soon be the source of 40 percent of Soviet military recruits. That will require great changes.

Soviet technological backwardness also has serious ideological consequences. Marxism-Leninism promised that socialist planning would solve problems of technological advance and economic growth that advanced capitalism could not, and that a socialist Russia would not simply follow the West but would lead it to a new, higher level of civilization, making Moscow into the Third Rome. But in actuality, even though Russia and Japan began industrializing at the same time and Japan has only half the population of the Soviet Union, Japanese GNP has pulled even with the Soviet Union's and is surging ahead. Japan exports advanced technology in a way that the Soviet Union cannot begin to do. Tokyo has become the Third Rome. This is difficult to explain to the Soviet people and will become more so as increasing numbers of Third World countries follow the Japanese path.

Gorbachev's ability to deliver on his promise to bring Soviet technology to world levels does merit a certain degree of skepticism. But the crucial question for America is the effect economic reform will have on Soviet foreign policy. Even if the reform does not deliver all that Gorbachev hopes it will by the year 2000, the changes it makes in foreign policy will have long been in place.

U.S. speculations about the foreign policy consequences of economic reform have focused on Moscow's need to limit military spending and hence to strike an arms control agreement with Washington. Clearly the Soviet Union will place great importance on curbing military expenditures, particularly counterproductive expenditures on weapons procurement and readiness. But Americans should not assume that an agreement with the United States is a prerequisite for this. The natural Soviet response to the seven U.S. strategic programs is a mobile missile that can be hidden—a need that would be filled by a slow, inexpensive deployment of the SS-25. The natural reaction to Reagan's SDI program is an all-out computerization effort: since American scientists say that computers and software are the bottleneck in the American program, they must be even more of a bottleneck for the Soviet Union. Finally, for there to be real savings in military expenditures, there must be real reductions in conventional weapons and troops. And these reductions depend more on developments with China and Western Europe than on those with the United States.

Indeed, the sacrifices needed to implement economic reform and even to reduce military spending are easier to justify in terms of national defense against America than on the basis of a claim that America can now be trusted. When Soviet moderates simultaneously overemphasize the danger of nuclear war, bash the United States, and call for a moderate policy toward it, they run into the same domestic political problems that U.S. moderates do.

From Gorbachev's perspective, the beauty of SDI is that it poses no near-term threat, and hence justifies no short-term military expenditures, yet it can be portrayed as a devastating long-term threat that can be met only by computerization and the necessary accompanying steps. Gorbachev can repeat what he said at Geneva about the U.S. ambition for world domination through control of space. For at Geneva, he also laid out his responses to the U.S. strategy: "Much of American policy with regard to the Soviet Union is based on the mistaken assumption . . . that the arms race exhausts the Soviet Union economically and thereby strengthens the hand of the United States of America . . . Maybe this has even reached the President himself." The implication here is that the Soviet Union should not play the president's game and be forced into matching every weapons development. "Americans are certainly very strong in certain areas of technology, particularly in computer sciences, in radio communication, and of course there's the desire for us . . . to gain some sort of superiority [there]." This is the area where Soviet resources will need to go.

A second consequence of economic reform, if the Soviet Union takes it seriously, is a major opening of the country to the outside world. The slavophile exclusiveness and autarky of the past 60 years has meant that Russian manufacturers—the Soviet equivalent of capitalism's hated businessmen—received complete protectionism from foreign competition. This has had all the consequences that any free trader would have predicted in terms of innovation, quality, and efficiency.

The countries that have industrialized most successfully in recent years—Japan and other Pacific Basin countries—have protected their domestic industries, especially early on, but have also followed an export strategy in order to compel their manufacturers to meet foreign competition abroad. They did this not after they had achieved technological superiority but rather while they were still relatively backward, in order to force manufacturers to raise the quality of their production to world levels. The Soviet Union must now follow a similar strategy if its technology is to improve. This will require Moscow to tolerate exposure to foreign ideas. Soviet businessmen can never succeed until Soviet society obtains a far better feel for the outside world than is now permitted.

Economic reform will also require the Soviet Union to move away from the bipolarism of recent decades to a multipolar policy. Bipolarism fit well with a conservative domestic strategy: ideologically, it was easier to handle than a multipolar policy; for an aging leadership, it was less demanding to conduct; it gave East European countries less maneuvering room. Perhaps most important, it made liberalization at home dependent on good relations with the United States—and that effectively restricted liberalization since relations with America were never going to be remarkably smooth, especially with Soviet Third World policy focusing on radical countries and its Middle East policy being totally anti-Israel. Indeed, to use Gorbachev's words, foreign policy was probably a continuation of domestic policy, motivated by the conservative implications it had for domestic affairs. Economic reform is likely to change that foreign policy because it will remove the factors that led to its formulation.

Many Americans still treat the signs of an impending multipolar policy by Gorbachev as evidence of a strategy to split Europe and Japan from the United States. This type of thinking belongs to the World-War-II era. In a nuclear age, breaking up NATO would not serve Soviet foreign policy interests, for the real danger to the Soviet Union—rockets coming over the North Pole—would not be decreased but would perhaps even be intensified by Amerian insecurity. Moreover, an independent West Germany might eventually become nuclear (Gromyko understood this well: "German revanchism" was a buzzword he used to defend his bipolar policy.) In addition, splitting NATO would rob the Soviet Union of its chief justification for stationing troops in Eastern Europe. The last thing Gorbachev wants is an opening to the West that loosens West Germany's tie to NATO and East Germany's to the Warsaw Pact, for a closer relationship between the two Germanys, which almost certainly is on the way, will be acceptable to Moscow only if the present military alliances are maintained, at least formally.

Thus a multipolar policy is not designed to break up the block system but rather to achieve other goals. It will facilitate the internal politics of reform by allowing Soviet leaders to argue that an opening to the West is an anti-American move and is necessary for defense. More importantly, it will fill economic needs. The only way the Soviet Union can adopt an export strategy while its technology is inferior is to export at low cost. The United States will respond with charges that the Soviet Union is dumping its products on the world market; furthermore, U.S. technological controls will interfere with a reciprocal trade of American technology. Western Europe, Japan, and the moderate Third World countries will better serve the Soviet Union's economic interests. The concessions Moscow will have to make to gain guaranteed access to markets there will be less onerous than those the United States would demand. They would involve things like an easier East German-West German relationship, giving the Kuril Islands back to Japan, granting these countries the right to invest in the Soviet Union, and shifting the emphasis of Soviet Third World policy to the larger, more moderate countries at the expense of the radicals.

Economic reform will also tend to reduce the general Soviet tendency toward secrecy, which will have indirect but nonetheless terribly important consequences for foreign policy. Paradoxically, the Soviet behavior that has really prevented many Americans from perceiving Moscow's competitive actions as normal has been not its foreign policies but its domestic ones. The Soviet Union's obsessive secrecy, as well as a number of bizarre and seemingly inexplicable domestic policies, are perfectly legal; but they have had disastrous consequences for U.S.-Soviet relations and for the effectiveness of the arguments of U.S. moderates.

The basic problem is the American public's deep ignorance of foreign countries and international relations. On a blank map, most Americans could probably not even identify the continents on which Afghanistan, Ethiopia, and Nicaragua are located. They simply know that some U.S. specialists on the Soviet Union assert that Soviet foreign policy is inexorably and monolithically expansionist. Other specialists may perceive more limited Soviet aims and therefore suggest the possibility of cooperation in the midst of competition, but the American public has no way of judging which of these images is correct.

The public does, however, have a very clear sense that Soviet leaders are enormously secretive. They hide all the details of their political life; they don't announce their military programs or provide information about them; they protect their borders so fiercely that they shoot down civilian planes like the KAL airliner. The real reason for secrecy, besides sheer inertia, was probably the Brezhnev generation's desire to look as though the country had achieved equality with the United States—to create a more threatening image than reality warranted. The American public has made the more normal conclusion: if the Soviet leaders are so secretive, they must have something to hide, and a prudent person assumes that that something is dangerous.

The Soviet Union's behavior is also quite alien in other respects. Suppressing people like Andrei Sakharov does leave a bad taste, but at least it makes some sense in terms of dictatorial control. But why is the Soviet Union against abstract art? What does it have against situation comedies or soap operas or game shows on television? Why does it not permit comic books or true romance novels or gossip columns or the dozens of other features of Western life that are very popular and contribute to political stability? Why keep barber shops, restaurants, and even farming nationalized when they function so poorly that way and when small private entrepreneurs are scarcely going to be a powerful class enemy?

It is easy to say that such behavior should be irrelevant to Soviet-American relations—no doubt, it should be. Yet when a public sees a powerful opponent acting in strange ways that do not even seem to serve its own self-interest, the questions inevitably arise: What is motivating those people? Is it not some kind of fanaticism that may lead to dangerous, inexplicable actions in foreign policy as well? A specialist may dismiss such fears as unjustified, but they are perfectly reasonable and will continue to prevail over any counterarguments. Rightly or wrongly, the American public will never believe that meaningful agreements are possible with such a peculiar leadership.

But much of that peculiarity, too, could change—and is already changing. This is why the public has been so interested in Mikhail Gorbachev's more Western style and in Raisa Gorbachev's appearance on television and her Western dress. By our standards, it is incredibly peculiar—even uncivilized—that we did not know whether Andropov still had a wife until she appeared at his funeral. The fact that Gorbachev travels with his wife like a normal Western leader provides an eagerly seized-upon bit of evidence on his general world outlook. One may argue that not too much weight should be put on such evidence, but, consciously or unconsciously, people have already placed enormous weight—too much weight, certainly—on the countervailing evidence that past Soviet leaders hid their wives from view. The public will never accept the moderates' argument that it is possible to treat the Soviet Union as a civilized power in international relations until its leaders behave in what we consider a civilized manner on "unimportant" matters.

In addition, Gorbachev has little of Brezhnev's (and Ustinov's) need to hide Soviet military failings and to exaggerate Soviet military strength. If he wants reform, he has an interest in saying that the Soviet military is adequate for any task today, but that it has enormous technological shortcomings that will create problems in the future. Any major movement away from the past's obsessive secrecy on military matters will have a major impact.

Similarly, any kind of market strategy that gives added independence to farmers or allows an expanded private service sector will alter the very alien and therefore threatening image that Americans have of the Soviet Union. The same is true of any kind of westernizing trend in Soviet culture. Already under Brezhnev, literature began treating love stories more honestly and even graphically, and detective stories became popular. There is every reason to believe that this process will accelerate under Gorbachev, eventually becoming quite visible. If, as growing signs indicate, Gorbachev is going to permit greater honesty about the Soviet past—including Stalin and Khrushchev—the change will have an even more dramatic impact on the West.

THE AMERICAN RESPONSE TO GORBACHEV

If the Soviet Union changes in the ways I have suggested, then obviously much will change in the way the United States responds to it. This evolution of American attitudes is likely to be reinforced by generational change, as leaders of the Reagan-Gromyko era pass the mantle of power on to younger individuals. Gorbachev was only 14 when nuclear weapons were first used; Gary Hart and Jack Kemp, among others, are roughly five years younger still. Their generation will find it much easier to abandon many anachronistic political assumptions dating from the prenuclear era.

We are accustomed to speaking of generational change in the Soviet Union, yet the one that will occur in America is just as important as the one that has put Gorbachev in power. Arthur Schlesinger has pointed out that the United States has had a 30-year political cycle, with reform movements arising at the beginning of the 1900s, and 1930s, and the 1960s. Similarly, President Coolidge in 1925, President Eisenhower in 1955, and President Reagan in 1985 all provided the country a needed breathing space—a vacation from troubles—in the wake of a national trauma.

To a large extent, this cycle has a generational base. The 50-year-olds who carried through the Great Society in 1965 had been student activists during the New Deal period; their own children were the 1960s college students. Today's 50-year-olds were 20 in 1955, during the materialistic Eisenhower period, and their children, whose views resemble those of their parents, are the largely nonactivist college students of today. As we move toward the 1990s, the Vietnam generation will be passing through its forties, and its children will be entering college. The 1960s' skepticism on military and foreign policy questions will be close to the surface and easy to evoke, especially if the Soviet Union shows signs of significant change.

Yet a "fresh start" in U.S.-Soviet relations will not occur automatically. We need to give serious attention to what such a start will involve. William Hyland, editor of Foreign Affairs, is right in asserting that "we have rarely thought out the concrete terms of a settlement with the Soviet Union [and] this amounts to a fatalistic abdication of policy."[5]

As already noted, the Reagan administration has to a large extent implemented the standard moderate program: a combination of competition and cooperation, dialogue and arms control negotiations, unofficial ratification of the SALT-II agreement, promotion of exchanges to increase understanding, and now (under moderate pressure, to be sure) a slow and "responsible" military buildup. In the process, Reagan has exposed this program for the collection of empty clichés that it is. The moderates must now move beyond it.

First, general talk about cooperation and competition needs to be replaced by hardheaded discussions of international relations in general. We must set aside the old isolationist assumptions about the illegitimacy of normal conflicts of interest, and must recognize the inherent ambivalence of international relations—the complex play of interests that a relationship with any country, "friend" or "foe," involves.

In the aftermath of World War II, U.S. politics had to find a way to cope with some of the idealism of such men as Cordell Hull and Henry Wallace, but today the greatest danger lies in the Manichean image of good and evil that the Reagan administration has used to depict U.S.-Soviet relations. In the past, this dualistic attitude has been expressed in extreme ways. Reagan, in his "evil empire" speech, praised as a "profound truth" a father's statement that "I would rather see my little girls die now still believing in God than have them grow up under Communism and one day no longer believing in God."[6] Perhaps this type of thinking will give way after several summit meetings between Reagan and Gorbachev. Yet the president's extremely selective choice of regional issues to bring up suggests that the administration continues to regard the Soviet Union as the focus of evil and source of all trouble and revolution in the world.

Fortunately, these Manichean views have thus far not been particularly dangerous, for President Reagan comes basically from the isolationist tradition of the 1930s and 1940s and keeps his administration's global unilateralists on a tight rein. Outside of Central America—which isolationists always treated as a U.S. domestic concern and where they frequently intervened—Reagan has shied away from dangerous foreign entanglements. He has followed a policy of limited U.S. involvement in Lebanon and in the Iran-Iraq war, which has reassured the public. His military budget has focused not on readiness and conventional weapons, but on a Fortress-America strategy, reminiscent of Herbert Hoover's and Robert Taft's, that emphasizes the navy, retaliatory strategic rockets, and, of course, a defensive shield in space.

The real danger of the Reagan-style Manichean worldview would come if it were held by a leader who did not share President Reagan's basic isolationist assumptions. Under a younger leader who took U.S. involvement in Korea and Vietnam for granted and was only unhappy that America did not win, the "crusade" that Reagan proclaims but does not actually conduct could lead to disastrous consequences.

When the United States was truly isolationist, it could afford to embrace a dualistic worldview: it could treat international relations as illegitimate except when they involved interventions against evil. But as a great power with global responsibilities, whose interests are increasingly tied with those of other countries, the United States must accept the reality that all nation-states are engaged in a struggle of power and influence. America carries on such a struggle, and so does the Soviet Union, and so do Iran and Japan and Great Britain and Canada. It is the nature of the world.

Of course, international relations are not simply a field of conflict. Japan and America's severe economic and trade disputes do not prevent their having a strong economic and security relationship. West Germany's installation of the Pershing-2 missiles did not disrupt an East-West German contract for West Germany to lay a cable to carry its commercial television into Dresden, East Germany. (The other parts of East Germany were close enough to receive West German TV through the airwaves.) Argentina's boycott of the Moscow Olympics did not interfere with Soviet-Argentine grain trade.

And so it is—or should be—in Soviet-Amerian relations. The United States cooperates with the Soviet Union in allocating broadcast frequencies, in defining fishing rights, in establishing safety rules at sea, and now (belatedly) in warning airliners on the Pacific route if they stray off course. The two countries tacitly cooperate in the Iran-Iraq War. Though the Soviet Union refused to cooperate with the United States during the Iranian hostage crisis, it has done so tacitly in the Iran-Iraq War to help prevent an Iranian victory. This kind of development should be supported and expanded upon. If Arbatov is right about a common U.S.-Soviet interest in promoting economic stability, then far wider cooperation in a number of areas is possible.

Generally, the United States should encourage the Soviet leaders' growing tendency to integrate their country back into the world community. Fanatical Marxism-Leninism in Moscow is dangerous to the world, and a mellowing of it makes the world safer. The unnatural subjugation of Eastern Europe, to cite one example, will ease only when the two-bloc mentality in the Soviet Union begins to break down. In particular, Soviet integration into the world economy should be encouraged. Soon the Soviet Union will be the only East European country not in the International Monetary Fund; perhaps this anomaly should be corrected.

Second, the moderates must adjust their thinking to the shift that has occurred in the relative importance of the economic and military components of national power and security. In particular, they must launch a vigorous attack on the exaggerated notion of the role military force plays in international relations today. The Reagan administration clearly believes that Soviet restraint in the Third World has resulted largely from such U.S. actions as invading Grenada or supporting the Nicaraguan contras. It attributes Moscow's return to the bargaining table to fear of the SDI program, and it perceives Soviet policy in Europe as trying to split the Western military alliance. None of this is correct. The United States has been winning in the Third World because of the superiority of its economic model and its ability to supply capital and technology; the Soviet Union returned to the bargaining table because it was losing the propaganda war in Europe; and as has been seen, Moscow is playing to Europe for domestic and economic reasons.

The nuclear age really has changed the relative importance of the military factor in international relations. When the threat comes across the North Pole, buffer zones are not terribly crucial. As the conservative Robert W. Tucker has pointed out, a nuclear power's military alliances endanger it more than they add to its security.[7] A Western Europe that can offer technology is more useful to the Soviet Union than a conquered Western Europe that must be communized and that provides not technology but political headaches.

Japan seems to be the country that has most fully grasped the rising importance of economic power in the nuclear age; accordingly, it has concentrated its resources in areas that maximize that power. The rest of the world—especially the United States—needs to learn from Japan. A buildup of the navy and strategic missile forces that produces a $200-billion deficit is a threat to national strength, not an augmentation of power. It creates tensions with other countries, keeps interest rates dangerously high, and curtails investment—and thus in the long run undercuts America's competitive position.

Finally, the moderates need to move beyond the old package of empty generalizations about arms control. Talk about negotiating arms control agreements is not enough; we need to talk about controlling armaments. The Reagan military buildup was compatible with the SALT-II treaty—a good indication of the relative irrelevance of even the most far-reaching arms control agreements of the 1970s. At that time, arms control was pushed by two conservative leaders, Nixon and Brezhnev, and two even more conservative foreign ministers, Kissinger and Gromyko, who were all trying to placate their respective liberal oppositions and legitimate a continuation of high military spending. Arms control has served to justify weapons as bargaining chips and to distract public attention to peripheral issues.

Thus, at the present time the United States has seven separate programs for the delivery of nuclear weapons: the MX, the Midgetman, the Pershing-2, cruise missiles (of which there are actually several types), the B-1 bomber, and Stealth bomber, and a new Trident rocket. America has an enormously expensive plan to expand its fleet of carrier groups—each capable of launching only 50 attack planes! It is sheer craziness. Yet public attention is now riveted on a few billion dollars of expenditures on SDI that will have at least a few useful technical spin-offs and that will almost surely never be funded in any major way. Meanwhile, enormous spending on the navy, nuclear delivery systems, and nuclear warheads proceeds without public challenge.

Congressmen are beholden to contractors—and even more to the work force of defense plants—within their respective districts; thus they will vote in a military expenditure even when they know it is a waste of money. This situation will change only if congressmen learn that they lose more votes by approving expenditures than by opposing them. Moderates must emphasize the fact that the Pentagon consists of bureaucrats just like civilian bureaucrats, who push unnecessary projects for selfish reasons. Moderates must call a spade a spade—the defense industry is a special interest—and must tell Washington that until it controls the U.S. military-industrial complex, Soviet leaders will act on the assumption that this complex controls the United States.

Just as the Soviet Union can cut military spending without an arms control agreement, so can the United States. Just as the mobile SS-25 is the correct Soviet response to the U.S. strategic programs, so is the Midgetman, combined with air-launched cruise missiles, the correct answer to Soviet first-strike weapons—but only if the Midgetman and cruise missiles replace existing weapons rather than supplement them. The military hates the Midgetman precisely because it fears it might be a replacement.

If moderates articulate these general positions skillfully, they will find that the tactical problems their traditional approach has produced will diminish. To talk about the inevitable and natural character of international conflict is to merit being labeled the realist side in the U.S. political debate. To express confidence in the enormous power of our economic system is to stand up for the United States. To hammer home the annual cost of our nuclear bomb program, the cost of seven delivery systems, and the cost of a carrier task force that puts only 50 attack planes in the air is to initiate a serious critique of the Reagan military budget. Concentrating on $500 toilet seats will not achieve the same purpose.

But above all, the moderates should begin speaking of the end of an era. They should say that much of what we have taken for granted for

40 years is not inevitable. Rather, these assumptions spring from the insecurity that was generated when U.S. and Soviet elites were thrust from being leaders of regional powers in 1939 to being heads of superpowers in 1945. The generation that has handled these past 40 years is to be commended for having avoided nuclear war, but it is time for new generations to lead the postwar world. It is time for the United States to become a self-confident participant in international relations: it certainly has the economic cards in its hand; and if it plays them right, its position can be much more secure than it is now.

Obviously, if Gorbachev does not go beyond skillful public relations to engage in skillful diplomacy, if he does not reduce the secrecy that makes the Soviet Union seem so alien and threatening, then the moderates are going to have a much more difficult time convincing a majority of the U.S. population. But it is wishful thinking to believe that this new Soviet leader will pose as little of a challenge to the United States as his predecessors did. If Gorbachev does make significant moves, demonstrating that he is entering a new era, the argument that the United States must either enter that era as well or else begin to lose will become absolutely compelling. Those American politicians who articulate a sense of a new future and express confidence in their ability to handle it will be those chosen to lead the United States forward.

NOTES

1. In December 1982, Andropov offered to reduce the number of warheads aimed at Europe from 950 to 498 (three each on 166 SS-20 missiles), contingent only on the United States not installing the Pershing-2 and cruise missiles. In the course of 1983, he improved his offer several times, finally agreeing to go down to 360 Soviet warheads. That is, the Soviet Union was offering to dismantle 590 warheads without any reduction of existing U.S. or allied forces. This position would have accepted a number of warheads well below the level that the West had tolerated in the 1970s—i.e., 600 warheads—without any decrease in the allied forces that had matched that level. It meant that the Soviet Union was doing what arms controllers said it would not do—proposing a unilateral reduction in which it would trade existing missiles for an American offer not to deploy new ones.

2. Seweryn Bialer and Joan Afferica, "Reagan and Russia," *Foreign Affairs*, Vol. 61, No. 2 (Winter 1982–83), pp. 257, 357.

3. The irrelevance of the Vietnam War, except in domestic American terms, becomes clear if one asks: what difference would it have made outside of Indochina if the United States had won? Except for domestic costs, no significant bad consequences have resulted from the defeat in Vietnam. As balance-of-power international relations theory would have predicted, neighboring countries did not act as dominos, but instead moved closer to America for protection. If the United States had won the war, it is difficult to see what international benefits would have ensued. It is the irrelevance of the result that makes the Vietnam War such an unnecessary tragedy.

4. *Time*, September 9, 1985.

5. William G. Hyland, "Paging Mr. X," *The New Republic*, June 18, 1984, p. 37.

6. *New York Times*, March 9, 1985, p. A-18.

7. Robert W. Tucker, "The Nuclear Debate," *Foreign Affairs*, Vol. 63, No. 11 (Fall 1984), p. 30.

15

How Vulnerable is the West?*

RICHARD PIPES

SOVIET GRAND STRATEGY

Soviet leaders claim, with unconcealed pride, that they approach every problem that confronts them in a scientific manner. By this they mean that they act neither on emotional impulses nor out of moral consider-ations, but always seek to determine dispassionately, first the laws that govern the business at hand, then the "objective factors" of the situation, and finally, where pertinent, the "correlation of forces" between the contending parties. In their dealings with foreign powers, they try to initiate actions or respond to the actions of others in accordance with a systematic assessment of the correlation of forces. Whether politics in fact lends itself to such scientific management is questionable; at any rate, frequent Soviet foreign policy failures suggest that the appropriate methodology has not yet been discovered. Never-theless, it is true that the individuals who make foreign policy in communist societies analyse and weigh more carefully the factors likely to influence the outcome of political or military initiatives than is the case with their democratic counterparts. This habit the communists first acquired in the revolutionary underground. Experience taught them long ago that, when engaging a superior opponent (and until they triumph, revolutionaries are by definition weaker than the governments they seek to overthrow), one must always act with utmost caution, paying close attention to the correlation of forces and underestimating rather than overestimating one's own strength. In as much as the trend of history is on the side of communism anyway, there is no point in precipitating events when circumstances appear unfavourable; one merely has to wait for the correlation of forces to shift to one's advantage.

We have no knowledge how the Soviet leadership assesses its strengths and weaknesses in the global correlation of forces. A hypo-thetical balance-sheet, however, might look as follows:

Soviet Strengths

• A unique geopolitical situation that assures the USSR of relative immunity from conquest by hostile powers and yet allows it to probe for

* Extract from *Survival Is Not Enough* by Richard Pipes, published in 1984 by Simon and Schuster, New York.

and exploit such opportunities for expansion as develop on the other side of its immensely long frontier with Europe and Asia;

• Virtually complete control of its population and resources, unconstrained by constitution, representative bodies, or overt public opinion, with the resulting ability to coordinate political, military, economic and ideological instrumentalities in a Grand Strategy;

• The opportunity to exploit to the fullest the internal differences in democratic societies without fear of being subjected to the same treatment; greater unity within its imperial bloc than is the case with the opponents' loose alliance of sovereign and democratic states.

Soviet Weaknesses

• An economy that, owing to the country's inherent poverty and an inefficient, heavily politicized method of organization, cannot adequately support the regime's global ambitions;

• A political system that for all its outward solidity is ill-suited to cope with emergencies, such as political succession or foreign failures; because its domestic authority rests largely on the population's belief that it is invincible, the regime always faces the risk that humiliation abroad will subvert its power at home;

• The danger that military involvement abroad may lead to a conflict with the United States and unleash nuclear war;

• The unpopularity of Soviet-style communism among the world's masses and the absence of an attractive culture or life-style.

This particular combination of strengths and weaknesses shapes Soviet Grand Strategy. Its relatively weak economy and its unappealing culture do not permit the Soviet Union to seek the kind of financial, commercial and cultural influence that greatly contributed to the successes of British imperialism. At the same time, fear of the political consequences of defeat on the field of battle, reinforced by the desire to avoid nuclear war with the United States, keeps the Soviet Union from resorting to military force in the brash manner of twentieth-century Germany and Japan. The Soviet regime has had to develop a special kind of imperialism, adapted to its own strengths. These, in the ultimate reckoning, are political in nature and consist in *the unique ability of communist regimes to impose tight control over their own domain while destabilizing the enemy's.* Given these realities, it is understandable that communist leaders should rely most heavily on political means (which, in their thinking, include military power used for purposes of intimidation) and prefer to commit to military operations by proxy forces rather than their own. This kind of imperialism calls for a protracted, patient and prudent but unremitting *war of political attrition.* Its purpose is to undermine the authority of hostile governments and the will of their citizens to resist, while maintaining their own base solid, impregnable, and in a permanent state of mobilization.

Political attrition can be accomplished in a variety of ways: by exploiting the "contradictions" in the enemy's camp; by playing on his fears, especially those of nuclear destruction; by redefining the political vocabulary and bending the rules of international conduct to one's own advantage; by isolating enemy countries from one another and from their sources of raw materials. It is the sum of these diverse measures that constitutes Soviet Grand Strategy.

The term *politics* is used in communist societies in a sense very different from that common in democracies. In the West, politics means civic activity—that is, the practice of administration or, more broadly, the art of governing. Communist theoreticians, however, have militarized politics and view it exclusively as a form of class warfare. This is how the subject is taught in Soviet school textbooks:

> In working out the strategic [or political] line of the Party under conditions of capitalism it is important, first of all, to define the *principal aim* of the working class at this stage and the *principal class enemy*, against whom it is essential at this point to concentrate class hatred and the striking force of all the workers in order to break his resistance.[1]

Noteworthy in this passage is the assumption that the objective of politics is "to break the resistance" of the opponent; this is essentially a military concept, and as such, it differs fundamentally from the view of politics prevalent in the West since the days of Aristotle, which sees its essence not in destruction but in cooperation. . . .

SOVIET POLITICAL STRATEGY

As previously mentioned, the logic of the situation—its particular blend of strengths and weaknesses—compels the Soviet Union to rely heavily in its Grand Strategy on political means. Political strategy, in turn, means first and foremost promoting and exploiting divisions in the enemy camp: driving wedges between citizens of democratic societies and their elected officials, aggravating relations among social classes as well as ethnic and religious groups, and sowing discord among allies. This classic *divide et impera* policy, which forms the essence of Soviet political strategy, was formulated as early as the 1920 Congress of the Communist International as "exacerbating the struggle in the camp of the bourgeoisie itself on the national and international scale."[2] Lenin often stressed the supreme importance of this technique. In a tract written in 1920 against the advocates of a "direct" assault on capitalism, he expressed his views in a particularly blunt manner:

[The] entire history of Bolshevism, both before and after the October Revolution, is *full* of instances of changes of tack, conciliatory tactics and compromises with other parties, including bourgeois parties!

To carry on a war for the overthrow of the international bourgeoisie . . . and to renounce in advance any change of tack, or any utilization of a conflict of interests (even if temporary) among one's enemies, or any conciliation or compromise with possible allies . . . is that not ridiculous in the extreme? . . .

After the first socialist revolution of the proletariat, and the overthrow of the bourgeoisie in some country, the proletariat of that country remains *for a long time weaker* than the [international] bourgeoisie . . . The more powerful enemy can be vanquished only by exerting the utmost effort, and by the most thorough, careful, attentive, skillful and *obligatory* use of any, even the smallest, rift between the enemies, any conflict of interests among the bourgeoisie of the various countries . . . and also by taking advantage of any, even the smallest, opportunity of winning a mass ally, even though this ally is temporary, vacillating, unstable, unreliable, and conditional . . .[3]

This strategy is designed to exploit clashes of opinion and of interest, which are the essence of democracy, to the advantage of a regime that tolerates neither—in other words, to turn constructive competition into self-destruction. That this technique must be employed by any power bent on conquering a Western country was noted with remarkable prescience a century and a half ago by the father of modern strategic doctrine, Karl von Clausewitz—"It is impossible," he wrote, "to obtain possession of a great country with European civilization otherwise than by aid of internal division."[4]

The *divide et impera* policy strives to sow discord among the allies as well as within each allied country by inflaming antagonisms and arousing mutual suspicions, using for this purpose political, military and economic inducements or punishments, as the situation requires. The following are some examples of this tactic as applied by the Soviet Union towards NATO countries:

• In signing business contracts for projects in the USSR and Eastern Europe, preference is given to countries which pursue an accommodating policy towards Moscow and are prepared to "de-couple" commercial relations from political ones; countries which are deemed unfriendly or (because of their resort to sanctions and embargoes) "unreliable" are penalized. Such contracts encourage political accommodation, but they also create a dependence of the countries concerned on the communist client. In Germany alone, some 300,000 jobs are said to be directly or indirectly linked to business with the Soviet Union and Eastern Europe. Since many of these jobs are in so-called "sunset," or declining industries, liable to go under without the benefit of sales to communist countries, aggravating unemployment, an economic dependence is created that no German government, regardless of its political preferences, can ignore.

• The Soviet Union has persuaded much of the United States business community that if Washington conducted a more "friendly" policy—that is, reconciled itself to its aggressive actions—they would receive lush export orders. The lure of these orders has transformed United States business leaders into the most vociferous neutralist lobby in the country.

• In countries with powerful communist trade unions, such as Italy and France, the Soviet Union takes advantage of their presence to threaten industrial unrest to firms that hesitate to enter with it into commercial agreements.

• The Soviet Union has for years exploited the yearning of West Germans for personal contacts with their families in East Germany to extract from Bonn an accommodating stance; it has used, to the same end, West Germany's desire for the eventual unification of its divided nation.

• France's fear of the supremacy of the "Anglo-Saxons" as well as of the Germans on the Continent is played upon to incite Paris to conduct an "independent" foreign policy.

• The Soviet Union interferes in democratic elections abroad by bestowing its blessing on candidates whose stand on international issues happens to suit its interests. They and their parties are depicted as forces for "peace," whose election will lead to the improvement of relations with Moscow and lower the risk of war (e.g. Richard Nixon in 1972; Giscard d'Estaing in 1973 and 1981; and the German Social Democratic Party in 1983).

• The USSR pressures the West to enter with it into "mutual security" accords, the most comprehensive of which was signed in Helsinki in 1975; these create the illusion that it shares with the United States responsibility for safeguarding the peace and integrity of the Continent as a whole, thereby undermining NATO and pushing Western Europe towards neutralism.

• Moscow increases or diminishes the flow of Jewish *émigrés* in accord with the status of overall United States–Soviet Union relations as a device for pressuring the American Jewish community to influence its government towards accommodation.

• The USSR offers support to terrorists of every political hue, right-wing as well as left-wing, sometimes both concurrently, in order to destroy in foreign countries the basis of law and order and thus either make them vulnerable to a communist power seizure or else drive them into the arms of a right-wing dictatorship, which enables native communists to assume leadership of the "united democratic front"; this practice by the Soviet client Bulgaria caused civil unrest to break out in Turkey a few years ago and nearly resulted in that country's political collapse.

Such instances of the application of the principle of *divide et impera* can be multiplied without difficulty from the experience of Europe and other regions; they implement Lenin's call for exploiting the "rifts" in the enemy camp. It is a devastating strategy when applied against democracies, because democracies cannot remain true to themselves unless they tolerate dissent among their citizens and disagreements within their alliances. Such dissent and such disagreements, however, offer Moscow infinite opportunities to interfere in their affairs by throwing its not inconsiderable weight to support now this, now that contending party. Confronted with another totalitarian state, such as Nazi Germany or Communist China, the Soviet leadership, unable to resort to this strategy, finds itself severely handicapped—prevented by the hostile regime's tight grip on its population from reaching over its head to the diverse social and political groups, it tends towards accommodation. Thus, after signing the non-aggression pact with Hitler in 1939, Stalin scrupulously refrained from interfering in internal German affairs. When in January 1940 Mussolini berated his ally for being too friendly with Moscow, Hitler responded that a basis had been created for an "acceptable" relationship with the USSR—"We no longer have cause [to complain] that any Russian department attempts to exert influence in internal German affairs."[*5] It goes without saying that the vulnerability of democratic societies to internal interference causes Moscow to favour the broadest kind of democracy for countries that it has an interest in weakening, in accord with the adage, "When I am the weaker, I demand from you liberty, because this is your principle; when I am the stronger, I deprive you of it, because this is my principle."

So much for political tactics. Above them stands the "general line" that determines the application of Grand Strategy to given historic circumstances. In Lenin's day, the general line focused on two targets: in the industrial countries, aggravating social strife and the competition for markets; in the colonial areas, inciting movements for national independence. This approach largely lost its utility after the Second World War. The extraordinary economic progress of Western societies under "Pax Americana" and the movements of social reform that accompanied it have in all Western countries reduced class consciousness as well as social strife. The modern Western working class can by no stretch of the imagination be treated as *proletariat* in the classic Marxist sense. This concept, which derives from the Latin *proles* ("offspring," defining a

* The Soviet government, indeed, showed a tolerance towards Nazism that it has never displayed towards the democracies. In a speech which he delivered on 31 October 1939, in the midst of furious attacks on England and France for waging war on Hitler, V. M. Molotov, Soviet Commissar of Foreign Affairs, declared preference for National Socialism to be a question of taste: "The ideology of Hitlerism, as any ideological system, can be accepted or rejected: this is a matter of political opinion" (*Pravda*, 1 Nov. 1939, p. 1).

class in ancient Rome whose whole wealth consisted of children), lost meaning in the advanced industrial countries as labour merged into the lower-middle class. Surveys conducted since the Second World War indicate that only a small minority of German workers think of themselves as workers, and many of them do not even know what the word *proletarian* means. In addition, everywhere in the industrial countries the proportion of manually occupied employees steadily declines as white-collar and service employees take the place of blue-collar workers. Any communist political strategist worth his salt would have to conclude that the objective trends of modern economies point towards an irreversible decline of labour as an isolated and aggrieved class and, consequently, that a strategy based on the exploitation of differences between the haves and have-nots in advanced industrial countries offers little scope. The same holds true of expectation of conflicts among "capitalist" countries for markets and sources of raw materials. In the 1920s Trotsky could still fantasize that economic rivalries would lead the United States and Great Britain to war. But nothing of the kind has ever occurred or even came close to occurring. The emergence after the war of multinational corporations has further smoothed competition among states over markets and resources. Those economic differences that continue to divide democratic societies—as, for instance, over tariffs or subsidies—are resolved peacefully through high-level negotiation; they hardly lend themselves to political exploitation by Moscow.

The old general line is no more appropriate to conditions in the post-war Third World. Since 1945, all the non-communist colonies have been emancipated, making agitation for "national liberation" irrelevant. Here and there it is still possible to stoke the fires of anti-Westernism (e.g. among the Palestinians and in Namibia) but these areas offer limited opportunity. Here too, therefore, new strategies had to be devised. We will now turn to the central theme of the current Soviet general line towards the West, which revolves around the related subjects of "peace" and "the bomb.". . .

The Soviet government exploits the peace theme in a variety of ways. Of these, two deserve particular attention: defining peace to mean acquiescence to Soviet demands; and creating a false sense of identity between East and West by making weapons rather than the people behind the weapons appear the main threat to peace. Moscow dominates the international discussion about nuclear weapons, because it is able to counter the babble of contentious and emotional Western voices with a single, steadfast voice of its own. The commissioning of its nuclear weapons is surrounded with such a thick veil of secrecy that even high Soviet officials are kept in the dark. This contrasts with comprehensive debates in Congress and the media in the United States about appropriateness for every proposed new nuclear system and, in

Western Europe, about their deployment. While in the West strategies for waging nuclear war are discussed openly in bloodcurdling detail— "limited nuclear war," civilian versus military targeting, weapons that destroy people but spare inanimate objects, and so on—in the Soviet Union these matters are left exclusively to the discretion of a small body of military experts. As a result of the imposition of near-total secrecy on its own nuclear deployments and strategies, Moscow is able to create the impression that it does not even consider such matters and builds weapons solely to protect itself from "nuclear maniacs."

It is in the interest of the Soviet Union to depict the nuclear weapon, however employed, as capable of destroying life on earth—regardless of whether this is objectively true or not. In order to keep this threat clearly in front of the Western public, it insists that not only can there be no limited use of nuclear weapons, as postulated by NATO's theory of "flexible response," but that any resort to these weapons will inevitably unleash a nuclear holocaust. This is not a strategic doctrine, since Soviet nuclear deployments clearly indicate that Moscow entertains a variety of its own "flexible responses"; it is, rather, a psychological device, a means of behavioural manipulation. It helps to establish the principle which is at the heart of the current Soviet political strategy towards the West, that good relations with the Soviet Union must become the supreme objective of Western policy. This principle is conveyed by a series of half-truths linked by a pseudo logic, the appeal of which is not to the mind but to the heart. It is designed to translate the natural dread that most people have of war in general and nuclear war in particular into an overwhelming anxiety that paralyses thought and will. The chain of casuistic reasoning runs approximately as follows: (1) nuclear war would destroy life on earth; (2) since life is the highest good, anything is preferable to nuclear war; (3) nuclear war can be avoided only if the interests of the Soviet Union and its bloc are respected; (4) the interests of the Soviet Union and its bloc are determined by the Soviet government; (5) any challenge to the wishes of the Soviet government, therefore, threatens nuclear war and extinction of life on this planet. From this sequence of reasoning, whose connections are anything but logical, it follows that every Soviet action, no matter how aggressive and immoral, need not be condoned but must be acquiesced to for the sake of the supreme objective, preservation of good relations with the Soviet Union, which alone makes it possible to preserve peace, which in turn ensures the survival of mankind.

The Soviet Union has achieved remarkable success with this specious argument. One can often hear Western intellectuals and politicians echo it with a conviction worthy of a better cause. Thus, Congressman Jonathan Bingham of New York has expressed the following sentiment:

Above all, we must remember that the Soviet Union remains the world's only other superpower—the only country in the world capable of destroying us. Maintaining good relations with the Soviet Union must be our *paramount* objective.[6]

On the face of it, the statement appears unexceptionally trite. But what is it really saying? That objectives of life other than physical survival, objectives which enabled our ancestors to bequeath to us the benefits of their civilization—among them, personal freedom, the rule of law, and human rights—must in our age take second place to "good relations with the Soviet Union"? That should other powers also acquire the capacity to destroy us, "good relations" with them will also have to become our "paramount objective"? That we must give the Soviet government carte blanche to perpetrate inside its country and abroad any barbarity as long as it refrains from firing nuclear weapons at us? It is doubtful that Congressman Bingham had thought through the implications of his words, they seemed such a reassuring string of clichés, but whether he knew it or not, he had adopted the Soviet definition of peace.

Another example of this mentality, in some respects even more appalling, comes from Carl-Friedrich von Weizsäcker, the current President of West Germany. The author is a distinguished scientist who has close connections with the leadership of the German Social-Democratic Party. He felt no compunction in saying, in what appears to be oblique criticism of President Reagan:

A policy which divides the world into the good and the evil, and which views the greatest power alongside which it is our destiny to live as the centre of evil is not a policy of peace *even if its moral judgments are correct.*[7]

What Mr Weizsäcker seems to be saying is that in relations with a nuclear power of the first magnitude, moral judgments have to be suspended or at least not voiced. Morality itself is subordinated to the cause of "peace," in the sense of getting along with "the greatest power"—that is, the Soviet Union. Inconsistently, Mr Weizsäcker does not condemn Soviet leaders for abusing the United States in incomparably more offensive terms; for some reason he does not consider abusive pronouncements when they emanate from Moscow as a disservice to the cause of peace. Such are the inconsistencies and immoralities one is driven into when one adopts the principle that survival is the supreme goal of individuals and nations.

Once the principle has been established that irritating or standing up to the Soviet Union must be avoided at all costs, no matter how grave the provocation, an important psychological battle has been lost. In this atmosphere, the Soviet Union is able to set the rules for the conduct of international relations in a manner that gives it licence to perpetrate any outrage short of launching nuclear weapons without having to worry about reactions other than opprobrium; and, if Herr von Weizsäcker has his way, even opprobrium will be silenced. Should this view prevail, the driving force behind the foreign policy of Western powers will no longer be the commitment to protect national interest or the values of Western civilization, but the naked terror of the caveman. Terror-driven fear, however, lends itself to political exploitation. The subject has not attracted much attention from scholars; among the few to have considered it is the Swiss writer Urs Schwarz. Mr Schwarz draws a useful distinction between fear proper (*Fürcht*), which he defines as a healthy response to an identifiable threat that produces a defensive reaction, and anxiety (*Angst*) which is a generalized condition of fear, focused on no particular threat, and, as such, liable to feed on itself and to paralyse the will. Referring to nuclear weapons, he says:

> That the danger in the technical sense is real and that the accumulated forces of destruction are monstrous, requires neither emphasis nor proof. One knows them and has every reason to be deeply concerned. But the attitude of the majority of the people towards these facts is not one of fear or of concern but of pronounced anxiety . . . It is precisely in this connection that the distinction between fear and anxiety assumes great significance . . . While fear . . . is an entirely desirable reaction to the threat of nuclear weapons, because it makes possible the reaction of deterrence and thereby prevents war, anxiety can produce the contrary effect.[8]

Andrei Sakharov has warned the West of the dangers of accepting the Soviet "rules of the game" in international relations. But as with much else that concerns this wise and brave man, he is praised and his counsel ignored. Manipulation of the international rules of conduct to its exclusive benefit, against a general climate of nuclear terror, is one of the most effective and least noted tools of Soviet foreign policy. Of the rules skewed in favour of the communist bloc the following may serve as examples:

• The so-called Brezhnev Doctrine, which insists that any country that has crossed the line separating "feudalism" or "capitalism" from communism must under no conditions revert to its previous status, whereas all non-communist social and political systems are subject to change of ownership at all times. This principle of one-way change, tacitly accepted by the West, ensures that the East-West competition over spheres of influence takes place exclusively at the expense of the West or third parties.

• In any region where they come under attack from communist guerrillas, non-communist governments (e.g. in El Salvador) are subjected to international pressure to negotiate with their armed opponents; when the same situation arises in countries under communist control (e.g. Nicaragua, Afghanistan, Angola) such pressures are absent.

• The Soviet Union claims that its interests extend to every region of the globe—in the words of Andrei Gromyko "today [1971] there is no question of any significance that can be decided without the Soviet Union or in opposition to it."[9] This claim allows Moscow to demand a voice in the solution of regional crises in any part of the world. At the same time, the Soviet Union denies other countries, the United States included, a comparable right; in high-level negotiation between the two countries, Soviet representatives insist that the agenda remain strictly confined to bilateral issues, which, in practice, means arms control.

• The Soviet Union claims the prerogative of engaging in unrestrained "ideological warfare" even under conditions of *détente*. This concept embraces hate campaigns against the United States, official pronouncements linking it with Nazi Germany, and predictions of the inevitable doom of the "capitalist" order. When, however, a Western statesman, such as President Reagan, refers to communism as a historic failure or the "focus of evil," outraged voices in the Soviet establishment and in the West complain of bellicosity and dangerous interference in the internal affairs of another "superpower."

• The Soviet Union demands and receives the right to present its views on international affairs in Western media; no comparable right is accorded to Western spokesmen in Soviet media.

• The Soviet Union is suffered to manufacture and deploy nuclear missiles with an unmistakable first-strike capability; when the United States commissions similar weapons, it is accused of "destabilizing" the nuclear balance and provoking war.

This double standard cannot be defended on grounds of either logic or equity; it is nevertheless widely accepted and rationalized by left-of-centre opinion in Western countries. The Brezhnev Doctrine goes unchallenged in the name of "realism." It would be "unrealistic," the argument runs, to try to alter the map of Eastern Europe or to remove Castro, even though these communist regimes are admittedly unpopular and maintain themselves in power by the force of arms. (Oddly enough, the principle of realism is not invoked in regard to Israel's presence on the West Bank or South Africa's in Namibia.) Communist guerrillas are said to embody irresistible forces of social progress, whereas their anti-communist counterparts stand for reaction. The one-sided Soviet access to Western media is defended as proof of democracy's superiority.

Soviet strategy has had much success in enforcing the principle that the West must present it with no proposal concerning East-West relations that Moscow has declared in advance to be unacceptable to it. As a consequence, East-West negotiations often take place within the Western camp, the contending parties arguing among themselves over the best terms that may reasonably be offered to Moscow. Proposals considered unacceptable to Moscow are rejected *a priori*, without a discussion of their intrinsic merits. An instance of such self-regulation occurred in the summer of 1983. During testimony before the Senate Foreign Relations Committee, the new director of the Arms Control and Disarmament Agency, Kenneth Adelman, came under pressure to define what weapons the Russians would have to give up to make it possible to cancel the MX programme. Mr Adelman objected that this question could not be meaningfully answered; but as the questioners would not relent, he volunteered that a dismantling of the Soviet SS-17, SS-18 and SS-19 systems would allow the United States to dispense with its new ICBM system.

How seriously Mr Adelman meant this answer to be taken need not detain us. What matters is that the discussion that ensued centred not on the question whether the proposal was sensible and fair, but whether it would be acceptable to the Soviet Union. Senator Charles Mathias reacted at once negatively: he said that the administration "has made impossible demands" on Moscow. Deputy Secretary of State Kenneth Dam, testifying in Congress, expressed the opinion that "to talk about eliminating an entire weapons system would go far beyond anything . . . the Soviets are willing to talk about."[10] By contrast, when the United States government made it known that it found entirely unacceptable Soviet proposals for a "nuclear freeze," no clamour was raised on either side of the Atlantic for the Soviet Union to give it up on the grounds of its "unacceptability" to the United States. In this case, whatever discussion took place concentrated on the merits of the Soviet proposal.

The impressive successes of the Soviet strategy of political divisiveness are in good measure explicable by the cooperation that it receives from witting and witless elements in the West.

Moscow has few reliable followers in NATO countries. In most of them, communist parties enjoy little influence; in the few where they do dispose of a significant following, the local leaders often openly take issue with Soviet policies. Here and there, communists manage to penetrate and capture the leadership of trade unions, church organizations, and other public bodies; they establish or support institutes that turn out pseudo-academic publications supportive of Soviet interests; they muster temporary alliances of "progressives" to oppose United States involvement in some Central America country or to pressure the United States to adopt a more "flexible" response to a Soviet arms proposal. If, however, the Soviet Union had to rely exclusively on these elements to advance its political strategy, it would scarcely be able to achieve much.

Of incomparably greater value to it are individuals and groups that have sympathy neither for communism nor for the Soviet Union, but who, for reasons of their own, often unconnected with security considerations, find themselves supporting Soviet causes and abetting Soviet political strategy. They are the "useful idiots" whom Lenin had long ago taught his followers to exploit.

Democratic societies are oriented towards the satisfaction of private interests; the public sector exists for, and justifies itself by, its ability to create optimal conditions for the pursuit of such interests. Ideally, it should have no interests of its own; the democratic state is meant to be a service organization. Under any circumstances short of armed conflict, the democratic state finds its citizenry loath to sacrifice private interests to those of national security. This makes it possible for the most bizarre informal alliances to be formed between Western groups and Moscow. An American businessman who receives orders from the USSR but cannot fill them because he is unable to obtain an export licence looks upon Moscow as a friendly customer and upon Washington as a foe. An American politician who wants public money to fund "social" programmes (an activity not unconnected with the garnering of votes) finds himself at one with Moscow in opposing increased United States defence expenditures. Rivals of the party in office derive malicious satisfaction from its foreign policy failures, since these vindicate their opposition and bring the time nearer when they may come to power. As long as East-West competition remains at an acceptable—that is, non-violent—level, major private interests in the West find it to their advantage to stress alleged similarities between East and West and to minimize the Soviet threat. In so doing, they are, in effect, making common cause with Moscow.

Weapon manufacturers apart, it is difficult to think of a group in the West that has a vested interest in bad relations with the communist bloc. And the production of military hardware is neither a significant nor a particularly profitable sector of Western economies, notwithstanding the mythology that surrounds the subject. The list of the 400 wealthiest Americans, published annually by *Forbes* magazine, carries no names of arms manufacturers; it indicates that the road to riches leads by way of oil, real estate, computers or cosmetics, not national defence. The so-called hard-line trend in United States foreign policy is almost exclusively ideological in motivation: it brings little, if any, profit. It is in the "soft-line" end of the spectrum that one can identify a wide range of self-interest. This interest can assume various forms, material and other.

To begin with the academic community. In the 1930s, university circles showed a great deal of sympathy for communism, but of this little remains. Western specialists on the Soviet Union in particular are, with few exceptions, highly critical of that country and regard sojourn there as hardship duty. Professional considerations, however, compel most of them to keep their opinions to themselves. A "sovietologist" feels that he must be able to travel to the USSR from time to time to consort with specialists there and to carry out research in libraries and archives. Since public criticism of the Soviet system or its actions may result in visa denials, the typical expert will not speak out on East-West relations other than in a most circumspect manner, balancing criticism of the one side with condemnation of the other. He will also strongly endorse cultural and scientific exchanges, even when these can be shown to be inequitable because he is eager to ensure for himself access to the countries in which he specializes.

In broader intellectual and academic circles an interesting ambivalence prevails in regard to this subject. Most Western writers, scholars and scientists look upon the Soviet regime and its clients with unconcealed distaste. They are disgusted with the suppression of freedom there and the persecution of their friends and colleagues. They readily sign letters and petitions protesting such uncivilized behaviour; some even go to the lengths of boycotting conferences held in communist countries. But there is always present, especially among self-styled social scientists frustrated in their ambition to gain the prestige accorded to genuine scientists, an undercurrent of resentment against their own societies for not treating them with the proper respect, and, related to it, envy of their counterparts in the East. Although they entertain no illusions about the price which the communist authorities exact, they begrudge the distinctions and privileges that faithful service to the *nomenklatura* brings with it, and of which they feel unjustly deprived. Such sentiments are quite common among Western academicians, although they are rarely expressed with the candour that the British historian A. J. P. Taylor displayed in his report on a visit to Hungary: "The treatment of [Hungarian] historians and other scholars fills me with envy," he confessed on his return—

> The Institute of Historical Research in Budapest has extensive quarters on Castle Hill and over 60 paid researchers on its staff. The comparable English Institute in London has modest quarters in the Senate House and no paid researchers. The Hungarian Academy has a palace all to itself just across from the Parliament House: colonnaded entrance and marble staircase. The Academy also owns country cottages, on Lake Balaton and in the mountains, which members of the Academy can use for free during the summer. The British Academy occupies a few rooms in Burlington House and possess no country cottages.

Professor Taylor cannot be ignorant that the colonnaded entrances, marble staircases, and country cottages that have aroused such envy in him must be paid for in directed research, censorship, and other forms of intellectual humiliation. Even so, he resents society for denying him the rewards he considers rightfully his; and he does so despite the evidence that he himself adduces that the Hungarian academics themselves do not seem aware "how well off they are," for it appears that during his visit most of them were out of the country on sabbaticals in England, the United States and Finland.[11]

Allowance must also be made for public groups and their patrons in the federal and state governments who draw on money raised through taxes (or paid for with deficits) to subsidize their programmes and pay their salaries. The powerful associations of teachers and health-care personnel, for example, have a vested interest in keeping the defence budget as small as possible, since that budget is in direct competition with their own for public funds. To keep defence budgets small, they minimize the Soviet threat, and represent the real danger to United States security as coming from inadequately financed social services. It helps to assess the quality of this argument by imagining how it would have sounded in the 1930s, when the Nazis were arming for war, had it been said of Poland, Britain or France that they were threatened not by the Wehrmacht, but by inadequately funded schools and hospitals. Self-serving and specious as this argument is, it has persuasive force, because it involves immense sums of money and affects the welfare of millions of voters.

The most unabashed voice in the West favouring accommodation with the Soviet Union, however, belongs to the business community. On the face of it, pro-Soviet sympathies on the part of a group that Soviet Union is committed to destroying may seem absurd, but it is a fact that only serves to emphasize the élitist character of the Soviet leadership and the affinities that élites feel for each other, notwithstanding ideological or national differences. The workers of all countries have never united as effectively as have their ruling élites, which constitute the only true international. In United States elections, as a rule, the most "liberal" candidates fare best in precincts with educated and affluent voters, whereas conservative ones draw their support from the poorer classes. This trend runs contrary to historical experience: conservatism has traditionally been the ideology of the privileged who have a vested interest in the status quo and oppose change. The Soviet *nomenklatura*, which is a rigidly conservative body, conforms to this pattern. Public-opinion polls further indicate that in the United States, the desire for accommodation with the Soviet Union is strongest among the educated upper-income groups, and declines as one moves down the educational and social scale, yielding among the lower strata to belligerent anti-communism. It surely is astonishing that Soviet emissaries are received with open arms by the National Association of Manufacturers and the

Chamber of Commerce, but dare not set foot in the headquarters of American trade-union organizations.*

This unnatural goodwill for the Soviet Union of those who stand to lose the most should it attain its ultimate objectives is most readily explained by commercial interests. The United States business community has always believed that the Soviet Union constitutes a vast potential market for its capital and goods. Its representatives beat a path to Lenin's Moscow as soon as the last shots of the civil war had died down, in search of profitable concessions and contracts.[12] Experience has never borne out these expectations. Because the Soviet government is chronically short of both capital and goods to sell in industrial countries, its hope for extensive trade with the West rests on receipt of loans, either issued or guaranteed by Western governments.

The United States government has not adopted the practice of European states in this respect; indeed, in the early 1970s it imposed stringent limits on the amount of credits the Import-Export Bank could extend to the Soviet Union. As a consequence, United States-Soviet trade has never come near the levels that its advocates in both countries had hoped for. In the 1970s, during the era of *détente*, the total non-agricultural trade between the two countries (imports and exports combined) hovered around one billion dollars a year. United States non-agricultural exports to the USSR between 1971 and 1981 averaged annually slightly over $500 million; even in the second half of the decade, when the USSR had begun to make large-scale agricultural purchases, exports barely reached $2 billion. Total United States imports from the USSR remained through this decade in the low hundreds of millions.[13] United States imports from the Soviet Union even before the Afghanistan embargoes (1979) were one half those from Trinidad and Tobago. In spite of this disappointing record, United States corporations continue to look toward significant expansion in trade with the USSR, once political relations are improved. Leading business executives stand in the forefront of organizations dedicated to promoting better relations between the two countries; they vigorously oppose punitive sanctions and embargoes; and they are the most vociferous champions of arms control and summit meetings. The *nomenklatura*, which realizes these facts very well, courts the business community with great zeal, not only

* The first (and, so far, last) occasion when a Soviet dignitary met with US labour leaders occurred in January 1959, when Deputy Prime Minister Anastas Mikoyan paid a visit to the AFL-CIO. In the spirit of bourgeois goodwill, *The New York Times* (7 Jan. 1959) reported that "although some embarrassing questions [were] raised there had been no heated exchanges," conveying the impression that the guest and hosts parted amicably. In reality, as is known from an eyewitness (John Herling in the *New Leader*, 2 Feb. 1959, 3–6), the encounter turned highly acrimonious as US labour leaders pressed Mikoyan about Soviet policies and practices. After heated exchanges, Mikoyan said: "The American trade-union leaders were more antagonistic to the Soviet Union than were the American capitalists whom I have met." This has always been the case.

because it hopes to reap economic benefits from this quarter, but also and above all because it regards "capitalist" businessmen as their most effective lever in Washington. In Western Europe, whose commercial relations with Moscow are much more extensive, the business and banking communities play a critical role in promoting the spirit of *détente* and pressuring for NATO's de-coupling of commercial dealings from political relations with the Soviet bloc.

Still, the number of business enterprises actually or even potentially involved in United States–Soviet trade is too small and their turnover too low to explain the commitment of the United States business élite to friendly relations with the Soviet Union regardless of the outrages which that country perpetrates or its hostile actions against the United States. The deeper causes for this phenomenon must be sought in social and cultural factors.

The modern corporate officer bears little resemblance to the classic bourgeois entrepreneur; he lacks the latter's spirit of individualism, his belief in himself and in his contribution to society, and his ethical values. He is a bureaucrat to whom stands open the path to potentially unlimited rewards, but whose personal status, as that of any salaried employee, is insecure. The corporation is his world; there is little connection between his personal morals and his work ethic. In these respects he has a great deal of affinity with a functionary of the *nomenklatura* with the difference that while he strives for higher profits, his Soviet counterpart strives for higher productivity. An American business executive instinctively understands a Soviet industrial manager, for, like him, he wants above all to get things done; like him, he views workers' demands as an impediment to higher production and profits, and intellectuals who talk of human rights as impractical dreamers. Today, the classic bourgeois can be found mainly in the younger branches of the economy, which risk-taking and private ownership continue to predominate. This type of businessman tends to be conservative in his politics. Executives of large, established and public corporations incline towards unideological pragmatism.

The other factor, even more imponderable, is snobbery. In the drawing rooms of New York's East Side, Georgetown, Cambridge or Beverly Hills, one is unlikely to meet with pro-Soviet sympathies; this sort of thing has long gone out of fashion. The occasional communist who turns up in these circles is treated as an eccentric, rather endearing if he happens to be rich—a millionaire communist is, after all, not unlike a missionary who champions cannibalism. But anti-communism is taboo. It is regarded as vulgar and low class, conjuring images of Senator McCarthy, the Moral Majority, and other unspeakable subjects. In contemporary America and Britain, anti-anti-communism has become an important indicator of social status. Such use of ideas as a device for separating the right from the wrong persons cannot be new, since three-quarters of a century ago Arnold Bennett had a character in one of his plays say that "it isn't views that are disreputable, it's the people who hold them."

That anti-anti-communism should have become a hallmark of superior social standing has probably a great deal to do with the shifting standards by which such standing is defined. As Hilton Kramer has pointed out, the diffusion of affluence and the democratization of life-styles which it has made possible, have debased, one by one, the tokens with the help of which the upper classes have traditionally distinguished themselves from their inferiors; art, sexual freedom, travel and good food are now accessible to the multitude and are, therefore, useless as status indicators. Politics is virtually the last reliable social indicator left. "There, as nowhere else, the appeals of snobbery remain sharply defined. Nothing else nowadays gives people of a certain taste such confident sense of the chasm that divides 'us' from 'them.' "[14] Since the common man, to judge by labour unions and mass-circulation newspapers, is patriotic and anti-communist, patriotism and anti-communism have become unacceptable to anyone with social aspirations. . . .

We have identified a number of factors in Western societies which create an atmosphere favourable to Moscow's strategy of political divisiveness. The resentment of intellectuals and academics of what they consider shabby treatment at the hands of their societies; the desire of businessmen to trade without political interference; the need of politicians and special-interest groups for funds from the defence budget; the quest of climbers for social symbols in a world where these have become scarce—all these combine to make influential segments of democratic society unwilling to face the threat to their country's security and prone to minimize it or even deny that it exists.

The power of these groups is much magnified by the influence they exert over the media. That the media, especially the prestige organs, are dominated by people given to anti-anti-communist views, people for whom the main danger to the United States comes from internal failures rather than from external threats, can be in some measure statistically demonstrated. In a 1979–80 survey, 240 editors and reporters of the most influential newspapers, magazines and television networks in the United States indicated that in the preceding two decades four out of five of them had voted for Democratic candidates; in 1972, 81 per cent had cast ballots for George McGovern, a Presidential candidate rejected by the voters in 49 of the 50 states.[15] The situation is similar in Europe; in West Germany, for instance, three-quarters of the journalists employed in television are described as left of centre.[16] Among members of the self-designated public-interest groups in the United States (e.g. consumer and environmental protection societies) the prevalence of such sentiments is higher still—96 per cent of the persons polled from such groups stated that they had voted for McGovern; they further expressed preference for Fidel Castro over Ronald Reagan by a margin of nearly seven to one.[17]

To derive maximal benefit from their convergence of interest with the inward-oriented, isolationist liberal establishment in the United States, Soviet foreign policy specialists have concocted an artificial language of international communication. Its purpose is to create the illusion that the totalitarian East and the democratic West not only have no quarrel but share a common destiny. The threat to democratic societies, this synthetic jargon says, comes not from communist regimes and their aggressive actions, but from nuclear weapons, the arms race and, above all, anti-Sovietism, which the two sides have an equal interest in liquidating. Once this language becomes assimilated by non-communist societies, the communality of language conveys the sense of a communality of interest. Much of the terminology currently employed in the West for East-West relations has either been coined by Soviet specialists or extracted by them from Western liberal sources, assigned the desired meaning, and frozen into mandatory clichés.

A veritable treasury of cant deployed for this specific purpose can be found in a recent book of interviews with Mr George Arbatov. The best-known (if not necessarily the most influential) Soviet expert on the United States, Mr Arbatov has paid many visits to this country, in the course of which he established close contacts with liberal intellectuals and *détente*-prone businessmen. His fluency in English and mastery of the American liberal patois have earned him among his American admirers the reputation of a man who speaks with the authentic voice of the Russian people. In *The Soviet Viewpoint* he draws on the whole gamut of newspeak to assure his readers that the United States and the Soviet Union have one common enemy, the "hard-liners" in Washington:

> The eerie thing about *The Soviet Viewpoint*, written in the form of several long interviews . . . conducted by Dutch journalist Willem Oltmans, is that Georgi Arbatov seems to be impersonating Cyrus Vance.
>
> What the book stunningly reveals is Arbatov's sophistication about American liberalism. He knows its peculiar gullibility, and he speaks its idiom with near-perfect nuance. No "running dogs" or "Wall Street lackeys" or "capitalist bloodsuckers" here; Arbatov utters the Leninist vision in terms that might have been lifted from *Foreign Affairs*.
>
> Soviet-American relations have need of *reciprocity*. We must seek *mutually acceptable solutions*. Let us avoid *confrontation*, but instead confront *new realities*, eschewing the while any *mood of nostalgia* that might lead to a *new cold war* (much as such a development might please *hard-liners in Washington*, who are fond of *saber-rattling*).

This is a time for *international cooperation*. We face *global problems*, such as the *depletion of natural resources*, which can't be dealt with through *old perceptions inherited from the cold war*.

Whether one likes it or not, we are chained together on this planet. We dare not treat the situation as a *zero-sum game*, or *continue to squander our resources through the arms race*. Not *if we are to avoid doomsday*. It is imperative that we pursue the *possibility of lessening tensions*, of *lowering the level of military confrontation*.

Despite our *different social systems* there are *overriding common interests, that call for cooperation*. *We are talking of human survival on this planet, of today's increasingly complex, fragile, and interdependent world*.

The real issue is the *quality of life*. If we are serious about *building a new society*, we must combine a genuine commitment to *social spending* with *a new, broader approach to human rights*.

Remember, *the Vietnam War torpedoed the Great Society*, and in a nuclear war, *there will be no winners*. Think of the *human cost*! Not only of *the war threatening humanity*, but of any *new massive military build-up*.

Any *significant improvement* in the *infrastructure* must be *viewed in the context* of the phenomena of *wide-spread alienation* and *social atomization* stemming from *McCarthyist witch-hunts*, and the *long-term trends* that culminated in *Watergate* with all its attendant *pressures for change* in the *military-industrial complex* whose *macho* posturing has thus far precluded *meaningful redistribution . . . social expenditures . . . purely internal Afghan development . . . .*

"There's hardly a sentence in this book, " the author of the review concludes, "that couldn't have been picked up on the narrow frequency band between *The New York Times* and the Institute for Policy Studies."[18]

On the face of it, such abuse of language may appear harmless—what, indeed, is linguistic pollution against the danger of nuclear war? But language does shape the framework within which people think and communicate; he who controls the vocabulary exerts powerful influence on the content of thought and speech. Thus, the absence from their authorized vocabulary of such terms as *Holocaust* and *Gulag* makes it difficult for citizens of the Soviet Union to discuss these phenomena in public. Oliver Wendell Holmes rightly classified "verbicide" as a major crime. . . .

Until the middle 1950s, linguistic regimentation was confined to the Soviet Union and foreign communist parties. Stalin did not attempt to impose his terminology on anyone outside his political control. Things have changed since his death. The appearance of the "bomb" made it possible for Soviet propagandists to argue that humanity shares one destiny, that is "chained together," in Mr Arbatov's phrase: coexistence of this sort calls for a common language. Over the past 30 years, a Soviet-type jargon has been spreading over the world; it pervades discussion of everything that touches on East-West relations and increasingly replicates the situation which prevails inside communist societies.

> By calling "autonomous" that which is powerless, "federated" that which is unitary, "democratic" that which is autocratic, "united" that which is schismatic, "popular" that which is imposed by terror, "peaceful" that which incites war—in brief, by systematically corrupting language to obscure reality—the Communists have made inroads into our sense of political reality. Language is, after all, the only medium in which we can think. It is exceedingly difficult to eliminate all the traditional connotations of words—to associate words like "For a lasting peace and a People's Democracy" with neither peace nor popular movements nor democracy.[19]

To disparage the United States–Chinese *rapprochement*, Soviet propagandists have put into circulation the condescending term "China card," and to denigrate United States' use of satellites to verify arms-control agreements they dub them "spies in the sky." Sometimes, Soviet language manipulation goes to ridiculous lengths, as when censors insist that Soviet publications refer to the army that is ravaging Afghanistan as "the limited contingent of Soviet troops in Afghanistan" and never in another way.

By formulating and consistently using terms applicable to international relations in the desired mode, Moscow accords them legitimacy even when they bear no relationship to anything real—terms such as "peaceful coexistence," "Zionist racism," or "Polish counter-revolution." The vocabulary of East-West relations, shared by Western liberals and the Soviet apparatus, serves the same purpose as the official jargon inside the Soviet Union. It focuses the discussion on matters that are desired but may or may not exist, and places out of bounds subjects that emphatically do exist but are deemed best unmentioned. It perverts one's perception of phenomena by attaching to them pejorative words when they are considered inimical, and positive ones when they are useful. Thus, the countries of Eastern Europe under the occupation of the Soviet army are labelled "People's Democracies." Such usage is not only deceptive but absurdly tautological: since "democracy" means "people's rule," a "people's democracy" is "people's rule by the people." Because "communism" evokes negative images in the West, it has been gradually supplanted with "socialism." For some time now, Moscow has been calling its bloc the "socialist camp," and this usage too has spread to Western media. The title General Secretary suggests a bureaucratic dictator, so for purposes of foreign dealings it has been replaced with that of President, which, in the Soviet context, is meaningless. How much easier it is, however, to meet and shake hands with the "President" of a "socialist country" than with the dictator of a communist one!

Liberal journalists not only have assimilated much of this vocabulary but also introduced refinements of their own, which are promptly borrowed by Moscow. They routinely call someone critical of the Soviet Union a "hard-line anti-communist," but never refer to anyone as a "soft-line pro-communist," even though every adjective demands its opposite. "Extremist," when applied to a person's views on the Soviet Union, invariably means anti-communist, a pro-Soviet "extremist" being unknown to journalism—the latter is a "moderate."

Linguistic manipulation leads to intellectual confusion, and as such it is dangerous. It enables Soviet political strategists to dominate the intellectual climate of East-West relations and to insinuate themselves into Western political discussions. It allows them to project false identities of interest between the two systems and to incite internecine conflicts of opinion as well as of interest within the Western community. It blurs the line between fiction and reality. If this is allowed to go on, the day may well come when Western citizens, like Stalin in his waning years, will be regaled with specially prepared films that show the world basking in peace, while "limited contingents of Soviet troops" are shooting their way into their homes.

WHO SHOULD BE IN CHARGE OF POLICY TOWARDS THE USSR?

The Department of State is widely thought of as the proper agency to conduct the foreign policy of the United States; an arrogation of this responsibility by another agency of the government is seen as a violation of both the constitutional division of powers and of good political practices. This view is incorrect on two counts. The constitution, in effect, charges the President with the conduct of foreign affairs, so no matter how much authority the President may decide to delegate to his Secretary of State, the ultimate responsibility is his. This means that the State Department cannot be the prime mover of foreign policy: constitutionally it is the agency that implements the President's will.

This holds true also for reasons of practical politics. The belief that the State Department is the proper instrument of foreign policy derives from the fallacious view that foreign policy is synonymous with diplomacy—which, as has been pointed out, is not the case. The Department of State is the branch of government specifically responsible for diplomacy in all its aspects, and this involves, first and foremost, the peaceful resolution of disagreements and conflicts with other sovereign states. This task has a great deal in common with law. And indeed, on closer acquaintance, the Department gives the impression of a giant law firm. Its staff of Foreign Service officers, many of them highly competent in the area of their responsibility, are professionally trained to reach agreements—a successful diplomat is by definition one who knows how to negotiate an agreement favourable to his country. Diplomats have an instinctive aversion to violence and an insurmountable suspicion of ideology; the one is to them evidence of professional failure, the other, a hindrance to accords. Foreign Service officers have as much taste for ideas and political strategies as trial lawyers have for the philosophy of law. They squirm at the very mention of the words *good* and *evil*, which in their professional capacity they regard as meaningless. Since ideas lead to ideology, they scorn ideas, contrasting them with "pragmatism," which in practice means muddling through from case to case, from crisis to crisis, without the need even to consider long-term objectives. They are capable of drafting meticulously crafted position papers setting out policy recommendations or options, without ever asking themselves what the ultimate purpose of these policies is to be. Their attitude towards the representative of even the most hostile power is somewhat like that of one attorney to another: they never allow anger, indignation or any other emotion to enter into their relationship, seeking instead to base it on mutual professional respect, safe in the knowledge that crises come and crises go, but lawyers stay on.

This sort of mentality serves diplomats well when the issues in dispute are specific and therefore negotiable—that is, when the parties quarrel not over the principles of law or the jurisdiction of the court, but over the facts of the case and their interpretation. Essentially, diplomacy is a device for settling disputes out of court, the court, in the case of international conflicts, being the battlefield. It is an irreplaceable method for resolving controversies over such issues as treaties, rescheduling of debts, fishing and water rights, and the myriad other issues among states that life constantly brings forth. But these issues embrace only a part, and not even necessarily the most important part, of international relations as practised in the twentieth century; the latter include also military power, ideology, and a host of other matters that are implicit in Grand Strategy and do not lend themselves to resolution by diplomatic means. As soon as international conflict is shifted to this ground, diplomacy is powerless. The natural reaction of diplomats under these circumstances is to minimize the phenomena they are incompetent to deal with, so as to reduce everything to manageable—that is, negotiable—terms, where their particular skills can come into play.

Because totalitarian regimes do not operate within a narrowly defined concept of foreign policy, the collective record of the world's foreign service in dealing with them has been most unimpressive. By virtue of their professional upbringing, diplomats could never take seriously the ravings of a Lenin, a Hitler or a Mao, and so they dismissed them as rhetoric behind which had to lie concealed the dictator's "real" demands, and concentrated on discovering what those alleged "real" demands were, in order to bring them to the negotiating table. Appeasement, whether of Hitler or of Stalin, so rampant in the foreign offices in their day, was due neither to stupidity nor to treason, but to a *déformation professionelle* of foreign offices. It is astonishing to read, for instance, in what cavalier manner British and American diplomats during the Second World War dismissed the flow of reports that the Nazis were engaged in a systematic programme of exterminating Jews, on the grounds that such things could not be.* One may expand this point and say that most of totalitarian politics, with its ideology, Grand Strategy, psychological warfare, and programmed brutality is outside the intellectual ken and therefore beyond the professional reach of diplomacy. It is, therefore, no service to the Department of State or the profession of diplomacy to charge them with responsibility for problems that they were never meant to cope with.

Thus, for both constitutional reasons and reasons connected with the peculiarities of totalitarian politics, the State Department is not the proper agency to formulate and execute foreign policy towards the Soviet Union or any other totalitarian state. These states play by different rules and must be dealt with accordingly. Since they employ Grand Strategy, to the extent that democracies are capable of coordinated foreign policies, these must be undertaken by the chief executive. In the United States, the natural locus for such coordination is the office of the President and his staff, the National Security Council. At the time of its founding in 1949, the NSC was formally and specifically charged with responsibilty for advising the President "with respect to the integration of domestic, foreign and military policies relating to national security"—which is precisely what Grand Strategy is supposed to accomplish. The National Security Council alone is sufficiently close to the President to know his thoughts and political interests. Because it is not a Department, with a large bureaucracy or an influential outside constituency, it is best qualified to coordinate the various branches of administration, which tend to advance contradictory interests and demands. And because it combines in miniature all the skills that go into a Grand Strategy—politics, economics, the military and intelligence—it possesses a unique capability of formulating the kind of foreign policy that the professional diplomat abhors but the current situation requires. The transfer, under President Reagan (on Secretary Haig's insistence) of the main foreign policy coordinating bodies (inter-agency committees) from the NSC to State has had a very detrimental influence on the administration's ability to translate the President's approach to East-West relations into concrete policy. At every occasion, State Department staff sought to water down attempts at developing a United States strategy. Its preference has been and continues to be for traditional

* See, for example, a report that the US Department of State rejected information of this nature received from the representative of the World Jewish Congress in Geneva, who in turn had obtained this information from a well-informed German industrialist, as "fantastic" and "unsubstantiated." (*The Washington Post*, 28 Sept. 1983, A2.)

"dialogues" with Moscow . . . . It has an abiding faith that agreements on small issues lead to accords on major ones, although the entire history of Soviet foreign policy shows this faith to be misplaced. Whenever the NSC sought to assert what clearly were the President's wishes, the alarmed Department of State would intercede, provoking political and jurisdictional disputes. This, of course, is nothing new; rivalry between NSC and State is embedded in the system. Every President seeks to resolve it, usually by making the Secretary of State responsible for foreign policy. It is an unworkable solution as long as there are in the world countries not heirs to that Western diplomatic tradition of which the Secretary of State is the American custodian—and this is likely to be for some time to come.

Soviet policy is conducted globally from the International Department of the Central Committee. This being the case, it would be desirable for the United States to create a counterpart institution to monitor Soviet activities globally. As of now, no such body exists: neither at the National Security Council, nor at the Department of State, nor at the Central Intelligence Agency is there a group of experts who follow from day to day the plans and activities of the International Department. The situation in the Department of State in this respect is remarkably antiquated, dating in conception to the nineteenth century. The principal political desks at State are organized on the geographic principle: the Soviet Union comes within the purview of the Assistant Secretary for European Affairs, who is also responsible for all of Western and Eastern Europe, and, as if this were not enough, Canada as well. An official responsible for this vast area, where are located most of the allies of the United States, must of necessity devote his attention mainly to relations with friendly states. He thus has neither the time nor the personnel to deal adequately with the central problem of United States foreign policy, which is the Soviet bloc.

To make matters still worse, because of the regional nature of the political desks, no one office at State is responsible for tracking the international communist movement as such: the Latin American desk follows Soviet activities in Cuba and Nicaragua; the African desk those in Angola; the Middle Eastern desk gathers information on Soviet activities in Syria and Lebanon. There is no overview and therefore no sense of Soviet Grand Strategy or of the fluctuating Soviet "line" in regard to broader issues, which are not primarily regional. The present arrangement ensures that the whole picture of Soviet global policy is broken down into disjointed fragments which the regional desks cannot properly interpret because they are not aware of the broader context into which they fit.

One way to remedy this shortcoming would be to appoint a State Department official, at the rank of Under-Secretary or Counsellor, to assume responsibility for monitoring East-West relations and Soviet strategy in their broadest sense in all the fields and in all the regions where they manifest themselves. Only in such a manner will the government feel the pulse of Soviet global activities and the Secretary of State be in a position to advise the President on an intelligent response to them. For this to happen, of course, the Secretary of State must first persuade himself that unlike the United States, the Soviet Union has a Grand Strategy that is not only pragmatic but also ideological, and not only regional but also global in scope.

NOTES

1. O. V. Kuusinen, et al. *Osnovy Marksizma-Leninizma: Uchebnoe posobie* [The Fundamentals of Marxism-Leninism: A Textbook], 2nd ed. (Moscow, 1962), p. 360.

2. Above, p. 6.

3. *"Left-Wing" Communism, an Infantile Disorder*, in *Collected Works* (Moscow, 1966), vol. XXXI, pp. 70–71.

4. *The Campaign of 1812 in Russia* (London, 1843), p. 184.

5. Hans-Adolf Jacobsen, *Der Zweite Weltkrieg* [The Second World War] (Frankfurt a/M, 1965), p. 57, p. 59.

6. With Victor C. Johnson, *Foreign Affairs*, Spring, 1979, p. 919. Emphasis added.

7. "Abschreckung—nur eine Atempause?" ["Deterrence: Only a Breathing Space?"], *Die Zeit*, No. 13 (26 March, 1982), p. 19. Emphasis added.

8. *Die Angst in der Politik* [Anxiety in Politics] (Düsseldorf and Vienna, 1967), pp. 61–62.

9. XXIV S'ezd KPSS: *Stenograficheskii otchet* [24th Congress of the CPSU: Stenographic Record] (Moscow, 1971), 1, p. 482.

10. Boston Globe, 24 June 1983 and *The New York Times*, 23 June 1983.

11. "Diary," *London Review of Books*, 17 Feb.–2 March, 1983, p. 21.

12. On the relations of US businessmen with the Soviet government, see Joseph Finder, *Red Carpet* (New York, 1983).

13. US Department of Agriculture, Economic Research Service, *USSR, Review of Agriculture in 1981 and Outlook for 1982* (Washington, DC, May, 1982), p. 13.

14. *The New Criterion*, No. 10 (June 1983), p. 3.

15. This survey, conducted by a Columbia University research institute and directed by S. Robert Lichter and Stanley Rothman, is reproduced in the *Congressional Record* of 23 March 1982, S2619–2622.

16. *Epoche*, May 1982, p. 7.

17. Survey conducted by Lichter and Rothman, summarized in *The Wall Street Journal*, 21 July 1983, under the rubric "Asides," p. 26.

18. Joe Sobran in the *Dartmouth Review*, III, No. 23 (16 May, 1983).

19. Ambassador Jeane J. Kirkpatrick, interview with George Urban, Radio Free Europe, Munich, Germany, July, 1983, p. 104.

16

Do We Still Need Europe?

ELIOT A. COHEN

For an American to suggest that we should investigate our strategic interest in Europe can sound positively subversive—tantamount to repudiating our commitment to Europe altogether, or denying Europe's value to American security. Indeed, one can make a strong case against a too-frequent investigation of the roots of the American commitment to Europe, or for that matter of any well-established foreign policy; this stricture carries particular force when we speak of an alliance as old, as firmly established, and as much in the American national interest as NATO. And yet such a reappraisal is due, and overdue. For the world has changed in many ways since the victorious statesmen and generals of World War II, in a massive departure from American tradition, advanced the first arguments for the commitment of hundreds of thousands of American soldiers to the peacetime defense of Europe.

The most obvious changes have occurred in the strategic environment, i.e., in the balance of power between the West and the Soviet Union. Since the early 1950's, when the founders of the Atlantic alliance established the current structure and basic policies of NATO, the Soviet Union has achieved nuclear parity, developed an increasingly powerful navy, and secured overseas bases and clients (Cuba and Vietnam, for example) unimaginable in 1950. The Soviet Union has also found itself confronted by new strategic threats, particularly from China, where a close alliance has been replaced by a bitter and, it would appear, enduring enmity. These developments, and others—including the withering of the Soviet Union's purely ideological appeal to Third World states—all argue for a reassessment of America's own strategic position vis-à-vis the Soviet Union and primarily in the central arena of confrontation, namely Europe.

A second reason for investigating America's strategic interest in Europe has to do with generational developments. The appearance of the "successor generation"—Americans and Europeans in their late thirties and early forties marked not by World II and the Berlin crisis but by Vietnam and the student revolts of the 1960's—has given rise to anxious inquiries about the basis of the alliance. Writers on both sides of the Atlantic seeking to reassure their readers and themselves have maintained that, although the level of annoyance among the partners has increased over the past decade, the alliance remains secure, and precisely because it is in the strategic interest of the United States that it be so. Others, however, are not so sure.

Finally we see a debate among Americans themselves over the future prospects of NATO. The chronic low level of tension which Europeans have noticed has also led many American observers to conclude that the nature of the alliance has changed. Such firm friends of Europe as Senator Sam Nunn of Georgia and former Secretary of State Henry Kissinger have suggested that the time may have come to reduce, perhaps substantially, America's military commitments to the alliance. A spirited American debate has thus begun over the place of Europe in American foreign policy.

Regrettably, lively prose rather than careful analysis has characterized that debate. On the one hand, Jeffrey Record, a prominent military analyst, declares flatly that we see before us "the manifest disintegration of NATO as a viable security organization warranting the present commitment of U.S. ground forces to Europe's forward defense." At the other end of the spectrum Robert Komer, a former senior defense official, condemns the "sin" of unilateralism, and argues in effect that nothing has changed in the American relationship with the continent over the past thirty-five years. To compound the difficulty, the interlocutors in these debates often conflate different definitions of the problem, opposing geostrategic concepts to geopolitical ones or stating the alternatives—Europe vs. the Pacific, going it alone vs. having allies, keeping resolutely to the sea vs. preparing to engage the Red Army on the continent—too starkly for useful discussion.

The art of strategic analysis does not, or should not, rest on such simple dichotomies, and in the real world statesmen do not make such bald choices. Rather, the question is one of degree—what priorities we assign in peace and war to different theaters of operations, how we structure forces to achieve their missions, and so on. Even in the most "unilateralist" view the United States will need allies, if only to project its power overseas; and even the most ardent advocate of "coalition defense" must admit that the United States as a great power has interests distinct from those of its European allies. Europe is extremely important to us, but so too is the Pacific region, specifically Japan. Command of the sea is the sine qua non of successful American containment of the Soviet Union and its allies, but (as England discovered in each of its wars against Spain, France, and Germany) command of the sea can accomplish nothing without continental power.

What follows, then, is an attempt to clarify America's strategic interest in Europe. In concentrating on the strategic question I hardly mean to dismiss or ignore economic or, perhaps even more important, ideological interests. Ideological and cultural affinities in particular have made the alliance both workable and worthwhile in ways that would be quite inconceivable in a coalition based on strategic commonality alone. We should remember, however, that America's initial commitment to Europe during World War II and, afterward, during the early 1950's, was regularly justified in terms of a strategic interest quite distinct from other and less potent interests. Although Secretary of State Dean Acheson at first made his case for the dispatch of a half-dozen American divisions to Europe in 1951 on the basis of our common culture, he went on to say, "But our policy does not rest solely upon these intangibles, important as they are." Rather,

> Outside of our own country, free Europe has the greatest number of scientists, the greatest industrial production, and the largest pool of skilled manpower in the world. Its resources in coal, steel, and electric power are enormous. It has a tremendous shipbuilding capacity, essential to control of the seas. Through its overseas connections, it has access to a vast supply of raw materials which are absolutely vital to American industry.

In short, Acheson made a strategic argument, one that was echoed by General Dwight D. Eisenhower and others, and which also reflected the opinions of the Joint Chiefs of Staff (JCS). The question we need to answer is, to what degree is this analysis still valid today?

II

It was quite clear following World War II and the dissolution of the allied coalition against Hitler that control of Western Europe would be, as the official historian of the JCS has written, "the foremost prize in the cold war." Europe was the epicenter of the world economy; indeed, it had given birth to that world economy. Although two world wars had devastated the continent, ruining industry and slaughtering millions, the fact remained that Europe still contained a skilled and energetic population and the basic material requirements for large-scale economic production. Moreover, Europe still controlled most of the non-European world, and the vital raw materials located there. British sway over the Persian Gulf safeguarded Middle Eastern oil; France and the Nether- lands controlled territories possessing similarly valuable raw materials.

Europe was thus *the* strategic stake for the United States in the immediate postwar period. With it in our camp, we could count on ultimate economic superiority over the Soviet Union: without it, we would have faced as bleak a political-military situation as that of the summer of 1940. Eisenhower put it simply: "If we take that whole complex with its potential for military exploitation and transfer it from our side to another side, the military balance of power has shifted so drastically that our safety would be gravely imperiled."

The importance of Europe as the main stake in the U.S.-Soviet competition escaped very few American statesmen and soldiers—hence the relative ease with which they could take the unprecedented action of stationing several hundred thousand American troops there to protect it from subversion and aggression during its period of recovery. Other areas of the world, including the Far East, had second priority—indeed, in the case of Japan, a priority considerably lower than that.

Europe recovered in due course from World War II, and today continues to constitute a strategic stake of the first order for the United States. Considered together, the West European states make up one of the three most productive regions of the world, accounting for some 17.3 percent of world gross national product (as opposed to 24.9 percent for the United States, 8.7 percent for Japan, and 13.8 percent for the Soviet Union). Yet a number of striking changes have occurred since the 1950's which considerably diminish the *relative* importance of Europe as a strategic stake.

Perhaps the most significant of these is the rise of Japan, and of the countries of the Pacific basin more generally. The Japanese economy, once smaller than that of any of the major European states, now far outstrips them, individually if not yet collectively. It has known a period of extraordinary sustained growth which gives no indication of stopping. The figures are most telling in the automobile industry: in 1960 Japanese automobile production stood at 165,000 units as opposed to Europe's 4,920,000; by 1980 Japan's production had leaped to 6,758,000, while Europe's had barely doubled to 9,450,000. Even more important from the point of view of long-term military-industrial potential is what has happened in electronics. American and Japanese companies lead in the development of computers, fiberoptics, and all of the associated technologies which have already begun to exert as profound an influence over military technology and warfare as did the introduction of the steam engine in ships or the internal combustion engine on land. Europe, on the other hand, has fallen seriously behind in the electronic revolution.

The reasons for Europe's relative economic decline since the early 1970's are too numerous and complicated to be explored in detail here. They include an expanding welfare state, low labor mobility, and the failure of the European Economic Community to promote real free trade, as opposed to the subsidization of various special interests. Europe's decline means, however, that it does not carry the same strategic economic weight that it did in the 1950's and early 1960's. Indeed, the loss of *Japanese* technological and human resources to the Soviet Union would now threaten the United States as much as the loss of Western Europe.

This is not to suggest that Europe has become unimportant from the point of view of American strategy. Rather, other areas have increased their importance substantially: Northeast Asia (including Japan and China), the Persian Gulf, and Central America.

Japan's importance from the military-industrial point of view is obvious. In addition, Japan's recent increases in military expenditure and its alignment with China against the Soviet Union both work to the American advantage. China has also become a strategic stake for the United States because of its ability to tie down large proportions of Soviet forces, and to divert large amounts of military investment from other areas. Sino-Soviet antagonism, barely envisaged at the beginning of the cold war, has become a major source of strategic advantage to the United States, and it is in America's interest to see that hostility continue. Approximately one-quarter of the Red Army's divisions face the Chinese. Although many of these are only at half-strength, and although the Soviets station approximately twice as many divisions in Eastern Europe and the European military districts of the Soviet Union, the creation and sustenance of the Far Eastern forces places an immense logistical burden on the Soviets.

Persian Gulf oil also remains critical for the functioning of the world economy. Whereas in the early 1950's and through the 1970's other powers (Britain and then Iran) helped police the Gulf, today the United States bears the brunt of ensuring the continuation of the flow of oil from that region. Despite the stimulus to oil exploration elsewhere and to conservation caused by the OPEC price rises of the 1970's, Europe depends on Persian Gulf sources for about a third of its oil, Japan, Australia, and New Zealand for over half of theirs. The United States has slowly begun to take the measure of what this commitment requires in terms of force structure, logistics, and deployments. In many cases it means the reallocation of funds and forces away from European contingencies.

In Central America the boiling up of revolution—home-grown, perhaps, but also fostered by outside powers—has restored some of the importance of that area as a strategic stake. The possibility of a turbulent southern border, massive population flows into the United States, and/or the creation of hostile Soviet client states will inevitably increase strategic concern with America's own backyard—a preoccupation absent from American strategic thinking since the fourth decade of this century—and create another potential drain on American military resources.

These three regions have emerged in addition to Europe as strategic stakes in the U.S.-Soviet competition. In all cases, their preservation or exploitation will require additional military expenditures and deployments, although not necessarily on the scale of those devoted to Europe.

III

In addition to its role as a strategic stake for the United States, Europe must also be considered in its role as a strategic *asset*, in particular a military asset. The European states possess, collectively, one of the greatest masses of conventional power in the world. Whether we are considering equipment or manpower, the European NATO states and the friendly neutrals of Europe possess more ground forces—in terms of numbers of soldiers, tanks, and so forth—than the United States. Yet in this area, too, enormous changes have occurred since the formation of NATO.

Over the years the European powers had gradually assumed most of the manpower burden of NATO defense, and integrated more countries into that defense. This was particularly true during the Vietnam war, when the Europeans increased their defense budgets in small increments even while the United States was drawing down forces in Europe in order to fight in Southeast Asia. Recently, however, the aggregate trends have been reversed, in particular as the Carter and Reagan administrations have made additional commitments to European defense. Today, for example, some 25 percent of NATO's 20,000 tanks are American; ten years ago the ratio was approximately 20 percent. The recent steady increases in the American defense budget (including the portion devoted to NATO), the program to modernize American armed forces, and, on the other side, the budgetary and demographic pressures facing the European allies will cause the overall relative contribution to Europe to diminish. (This assumes no major increases in European defense spending, a premise which seems reasonable enough.)

Even more significant in terms of long-term trends are qualitative changes like the virtual disappearance of European states (with the exception of France) as transoceanic powers and the diminution or disappearance of colonial contributions to Western power. To be sure, American statesmen in the immediate postwar period regarded European control of colonies overseas as a diversion from continental defense; this was particularly true of the American approach to France in the 1950's. A more sober recalculation in the 1970's suggested that the United States should not have expected so much of a military return on European decolonization; in fact, decolonization imposed political-military costs as well as yielding benefits.

In the early part of the cold war it was expected that American allies would help bear the burdens of defense outside Europe. Indeed, in 1951 the Army Chief of Staff, General J. Lawton Collins, could point to the participation of French, British, Turkish, and Dutch soldiers in the

Korean war as evidence of such contributions. But following Korea, the willingness of our European allies to fight outside Europe for common interests eroded quickly. Somewhat more slowly, but nonetheless inexorably, the ability of European states engaged in extra-European politics to project force also dwindled. Great Britain and France in particular, which had exercised substantial regional influence through the use of forces deployed in Africa, Asia, and the Middle East, gradually withdrew those forces as they granted independence to their former colonial dominions.

The British and French governments made (and continue to make) some effort to retain strategically mobile light forces for deployment overseas, but such efforts are of necessity small. In the Falklands war of 1982 and the Zaire intervention of 1978, the respective British and French forces required American logistical support in order to conduct relatively small operations overseas. In each case the operation succeeded, but each case also demonstrated how far these two powers had sunk even from the efforts of which they had been capable in 1956 at Suez.

To be sure, the European powers retain some forces uniquely suited to operations in the Third World, and some will to use those forces. The shadowy British involvement in Oman is one example; France's deployments in West Africa and Djibouti are another. At the lowest levels of conflict the European powers can thus make significant contributions to American power. But once one considers larger requirements—the projection of substantial air and naval power, the dispatch of expeditionary forces, or the rapid arming or rearming of a Third World ally—European capabilities appear far more modest. Moreover—and this is crucial—European states are and will no doubt remain unlikely to participate in major military operations outside the NATO area.

As for the independent European nuclear forces of France and Great Britain, these do make an additional contribution to the overall strategic balance between West and East, although the measure is hard to quantify. These forces do not merely increase the "target sets" of Soviet nuclear forces; far more importantly, they complicate Soviet planning of an attack against the West by presenting multiple centers of decision, each of which could destroy a substantial proportion of Soviet society. The rising cost of effective nuclear delivery systems, however, and the prospect of increasingly effective anti-missile defenses, call their future utility into some doubt.

IV

Whatever our assessment of its role as a strategic stake and a strategic asset, Europe is also of interest to the United States simply by virtue of its location. European bases are important for the conduct of strategic nuclear war against the Soviet Union; Europe is a point of access to the restive satrapies of Eastern Europe, the most sensitive parts of the Soviet empire; Europe holds naval chokepoints for denying the Soviet fleet access to the Atlantic Ocean and Mediterranean Sea; finally, Europe is a point of access to strategic positions in the Third World.

That Europe contains the most extensive array of American overseas bases has long been known. Often forgotten, however, is that throughout the 1950's and early 1960's the United States depended on European bases in order to be able to conduct *any* military operations—above all, nuclear operations—against the Soviet military-industrial heartland. During the 1950's the limited range of the B-47, the main weapon of the Strategic Air Command, required bases in European or European-controlled countries. As an interim measure until intercontinental ballistic missiles were developed, intermediate-range Thor and Jupiter missiles were deployed in Italy and Turkey, and U-2 reconnaissance planes were staged from European airfields. In the early days of submarine-based nuclear forces, American submarines also had to operate within short ranges of their targets—in other words, off European coastlines.

Thus, in the early stages of the cold war American intelligence-gathering and strategic forces depended heavily on the security of European bases. But this has changed. The development of a genuine intercontinental bomber (the B-52), landbased intercontinental ballistic missiles (the Titan, followed by Minuteman), and increasingly long-range sea-launched ballistic missiles (the C-4, with a range of three times that of the early Polaris missiles) has meant that American strategic forces can operate without using European bases.

Additionally, the tremendous growth in the use of satellites for various kinds of intelligence-gathering has reduced some of the utility of West European bases. Although the invention and deployment of the cruise missile may in part renew Europe's importance as strategic geography, since cruise-missile carriers will have to operate in close proximity to Europe in order to strike at Soviet targets, the fact remains that the central strategic forces of the United States no longer require European basing or find themselves greatly aided by it.

In quite a different way, however, Europe retains geostrategic significance as a point of access to the Soviet Union itself, and its empire. Traditionally, NATO planners have viewed this as more of a vulnerability than a potential asset, although some have suggested that more might be done to exploit the proximity of a restive population to the west of the Soviet Union; Samuel P. Huntington, for instance, has suggested that the United States could use the threat of a retaliatory offensive into Eastern Europe to deter Soviet attacks on NATO, a strategy which, if adopted, would require the continuation of a substantial land-based force in Central Europe.

One might argue that a free and independent Western Europe under the aegis of American military power exercises, by virtue of its very existence, a corrosive effect on the Soviet empire in Eastern Europe. Television and radio broadcasts, in addition to commercial and tourist travel across the Iron Curtain, serve to remind East Germans, Czechs, Hungarians, and Poles of the ties which once bound them to the countries of the West.

In two locations, the far north and along Turkey's northern border, NATO has land borders with the Soviet Union itself. The Soviets' preoccupation with territorial integrity leads them to place great emphasis on protecting their borders. As a result, these borders create both dangers and opportunities for the United States. Dangers, because of the possibility of an accidental clash of U.S. or allied and Soviet forces; opportunities, because they force the Soviet Union to divert military resources to defend its border regions.

A third source of geostrategic interest arises from consideration of maritime power. The steady growth of the Soviet navy and Soviet naval aviation since the mid-1960's has focused attention on the problem of securing NATO's sea lines of communication. In addition, the growing range of Soviet sea-launched ballistic missiles (from 1,400 km in the mid-1960's to 8,000 km or better today) enables the Soviets to create submarine "sanctuaries" off NATO's northern flank. In order to maintain an orderly flow of reinforcements and goods to Europe in the event of a war—in other words, in order to preserve Europe as a strategic stake—American and allied forces must attempt to hold back Soviet forces along the chokepoints of the northern flank, if not to push them back to their bases on the Kola peninsula. The obvious implication is that American anti-submarine forces will have to operate more in the northern area than had previously been planned. A similar chokepoint in the southern flank—the Dardanelles—is vital for control of the Mediterranean.

The final point of strategic geography has to do with access to the Third World. European bases are physically well structured to support operations in various parts of the Third World, but are not necessarily *politically* well-situated to do so. Here the lessons of the 1973 Middle East war are significant: American attempts to use European bases in contingencies other than an all-out war between NATO and the Warsaw Pact may meet opposition or even a veto by the host country. More importantly, Europe no longer controls bases *in* the Third World which would be useful in the event of conflict. In the 1950's, European-controlled outposts in North Africa (especially Morocco), the Middle East (Algeria and Egypt), and the Far East (Aden and Singapore) offered valuable supplements to the American basing network; today the United States finds itself painfully reestablishing a basing network by negotiating new, bilateral arrangements with Morocco, Kenya, Somalia, and Oman.

In addition, the rise of new areas of concern in the Third World changes the relative utility of certain European basing areas. In particular, eastern Turkey has become increasingly important for the projection of military power into the Persian Gulf. Newly constructed air bases in that region, although not specifically designated for the purpose, could help the United States Air Force slow a Soviet invasion of Iran. Equally importantly, bases in Turkey serve as a useful threat to the southern flank of the Soviet Union. Turkey's numerous, hardy, and disciplined armed forces lack modern military hardware. Insofar as the United States can remedy that need (which is huge), it will create an increasing southern-flank threat to the Soviet Union.

V

Finally, in calculating the American strategic interest in Europe it is necessary to determine not only the value of Europe as stake, asset, and geographical location, but also the cost to America of maintaining its commitment to its European allies. That is to say, to what extent is Europe a strategic liability?

Europe has always had first claim on American military resources. But when in the 1970's and 1980's efforts were made to calculate the size of that commitment, the results astonished even its advocates. According to one General Accounting Office calculation, 56 percent of U.S. military spending went to cover European contingencies; total American expenditure on NATO amounted to slightly more than that of the other members of the alliance combined.

To be sure, all such attempts to calculate in purely monetary terms the price of America's commitment to Europe face serious accounting problems: how, for example, should one assess the cost of forces stationed in the United States and dedicated to NATO, yet capable of being given other missions?

Moreover, it must be recognized that even if American troops stationed in Europe were reduced in number, American force structures might remain as large as they are, or become even larger. A more fruitful line of inquiry would ask: (1) What are trends in Europe's claim on American military resources? (2) What effects has the European commitment had on the size and composition of American forces? (3) What effects has the European commitment had on the intangible elements of force structure—doctrine, orientation, and habits of thought?

The first of these questions is easily answered. Europe absorbs a greater proportion of U.S. conventional forces in 1985 than it did in 1964, before the Vietnam war. Although absolute numbers of U.S. forces stationed in Europe have declined since the early 1960's, as a proportion of U.S. forces stationed abroad they have increased steadily. Over two-thirds of American soldiers, sailors, and airmen stationed overseas serve in Europe, and an increasing percentage of those serve in Germany. U.S. forces in the Pacific, by contrast, have declined both in real terms and proportionate to U.S. forces overseas and U.S. forces overall. The initial commitment to Europe of some 300,000 men came from an overall armed force of 3.25 million. A similar sized force today comes from an overall force almost a third smaller. Trends in deployment of key items of equipment point in the same direction.

Over time, the strategic commitment to Europe has more and more sharply affected American force structures at home as well. The "heavying" of Army divisions in response to increased preparation for European contingencies has been one aspect of this. Increasingly, U.S. reserve forces and even the Marine Corps (not traditionally a Europe-oriented force) have found themselves assigned to European missions, with corresponding effects on doctrine and organization.

The most obvious manifestation of the increasing commitment of American military resources to Europe lies not in the numbers of troops stationed there in peacetime but in those committed to its defense by American war planners. Current plans for a crisis envision an extraordinary deployment of ten divisions in ten days to the European front lines, with four divisions drawing their equipment from POMCUS (Prepositioning of Materiel Configured to Unit Sets) stocks warehoused in Europe. The strategic awkwardness of this arrangement should be apparent: POMCUS is costly, and offers lucrative targets to Soviet air and special forces. More than one knowledgeable observer has asked whether the forces scheduled to pick up this equipment will find it intact, find it operable, or be able to organize themselves and deploy in an orderly fashion from assembly points under attack.

The overstretch of American forces caused by the advent of the All-Volunteer Force, the emergence of new military commitments (particularly in the Persian Gulf), and the decay of alliance structures has led American planners to assign extremely demanding missions to the reserves. To meet the increased mobilization commitment to Europe, the United States Army has created a force structure that depends on reserve forces in order to undertake any major military campaign.

The results are twofold. First, reserve units must now prepare for early commitment and hence maintain high readiness for all-out combat. Not only do the history and logic of the American reserve system make one doubt that reserve units can attain the requisite efficiency; what this also means is that the most capable reserve units cannot serve (as they have traditionally and most usefully served) as a framework for a vastly increased force structure in wartime. By assigning the most efficient and well-equipped reserve forces to early European deployment, the United States runs the risk of finding itself stripped of a central strategic reserve after mobilization, and without a cadre of experienced units and soldiers to train and stiffen new, draft-based armies. Second, a reserve-dependent force structure oriented toward Europe will prove awkward for use in lesser contingencies (in the Persian Gulf, for example); for domestic political reasons, any President would hesitate to call out reserve forces for such purposes.

The European orientation of U.S. forces, particularly the Army, detracts from our ability to cover other contingencies adequately. More precisely, the need to prepare for a massive and early commitment to a land war in Europe distorts planning for both hot and cold war with the Soviet Union and other powers in other regions. With the exception of the Pacific Command, other regional commands—Central Command, for example, responsible for the Middle East and the Persian Gulf in particular—have no forces under their peacetime control, because such forces have dual (European and non-European) missions. Even the Army's new light divisions must prepare for a European role in addition to Third World contingencies. The emphasis on Europe extends to training and equipment as well: the military deemphasizes skills such as counterinsurgency that do not apply to the European scenario.

Europe acts as a strategic liability in other ways, too, primarily by exercising a restraining effect on American actions. This has been most noticeable in the Middle East, where American and Europrean policies have been at odds, but it holds true in other areas as well (the Strategic Defense Initiative, for example). If, on balance, U.S. and European interests overseas conflict less than they have done in the past, that is simply because European interests overseas have contracted so sharply. Where interests do clash is with regard to Eastern Europe and the Soviet Union. The Europeans, far more dependent on trade generally than the United States, and hard pressed to compete in world markets with the United States and Japan, find the Eastern-bloc markets increasingly attractive. At the same time the United States, fearful of Soviet attempts to steal or purchase Western technology, has attempted to impose restrictions on the kinds of trade its partners conduct with the Soviet empire.

In a larger sense, the Europeans have yet to experience the same disillusionment with détente that Americans have. Despite the invasion of Afghanistan and the imposition of martial law in Poland, the European states remain reluctant to resume the kind of conflict which divided the continent during the 1950's. One reason is that Western Europe benefits from closer economic ties to Eastern Europe. At a psychological level Europeans have also enjoyed the generally more relaxed political atmosphere that has pervaded the continent in the wake of détente and have hoped to insulate themselves from the atmosphere of East-West hostility which set in again in the late 1970's.

To sum up: over the past thirty years, America's commitment to Europe has absorbed an increasing proportion of U.S. military power, broadly defined. That commitment is most noticeable in the central region of Europe, although its effects have been felt to a lesser degree along the flanks as well. More importantly, the commitment has exercised an ever-growing influence on doctrine and organization. Demographic and fiscal trends—declining pools of draftable young men and stagnant European defense budgets—promise to augment the American role still further. This will hold true all the more if, as appears likely, the United States continues to dominate the next generation of military technology. Finally, all this has been happening while U.S.-European interests have increasingly diverged, or at any rate while the focus of divergence has moved from the periphery—the former colonial world—to the center, the very heart of East-West relations.

VI

What do we learn from this analysis? Broadly speaking, three changes have occurred over the history of the Atlantic alliance.

The first is Europe's relative decline as a strategic stake and asset in the competition with the Soviet Union, although the decline has by no means been precipitate or steep: the preservation of a free and allied Western Europe remains overwhelmingly important to the United States, and its forces remain a major asset in the overall balance between the United States and the Soviet Union.

The second is that Europe has become more of a strategic liability to the United States, less for reasons intrinsic to Europe than because of transformations elsewhere, including the rise of new areas of strategic concern (particularly the Persian Gulf and Central America) and the expansion of Soviet power.

Third, from the point of view of strategic geography it is the flanks of NATO that are becoming increasingly important, primarily because of the rise of Soviet maritime power, because of changes in military technology, and because of threats in the Persian Gulf.

These changes are all long-term and slow in nature; they constitute a kind of tectonic movement beneath the surface of policy debates. It is striking, however, how little systematic attention has been paid to them. Current force postures and commitments still represent a cumulative set of marginal additions to a strategic policy established some thirty-five years ago. It is natural that policy be made that way (in the United States, at any rate), but the process is not without its perils.

Can we do anything about these structural changes in our strategic interests without causing catastrophic political damage to the alliance? That is not an easy question to answer. What we can do, at least, is to make an effort to *understand* those changes, and their implications, in order to prepare ourselves to take remedial action in the event of some major break in the continuity of alliance politics or international relations more generally—say, the defection of Greece from the alliance, or Soviet intervention in Iran.

One such implication is the need to emphasize the flanks of NATO more than the central front. The latter was a major source of worry in 1951 when American troops were seen as necessary to stop (or at least slow) a Soviet army poised to overrun a disarmed Germany and a war-enfeebled Western Europe. The great shifts since then—the rearmament of Germany, and the opportunity for a defense conducted with European reserve forces behind prepared fortifications and barriers— militate against pouring more resources into what is, after all, the region least likely to see a war. Instead, marginal resources could be devoted to Norway and above all to Turkey, the only country in NATO with no manpower shortage and with a long record of adherence to the alliance even in the face of poor treatment by it. It is, after all, on the periphery that the great wars of the past have broken out, and it is on NATO's flanks that one can most easily imagine military confrontations between the two sides.

A second implication is the need to reduce the dependence of Europe on immediate reinforcement by U.S. land-based forces. Military logic suggests the peculiarity (at the very least) of a strategy which relies heavily on the appearance within a week of massive armies from a power thousands of miles distant from the main battle front. Such a dependence is as politically unhealthy as it is militarily tenuous. The primary responsibility for Europe's defense on the ground must rest with Europeans.

Third is the need to encourage, as far as possible, the development of European defense entities. This may take a variety of forms: encouraging the revival of the West European Union; aiding, if need be directly, the creation of all-European (as opposed to national) arms industries; and minimizing the pressure the United States puts on Europeans to act where they will be least united, i.e., overseas. The stronger the European common defense—including ultimately a broader nuclear force than those of Britain and France—the less difficult it will be for the United States to adjust the balance between the forces and strategy on the one hand and its political commitments on the other.

Above all, the United States must face the realities of its own strategic position, which has changed in major ways since the 1950's. The durability of the Atlantic alliance is both a source of strength and a temptation to the belief that the strategic equilibrium has remained unaltered. That belief is mistaken. We can, however, recognize that new strategic realities exist without concluding that we must discard old instruments of security. Indeed, only through such a recognition will we avoid the further enfeeblement of a coalition as venerable, and valuable, as the Atlantic alliance.

17

The Evolution of the U.S.-Japan Alliance

WILLIAM C. SHERMAN

In the fall of 1945 Japan lay in ruins, and the United States entered the country as victor and occupier. Forty percent of Japan's urban areas had been destroyed, production in both the agricultural and manufacturing sectors was only 60 percent of 1933 levels, and more than 25 percent of Japan's physical capital stock had been lost to direct war damage. Few Americans then would have dared to predict that just more than 30 years later, Japan would be the world's second largest economy, a global leader in technology, and a major source of private capital and offical development assistance for the nations of the world. But on the day that he accepted Japan's surrender, General Douglas MacArthur broadcast a report to the American people. Speaking with the authority of his long experience in Asia, MacArthur forecast a future for Japan:

"The energy of the Japanese race, if properly directed, will enable expansion vertically rather than horizontally. If the talents of the race are turned into constructive channels, the country can lift itself from its present deplorable state into a position of dignity."[1]

In 1945 even fewer would have dared to predict also that these two wartime enemies would forge during the next four decades one of the world's strongest and healthiest alliances, and one that continues to grow in importance not only to the United States and Japan themselves, but also to the world. In his landmark speech at the Shimoda Conference on 2 September 1983 exactly thirty-eight years to the day after MacArthur's broadcast to the American people, Secretary of State George P. Shultz said that something "remarkable" has happened in our relationship. An increasing Japanese perception of Japan's global responsibilities; a resurgence of American confidence and of confidence in America; our combined influence on events; and the fact that what we do together has worldwide ramification, have turned our bilateral partnership into a global relationship. "We are faced now with unprecedented opportunities to act as partners on a global scale," said the Secretary, "and we have an obligation to grasp those opportunities and to use them for the advantage of present and future generations of the entire world."[2]

An equally remarkable and positive transformation has taken place in American popular attitudes towards Japan as well—although it is hard to tell that from a perusal of current literature. A glance at recent American magazines and books could lead one to believe that the United States and Japan are again on a collision course: Trade War, Chip Wars, The Japanese Conspiracy: The Plot to Dominate Industry Worldwide and How to Deal with It, and Japan Against the World, 1941–2041: The One Hundred Year War for Supremacy are among the most recent book titles, and the pages of American newspapers regularly highlight the latest problems in our trade relations. Publishers apparently believe that this is what will sell, and editorial standards and reality are often thrown to the wind in the process. A recent article in a prestigious business magazine authoritatively stated that Japan "is still virtually shutting out U.S. agricultural imports"[3]; yet the reality is that Japan is America's best customer for food products—bar none—and buys nearly $7 billion per year from us.

The truth is that the American people have a far more positive attitude and a lot more common sense about Japan than many people in Washington give them credit for. In a spring 1984 Gallup poll of the American people, Japan ranked third among twenty-two countries and almost equal to Great Britain both in terms of importance to the United States and on a like/dislike scale. (Canada was number one.) In a January 1984 poll the American people were asked to cite the reasons for our trade deficit with Japan, and the four most prevalent answers were: (1) Japanese products are less expensive; (2) American wage rates are too high and lower our manufacturers' competitiveness; (3) Japanese products are superior in quality and reliability; and (4) Japanese work harder to sell their products in America than do Americans in the Japanese market. Only by the time they got to reasons five and six did they mention the causes usually cited by those who knock on our doors in Washington: that Japan has unfair trade barriers which keep U.S. products out of the Japanese market, and that the Japanese government helps Japanese industries to export through subsidies and other measures. Finally, in a January 1984 survey of 5,000 individuals selected from Who's Who, the respondents believed by a margin of 67 to 21 that

Japan's emergence as one of the world's largest economic nations represents a benefit rather than a threat to the United States.*

Most long-time participants in the conduct of the United States–Japan relationship believe that the state of our alliance has never been better than it is today. One senior Japanese political leader recently told a departing officer at our embassy in Tokyo that "our overall relationship is so good, that it's frightening." Those of us who have been involved in this relationship over the past three decades know that this happy state of affairs has not always been so; we have witnessed and participated in many turbulent and emotional encounters between our two countries that have strained the alliance. We also know that there are many both in America and Japan who believe that today's situation cannot last, and who are looking for indicators of future disaster. After so many years of trade frictions and troubles over defense and security issues, they have a difficult time imagining a relatively problem-free, "Golden Age" for U.S.-Japan relations. It reminds me of a story told by an American correspondent in Tokyo about his interview with Masayoshi Ohira, then secretary-general of the Liberal Democratic party, after Jimmy Carter came into office in 1977. "I asked him what he thought about President Carter's promise that America would consult closely with Japan before taking any actions and would deliver no more shocks," said the reporter, "and Ohira said if the Americans did all that, then U.S.-Japan relations would become very boring!" A similar disbelief exists among the many who have made a career out of U.S.-Japan trade problems—whether reporters, government officials, lawyers, or lobbyists. As one set of problems is resolved, there always seems to be a set of issues in reserve to put on the front burner of our relationship. They, too, cannot envision a future in which the problems that arise in U.S.-Japan trade—and it is inevitable that there will be problems in any economic relationship of the magnitude and complexity of ours—will be handled in a routine fashion, out of the political and public spotlight. Indeed, until relatively recently our tendency (unfortunately shared by the Japanese) to deal with our relationship on an issue-by-issue basis has been a flaw in the strategy that has governed our handling of U.S.-Japanese relations.

What is it that has happened in our relationship to transform it over the past thirty-nine years to its present excellent state? Our natural instinct is to look for significant turning points, personalities, major

---

* It is interesting to note that in the same poll of elite attitudes, the respondents believed quite strongly that their generally favorable views of Japan were not shared by their fellow Americans. An overwhelming 84 percent of the respondents said that the U.S. public was "not well-informed" about Japan. As for the U.S. public's attitude toward Japan and its international role, only 43 percent felt that the American citizenry was friendly, while 33 percent believed that they were "suspicious."

events, and key policy statements. Certainly these exist, but more often than not they are the symbols and manifestations of what has been taking place both within and between the two countries, rather than their causes. The process of change in postwar U.S.-Japan relations has not been cyclical, but rather one of linear development and cumulative growth, much like Japanese history itself: While there have been major "battles," heroes, and the shocks of external events, more often it has been the nondrama of incrementalism and slow organic growth.[4] Perhaps a few recollections from my own experience in Japan over the past three decades would serve to dramatize the kinds of basic changes that have taken place.

I first went to Japan shortly before the Treaty of Peace entered into force in April 1952, posted as one of our vice-consuls in Yokohama. In hindsight, it was one of the more dramatic years of Japan's postwar era, one that both laid the initial foundations of the postwar U.S.-Japan relationship and signaled the problems and concerns of the next decade. Japanese GNP stood at only $16.3 billion, only slightly more than 1 percent of what it is today. Total U.S.-Japan trade that year was $622 million, again only 1 percent of what it is today, and it was overwhelmingly in America's favor. Japan desperately needed to sell goods abroad in order to pay for the basic commodities it required to survive and recover. One of my duties was to scour Yokohoma and its consular district, trying to find anyone who made something that could be sold in America—paper flowers or handicrafts—and encourage them to try to export it to the United States. We even offered free advertising in a Commerce Department publication. In 1952, as throughout the 1950s, one of our major concerns was Japan's economic viability, and whether it would be able to stand on its own without American assistance. And if it could not, then what were the implications for internal political stability in Japan and our nascent security relationship?

The year 1952 was a watershed year in terms of the bilateral relationship as well. The San Francisco Peace Treaty and the U.S.-Japan security treaty both went into effect in April, and just two months earlier, the United States and Japan signed an administrative agreement that established the terms for the establishment and operation of post-Occupation U.S. bases in Japan. Pent-up feelings and opposition to both the peace treaty and the security arrangements with the United States led to violent anti-American demonstrations on May Day; two demonstrators were killed, many others wounded, and hundreds arrested. A number of American vehicles were burned in demonstrations near our embassy in Tokyo. Later in the year the Soviet Union vetoed Japan's first attempt to gain entry into the United Nations. For the next two decades major differences of political opinion in Japan over these issues—Japan's foreign policy orientation, the alliance with the United States, and the presence of U.S. military bases in Japan—dominated our relationship. The foundations of the alliance were there, but they were on potentially unstable ground. The Japanese government was constrained by a militant opposition and a large segment of hostile public opinion to take the "lowest posture" possible, to resist any international role, and to be extremely cautious with respect to security cooperation with the United States. Almost every adult American has a series of images from 1960 in his memory—hundreds of thousands of Japanese marching in the streets to protest the signing of a revised security treaty, police entering the Diet to carry the Speaker of the Lower House through throngs of angry opposition legislators determined to prevent him from reaching his seat, White House Press Secretary Jim Hagerty being rescued from a mob rocking his car at Haneda Airport, the forced cancelation of President Eisenhower's visit while he was enroute to Japan, and the resignation of Prime Minister Kishi on the same day that the Security Treaty was ratified.

Just one year later in June 1961, the first picture of a changed U.S.-Japan relationship emerged during Prime Minister Ikeda's visit to Washington. The United States began to take a broader view of its relationship with Japan that went beyond its interest in mutual-security arrangements and internal political stability. Japan's economic recovery now was well on track, it agreed to repay American economic assistance, and Ikeda announced his plan to double Japan's GNP within ten years. The two countries then proceeded to establish a Cabinet-level Committee on Trade and Economic Affairs, the U.S.-Japan Committee on Scientific Cooperation, and the U.S.-Japan Culture Conference (CULCON). President John F. Kennedy sent an ambassador to Japan whose manifest intellectual credentials, broad knowledge and understanding of Japan and its potential excited the Japanese people and educated the Americans. A new and increasingly important economic relationship began to develop between the two countries. Although Ikeda had an income-doubling plan for Japan's GNP, U.S.-Japan trade would in fact quadruple by the end of the decade; furthermore, by 1965 the balance of trade would swing in Japan's favor. But in foreign affairs, however, the United States did not yet envisage Japan's playing a major role in Asia, let alone the world. "The real contest in Asia," President Kennedy wrote in *The Strategy of Peace*, "is between India and China—a contest to determine which country will serve as the model for Asia's future development."[5] In Kennedy's Public Papers for 1961–63, Japan is cited sixty-two times in the index; China draws ninety-four references, and India ninety-seven. (Two decades later, the indices to the Reagan Public Papers for 1981–82 show thirty references to Japan, eighteen to China, and only ten to India.)

By the time I returned to Japan near the end of the decade, it was a country transformed. No longer would we be concerned about Japan's economic viability (and certainly no longer would I need to encourage Japanese companies to export to the United States). If anything, the opposite was true: with Japanese automobiles, textiles, steel, and consumer electronics now finding major markets abroad, and especially in the United States, American businessmen were becoming concerned, and the administration in Washington echoed the concern. But in Japan, it was not concern that I saw on the faces of the Japanese people during my many visits to the Osaka Expo '70 site, it was pride. With flags unfurled, Japan was announcing its new presence to the world, proud of its economic accomplishments and political tranquility.

The decade of the 1970s was without question the most turbulent and potentially disruptive period in United States–Japan relations since World War II, and the one that brought tremendous changes within both countries and in their relationship with each other. To the Japanese, the surprise U.S. opening to China, the "dollar shock," and the soybean embargo which followed each other in close succession all signified an American insensitivity to Japan's interests and negated the very concept of partnership. The war in Vietnam, which relied heavily on U.S. bases in Japan even after with the withdrawal of American forces in 1973, brought continued political protests in Japan and questioning of the security relationship by opposition parties, the press, and substantial sectors of the public. Demonstrations in front of the embassy were commonplace. Within Japan, there were major economic and political changes. The oil crisis in 1973 revived Japan's historic fears of vulnerability; and when oil price hikes were combined with Japanese inflation, higher wage rates, and the rise of the so-called newly industrialized countries (NICs) Japan found that it no longer could compete internationally on the basis of resource-intensive, lower-wage products. Domestic politics entered a period of crisis and unpredictability; Japan had six prime ministers between 1970 and 1980. Japanese terrorists committed a massacre at Lod Nol, blew up Mitsubishi headquarters in Tokyo, and hijacked airplanes. The primary focus in the U.S.-Japan dialogue turned to economics and especially trade, and the United States engaged in a concerted and often painful effort to break down Japan's barriers to trade and investment. At several points during the decade, major crises in the trading relationship erupted, which like the security crises of earlier decades threatened to shake the very foundation of the alliance. Each time, however, both sides would pull back when the "conservators" of the relationship—Japan experts public and private—were able to engage the senior administration leadership in a recognition of the fundamental importance of the relationship. Unfortunately, each new generation (or some might say, each new administration) had to learn this lesson anew for itself.

A history of alliances no doubt would show that many alliances weaken over time, that allies part ways or even become adversaries, and that alliances break up when the conditions that brought the two countries together no longer exist. This phenomenon was codified by Lord Palmerston's well-known statement that his majesty's government had "no eternal allies and no perpetual enemies. Our interests are eternal." The remarkable feature of the United States–Japan alliance has been its ability to adapt over time to changing circumstances and, like a steel sword, to emerge even stronger from the fires in which it has been tempered. We have always in the last analysis been able to recognize our strong and abiding interest.

This look at pictures from the past helps to explain why the United States–Japan alliance today rests on such firm footing:

—In our defense relationship, the existence of the Self-Defense Forces, the Treaty of Mutual Cooperation and Security and the presence of U.S. military forces in Japan today are accepted by the great majority of the Japanese people and the political parties that represent them. Furthermore, over the past few years it has become more and more apparent that the Japanese government is actively enhancing its defense effort, and within the restraints of its Constitution, assuming defensive roles and missions that support our mutual goals.

—In our overall economic relationship, both countries have built up an enormous and positive stake in trade and investment with each other, and in working together to strengthen the world trade system and promote general economic development. While problems remain, over $80 billion worth of trade in goods and services flows smoothly between the two countries, and Japan each year leads the list of countries making new investments in the United States. In the meantime, our two countries lead the world in calling for a new international trading round, in developing new technologies, and in providing economic assistance and private capital to the developing nations.

—As Secretary Shultz indicated in his Shimoda speech, Japan is assuming a greater and more active international, political, and diplomatic role in close partnership with the United States, a move that we welcome.

—As the public opinion polls cited above indicate, there is an increasingly broad awareness in the United States that our relationship with Japan not only is extremely important, but also produces more benefits than costs for the United States. In the process, an informed and vocal constituency of Americans from all sectors of our society who have familiarity with Japan and an interest in the alliance has begun to develop.

—Along with the concern that many have about Japanese competition, there is also a deep admiration among most Americans for Japanese accomplishments, and particularly for Japanese product design and technology. Most Americans appear to believe that the challenge of Japanese competitiveness must be met through the marketplace and not through protectionism.

—Finally, after the turmoil of the 1970s, both countries are enjoying periods of relative political stability, allowing them to focus more confidently on both economic development and foreign affairs.

Will this all last? How firmly based are U.S.-Japan relations today? In connection with its recently completed report, the United States–Japan Advisory Commission—a distinguished panel of U.S. and Japanese leaders appointed to survey the present state of the relationship—asked scholars in Japan and the United States to work independently to produce long-term illustrative scenarios about how our relations might develop in the future. The commission's report outlined three alternative futures: continuation of the present relationship, a worst-case scenario, and a best-case scenario.[6]

The present relationship, the commission found, is characterized by a pattern of continued security cooperation and constantly increasing economic interaction, with chronic and growing frictions over economic issues. In this present relationship, growing resentment on both sides, primarily over trade issues, makes it politically difficult for leaders to cooperate as fully as they might in a more friendly atmosphere. Political pressures against compromise grow, and more and more trade disputes are apt to be marked by tough tactics, polemic rhetoric, and brinksmanship.[7] Thus, the commission's major conclusion was that while the United States–Japan relationship fundamentally is on the right course, the current, too often confrontational pattern of interaction between the two countries is eroding goodwill and mutual trust.[8] This pattern, the commission says, is unlikely to disappear soon.[9]

The commission's worst-case scenario would grow out of the conditions of the previous scenario, in which more openly nationalist sentiment gained the upper hand in each country. In this scenario, growing resentment in Japan against American trade demands or actions that Japan regarded as unreasonable or unfair could lead to a government in Japan less disposed toward cooperation with the United States. At the same time, major protectionist measures might be enacted in the United States, such as an import surcharge on all Japanese products or local-content legislation. Alternatively, there might be an effort to attenuate our defense ties or modify our security treaty. While this scenario seems highly implausible, the commission concluded that it is not altogether out of the question.[10]

The commission sees the plausible path to the best-case scenario coming not through any single, major event which makes the benefits of closer cooperation immediately evident but rather through the continued accretion of small-scale measures in government and private-sector cooperation—not in fact a major departure from the long-term present trend.[11] By implication, the contrast to the two previous scenarios relates not to the substance of individual issues but to the way the relationship is conducted and the willingness of the two countries to focus on broader concerns.

These, of course, are not the only scenarios. There are an infinite number of permutations, and external events that could influence their unfolding cannot be predicted. But the three cases form a useful matrix and it is surely in the interest of the United States to encourage the more positive outcome. Given the importance of both countries to the world, successful management of the relationship is a major political challenge to leadership.

The style of the relationship, the development of a broader public understanding of the vital importance of the United States–Japan alliance, and the continuing need on both sides of the Pacific to prevent the fabric of the relationship from becoming damaged by short-term, narrowly focused controversies are matters of truly national concern. "If some economic frictions are inevitable," the commission reported, "frictions of the scale, frequency, and bitterness of those currently dominating the U.S.-Japan relationship are not."[12] It is up to us to develop the wisdom, the patience, and, above all, the institutions that assess, analyze, and channel these problems to resolution in quiet, equitable, and noncontroversial ways.

NOTES

1. GHQ, SCAP, Press Release, "Text of Speech by the Supreme Commander for the Allied Powers Broadcast to the American People on V-J Day," 2 September 1945, as cited in *Reports of General MacArthur, The Campaigns of MacArthur in the Pacific*, vol. 1, prepared by his General Staff. (Washington, D.C.: Government Printing Office, 1966), 455, 458.

2. "Japan and America: International Partnership for the 1980s." An address by Secretary of State George P. Shultz before the sixth Shimoda Conference, 2 September 1983, or *Current Policy* 506.

3. Anne B. Fisher, "Can Detroit Live without Quotas," in *Fortune*, 25 June 1984, 24.

4. John Whitney Hall, *Japan from Prehistory to Modern Times* (New York: Delacorte Press, 1970), 3–4.

5. John F. Kennedy, *The Strategy of Peace* (New York: Harper and Brothers, 1960), 141–2.

6. "Challenges and Opportunities in United States–Japan Relations: A Report Submitted to the President of the United States and the Prime Minister of Japan by the United States–Japan Advisory Commission, September 1984." (Washington, D.C.: U.S. Government Printing Office, 1984), 17–24.

7. Ibid., 20–21.

8. Ibid., 3.

9. Ibid., 21.

10. Ibid., 21–22.

11. Ibid., 23–24.

12. Ibid., 24.

18

International Bargaining
and Domestic Politics:
U.S.-China Relations Since 1972

ROBERT S. ROSS

Introduction

The interplay between domestic and international politics and the international behavior of states is a source of debate among scholars of comparative foreign policy. Often, the literature presents a skewed picture: one analytical perspective is overemphasized so that the explanatory value of the other is greatly underrepresented. Such is the case in much of the writing on Chinese policy toward the United States since 1972, particularly concerning the sources of conflict in the otherwise mutually beneficial U.S.-China relationship. The most difficult task has been to integrate our admittedly insufficient knowledge of Chinese domestic politics with the analytical conclusions suggested by the dynamics of U.S.-Soviet-P.R.C. triangular politics.

Despite the dearth of knowledge of Beijing politics, a number of specialists have produced important scholarship and reached significant conclusions concerning the impact of domestic China on the P.R.C.'s foreign policy. Notwithstanding these important contributions to our knowledge of Chinese policy making, there has been a trend to give undue emphasis to Chinese domestic politics in explaining instability in U.S.-China relations, particularly concerning the recurring conflict over Taiwan. It has been argued that, because reunification of Taiwan with the mainland is such a nationalistic issue, any Chinese leadership that cooperates with the United States is subject to intense criticism. Thus, unless the U.S. respects Chinese sensitivities, Beijing will adopt a rigid and hostile policy, and Taiwan will remain a contentious issue in U.S.-China relations. It has even been said that Washington's Taiwan policy could lead, or already has led, to a more conciliatory Chinese policy toward the Soviet Union due to the pressures of domestic politics on individual leaders such as Deng Xiaoping.[1]

This approach carries implicit assumptions concerning the role of Taiwan in the foreign policy of the People's Republic, the leadership's attitudes toward the Taiwan issue, and the sources of Beijing's U.S. policy, which fail to consider fully the restraints on P.R.C. policy imposed by the international environment. One fallacy is the assumption that the P.R.C. leadership is divided over the Taiwan issue—that if "rational" leaders such as Deng Xiaoping were free from domestic political opposition, they would not let the Taiwan issue interfere with U.S.-China relations. Actually, Deng Xiaoping and his colleagues are no less interested in the reunification of Taiwan with the mainland than are other Chinese politicians. Second, excessive attention to domestic politics fails to recognize the P.R.C. as a goal-oriented actor. Taiwan is a strategically located island (at one time called by American statesmen an "unsinkable aircraft carrier"), which could pose a threat to China if it were allied with an adversary, or which could enhance China's political position if it were controlled by the P.R.C. For this reason alone, Chinese leaders agree on the need to recover Taiwan. Finally, the importance of the international environment in Chinese policy making is suggested by the P.R.C.'s passivity concerning Taiwan from 1972 to 1978. Even though the United States was unwilling to compromise on its recognition of the Guomintang as the government of China, and despite intense succession politics in Beijing, it was during this period that Chinese leaders assured Washington that Taiwan was not an important issue, and that the two sides should concentrate their attention on dealing with Soviet "hegemonism."[2]

In this paper, I explain the ups and downs in U.S.-China relations since the Shanghai Communiqué as primarily a function of shifting "patterns of relations" in the strategic triangle: the trilateral pattern of relations in a particular era has been the dominant influence on China's U.S. policy. By affecting the bargaining relationship between the two countries, the pattern of relations also affected the strategy of China's goal-oriented behavior—in this case, reunification of Taiwan with the mainland. This approach does not reject the role of domestic politics in the formation of the P.R.C.'s foreign policy. On the contrary, domestic politics are influential in the P.R.C.'s foreign policy formation. But it is important to isolate the role of domestic politics within the constraints of international politics and to examine how various triangular patterns of relations set the parameters of the policy debates and thus influence the shifting salience of the Taiwan issue in the domestic political arena.

Triangular Patterns of Relations and Bargaining Among Strategic Partners

Systems theory explains the impact of a particular political structure on the behavioral patterns of states. As Kenneth Waltz has argued, "systems theory explains changes across systems, not in them. . . ."[3] Such theories have proved to be extremely powerful in explicating the long-term and fundamental dynamics of international politics, such as recurring balances, and in calling attention to differences in behavioral patterns of states under different international structures. Nevertheless, recurring patterns of behavior in international politics are the result of more variables than the "ordering principle" and the number of major powers in the system. Although he admits that alliance patterns may have a high explanatory value, Waltz argues that they have no place in a systems theory.[4] He may be correct, but that does not free us from the task of determining the influence of alliance patterns on state behavior.

When there are more than two major powers, the pattern of relations between them may vary considerably.[5] The contemporary world is bipolar; only the United States and the Soviet Union have comparable nuclear capabilities. Nevertheless, since President Nixon traveled to China in 1972 and signed the Shanghai Communiqué, international politics have reflected many of the characteristics of a multipolar balance-of-power system. Although the P.R.C. lacks a comparable nuclear inventory, its population, size, and resource base compel the superpowers to consider it a significant actor affecting their vital interests. Some European nations may have similar attributes, but the flexibility and unpredictability of U.S.-Soviet-P.R.C. relations creates the multipolar dynamics of the strategic triangle.[6]

Within this triangular relationship, there is a variety of possible forms of relations, depending upon "systemic *patterns* of exchange relationship" and the roles of the actors within each pattern. Three possible patterns have been identified. The most easily recognized of these is the "romantic triangle," whereby a "pivot" or "swing" state has a détente relationship with both of the other actors in the triangle.[7] The animosity between the two other actors makes them dependent upon friendship with the pivot for their security. The pivot is able to use to its advantage its suitors' fear of the abandonment and isolation that would develop from improved relations between the pivot and a suitor's adversary. Dependence is thus a function of the realignment alternatives of one's partner.[8] Put differently, dependence is a function of "asymmetrical strategic interests." Where one actor is more concerned than the other that its partner's strategic assets may enhance its adversary's capabilities due to realignment, relative fears of abandonment are affected. As Glenn Snyder has observed, such asymmetry explains why the more powerful actor in a dyad often has little influence over its weaker partner.[9] Détente generates uncertainty concerning the reliability of a partner and raises the possibility of a deeper, more cooperative relationship—a "stable marriage" in Dittmer's terms—which would undermine the security of the isolated state.[10]

There has been excellent work assessing the impact of such asymmetries in triangular relations on crisis behavior.[11] There have also been studies of the impact of such asymmetries on relations between adversaries in the strategic triangle.[12] Comparatively little work has been done, however, on the impact of shifts in the pattern of relations—"interaction change" in triangular politics—on relations between security partners. The existing studies on conflict between allies are primarily concerned with differences that arise on policy toward their common adversary.[13] Little has been written concerning the bargaining process on conflicting "particular interests" in bilateral relations in the context both of shared "general interests" vis-à-vis an adversary and of the triangular pattern of relations in the particular era.[14]

When there are shared general interests toward a common adversary as well as conflictual particular interests, as is the case in U.S.-China relations, each side must decide on a bargaining strategy concerning the conflictual issues. This strategy is, for the most part, a function of each state's position in the triangular pattern of relations. The changing pattern of relations establishes the range of choice, either severely restricting or expanding a state's bargaining power. The general interest will dominate the course of the relationship along the amity/enmity continuum; the pattern of relations will determine the cost to each state in terms of the compromises it must make on the conflictual bilateral interests. Enhanced bilateral conflict raises the possibility that détente between one's strategic partner and one's adversary might occur during a crisis, leading to abandonment and reduced security of the isolated state.[15] The likelihood of this, a function of the pattern of relations, affects a state's bargaining strategy and its willingness to create conflict with its ally. In the case of China and the United States, that is the primary explanation for their changing relations since 1972 with regard to their most conflictual particular interest, Taiwan. Indeed, it is important to recognize that Taiwan has been an object of U.S.-China bargaining since the Shanghai Communiqué. The two governments have had different preferences for the diplomatic, political, and military relationship between the United States and Taiwan since 1972, and China's bargaining strategy has changed over time.

Emphasis on triangular patterns of relations allows for consideration of the role of domestic politics in U.S.-China relations. Domestic politics is part of the "internal setting" of the process of foreign policy making.[16] The multiple roles of decision makers—as representatives of their states in international politics and as contestants for power in domestic politics—sometimes call for contradictory behavior. In extreme cases, a decision maker's domestic interests may prevail to such an extent that the state will not adequately respond to international pressures. Within the P.R.C., politics may affect policy insofar as Taiwan is a politically sensitive issue. Alternatively, China's leaders may simply have different perceptions of the relative bargaining strengths of the actors in the triangle or of their value as strategic allies.[17] Domestic politics may thus shape foreign policy insofar as leadership instability and change leads to policy change. Scholars have identified competing policy alternatives among the Chinese elite.[18]

Although domestic politics influences foreign policy formulation, the international strategic environment sets the "outside limits" of a state's bargaining position.[19] Chinese domestic politics may not have altered the fundamental character of China's U.S. policy in terms of the value attached to either a cooperative or conflictual relationship, but it may affect the timing of policy changes, hastening or slowing a particular trend. Domestic politics may also affect the tenor of a relationship within the pattern of relations dominant during a particular era: leaders may say or do things which serve their domestic needs, but which are not intended to alter their foreign policy line. It is therefore important to consider the intended audience of a policy statement.

Emphasis on triangular structures and range of choice suggests a "second image reversed" analysis of the interplay between international and domestic politics.[20] The international environment establishes the range within which debate over foreign policy can take place. As the pattern of relations of the strategic triangle has shifted since 1972, altering China's bargaining relationship between the superpowers, the content of the Chinese debate—and, thus, the role of Chinese domestic politics in China's foreign policy formulation—has changed.

Triangular politics, bargaining, and domestic politics are the three elements essential to understanding China's foreign policy toward the United States over Taiwan since 1972. Nevertheless, it is difficult to specify the exact mix of the international and domestic environment; during any particular era, the mix will be different. Still, the restraints can be generalized, delineating the range of choice, while the immediate situation is more susceptible to temporal political circumstances.

The Quiet Years, 1972–1979:
The Impact of Triangular Relations

In the early 1970s, the strategic triangle had yet to become salient in international politics. China's "dual adversary policy," entailing intense hostility toward both the superpowers, reinforced strategic bipolarity as both superpowers were denied the benefit of an alliance with the P.R.C. This situation proved untenable with regard to China's security demands as the dangers of isolation became clear following the 1968 Soviet invasion of Czechoslovakia and during the P.R.C.'s brief, yet dangerous, border war with the Soviet Union in 1969. Isolation and the resulting escalated threat posed by the Soviet Union coincided with the U.S. retreat from Indochina, encouraging Chinese leaders to seek a rapprochement with the United States. Prime Minister Zhou Enlai reportedly recognized that a continuation of the dual adversary policy would "plunge new China . . . into international isolation."[21] The P.R.C.'s efforts culminated in the Shanghai Communiqué, signed during President Nixon's visit to China in 1972.

Diplomacy successfully reduced the leaders' perception of isolation and their fear of Soviet pressure.[22] The image of the leader of the United States traveling to China and meeting with Chairman Mao Zedong did much to reassure China that it no longer stood alone against the "polar bear" to the north. Nevertheless, reduced international isolation also brought into play triangular influences on China's bilateral relations with the United States. Whereas Beijing had earlier simply refused to negotiate its differences with Washington, preferring to weaken the United States through a war of attrition by proxy in Indochina, it now became susceptible to the give-and-take of bargaining relationships in triangular politics.

During this period, the pattern of relations was that of a "romantic triangle." The United States held the pivot position, pursuing détente with the Soviet Union and China, while the latter two states were engaged in an unrelenting cold war. From the perspective of the P.R.C., the United States was on the defensive, nursing the wounds received from its involvement in the Vietnam War and its domestic instability, while the Soviet Union was on the offensive, seeking to "fill the vacuum" left by the American retrenchment. In late 1973, Mao feared that the Watergate disruptions might undermine Washington's ability to resist Soviet expansionism.[23] Deng Xiaoping stated at the United Nations early in 1974 that of the two superpowers, the Soviet Union was "especially vicious."[24] In 1975, in the aftermath of the fall of Saigon, Mao characterized the United States as strategically overextended *"trying to catch ten fleas with ten fingers,"* and told Henry Kessinger that China no longer considered the United States as a "paper tiger" but as a "wounded tiger"[25]—a conclusion that did not change during the first half of the Carter administration. In 1978, Chairman Hua Guofeng insisted that the Soviet Union was the "most dangerous source of a new world war" and *Renmin Ribao* (People's Daily) reported that "The Soviet Union Is Bent on Utilizing America's Lack of Will."[26]

Fearful of the Soviet threat, the P.R.C. attempted to offset Soviet power by associating itself with the United States. Various statements by Chinese leaders and the media explained that, due to the more dangerous nature of the Soviet Union, China must use the United States to reduce its own insecurity. In 1973, Premier Zhou quoted Mao's statement that China " 'must not fight two-sided; it is better to fight one-sided.' "[27] In later 1977, *Renmin Ribao* argued that if Chinese leaders "indiscriminately put the two superpowers on a par and fail to single out the Soviet Union as the more dangerous instigator of world war, we would only be blunting . . . revolutionary vigilance . . . and blurring the primary target in the struggle against hegemonism."[28]

Reliance on the United States put China in an extremely disadvantageous position. Because America held the pivot position in the romantic triangle, Chinese leaders lived under constant fear of abandonment by the U.S. and renewed isolation in the face of the dangerous Soviet Union. That apprehension was not without basis. In 1973, for example, Nixon and Brezhnev had signed an agreement stipulating that the U.S. and the U.S.S.R. enter into "urgent negotiations" if relations between both of them or between either side and a third party "appear to involve the risk of nuclear conflict."[29] The P.R.C. was a likely third party of such "collusion."

The fear of abandonment and isolation is clearly reflected in statements by the Chinese leadership. In 1973, Premier Zhou Enlai reported that the superpowers were "colluding" and that "the West always wants to urge the Soviet revisionists eastward to divert the peril towards China."[30] In the same year, Chairman Mao and Premier Zhou met with Henry Kissinger on different occasions and expressed fear of a U.S.-Soviet condominium, and that détente might free Moscow to increase its pressure on China. Mao insisted that the U.S. "resist the temptation to 'push the ill waters eastward.' "[31] The Helsinki conference in 1976 and the so-called Sonnenfeldt doctrine further deepened the P.R.C.'s apprehension. Chinese Foreign Minister Qiao Guanhua told the U.N. General Assembly that

> There are always some people in the West who want to urge social-imperialism eastward and divert this peril towards China, thinking it best if all is quiet in the West. The "European security conference" reflected such a Munich line of thinking. . . . Some people take the lead in appeasing and making concessions to the expansionists, attempting to shift this strategic focus by recognizing their sphere of influence. . . .[32]

The P.R.C. was not encouraged by U.S. foreign policy in the first half of the Carter administration. *Renmin Ribao*, alluding to Carter, charged that "certain leading figures" in the U.S. ruling elite, similar to such "advocates of appeasement" as Neville Chamberlain, were trying to "divert the Soviet peril to the east, to China."[33] When the Soviet Union intensified its encirclement of China by increasing its influence in Vietnam and Cambodia, Hua Guofeng voiced similar fears.[34]

Clearly, then, Chinese leaders were dependent upon the United States for security against the Soviet Union and feared that U.S.-Soviet détente might develop to China's disadvantage. The fact that they regarded their security relationship with the United States as tenuous, at best, affected China's bargaining position. Fear of abandonment and isolation undermined China's ability to threaten the United States if Washington did not accede to the P.R.C.'s demands, for a break with the U.S. would mean a return to the isolation of the dual-adversary policy. The United States, on the other hand, could risk a break with China, because détente with the Soviet Union had minimized America's isolation. This asymmetrical relationship so diminished China's bargaining strength that Beijing preferred to shelve the disputed issues rather than having to bargain from a position of weakness. Geng Biao, head of the International Liaison Department of the Central Committee of the CCP, reportedly made just this point by arguing that if

> we put the two superpowers together and deal with them one after another, the outcome will be unthinkable. Therefore, for the sake of survival, we

must, in the first place, give one up and win the other over. From the strategic point of view as a whole: if we shelve the China-U.S. controversy, we will be able to cope with one side [the Soviet Union] with all-out efforts. . . . Therefore, striving to foster good China-U.S. relations to diminish one enemy . . . [is] put forth in accordance with the requirements of the situation.[35]

He explained that only when Chinese leaders regarded "the time as ripe" would the P.R.C. tell "Uncle Sam . . . [to] pack up your things and go."[36] Earlier, Qiao Guanhua had also argued for the necessity of conflict-free U.S.-China relations, urging that China should treat the two superpowers separately; "otherwise, if we push too hard, they may be forced to unite" and increase China's foreign policy difficulties.[37]

Such statements reflected actual Chinese policy toward the most conflictual issue in the relationship—the status of Taiwan. At no time between the Shanghai Communiqué and 1979 did the P.R.C.'s diplomats ever suggest that the U.S. downgrade its ties with Taiwan as a precondition of continued good relations. On the contrary, Chinese leaders emphasized again and again that the Taiwan issue was not crucial to stable relations; they repeatedly overlooked developments in U.S.-Taiwan relations.

In February 1973, Zhou Enlai surprised Henry Kissinger when he accepted the latter's casual suggestion that the United States establish a liaison office in Beijing and offered reciprocity. Washington had assumed that the P.R.C.'s envoys would never appear where Taiwan officials served in an official capacity. But, because China wanted to move ahead in the relationship, it did not press for U.S. concessions on Taiwan. Later that year, Mao told Kissinger that "we can do without Taiwan for the time being, and let it come after one hundred years. . . . Why is there the need to be in such great haste?" He further offered, "As for your relations with us, I think they need not take a hundred years. . . . But that is to be decided by you. We will not rush you."[38]

In 1975, despite the absence of formal improvement in relations, the Chinese still wanted President Ford to visit the P.R.C. Fearful that the trip might be cancelled because of America's desire to avoid the P.R.C.'s polemics, Beijing emphasized its patience regarding Taiwan and assured Washington that it wanted the President's visit to take place regardless of the lack of progress toward normalization. When Ford arrived, Deng Xiaoping emphasized that normalization would have to take place "eventually." Ford noted that Deng "seemed in no hurry to press for full diplomatic recognition or the termination of our long-standing commitments to Taiwan."[39] U.S. congressional delegations visiting the P.R.C. in 1975 reported similar attitudes.[40] This situation also characterized the early years of the Carter administration. In 1978, Hua Guofeng insisted on Chinese conditions for normalization, but suggested that in the absence of normalization the P.R.C. still hoped to "increase contacts . . . and promote mutual understanding" between the two countries.[41]

The foreign policy makers' avoidance of conflict is also reflected in P.R.C. media and Foreign Ministry materials. *Xinhua's* attack on Senator Goldwater's March 1976 statement of support for Taiwan was a rare exception, as was strident impatience over the Taiwan issue on the part of Chinese officials during Senator Hugh Scott's visit to Beijing in July of that year. A low-level protest in 1975 against Washington's cancellation of a visit by a Chinese singing group because of its selection of a song calling for the liberation of Taiwan was the first authoritative statement critizing U.S. Taiwan policy since 1972. The only high-level criticism during this period—a Foreign Ministry attack on American "connivance" with *Tibetan* "traitors" residing in the United States[42]—only underscored the P.R.C.'s usual silence on the role of Taiwan in U.S.-China relations.

Beijing's patience on the Taiwan issue was not due to U.S. respect for Chinese sensitivities or progress in distancing itself from Taiwan. Although the United States had removed its last offensive weapons from the island by May 1975, other acts reaffirmed its commitment to Taiwan. Between 1973 and 1975, Washington appointed a senior diplomat to serve as ambassador to Taipei, permitted Taiwan to open two additional consulates in the United States, failed to complete the withdrawal of U.S. troops from Taiwan, and sold additional military hardware to Taiwan on credit. When Saigon fell to North Vietnamese forces in April 1975, President Ford, in a clear reference to the U.S.-Taiwan Mutual Defense Treaty, declared that it was his "aim" to "reaffirm our commitments to Taiwan." Although the P.R.C. appeared unhappy with these developments, and U.S.-China relations remained stagnant, it failed to press the point.[43] The one instance in which China did challenge the U.S. on the Taiwan issue occurred in 1977, in the aftermath of Secretary of State Cyrus Vance's visit to Beijing. Chinese leaders were angry, not because of lack of progress toward normalization, but because Washington gave the impression that China had compromised on its normalization conditions.[44]

That its strategic vulnerability in the romantic triangle was Beijing's primary concern is reflected in the actual focus of the P.R.C.'s diplomacy. Rather than harping on U.S.-Taiwan relations, Beijing relentlessly criticized U.S. policy toward the Soviet Union and the detriments of détente, seeking to encourage Washington to abandon détente in favor of a more aggressive global policy. If successful, the Chinese policy would reduce the probability that the U.S. would abandon the P.R.C., and thus would improve Beijing's bargaining position in U.S.-China relations.

When Kissinger met with Zhou Enlai in 1973, the Chinese Premier skirted the Taiwan issue and concentrated on Soviet policy. When he visited China in 1975, Kissinger was subjected to a long diatribe on America's alleged lack of resolve in dealing with the Soviet Union. Mao insisted in his conversations with President Ford that Washington had to stand up to Moscow's attempt to achieve hegemony, and that the U.S. had to maintain its strategic role in East Asia. Deng asserted that resistance to Soviet ambitions was "a more important question" than Taiwan. During the Carter administration, the P.R.C. continued to equate U.S.-Soviet détente with U.S. appeasement, and gave little attention to Taiwan.[45] The common elements during this period were patience regarding bilateral conflicts and vociferous opposition to U.S.-Soviet détente. Once détente began to crumble and the United States lost the pivot position in the U.S.-Soviet-P.R.C. triangle, China shifted the focus of its criticism to more conflictual bilateral issues.

The Quiet Years and Chinese Domestic Politics

Although the international environment of foreign policy making explains a great deal of China's U.S. policy, Chinese domestic politics also affected U.S.-China relations after the Shanghai Communiqué. Our problem lies in determining the influence of domestic politics in the context of the limits of choice imposed by the pattern of triangular politics.

Zhou Enlai's and Mao Zedong's decision to seek rapprochement with the United States was not universally popular among the Chinese elite. Jiang Qing, Mao's wife, believed that China's U.S. policy was both unnecessary and too conciliatory; she insisted that "although we do not have 'white friends,' 'big friends' and 'wealthy friends,' we are not isolated." She argued that China's dual adversary policy was not dangerous and that the P.R.C.'s relations with Third World countries were sufficient to deter the Soviet Union from infringing upon Chinese interests. Hence, she saw little need to establish close relations with the American "imperalists": "It is impossible to attain the final victory of the socialist revolution by departing from national independence and development of the national economy. It is on this point that we are different from the opportunists."[46] Zhou, however, did believe China was isolated and he thus sought "friends" whom Jiang considered unacceptable. When Jiang Qing and her colleagues, the so-called "Gang of Four," were ousted following the death of Mao, elite opposition to China's U.S. policy remained. In 1977, the Chinese media reflected two foreign policy themes. One emphasized that the P.R.C. should lean to the West; the other emphasized self-reliance and unity with the Third World, in opposition to both the United States and the Soviet Union.[47] Taiwan was often the focal point of the opposition, as some leaders were impatient with the lack of progress toward unification.[48]

In the debate within the leadership, the political opposition used the Taiwan issue to criticize Beijing's foreign policy makers. It also influenced the content of China's media. In the midst of the 1973–1974 anti-Confucius campaign which aimed to weaken Zhou Enlai's political power, and for some time thereafter, the media intensely criticized Western and American societies. Implicit in this criticism was an attack on Zhou Enlai's policy toward the United States.[49]

It is suggestive, however, that both the media and Chinese leaders never directly attacked U.S.-Taiwan relations. The circumspect nature of the assault underscores the limited impact of the opposition and of its policy preferences. Indeed, there is no evidence that those opposed to China's U.S. policy after the Shanghai Communiqué had any direct role at all in the policy-making process.[50] It seems that the consensus among those actually involved in making foreign policy was that implicit Chinese alignment with the United States was essential given China's international circumstances, and that the Taiwan issue should not be a subject of U.S.-China negotiations. The potential for conflict with the United States, and resultant isolation, effectively squelched the competing foreign policy options. The romantic triangle, with Washington holding the pivot position, shaped the debate in Beijing; dependence on the U.S. restricted the viability of alternative policy options, undermining the influence of those leaders who criticized existing policy.

That international politics influenced domestic Chinese political interactions does not negate the role of domestic politics in foreign policy. Although Jiang Qing and her supporters were unable to bring about China's detachment from the United States, the political impact of their criticisms was sufficient to deter Zhou Enlai from seeking compromise and made marginal incremental improvement politically difficult. Here we see the impact of Chinese domestic politics on U.S.-China relations between 1972 and 1978. Zhou Enlai made this quite clear to Henry Kissinger. Zhou understood that compromise on Taiwan would make U.S.-China ties unpopular in China, thus undermining the security relationship, and proposed that the two sides maintain the status quo on the Taiwan issue.[51] Chinese domestic politics similarly affected President Ford's visit to the P.R.C. in late 1975, obstructing further improvement in U.S.-China relations regardless of American intentions. According to Michel Oksenberg,

> from 1974 through 1976, as Zhou Enlai's political position eroded under attacks from the radical "Gang of Four," the Premier's ability to protect and advance the issues under his control weakened. By 1975, it was impossible for him or for Deng Xiaoping to bring fresh initiatives to the relationship with the United States.[52]

When Secretary of State Cyrus Vance visited China in mid-1977, it was clear that Deng Xiaoping was in no mood to make concessions. He had lost his position in April 1975 and had yet to consolidate his power within the post-Mao leadership. Although he did not yield to domestic pressure to raise conflictual issues, neither could he appear willing to compromise. Thus, he challenged the U.S. position—that the visit was a success and that the P.R.C. was flexible on the Taiwan issue and the terms of normalization—declaring that Vance's mission had caused a "setback" in U.S.-China relations.[53]

Because of the impact of the international environment, domestic pressure did not succeed in bringing about the adoption of a hard line. A stable relationship was sufficient to avoid damaging criticism. Perhaps most revealing was Hua Guofeng's apparent shift in policy preference between the time he was first in power following the death of Mao and the purge of the "Gang of Four," and the later period from mid- to late-1977, when Deng Xiaoping assumed greater responsibility for Chinese foreign policy. Initially, when Hua was responsible for Chinese foreign policy, he was quick to express support for maintaining the status quo in U.S.-China relations.[54] Although there had been a transition in leadership, policy remained the same. As responsibility for policy shifted to Deng Xiaoping in 1977, policy also remained the same, but Hua Guofeng's position shifted. He now called for P.R.C. equidistance between the superpowers and attacked Deng Xiaoping on the Taiwan issue.[55]

U.S.-China politics during this period also reflected the problem of a dual audience. When Alexander Haig traveled to Beijing in January 1972, Zhou Enlai used the occasion to defend himself against domestic charges of weakness toward the "imperialists." At a midnight meeting with Haig, in the presence of various Chinese "cabinet members," the Chinese press, and television cameras, Zhou "launched into a vitriolic denunciation of the United States." When Haig protested, Zhou "clapped his hands," the cabinet and the journalists departed, and the two statesmen held a serious discussion until three o'clock that morning.[56] Zhou had his footage for the domestic audience and could now talk business with the representative of "imperialism." Other government and media statements undoubtedly served similar purposes; they certainly did not reflect a new challenge to the status quo in U.S.-Taiwan relations.

It thus appears that from 1972 to 1978, the P.R.C.'s leaders consistently adopted their predecessors' foreign policy, while those out of power—regardless of their preference when in power—consistently criticized the established policy. Demands for a less aligned policy toward the United States apparently had domestic political purposes which inhibited new initiatives, but which did not promote initiatives that sought to force the Taiwan issue or to distance the P.R.C. from the United States. The consistency of policy, the lack of initiative, and the role of the domestic opposition were the result of the limits of choice imposed by China's weak bargaining position in the U.S.-Soviet-P.R.C. triangle, which was in turn a product of the era's pattern of relations.

The Collapse of Détente and the New Era in U.S.-China Relations

The pattern of the triangular relations of the 1970's began to change in the middle of the Carter administration. The first steps had occurred in 1975, following Soviet-Cuban cooperation in Angola and the fall of Saigon. Later developments in Ethiopia aggravated Washington's suspicions that even minimal cooperation with the Soviet Union might not be possible. Although the Carter administration initially pursued cooperation between the United States and the Soviet Union, it gradually became less sanguine about Moscow's intentions. Deployment of Cuban troops in the Horn of Africa in mid-1977 and difficulties of reaching an arms control agreement with Moscow encouraged a more confrontational policy. The discovery of Soviet combat troops in Cuba and the Soviet invasion of Afghanistan ultimately changed Washington's policy.[57] U.S.-Soviet détente died on the battlefields of Afghanistan.

As the Soviet Union came to appear more ominous, China grew more valuable to the United States as a strategic ally. National Security Advisor Brzezinski's visit to China in May 1978 was impelled by his belief that the Soviets' "misuse of détente" had made a "strategic response . . . necessary."[58] Normalization of relations in late 1978 merged with other aspects of U.S. China policy to cause a strategic tilt toward China. It was clear that the United States now sought a "stable marriage" so as to better contend with Soviet U.S. policy. In August 1979, when Vice President Mondale visited Beijing, the P.R.C. received most-favored-nation status, Export-Import Bank credits, investment guarantees, and access to U.S. technical services, none of which were available to the Soviet Union.[59] In January 1980, in response to the Soviet invasion of Afghanistan, President Carter instructed Secretary of Defense Harold Brown that during his visit to Beijing he should propose U.S. sales of nonlethal military equipment to the P.R.C., including ground telecommunication stations that could receive data (with military uses) from U.S. satellites. These developments reflected the end of American evenhandedness between Moscow and Beijing and the beginning of a U.S.-China military relationship that was "traceable to the rapidly growing Soviet military might . . . and to Soviet intervention in southern Africa, the Horn of Africa, Indochina and Afghanistan."[60]

In response to these changes in U.S. policy, the Chinese media increasingly depicted the United States as rising to the challenge of Soviet "hegemonism" and abandoning appeasement. In 1979, before the Soviet Union invaded Afghanistan, *Shijie Zhishi* (World Affairs) observed that the United States had begun to carry out "certain adjustments in its strategy toward the Soviet Union." In U.S. Soviet policy, "the trend of taking the 'offensive while being on the defensive' is gradually increasing."[61] Zhuang Qubing of the Foreign Ministry's Institute of International Studies argued in *Shijie Zhishi* that the supporters of appeasement are decreasing and that there are "more and more people who advocate that the U.S. administration should 'change course,' revise its strategy . . . and 'seek peace through strength,' [and] increase the military budget . . . in order to . . . realistically and effectively deal with Soviet 'global' expansion." Nevertheless, it was too early to determine the course of U.S. policy, for "there is still so much debate in the U.S. that no concensus can be reached, and recently this debate has further sharpened."[62]

Washington's response to the Soviet invasion of Afghanistan reinforced the Chinese leaders' perception of a new anti-Soviet direction in U.S. policy. Zhuang Qubing now wrote that there was a clear change in U.S. Soviet policy and that the United States had "adopted several measures to resist the Soviet Union which it had not previously adopted," including establishing strategic relations with China. He also predicted that "from now on, the United States and the Soviet Union will unavoidably open a new round of the arms race, and the global rivalry between the two sides will further sharpen."[63] *Renmin Ribao* maintained that the increase in the U.S. defense budget "marks a major change in U.S. defense policy." Moreover, Washington "altered its position of avoiding military involvement in 'regional conflicts' and has put forward . . . the 'Carter Doctrine' . . . with a view to protecting U.S. interests in the Middle East and the Persian Gulf. . . ." Overall, *Renmin Ribao* was pleased that the United States now held a "realistic appraisal" of the Soviet Union. Détente was now a thing of the past, as

> it is quite impossible to return to the bygone situation of East-West relations. Antagonism will be the main feature in the relations between the two countries in the foreseeable future. . . . the tendency toward intensive contention . . . is irreversible."[64]

Similar analyses appears throughout the year—to the effect that the Soviet Union had "fallen into unprecedented isolation," that superpower contention in the Mediterranean was "still sharpening," and that future Soviet-American arms control agreements were highly unlikely.[65]

Chinese leaders were no longer so concerned about the prospects of expanded Soviet-American détente and anti-P.R.C. collusion, or afraid of U.S. abandonment of China. Despite its implications of Soviet "encirclement" of China, Moscow's invasion of Afghanistan was a clear plus for Chinese interests, for it altered U.S.-China dependency relations. In late 1980, Deng Xiaoping maintained that Washington "alone is not in a position to deal with Soviet hegemonism. The Soviet challenge can only be coped with if the United States strengthens unity with its allies and unites its strength with all the forces that are resisting the Soviet challenge. . . ."[66] In view of Washington's intentions, it was ironic that the U.S. quest for a stable marriage reduced the P.R.C.'s dependence and altered the U.S.-China bargaining relationship so that Beijing no longer feared the implications of conflict with the United States. But such was the nearly inevitable outcome of the shift in the triangular pattern of relations. The result was actually increased instability in U.S.-China relations, as Deng Xiaoping and other Chinese leaders emphasized independence from the United States and pressed China's interest in reducing the cost to Beijing of good U.S.-China relations in terms of Taiwan's relationship with the United States.

Chinese policy toward the Taiwan issue was further influenced by Beijing's involvement in negotiations with the Soviet Union. No longer so fearful of abandonment by the U.S. and of Soviet expansion, Beijing had greater confidence in talking with Moscow. Chinese leaders had flirted with the idea of conducting serious negotiations with the Soviet Union before 1979,[67] but they were unable to turn such ideas into policy, for their fear of isolation weakened their bargaining position vis-à-vis the Soviet Union. Now that America had committed itself to China, the P.R.C. could seek a reduction in Sino-Soviet tensions from a strengthened position.[68]

In early April 1979, China informed the Soviet Union that it would not renew the 30-year Sino-Soviet treaty of 1950. Simultaneously, it offered to open negotiations with Soviet leaders. A short time later, Beijing suggested that the two sides conduct general negotiations with no preconditions. Through October 17, there were five preliminary meetings and six sessions at the deputy foreign ministerial level. Although the talks did not yield any concrete achievements, they were the first serious Sino-Soviet negotiations in 15 years.[69] Even though the Soviet invasion of Afghanistan obstructed progress, Chinese leaders continued to signal their interest in moderated Sino-Soviet tension. They waited nearly three weeks after the invasion to suspend negotiations, feebly arguing that the new circumstances were "apparently" inappropriate. In early February 1980, Chinese leaders met as scheduled with their Soviet counterparts to discuss arrangements for river navigation.[70] Thus, in 1979, concurrent with the deterioration of Soviet-U.S. détente and the Carter administration's quest for a stable marriage with China, a small but significant change took place in relations between Beijing and Moscow. The contrast is striking between these developments and the situation a mere three years earlier, when Moscow sought improved relations after Mao's death and was rebuffed by Chinese leaders.[71]

Under these conditions, progress toward the unification of Taiwan and the mainland now became a major component of the P.R.C.'s policy. China was no longer content to wait indefinitely, but initiated a policy designed to expedite the process. The change was evident in

Deng Xiaoping's speeches. In January 1980, in an important speech, Deng announced that in the 1980s, "we must work hard to achieve" reunification in Taiwan with the motherland, and "even though there will still be complications of various sorts, . . . from [the] beginning it is a great issue that will be placed on our agenda."[72] In May of the same year, he stated that peace in Asia would be served if Taiwan "returned to the motherland at an earlier date. . . ."[73]

The first Chinese initiative followed President Carter's decision of June 1980 to allow U.S. companies to discuss the sale of the so-called FX jet fighter to Taiwan.[74] Although the United States had sold advanced weapons to Taiwan in the mid-1970s and had made clear that it would continue to sell defensive weapons to Taiwan after normalization,[75] the P.R.C.'s leaders, for the first time since the Shanghai Communiqué, strongly challenged U.S. policy. A *Xinhua* commentary criticized the decision, as well as transfers of large amounts of military equipment to Taiwan in 1979 and 1980, warning that U.S. arms sales to Taiwan were "harmful" to U.S.-China relations and were "bound to aggravate tension in the Taiwan Strait. . . ." It issued a "strong demand" that the United States "stop forthwith its arms sales to Taiwan."[76] Such forceful language concerning Taiwan had not been heard since 1972.

A similar situation occurred later in 1980 when Washington granted diplomatic immunities and privileges to representatives of the Taiwan government. U.S. Ambassador Woodcock was summoned to Beijing's Foreign Ministry, where he received a protest note expressing the P.R.C.'s "unhappiness and concern" regarding U.S.-Taiwan relations. An authoritative Commentator article in *Renmin Ribao* insisted that this policy was "completely unacceptable" because it reflected a "two-China" policy. The paper suggested that U.S. failure to accept the P.R.C.'s demands might lead to greater U.S.-China conflict and would be harmful to cooperation against Moscow. The decision of whether or not to pursue continued development of U.S.-China relations or "reverse them" was said to be of "major strategic importance" to U.S. leaders.[77] For the first time since rapprochement, the P.R.C. was threatening the U.S. with a "reversal" of relations if Washington did not alter its policy.

During the 1980 presidential campaign, Beijing criticized Ronald Reagan's promise to resume official relations with Taiwan. *Renmin Ribao*, reflecting China's heightened confidence that it was no longer dependent on the U.S. and that U.S. abandonment of the P.R.C. was less likely than before, declared that "those who think that China is willing to develop ties with the United States because China needs its help, or that China, in order to maintain its relations with the United States, will eventually swallow the bitter pill prepared by Reagan are daydreaming and miscalculating."[78] A *Renmin Ribao* commentary added that if Reagan's proposals were carried out, there would be a "grave retrogression in Sino-U.S. relations" and his policy would have a "serious harmful effect on the struggle against hegemonism. . . ."[79] Although these and similar articles were directed at Reagan, together with P.R.C. objections to U.S. arms sales to Taiwan and to the granting of diplomatic immunities and privileges to Taiwan representatives, they conveyed to both Reagan and President Carter Beijing's new strategic outlook and the new aggressiveness in China's Taiwan policy.[80]

Thus, the P.R.C. adopted a more aggressive U.S. policy during the latter part of the Carter administration in response to changes in the triangular pattern of relations and in U.S.-China relations. The Reagan administration's policies furthered these changes and led Beijing to increase its pressure on the United States to weaken its relationship with Taiwan. As in 1979 and 1980, it was U.S. Soviet policy and its implications for triangular politics that most affected China's bargaining position and its attitude toward the Taiwan issue.

Ronald Reagan entered office with a record of hostility for the Soviet Union, and his arms control position and proposed defense budget indicated an intention to challenge, rather than to appease, Moscow's alleged ambitions. Chinese leaders were keenly aware of the shift in policy. In *From Hollywood to the White House*, one analyst observed that Reagan "criticizes the past few administrations . . . , emphasizing that détente is only a 'fantasy,' that the cold war never ended, and that peace cannot be achieved through concession and compromise." He "takes practically every problem as part of the U.S.-Soviet struggle for hegemony" and believes that East-West competition is "unavoidable" and "continually intensifying."[81] *Shijie Zhishi* observed that the new administration *"clearly states that it takes resistance to Soviet expansion as the central link of its foreign policy."* Although the Carter administration responded to the Soviet invasion of Afghanistan with a "new policy of containment , . . . it did not put forward a set of new strategic concepts." By contrast, Reagan and his associates "stress that the Soviet Union is 'the root cause of all troubles.'. . ." In all, "an important change" had taken place.[82] In 1981, *Xiandai Guoji Guanxi* (Contemporary International Relations) maintained that, compared to Carter, Reagan "has paid greater attention to increasing . . . military strength to engage in global struggle with the Soviet Union" and that he believes that the United States "must speed up military preparation" to deal with increased Soviet power.[83] Reagan's electoral victory was explained as America's response to the "new low" in its international position and to the possibility that it would become a "second-class power, militarily inferior to the Soviet Union." Americans sought a "new leader" to end the "trend to their country's declining position in the world." Reagan's victory was a result of this "historical setting."[84]

By the middle of 1981, Chinese leaders were convinced that there was no possibility that U.S.-Soviet relations would improve. When Reagan expressed a desire to open discussions with Moscow on theater nuclear forces in Europe, *Renmin Ribao* saw it as a mere propaganda ploy: "It makes no difference" whether or not the two sides hold talks, "since the struggle is in any case going to continue."[85] In November, on the eve of the talks, a *Renmin Ribao* News Analysis noted that the Reagan administration "has not acted with weakness" in response to Soviet deployments of the SS-20 missile; rather, its plans to deploy the Pershing II missile in Europe "dealt a heavy blow" to the Soviet Union.[86] China's confidence in continued U.S.-Soviet hostility and its skepticism of Reagan's calls for negotiations continued throughout 1982. By June of that year, a *Renmin Ribao* Special Commentary declared that an arms race was well underway and that "it cannot be stopped even if both sides wished to" stop it. The superpowers' arms race and their "tit-for-tat war preparation activities have become increasingly more intense and dangerous."[87] Chinese leaders, who had once been preoccupied with détente and with an alleged U.S. plan to divert the Soviet threat eastward, were now confident that the new Soviet-U.S. cold war would continue unabated.

Thus, the changes in Soviet-U.S. relations in 1979 and 1980 intensified under the Reagan administration. The U.S. had irrevocably lost the pivot seat in the strategic triangle; there was no longer any possibility of restoring détente with the Soviet Union, and there was even less possibility of isolating the P.R.C. because the U.S. needed China as an ally. Moreover, Beijing's growing sense of independence was enhanced by the Soviet Union's foreign policy. Its occupation of Afghanistan and military and economic support for Cuba and Vietnam, instability in Eastern Europe, and domestic economic troubles weakened Soviet expansionist capability. Although the struggle against hegemonism could not be abandoned, the threat was less immediate.[88]

Chinese confidence was reflected in Beijing's changing global posture. In the 1970s and during most of the Carter administration, Chinese leaders had stressed the importance of close relations with the United States in order to resist Soviet hegemonism; beginning in 1980 and increasingly in 1981, Beijing de-emphasized its strategic relationship with Washington, accentuated the evils of both the superpowers, and stressed China's common interests with third-world countries in opposing superpower hegemonism.[89] China now perceived itself as less dependent on the United States for its security vis-à-vis the Soviet Union, and therefore ended its almost total support for U.S. foreign policy.

Beijing's increasing independence encouraged Chinese leaders to attempt once again to alleviate Sino-Soviet hostility, further improving China's position in the U.S.-Soviet-P.R.C. triangle. In June 1981, *Renmin Ribao* suggested a resumption of border talks. Later in the year, in a favorable response to Moscow's overtures, China and the Soviet Union signed a railway transport agreement.[90] Progress was slow but unmistakable. In April 1982, the two sides agreed to resume border trade and to increase the value of two-way trade by 45 percent, thus reaching the highest level since 1967. Moreover, Chinese propaganda ceased referring to Soviet leaders as "revisionists," thereby making compromise less of an ideological heresy.[91]

After 1979, the issue of arms sales to Taiwan was the primary source of the P.R.C.'s discontent with the United States. China now no longer simply opposed the sale of the FX war plane, but all arms sales to Taiwan. Beijing basically insisted that Washington relinquish its position that it alone would determine the nature of U.S.-Taiwan military relations; it sought to participate in defining and limiting the terms of U.S. arms sales to Taiwan. The negotiations reveal the impact of the triangular pattern of relations on Beijing's bargaining strength, on its U.S. policy, and on the nature of the U.S.-China relationship.

Beijing started by indicating that it did not fear isolation or U.S. abandonment. *Guoji Wenti Yanjiu* (International Affairs), the journal of the Foreign Ministry's Institute of International Studies, noted that China's dependency on the U.S. had changed in recent years. It declared that members of the U.S. elite held an

> old outlook: so long as the United States opposes Soviet expansionism, China will not care very much about the Taiwan issue. . . . If some people still believe that Sino-U.S. relations can only be based on opposition to other countries' hegemonic acts, if this is not a retreat, then what is? If they believe that China will agree to this retreat, if this is not a dream, then what is?[92]

Because the P.R.C.'s Soviet policy is beneficial to U.S. strategic interests, "it is especially ridiculous to say that China has more reason to look to the United States for help."[93] Beijing and Washington no longer experienced "asymmetrical strategic interests," and Chinese leaders were confident that the new administration, due to its own preoccupations with the "Soviet threat," would seek to avoid a deterioration in U.S.-China relations.

This confidence helped to shape an aggressive policy toward U.S.-Taiwan relations. For the first time since the Shanghai Communiqué, Chinese leaders threatened to withhold their cooperation if Washington did not comply with the P.R.C.'s demands. *Guoji Wenti Yanjiu* pointed out that in the 1950s, Moscow mistakenly believed that China's dependence on the Soviet Union meant that Beijing would have to tolerate Soviet demands; the result was the Sino-Soviet conflict. In suggesting that such a situation might develop in U.S.-China relations, the article warned that, for those who have made similar miscalculations concerning Chinese policy toward the U.S., "this history should have educational significance."[94]

When Washington attempted to moderate Beijing's stand by balancing arms sales to Taiwan with arms sales to the P.R.C., Chinese leaders refused to buy U.S. arms and threatened further hostile action. During Secretary of State Haig's visit to Beijing in June 1981, Foreign Minister Huang Hua mentioned the possibility of a "rupture" in the relationship, and Deng pointed out that Chinese patience was limited. U.S.-China relations, he warned, might deteriorate if Washington failed to moderate its stand on the issue. Moreover, during Haig's stay in Beijing, *Renmin Ribao* proposed a Sino-Soviet border agreement. The day after he left China, the P.R.C. media threatened to downgrade relations if the arms sales issue was not resolved, repeating the analogy between the Sino-Soviet conflict and the current instability in U.S.-China relations.[95] When the U.S. persisted in trying to offset arms sales to Taiwan with arms sales to the P.R.C., Chinese leaders reinforced their warnings.[96]

China increased the pressure in later October, when Premier Zhao Ziyang met with President Reagan in Cancun. Zhao pointed out that the arms sales issue obstructed developing strategic relations. Huang Hua was more explicit. In a meeting with Haig, he demanded that the U.S. "specify the period to time over which it intended to sell arms to Taiwan, undertake that sales in any given year would not exceed the level of the Carter years, and indicate that sales would decline year by year and then cease." On a visit to Washington a short time later, he issued an "ultimatum": that the U.S. specify the date when arms sales to Taiwan would cease. He suggested that high-level talks be conducted to work out an agreement.[97] For the first time since U.S.-China rapprochement, China was on the offensive and the United States was on the defensive.

Negotiations began that December. They often involved strident exchanges and escalated pressure tactics as neither side compromised quickly. When the Netherlands ignored the P.R.C.'s warnings and sold two submarines to Taiwan, the P.R.C. downgraded Sino-Dutch relations to the liaison level. In so doing, Beijing appeared to back itself into a corner, leaving itself no choice but to respond similarly to U.S. arms sales to Taiwan. A commentary in *Guoji Wenti Yanjiu* noted that the Sino-Dutch situation was "not without a relationship to U.S. arms sales to Taiwan" and warned, "whether or not China-U.S. relations also retrogress depends on . . . [U.S.] determination to resolve the issue of arms sales to Taiwan." Moreover, Chinese "tolerance has a definite limit. . . . China-U.S. relations are currently seriously threatened. This is completely caused by the United States." The commentary also recalled the Sino-Soviet split and ended with the ominous declaration that "the Chinese side strives for a good future, but it is also prepared for a bad outcome."[98] Eventually, the two sides signed the August 17 Communiqué. Although China backed away from its original negotiating position which had called for a precise date when arms sales would terminate, the new agreement restricted U.S. arms sales to Taiwan, bringing China closer to its goal of completely severing the military relationship between the U.S. and Taiwan.

The negotiating process revealed China's confidence in its ability to threaten the United States, as well as Washington's fear that China would carry out its threat, thereby undermining the strategic relationship with China. When Reagan altered U.S. Taiwan policy with provocative and contentious pronouncements, China countered with more than mere diplomatic ripostes—a response that was too aggressive if it merely sought to pressure Reagan to return to the policy of the Carter administration. While the first signs of tension had appeared during the Carter administration, Reagan's statements provided the diplomatic justification for the P.R.C. to seek an ambitious change in the U.S.-Taiwan relationship. Beijing calculated that its greater independence made it threats credible, and that the Reagan administration's concern for Soviet expansionism would lead it to protect strategic cooperation with China at the expense of a compromise in U.S. Taiwan policy. This proved to be a correct evaluation.[99]

Chinese Domestic Politics and
U.S.-China Conflict

What was the role of Chinese domestic politics in the P.R.C.'s new policy toward relations between the United States and Taiwan? As had been the case between 1972 and 1978, there were leadership differences over U.S. policy. Some Chinese leaders were opposed to Deng Xiaoping's policy of strategic alignment with the U.S. and believed that Deng, like Premier Zhou before him, had unnecessarily compromised China's position on Taiwan.[100] In January 1982, Vice Premier Li Xiannian, for example, denied that there could be close relations between China and the U.S., declaring that the Chinese people "know very well that the United States is still an imperialist country."[101]

It is significant that the new policy debate apparently had a different impact from that of the earlier period. While domestic opposition between 1972 and 1978 led to a lack of policy initiative, policy has become more aggressive since 1979, as preferred by Deng Xiaoping's critics. It has been persuasively argued that Deng was inclined to play down the Taiwan issue rather than press the U.S. to accommodate itself to the P.R.C.'s interests, but that he reluctantly took a hard line in response to criticism from his political adversaries.[102] Why did domestic politics have such a strong impact during this period?

It is not sufficient to argue that Deng adopted a hard line toward the U.S. because his political power was vulnerable to charges of being "soft" on the Taiwan issue.[103] Zhou Enlai pursued a similar policy and was exposed to similar criticism, yet he did not change his line. Zhou's steadfastness is significant because, for practically the entire period from 1973 to his death in January 1976, he was the focus of one anti-rightist campaign after another. Deng Xiaoping, on the other hand, though he did not have complete freedom of choice, was less susceptible to the threats of the opposition in the post-normalization period. In view of Deng's relative political security in contrast to Zhou's somewhat more precarious position, more than the existence of political opposition must be considered in order to adequately explain Deng's apparent willingness to pursue the policy option preferred by his rivals.

As in the situation before 1979, the "second image reversed" perspective makes clear that international politics after the romantic triangle period influenced the role of domestic debates on Chinese policy. As Chinese leaders realized the evolution of the pattern of relations, the viability of adopting a hard stance toward the United States undermined the policy makers' ability to maintain the status quo, especially on a topic such as Taiwan. On a less emotional issue, criticism might be rebuffed. But once change in policy was an option, Taiwan became a vulnerable point for Deng despite his relative political stability.

That is what explains the shift in Deng's attitude. While he called for reunification with Taiwan in 1979 and 1980, he also promoted closer U.S.-China relations and an anti-Soviet alliance on the part of the Western powers, China, and the third world; he was a reluctant spokesman for China's Taiwan policy.[104] In mid-1981, however, he dropped his pro-U.S. stance and forcefully threatened the U.S. with downgraded relations if the two sides failed to resolve the Taiwan issues.[105] His ultimate commitment to a hard-line policy reflected more than mere domestic political pressure; Deng was no longer responding to domestic politics when he spoke on Taiwan, but expressed a new policy preference.

This also explains the continuity in Chinese policy after the immediate crisis was resolved with the August 17 Communiqué, and after Reagan moderated his language so as to stop supplying ammunition to Deng's domestic adversaries. The logic of the primacy of domestic politics suggests that relations should now have resembled those of the more placid 1970s. Yet this was not the case, as China continued to emphasize its dissatisfaction with various aspects of U.S. foreign policy through 1982 and into 1983. Rather than simply find a new explanation for such continuity in policy,[106] it is best to see continuity in cause: conflict in U.S.-China relations was caused by the leadership's recognition of China's new bargaining power. China's passivity was the product of one era; its ambition was the product of the era that followed.

During the earlier period, Chinese domestic politics may have slowed the process of consolidating relations; after normalization, it speeded the process of developing conflict. In response to domestic opposition in 1979 and 1980, Deng and his colleagues apparently initiated the diplomatic offensive toward America's Taiwan policy before they recognized its international political validity. Deng did not actively participate in China's new U.S. policy until 1981. Had the P.R.C.'s leadership been free of domestic constraints, it might not have changed China's U.S. policy so quickly; Deng's learning process might have taken longer to develop.

Deng's acceptance of his adversaries' general policy preference did not end the significance of Taiwan as a political football. Reagan's often extreme statements demanded a response from China's leaders regardless of their policy preferences; no Chinese leader could at that time appear to acquiesce to American statements that suggested a "two-China" policy. Hence, many of Deng's sharp attacks on the United States may have served his domestic needs rather than fit into a well-thought-out tactical plan for bringing about U.S. pliability. That does not mean that Deng did not seek to pressure Washington or that he accepted the status quo in U.S.-Taiwan relations; it does mean that the appearance of China's day-to-day tactics may have been skewed by domestic influences.[107]

Thus, during the period of the new U.S.-Soviet cold war, Chinese domestic politics was an important factor shaping the character of U.S.-China relations. Although domestic politics cannot adequately explain why China's policy changed, it does explain why policy changed at a particular time, and why China appeared to be more bellicose at one time than at another. The particular pattern of triangular relations defined the nature of the U.S.-China relationship, set the parameters of the Chinese domestic debate over its foreign policy, and established the limits of the influence of Chinese politics of Beijing's policy toward the United States.

Conclusion

The changing nature of both the pattern of relations of the strategic triangle and China's domestic situation has brought about changes in the P.R.C.'s policy toward the United States since the Shanghai Communiqué. Within the context of shared general interests, China has developed different strategies for dealing with the conflictual particular interest of Taiwan and for seeking to alter the status quo in U.S.-Taiwan relations. Changes in the pattern of relations in the strategic triangle have been the determining factor in shaping the P.R.C.'s policy. China preferred to ignore U.S.-Chinese differences over Taiwan for most of the 1970s; but when the United States lost the pivot position in the triangle as the new cold war developed in U.S.-Soviet relations, China gained the confidence required to bring the Taiwan issue to the negotiating table in a forceful and sometimes belligerent manner.

These conclusions suggest that one key to the P.R.C.'s compliance with Washington's preferences in U.S.-Chinese relations lies in moderate U.S.-Soviet relations. When relations between Moscow and Washington deteriorated, China went on the diplomatic offensive. China is likely to continue to emphasize its independence from the United States as long as the superpowers are unable to moderate the nuclear arms race and their global conflict. The August 17 Communiqué did not signal an immediate end to China's aggressive U.S. policy, to its effort to ameliorate Sino-Soviet relations, or to its diplomatic emphasis on the third world.[108]

The implication of this approach is that there is a secondary role for Washington's bilateral China policy in efforts aimed at affecting the character of U.S.-Chinese relations. Once the U.S. lost the pivot position, efforts to placate the P.R.C. were likely to encourage Chinese leaders to believe in the efficacy of their bargaining power, to believe that "the U.S. needs China more than China needs the U.S." Nevertheless, there was probably little the United States could do to prevent the shift in U.S.-China relations and the attendant compromises over Taiwan. The decline in U.S.-Soviet relations, which began during the Carter administration, could not be prevented by Washington alone, and it was this end of détente that changed the U.S.-Chinese bargaining relationship.[109]

Since mid-1983 the tension in U.S.-China relations has been reduced despite continued differences and lack of new compromises over Taiwan, trade, and security relations. What explains this apparent shift to a third period in U.S.-China relations? Apparently President Reagan's confidence in U.S. strength vis-à-vis the Soviet Union after increased U.S. military spending and his emphasis of the role of Japan over the P.R.C. in U.S. security policy in the Pacific have reduced China's bargaining leverage.[110] Nevertheless, continued U.S.-Soviet conflict and a reduction in Sino-Soviet tension still result in the P.R.C.'s independence from the U.S. Recent U.S.-Chinese relations therefore appear to be characterized by a more equal bargaining relationship.

Chinese domestic politics have played an important role in the P.R.C.'s policy toward the U.S. Both during the period when China's bargaining position was weak because of Washington's pivot position and later, when the demise of détente encouraged P.R.C. initiatives on the Taiwan question, China's leaders were under the constraint of domestic political exigencies. The relative importance of domestic politics has been a function of the range of choice allowed by the pattern of triangular politics. When the range of choice was narrow, domestic politics had a small impact on China's U.S. policy. When the choices expanded, domestic critics wielded greater influence on foreign policy making. Patterns of triangular relations explain *why* changes occurred in

China's U.S. policy; domestic politics explains why those changes occurred *when* they did.

On some occasions, Chinese leaders were compelled to respond publicly to their critics on the Taiwan issue in order to protect their political power. The dual audience problem was thus a factor in U.S.-China relations. Understanding the immediate short-term relationship between China's domestic politics and its U.S. policy is crucial to Washington officials concerned with formulating policy toward the P.R.C.; they must determine whether the fundamental direction of China's foreign policy is undergoing change in response to changes in its bargaining power, or whether belligerent statements arise primarily from domestic pressures and do not suggest a policy change. The potential for unnecessary but significant conflict lies in the possibility of misperceiving hostile Chinese statements as aimed at Washington, when in fact both triangular and Chinese politics suggest that such statements may be aimed at domestic constituencies.

Theories of the connection between alternative patterns of triangular relations and relative bargaining strengths in bilateral relations have proved valuable in understanding the sources of conflict and cooperation since the Shanghai Communiqué. The present essay is merely a first cut at a complex multilateral phenomenon. A complete study of the dynamics of triangular politics requires a full analysis of the P.R.C.'s Soviet policy and of Soviet and U.S. foreign policy toward China and toward each other. The relationship between domestic political dynamics in the Soviet Union and the United States and their respective foreign policy making processes must also be investigated.

Only brief mention has been made here of the role of diplomacy in determining the course of bilateral politics under any given pattern of triangular relations. There has been a tendency in the international politics literature to stress structure at the expense of overlooking the crucial role of diplomatic ingenuity—a tendency similar to that of emphasizing domestic politics over structure in the literature on Chinese foreign policy. The problems of generalizing on the role of diplomacy in mitigating the impact of structure are significant. But the potential rewards are just as significant. Knowledge of how U.S. and P.R.C. diplomatic behavior—such as provocative American statements suggesting a two-China policy—has shaped conflict and bargaining under a given triangular pattern of relations would provide a more complete analysis of the politics of the strategic triangle. The present study, however, has been confined to an analysis of the interplay of domestic Chinese politics with the bargaining restraints imposed by various patterns of triangular relations. Building on theories of structure and bargaining in international politics and our knowledge of Chinese foreign policy and domestic politics, it represents one step in the process of fully explaining the dynamics of the strategic triangle.

NOTES

1. For various interpretations of the interplay of U.S. Taiwan policy, P.R.C. domestic politics, and China's Soviet policy, see, for example, Robert A. Manning, "Reagan's Chance Hit," *Foreign Affairs* 54 (Spring 1984), 83–101, at 93; William Barnds, "China in American Foreign Policy," in Barnds, ed., *China and America: The Search for a New Relationship* (New York: New York University Press, 1977), 224–25; Carol Hamrin, "China Reassesses the Superpowers," *Pacific Affairs* 56 (Summer 1983), 209–31, at 224–27; Alexander Haig, Jr., *Caveat: Realism, Reagan, and Foreign Policy* (New York: Macmillan, 1984), 200.

2. For an overview of U.S.-China relations, see the memoirs of U.S. statesmen: Henry Kissinger, *The White House Years* (Boston: Little, Brown, 1979); Henry Kissinger, *Years of Upheaval* (Boston: Little, Brown, 1982); Richard Nixon, *RN: The Memoirs of Richard Nixon* (New York: Grosset & Dunlap, 1978); Gerald Ford, *A Time to Heal* (New York: Harper & Row, 1979); Zbigniew Brzezinski, *Power and Principle* (New York: Farrar Straus Giraux, 1983); Cyrus Vance, *Hard Choices: Critical Years in America's Foreign Policy* (New York: Simon & Schuster, 1983). For an overview of the Carter years, see Robert G. Sutter, *The China Quandary: Domestic Determinants of U.S. China Policy, 1972–1982* (Boulder, CO: Westview Press, 1983). On Chinese policy debates, see Harry Harding, "The Domestic Politics of China's Global Posture," in Thomas Fingar and The Stanford Journal of International Affairs, eds., *China's Quest for Independence: Policy Evolution in the 1970s* (Boulder, CO: Westview Press, 1980); Kenneth Lieberthal, *Sino-Soviet Conflict in the 1970's: Its Evolution and Implications for the Strategic Triangle* (Santa Monica, CA: Rand, 1978). For a discussion of the fallacies of reliance on domestic politics, see Michael Ng-Quinn, "The Analytic Study of Chinese Foreign Policy," *International Studies Quarterly* 27 (June 1983), 203–24, at 211–22.

3. Waltz, *Theory of International Politics* (Reading, MA: Addison-Wesley, 1979), 71.

4. *Ibid.*, 98–99. Morton Kaplan, in *System and Process in International Politics* (New York: John Wiley and Sons, 1957), includes alliance patterns in systems theory.

5. The "pattern of relations" is discussed in Glenn H. Snyder and Paul Diesing, *Conflict Among Nations: Bargaining, Decision Making, and System Structure in International Crises* (Princeton: Princeton University Press, 1977), 463.

6. On the multipolarity of contemporary international politics, see *ibid.* For a perspective emphasizing Chinese behavior as a product of bipolarity, see Michael Ng-Quinn, "International Systemic Constraints on Chinese Foreign Policy," in Samuel S. Kim, ed., *China and the World: Chinese Foreign Policy in the Post-Mao Era* (Boulder, CO: Westview Press, 1984).

7. The romantic triangle and the pivot state are discussed in Lowell Dittmer, "The Strategic Triangle: An Elementary Game-Theoretical Analysis, *World Politics* 33 (July 1981), 485–515, at 489 (emphasis in original). The swing position is discussed in Snyder and Diesing (fn. 5), 465. Dittmer argues that a "stable marriage pattern," characterized by amity between two states and enmity between these two and the third state, has characterized Sino-American relations since 1978. I will show below that this pattern is highly unstable, due to the implications on dependency relations of one state's quest for a stable marriage. Dittmer analyzed a third form of triangular relations, *"ménage à trois,"* which will not be discussed in this paper.

8. Glenn H. Snyder, "The Security Dilemma in Alliance Politics," *World Politics* 36 (July 1986), 461–95, at 471–73; also see Dittmer (fn. 7), 510.

9. Snyder (fn. 8), 471–73.

10. Dittmer (fn. 7), 489; Snyder and Diesing (fn. 5), 465.

11. See, for example, Snyder and Diesing (fn. 5).

12. Henry Kissinger argues that Soviet fear of greater U.S.-China cooperation moderated Mocow's arms-control policy. See Kissinger (fn. 2, 1979), 766–68, 836–37.

13. The standard work remains George Liska, *Nations in Alliance: The Limits of Interdependence* (Baltimore: The Johns Hopkins University Press, 1962). The importance of "interaction change" is noted in Robert Gilpin, *War and Change in World Politics* (New York: Cambridge University Press, 1981), 43–44.

14. The terms are from Snyder (fn. 8), 464–65.

15. Snyder and Diesing (fn. 5), 436, 465. Also see Fred Charles Iklé, *How Nations Negotiate* (New York: Harper & Row, 1964), 30. Third-party behavior affects decisions to

go to war. See also Bruce Bueno de Mesquita, *The War Trap* (New Haven: Yale University Press, 1981); Geoffrey Blainey, *The Causes of War* (New York: The Free Press, 1973).

16. Richard C. Snyder, H. W. Bruck, and Burton Sapin, "The Decision-Making Approach to the Study of International Politics," in James N. Rosenau, ed., *International Politics and Foreign Policy* (Glencoe, IL: Free Press, 1961), 188–90; Kaplan (fn. 4), 108, 158; Snyder and Diesing (fn. 5), 354–55.

17. *Ibid.*, 526, 530.

18. See, for example, Kenneth Lieberthal, "The Foreign Policy Debate in Peking as Seen through Allegorical Articles," *The China Quarterly*, No. 71 (September 1977), 528–54.

19. Snyder and Diesing (fn. 5), 526.

20. See Peter Gourevitch, "The Second Image Reversed: The International Sources of Domestic Politics," *International Organization* 32 (Autumn 1978), 881–911. Also see Snyder and Diesing (fn. 5), 530.

21. *Xinhua*, March 4, 1978, in *Foreign Broadcast Information Service, People's Republic of China, Daily Report* [hereafter cited as *FBIS/DR*], March 6, 1978, p. E25.

22. Robert G. Sutter, *China Watch: Toward Sino-American Reconciliation* (Baltimore: The Johns Hopkins University Press, 1978), 111–12.

23. Kissinger (fn. 2, 1982), 690.

24. *Speech by the Chairman of the Delegation of the People's Republic in China, Teng Hsiao-Ping, at the Special Session of the U.N. General Assembly* (Beijing: Foreign Languages Press, 1974), 4.

25. Editorial Department of *Renmin Ribao* [hereafter cited as *RMRB*], *The Theory of the Three Worlds* (New York: Books New China, 1977), 46 (emphasis in original); *New York Times*, October 24, 1975, p. 6.

26. *Documents of the First Session of the Fifth National People's Congress of the People's Republic of China* (Beijing: Foreign Languages Press, 1978), 101; *RMRB*, April 18, 1978, *FBIS/DR*, April 27, 1978, p. A3 (upper case in original).

27. "Chou En-lai's Reports on the International Situation," *Issues and Studies* (Taiwan) 13 (January 1977), 113–27, at 127.

28. *The Theory of the Three Worlds* (fn. 25), 29–30.

29. Lieberthal (fn. 2), 99–100.

30. *The Tenth National Congress of the Communist Party of China (Documents)* (Beijing: Foreign Languages Press, 1973), 23–24.

31. Kissinger, (fn. 2, 1982), 55, 67, 690.

32. *Xinhua*, October 5, 1976, *FBIS/DR*, October 6, 1976, p. A3. Also see Beijing Domestic Service, May 22, 1976, *FBIS/DR*, May 24, 1976, pp. A11–12.

33. Jen Ku-ping, "The Munich Tragedy and Contemporary Appeasement," *RMRB*, November 26, 1977, in *Peking Review*, Vol. 20, No. 50 (December 9, 1977). Also see, for example, *The Theory of the Three Worlds* (fn. 25), 47–48.

34. *Documents of the First Session* . . . (fn. 26). 101.

35. "Keng Piao's Talks on 'A Turning Point in the China-U.S. Diplomatic Relations,'" *Issues and Studies* (Taiwan) 13 (January 1977), 129.

36. *Ibid.*, 130–31.

37. "Ch'iao Kuan-hua's Address, May 20, 1975," *Issues and Studies* (Taiwan) 11 (December 1975), 95.

38. Kissinger (fn. 2, 1982), 60–63, 691–92.

39. A. Doak Barnett, *China and the Major Powers in East Asia*, 206, 383–84, n. 143; Sutter (fn. 2), 38; Ford (fn. 2), 337.

40. Sutter (fn. 2), 24–25.

41. Hua's statement is in *Documents of the First Session* . . . (fn. 26), 111–12.

42. Sutter (fn. 2), 21, 24–25, 46; Barnett (fn. 39), 384, n. 144.

43. The ambassador was Leonard Unger. On this and other aspects of U.S.-Taiwan relations, see Barnett (fn. 39), 205–07, 223–25, 383, n. 142.

44. Vance (fn. 2), 79–83.

45. Kissinger (fn. 2, 1982), 47; Sutter (fn. 22), 115–16, Ford (fn. 2), 336–37; *FBIS, Trends in Communist Media*, October 27, 1977, pp. 1–4, and November 30, 1977, pp. 8–10; *Xinhua*, May 20, 1978, *FBIS/DR*, May 22, 1978, pp. A2–3. On the Carter period, see the discussion of Brzezinski's May 1978 visit to China, in *FBIS, Trends in Communist Media*, May 24, 1978, pp. 1–2.

46. "Chiang Ch'ing's Address to Diplomatic Cadres," *Classified Chinese Communist Documents: A Selection* (Taipei: Institute of International Relations, 1978), 538–39.

47. William DeBerard Mills, *Sino-Soviet Interactions, May 1977–June 1980*, Ph.D. diss. (University of Michigan, 1981), 76–77, 102–07, 138–41.

48. Zhou often encountered criticism over Taiwan. See "Chou En-lai's Report on International Situation, March 1973," *Issues and Studies* (Taiwan) 13 (January 1977), 113–27, at 126; Kissinger (fn. 2, 1982), 679–81, 684.

49. See Sutter (fn. 2), 35; Lieberthal (fn. 2), 112–13, Barnett (fn. 39), 205.

50. Ng-Quinn (fn. 2), 212–15, overstates the case, I believe, when he argues that debates over Chinese foreign policy remained merely debates, solely reflecting attempts to secure domestic political support, and never influencing foreign policy outputs.

51. Kissinger (fn. 2, 1982), 679–81, 684.

52. Oksenberg, "The Dynamics of the Sino-American Relationship," in Richard Solomon, *The China Factor* (Englewood Cliffs, NJ: Prentice Hall, 1981), 72–73.

53. Michel Oksenberg, "A Decade of Sino-American Relations," *Foreign Affairs* 61 (Fall 1982), 175–95, at 182–83; Vance (fn. 2), 82–83; *New York Times*, September 7, 1977, pp. 1, 2. In 1977, Oksenberg was responsible for Chinese affairs on the National Security Council.

54. See, for example, the statement of the Central Committee of the CCP, the Standing Committee of the National Peoples' Congress, the State Council, and the Military Commission of the CCP, *Xinhua*, November 2, 1976, *FBIS/DR*, November 2, 1976, pp. A1-2; Chiao Guanhua's speech to the U.N. General Assembly, *Xinhua*, October 5, 1976, *FBIS/PRC*, October 6, 1976, pp. A1–6; *Agence France Presse*, November 1, 1976, *FBIS/DR*, November 2, 1976, pp. A2–3. Also see *FBIS, Trends in Communist Media*, September 22, 1976, p. 7; October 6, 1976, pp. 10–11; November 3, 1976, pp. 6–7; November 17, 1976, p. 7.

55. Mills (fn. 47), 76–77, 82–85, 132–33.

56. Haig (fn. 1), 201–02.

57. On Carter's changing Soviet policy, see Brzezinski (fn. 2).

58. *Ibid.*, 203–04; Vance (fn. 2), 116.

59. Sutter (fn. 2), 83–84.

60. Oksenberg (fn. 53), 191. On Brown's visit, see Sutter (fn. 2), 86.

61. Zeng Qing, "Meiguo dui Su zhanlue de dongxiang" [The trend in U.S. strategy toward the Soviet Union], *Shijie Zhishi*, No. 6 (March 16, 1979), 5. Unless otherwise noted, translations are by the present author.

62. Zhuang Qubing, "Meiguo dui Meisu junshi liliang duibi de jizhong kanfa" [Various U.S. views of the U.S.-Soviet balance of military strength], *Shijie Zhishi*, No. 2 (January 16, 1979), 14–15. Also see, example, Chen Xiong and Yao Mei, "'Lianggeban zhangzheng' yu 'yigeban zhanzheng'" [Two-and-a-half war and one-and-a-half war], *Shijie Zhishi*, No. 23 (December 1, 1979), 3–5; Fang Zhidan, "Illusion and Reality," *RMRB*, May 14, 1979, *FBIS/DR*, May 24, 1979, pp. A1–4; Bu Qing, "Contention in the Persian Gulf," *RMRB*, August 7, 1979, *FBIS/DR*, August 15, 1979, pp. A1–2.

63. Zhuang Qubing, "Meiguo dui Su zhengce de xin quxiang" [The new trend in United States policy toward the Soviet Union], *Shijie Zhishi*, No. 3 (February 1, 1980), 2–3; Hu Zhengqing and Zhuang Qubing, "Meiguo weishenma xiuding hezhanlue" [Why did the U.S. revise its nuclear strategy?], *Shijie Zhishi*, No. 18 (September 16, 1980), 10–11.

64. Juan Xiang, "New Development of U.S. Military Posture Toward the Soviet Union," *RMRB*, March 25, 1980, *FBIS/DR*, March 27, 1980, pp. B1–4.

65. See, for example, Commentary, "New 'Proposal,' Old Tricks," *Xinhua*, May 24, 1980, *FBIS/DR*, June 3, 1980, pp. C1–2; Zhang Qihua, "The European Security Conference and the Security of the Mediterranean," *RMRB*, September 12, 1980, *FBIS/DR*, September 22, 1980, pp. A3–5; Fang Min, 'The Unpredictable New Round of U.S.-Soviet Nuclear Talks," *RMRB*, October 15, 1980, *FBIS/DR*, October 23, 1980, pp. A2–3. Also see Li Dai, "Afuhan shijian qiangdongle quanshijie" [The Afghanistan incident affected the whole world], *Shijie Zhishi*, No. 6 (March 16, 1980), pp. 2–5.

66. Jonathan Pollack, *The Lessons of Coalition Politics: Sino-American Security Relations* (Santa Monica, CA: Rand, 1984), 76–77.

67. On the nuances of China's Soviet policy, see Lieberthal (fn. 2); Harding (fn. 2).

68. For early, relatively sanguine views of the Soviet Union, see Chen Xiong, "Dangqian Sumei zhanlue taishi" [The current Soviet-U.S. strategic situation], *Shijie Zhishi* No. 12 (June 16, 1979), 1–5; "New 'Proposal,' Old Tricks" (fn. 65).

69. See William Hyland, "The Sino-Soviet Conflict: Dilemmas of the Strategic Triangle," in Solomon (fn. 52), 141–45: *Kyodo News Service*, October 18, 1979, *FBIS/PRC*, October 18, 1979, p. C1.

70. Mills (fn. 47), 248–50.

71. Hyland (fn. 69), 140.

72. *Deng Xiaoping Wenxuan* [Selected works of Deng Xiaoping] (Beijing: Renmin Chubanshe, 1983), 203–04.

73. *Xinhua*, May 14, 1980, *FBIS/DR*, May 14, 1980, p. D2.

74. "FX" was the name of two models of aircraft considered for sale to Taiwan. On the issue involved, see A. Doak Barnett, *The FX Decision: "Another Crucial Moment" in U.S.-China-Taiwan Relations* (Washington, DC: The Brookings Institution, 1981); Sutter (fn. 2), 81.

75. See Vance (fn. 2), 117; Brzezinski (fn. 2), 231.

76. Commentary, "Do No Harm to Sino-U.S. Relations, " *Xinhua*, June 20, 1980, *FBIS/DR*, June 23, 1980, pp. B2–3. Also see *FBIS, Trends in Communist Media*, June 25, 1980, pp. 7–8. For a later indirect threat of greater conflict with the U.S., see the pro-P.R.C. Hong Kong newspaper *Wen Wei Po*, October 22, 1980, *FBIS/DR*, October 27, 1980, pp. U1–2.

77. On the protest note, see *Xinhua*, October 15, 1980, *FBIS/PRC*, October 16, 1980, p. B1; *Agence France Presse*, October 11, 1980, *FBIS/DR*, October 14, 1980, p. B1. The Commentator article cited is "An Inadvisable Move" *RMRB*, October 9, 1980, *FBIS/DR*, October 9, 1980, pp. B1–2. *Shijie Zhishi* issued a similar warning; see Wen Fu, "Sunhai Zhongmei guanxi de Meiguo 'yu Taiwan guanxifa'" [The United States "Taiwan Relations Act," which harms U.S.-China relations], *Shijie Zhishi*, No. 21 (November 1, 1980), 14–15. For additional information, see *FBIS, Trends in Communist Media*, October 16, 1980, pp. 1–3.

78. Zhou Lifang and Zhou Cipu, "George Bush's Difficult Mission, *Xinhua* August 23, 1980, and *RMRB*, August 24, 1980, *FBIS/DR*, August 25, 1980, pp. B2–3.

79. Benkan Pinglunyuan [*RMRB* Commentator], "Ligen xiang ba Zhongmei guanxi yinxiang nali?" [Where does Reagan intend to lead Sino-U.S. relations?], *RMRB*, August 28, 1980.

80. Also see Pollack (fn. 66), 67–68.

81. Yi Bianzhu, *Cong Haolaiwu dao Baigong* (Beijing: Shishi Chubanshe, 1981), 56–59.

82. Zhuang Qubing, "Ligen de waijiao qiju" [Reagan's diplomatic chessboard], *Shijie Zhishi*, No. 6 (March 16, 1981), 2–3 (emphasis in original). On Reagan's arms control policy, see Strobe Talbott, *Deadly Gambits* (New York: Harper & Row, 1984).

83. Wang Qianqi, "Ligen zhengfu de junshi zhanlue [The military strategy of the Reagan administration], *Xiandai Guoji Guanxi*, No. 1 (October 1981), 22. Also see Gao Bo and Yu Lei, "Sulian nanxia zhanlue ji qi mianlin de zuli" [The Soviet strategy of thrusting southward and the impediments it faces], *Xiandai Guoji Guanxi*, No. 1 (October 1981), 12–15.

84. Jin Junhui, "Ligen zhengfu de duiwai zhengce" [The foreign policy of the Reagan administration], *Guoji Wenti Yanjiu*, No. 1, (January 1982), 3.

85. Yuan Xianlu, "A New Round of Struggle, *RMRB*, September 27, 1981, *FBIS/DR*, September 28, 1981, pp. B1–2.

86. Fang Min, "On the Eve of the U.S.-Soviet Nuclear Talks," *RMRB*, November 30, 1981, *FBIS/DR*, November 30, 1981, pp. A1–2.

87. Lu Shipu, "A New Round of the Arms Race Between the Soviet Union and the United States," *RMRB*, June 2, 1982, *FBIS/DR*, June 3, 1982, pp. A1–3. Also see Chen Weibin, "A Prolonged and Fruitless Process," *Xinhua*, January 12, 1982, *FBIS/DR*, January 13, 1982, p. A1; Fang Min, "Reasons for Reagan's Disarmament Statement and His Stand," *RMRB*, April 7, 1982, *FBIS/DR*, April 8, 1982, pp. B1–3; Fang Min, Special Commentary, "U.S. Dual Tactics Toward the Soviet Union," *RMRB*, June 29, 1982, *FBIS/DR*, June 29, 1982, pp. B1–3.

88. See A. Doak Barnett, "China's International Posture: Signs of Change," in Richard Bush, ed., *China Briefing, 1982* (Boulder: CO: Westview Press, 1983), 90.

89. *Ibid.*, 93–96.
90. See Barnett (fn. 74), 29; Donald Zagoria, "The Moscow-Beijing Detente," *Foreign Affairs* 61 (Spring 1983), 853–73, at 856. Also see Barnett (fn. 88), 92–93.
91. "Quarterly Chronicle and Documentation," *The China Quarterly*, No. 91 (September 1982), 564–65; Barnett (fn. 88), 90.
92. Zhuang Qubing, Zhang Hongzeng, and Pan Tongwen, "Ping Meiguo de 'yu Taiwan guanxi fa'" [Criticize the U.S. 'Taiwan Relations Act'], *Guoji Wenti Yanjiu*, No. 1 (July 1981), 21–27, at 25.
93. *Ibid.*, 26. Also see Commentary, "A Key Link in the Development of Sino-U.S. Relations," *Xinhua*, June 18, 1981, *FBIS/DR*, June 19, 1981, pp. B1–2.
94. *Guoji Wenti Yanjiu* (fn. 92), 26.
95. Haig (fn. 1), 204–05, 206–07; Barnett (fn. 74), 29. On China's response to U.S. policy of evenhanded arms sales, also see, for example, Hua Xiu, "China Won't Accept U.S. 'Balanced Arms Sales,'" *Beijing Review*, Vol. 24 (June 22, 1981), 11–12.
96. See Deng's statement in Pollack (fn. 66), 89. For additional Chinese warnings, see Haig (fn. 1), 208.
97. Haig (fn. 1), 209–10.
98. Speical Commentator, "Zhongmei guanxi de zhengjie hezai?" [Where lies the crux of Sino-American relations?], *Guoji Wenti Yanjiu*, No. 2 (April 1982), 6–7.
99. Haig (fn. 1), 211–15. This has been confirmed in discussion with former Reagan administration officials. Also see Banning Garrett, "China Policy and the Constraints of Triangular Logic," in Kenneth A. Oye, Robert J. Lieber, and Donald Rothchild, eds., *Eagle Defiant: United States Foreign Policy in 1980s* (Boston: Little, Brown, 1983), 237–71.
100. See Kenneth Lieberthal, "Domestic Politics and Foreign Policy," in Harry Harding, ed., *China's Foreign Relations in the 1980s* (New Haven: Yale University Press, 1984), 55–66; Hamrin (fn. 1); Barnett (fn. 74). Also see *FBIS, Trends in Communist Media*, August 6, 1980, pp. 3–5.
101. Cited in Lieberthal (fn. 100), 65.
102. Hamrin (fn. 1); Lieberthal (fn. 100), 55–66.
103. Hamrin (fn. 1); Lieberthal (fn. 100); and Barnett (fn. 74).
104. Indeed, in his January 1980 speech placing reunification on the agenda for the 1980s, Deng suggested that combatting hegemonism was of greater importance; see *Deng Xiaoping Wenxuan* (fn. 72), 203–04. Also see Mills (fn. 47), 251; A. Doak Barnett, *U.S. Arms Sales: The China-Taiwan Tangle* (Washington, DC: The Brookings Institution, 1982). For Deng's remarks on U.S.-China relations, see "Deng fuzongli tong Meiguo guangbo dianshijie de tanpan" [Vice Premier Deng's talk with people in U.S. television circles], *Shijie Zhishi*, No. 5 (March 1, 1979), 1–4.
105. Pollack (fn. 66), 89.
106. Hamrin (fn. 1), 226–27.
107. See, for example, Barnett (fn. 74). For a critique of the argument that Reagan's policy errors can explain the deterioration of relations, see Steven I. Levine, "China and the United States: The Limits of Interaction," in Kim (fn. 6), 123–25.
108. On U.S.-China relations, see *ibid.*, 118–31. For Sino-Soviet relations, see Chi Su, "China and the Soviet Union: 'Principled, Salutary, and Tempered' Management of Conflict," in Kim (fn. 6), 136–41. China's third-world posture is discussed by Harry Harding, "China's Changing Roles in the Contemporary World," in Harding (fn. 100), 195–201.
109. Also see Dittmer (fn. 1), 504–07.
110. For a harsh P.R.C. response to the shift in Reagan's Asia policy, see Zhang Jia-lin, "The New Romanticism in the Reagan Administration's Asian Policy," *Asian Survey* 10 (October 1984), 997–1011. For P.R.C. analyses of U.S. assertiveness and confidence in world affairs, and its recent "ascendency over the Soviet Union," see, for example, Jin Junhui, "Reagan's Diplomacy: An Overview," *Beijing Review* 28 (June 17, 1985), 21–25; Zhou Jirong, Wang Baoqin, and Gu Guanfu, "Sumei zhengba taishi de bianhua yu qianjing" [Change and the prospect for the Soviet-U.S. struggle for hegemony], *Xiandai Guoji Guanxi* 6 (March 1984), 1–6; Huang Su'an and Li Changjiu, "Meiguo jingji liliang de huifu yu duiwai zhengce" [U.S. economic recovery and foreign policy], *Guoji Wenti Yanjiu* 3 (July 1985), 1–7.

THE GLOBAL BALANCE OF POWER: CAN THE GREAT POWERS RULE THE WORLD?

19

Dateline Middle East: The Dangers of Disengagement

CHARLES McC. MATHIAS, Jr.

The Reagan administration's Middle East policy, or what is left of one after Lebanon, failed peace talks, shelved arms sales, and a questionable obsession with Libyan leader Colonel Muammar el-Qaddafi, brings to mind one of Mark Twain's maxims about learning through experience. A cat that sits down on a hot stove lid, said Twain, "will never sit down on a hot stove lid again—and that is well; but also she will never sit down on a cold one."

During a 3-week trip to the Middle East in February 1986, I found telltale signs that in the last few years the United States has, like Twain's cat, learned the wrong—or too many—lessons from its recent experiences. Once or twice burned, by assorted failures and catastrophes in Lebanon and by the lack of response to President Ronald Reagan's 1982 peace initiative, the United States seems reluctant to come near the source of the pain with anything like the full-fledged commitment that previous administrations thought necessary to ward off potential conflicts and promote peaceful solutions in one of the world's most critical regions. Fear of failure and the distractions of terrorism and falling oil prices have only added to the problem. Call it benign neglect, call it lack of interest at the highest levels not only of the executive branch but also of Congress, the results are the same: an erratic policy toward the region's many problems and a disturbing erosion of U.S. influence.

America's loss of influence has not translated yet into significant gains for the Soviet Union or radical Islamic fundamentalist forces. Several factors suggest that there is no immediate danger that a major conflict will break out—apart from a sudden escalation of the ever dangerous, ever underestimated Iran-Iraq war. But continued slippage of U.S. interest and influence threatens to allow events rather than policies to take control of the Middle East, undermining the stability of America's friends while emboldening its enemies.

America's level of interest in the region, measured especially in terms of constant public and private presidential and cabinet-level attention, has diminished in the last 3 years. Acts of terrorism refocus U.S. attention from time to time, but for the most part, Washington is no longer fully engaged. Middle Eastern leaders, both Arab and Israeli, sense this shift and now are confused about America's real intentions.

Despite the unprecedented warmth of their ties with the United States, Israeli leaders can hardly look with equanimity on the prospect that the Soviet Union gradually will gain influence in the Middle East. They should therefore be concerned about policies, or policy vacuums, that encourage and accelerate that development.

Many moderate Arabs are worried or angry, and do not hesitate to say so. Surveying recent actions in Washington that ranged from standoffishness on Arab-Israeli peace talks, to the failure of arms sales, to Reagan's praise of the October 1985 Israeli raid on Tunis, one Jordanian leader observed, "[Israeli Prime Minister] Shimon Peres is doing more to educate his people to the need for peace than the U.S. government is doing to educate its own." Even some Israelis are puzzled by the U.S. attitude. "Reagan's approach to Israel is avuncular rather than paternal," said one Israeli official. "He loads us down with sweets but never takes the time to talk to us about our problems."

The recent evolution of U.S. Middle East policy—especially in regard to the Arab-Israeli conflict—is by no means due to any single cause or person. But there is little doubt that the painful experience of Lebanon played a central role. Statements by Reagan just before and just at the end of America's intervention illustrate the shift dramatically.

Setting out his bold and widely praised peace initiative on September 1, 1982, the president declared: "The story of the search for peace and justice in the Middle East is a tragedy of opportunities missed. . . . For if we miss this chance to make a fresh start, we may look back on this moment from some later vantage point and realize how much that failure cost us all." By early February 1984, the horizon was measurably darker. "If we get out [of Lebanon]," the president told the *Wall Street Journal*, "it also means that the end of any ability on our part to bring about an overall peace in the Middle East. And, I would have to say that means a pretty disastrous result for us worldwide."

Employing hyperbole as tactic more than as unintended prophecy, the president obviously overstated the case. Withdrawal from Lebanon, executed just days after this latter statement, did not foreclose U.S. options in the region. After a period of reassessment triggered by the Lebanon fiasco and by the March 1984 outburst of King Hussein of Jordan about American credibility, the administration renewed its diplomatic and other efforts, including arms and economic aid packages. With a more flexible Israeli government headed by the Labor Alignment's Peres, both the administration and Hussein saw a window of opportunity.

Looking back at the results, however, and anticipating the window's closing when the Likud bloc's Yitzhak Shamir becomes prime minister in the Israeli government's game of musical chairs this October, several causes for the failure of the most recent initiatives become clear. Certainly the intransigence of the Palestine Liberation Organization (PLO) and the Palestinians' identity crisis were leading obstacles to progress. The excessive caution of other parties, notably Saudi Arabia, also created difficulties. But one also witnessed a more tentative American role, in both the executive and the legislative branches. The new diplomatic course veered from consistent U.S. policy over the last decade, recalling former Secretary of State Alexander Haig, Jr.'s image of a ship without a helmsman—or a cat timidly tiptoeing around a stove whose temperature is still undetermined.

This more limited engagement reflects a growing desire in the United States for a lower profile in the Middle East. Its conflicts, so the argument goes, are irreconcilable (at least by Americans), U.S. oil needs are dwindling, and America's efforts are a lightning rod for terrorists. The United States, therefore, should become fully engaged only when the various forces in the region show themselves to be better prepared for major concessions.

This attitude, however, has proved foolhardy in the past and will be even more costly in the future. No matter how frustrating the efforts, the alternative to trying to shape developments in America's direction would be to allow hostile forces to exploit the Middle East's deep political divisions and myriad social and economic problems. Like it or not, the United States is a global power with far-flung interests and long-standing commitments to countries and peoples in the Middle East.

The U.S. need for Persian Gulf oil may be less today than a decade ago, but does anyone want to gamble that this will be true in the 1990s? Even if American needs remain low, America's closest allies are likely to remain dependent. Japan today imports 60 percent of its oil from the

Middle East and Western Europe, 20 to 25 per cent, and the United States has agreed to share petroleum in the event of a shortage.

Moreover, America's support for Israel stems from the deepest shared values and interests. Israel's strategic role in the eastern Mediterranean is incalculable. Yet the cost of continuing American defense and economic assistance, which is directly related to the failure to resolve or ease Arab-Israeli tensions, threatens to reach unhealthy and politically unacceptable levels.

In addition, the growing danger of destabilization in moderate Arab countries such as Egypt dictates an active and pragmatic American stewardship of the peace process. Progress toward settlement of the Arab-Israeli conflict, even by starting with secondary issues such as the Egyptian-Israeli dispute over a strip of territory at Taba in the Sinai peninsula, can offset social and economic dynamics that threaten to set off an Islamic fundamentalist—and anti-American—explosion.

Thus with the collapse of direct and indirect talks among the United States, Israel, Jordan, and Palestinian representatives earlier this year, a golden opportunity for progress went by the board. A divided and confused Palestinian leadership proved impotent. But what better conditions to press hard for real advances could have existed: a popular, second-term American president, a pragmatic Israeli leader, a willing Jordanian monarch, and limited Soviet influence? Syria, although committed to achieving strategic parity with Israel, remains considerably short of this goal, and more radical fundamentalist forces are as yet marginal actors.

Whatever other crises distract Washington, and they abound, the Middle East stands out as one of the few regions of the world where the U.S. focus must be constant and the energies of American leadership fully engaged. The Middle East remains one of the few areas of the world where peace, as the Harvard University political scientist Stanley Hoffmann wrote in *Primacy or World Order* (1978), is "inseparable from our welfare." The region will not become less relevant to U.S. national interests because it is less amenable to American influence.

Former Israeli Foreign Minister Abba Eban cogently described America's predominant role in the Middle East—and the responsibility that goes with it—in his 1983 book *The New Diplomacy*:

> The United States is today the guarantor of Israel's security and economic viability, the protector of the Gulf oil states, the source of the region's development aid programs, the friend and supporter of Egypt, Lebanon, Jordan, and Saudi Arabia, and the assiduous conciliator whenever regional tension threatens to burst into flame. To balance the picture we must recall that the United States is also the main target of Iran's passionate hostility and Libya's rancor as well as Syria's hostility. No nation in the Middle East is totally satisfied with American policy, but none of them can begin to define

its own diplomatic and strategic direction without taking the United States as the central theme of its preoccupation.

In contrast, America's principal adversary, the Soviet Union, is currently limited to supplying arms to several Arab countries, mainly Syria and Iraq. And the bloody January 1986 coup in South Yemen served to remind any leaders interested in closer ties of the ultimate risks of Soviet clientism. Despite Soviet efforts to capitalize on Washington's problems in the region, the United States remains today the "guarantor," the "protector," the source of aid, the friend, and the "assiduous conciliator."

Yet in my talks with national leaders, academic experts, and business leaders in Egypt, Israel, Jordan, Saudi Arabia, and Syria, serious doubts were voiced about America's ability to continue fulfilling all of these roles. The perceptions of Middle East leaders that point to a loss of U.S. influence and credibility fall into four general areas: the peace process, defense relationships, economic support, and the tangled problem of terrorism. No one pins the blame for the unraveling of the Hussein-Arafat-Peres talks solely on the United States. Thanks to Hussein's candor, PLO Chairman Yasir Arafat gets the credit. Nevertheless, leaders on all sides question whether the Reagan administration has thrown its full weight into the process.

All sides agree that Assistant Secretary of State for Near Eastern and South Asian Affairs Richard Murphy worked with vigor and dedication to bring about face-to-face negotiations between Israel and a joint Jordanian-Palestinian delegation. But American deference to Israel over the names of possible Palestinian representatives and uncertainty over the international framework, combined with the humiliating failure in Congress of the Jordanian arms package, convinced Jordan that U.S. efforts enjoyed only modest support at the highest levels in Washington.

Past presidents were willing to take significant risks both domestically and internationally to pursue peaceful solutions in the Middle East. Speaking to the nation on September 1, 1982, Reagan paid tribute to his predecessors: "For more than a generation, successive United States administrations have endeavored to develop a fair and workable process that could lead to a true and lasting Arab-Israeli peace." Yet during what many observers saw as an opportune period earlier this year, the man on the line was Murphy, not Reagan or Secretary of State George Shultz.

Israelis say that America is often ineffective at pressuring Arab leaders to make needed concessions, but many Egyptians, Jordanians, and Saudis say that the United States has moved so close to Israel in its "strategic partnership" that Washington has little leverage in Jerusalem. One Jordanian, speaking anonymously, insisted that the Peres government would have accommodated itself had the United States accepted several Palestinians for negotiations, and even held unofficial talks with them. He maintained that Peres made protests only for domestic consumption.

Jordanians, and to a lesser extent, Saudis, are even more irritated at what they see as halfhearted administration support for proposed arm sales, a second major area of U.S. influence. Sensing a double standard, moderate Arab leaders recently have displayed a certain resignation about American aid to Israel, a resignation that goes beyond anger. Yet they regard the failure of recent sales to their countries as a sign of a significant lessening of interest by America, not only because of the losses themselves, but also because of the administration's timid lobbying efforts. These leaders believe that the United States should make such decisions solely on the basis of long-standing security relationships and U.S. strategic interests in the region, without snarling the proposals in the question of peace talks.

Although Hussein has kept his thoughts to himself, it is not hard to imagine his conclusions as he watched the full-court press for $100 million for the *contra* rebels fighting Nicaragua's Sandinista government only a few weeks after the full-scale retreat on a $1.9 billion arms sale that was promised on three occasions by Reagan. Although warning that they may be obliged to turn to the Soviets for more weapons, as Hussein did in 1984, the Saudis are more diplomatic about the subject. But their leaders, if not financially strapped like Hussein, are equally concerned. Moreover, there is considerable unease under the surface in Egypt and in Jordan about the impact on U.S. foreign aid of the Gramm-Rudman-Hollings budget-balancing law.

Terrorism is not lightly discussed in a region where leaders and their families are at risk daily. Israeli officials must treat terrorism as a constant threat throughout the country. Hussein has been the target of more than a dozen assassination attempts. And Egyptian police have defused several Libyan terrorist plots. The March 2, 1986, murder of the popular Palestinian mayor of the West Bank city of Nablus, Zafer al-Masri, showed how extremists can sidetrack promising political initiatives and polarize competing forces.

Terrorists of varying factions have, in fact, achieved considerable success because they have distracted America and others in the region from the principal issues: peace and the security and economic well-being of Israel and the moderate Arab states. Terrorism has focused U.S. attention on Qaddafi, who is, in the larger scheme of things, a marginal force. In fact, one of the most constant criticisms of U.S. policy in Arab capitals is that Washington plays into the Libyan ruler's hands by paying so much attention to him. Some observers are more cynical: "You promote Qaddafi to embarrass and divide the Arab world," one Arab official remarked.

The ultimate consequences of the Gulf of Sidra confrontation and the subsequent raid on Tripoli and Benghazi cannot be foreseen. Any sense of triumph, however, needs to be balanced by the prospect of accelerating terrorism and further strain in U.S. relations with Arab states. Moderate Arabs might not disagree with a policy of force on one front if it were matched by a full-fledged diplomatic offensive on the other.

An Educational Process The Middle East recently has witnessed some positive developments that, though overshadowed by the overall perception of stalemate, still offer material grounds for hope and progress. Despite recent setbacks in peace talks, at least the discussion now focuses on negotiations. There is little talk of war—at least in the short term. Israel is for all practical purposes accepted as a fact of life by much of the Arab world, not regarded as something that can be wished or driven away. Arab leaders, themselves divided and distracted by internal and intra-Arab conflicts, argue not about whether they should negotiate, but about how. An educational process takes a long time, but academics and other people not immersed in daily decision making see room for optimism. Israeli television news is seen regularly in Jordan, and moderate Palestinians are seen defending the PLO on Israeli television. Political debate is as lively as ever in the Israeli press and is becoming more so in the Arab world, especially in Egypt.

Israeli policies in the West Bank remain extremely controversial, most recently because of an increase in the numbers of detainees that authorities attribute to a rise in terrorism. But the pace of settlements has declined under Peres. And policy tentatively aims at encouraging more Palestinian self-rule, particularly in less sensitive areas such as education, housing, and commerce. The possibilities of this shift were brutally set back by the murder of Masri, who had told me 2 weeks before his death that he sought "a solution short of what we want, but better than we've had."

Against tough odds, Hussein appears determined to make Jordan a modern, progressive state. And Egypt's democratic opening holds promise despite the country's staggering social and economic problems. Recently, the lessons of a free press hit home dramatically. Efforts to cover up the October 5, 1985, murder of seven Israelis by an Egyptian policeman and the bloody storming on November 24, 1985, of an Egyptair jetliner that had been commandeered by terrorists to Malta backfired. But open reporting of the February 1986 security police riots set the stage for an unusually decisive—and publicly supported—response by President Hosni Mubarak.

Yet whether one's analysis reflects optimism or pessimism, it is clear that America simply must repair to its tried and true position as an actively engaged global power that recognizes its vital political and economic stakes in Middle East stability and, someday, peace. Only a policy of leadership, continuity, and balance can sustain what Eban has called America's "central" position and can shape developments in the interests of the United States and of most of the area's countries.

Leadership means full-fledged attention at the highest level to the region, to negotiations, to arms and economic aid proposals, and to the views of America's friends and allies there. Occasional activism behind the scenes is not enough; Washington needs to be perceived as keenly interested in and supportive of its friends and allies. Moreover, leadership and attention must emanate from Congress as well as from the executive branch. Too often, members of Congress engage in freewheeling activities for domestic political gain with little thought of the effect on the U.S. position in the region.

More travel throughout the region by members of Congress would help. As Samuel Johnson observed, the "use of traveling is to regulate imagination by reality, and instead of thinking how things may be, to see them as they are." It is considerably easier to see things as they are when flying over the Ras Tanura oil terminal in Saudi Arabia, where the Iran-Iraq war rages over the horizon; when looking from a hill east of Tel Aviv toward former Jordanian territory on the West Bank, where Israeli soldiers can be seen protecting an isolated Israeli settlement defiantly placed in Arab-populated Hebron; or when standing in the mist on the parapets of a 12th-century Crusader fortress on the Syrian-Lebanese border, knowing that not far away five Americans may be held hostage.

To help see things as they are, debate in this country about the Middle East can be raised to a higher, more candid plane. The debate over fundamental policy questions is often more vigorous in Jerusalem than in Washington.

With the renewal of America's commitment, the foundations of U.S. policy must be reasserted: the security of Israel, the stability of moderate Arab states, steady, purposeful movement toward a solution of the Palestinian problem, and limitation of Soviet activity. Because these interests and objectives are so complex, it is essential to resume the practice of appointing a topflight presidential emissary, an experienced and skillful negotiator such as former Secretary of State Henry Kissinger or former special presidential envoy Sol Linowitz, to reactivate U.S. policies.

Above all, the United States cannot afford to be discouraged by recent setbacks and must always be prepared with alternative initiatives if one track proves futile. Because of the diversity of U.S. interests and the complexity of forces in the region, Washington must move on many fronts simultaneously. Conciliation between Israel and Egypt can be promoted aggressively and independently. The Camp David accords are still the cornerstone of peace in the region, and it is extremely important to broaden that foundation so that Egypt will be seen as a pacesetter and not a traitor by the Arab world.

Washington should communicate more frequently and more directly with Damascus. A tendency to ignore Syria, which former French Prime Minister Pierre Mendès-France called "the key" to the Middle East, only plays to its aloof leader's strengths and vision of Syria as the ultimate spoiler. Although now bogged down in Lebanon, Syrian President Hafez al-Assad appears determined to regain military parity with Israel. U.S.-Syrian contacts still offer some hope of gaining the release of the American hostages in Lebanon, as demonstrated already in the June 1985 TWA hijacking, and create on opportunity to open channels that could prove useful should an Israeli-Syrian clash loom larger.

Last, America must do what it can to help solve the Palestinian question, the most important obstacle to peace. This issue lies at the heart of the intractable conflict in the region and will not go away. Nor should it be wished away.

If the United States favors self-determination in Manila and Managua, it can hardly oppose it in Jericho. As Reagan noted in 1982, "the departure of the Palestinians from Beirut" dramatized "more than ever the homelessness of the Palestinian people." According to the president, the Camp David accords pledged that any final disposition of the West Bank and the Gaza Strip should satisfy "the legitimate rights of the Palestinians and their just requirements." Although "self-determination" has become a code word for an independent Palestinian state, it is possible to work out a formula that embodies those principles short of establishing such a state. Creation of a Palestinian entity in confederation with Jordan would constitute a logical, feasible first step in what is bound to be an arduous process with an undetermined outcome. Some prominent Palestinians are willing to accept that limit on their immediate political goals.

While insisting that Palestinians recognize Israel's right to a secure future, the United States also must make clear its full opposition to any further Israeli settlements in the territories occupied after the 1967 war. Traditionally, Washington has never linked aid to Israel with Israeli cooperation, but it is contrary to historical experience for one country indefinitely to help finance policies carried out by another country that conflict so fundamentally with the donor's values and policies. Strong public and private statements from the president and the secretary of state should leave no doubt about the U.S. conviction—and policy—that settlements seriously jeopardize peace prospects. Aside from the serious question they raise about the future of democracy and Jewish identity in a state with a potential Arab majority, such settlements frequently involve the expropriation of Arab land and clearly hinder the peace process.

The Camp David accords offer a realistic framework to address the concerns of both Arabs and Israelis. Despite today's cool Egyptian-Israeli relations, the peace treaty they signed must not be taken for granted. In the meantime, the United States can continue to play a helpful role through its "quality of life" program in the occupied territories. Palestinians tend to be suspicious of grand speeches about "autonomy" and "devolution," but they welcome specific projects such as health care programs, agricultural assistance, and marketplaces now being aided by the U.S. Agency for International Development. In addition to current U.S. assistance to the Middle East, Israelis, Jordanians, and Palestinians would all welcome an increase in the $14 million provided this year by Washington for West Bank and Gaza programs.

In all these areas, the question of timing remains critical. Despite current difficulties, the present moment still has the advantages already mentioned: a second-term American president, the flexible policies of the current Israeli coalition, the relative stability of surrounding Arab states, and the limited influence of the Soviet Union. Perceptions of a decline in American influence become all the more distressing in a period when the United States seems to have an urgent, paramount interest in moving toward settlement of critical problems. The possible growth of Islamic fundamentalism and the spread of nuclear weaponry in the region, combined with conflicting goals of the superpowers, serve as sobering considerations.

Robert Neumann, former U.S. ambassador to Afghanistan, Morocco, and Saudi Arabia, likes to recall advice given by Charles de Gaulle before his return to power in 1958 to deal with France's Algerian crisis. Given issues of such intense complexity and historical burdens, de Gaulle argued, a process of negotiation—of healing—had to be very slow and based on subtle psychological changes. And each step in the process, de Gaulle remembered, had to be built on the previous one, carefully but courageously.

In regaining momentum for a productive Middle East policy, America, too, must take risks for peace—with courage, with care, and with maximum effort—so that it can one day look back on the triumph of peace and justice in the Middle East instead of on a series of lost opportunities.

20

Paying Less Attention to the Middle East

RICHARD N. HAASS

FEW ideas have been more influential in the shaping of American foreign policy in the Middle East than that which can be summed up in the shorthand phrase, "territory for peace." For nearly two decades, virtually everything that has been thought or said about this region has been informed by United Nations Security Council Resolution 242, with its call for the "establishment of a just and lasting peace in the Middle East"—a peace to be brought about by Israel's returning most if not all of the territories it conquered in the 1967 war in exchange for the recognition of its neighbors and the right to exist.

Implicit in American acceptance of the territory-for-peace model is the belief that the status quo—that is, a Middle East with Israel in possession of the West Bank and the Gaza Strip, the Golan Heights, and a unified Jerusalem—is not only unjust but inherently unstable, and hence threatening to American interests. It is argued that U.S. strategic, political, and economic interests in the Arab world will suffer so long as the United States is seen as supporting Israel and its conquests. Moreover, many believe that the Middle East, possibly more than any other part of the world, has within it the seeds of a dangerous confrontation between the U.S. and the Soviet Union. Also associated closely with the territory-for-peace idea is the notion that significant diplomatic progress in the region requires U.S. leadership. Many observers contend that the situation will get worse if it does not get better, and the only way for it to get better is for the United States to take an active role in brokering a settlement between Israel and its Arab neighbors.

In 1985, adding urgency to these related themes were the uncertain future of Arab moderates like Jordan's King Hussein and, recently, the brief remaining tenure of Prime Minister Shimon Peres of Israel, who is soon scheduled to transfer the reins of leadership to Foreign Minister Yitzhak Shamir, a man believed to be far less flexible on the matter of a possible trade of territory for peace. For these reasons we have seen over the past year considerable U.S. interest in the so-called "Jordanian option"—i.e., the attempt to persuade King Hussein to step forward and negotiate directly with Israel on behalf of the Palestinians. Others have suggested bringing Syria or the Soviet Union or the Palestine Liberation Organization (PLO) directly into the process, possibly by holding an international conference. What all such proposals have in common is the premise that the United States must and can act to promote reconciliation between Israel and at least some Arab leaders, and that the interests of no responsible party are served by the further passage of time.

These ideas are not new. The past eighteen years are rife with examples of various schemes to bring about "progress" in the Middle East. One such scheme, in the first Nixon administration, was the Rogers Plan for a comprehensive settlement of the entire Middle East question along the lines of UN Resolution 242; another was the Carter administration's joint call with the Soviet Union in October 1977 for a Geneva conference on the Middle East. Both the 1978 Camp David Accords and the 1982 Reagan Plan constituted blueprints for an overall settlement of the region. Even our efforts in Lebanon in recent years, whether they have taken the form of sending special negotiators or of sending the Marines, have been presented as necessary demonstrations of our ability to foster diplomatic progress in the Middle East, thereby paving the way for a more comprehensive effort to follow.

Yet despite the continuing allure of territory-for-peace as a diplomatic paradigm, the fact remains that with the important exception of what was achieved by the Camp David Accords, no exchange of territory for peace has actually taken place. Moreover, although Jordan has often flirted with the idea of negotiating directly with Israel, neither it nor Syria, the two countries claiming territory which Israel occupies, has offered to make peace. Israel, meanwhile, has annexed Jerusalem and the Golan Heights and settled large parts of the West Bank. And as for the future, candor requires acknowledging that the territory-for-peace paradigm stands little chance of being realized.

To understand why, we need to look at developments in both Israel and the Arab world. Within Israel, one can point to a host of factors: the national confidence which erupted in the wake of the 1967 war but which discouraged Israelis from ardently pursuing new territorial and political arrangements; the brooding and self-doubt which then emerged following the 1973 war, and which intensified sharply after the Lebanon conflict, reducing any propensity to "take risks for peace"; the decline in the strength and appeal of the Labor alignment, and the parallel rise of a nationalist Right and of militant religious sentiment; the attachment to "Judea and Samaria" which made it all but impossible for former Prime Minister Begin to contemplate replicating on the West Bank what he did in Sinai; and, most recently, the disillusionment with an Egypt which has proved reluctant to translate its peace accord with Israel into genuinely full relations.

Israeli politics in the mid-1980's are thus a far cry from what they were just fifteen years ago, when the Labor party, to considerable public approval, could espouse various plans for returning much of the West Bank to Jordan. At issue today is not whether the Jordan River forms

Israel's eastern defense boundary but whether it ought to form the country's eastern political boundary as well. With time, the choice facing Israel could well become whether it should annex the West Bank and Gaza Strip, people and all, or annex them without their Arab inhabitants. For a variety of reasons Israel is unlikely to take such drastic action, but it is also unlikely to support anything that approximates the territory-for-peace model, as there is no longer a consensus in the country for doing so; indeed, any attempt by the government to implement a substantial exchange of territory would encounter armed resistance from the settlers and their supporters. As a result, Israel is likely to avoid confronting what has become *the* national question.

Of course the decline in Israeli support for an exchange of territory for peace is in part a response to developments in the Arab world. Only Sadat was able to capitalize on the Arab "victory" in the 1973 war to negotiate with Israel. The universal Arab rejection of Egypt, and Sadat's subsequent assassination, bode ill both for long-term Egyptian-Israeli ties and for the prospect that any other Arab leader would risk as much for peace. That relations with Egypt never improved beyond the rudimentary level exacerbated matters.

Among other Arab leaders, Jordan's King Hussein, too weak to stay out of war in 1967, proved too weak to opt for peace in its aftermath. He has come to the brink often, only to pull back; while his caution is understandable, it makes him a poor partner in any peace process. His neighbor to the north, Hafez al-Assad of Syria, is an even worse partner, if for different reasons: he has refused to compromise on his demand for the complete return of the Golan Heights, and as the self-proclaimed leader of the Arab world he has also refused to compromise on Israel's complete relinquishment of the West Bank and Gaza. Saudi Arabia, an important behind-the-scenes actor, has used its considerable economic resources to support both Jordan and Syria; there is no evidence to suggest that the Saudis are a force for compromise in the region. The only other Arab state of consequence in this context—Iraq—has had its hands full contending with the bitter fruits of its ill-conceived invasion of Iran.

Two other factors affecting Arab politics also explain why territory-for-peace has fared poorly. The first has to do with the USSR. The Soviets have been intent upon strengthening Syria's might and thereby their own influence over Damascus and in the region generally; out of similar considerations they have aided the PLO and wooed Jordan's Hussein. At the same time the Soviets have refrained from resuming diplomatic relations with Israel, broken in 1967, despite the fact that Israel has made such recognition a prerequisite to sitting down with the Soviet Union at an international conference or anywhere else. Soviet policy toward the region has consisted of criticizing American peace-making efforts and giving armed support to several of the key Arab protagonists; the principal result of this approach has been to maintain the perception in the Arab world that a military option still exists and that time works for rather than against the radical Arab cause.

Even more important as an explanation of the current stalemate has been the politics of the PLO. It is more than a decade since the PLO received, from the Arab leaders who gathered in Rabat in the fall of 1974, an exclusive mandate to represent the Palestinian people. In retrospect, the collective Arab decision is noteworthy for nothing so much as ensuring that Jordan would not become a viable negotiating partner with Israel. The principal Palestinian leader, Yasir Arafat, has used the bulk of these past twelve years to gain international support for his cause, to strengthen the PLO's military arm, and to meet internal challenges to his authority. He has refused to recognize Israel or entertain the possibility of some form of Palestinian entity in the occupied territories. He has also refused to give up the instrument of terror. However understandable any or all of these decisions may be in light of the movement's aims and internal dynamics, they have made the PLO an organization with the power to undermine but not to contribute to the prospects for peace.

Recent activity only confirms the thesis that the Middle East is not ripe for movement toward an exchange of territory for peace. For much of the past year, attention has focused on whether King Hussein and Yasir Arafat, in the wake of their February 1985 pact, would steer themselves either to a "Jordanian option," in which Jordan, together with Palestinian representatives acting with the PLO's blessing, would negotiate directly with Israel, or a PLO option, in which the PLO would finally renounce terror, accept 242 (which it has heretofore refused to do), and recognize Israel's right to exist, thereby earning a place at the bargaining table. Although Israel's own willingness to explore the second option has been and remains questionable, the PLO never tested the issue, opting instead for the hijacking of the *Achille Lauro*. In February of this year Hussein finally terminated the common effort with the PLO but at the same time refused to move forward on his own. American, British, and intra-Arab diplomacy had once again came to naught.

The PLO's behavior was not the only bad news for Hussein. Israel's raid on PLO positions in Tunisia last October was a major embarrassment to him, as was the inability of the Reagan administration to convince a majority in Congress to permit a major ($1.9 billion) arms sale to Jordan. At the first Reagan-Gorbachev summit, the Middle East hardly came up. It is thus not altogether surprising that Hussein has turned away both from the PLO and from Washington to Damascus. There he has found a willing partner, as Assad means to demonstrate that there can be no peace without his full participation and support.

(The United States unexpectedly appeared to endorse this turn of events; on December 5, 1985 the State Department declared U.S. support for Syrian participation in the peace process, adding pointedly that implementing Resolution 242 would mean Israel's return of the Golan Heights.) Yet if history is any guide, increased Syrian prominence will not be a boon for peace prospects. It may be difficult to make peace without Assad, but given his pretensions to establishing Syrian primacy in the region, it may well be impossible to make peace with him.

It is, in sum, hard to escape the conclusion that the territory-for-peace idea has run its course. Jordan is unwilling and perhaps unable to go it alone, while neither the PLO nor Syria is a promising participant in any diplomatic exercise. And as for Israel, although a more forthcoming Arab approach toward the principal issues of the Middle East would almost certainly moderate that country's often fickle public opinion, the maximum that Israel could be expected to propose in any peace package would fall short of the minimum any Arab state or the PLO could be expected to accept.

But if the basic paradigm is moribund, what about its two associated notions: that the current situation is inherently unstable and prejudicial to American interests, and that American activism is required not only to move diplomacy forward but to prevent the situation from worsening? As is often the case with conventional wisdom, neither of these propositions survives inspection.

Despite the absence of movement toward the goal of territory for peace, with Egypt removed for the foreseeable future from the list of potential confrontation states it is difficult to envision a realistic military option for the Arabs. Lebanon will remain preoccupied with its own internal struggles, Jordan is too vulnerable to Israeli aircraft and armor, the PLO lacks any significant military capacity after its losses in Lebanon, while the non-adjacent Arab states lack the means to project military power across the distances involved. Only Syria has the ability to engage Israel militarily, and although at some point there may be some logic for doing so—perhaps to distract actual or potential domestic political opponents, or to create a sense of crisis in the hope that the superpowers would feel compelled to step in and "impose" a settlement to Syria's liking—the reality is that Syria would lose badly in what would be a one-front war. Moreover, whatever the United States and the Soviet Union could do to manage a crisis would certainly fall far short of creating a new regional configuration. This is not to say that there will be no terrorist incidents or Israeli-Syrian clashes over Lebanon or war jitters; but full-scale war is less likely.

What is emerging in the Middle East, then, is a state of no peace–no war, a military standoff brought about by military facts and strengthened by tacit understandings among the principal protagonists.

How will U.S. interests fare in such a Middle East? Although it is often assumed that our relations with the Arab states will suffer, history suggests otherwise. The United States has consistently been able to engage in substantial economic, political, and military dealings with the Arab states of the Middle East despite their unhappiness over American diplomatic and military support for Israel. Arab oil and American goods, services, and technology have been traded, and political-military cooperation has grown between the United States and countries as varied as Egypt, Jordan, Oman, and Saudi Arabia. U.S. relations have even improved with Iraq, which, in view of its struggle with Iran, no longer has the luxury of keeping the United States at arm's length; many of the smaller Gulf sheikdoms may soon find themselves in similar straits. In the Middle East and beyond, the world teems with examples of states able to conduct a wide range of mutually beneficial business dealings notwithstanding deep political divides.

But, it may be asked, even if U.S. interests can be sustained in a Middle East in which Israel continues to occupy territories taken in war, does it not benefit us to be *seen* to be active diplomatically in behalf of territory-for-peace? There is something to this notion, for the United States does garner some credit around the world when it is perceived as working toward a Middle East settlement. It was, after all, American diplomatic efforts that were central to the disengagement agreements between Israel and both Egypt and Syria after the October 1973 war and to the success at Camp David. Moreover, the promise of peace provides a *raison d'être* for Arab "moderates," who have earned this title largely on account of their own perceived willingness to recognize and live peacefully alongside Israel. In the absence of a U.S.-led peace "process," many of these Arab leaders may come to feel abandoned, and a Middle East in the grip of such feelings could become more likely to slide into war.

Yet there are stronger reasons for the United States *not* to go on pressing for the basic paradigm of territory-for-peace. Among Israelis, such a policy will only antagonize and possibly embolden those who claim the United States cannot be trusted and that Israel must as a result take dramatic or decisive steps—i.e., annexation of the territories—to ensure its own long-term security. Among Arabs, heightened U.S. efforts will over time produce more frustration than satisfaction as it inevitably becomes clear that we cannot deliver what they want. In the process we will be wasting precious diplomatic resources, not the least of them our reputation as a sometimes effective arbiter of regional disputes. Most important, visible U.S. efforts aimed at a comprehensive Middle East settlement will help perpetuate the escapist and self-serving illusion in the Arab world that the key to regional settlement lies not in Arab willingness to compromise but in American willingness to pressure Israel. So long as this view dominates, we cannot expect those most directly affected to act responsibly.

Still, eschewing activism does not constitute a policy. What, then, can and should the United States do to help avoid large-scale regional conflict and a U.S.-Soviet confrontation, to maintain access to resources and markets, to limit the scope for terrorism, and to expand political-military ties?

The United States can and should adhere closely to the position that peace in the Middle East lies mainly in the hands of the leaders and peoples of the region. While there is nothing to gain (and possibly a good deal to lose) from explicitly repudiating the territory-for-peace formulations of Camp David and the 1982 Reagan Plan, and similarly nothing to gain from renouncing UN Resolution 242, there is also little to be gained from actively championing these approaches. American officials would do better to continue making clear our opposition both to Israeli annexation of the West Bank and Gaza Strip—for this would unnecessarily antagonize Arab states and peoples and possibly bring renewed violence to the region without materially improving Israel's security—and to Palestinian "self-determination," which, as a short-hand for statehood, aims to bring into being an entity wholly unaccept-able to Israel and arguably contrary to our own interests.

Some observers believe the United States has a strategic as well as a moral imperative to support Palestinian self-determination. But the United States has never supported the principle of self-determination unconditionally; factors of history, viability, and national interest have always entered into the calculation. A Palestinian state limited to part of the West Bank would almost certainly lack viability. It would pose a potential threat to both Israel and Jordan. Moreover, Palestinian leaders, and the PLO in particular, have compromised their claim to self-determination by their failure to recognize Israel or renounce terror. Under these circumstances it is absurd to expect the United States to support the Palestinian demand for self-determination.

Overall, we would do better to avoid focusing on political arrange-ments for the West Bank and emphasize instead our interest in promot-ing a mixture of home rule and functional ties between Palestinians and both Jordan and Israel. At this point, the best hope for the Palestinians lies not in summits or international conferences but at the more mundane levels of political and economic life which they themselves can somewhat control. Despite such setbacks as the March 1986 assassina-tion of Nablus Mayor Zafer el Masri, Israel can be encouraged by us to move forward with its policy of "devolution" for key West Bank towns, an approach which has the virtue of improving people's lives while developing a local leadership class and keeping open ultimate questions of political status.

Ironically enough, a model for the people of the West Bank may be found in the condominium arrangements recently entered into by the United Kingdom and the Irish Republic, in which the latter was granted a degree of influence over the affairs of Northern Ireland in the context of continued British sovereignty there. Analogously, some mix of Palestinian, Jordanian, and Israeli influence in the occupied territories could well prove to be the most desirable outcome in the near term for the local inhabitants. There is sense in confronting only those issues for which a consensus may be fashioned, while postponing those which are simply too difficult to address. For the foreseeable future, the Palestinian predicament is one that cannot be solved, only managed.

A second but no less important tenet of U.S. Middle East policy ought to be nurturing of Israeli-Egyptian ties. More than any other development, the return of the Sinai and the creation of an accepted border between Israel and what was (and some day again could be) the most militarily capable Arab state have transformed the regional political landscape. U.S. policy must therefore concern itself with promoting the stability of the Mubarak regime and instilling a pro-Western attitude (including, if possible, tolerance for Israel) among the elite.

At present, Israeli-Egyptian ties are foundering; dissatisfaction, and disaffection, are rampant in both countries. There is no Egyptian ambassador resident in Tel Aviv, there are minimal high-level contacts, almost no travel by ordinary Egyptians to Israel, and no settlement of the status of Taba, a small parcel of land on the border which Egypt claims and Israel still controls. Meanwhile the Mubarak government's relations with the United States and Israel are the object of mounting hostility among Egypt's leftists and Muslim fundamentalists alike. In Israel, the relationship (or lack of one) has engendered considerable bitterness about what can be expected from the Arabs even in the best of circumstances.

The United States can act to arrest this deterioration by ensuring the flow to Cairo of substantial economic and military assistance (including military education and training), by expanding trade, investment, and educational and cultural ties, and by continuing to throw our diplomatic resources behind a settlement of the small but acrimonious Taba dispute. These objectives, along with a strengthening of the Egyptian-Israeli dimension of the Camp David Accords, merit U.S. attention more than the attempt to broker yet another deal among Jordan, Israel, and the PLO.

It would also be useful for the United States to resume a limited dialogue with the Soviet Union on the Middle East, for the simple reason that there is something to be gained by both Washington and Moscow in having a better understanding of each other's interests and intentions. Such knowledge can help avoid crises or, if crises occur, facilitate their management. Dialogue between the two powers might also take in the issue of the potential proliferation of chemical and nuclear arms in the region.

But U.S.-USSR dialogue ought not to be portrayed as more than it is, and certainly should not be translated into American support for an international conference on the Middle East. A gathering at which the key parties to the Middle East dispute would meet in order to provide cover for Israel and Jordan (with the PLO's blessing) to go off and negotiate the future of the West Bank and Gaza will never take place. A more realistic scenario would be one in which the Soviets, having resumed relations with Israel and thereby earned a right to attend, would, with Arab help, put the United States representative in the unenviable position of having to choose between distancing himself from Israel, in order to curry favor with the Arab participants, or siding with Israel at the expense of the opprobrium of the majority; in neither case are our national interests likely to be improved.

Lastly, we must expect that terrorism will continue to pose a direct threat to Western interests in the region. This would be true even if a settlement could be reached along the lines of the territory-for-peace paradigm, since certain Arab leaders would be content with nothing less than Israel's disappearance. In the absence of such a settlement, there is certain to be even more terror. Providing counterterrorist assistance to friendly governments would help here. Out of concern for self-preservation, Arab leaders can be counted on to cooperate with us despite their unhappiness at our support for Israel. But raising the salience of the terrorism issue will have its desired effect only if (as in the bombing of Libya last April) we make good on our rhetoric; a policy of bluster and inaction is worse than no policy at all.

These four elements—reduced involvement in schemes intended to produce a solution of the Palestinian problem, much less a comprehensive settlement of the Middle East; greater attention to the Israel-Egypt relationship; a continued but narrow dialogue with the USSR; and increased action against terrorism—will not bring peace to the Middle East. Nor will they ensure that all American interests will prosper. But they do comprise a valid approach to the region, one that will allow the United States to promote its political, economic, and strategic interests in an environment free of major conflict.

A more modest posture for the United States in the Middle East need not be permanent. We could resume a more active diplomacy—indeed, we should declare our readiness to do so—as soon as the necessary prerequisites for progress are seen to exist. As experience has shown, American diplomacy can play a crucial role in the Middle East, but only when the desire to negotiate and compromise is to be found among the local protagonists. As for when such a desire will emerge, what may be required first is a major event like the passing of Assad from the leadership of Syria, or of Arafat from the de-facto leadership of the Palestinians. In the latter case, opportunities might well develop for the emergence of a legitimate popular Palestinian leadership. Nor is it out of the question that a Palestinian state may arise, not west of the Jordan River but east, in the Hashemite kingdom of Jordan where even today Palestinians constitute a majority.

Today's facts, in short, may not be tomorrow's. The only thing that is certain now is that the Middle East is not ripe for any grand American initiatives. But this is no reason for despair. Indeed, the long-term interests of the United States, Israel, and conceivably even the Palestinians themselves might be served by a little less attention from Washington. One hopes that the current "period of reflection," declared by the Reagan administration in the wake of King Hussein's termination of his effort to create a common approach with the PLO, will be a prolonged one. We have seen what territory-for-peace can do; the time has now arrived for a different approach to the Middle East.

21

The Race for South Africa

PAUL JOHNSON

The campaign of economic attrition now being waged within the United States against the Republic of South Africa, which is summed up in the word disinvestment, is an outstanding example of the power of political propaganda. That the United States, the richest country in the world, should deliberately set about destroying the economy of what is in some respects still a developing nation is an absurdity in itself, and a cruel absurdity. Such a policy might make some kind of brutal sense, in terms of *Realpolitik*, if it were to America's economic and political advantage to wreck the economy of South Africa. In fact the reverse is true. The United States has absolutely nothing to gain, and a good deal to lose, if disinvestment inflicts radical damage. The truth is, the campaign makes no practical sense at all, as South Africans of all shades of political opinion—except the men of violence—have tried to explain to the American public. In no sense is it justifiable. It is, however, explicable on the assumption that the South African regime is a unique moral evil, whose wickedness is so great that the necessity for its destruction transcends all the rules governing relations between states and, indeed, the dictates of elementary common sense. That, in fact, is the assumption behind the campaign; and that is its moral basis.

Therein lies the triumph of propaganda. For South Africa is not unique. In many fundamental respects it is a typical African country. The problems which confront its government, and the way it responds to them, are typical too. Let us look at six ways in which the Republic is an African archetype.

First, like every state in Africa, it is undergoing a very rapid population increase. Africa is the last of the continents to experience what is termed the population explosion. It occurred first in 19th-century Europe, which accounts for the phenomena of European emigration and colonialism. It then spread to Asia and South America, both of which (like Europe after 1918) are now emerging from the phase of fast growth. In Central America the "explosion" is at its height and that is one prime reason for the turmoil we find there. In Africa it is just beginning, but the curve of population growth is rising steeply and it is already producing Malthusian countereffects in the form of over-cultivation, droughts, famines, and wars. So far, South Africa has avoided the worst of these, but it is feeling intense population pressure like every other African country.

Demographic growth exacerbates what is the most important single characteristic of the African continent: its lack of racial, cultural, and linguistic unity. No other continent is so fragmented. Before colonialism intervened, Africa was beginning to evolve larger units by a process of tribal imperialism, and the effect of the colonial century was to accelerate the process and to transform many thousands of tribal societies into about fifty superficially modern states, which are now independent. Scarcely one is homogeneous. Even small states like Rwanda are riven by racial fissures. In the first quarter-century of independence these divisions have produced appalling civil wars in Nigeria, the Sudan, Chad, Zaire, Uganda, and elsewhere.

Here is the second respect in which South Africa is typical. It is a large African country and because it is large its racial problems—like those of Nigeria, Zaire, and the Sudan, for example—are particularly complex. At the level at which disinvestment is debated in the United States, the Republic is seen as divided between whites and blacks. The reality is much more complicated.

The largest racial group is the Zulu, with 5,412,000 people. In a way it is more a national than a simple racial group, because it is divided in turn into about 200 tribes, each subdivided into clans. The next largest are the whites, with 4,454,000, but these too are composed of diverse ethnic groups—Dutch, French, English, and German—and have two distinctive cultures and languages, Dutch-Afrikaans and English. The figure also includes other important subgroups, such as the large Jewish community, Portuguese, Greeks, Italians, and "Rhodesian Whites." Third in size are the Xhosa, with 2,685,000, followed by the mixed-race group officially called Coloureds (2,556,000), the North Sotho (2,265,000), South Sotho (1,793,000), and Tswana (1,216,000).

In addition to all these, there are seven other main groups, ranging from the Shangaan, with nearly 890,000 and the Asians with 780,000, to the Venda, with 185,000. This last is the most homogeneous group, but even it has 27 distinct tribes. The Asians are divided into Hindus (65 percent), Muslims (21 percent), Christians, Buddhists, and other cultures. As for language, there are four major and 23 minor African ones.

This analysis, moreover, excludes the people of the quasi-independent states created within South Africa: Transkei with 2,500,000 people, Bophuthatswana with 1,300,000, Ciskei with 636,000, and Venda with 358,000, making about 4,800,000 in all.

The third way in which South Africa is typical is that population pressure on the land is driving people into the towns, and especially into the big cities. All over Africa traditional rural societies are breaking up. Towns like Lagos (Nigeria), Johannesburg (South Africa), Dakar (Senegal), Nairobi (Kenya), Khartoum (the Sudan), Kinshasa (Zaire), and Harare (Zimbabwe) are expanding at terrifying speed. Most of the new arrivals live in shantytowns. The statistics of crime, and especially murder, are deeply depressing. No place in South Africa can rival the murder rate in Lagos or half-a-dozen other big black African cities, but the 1984 figures were pretty alarming all the same: in just four police districts in the Rand (the gold-mining region which includes Johannesburg) there were over 2,700 killings last year. Soweto, perhaps the best known of the black townships in the Rand, had 1,454 killings classified as murder. The average police district has between three and seven murders a day. The number of reported rapes is also enormous.

These burgeoning and ultraviolent giant cities pose growing problems to the authorities in all African countries, and here again South Africa is typical. Governments have found that, unless they respond ruthlessly, the shantytowns quickly become no-go areas for the police and are ruled or partitioned by rival gangs; soon the whole city becomes ungovernable.

So governments respond with what has become the curse of Africa—social engineering. People are treated not as individual human beings but as atomized units and shoveled around like concrete or gravel. Movement control is imposed. Every African has to have a grubby little pass-book or some other begrimed document which tells him where he is allowed to work or live. South Africa has had pass-laws of a kind since the 18th century. They have now spread all over the African continent, and where the pass-book comes the bull-dozer is never far behind.

Virtually all African governments use them to demolish unauthorized settlements. Hundreds of thousands of wretched people are made homeless without warning by governments terrified of being overwhelmed by lawless multitudes. In the black African countries bordering on the Sahara, the authories fight desperately to repel nomadic desert dwellers driven south by drought. When the police fail, punitive columns of troops are sent in.

South Africa has the most efficient (though not the largest) repressive apparatus on the continent, much admired and imitated by other African governments, who buy South African police hardware when they can. All these security forces are ruthless and liable to act with unpredictable violence. But many are ill-paid and undisciplined, unlike the South African police, and therefore far more savage. The bloody cost of social control and engineering in black Africa goes largely unreported. South Africa, by contrast, has a large, varied, and in many ways excellent press, so we know exactly what goes on there.

African social engineering is, perhaps inevitably, given the lack of homogeneity, conducted on a racial basis. Here again South Africa is typical. All African states are racist. Almost without exception, and with varying degrees of animosity, they discriminate against someone: Jews, or whites, or Asians, or non-Muslim religious groups, or disfavored tribes. There is no such thing as a genuinely multiracial society in the whole of Africa. There is no African country where tribal racial origins, skin color or religious affiliation are not of prime importance in securing elementary rights.

African countries vary in the extent to which their practice of discrimination is formalized or entrenched in law codes and official philosophies. Most have political theories of a sort, cooked up in the political-science or sociology departments of local universities. Tanzania has a sinister totalitarian doctrine called Ujaama. Ghana has Consciencism. There is Zambian Humanism, Négritude in Senegal, and, in Zaire, a social creed called Mobutuism, after the reigning dictator. All these government theories reflect the appetites of the ruling racial groups.

Apartheid, cobbled together in the social-psychology department of Stellenbosch University, is a characteristic example of the distinctively African brand of political theory which has developed in the last half century. Apartheid is not a concept which divides the Republic from the rest of Africa: on the contrary, it is the local expression of the African ideological personality. No continent has ever suffered more at the hands of its politically-minded intellectuals, and here again South Africa is very typical.

Those, then, are six important ways in which the Republic is a characteristically African state. But in four respects it does differ from its neighbors, and these must be examined too.

The first concerns its wealth: South Africa has by far the richest and most varied range of natural resources of any African country. Its settlements were originally poor, wholly agricultural, largely pastoral; but since the discovery of diamonds in quantity in the 1860's it has emerged as the richest depository of minerals in the world, exceeded in quantity only by the Soviet Union. About 85 percent of what it mines is exported. It is the largest world supplier of gold, platinum, gem diamonds, chrome, vanadium, manganese, andalusite metals, vermiculite, and asbestos fibers. It is the second largest supplier of uranium and antimony, and among the top ten suppliers of nickel, copper, tin, silver, coal, and fluorspar. South Africa's mineral reserves are prodigious and seem to expand *pari passu* as world demand makes them worth exploring and exploiting. Even as things stand, the country is known to have 86 percent of the West's platinum-group metals, 64 percent of its vanadium, 48 percent of its manganese ore, 83 percent of its chrome ore, and nearly 50 percent of its gold.

There are a number of critical metals in which South Africa's only real rival is the Soviet Union. The two countries between them control 99 percent of the world's platinum, 97 percent of its vanadium, 93 percent of its manganese, 84 percent of its chrome, and 68 percent of its gold. There are many other metals in which the two are paramount. It is impossible to name any country or class or racial group which would materially benefit from the destruction of the South African economy, with one notable exception. The Soviet Union would be an outstanding beneficiary if South Africa's mining industry were put out of action and, still more, if it were placed in hands the Soviet government could control.

The second way in which South Africa differs is that its mineral wealth has become the basis of a modern economy—the only modern economy in the whole of Africa. South of the Sahara, South Africa has less than 25 percent of the population, but it has nearly 75 percent of the total Gross National Product. The core of its economy is mining. Again after the Soviet Union, it has the largest mining industry in the world, employing over 700,000 people as opposed to 470,000 in the United States, 140,000 in Canada, and 70,000 in Australia. In many important respects the South African mining industry is the most efficient and technically advanced in the world.

The strength of the mining industry accounts for the third way in which South Africa differs. Except for the Ivory Coast, Kenya, and Malawi, all the black African states have experienced falls in real incomes per capita since independence. But only in South Africa have the real incomes of blacks risen very substantially in the last quarter-century. In mining, black wages have tripled in real terms in the last decade and are still rising, despite the recession through which the South African economy has been passing since the second quarter of 1984.

This helps to account for the fact that there are more black-owned cars in South Africa than there are private cars in the whole of the Soviet Union. The Republic is the first and so far the only African country to produce a large black middle class. In South Africa the education available to blacks is poor compared to what the whites get, and that is one of the biggest grievances the black communities harbor; but it is good compared to what is available elsewhere on the continent. The number of blacks matriculating (i.e., completing secondary education) is about to pass the white total, and so, more surprisingly, is the number of black South African women with professional qualifications—now over the 100,000 mark and rising fast. Almost certainly there are now more black women professionals in the Republic than in the whole of the rest of Africa put together.

Thanks to mining, again, this modest but rising prosperity is not confined to blacks born in South Africa. About half of South Africa's black miners come from abroad, chiefly from Mozambique, Malawi, Lesotho, Swaziland, and Botswana. Most of their wages are remitted. About 10 million people, in half-a-dozen countries, are financially dependent on South Africa's mining industry, and its breakdown would thus be an unimaginable catastrophe for the whole of southern Africa. Black Africans, like other people, vote most sincerely with their feet. South Africa is the country where they most want to work and (if open to them) live in.

That is one reason Bishop Tutu of Johannesburg was manifestly wrong when he declared last year that South African blacks would welcome a Soviet occupation. The Soviet Union has often been admired from afar, but no one goes there to work in its mines. Nor do South African blacks emigrate, legally or illegally, to neighboring black-run countries like Angola, Mozambique, or Zimbabwe. The security fences South Africa is now rather anxiously erecting are designed to keep intended immigrants out, not—like the Berlin Wall—to keep people in.

The fourth way in which South Africa differs from the rest of the continent is that it is in many respects a free country. Every other African country has become, or is in the process of becoming, a one-party state. None of them subscribes in practice, or in most cases even in theory, to the separation of powers. Both the rule of law and democracy are subject in South Africa to important qualifications. But it is the only African country where they exist at all. The emergency and security powers enjoyed by the South African government are so wide and draconian that they almost make us forget that the judiciary is independent—very much so—and that even non-whites can get justice against the state, something they are most unlikely to secure anywhere else on the continent. The courts are cluttered with black litigants suing the police, the prison authorities, or other government agencies, or appealing against sentences. For instance, the circumstances in which the black leader Steve Biko died in detention have been subjected to a degree of minute scrutiny in the courts which would be rare even in America, and quite impossible anywhere else in Africa.

South Africa has a parliamentary constitution with a limited franchise, rather as Britain had in the early 19th century. Like Britain then, and unlike the rest of Africa now, it has been moving toward democracy rather than away from it. The new constitution introduced last year gives parliamentary representation, though on separate rolls, to both the Asian and the Coloured communities. Asian and Coloured ministers now serve in the government. No one doubts that the blacks, who already have the vote in local government elections, will get it in some form in central government elections. The claim by opponents of the regime that these changes are simply cosmetic is evidently not shared by the extremists of the African National Congress (ANC), who have been doing everything in their power to murder or terrorize non-whites who participate in elections.

There is also overwhelming evidence that South Africa has been moving away from apartheid. Some of it was always a dead letter; other aspects are no longer enforced. The fact that over 10 million blacks live and work in areas officially designated white shows that the physical core of apartheid has been surrendered. Now the scrapping of Section 16 of the Immorality Act, which made interracial sex illegal, and of the Prohibition of Mixed Marriages Act has destroyed its emotional core. It is quite clear that P.W. Botha, who became President (in the U.S. sense) under the new constitution, is convinced that apartheid has to go and has been dismantling it almost by stealth to avoid panicking the bulk of the regime's followers.

The view of Alan Paton, South Africa's greatest writer, now eighty-one, as expressed to the South African weekly, the *Financial Mail*, earlier this year, is worth quoting:

Since Union [1910] I've observed all our prime ministers closely, except Louis Botha, who died when I was about sixteen; and I certainly think the most astute of them all is this current chap who is now our state president. There's a word that I've decided to cut out of my vocabulary, and that's "cosmetic." I believe that P.W. Botha with his whole heart wants to remain part of the West. And I think that P.W. realized that if we were once dropped by the West, it would be the end of us, and especially the end of the Afrikaner. . . . P.W. has said things that no prime minister has said before—not one, not even Louis Botha or [Jan] Smuts. He said that he wanted a future for every child in this country, white, black, or brown. He said that if these people are good enough to go and fight on our border, they are good enough to have a place at home.

What is happening within the political system is that the real supporters of apartheid are moving out of the regime's National party and into the opposition Conservative party of Dr. Andries Treurnicht; and their places in the National party are being filled by more liberal English-speaking voters. The true voice of apartheid now comes from the Conservatives, isolated from power at the Right end of the spectrum. The voice of the regime itself is the voice of change.

At the end of February this year, Treurnicht proposed a motion in parliament rejecting the government's intention to extend the existing political integration and power-sharing to include blacks, and affirming that the only meaningful solution for South Africa was partition, a logical extension of apartheid. He used the same arguments which, until quite recently, were the stock government defense of the system.

Even more significant was the speech rejecting the motion from Chris Heunis, Minister for Constitutional Development and a key figure in the reform process. He said that Treurnicht "is not seeking self-determination for all groups . . . [but] only for the whites, and in his terminology this means domination." Peaceful coexistence on this basis was impossible and violence was certain. The basic difference between the government and the Conservatives, Heunis added, was that the government "accepted the implications of South Africa's multinationalism," of "our multi-ethnic society," and these were that "we are not just one nation here which can exclude and push all the others around." To refuse to accept these implications was "to flee from reality" and "to bury the head in the ground like an ostrich."

Where have we heard all these phrases and arguments before? Why—until recently they were hurled at the regime by its English-speaking liberal opponents.

At the rate things have been moving, apartheid could be dead and officially buried in five years. If so, I like to think that South Africa will be only the first African state to recognize that its particular "ism" cannot work, and the repudiation of apartheid will be followed by the dissolution of similar ideologies elsewhere on the continent.

Certainly any acceptance of power-sharing by the Republic will have a beneficial effect on its neighbors, especially if it can be carried out peacefully. In many ways South Africa is the natural leader and former of opinion, at any rate in the southern half of the continent. The Republic had a baneful and destructive influence during the 1950's and 1960's, when apartheid was riding triumphant, and undoubedtly contributed to the spirit of intolerance and violence which destroyed civilized government in so many of the new black states during these decades. If South Africa is sickening of social engineering and the ideological superstructure built upon it, it may mean that this dark period in African history is drawing to a close, and that the Republic will lead other African nations to better ways of conducting their affairs.

Against this historical background, and what amounts to a watershed in African development, what is the campaign for disinvestment likely to achieve? It could have one of two effects. By far the more likely, in my opinion, is that it will ultimately strengthen both the regime and the South African economy. Economic sanctions are remarkably ineffective against a strong modern economy; often they merely enforce improvements, in quite unexpected ways. South Africa was traditionally a colonial economy which exported commodities and imported manufactures. The sanctions imposed over the last quarter-century have simply hastened its progress toward economic self-sufficiency.

The arms embargo, now more than two decades old, merely led to the creation of an indigenous arms industry. South Africa exploited the advanced technology of its mining industry to become a world leader in the manufacturer of conventional explosives, rivaling the hitherto unchallenged supremacy in this field of Sweden and the U.S. It also specializes in mine-resistant armored-security vehicles, in which it has outstripped all its competitors. From an importer of arms it has become an exporter, selling its products all over the world but expecially to other African governments, whose needs are similar. In fact the United Nations, which once instructed its members to stop selling arms to South Africa, is now driven to beg them to stop buying arms from the Republic.

The oil embargo produced similar results. South Africa, as it happens, does not find much difficulty in buying oil these days. But to make itself more than 85-percent self-sufficient in energy, it has created a synthetic-fuel industry whose chief component, Sasol, the semi-public coal-into-petroleum firm, is now the world leader in this technology. This has involved modernizing and expanding the coal industry, and as a by-product South Africa has created the lowest-cost coal-export trade in the world. It has captured a huge slice of the Japanese market and even exports coal at a profit to the United States.

These two examples (there are many others) suggest that disinvestment will not work. As long as investment in South Africa, especially in mining, remains highly profitable, capital will find its way there, whatever the U.S. banks and multi-nationals decide. The only change will be a growth in South African financial institutions, with Johannesburg doing for itself what at present is done by others. The net result will again be a broadening of South Africa's economic base by adding a strong financial sector, the elements of which already exist. The loser will be the United States economy.

There is, however, the possibility—I put it no higher—that the disinvestment campaign will succeed in inflicting substantial damage on South African industry, especially mining. In that case, we must then ask ourselves who the victims will be. Who will suffer?

It will not be the supporters of apartheid. They are, for the most part, small farmers, impervious to outside economic pressure. They are isolationist by instinct and by historical tradition. Their forebears undertook the Great Trek, away from Britain's Cape Colony and into the wild interior, precisely to escape from the world, to make themselves independent of it. They are far more isolationist than any prewar American Republicans. Their image of security is the *laager*, the circle of wagons drawn close together to keep alien forces out of their warm, inbred, Calvinist society. They regard Johannesburg and its business and financial palaces as Sodom, the city of Satan. Anything which damages the money-power is welcome to them.

Hence a successful campaign of disinvestment would simply drive the Afrikaners back into the *laager* and into the waiting arms of Dr. Treurnicht and his Conservative party. The forces of reform within the regime would lose their electoral base and the reform movement itself would come to a halt; perhaps be put into reverse. The political consequences of disinvestment would thus be the opposite of what its supporters claim. Those South African whites who support apartheid have always argued that big business and international finance were dragging the country along the calamitous path to multiracialism: the disinvestment campaign, if successful, would prove them right.

They *are* right, of course. The primary opponent of apartheid in South Africa—its only effective opponent, in practice—is capitalism. For it is a mistake to regard apartheid as the extreme right-wing end of the political spectrum. It is more accurately described as ethnic socialism, a system which necessarily involves state interference in every aspect of economic activity, a huge state sector, an ever-growing state encroachment on the national income, and a mass of restrictive laws which inhibit the operations of the free market. Capitalism is incompatible with apartheid for broadly the same reasons it is incompatible with feudalism: it cannot coexist with a social and political system based on inherited racial caste, which forbids freedom of movement and a free market in labor, and subordinates all business decisions to the needs of a primitive world view.

Hence it is the nature of capitalism in South Africa to destroy apartheid, and that is precisely what it has been doing. If we look at the aspirations of South African blacks, not as imagined in theory and from the outside but as they actually exist, we find that black priorities center on five practical objects. These are, in probable order of importance: better education for their children; rights of citizenship; the right to own property, especially house title, anywhere in the country; the end of Influx Control—that is, freedom of movement and residence; and a natural corollary of the last three demands, freedom from excessive police supervision. On each and all these demands, and in their overall aspiration, the blacks have the vigorous support of virtually the whole business community.

There is, in fact, a common interest for blacks and business to dismantle apartheid. This common interest is paradoxically underlined by the disinvestment campaign. For if it succeeds, both will be victims.

That business, and especially the mining industry, will suffer is obvious enough. The new very-deep-level gold mines, for instance, absorb colossal quantities of investment cash. To sink a single shaft can cost over $1 billion. On the other hand, one big mine can employ 20,000 people or even more, three-quarters of them blacks.

If mines close or reduce production, the first to be turned away will be black immigrants. The effect on the economies of such countries as Mozambique, Botswana, and Malawi will be serious: they are poor enough already, and heavily dependent on foreign currency earned by such export of labor. If disinvestment does enough damage, South African blacks will lose their jobs too. There is a simple calculation: of every hundred jobs disinvestment destroys, between 70 and 80, and possibly more, are held by blacks, and these are the best-paid black industrial jobs on the whole continent.

I have no doubt that this is exactly the effect which some of those who support the disinvestment campaign wish to achieve. It is certainly the aim of the African National Congress, which is no longer interested in reform or a negotiated, gradualist settlement, but seeks a solution by force. The ANC and its followers believe that mass unemployment will increase the "revolutionary consciousness" of blacks.

The present situation in South Africa can thus be seen as a race. On the one hand, there are those within the regime, and the white liberals outside it, who want to dismantle apartheid and build a system of multiracial power-sharing. They know they are engaged in a race, but they must move slowly, because they have to carry the bulk of the Afrikaners with them. On the other hand, there is the ANC, which is racing to destroy the moderate elements within the Asian, Coloured, and above all the black populations before they can be integrated into the reformed regime. Its terror campaign, which was brought to a head by young people under ANC influence, and which provoked the declaration of a state of emergency in July, has been aimed very largely at non-white moderates. Its object has been to murder as many of them as it can, and to frighten the rest into noncooperation. It is strongly reminiscent of the campaign waged by the National Liberation Front against Arab moderates in French Algeria, and of the efforts by the

Grand Mufti and his killers to destroy the forces of Arab moderation in prewar Palestine.

Both these earlier terror campaigns succeeded, and it is possible that the ANC, helped along by disinvestment, will eventually succeed as well, in spite of harsh emergency measures adopted by the government. In that case, the black extremists will have won the race, the attempt to move away from apartheid will be abandoned, and South Africa will face a future of continuing and increasing violence. But it will be a future in which a refortified and emotionally strengthened regime of apartheid will almost certainly stay on top, using whatever force is necessary.

22

Sanctions and South Africa

COSMAS DESMOND

This article sets out to describe and analyse the causes and effects of the phenomenal growth in the South African divestment campaign and the increasing calls for sanctions in the United States and other parts of the world.

The campaign in the US for the divestment of holdings by universities, churches, cities and States in companies with South African interests and for the ending of bank loans is by no means new. Church and other groups have been taking shareholder action at company AGMs for the past ten years, without any great success; though there has been a regular trickle of cities and States passing legislation to prohibit or at least to limit the investment of public funds in companies with South African interests, starting with the city of Cotati, California, in 1978. The first State action was taken by Nebraska in 1980, followed by Massachusetts, Connecticut, and Michigan in 1982.

The campaign, however, took on a completely new complexion at the end of 1984; it began to attract nationwide support and to have more marked success. Timothy Smith, a long-time campaigner and Executive Director of the Inter-Faith Center on Corporate Responsibility, commented, 'A number of banks have turned the corner on South Africa.'[1]

Washington Notes on Africa (Winter/Spring 1985) lists a number of factors which led to the formation of the Free South Africa Movement, which was established at the end of 1984 to coordinate the efforts of political, labour, church and academic organisations and to spearhead the nationwide campaign:

Events in South Africa in 1984: the widespread unrest and police violence leading to over 200 deaths and 4000 arrests, centred around the imposition of the new Constitution;

The award of the Nobel Peace Prize to Bishop Desmond Tutu, which focused worldwide attention on apartheid;

The US Presidential candidacy of Jesse Jackson, which brought the issue of South Africa into the arena of national political debate;

The re-election of President Reagan, which brought the prospect of four more years of 'constructive engagement';

The failure of the Export Administration Act, which included proposals for sanctions against South Africa and which was passed by the House of Representatives but defeated in the Senate;

The success of anti-apartheid action at grassroots level, which had been going on for many years.

The first major demonstration and arrests took place outside the South African Embassy in Washington DC on 21 November 1984. Since then demonstrations have taken place on every weekday, leading to the arrest (by August 1985) of some 3000 people, including twenty-two Congressmen and numerous other eminent people. The demonstrations have not been confined to Washington. As *Time* magazine (5 August 1985) commented:

> More than any other issue since the Vietnam War, the question of apartheid has touched off a wave of public protest and voluntary arrest in the US that is far from being confined to Washington. While demonstrators have been taking to the streets of the capital others across the country have sought to pressure state and local governments, universities and colleges to rid themselves of holdings that involve US and foreign companies with interests in South Africa.

By August 1985, six States and twenty-six cities had passed some form of divestment legislation, while such legislation was pending in another twenty-five States and in numerous cities. Some forty universities had taken similar action, though in most cases, as is true also of some States, the divestment proposals were conditional upon the companies taking some action, such as achieving a satisfactory rating according to the Sullivan Principles (see appendix). The demands made by the Sullivan Principles, which are mainly concerned with desegregation and equal treatment in the workplace, have to a large extent been overtaken by events. Local South African businessmen are in fact making more radical political demands, such as common South African citizenship, repeal of the Pass Laws, and participation in national political life. Little is to be gained, therefore, from such conditional divestment.

In US usage, 'divestment' refers to the action of shareholders disposing of their holdings in companies; 'disinvestment' refers to companies withdrawing their capital from South Africa. Divestment is not an end in itself and it has no direct effect on South Africa. Its purpose is not to make the individual and institutional shareholders feel good, but to put pressure on the companies concerned to disinvest. This pressure is not purely financial; after all, others will no doubt purchase the shares disposed of. Although US companies derive only a proportion, and in the case of the giant multinationals only a very small proportion, of their profits from South Africa, the damage done to their image by the exposure and criticism of their involvement in South Africa might well affect profitability of their other operations. Companies might well decide therefore that, whatever the profitability of their South African involvement, their continued presence is not worth the effort. The campaign has at least succeeded in making companies spend a great deal of time and effort, which to them means money, on justifying their South African operations. As one US company executive observed, 'Although we get 10 per cent of our profit from South Africa, it's taking up 50 per cent of boardroom time.'[2]

According to *The Economist* (London) (30 March 1985) 'The total of sales of stock in South African-linked companies instigated by the anti-apartheid movement over the past year is probably past the $5 billion mark'. How much effect this has had on the companies concerned it is impossible to gauge; though since 1980, thirty US companies have withdrawn from South Africa while only eleven have gone in. Others, like Ford and Coca-Cola have cut back their holdings in South African companies to less than 50 percent. Even the British banks, Barclays and Standard Chartered, which have completely dominated the South African banking scene for decades have now reduced their holdings to well below 50 per cent. The companies themselves claim that their actions are based on purely commercial considerations. But those considerations are in turn determined by the political situation to which the campaign has been drawing attention for many years.

Most of the divestment has been carried out by city and State pension funds. (With a value of over $1 trillion, US institutional portfolios are one of the largest sources of capital in the world, and they are now realising that this gives them a great deal of power). While the motivating cause has been disapproval of apartheid, the trustees have also been able to show that divestment from companies with South African interests is not financially detrimental to their Funds, as they must do in order to comply with the trust laws. The governor of the State of Massachusetts, which was the first State to divest completely from South African-linked companies, disposing of an estimated $130 million worth of shares, commented, 'Divestment makes not only a strong moral statement against apartheid but divestiture has proven to have had no significant impact on our pensions earnings.'[3] Several studies have shown that portfolio performance would be no worse, and in some cases would be better, without South African involvement. Robert Schwartz, the leading exponent of socially responsible investment has written:

> As an investment adviser, I do not analyze moral or political issues but rather concern myself with the hard data necessary to make responsible financial decisions. In the case of South Africa-related investments, the facts are clear. Divestment should not be ruled out on financial grounds. The final consideration is not its effect on your investment portfolio but its effect on apartheid.[4]

Some more cynical observers see this as reason for dismissing the campaign as simply an opportunity 'to redress affluence with a little nostalgic protest . . . any noble posture, so long as it's cost free'.[5] But in challenging the conventional wisdom about the financial advantages of investing in South Africa the campaign is also challenging the political and moral assumptions on which that 'wisdom' is based.

There is very little real pressure on the companies voluntarily to withdraw completely from South Africa for anything resembling moral reasons. The campaign has, however, helped to create a political climate in which it was possible and politic for both Houses of Congress to pass legislation which would prohibit new investment and provide for some form of sanctions. In the House of Representatives fifty-six Republicans joined the Democrats in supporting an anti-apartheid Bill which would prohibit new loans to the South African government and state corporations, new investment, the sale of computers and nuclear technology as well as the sale of Krugerrands. The Senate agreed to a milder package; at the time of writing it was expected that the two would meet shortly to coordinate their strategy and that they would agree on proposals for a limited form of sanctions which President Reagan, in view of the worsening situation in South Africa, would find difficult to veto.* The US representative who met 'Pik' Botha on his European visit following the declaration of the state of emergency was reported as having told him 'that the "emotional climate" in the US would not permit the presidential veto unless there was "accelerated movement" toward the dismantling of apartheid.'[6]

Even the House of Representatives' proposals called only for an end to new investment in South Africa, which is presently insignificant and has been declining in importance for many years. Much of the growth of foreign investment has been attributable to the reinvestment of profits which, from 1960, in the wake of the Sharpeville massacre, until February 1983 when exchange controls were lifted, could only be repatriated at a discount of up to 40 per cent. Total foreign investment has in any event been shrinking in real terms for the past few years and US investment has fallen in absolute terms. It reached a high of $2.8 billion in 1982 and fell to $2.2 billion in 1984. During the whole of 1981 and 1982 no more than $100 million of new US capital was invested. Since the abolition of exchange controls more money is leaving South Africa in the form of dividend payments than is entering for capital investment.

Companies invest in South Africa (as they do elsewhere) in order to make a profit; not in order to benefit the South African economy as a whole nor to improve the lot of blacks in particular. It can be argued *a priori* therefore that their withdrawal would harm them more than the South African economy or the black population. They will only withdraw when it is in their financial interests to do so, either because of the

* In October 1986, Congress overrode the President's veto of a limited sanctions bill against South Africa.

state of the economy or because public disapproval is affecting their profitability in other areas. Both these factors are already exerting some influence, as evidenced by the decline in new investment and the withdrawal of some companies. South Africa, while still a highly profitable field for investment in some sectors, particularly mining, is no longer the happy hunting-ground that it was until a few years ago. It was reported that Frost Sullivan, a New York risk consultant, had dropped South Africa from ranking as one of the safest of the world's economies to 'a par with some of the higher risk Third World countries.'[7] The Investor Responsibility Research Centre in Washington states that 'From a 31 per cent after-tax rate of return during 1980, a particularly good year for the South African economy, American companies realised an average return of only 7 per cent in 1982 and 1983'. It is not surprising, therefore, that in the first quarter of 1985 R2.9 billion of foreign investment, more than the total for 1984, was withdrawn from South Africa.

Current returns on investment are not, however, the only consideration. Much of the foreign investment in South Africa is now in the form of immovable assets which it would be physically impossible to remove and financially suicidal to dispose of locally. In any event, there is no reason to suspect that the South African government would hesitate to reintroduce exchange controls to prevent any major outflow of capital. Many companies are, therefore, obliged, in financial terms, to stay there however low the rate of return on their investments. Further, the major corporations have only a relatively small proportion of their assets in South Africa. A drop in the return on these will not have a dramatic impact on their overall performance. By staying in South Africa they not only hope, but are actively seeking to ensure, that the drop will be only temporary by ensuring that the present system survives.

Even in the unlikely event of the divestment campaign succeeding completely and causing all US companies to withdraw, the South African economy and apartheid would survive. It is true, as some opponents of disinvestment point out, that 'the divestment lobby is working on a tiny margin of the South African economy.'[8] (The investment lobbyists, however, use contradictory arguments: they argue *against* disinvestment on the ground that foreign investment is so insignificant that its withdrawal would have no effect. On the other hand, when arguing *for* investment they claim that it has had a very significant effect and that its withdrawal would be most harmful to the black population.) But the arguments for disinvestment are not solely, nor indeed primarily, economic. They are political. What is needed in South Africa is radical political change. Foreign investment because of its nature helps to preclude that change, since its role is to preserve the present system. In doing so there is no way in which it can, as its advocates claim, benefit the black population, since it is that system which is the cause of the problems, not simply bad working and living conditions and the denial of human rights, which are the necessary consequences of the system.

The campaign, like the House of Representatives' proposals, is also concerned with ending bank loans, which, as the South African Finance Minister confirmed in March 1984 were 'becoming of relatively greater importance to South Africa than equity investment.'[9] Eva Militz's work, *Bank Loans to South Africa Mid-1982 to End 1984*, 'identified a total of 202 banks of eighteen nationalities that provided ninety-eight new loans totalling US $4244.1 million to the minority regime, its parastatal institutions and private companies'. US banks accounted for 27 percent of this. Most of the leading banks now have a policy of not making loans to the South African government and its agencies; others have restrictive policies. The most notable 'convert' perhaps was Citibank, the world's largest private bank and the US's largest lender, which announced in February 1985 that it would no longer take part in loans to the South African government nor would it sell Krugerrands. Citibank had been subject to considerable pressure from divestment campaign:

> By March 1981 over thirty Protestant and Roman Catholic bodies had affirmed the pledge to buy no further bonds and CD's from Citibank. Other organisations like the famous Harvard University joined in and divested from Citibank. . . . the City of New York in 1984 began to withdraw pension money from banks and companies that deal with South Africa and a measure calling for further divestment was introduced in February 1985. . . . (Citibank is said to manage up to $3 billion a year on behalf of New York.)[10]

Citibank's announcement was, therefore, hardly surprising or coincidental. Wells Fargo and the First National Bank of Boston have gone further and have said that they will also not make loans to the private sector in South Africa.

Partly, at least, as a result of the campaign, there has been a fall in US bank loans to the public sector from $623 million in 1982 to $343 million in September 1984. There has, however, been a dramatic increase in loans to the private sector; these could easily be channelled to the government and its agencies and it at least leaves other avenues open to them. US lending to private institutions other than banks increased from $496.2 million in June 1981 to $1.1 billion in September 1984 and lending to banks from $1.08 billion to $3.55 billion over the same period.

The stated aim of the Free South Africa Movement is the end of apartheid and a change in US policy. While it is already having some effect on the latter, its effect on the former is, and will remain, minimal, though not necessarily irrelevant. What North Americans mean by 'an end to apartheid' and what black South Africans mean by it are two very different things. Although the whole movement should not be dismissed, as it is by some of its more strident opponents, as simply a self-indulgent expression of 'bleeding-heart liberalism', it does tend to be little more than an extension of the US civil rights movement and to treat apartheid merely as a particularly iniquitous form of denial of individual human rights based on racism. For black South Africans apartheid is a total politico-economic system which must be completely destroyed and not tampered with by the granting of 'concessions' concerning freedom of movement, trade union rights, etc. (Black political activists have tended for many years not even to refer to 'apartheid'; they speak of 'the system'.)

Many among both the proponents and opponents of foreign investment talk glibly about its positive or negative effects without showing any real understanding of what apartheid is or of the nature of the relationship between foreign investment and the apartheid system. If apartheid were simply about the practice of racial discrimination there would be equally valid, and insoluble, arguments for the use of investment as a carrot or disinvestment as a stick in order to persuade South Africans to change their ways. If apartheid were simply about separate park benches, separate shop entrances, separate schools, separate hospitals, separate buses, separate sports facilities—all on the basis of skin colour—it would still warrant universal condemnation. It is all that, but it is also much more. If that were all it was, the South African government could claim, as it does, that things were changing: there are now integrated hotels and restaurants (seventy-four and thirty-four respectively in the whole country) integrated sports teams (a token black has been chosen for the Springbok rugby team) and some integrated beaches (though swimming pools remain 99 per cent segregated).

South Africa is certainly racist. Racism exists not only on an interpersonal level as it does in most countries; it is institutionalised and even constitutionalised. Racism is enshrined in the social structures, the law and the Constitution. Their racial classification affects every aspect of people's lives: their right to vote, where they may live and work, whether they may live together as a family, the quality of their education, the size of their income and even where they may be buried.

Apartheid is not, however, simply about segregation. Social, geographic and political separation is only one of the many means used to achieve the aim of retaining economic wealth and political power in white hands. Apartheid means inequality and control. No one who is committed to the capitalist system would willingly forgo such an efficient method of protecting their material interests. Botha, Reagan and Thatcher possibly understand this better than some of the critics who are concerned only with the inhumanity of the means used.

Racial discrimination is never simply an end in itself. In South Africa it is a means towards the end of retaining political power, and consequently economic wealth, in the hands of the white minority. Apartheid and white economic development do not merely exist side by side; they have a symbiotic relationship. The South African government does not implement apartheid for purely ideological reasons, regardless of the economic consequences; it implements apartheid precisely because of these consequences, which are in the material interests of whites, including foreign investors. Apartheid, far from being a burden on the economy, has served it well. As F A Johnstone has noted:

> Given the vast economic growth and industrialisation which has taken place in South Africa during the twentieth century, and given the concomitant continuity and consolidation of the system of racial domination, it clearly makes little sense to begin by characterising the relationship between this system and the economic system as essentially 'dysfunctional'. Still less sense does this view make in view of the extensive determination of the system of racial domination by property owners, notable in such forms of racial discrimination as the coercive labour controls of the contract system, the pass system and the compound system and the various discriminatory property laws.[11]

It was foreign capital, mainly British, which enabled the gold and diamond mines, the foundations of the South African economy, to be developed in the first place. Such investment would not have been profitable, and therefore would not have been made, were it not for the existence of a vast, and extremely cheap, labour force. This labour force did not come into existence purely by chance; it had been deliberately created. There is nothing inherently exploitable about black workers. They were made exploitable by military conquest and the denial of political rights. They were forced to sell their labour *extremely* cheaply by the imposition of a tax when the only source of cash in an otherwise subsistence economy was working in the mines. Apartheid, albeit under a different name, served the interests of foreign capital from the start, and it continues to do so. Foreign investors are not therefore merely engaging in the morally reprehensible act of benefiting from an evil system. They are an essential part of that system. They could not survive very profitably without it; it could not survive without them.

Although foreign investment now accounts for only a small proportion (3.8 percent) of new fixed capital formation in South Africa, the State President P W Botha, for one, is under no illusions about its strategic importance. It was important he said, 'because it supplemented domestic savings to finance investment, favourably affected the balance of payments and often involved the transfer of technological know-how and sometimes the immigration of managers and highly qualified technical people'.[12] The basic contradiction of the apartheid system is that there is one economic system, which is dependent on blacks both as workers and as consumers, but a plural political system which denies blacks any effective power. The greater the economic dependence on blacks, the greater the pressure for a new political dispensation. To survive, apartheid must decrease its dependence on black labour and defuse the threat posed by the presence of blacks in 'white areas' by forcibly 'resettling' them. Foreign investment, because of its capital intensive nature, and, just as importantly, because of the 'technological know-how and highly qualified technical people' referred to by Botha, furthers this process and so lessens the pressure for political change. Disinvestment would obviously have the opposite effect.

While the withdrawal of foreign companies would have a deleterious effect on the small proportion of the workforce directly employed by them it would be beneficial to the majority since foreign investment destroys more jobs than it creates. The mechanisation of agriculture, for example—with the aid of foreign technology—has led to the 'resettlement' of 1.1 million blacks who were rendered 'superfluous' on white farms. As the South African economist Michael de Klerk has pointed out:

> . . . instead of investing the lion's share of our capital resources in industrial jobs which cost R5400 each to create, we should be investing much more in small-scale agriculture where jobs cost perhaps one-tenth of that amount to create. Such a redistribution of land and capital would help increase rural incomes and so attract the men who are critically lacking in black agriculture back to the rural areas. Agriculture is also one of the few remaining areas of economic activity where labour-intensive techniques are still competitive. . . . The distribution of power and wealth in South Africa, and *our involvement in the Western economic system*, has caused our economy to develop along almost entirely contrary lines, and this is perhaps *the single most important cause* of the high level of structural unemployment in the Republic.[13] (emphasis added)

He points out that among the causes of increasing capital intensity are 'the nature of foreign investment in the country' and 'the notion that development means using the latest overseas techniques.'

The argument for disinvestment, therefore, is not, or should not be, based on a moralistic self-righteousness; 'These people are so evil that we will have nothing to do with them.' Disinvestment and other sanctions should not, I believe, even be described as 'punitive'. Investors are necessarily party to the 'crime of apartheid'. The UN Convention on the Suppression and Punishment of the Crime of Apartheid states:

> International criminal responsibility shall apply, *irrespective of the motives involved* (emphasis added) ,to individuals, members of organisations and institutions and representatives of the State, whether residing in the territory of the State in which the acts are perpetrated or in some other State whenever they
> (a) Commit, participate in or conspire in the commission of the acts mentioned in Article II of the present Convention;

(b) Directly abet, encourage or cooperate in the commission of the crime of apartheid

Among the acts mentioned Article II is: '(e) Exploitation of the labour of the members of a racial group or groups, in particular by submitting them to forced labour.' Investors and other collaborators should, therefore, be concerned about their own 'criminal responsibility' in addition to that of the South African government. Refraining from incurring that responsibility is in one's own interests, not just a means of punishing others. By disinvesting companies do not simply wash their hands of the problem; they cease to play an important part in maintaining the system. To stop doing evil is a positive action. Disinvestment can only be viewed as a negative action if South Africa's racist policies are considered to have their own existence independently of the economic system. As we have seen, the only explanation for the apartheid system, both historically and in the present context, is in that it serves the political and economic interests of the whites. It is a contradiction in terms, therefore, to seek to change apartheid by participating in the present economic system. The 'Oppenheimer thesis' that economic growth, fuelled by foreign investment necessarily leads to positive political change, has clearly been discredited by experience. Repression has steadily increased throughout a period of massive economic growth. Today, after 150 years of foreign investment, there is in South Africa a state of emergency, widespread killings and arrests, and treason trials; the position of blacks is worse than it has ever been. The cosmetic changes that have been introduced have served only to entrench white rule; the new Constitution and the tricameral Parliament are prime examples of this. Foreign investment certainly makes a contribution to economic growth, a bigger one than those who seek to minimise its role so as to justify their continued presence there will admit. According to South Africa's Finance Minister, Barend du Plessis, 'South Africa could manage long-term growth of about 5.5 per cent a year with the help of heavy foreign investment. But if the country has to manage on its own resources, its viable growth rate is about 3.5 per cent a year.'[14] But there is no evidence of blacks benefiting from that growth. Disinvestment would change the nature rather than the extent of the growth, but at the same time, by increasing the dependence of the economy on black labour rather than foreign capital, it would heighten the basic contradiction of apartheid. How that contradiction is resolved is a question for black South Africans.

The pro-investment lobby would have us believe that any form of external pressure on South Africa is counter-productive because such is the Afrikaner mentality that they would react like cornered animals. Apart from being a blatant example of Anglo-American arrogance and racial stereotyping, the argument is clearly false. Even Dr. Verwoerd, the architect of Grand Apartheid and the most doctrinaire and intransigent of all Afrikaner leaders, admitted that he had to bow to foreign pressure. When introducing his plan for separate 'homelands' in 1962, he said in Parliament, 'This is not what we would have liked to see. It is a form of fragmentation that we would not have liked had we been able to avoid it. In the light of the pressure being exerted on South Africa, there is however no doubt that this will have to be done, thereby buying for the white man his freedom and the right to retain his domination in what is his country'. There is also a warning here. Verwoerd was not prepared to be diverted from his primary aim; he was only willing to adapt the means of achieving it in order to placate foreign opinion. Botha has been adopting the same strategy. In his policy speech of August 1985 he made it quite clear that he had no intention of sharing effective political power with blacks, but he did at least feel constrained to make the effort, bungled though it was, to respond to overseas pressure. He knew that the measures would be dismissed by blacks and had he been addressing his own supporters he would have made the speech in the Transvaal and in Afrikaans rather than in Natal and mainly English. This, however, is an argument for applying more pressure not less. More recently, the mere threat of very limited sanctions sent the Foreign Minister, 'Pik' Botha, scurrying to Europe to assure the US, Britain and West Germany of P W Botha's good intentions.

The Nationalists themselves are well aware of both the political and economic importance of foreign investment. They go to great lengths to encourage it; and to even greater lengths to discourage the advocacy of disinvestment. They realise that the more Western capital, in the form of bank loans and direct investment, that is tied up in South Africa the greater the West's interest in giving them political support. It is concern for the protection of these interests, rather than any concern about the effects on the black population, that leads one or other of the major powers inevitably to veto any action against South Africa proposed by the UN. (It is for this reason that disinvestment by companies of North American, British and French origin is of primary importance. Even if companies from other countries, such as Japan, Israel, etc, were to take their place, these countries could not acquire a vested interest in exercising a veto which they do not possess.) The advocacy of disinvestment by a South African, even if it takes place outside South Africa, is defined by the Internal Security Act as a crime of 'subversion', carrying a maximum penalty of twenty years imprisonment. This consideration alone should dispel any argument about which section of the population benefits from such investment. Even those black workers employed by US companies and who thus have their own vested interest in foreign investment recognise that it is the government and the whites who benefit most. A recent survey of such workers which has been widely quoted as showing that 71 per cent of them favoured foreign investment also showed that only 26 per cent considered that it helped blacks, while 44 per cent thought it helped the government and 30 per cent the whites.

Disinvestment would, therefore, have some economic impact; though a different one from that usually suggested by either the proponents or opponents of investment. The question is not whether foreign investment is of direct economic benefit to blacks or not, but whether it contributes to political change. Disinvestment, despite its relative insignificance in narrow economic terms, would remove an essential prop to the system and allow blacks greater opportunity, because of the system's increased economic dependence on them, to exert pressure for political change. In more basic terms, blacks do not need Westerners to hold their hand, but it would help if we got off their backs. Nobody claims that disinvestment alone would bring about radical political change in South Africa, but not only does it makes its own contribution, it also prepares the way for other actions, particularly for more wide-ranging sanctions, since Western countries would then have less to lose as a result of such actions.

Even if it is accepted that total disinvestment will not take place, certainly not if it is left to the companies themselves, the campaign still has some validity. On the psychological level, it is a gesture of solidarity with, and a morale boost to, black South Africans who are the primary agents of change; while it has the opposite effect on the white supporters of the system. Despite what the amateur psychologists in the investment lobby say, white South Africans, whether Afrikaners or English-speaking, *are* concerned about being treated as pariahs. The fact that black political leaders, with the exception of Chief Buthelezi, have consistently called for such action should in itself be a sufficient justification for the campaign. All concerned might do well to show more trust in the judgement of those who are in the forefront of the struggle.

The campaign also helps to create the right political climate for government action against South Africa. The leader of a black-led lobbying group in Washington, for example, was quoted in *Time* magazine as saying, 'Many Americans knew nothing about apartheid before the demonstrations began. Now there is a new understanding of South African repression. 'Such an understanding is a necessary, though by no means sufficient, prerequisite for government action. Without the campaign there would not even be the present threat of sanctions, which has been sufficient to have some influence on Botha's promise of future reforms. If, as anticipated, Reagan does approve some form of limited sanctions it will be an important political gesture and will put pressure on Britain at least to make a similar gesture. And at the moment nobody is really talking about anything more than a gesture.

Effective sanctions are not yet even on the agenda in the US or Britain or for that matter in any Western country. The divestment campaign has at least put the issue of South Africa on the agenda.*

The disinvestment campaign has not been confined to the US, though it is probably better organised and has more resources there than elsewhere; and for the first eight months of 1985 the US was certainly the dominant force in the campaign. There were, as has been mentioned, a number of reasons for this, some positive some negative, and its importance both in relation to bringing about change in South Africa and to influencing the rest of the world should not be exaggerated. The widespread support given to the campaign in the US has doubtless added impetus to the campaign in other parts of the world, but the only real question is whether US policy will have any influence on British policy. Some countries, however, were already ahead of the US, while others, in the wake of the declaration of the State of Emergency, have leap-frogged over them.

India severed all economic links with South Africa as long ago as 1947. The South African Minister of Economic Affairs reported to the House of Assembly in 1962 that boycotts of South Africa had been imposed by the USSR, China, Malaysia, Antigua, Barbados, Jamaica, [British] Guyana, Suriname, Ethiopia, Ghana, Liberia, Nigeria, Sierra Leone and the Sudan.[15] Other countries have imposed more limited sanctions: Norway decided in 1976 not to grant foreign exchange licences for investment in South Africa; Sweden banned new investment in 1979. Following the declaration of the State of Emergency on 20 July 1985, Canada, Australia, and all the members of the EEC, with the exception of Britain and West Germany, took some action. Brazil, which has a balance of trade surplus with South Africa, prohibited the export of arms, crude oil and petroleum derivatives and banned all social and cultural contacts. The most significant action was that taken by the French government which withdrew its ambassador and banned new investment. French new investment is very small, less than $15 million in 1984; nothing was said about its far more extensive trading links.

The divestment campaign is primarily a politicising and mobilising force; any disinvestment it achieves, and it is having some success, is a bonus. Effective action can only be taken by governments, and really effective action by the UN by means of comprehensive mandatory sanctions. An overwhelming majority of member States of the UN are in favour of at least some mandatory sanctions, beyond the existing mandatory arms embargo. In 1979 the General Assembly passed a resolution calling for a cessation of new investment: 'The General Assembly, convinced that a cessation of new foreign investment in, and

---

* The President was forced to accept limited sanctions by the congressional override of his veto.

loans to, South Africa would constitute an important step in international action for the elimination of apartheid, as such investment and loans abet and encourage the apartheid policies of that country . . . urges the Security Council to . . . achieve the cessation of further foreign investment in, and financial loans to, South Africa'. The Security Council has yet to impose such a moratorium.

Regular calls for mandatory sanctions are made in the General Assembly. In the 1984 vote there were only two votes against (compared to sixteen in 1983) and ten abstentions. In July 1985 not even Britain and the US vetoed the Security Council resolution on voluntary sanctions; though they had used their veto on an earlier one calling for mandatory sanctions.

In the past the South African economy has been considered impervious to sanctions, with the possible exception of oil, but in recent years it has become increasingly vulnerable. In 1982 and 1983 the economy experienced 'negative growth'. Despite some growth in 1984, the index of leading indicators fell 17 per cent in January and 13 per cent in February 1985; the prime borrowing rate of interest was 25 per cent in mid-1985, while inflation was at 61 per cent. The international finance community's disappointment with Botha's policy speech in August 1985 was reflected in the fall of the rand to a record low of $0.38 compared to $1 a year previously. In the past South Africa has had no difficulty in repaying loans since the international banks were always willing to make further loans because of their faith in the strength of the South African economy. Political factors have now changed that. On 27 August 1985 the Governor of the South African Reserve Bank in his annual report gave a number of reasons for the economy being in better shape than it had been in the previous year. Yet later that same day the Finance Minister announced the closure of the foreign exchange and shares markets. Four days later South Africa froze repayment for four months of $12 billion of short-term loans out of a total foreign debt of $17 billion. As the *Financial Times* (2 September 1985) commented, 'the crisis was brought about almost entirely by political rather than economic pressures'.

Even before the most recent unrest, South Africa had been described as being 'in the grip of a financial and economic crisis.' (M N Naidoo, unpublished paper) Naidoo points out that in 1984 South Africa devoted at least 27.8 per cent of its budget to defence, much of it going towards meeting the extremely high costs of the illegal occupation of Namibia, and a further 18 per cent on oil because of the high cost of its oil-from-coal process and the 'incentive payments' it has to make in order to circumvent the OPEC oil embargo. There were also other factors, as Militz points out, including the prolonged drought, the fall in the gold price and the rise of the dollar. The myth of South Africa's economic invulnerability has therefore been shattered. If UN mandatory economic sanctions were added to all these other factors there is no doubt that the economy would be crippled, though obviously this would not happen overnight. The object of the exercise, however, is not to bring economic chaos but political change. And this, not by frightening the Nationalists into agreeing to such change but by making it impossible for them to retain the necessary political control which relies on Western economic and political support. Without that support the nationalists could not continue to exclude blacks from the political process while at the same time becoming more economically dependent on them.

An end to bank loans and investment would, as has been noted, have some impact, though only a minor one. The main area in which such action would be effective remains that of oil. South Africa claims that half of its oil needs are now met by its oil-from-coal process at its Sasol plants, 'but it appears that figures are inflated to boost white morale. Only 18 per cent of the country's oil needs are provided by the Sasol plants'.[16] Despite the oil embargo imposed by all the OPEC countries, South Africa continues to import 200,000 barrels of oil per day; without this, in addition to the effect on industry, the defence force and the police would simply not be able to function. A ban on the export of technology, particularly computer and nuclear technology, would also have a major effect. The Managing Director of Burroughs, South Africa, has said, 'The economy would grind to a halt without access to the computer technology of the West'.[17] South Africa's nuclear programme—there is no doubt that it has the capability of producing nuclear weapons and has most probably already done so—depends particularly on French collaboration in supplying materials and on the recruitment of British scientists. These actions alone would have a major impact, but to make a significant contribution towards real change in South Africa sanctions need to be not only mandatory but also comprehensive. Both politically and morally if some sanctions are effective and right, any collaboration is counter-productive and wrong.

The only obstacle—and at present it appears to be an insuperable one—to the imposition of UN mandatory sanctions is the use of the veto in the Security Council by Britain and/or the US or possibly even by France. Both the US and Britain are concerned only with modifying apartheid, with smoothing off the rough edges so that it will be 'acceptable'. They would prefer a capitalist South Africa, even if it is racist, to a non-racist one which is also likely to be socialist. Both countries, but particularly Britain, would also incur financial losses from the imposition of sanctions. The likely US ban on new investment, for example, would affect fewer than 300 companies, whereas a ban on all trade would affect 5700.* The US is South Africa's largest export market, with Britain fourth; they are second and fourth respectively as sources of

* The October 1986 Congressional action included a ban on new investments, the cancellation of landing rights for South African Airways, and the prohibition of US import of steel, coal and iron from South Africa.

South Africa's imports. In relation to its total economy the US involvement with South Africa is insignificant; its imports from South Africa, for example, account for only 0.78 per cent of its total imports. Even its supposed dependence on South African minerals is grossly exaggerated:

> The sub-committee on Africa of the Foreign Relations Committee of the United States Senate, under the chairmanship of Senator George McGovern, published in 1979 a two-year survey of America's dependence on South Africa's minerals. This survey showed such dependence to be substantially one of habit rather than necessity: alternative sources of key minerals existed in Australia, Brazil and other countries. It was later pointed out by Robert S McNamara that it would be in America's interests to develop such alternative sources. Evidence before congressional and other committees of enquiry had indicated that in some sectors the West's own mineral development has been stultified by the long-held belief, fostered by the South African lobby, that only the South African grade of the relevant mineral was suitable for American industrial and military needs. Chrome is an example.[18]

In Britain's case the links are relatively far more significant. Britain's £5 billion of direct investment in South Africa represents 10 per cent of its total overseas investment and combined with its indirect investment of at least £6 billion provides some 45 per cent of foreign investment in South Africa. According to the United Kingdom South Africa Trade Association (UKSATA), a body not entirely devoid of its own vested interests, gross income for Britain from South Africa in 1982 was around £3.5 billion. UKSATA also maintains that breaking all links with South Africa would result in the loss of 250,000 jobs in Britain. Others (see Rogers and Bolton *op. cit.*) say that this is a gross exaggeration and that the figure could be as low as 10,000. Rogers and Bolton also confirm the findings of the US inquires about the availability of other sources of minerals and the possibility of other minerals being substituted. Further, in recent months there has been a growing body of opinion, especially within the British Labour Party, that one of the major causes of unemployment in Britain is the lack of capital for investment in industry as a result of the increase of overseas investment. Withdrawal of investment from South Africa could, therefore, provide capital for the creation of employment in Britain and thus offset any job losses which would result from other forms of sanctions.

As long as a Conservative government remains in power there is no likelihood that Britain would support mandatory, comprehensive UN sanctions. The Labour Party is committed to sanctions, though nationalist elements within it might baulk at comprehensive sanctions for which Britain would have to pay a price, at least in the short term. In any case, one veto is sufficient to prevent the imposition of mandatory sanctions; there is no doubt that the US would provide this. Public opinion in the US is undoubtedly in favour of improvements being made in South Africa and, as I have said, this will surely lead to the imposition of minor sanctions, which in turn will have some influence on 'reform', but it is not likely to support the overthrow of a white capitalist government in favour of a predominantly black socialist one.

Despite its widespread support and its limited success, there is an obvious danger that the divestment and sanctions campaign may be hijacked, if it has not been already, by those who have a vested economic and political interest in South Africa staying within the capitalist fold. The primary aim of US policy is to prevent South Africa, and with it ultimately the whole of sub-Saharan Africa, from falling within the communist sphere of influence. It has been seeking to do this through 'constructive engagement', but it would be willing to use other means, including limited sanctions, in order to achieve it. In other words, the campaign could be used as a means to enable the US to determine the nature, and control the pace, of change in South Africa.

Change will eventually come in South Africa, with or without the aid of sanctions. Sanctions are not, and never will be, the dominant factor. Although Reagan and Thatcher will doubtless remain deaf to mounting international call for stringent, even comprehensive, sanctions, the call in itself, as we have seen, has important psychological, political and economic effects. It may be a case of taking part being more important than winning. Nevertheless, the stronger the sanctions that are applied the more they may hasten the day and possibly lessen the bloodshed. If those countries, particularly African ones such as Nigeria, which support sanctions were to make their own trading and other links conditional upon countries severing all links with South Africa, even the major powers might find that the cost of maintaining such links is greater than the cost of sanctions. Even in terms of their own self-interest, the rest of Africa combined is more important to South Africa's trading partners than South Africa alone. The complete isolation of South Africa is, therefore, not possible on economic grounds. But America has shown in the past that it does not count the cost, in terms of money or even lives, of combating what it perceives to be the threat of communism. There is no evidence to suggest that a predominantly black South African government would be communist, but Reagan and others will doubtless believe Pretoria's propaganda which labels everybody who calls for radical change in South Africa as a 'communist.'

The longer sanctions are delayed the more irrelevant they become; all the arguments will be drowned in the sound of violence. Black South Africans are quite clearly not sitting idly by waiting to see what contribution the West is going to make before they begin the revolution; they have already started without us. If trading and other links are as important as the pro-South Africa lobby maintains it will be imperative to have those links with any future government in South Africa. It could, therefore, be argued *ad hominem* that it is in the West's own best economic interest to impose mandatory, comprehensive sanctions now, whatever the cost; otherwise it will lose even more when South Africa goes up in flames and subsequently a predominantly black government, which is not interested in maintaining links with those who found it so profitable to collaborate with their oppressors, attains power.

APPENDIX

1) *Notes on the Sullivan Principles*:

Leon Sullivan, a black American preacher and now a director of General Motors, first published his code of conduct for US companies in South Africa in 1977; it has been amplified on a number of occasions since then. It consists of six basic principles;

I Non-segregation in all eating, comfort and work facilities.

II Equal and fair employment practices for all employees.

III Equal pay for all employees doing equal or comparable work for the same period of time.

IV Initiation of and development of training programs that will prepare, in substantial numbers, blacks and other non-whites for supervisory, administrative, clerical and technical jobs.

V Increasing the number of blacks and other non-whites in management and supervisory positions.

VI Improving the quality of employees' lives outside the work environment in such areas as housing, schooling, recreation and health facilities.

The 1984 revision added some points on 'Increased dimension of activities outside the workplace', including support for freedom of movement and for the recension of all apartheid laws.

2) *A number of organisations in the US, including the following, provide information in various forms on the divestment issue*:

Investor Responsibility Research Center, Inc (IRRC)
1319 F St NW Suite 900
Washington DC 20004.

Interfaith Center on Corporate Responsibility (ICCR)
475 Riverside Drive
Room 566
New York NY 10115

American Committee on Africa (ACOA) & The Africa Fund
198 Broadway
New York NY 10038

3) *Regular US publications which monitor the divestment campaign include the following*:

Labor and Investment, published 10 times a year by IUD Publications Office, 2457 E Washington Street, Indianapolis, Indiana 46201 ($70).

South Africa Review Service Reporter, quarterly publication of the IRRC.

Washington Notes on Africa, published quarterly; available from 110 Maryland Avenue NE, Washington DC 20002.

The Corporate Examiner, published 10 times a year by ICCR.

ACOA Newsletter, published by American Committee on Africa.

BIBLIOGRAPHY

B Baldwin and T Baldwin, 'Economic action against Apartheid', The Africa Fund, New York, 1984.

H Barnes and F Cheru, 'A history of ICCR resolutions in South Africa', ICCR, 1984.

Committee on Mission Responsibility Through Investment, 'US corporations and banks in South Africa', New York, 1984.

D Hauck, et al, 'Two decades of debate: the controversy over US corporations in South Africa,' IRRC, 1983.

ICCR, 'What the banks say on South Africa', 1985.

IRRC, 'Foreign investment in South Africa', 1984.

Litvak, et al, 'Divesting from South Africa: a prudent approach for pension funds'. Conference on Alternative State and Local Policies, Africa Fund, 1981.

National Action/Research on the Military/Industrial Complex. 'Investing in apartheid', Philadelphia, 1984.

B Rogers and B Bolton, 'Sanctions against South Africa: exploding the myths', Christian Concern for Southern Africa, London.

UN Economic and Social council, 'List of transcendental corporations which operate in strategic sectors of the South African economy', 1983.

Leaflets

'Economic disengagement and South Africa: the effectiveness and feasibility of implementing sanctions and divestment', ACOA, 1984.

'Make It Massachusetts—not in South Africa: how we won divestment legislation', ACOA, 1983.

'Divesting from apartheid: a summary of state and municipal legislative action,'ACOA, 1983.

'The Sullivan Principles: no cure for apartheid', ACOA, 1980.

'US dollars in South Africa: context and consequences', ACOA, 1978.

South Africa Review Service, reports on individual US Companies, IRRC.

NOTES

1. *Rand Daily Mail* (Johannesburg) 10 April 1985.
2. *Financial Times* (London) 2 August 1985.
3. F Chen, 'The financial implications of divestment: a review of the evidence,' Interfaith Center on Corporate Responsibility, (hereafter ICCR), New York, 1984.
4. *New York Times*, 6 June 1985.
5. *Business Day*, 23 May 1985.
6. *Financial Times* (London) 12 August 1985.
7. *Sunday Times* (London) 28 July 1985.
8. *The Economist* (London) 30 March 1985.
9. *Financial Mail* (Johannesburg) 17 August 1985.
10. See E Militz, 'The International Campaign to end loans to South Africa', World Council of Churches, 1985.
11. Frederick A Johnstone, *Class, Race and Gold* London: Routledge and Kegan Paul, 1976.
12. South African Institute of Race Relations, *Survey of Race Relations 1983*, p 109.
13. Charles Simkins and Cosmas Desmond (eds), *South African Unemployment: A Black Picture*, Pietermaritzburg: University of Natal Press, 1978, pp 37–8.
14. *The Economist* (London) 27 July 1985.
15. C Child, 'Apartheid, economic collaboration and the case for United Nations comprehensive sanctions against South Africa', UN Centre Against Apartheid, 1984.
16. D Woods, *Apartheid—The Propaganda and the Reality*, London: Commonwealth Secretarial, 1985.
17. S Baldwin et al., *Pension Funds and Ethical Investment*, New York: Council on Economic Priorities, 1980.
18. Woods, *op. cit.*

ARMS: THE CRISIS IMPOSED BY TECHNOLOGY

23

The Present Danger

NOAM CHOMSKY

The recent growth of concern over the danger of nuclear war has been dramatic and impressive. It is also eminently realistic. Any sane and rational person who considers the scale and character of contemporary military power, the current vast expansion of the military arsenals of the superpowers, and the proliferation of armaments throughout the world would surely have to conclude that the likelihood of a global catastrophe is not small.

One might argue, in fact, that it is a miracle that the catastrophe has not yet occurred. According to a Brookings Institutions study by Barry M. Blechman and Stephen S. Kaplan, from November, 1946, to October, 1973, there were nineteen incidents in which U.S. strategic nuclear forces were involved (we do not have the record since, nor the record for the USSR and other powers). That means, to put it plainly, that every U.S. president regarded the use of nuclear weapons as a live policy option. The examples are instructive. Here are a few:

1. In February, 1947, long-range bombers assigned to the Strategic Air Command (SAC) were flown to Uruguay in a show of force at the time of the inauguration of the president of Uruguay.

2. In May, 1954, SAC bombers were flown to Nicaragua as part of the background planning for the successful CIA coup in Guatemala in June.

3. In 1958, U.S. strategic nuclear forces were involved in the U.S. intervention in Lebanon. According to the report of Wilbur C. Eveland, who was present as a mediator under CIA auspices, the use of nuclear weapons was threatened if the Lebanese army attempted to resist. Rockets with nuclear warheads were available had fighting developed.

4. In 1962, according to memoirs of participants, the "best and brightest" estimated the probability of nuclear war at one-third to one-half at the peak of the Cuban missile crisis, but were unwilling at that point to accept a settlement that would have resolved the crisis peaceably, with complete withdrawal of Russian missiles from Cuba. The barrier to this settlement in the view of administration planners was that it entailed simultaneous withdrawal of U.S. missiles from Turkey— obsolete missiles, for which a withdrawal order had already been issued (but not implemented) before the crisis erupted, since they were being replaced by Polaris submarines.

We can learn a good deal by studying these nineteen cases in detail— and they are not the only ones when the use of nuclear weapons was seriously considered and possibly threatened. Other powers have also issued nuclear threats, for example, the USSR at the time of the Israeli-French-British invasion of Egypt in 1956, and apparently Israel in the early stages of the October, 1973, war, when Egypt and Syria attacked the Israeli occupying army in the Sinai and Golan Heights. Furthermore, there have been numerous occasions when radar misidentifications, computer failures, or programming errors have produced false alarms of Soviet nuclear attack and only human intervention aborted the programmed reaction. It is reasonable to assume that the same (or worse) is true for the Soviet Union and that the future will be even more hazardous than the past in these respects, as the time span for human intervention is reduced. Those who speak of the likelihood of nuclear war are hardly alarmists. To reduce this likelihood is imperative. The question is: What directions should such efforts take? How should energies be distributed if they are to be maximally effective in averting this catastrophe?

We may realistically assume that any military conflict between the superpowers (and others, in the not-too-distant future) will quickly become a nuclear conflict, and an unlimited one. While there are elaborate scenarios assuming the contrary, they hardly can be taken very seriously. The central questions, then, reduce to these: What are the likely sources of superpower conflict? What can be done to reduce the likelihood of such conflict?

Some years ago it was perhaps realistic to suppose that Europe was "the tinderbox," but such a judgment hardly appears accurate today. Brutal repression will no doubt continue under Soviet rule, but it is extremely unlikely that it will lead to Western intervention; the day is long past when the U.S. was actively supporting guerrilla armies established by Hitler in the Carpathian mountains or attempting to carry out coups in Albania as part of its "rollback strategy," though it may be that the Reagan administration harbors dangerous fantasies on this score. It is also hardly likely that the USSR would intervene within Western domains, even at or near its borders, any more than it has in the past: e.g., when the U.S. was engaged in destroying the former anti-Nazi resistance in Greece in the late 1940s, or backing the restoration of fascism in Greece in 1967, or supporting a ruthless military dictatorship in Turkey since 1980. Nor is it likely that either superpower will attack the other directly. Judgments necessarily must be speculative, but prospects such as these appear to be highly remote contingencies.

But war may very well break out elsewhere, engaging the superpowers. Possible examples, by no means remote eventualities, are all too numerous:

1. Secretary of the Navy John Lehman recently observed that a U.S. attempt to impose a blockade on Cuba and Nicaragua might lead to a U.S.-Soviet naval war. The Navy "cannot conceive that a naval conflict which engaged Soviet forces could be localized," he stated; "It is instantaneously a global war." He added that he envisioned a conventional rather than nuclear war, but this is hardly credible. These possibilities are not far removed. Since the summer of 1981 the U.S. has been conducting major war games and large-scale maneuvers in the Caribbean area, obviously aimed at Grenada, Cuba, and Nicaragua. And only a strong public reaction in the U.S. prevented moves toward blockade and perhaps direct U.S. military intervention in El Salvador in the early months of the Reagan administration, in my view.

2. The 1979 Chinese invasion of Vietnam, surely with at least tacit U.S. backing, might well have elicited a Russian response and U.S. countermoves, bringing the superpowers into conflict. A recurrence is not out of the question. Vietnamese troops are in Cambodia, and the U.S. and China are supporting Pol Pot as part of the policy of "bleeding Vietnam."

3. The U.S. is now committed to arming the military dictatorship of General Zia in Pakistan, allegedly to protect Pakistan from Soviet expansionism. It is difficult to imagine that the USSR would invade Pakistan; and if it were insane enough to do so, the arms being sent hardly would serve as a deterrent. The arms very likely will be used for internal repression, as in the past—for example, in the mid-1970s, when U.S. equipment supplied by the shah was used by the Pakistani army in attacking the Baluch, who now appear somewhat ambivalent, not surprisingly, about the Soviet presence in Afghanistan. Interviewing the "triumvirate" of Baluch leaders, Selig Harrison found that each was

thinking of the possibility of seeking Soviet support in response to U.S.-backed government repression: "If the Americans pump weapons into the Punjabis, obviously we have to stretch our hands to another superpower," one stated. Further repression might well lead to a call for Soviet assistance, triggering renewed cries of a Soviet "march to the Gulf" and a U.S. reaction, leading to a superpower conflict. Arms to Pakistan will also fuel the Indo-Pakistan arms race, with nuclear weapons on the horizon. It is also likely that the heavily armed Pakistani military dictatorship will come to serve as part of the elaborate base structure for the U.S. Rapid Deployment Force, designed for intervention in the Middle East, while Pakistani troops protect the Saudi monarchy against possible domestic insurgency.

4. The Iraqi invasion of Iran and the recent reversal of fortunes in Iran's favor have created a situation of great instability, in some ways reminiscent of Afghanistan in early 1978 before the Russians won that particular skirmish in the Great Game, but with much higher stakes and far greater dangers. The superpowers no doubt are maneuvering to pick up the pieces, and others are also hovering in the not-so-distant background, in particular Israel, which desires that Iraq break up into separate states and that a post-Khomeini military coup in Iran restore the Irano-Israeli alliance of earlier years. U.S. support for the Turkish military dictatorship is motivated in part by plans to use eastern Turkey as an intelligence center and a base for projection of American power in this region. The USSR presumably is making similar preparations along its own southern border. Again, the possibility of a superpower conflict is not negligible.

The Middle East, for obvious reasons, is the most likely candidate as the trigger that will set off a nuclear war. General Thomas Kelley of the NATO southern command (AFSOUTH) observed plausibly that "If we have a WWIII, it will probably start here in the Mediterranean when a local conflict burns out of control." The largest recipients of U.S. military aid for Fiscal Year 1983 are, in order: Israel, Egypt, Turkey, Spain, Pakistan, Greece. A prime concern in each case is to strengthen U.S. dominance in the Middle East. In addition, the U.S. is selling vast quantities of arms to Saudi Arabia and, as already noted, is developing a base structure ringing the Gulf region for U.S. intervention forces. While the official justification is the threat of Soviet aggression, a more reasonable interpretation is that the perceived threats are indigenous to the region, including the threat of local uprisings against the regimes of the oil-producing states that are, for the most part, closely allied to the U.S. and see themselves as dependent on U.S. power to defend them against radical Arab nationalism. General Kelley's speculation is a realistic one, if we understand "Mediterranean" to mean "Eastern Mediterranean extending to the Gulf."

THE MEDIA AND THE MESSAGE

There are other examples of situations in which local conflicts or outside intervention may come to engage the superpowers, leading to global nuclear conflict. The rational conclusion from a survey of possible cases of this sort is straightforward: If we desire to avert nuclear war, our primary concern should be to lessen tensions and conflicts at the points where war is likely to erupt, engaging the nuclear powers. The size of nuclear arsenals is a secondary consideration.

Even if nuclear arsenals were vastly reduced, a nuclear interchange would be a devastating catastrophe; in fact, if they were reduced to zero, the capacity to produce nuclear weapons would not be lost and they would soon be available, and would be used, in the event of superpower conflict. Furthermore, the relation between the size of nuclear arsenals and the likelihood of the use of nuclear weapons is not an entirely simple one. Recall that on the one occasion when nuclear weapons were used to massacre civilians, there were exactly two available—and if two more had been available, in the hands of the Japanese enemy, it is quite likely that there would have been no atom bombing, for fear of retaliation. Nuclear deterrence probably does work, to some extent at least—a fact that cannot be lightly dismissed.

Suppose that reduction of the deterrent capacity would tend to increase the aggressiveness of one or the other of the superpowers—not an unlikely consequence. Then it would increase the likelihood of superpower conflict and, with it, the likelihood of nuclear war. It is not obvious that the prospects for peace and survival are enhanced by efforts to eliminate or radically reduce nuclear arsenals that do not form an integral part of a more general program to constrain state violence.

We should note, in addition, that the distinction between nuclear and conventional weapons is too crude. In the latter category there is an important difference between, say, antitank weapons designed for deterrence in Europe and attack carriers or the Rapid Deployment Force (which has nuclear capability as well). Intervention capacity constitutes a large component of the U.S. military budget, though it is often disguised in the official rhetoric of "deterrence." It may increase the danger of nuclear war even more than a new generation of nuclear monsters. More crucial still are policies the U.S. has pursued that contribute to tensions that may lead to war, engaging the superpowers. The U.S., of course, is not alone in this respect, but it cannot be stressed too often that it is U.S. policies that American citizens can hope to influence directly—a consideration that is of obvious significance in a democratic society, where the public can exert some influence on foreign policy.

There has been much discussion within the disarmament movement as to whether to concentrate solely on controlling the nuclear arms race or whether to include also an "anti-intervention plank" in programs and organizing objectives. The argument against extending the scope of activities to include interventionism, which has often prevailed, is based on two assumptions: first, that the consequences of nuclear war would be so horrendous that other issues pale by comparison; and second, that a "single-issue" focus will draw broader support.

The second point is arguable. At least with regard to elite groups, the argument probably holds true. It is difficult, for example, to imagine that the movement would retain its remarkably favorable media image—quite unusual for popular movements of protest—if it were to concentrate on the broad range of issues that fall under the rubric of "intervention." With such a shift of direction, the movement no longer would be "sober" and "responsible" but would become "violent," "extremist," and "emotional" in the ideological organs. This fact might in itself arouse a certain skepticism as to the nature of the movement. In general, a favorable media image is restricted to those who do not challenge power and privilege in any serious way. It is important to avoid being seduced by unaccustomed favorable attention in the mainstream ideological institutions and to think clearly about the appropriate distribution of effort if the movement is to be effective in realizing its goals. Nevertheless, though this tactical judgment may indeed be accurate with regard to elite groups, I suspect that it is wrong with regard to the population at large.

Activists in the disarmament movement should ask themselves whether they are not, in fact, holding back the popular forces that they see themselves as mobilizing. To cite one suggestive example: The Boston Jobs with Peace group succeeded in placing on the November, 1981, ballot a resolution urging that "the City Council call upon the U.S. Congress to make more federal funds available for local jobs and programs—in quality education, public transportation, energy-efficient housing, improved health care, and other essential services—by reducing the amount of our tax dollars spent on nuclear weapons *and programs of foreign military intervention*" (my emphasis). The resolution carried every ward in Boston, winning 72 per cent of the vote citywide. It received the backing of the Justice and Peace Commission of the Catholic Archdiocese in Boston, as well as support from labor and ethnic groups, among others. This was the result of a relatively small organizing effort, but evidently it touched a sensitive nerve; and though the anti-intervention issue was not the central focus of the campaign, it was quite clearly and explicitly included.

But it is the first argument that is most seriously flawed. In fact, it quite misses the point. Let us accept the assumption that prevention of nuclear war should dominate all other concerns—an assumption that might not be regarded as obviously correct by a substantial part of the human race, notably the millions who die of starvation every year. It then follows, as discussed earlier, that a prime concern should be the class of issues that fall broadly within the rubric of "anti-intervention" and, more generally, foreign policy initiatives concerning the Third World, where a nuclear war is most likely to break out. Consideration of other related questions seems to me to reinforce this conclusion.

Before turning to these, let me emphasize that I am restricting attention here to the U.S. disarmament movement. The movement in Europe should be considered in a rather different framework. It forms part of the long-term process in which Europe is slowly extricating itself from the bipolar world system established as a result of World War II, which has been eroding in the past years, to the discomfiture of the superpowers.

It is worth noting that the European movement has received a fair amount of harsh criticism in the U.S. media, perhaps reflecting an appreciation of the fact that it does pose a serious challenge to American power. At times, this criticism has taken on a remarkable tone—for example, an article in the *New York Times Magazine* by John Vinocur, chief of the *New York Times* bureau in Bonn, on the antinuclear movement in West Germany. West Germany is affected by a serious "malaise" in his view: "something has shaken loose" in the country, as reflected by the fact that "more young people favor an attempt at achieving neutrality than favor continuing a military alliance with the United States." "Public feelings of Angst and loss of control have led to increased pacifism," and for a significant part of the population, "a furious embrace of the illusions—or, at least, the serious miscalculations—of the last 10 years," in particular, the belief in the possibilities and importance of détente. There is "a crisis of national identity—a reality crisis, really—because it expresses fear and anger about the nation's being locked into the facts: its loss of unity and of total independence as a result of World War II." These irrational currents have recreated the "traditional notion of a German middle way between the West, often denounced as mercantile and impure, and Eastern Europe, seen as more romantic and less corrupt." With the collapse of détente, "there is hurt pride, frustration, anger and a more intense nationalism. With them come great emotion and a weakened hold over the rational—both very unhappy filaments in the Germans' past." One indication of this "weakened hold over the rational" is the belief that the U.S., as well as the USSR, poses dangers to world peace, an illusion that affects "the so-called peace movement." Throughout, Vinocur describes this so-called peace movement as a symptom of a general disease, a "problem" that the West Germans must somehow overcome themselves in a country whose "agonies are deep," and irrational.

In this "malaise," Vinocur perceives signs of a revival of the Hitler era. As his evidence, he cites a press report

> that people opposed to the Frankfurt Airport Authority's building a new runway through a wooded area think the plan is a NATO-United States plot. The mood is captured in a remarkable admonition—the vocabulary could have come out of a Hitler-era time capsule—tacked to a tree in the controversial woods: "Tremble before this tree. It was holy to your forefathers. Doing anything against the tree is a sign of an inferior people and base individual morality."

But all is not lost. Chancellor Helmut Schmidt "still represents pragmatism and a pro-Western orientation in the country" and, according to a confidant, feels "that the country's mood, sour and Angst-ridden, comes in part from an insufficient exercise of authority on all levels"— an impression that Vinocur appears to share. Note that this concern over "an insufficient exercise of authority on all levels" does not evoke memories of the Hitler era, in contrast with concern to save trees.

Once again, it is interesting to compare the generally favorable media treatment of the American disarmament movement, in the *New York Times Magazine* and elsewhere, with Vinocur's lament over the irrational concern for peace and détente and the equally irrational belief that both superpowers, not just the Russians, exhibit threatening behavior. His reaction perhaps can be understood as a manifestation of a fear that "the so-called peace movement" in Europe constitutes part of a long-term development toward a more independent role in world affairs for a European community of nations that might, if recent trends persist, become a really serious rival to the United States, with an economy on the scale of our own, a high level of education and technology, independent access to resources and raw materials, and interests that do not necessarily coincide with those of dominant groups in the U.S. and, in fact, are increasingly in conflict with them.

Mary Kaldor is, I think, quite right when she argues in *The Nation* that a motivating force in the European peace movement is "the sense within the movement of political emancipation," a sense that is international in scope and is "related to a growing awareness of European identity": "For the peace movement, the idea of a Europe free of military blocs and free from the artificial division of the continent—seen to have been imposed by the superpowers—is at least as important as the demand for denuclearization." The significance of such proposals as "no-first-use," she argues plausibly, is that if it is "seen as a way of *deemphasizing* the role of nuclear weapons in NATO and hence loosening the relationship between the United States and Western Europe, this might help to initiate a very different kind of reciprocal process, one that could eventually lead to the detachment of both halves of Europe from the superpowers." This aspect of the "no-first-use" policy, she notes, was completely ignored (not very surprisingly) by the "four eminent members of the American establishment—Robert McNamara, George Kennan, McGeorge Bundy and Gerard Smith" in their "widely publicized proposal for a 'no-first-use' nuclear strategy for NATO" in the Spring, 1982, issue of *Foreign Affairs*, just as they overlooked "the political nature of the demand for a nuclear-free Europe," namely, the "sense of emancipation" it reflects. Various important questions arise in this connection that are surely related to those that specifically concern the American disarmament movement and to the shape of the future world more generally.

As this discussion indicates, it is misleading to isolate concerns over the size and character of nuclear arsenals from a much broader nexus of issues. It is also important to bear in mind that strategic nuclear forces and "conventional forces" tend to grow in parallel, and for good reasons. The real function of the strategic weapons systems sometimes can be discerned in pronouncements of planners, for example, in the January, 1980, statement to Congress by President Carter's secretary of defense on the proposed military budget. "The programmed rates of growth," he argued, "are needed for two basic reasons." One is "the sustained expansion in the Soviet defense effort," and the other is "the growth in international turbulence, illustrated by recent developments in the Caribbean, Southeast Asia, Korea, Afghanistan, and Iran." The U.S. thus faces "simultaneous demands." "Our strategic nuclear capabilities," he said, "provide the foundation on which our security rests. . . . With them, our other forces become meaningful instruments of military and political power."

This is the heart of the matter. In fact, for each superpower, strategic nuclear capacities provide a protective cover for programs of state violence that it undertakes or supports in its own domains.

PROLIFERATING FACTORS

What, then, are the proper directions for the disarmament movement? It should, certainly, be concerned with controlling and reversing the strategic arms race. It should also be concerned with the proliferation of nuclear weapons; with the vast arms sales of the major (and some minor) powers, which are placing enormous means of destruction in the hands of states that will use them for internal repression or aggression; and with the fact that so-called "conventional arms" are reaching a point of destructiveness not far below that of nuclear weapons, so that "small" or "limited" wars will be extremely costly in human lives.

But there are other issues that cannot be dissociated from this complex and that are in many respects even more crucial: the domestic factors that drive the arms race, the dynamics of the cold war and its impact on many millions of people, the extraordinary dangers (and horrors) of superpower intervention, the policies that contribute to maintaining or inflaming conflicts and tensions throughout the world, which, apart from the cost to victims, are the most likely cause of a potential final holocaust.

The drift toward this final solution has a seemingly inexorable quality. The factors and powers involved appear to be out of control, beyond our ability to influence or constrain them. We can only hope that this perception is false.

24

The Case Against Arms Control

SEYMOUR WEISS

In one sense the case against arms control is not difficult to make. One might simply ask just what evidence exists that recent nuclear-arms-limitations agreements with the USSR have actually contributed to U.S. security. Yet in spite of the fact that no such evidence can be found, emotional attachment to the hoped-for benefits, together with the presumption that arms control is politically attractive, has created what Albert Wohlstetter has sardonically described as the mad momentum of arms control. It is this emotional attachment that makes the task of rational assessment more difficult. There is an undeniable and under-standable yearning among our people, reflected in Congress and certainly echoed by our allies, for a cessation of the tensions that have accompanied the years of confrontation with the USSR.

That yearning nevertheless sometimes takes forms which misperceive reality: the idea, for example, that arms control is necessary to stop the "arms race"; or that it helps to avoid wasteful military expenditures; or that it is essential to the prevention of nuclear war. Each of these pleas on behalf of arms control has been made (and no doubt will be made over and over again). But can these problems—the arms race, wasteful military expenditures, or the drift toward nuclear war—be attenuated or corrected by arms control?

To begin with the arms race: arms control cannot stop it for the simple reason that in no real sense has there been any such thing as an arms race. As Assistant Secretary of Defense Richard Perle stated in recent congressional testimony, the number of U.S. nuclear weapons has been "declining rapidly" for two decades. Thus the U.S. has over 8,000 fewer warheads and a fourth less megatonnage today than it had in the 1960's. This reduction in U.S. inventories has been the result of a modernization program, designed in part to put safer as well as more effective weapons in the U.S. inventory. It is not the product of agreements reached with the Soviet Union.

In any case, during the same period, which also marked the apex of détente and arms control, the Soviet Union, for its part, has added enormously both to the quantity and quality of its nuclear arsenal. A U.S. government study conducted in the late 1970's compared 41 categories of U.S. and Soviet nuclear capabilities (warhead numbers, megatonnage, delivery systems, and the like) for the year 1962 (the Cuban-missile-crisis period) with the late 1970's and early 1980's. It found the U.S. ahead significantly in every category in 1962 and behind in all but two by the late 1970's (with the lead in those two projected to disappear in the early 1980's).

There has, in short, been no arms race so far as the United States is concerned; conversely, arms control has not prevented the Soviets from forging ahead in their military programs.

How about saving money? Have past agreements not saved otherwise needless expenditures for arms, and might not additional savings be achieved through arms control in the future? The answer is a clear "no" to the former and an "almost certainly not" to the latter. Take the jewel in the arms-control crown, the ABM Treaty of 1972. One argument advanced at the time this agreement was negotiated was that it would spare the nation a wasteful and massive expenditure for a ballistic-missile defense. Some estimated that such a system might cost as much as $10 billion; other estimates ran considerably higher. Moreover, by precluding ballistic-missile defenses, each side would be saved the expenditure that would otherwise be required for offensive forces designed to overcome these defenses. The nation got an ABM treaty, but did it save itself the projected expenditures? It did not.

It is true that projected expenditures were cut back when we failed to finish the deployment of the ABM defense that was under way. At least in part as a result of that decision, however, we are proposing to spend tens of billions on the MX missile and perhaps tens of billions more on the so-called Midgetman missile in order to avoid the total vulnerability of our ICBM force—the very problem which the ABM system was expressly designed to solve. Furthermore, President Reagan has suggested that we reopen the issue of strategic defense, and specifically of ABM defense. While a sound suggestion on the merits, such a program, if adopted, could cost additional billions over time. Thus, it is possible that had we deployed an ABM defense in the early 1970's, we might have had a less costly, and not incidentally a more effective, defense posture than is now the case. (Surprisingly, some of the most vocal supporters of arms control advocate the adoption of a launch-on-warning strategy as a means of overcoming the vulnerability of our land-based forces. While this would indeed preclude the necessity for costly new programs of the MX or Midgetman type or of ABM's designed to protect such land-based systems, the danger to U.S. security of relying on such an unstable strategy ought to be apparent. The "cost" to the nation's security of such a strategy must surely be deemed to outweigh the costs of reconstituting our land-based forces whose vulnerability was in some measure increased by earlier arms-control agreements.)

In general, as most students of the subject will testify, savings have not resulted from arms-control agreements with the Soviets. Indeed, some have charged that arms control actually results in larger expenditures. For one thing, in order to gain the support of those directly responsible for providing for U.S. military security and who worry about the effect of arms control on the capacity for self-protection, other new and costly military programs must be promised. In addition, expensive new intelligence-monitoring systems must be developed. (It is arguable that certain military and intelligence programs might not have gained approval on their own merits without the pressures to provide for special safeguards generated by arms-control proposals.)

Finally, arms control, by constraining the kinds of systems we can have, as well as the numbers, increases the difficulty of providing for our security. Unless there is a commensurate reduction in the forces on the other side, the effect may be to raise the cost or endanger the security or both. The record clearly demonstrates that there has not been such a reduction.

The charge that the alternative to arms-control agreements is nuclear war would hardly warrant refutation were it not voiced at one time or another, directly or by implication, by a host of esteemed statesmen. On sober reflection, it is probable that so sweeping an assertion is not intended to be taken literally. Yet in the heat of political battle, when cherished policy objectives are being contested, extravagant statements do tend to be made.

In reality, the relationship between arms-control agreements and the avoidance of nuclear war is complex. Some even maintain that an inverse relationship exists—that arms-control agreements, by making it more difficult to provide for our security, may thereby have increased the ultimate danger of war. One need not go so far. Still, the positive relationship between recent agreements designed to limit nuclear arms and the prevention of nuclear war itself is anything but clear and direct.

It is, then, not hard to fault arms control on the merits. Nevertheless, no U.S. President has come out flatly against arms control. Why? There are several reasons having greater or lesser weight, depending upon the individual President. First, arms control is thought to be so politically popular (a notion fanned by the media despite polls which seem to demonstrate deep suspicion on the part of the public over agreements made with the Soviets) that no one seeking office can afford to oppose it in principle. Secondly, European support of and pressure for arms control must be reckoned with if the U.S. wants a politically viable alliance. Thirdly, no President can possibly take office without feeling the heavy burden placed upon him by the very existence of nuclear weapons, and he is therefore predisposed to embrace the view that arms control at least offers some hope of relief from a risky and burdensome arms competition.

Every recent President, every national leader, whether of liberal or conservative persuasion, has thus announced in favor of arms control. Some may have demurred on the terms of particular proposals, as was the case, for example, during the SALT II debates, but none challenged the principle. None rejected the notion that arms control was good (most said "essential"); the key was to find the right formula. But the unfortunate truth is that there can at present be no "right formula."

The reason lies in the nature of our conflict with the Soviet Union. Arms control is no more an end in itself than the national-defense efforts which nations undertake to provide for their security. Each is a means to an end. (Thoughtless advocates of nuclear arms-control agreements frequently lose sight of this fact; for such people arms control is an imperative, unlinked to other aspects of the U.S.-Soviet relationship.)

The development of a nation's military forces, moreover, is an expression of a national concern for the preservation and advancement of a vision of the national interest. What gives impetus to the development of military power is the existence of *seriously opposed* national interests. The U.S. force posture is not designed to cope with Canada or France or Japan, even though we may have some differences with these nations. For these differences are minor compared with our common interests. This is not so for the Soviet Union. In addition to pursuing interests inimical to our own, the USSR is a major military power. The constitutional requirement to provide for the common defense and protect the national welfare could in consequence not be fulfilled without offsetting military capabilities.

But could it not be argued that this is precisely what makes seeking arms-control measures a practical imperative? Cannot limitations of arms by each of the two sides substitute for a build-up? Exactly the contrary is true. The Soviet Union, at enormous material and political expense, has developed a massive conventional, theater-nuclear, and strategic-nuclear arsenal in order to advance its view of a desired international order, one dominated by Moscow. For the Soviets see military power as a precondition to maintaining a "favorable correlation of forces." Whether it is the physical suppression of freedom in Eastern

Europe, the invasion of Afghanistan, the projection of Soviet forces and equipment into the Syrian-Middle East tinderbox, the use of proxies in the Third World to foment and support revolution (in the Soviet lexicon, "wars of national liberation"), or simply the exercise of political black-mail against Western Europe, military power plays the key role in advancing the Soviet view of a desirable international order.

Given all this, what is the basis for believing that the Soviets will ever agree to limit or reduce the very military power they require to maintain and advance their national objectives? What leads us to imagine that the Soviets might be willing to negotiate away their hard-won military advantages in an arms-control agreement? Why would the Soviets hand over at the negotiating table what they see no prospect of being forced to surrender in the ongoing political contest with the West, or—should it come to that—in a contest of arms?

Nothing suggests any such outcome—certainly not the recent history of U.S.-Soviet arms-control negotiations. On the contrary, those nego-tiations and the few significant agreements that have emerged from them point to precisely the opposite conclusion. The Soviet Union will sign arms-control agreements with the West only if such agreements are consistent with its fundamental political objectives—that is, only if they contribute to the extension of Soviet power and influence, normally at the direct expense of the West.

Past agreements have been used by the Soviets to achieve this end in a variety of ways:

• They have been designed to sow political discord between the U.S. and its allies, in the hope of promoting the dissolution of the postwar Western alliance. If an agreement can properly be seen as limiting U.S. power to support friendly states desirous of resisting the extension of Soviet power, it has served a vitally important Soviet objective. This is especially pertinent in the case of nuclear weapons, the U.S. having made solemn political commitments to employ them, if required, in defense of allies.

• If an agreement can lull the U.S. into believing that arms control reduces—or even removes—the need for self-help military measures, this contributes to Soviet purposes. In a strikingly candid warning, the Soviet leader Brezhnev told President Nixon at the time of the signing of SALT I that the USSR intended to maximize its military power within the constraints permitted by those accords. Mr. Nixon, in revealing this Soviet warning to the American people, no doubt hoped that, being so forewarned, the Congress and the public would respond by maximizing the military programs permitted the U.S. It was a vain hope, revealing a lack of comprehension of the mind set of Western society. There never was a realistic possibility that Congress, once a highly publicized and much lauded "arms-control" agreement was concluded with the USSR, would appropriate vast sums for military preparedness. And so the predictable happened. While the USSR, true to Brezhnev's word, developed a military arsenal of unprecedented dimensions during the late 60's and 70's, a period paralleling the SALT negotiations, the United States failed to keep pace, thus permitting the military balance to shift adversely both in fact and in the perception of most of the world.

• If an agreement disrupts the development of U.S. military technology while permitting the Soviets to close an important gap, it also serves Soviet purposes. One agreement which has had precisely this effect is the ABM Treaty of 1972. At the time of its signing, the U.S. held a major technological advantage in ballistic-missile defense. In the decade since the signing, the Soviets have pursued a massive development program in, and at least a partial deployment of, ballistic-missile defense. U.S. efforts during the same period limped along at a pitifully inadequate level. (Why, it was repeatedly asked by the Congress and the press, should we invest in ABM research and development when deployment of an ABM system was prohibited by treaty?) The result is that, by most public accounts, the Soviets are now capable of deploying an extensive ballistic-missile defense far more rapidly than is the U.S. Thus was the ABM Treaty utilized by the Soviets to nullify an important U.S. lead in military technology.

• If an arms-control agreement is clearly either unverifiable or unenforceable, it serves Soviet purposes. The U.S., by virtue of the nature of its society, can be expected to adhere to strict interpretation of the terms of agreement. Indeed, examples abound whereby the U.S. exercised self-denial, fearing that a proposed arms development or production initiative *might* lead to an interpretation of inconsistency with an arms-control agreement. The Soviets, by contrast, have blatantly violated agreements. While insisting on arms-control provisions that are ambiguous, thus making verification inherently difficult, they are, in the last analysis, disdainful of the requirement to adhere even to *un*ambiguous agreements. Yet no U.S. administration has acted forcefully in the face of such violations. Even the Reagan administration, which to its credit has charged the Soviets with violations of treaty obligations, has not taken action to follow up on this charge. For the suggestion of retributive action would invoke the wrath of arms-control advocates who would deplore such action on the grounds that it would worsen U.S.-Soviet relations, as if it were the act of discovering Soviet cheating that was reprehensible rather than Soviet perfidy itself. It would appear that the Soviets' knowledge of the Western democratic process leads them to conclude (accurately) that Washington will resort to rationalizations of Soviet misbehavior to preserve arms-control agreements (and, when selling such agreements, will portray them in fictitiously favorable terms).

Can this deterioration be arrested? It is difficult to say. Arms control in the West has developed a dynamism and momentum of its own. Because of the false hopes concerning its putative benefits, most segments of Western society, ignoring the history of past agreements, call for more, not less, arms control. If SALT I worked contrary to our interests, negotiate SALT II. If the Soviets violate the Biological Arms Treaty, negotiate another treaty on any one of several subjects. If, as is occasionally the case, a U.S. proposal is advanced which might have the effect of reducing a Soviet military advantage and which is thus predictably rejected by the USSR, the cry goes up for more U.S. "flexibility" (a euphemism for making additional concessions to the Soviets).

Are there, then, any conditions that would permit an equitable agreement to limit nuclear arms? Two suggest themselves: first, fundamental Soviet political objectives might change. That is, the Soviets might abandon their quest for the advancement of a "socialist" international order responsive to Moscow. Clearly this is not a realistic prospect. Second, the U.S. might establish so formidable a level of military power that the Soviet Union would have no other alternative than to seek genuinely equitable agreements. This too seems remote. U.S. efforts to reestablish military might have a long way to go, despite the large defense budgets of the Reagan administration. (The notion that the U.S. might even try to reestablish military superiority, a condition which prevailed up until the mid-to-late 60's, is denounced by the U.S. press for reasons which remain obscure.) Moreover, the Soviets will try very hard to maintain military advantages where they have them. It is by no means clear that they would be unable to measure up in such a competition.

But if, in the broader sense, U.S. and Soviet political objectives are in radical conflict, what of those more narrowly defined interests that are presumed to emanate from successful arms-control negotiations—stability and equivalence?

Stability has generally been taken to apply to two issues: the so-called arms race and the management of crisis. As we have already seen, the arms race is largely an American illusion. American interest in and efforts at constraint are not shared by the Soviets. (Former Secretary of Defense Harold Brown once noted that "Soviet defense spending showed no response to U.S. restraint. . . . When we build, they build, when we cut, they build. . . .") The Soviet interest in constraint seems to be limited to U.S. military technology. In any event, more than a decade of arms control has seen the Soviet Union, with a much smaller GNP than the U.S. in a wide range of military (including nuclear) armaments. It would appear that the Soviets do not see such competition as fundamentally destabilizing.

Even less do they appear to share U.S. concern with crisis stability. Years of effort to persuade the Soviets that fixed MIRVed ICBM's are inherently destabilizing have been unavailing. U.S. analysts have emphasized that during a time of intense crisis such fixed systems would be so vulnerable to preemptive attack that the temptation would be great to fire the missiles before they could be destroyed. Moreover, once dispatched toward their targets, these missiles, unlike bombers, are not recallable. The Soviets, however, have shown little propensity to acknowledge the validity of these arguments, perhaps because they are not entirely unhappy with the vulnerability of our ICBM's to a preemptive strike.

Nor is seeking equivalence between the two strategic forces an apparent Soviet interest. In the SALT I negotiations, according to Ambassador Paul Nitze, the U.S. recognized that the asymmetrical characteristics of the U.S. and Soviet strategic systems would require the two sides to develop certain formulas which, if accepted, would create equivalence between their respective military capabilities. But the negotiations demonstrated that the Soviets did not share the U.S. desire to seek such an equivalence. Instead the Soviets sought a condition they described as "equal security." As defined by the Soviets, equal security meant that they must be permitted military forces in the aggregate superior to those maintained by *all* other potential adversaries. So defined, "equal security" is closer to the now outdated U.S. concept of strategic superiority than the U.S. arms-control concept of strategic equivalence.

We have seen that fundamentally incompatible political objectives logically preclude arms-control arrangements which by U.S. standards are fair to both sides. Yet it now appears that even on narrower grounds involving arms-control objectives like stability and equivalence, there is little reason to project a commonality of interest. As George Kennan once said:

> There is no use trying to swing Russians into line by referring to common purposes to which we may both have done lip-service at one time or another. . . . For them it's all a game. And when we try to come at them with arguments based on such common professions, they become doubly wary.

Suppose, for the sake of argument, that the case made here against arms control is essentially correct. The indictment would be a powerful one. The only possible conclusion one could draw would be that contemporary nuclear arms-control agreements with the Soviet Union have been contrary to U.S. national interests. Even so, no issue as complex as this one is likely to lead to so simple and direct a conclusion. Might there be a consideration not yet addressed that would impart to the arms-control efforts of the last two decades something more than a passing redeeming value? May it not be that even if the agreements were "flawed" in some respects, *the process itself* was—and is—of great value? For whatever one may think of the substantive merit of any particular agreement, the process keeps U.S. and Soviet officials in direct contact, exchanging views on nuclear strategy, weapons capabilities, and the intentions of the two sides. Surely, in the nuclear age, nothing can be of greater importance than the continuing contact that the arms-control process provides.

But is it really true that a better comprehension of an adversary's purpose offers promise of more tranquil relations? Not necessarily. Reviewing the history of the early 1930's, especially the arms-control efforts made at the time, one discovers that despite ample contact and a continuing process, Europeans whose vital interests were being challenged nevertheless deluded themselves about the purposes of the Third Reich. As Richard Perle wrote in 1981:

> After all, the political and bureaucratic elite in prewar Britain believed itself to be clear-eyed and hard-headed in matters of international politics and diplomacy. Its members believed in arms control and thought that it could stabilize the military balance in Europe in the 1930's. But they approached arms control with claims of prudence and caution that ring not so very different from those heard during the 1970's.

For example, Perle points out, the British Imperial Defense Committee in 1932 declared:

> The military forces of the nations . . . should be limited in such a way as to make it unlikely for any aggressor to succeed with a "knockout blow." The committee went on to urge an end to what is called "disarmament by example," a notion that Paul Warnke could be found advocating some forty-five years later.

Yet when the British government proposed a modest increase in the Royal Air Force over a five-year period beginning in 1934, "the Labor and Liberal opposition brought a censure motion regretting that: 'His Majesty's Government should enter upon a policy of rearmament . . . certain to jeopardize the prospects of international disarmament and to encourage a revival of a dangerous and wasteful competition.' "

Additional examples from British history in the 1930's could be cited, but the message is clear. It appears not only possible, indeed it may be the norm, for Western democracies to understand that they are confronting a serious adversary, to observe concrete evidence of military preparation whose purpose (given the opposed political objectives of the two sides) can only be political intimidation or aggressive military action, and yet to rationalize all this away. Such self-delusion is not surprising when the consequences of facing reality are so challenging and require hard sacrifice and courageous political leadership. How much easier it is to project an image of hope for a brighter future, free of these burdensome considerations. Under such circumstances, arms control has been, and continues to be, a longed-for panacea.

Self-delusion of the sort described here has little or nothing to do with lack of information due to inadequate contact with the adversary. British officials up to and including the Prime Minister met repeatedly with Hitler and his associates, but proximity did not breed a general comprehension of reality. Conversely, Winston Churchill required no intimate contact to perceive the truth. Here we have the sense of the matter. The process itself offers little hope for benefit when the parties bring divergent purposes to the table.

But still, is it not better to "talk than fight"? Consider the answer of Dean Acheson to this question:

> I have heard people who should know better . . . say happily, "As long as they are talking they are not fighting." Nothing could be more untrue; they are fighting. . . . To our minds international conferences and international negotiations are so completely means for ending conflict that we are blind to the fact that they may be and, in the hands of experts, are equally adapted to, continuing it. . . . "There is no alternative to negotiations with the Russians" is the constant theme of a well-known columnist and a prominent politician in this country. . . . This is, of course, silly. For if there is no alternative, and if the Russians will only negotiate, as is now the case, on their own terms, then there is no alternative to surrender. . . .

Nothing that has happened since has affected the truth of these words, and much that has happened since has strengthened the case against arms control. It does not serve our security, it does not save money, and it does not lessen the risk of war. Arms control is certainly politically popular, but it is just as certainly the repository of false and dangerous hopes.

25

The War for Star Wars

GEORGE W. BALL

1.

In a speech to the nation on March 23, 1983, President Reagan announced his Strategic Defense ("Star Wars") Initiative, which, he said, "holds the promise of changing the course of history." The abrupt broadcasting of that unexamined project to the nation—and to the world—was, in my view, one of the most irresponsible acts by any head of state in modern times.

To fulfill his objective of "providing new hope for our children in the twenty-first century," the President called on the American scientific community to "turn their great talents . . . to the cause of mankind and world peace, to give us the means of rendering . . . nuclear weapons impotent and obsolete." Once our scientists had developed an infallible nuclear defense, "no longer would our countrymen have to rely on retaliation to protect them from nuclear attack."

That, he implied, was as it should be, since "the human spirit must be capable of rising above dealing with other nations and human beings by threatening their existence"; and, in any event, he asked rhetorically, "wouldn't it be better to save lives than avenge them?" "What if free people could live secure in the knowledge that their security did not rest upon the threat of instant retaliation to deter Soviet attack, that we could intercept and destroy strategic missiles before they reached our soil or that of our allies?"

He spoke with such intensity of conviction as to sound more like a prophet than a president, evoking a state of grace for all mankind in the language of biblical rhapsody, and five months later he reaffirmed his beneficent intentions by suggesting at a press conference that the United States might even give our missile defense technology to the Soviets. Because each side would then be protected against the other, humanity would no longer have to live under the threat of nuclear extermination.

Although the President announced his decision with breathless awe, there is, in fact, nothing new about the idea of developing an antiballistic missile (ABM) system, or, as it is now fashionable to call it, a ballistic missile defense. Such a proposal was first examined and debated more than thirty years ago, and in the latter 1960s there was mounting pressure to develop ABM technology. President Lyndon Johnson, reluctant to embark on an extravagant program that would almost certainly be overwhelmed by developments on the offensive side, preferred to checkmate such a step through negotiations. Finally, in 1972, President Nixon, after consideration of all aspects of the question and with the approval of Congress, reached agreement with the Soviets on the ABM treaty which provided for a mutual renunciation of all but token missile defenses.

Now in a few sentences President Reagan reversed a major American nuclear policy. What are some of the implications of that action? He initiated a project that, if successful, would require renunciation of the ABM treaty with the Soviet Union, which most informed observers regard as one of the two most important measures yet achieved to limit nuclear arms. In addition he set in motion forces that seem almost certain to trigger a furious acceleration of the nuclear arms race, eliminate the last hope of controlling the weapons spiral through agreement, and seriously jeopardize the confidence and support of our NATO allies.

Taken after only the most cursory consultation and preparation, the surprise announcement of a decision "to change the world" seems quite out of character for a democratic leader. One might expect such a whimsical antic from an absolute monarch, as for example when Czar Nicholas II and Kaiser Wilhelm II produced on their own the ill-conceived Treaty of Björkö, which their horrified ministers then forced them to repudiate; or when the Kaiser impetuously dispatched the famous Kruger telegram. But one expects far more prudence from a president of the United States, especially when he is dealing with the agonizing issue of nuclear weapons and hence the fate of the world.

The President's proposal did not seem bizarre to a public used to science fiction and conditioned by long exposure to Buck Rogers, *Star Trek*, and Darth Vader to regard outer space as a natural environment for war and counterwar. The President had told us that the Soviet Union is an "evil empire" and he was now warning America that the "empire" might "strike back." Nor was it unexpected that the speech touched many Americans. It is heartwarming to think that our weapons would no longer be used to kill people but only to shoot down weapons of the adversary.

It all seemed too good to be true—and, of course, it was. If there was nothing new in President Reagan's central concept, there was also nothing new in his support for nuclear defense systems. Long before becoming president he had repeatedly shown his aversion to our need to depend for security on mutual deterrence—or Mutual Assured Destruction (MAD) as the doctrine was called. Indeed, as he later said explicitly, the entire idea of maintaining deterrence through the threat of retaliation was "immoral"—unconsciously repeating a major theme of both the European and American peace movements that he roundly condemned.

That two equally strong adversaries might live in peace by maintaining an uneasy equilibrium through agreement is clearly too exotic an idea for Ronald Reagan's thinking. Bargaining with the Kremlin was, he seemed to feel, more political shadow play than the means to an enduring peace. "How," he has asked, "do you compromise between good and evil? . . . How do you compromise with men who say . . . there is no God?"

So he had opposed not merely the ABM treaty but every arms control agreement America has ever made with the Soviet Union and he seemed fully convinced that, instead of seeking elusive security through agreements with a nation he despised, we should rely only on military might and a "technical fix." The prescription for security that emerged was the ultimate expression of that view: we should build overwhelming military power by piling one offensive weapons system on another, and at the same time we should contrive defensive systems to "render" such weapons "impotent and obsolete." He seems quite oblivious of the inherent contradiction.

Defense by physical means can be either passive or active but Reagan no longer shows interest, as he once did, in safeguarding the population through vast shelter programs. His obsession now is with active defense through the development of mechanisms for destroying enemy missiles before they reach American soil.

He has undoubtedly been encouraged in that conclusion by conversations that began in 1981 with a group gathered together at the Heritage Foundation which included such right-wing industrialists as Karl R. Bendetsen, the beer magnate Joseph Coors, and the late Justin Dart, who were often referred to as members of Reagan's Kitchen Cabinet. Technical advice was provided by Dr. Edward Teller and Lieutenant General Daniel O. Graham, formerly director of the Defense Intelligence Agency.

By the end of 1981, however, Graham and Teller disagreed over the most desirable way to install space defense, and the Kitchen Cabinet apparently took Teller's side. As a result of that disagreement, Graham organized a private study with the pretentious name "High Frontier," financed by contributions from right-wing sources. The report it produced outlined in some detail a proposed missile defense system.

The argument between Graham and Teller was over whether the United States should go forward quickly to try to build a space defense with existing technology (Graham's view) or should delay a commitment to a space defense system until our scientists had developed new technology (Teller's view). Impatient to get on with deployment, Graham was critical of Teller, while Teller asserted that even though Graham's High Frontier project might be built for a hundred billion dollars, "The Soviets can get rid of High Frontier for ten billion dollars." Despite Teller's disapproval, Graham's High Frontier study seems to have impressed the President.[1]

Made over an eighteen-month period prior to the President's speech, at a cost of $500,000 provided by private sources, the study called for a three-layered defense. The first layer, using existing technology, would consist of 432 United States space satellites armed with non-nuclear missiles—including chemical lasers—that would intercept Soviet missiles shortly after launch. As a backup, a second group of non-nuclear missiles would protect each US missile site from Soviet warheads that managed to get through. These two tiers, Graham claimed, could be put in place in six or seven years. Then four or five years later a third layer might be added consisting of particle beam weapons and other Star Wars defenses.

General Graham expounded the High Frontier gospel in conceptual language remarkably close to that used in the President's announcement. The High Frontier plan would replace the "ludicrous notion" of deterrence by Mutual Assured Destruction (MAD) with the concept of "assured survival." Mutual assured destruction was, Graham asserted, a "time-worn and morally bankrupt doctrine." By providing "strategic defenses" the High Frontier system would render the intercontinental ballistic missile "practically obsolete."

The High Frontier study was reviewed in the Pentagon by a panel led by the undersecretary of defense, Dr. Richard B. DeLauer, which found against it. As a result, on November 24, 1982, Secretary of Defense Caspar Weinberger wrote General Graham that neither he nor DeLauer believed that there was technology available to support the policy called for by the report and hence both were "unwilling to commit this nation to a course which calls for growing into a capability that does not currently exist." In April a background study for a panel analyzing space-based weapons for the Congressional Office of Technology Assessment described the High Frontier proposal as "a defensive system of extremely limited capability" to intercept current Soviet missiles. The study added that if the Soviets should upgrade their booster rockets with quicker burning systems, the system would have "no capability . . . even with no Soviet effort to overcome the defense."

Those negative findings did not seem to discourage the President. He still continued to refer to the High Frontier report and it no doubt had a part in his decision to put forward his Star Wars program. After all, in spite of their disagreement over procedures, both Teller and General Graham shared the belief that America could build an effective anti-missile defense. The President did not seem to know—or he did not care—that few scientists held that view. It was for him an article of faith that limitless scientific virtuosity was a special attribute of our national genius. It was that faith, rather than any factual analysis, that led him to reverse normal procedures, announcing his decision to the world before, not after, he ordered studies of its feasibility. Nor did it seem to bother him that the project he announced was opposed until the last minute by his secretary of defense and other principal members of his government.

When the President decided to announce his new initiative few were told except for the speechwriters. Neither of the two officials who together supervise most of the government's ballistic missile defense research—John Gardner, director of Defensive Systems at the Pentagon and Richard Cooper, director of the Defense Research Advanced

Projects (DARPA)—was consulted or informed. Dr. Richard DeLauer, the leading Pentagon expert on the missile defenses, knew nothing of the speech until the day before its delivery and thus, in his own words, "had no major input."

As George A. Keyworth, the President's own science adviser, is reported to have remarked: "This was not a speech that came up; it was a top-down speech . . . a speech that came from the President's heart." Dr. Keyworth, a protégé of Edward Teller's from the Los Alamos Laboratory, is reported to have given the project only weak support while the Joint Chiefs of Staff provided little more than the suggestion that they would favor a somewhat more intensive program for investigating strategic defense; they made no formal recommendation to go forward along that line.

Even granting that the President had devout faith in his proposal, why did he abruptly announce it with so much fanfare after so little study or consultation? Presumably the dictates of theater triumphed over statesmanship; surprise was exploited at the sacrifice of prudence. Of course, some cynics have doubted that the President was driven by idealism to unveil a long-cherished private vision, and they attributed his timing to a more sordid calculation; they intimate instead that he timed the introduction of Star Wars to make more palatable the vast expenditures he was seeking for his military budget and particularly for the MX missile. Alexander M. Haig, Jr., in a speech made in 1984, put heavy emphasis on the desire of the President's staff for a "big PR splash that would make the President look like the greatest leader in America." The President's announcement, he said, "had been poorly timed and prepared." Whatever the President's motives, the administration promptly closed ranks. Although the project clearly had many closet opponents there was now a mass conversion reminiscent of that decreed by King Ethelbert of Kent in the sixth century.

Yet not even the most faithful and vocal supporters of the President's vision could conceal their disbelief in his extraordinary proposal that America might "share" with the Soviets the defense technology it developed. That idea had first been put forward by the President at a press conference—quite possibly on the spur of the moment—and it was, they imply, merely the eccentric musing of a lovable leader, a benevolent quirk to be indulgently overlooked. Indeed the undersecretary of defense, Fred C. Ikle, has bluntly pointed out the fantasy nature of the President's promise; the United States would, he said, be prepared to share the technology "when the Soviets agree to abolish all offensive systems" or—to borrow one of Chairman Khrushchev's more earthy figures of speech—when shrimps learn to whistle.

2.

Far too much of the public discussion of the Star Wars proposal has centered on technical arguments and speculation and far too little has concerned the project's political and strategic implications. Yet one needs at least a rudimentary appreciation of the technological problems to comprehend the enormous complexity of any defensive system, its obvious vulnerability to enemy attack or evasion, and the vast expenditures required even before testing and deployment begin.

Scientists seem agreed on at least one point: that there are three phases in a ballistic missile's trajectory where attack might be at least theoretically possible. The first is the so-called boost phase when the bus laden with individually targeted (MIRVed) warheads is being hoisted through the atmosphere and into space by first-stage and then second-stage rockets that burn out and fall away. There would be obvious advantages in timing defensive attacks during the boost phase since all the multiple warheads carried on a single rocket could then be destroyed by a single attack. Moreover only in the boost phase does the flaming of the rocket emit an intense infrared signal that should greatly facilitate detection.

On the other hand, there are formidable—and perhaps insoluble— technical problems in destroying rockets during this first phase. To be effective a ballistic missile defense would have to be near enough to the target to be able to attack about 2000 Soviet boosters within three to five minutes after they emerge from their silos or submarine hatches and before they move outside the atmosphere and release their independently targeted warheads. The only weapons so far conceived that would be fast enough to warrant consideration for this purpose are lasers, particle beams, and so-called "smart rocks"—kill projectiles equipped with homing sensors—fired either from rockets based on satellites or from hypervelocity electromagnetic rail guns.

In order to put the weapons near enough to the Soviets' silos or to their nuclear submarines, one proposal is to build and launch into space a large fleet of so-called orbiting battle stations (each weighing approximately 100 tons) revolving around the earth in sufficient numbers to assure that enough of them would be over the launching area at any moment to attack Soviet rockets with their lasers or particle beams.

An alternative under consideration is to build many earth-based lasers whose beams would bounce off relay mirrors, orbiting at 24,000 miles above the earth, onto "fighting" or "mission" mirrors in low orbit. These would then redirect the energy beams at the rising enemy boosters. The mirrors would have to be kept optically perfect and capable of changing their angles with complete accuracy in fractions of a second under the direction either of their own sensors or of battle management satellites in geostationary orbit 24,000 miles above. Since prepositioned mirrors would be easy targets, some preliminary thought is being given to mirrors that would be carried collapsed on rockets and would be "popped up" at the first warning of an enemy attack.

Another variant is the possibility of "popping up" laser interceptor weapons mounted on rockets during the three to five minutes of the boost stage. X-ray lasers powered by a nuclear explosion are the only weapons light enough to be considered for such interception. Since the earth is round, the interceptor weapons would have to be fired from submarines off Siberia or close to the Soviet Union; a Soviet silo in Siberia cannot be seen by an interceptor popped up from Alaska until that interceptor has risen to an altitude of 1000 kilometers—by which time the Soviet missile would have completed its boost phase.

Once the boost phase is completed and the missile is in "midcourse," the target to be destroyed is no longer a single missile. One Soviet SS-18 might release ten or more warheads together with a hundred or more decoys and quantities of other so-called penetration aids, such as chaff and clouds of infrared-emitting aerosol. Thus a thousand Soviet launching silos could present our defenses with hundreds of thousands of potential targets.

Finally, there is a possible so-called third phase or terminal defense— which means destroying the warheads after they reenter the atmosphere and come as close as a quarter of a mile to the target. But the Soviets could set their warheads to detonate as soon as they sense interception, and interception even as high as ten miles' altitude could effectively devastate the cities we are trying to protect.

All of this is, of course, a crude and rudimentary description intended to suggest only a tiny fraction of the technical problems that must be resolved to mount even a partial defense against Soviet ballistic missiles. Moreover, even if we did succeed in building these enormously complex mechanisms we would still have to develop defenses against Soviet cruise missiles or bombers that do not operate in outer space but can fly under US radar. Notwithstanding such evident pitfalls, the danger remains that, in their eagerness to tackle the manifold problems of the Star Wars project, some scientists may be tempted to express more optimism than is justified by the hard realities. Meanwhile there is serious confusion within the administration itself.

Once the ritual conversion had occurred and faithful adherence to the President's proposal had become, in the words of one administration official, a "loyalty oath," exegetes of the President's text quickly surrounded it with conflicting heresies. Thus today administration spokesmen are rushing frenetically around the world expounding their own variants of the true faith, leaving the President as almost the sole apostle of the doctrine in its pristine form.

Even Secretary of Defense Caspar Weinberger—while defending the President's proposal with the excessive zeal of a last-minute convert—still interprets it as implying a quite different objective from what the President intended. "If we can get a system," he says, "which is effective and which we know can render their weapons impotent, we could be back in a situation we were in, for example, when we were the only nation with a nuclear weapon."

Thus, although repeating, as part of the orthodox ritual, that we will somehow achieve a "thoroughly reliable and total" antiballistic missile defense capable of protecting our cities, he interprets the President's vision not as abolishing nuclear competition by mutual neutralization, but rather as assuring an American nuclear monopoly. Far from construing the President's announcement as calling for a world in which all nuclear weapons are neutralized, he sees it as producing a "situation" in which the United States alone can rattle the atom and thus be in a position to impose its views on the Soviet Union.

But if Weinberger continues to hold firm to the thought that we can develop a "thoroughly reliable and total" missile defense system capable of ridding our people of the need to rely, for security, on deterrence, he is almost the only high-level American official to do so; others have been content to rationalize more credible prospects. Thus a central schismatic line divides those few who still take the President's vision literally from those who favor partial missile defense systems for quite different reasons.

The first foreshadowing of these heresies was contained in reports commissioned by the President himself. Although Ronald Reagan made almost no effort to check the wisdom, or even the feasibility, of his proposal before its dramatic unveiling, he afterward appointed two panels to study various phases of the project and a third interagency group to integrate those studies. The panels conducted their assessment of the project between June and October 1983.

James C. Fletcher, former and present administrator of the National Aeronautics and Space Administration, who chaired one panel, the "Defensive Technology Study Team," commented, in summing up his panel's findings, that even the most effective ballistic missile defense could never defend the total US population. "Total is one thing, substantial is another. . . . What you want is to minimize the casualties. There is no such thing as a nuclear umbrella."

Frederick C. Hoffman, a protégé of Albert Wohlstetter's who heads the California think tank called Pan Heuristics, led the second panel devoted to "Future Security Strategies." It was largely composed of weapons-industry representatives and established Pentagon consultants. That panel was even more skeptical than Fletcher's about the prospect of total defense; indeed it devoted most of its analysis to the development of strategic rationales for partial or "intermediate" systems designed not to safeguard the American population but to protect land-based missile silos and other military targets. Rather than concentrating on fulfilling the President's purpose of doing away with dependence on deterrence, the panel justified these partial measures as "strengthening deterrence" on the ground that such defenses of limited capacity could "deny Soviet planners confidence in their ability to destroy a sufficient set of military targets to satisfy enemy attack objectives."

That now forms the distinctive doctrine for the new set of heresies. Although paying occasional lip service to presidential orthodoxy whenever they remember to do so, most administration spokesmen implicitly reject the idea that the Star Wars project even seriously contemplates the defense of cities or that it will relieve endangered humanity from the need to rely on the "immoral" concept of deterrence. Under the new heterodoxy, the Star Wars project has become merely another—although obviously an extremely doubtful and costly—way of augmenting deterrence.

This strange duality is now evident in most of our official statements, to the confusion of our allies. Thus during a London press conference at the beginning of February Secretary Weinberger spoke of a "thoroughly reliable defense," while, in the same city during the following week, Kenneth L. Adelman, the director of the US Arms Control and Disarmament Agency, defended the achievement of "a less than perfect" defense as a means of reducing the risk of nuclear war by increasing the enemy's uncertainty.

That theme has also been echoed by the recently appointed principal negotiator for the current Geneva arms control talks, Max M. Kampelman. As coauthor of an article that appeared almost simultaneously with his appointment, he invented new gobbledygook to compound the confusion. We needed to explore, he and his coauthors proposed, a new third option called the Strategy of Mutual Security or "mutual assured survival." This, they asserted, must replace the doctrine of Mutual Assured Destruction, since after all, the "proper role of government is to protect the country from aggression, not merely avenge it." They attempted to justify their proposal, however, not by arguing that it would end the need to rely on deterrence, but by claiming that "the combination of defense against space missiles with retaliatory defense in reserve *enhances deterrence*."[2]

Fred C. Ikle, the undersecretary of defense for policy, has tried to make a potable highball out of all this muddy water. Appearing before the Senate Subcommittee on Strategic and Theater Nuclear Forces on February 17, 1985, Ikle first made clear the firmness of the administration's commitment to Star Wars. Implicitly dismissing the justification advanced by some apologists that the Star Wars proposal was needed to provide a potential bargaining chip in the forthcoming arms talks at Geneva, he said categorically: "The Strategic Defense Initiative is not an optional program, at the margin of the defense effort. It's central."

When asked whether the program would be designed to protect cities or only American missiles he replied that at first the system would be designed to protect the missile fields that are the presumed target of Soviet military planners. However, he suggested, in the next century it might be expanded to protect cities as well. Thus wretched mankind must live for at least the next two or three decades in the purgatory of Mutual Assured Destruction; only many years after the turn of the century can it hope to gain entrance to the heaven of what the President calls "Mutual Assured Security."

Into all this blathering Paul H. Nitze, a weary veteran of the nuclear defense arguments of twenty years ago, has bravely sought to inject a note of coherence. Since Mr. Nitze is a principal adviser to the secretary of state for the forthcoming disarmament talks and since his experience with arms control matters is unequaled in the administration, his words carry impressive authority.[3]

Under current United States strategy, as Nitze propounds it, the United States would continue to press for radical reductions in nuclear arsenals of both sides, while at the same time continuing (as it has, in fact, been doing for some years) to pursue research in strategic defensive systems. But the United States would begin to place greater reliance on defensive systems only if it finds that the technologies can produce "survivable" systems; otherwise "the defenses would themselves be tempting targets for a first strike" and that, he said, "would decrease, rather than enhance, stability."

Nor would our government regard a defensive system as feasible, Nitze said, unless it should prove to be clearly "cost-effective at the margin"—that is, "it must be cheap enough to add additional defensive capability so that the other side has no incentive to add additional offensive capability to overcome the defense." "If this criterion is not met," he continued, "the defensive systems could encourage a proliferation of countermeasures to overcome deployed defenses, instead of a redirection of effort from offense to the defense." (Henry Kissinger, for his part, recently commented that "the criteria . . . Paul Nitze has laid down for building a strategic defense system seem unlikely to be met.")[4]

Nitze then summed up the new American nuclear strategy, by insisting that it was, in fact, "wholly consistent with deterrence. . . ." In fact, he insisted, *In both the transition and ultimate phases deterrence would continue to provide the basis for the US-Soviet strategic relationship"* (emphasis added).

Not only does Nitze thus categorically deny the central thesis of the President's concept—that the Star Wars project would enable the American people to be secure without further reliance on deterrence— he also ignores another tacit premise of the President's approach that the only way to achieve security is by offensive and defensive military might. Instead he envisages US security as an objective to be accomplished through a concerted effort with the Soviets under which each side would develop its defenses while reducing its offensive arsenals. Diplomacy, in other words, is still at the heart of his strategy.

In contrast to these heretical views the President seems to be living at a different time and in a different world, for he continues to espouse his original proposal and to justify it with the same idealistic litany. As recently as the middle of February he was still talking about relieving Americans of the need to rely on "MAD—Mutual Assured Destruction," which in his view is immoral. "Why don't we have MAS instead—Mutual Assured Security," a catch phrase he seems to have borrowed from the article by Max Kampelman I have mentioned. In other words, he still justifies his proposal as ridding mankind of reliance on deterrence.

No one seems willing to tell the President that, in his exuberant faith in the wisdom of his doctrine, he is making a false representation to the American people. Were he a private citizen seeking to finance his project on such representations the SEC would immediately put a stop to it.

3.

During the early years of the administration one might have forgiven Ronald Reagan's performance, since it took him many months to realize that, as president, he could not speak with the same cavalier disregard for the facts as when he was making speeches for General Electric. Even after four years he seems not always to recognize that the words of a president are a powerful instrument to be used with scrupulous restraint; otherwise they may deeply prejudice the objective debate needed for a judicious determination of policy and, by their reverberations around the world, produce complex and destructive reactions in different parts of the globe.

As president, however, Ronald Reagan has either overlooked or deliberately ignored these hazards. Not only did he take his own advisers and the Congress by surprise, it seems never to have occurred to him or to his advisers that America was obligated to give advance notice to our principal NATO allies before it announced a drastic change in American nuclear policy that could deeply affect their security.

Had the President consulted the European leaders in advance he would no doubt have been told that they did not share his desire to neutralize nuclear weapons. Unlike Americans who never felt menaced by external attack until nuclear weapons were devised and now wish that had never happened, most Europeans devoutly believe that the invention of nuclear shells and missiles has provided their one hope of breaking the cycle of wars that have ravaged their continent two or three times a century. Moreover, the whole concept of NATO defenses is postulated on the deterrent effect of a nuclear response; and Europeans fear that were such weapons neutralized, Soviet conventional forces might overrun Europe.[5]

Although that concern is fundamental it is still not the sole issue worrying our NATO allies. Some are concerned that the result of America's building an effective missile defense would be to "decouple" our strategic missile force from the defense of Europe; or in other words they fear that, in case of a Soviet attack on Europe, America might sit safely behind its protective shield and let Europe be incinerated. To be sure, that reflects more paranoia than logic since until now the greater European fear was that an America exposed to Soviet attack would not risk New York to save Paris or London or Düsseldorf.

Another European worry is that once America felt protected against attack, it would not be willing or able to extend its defensive shield to Europe or that, in response to America's ABMs, the Soviets would build a defensive system of their own that would render useless the independent French and British deterrents.

All these are understandable concerns. Yet there is a mitigating factor—the hope in some European quarters that, if the United States should go ahead with a vast research program, European firms might share in the effort and thus benefit from a fallout of American technology. That attitude has led one shrewd and worldly American bureaucrat to remark that, although he agreed that European government support of Star Wars could not be bought, it still might "be rented."

In sum, European leaders remain uneasy and if they become convinced that the United States is seriously going ahead with the President's project, they will increasingly manifest suspicions and resentments that could help erode the fundamental confidence on which the NATO structure depends.

At home, the President's call for a missile defense system has been captured and perverted by various interests who, for reasons of religion, ideology, or profit, would like to speed up the arms race and, therefore, strongly oppose all efforts to reach a *modus vivendi* with the Soviets that would enable the two sides to halt or reverse it. Now that he has given those diverse groups a common rallying cry, they are mounting powerful pressure to railroad his proposal through Congress—even though they are on the whole antipathetic to his central objective.

Among other elements promoting their own special version of the President's proposal are the secular fundamentalists who style themselves neoconservatives. Among the most vocal members of this group are the intellectuals who are attached to conservative think tanks or who regularly fill the columns of such right-wing journals as *Commentary*, *Policy Review*, and *Public Policy*.

Since they share a vigorous repugnance to dealing with the Kremlin, the leading secular fundamentalists are now joining in a loud and well-orchestrated chorus, proclaiming that all past efforts at nuclear arms control have been futile and that most such efforts have benefited the Soviet Union against the interests of the United States. Such tendentious attacks ignore the manifest benefits of the Partial Test Ban Treaty and disparage SALT I because its renunciation of ABM interferes with the fundamentalists' desire to build more missiles and thus pursue their unavowed but evident desire for nuclear superiority, even though such superiority can only be illusory. They fail to acknowledge that the SALT II treaty, whose confirmation they opposed, was intended primarily to impose temporary limits on the arms race until SALT III could bring about real reductions. With more passion than logic they attempt to foreclose the possibilities of negotiations before they begin.

Thus in answer to the question posed by *Policy Review*, "Have control negotiations with the Soviet Union benefited the United States?" Professor Richard Pipes, a prominent advocate of the hard-line right wing who served in the National Security Council during the first years of the Reagan administration, answered that on the whole "such negotiations have been a failure." Irving Kristol asserted the negotiations "have only benefited the Soviet Union." Richard Perle, assistant secretary of defense and perhaps the most powerful influence on administration arms control policy, states: "I don't think the negotiations have helped us in the main."[6]

Simultaneously, Norman Podhoretz, the editor of *Commentary*, has written that "we find no rational justification for the faith in arms control." It is, he insists, "the great superstition of our time" that "can easily prompt action whose unintended consequence will be to bring about the very thing it is meant to avoid—including the abandonment of the Strategic Defense Initiative which, unlike the doomed delusions of Geneva, really does hold out the rational hope of an eventual escape from the threat of nuclear war."[7]

The leitmotif running through all these statements is the obsessive urge to build up our nuclear arsenal and to reject efforts to halt the arms spiral through diplomacy. Just how these militant intellectuals conceive that the process will finally end is the great unanswered question. Can we, as some seem to imply, drive the Soviets beyond the limits of their resources to ultimate exhaustion? Or, by outspending them, can we—to borrow a phrase recently hallowed by presidential use—force them to cry "uncle"? Neither possibility seems likely.

If we continue to build more and more nuclear weapons and the Soviets neither become exhausted nor submit, what then? That question seems never to concern the secular fundamentalists, even though an endless arms spiral could well turn into a cyclone. Nor do their fellow Soviet-haters, the religious fundamentalists, seem at all disturbed by the prospect of a cataclysmic collision. Because they regard the Soviet Union as the Beast of Revelations, they seem not to fear the final battle of Armageddon, since they know that just before it begins they, the elect, will ascend to Heaven to join Christ in Jerusalem where he will reign forever.[8] But the secular fundamentalists have no such comforting prospect; they are doomed to roast along with the rest of us.

America's right-wing intellectuals are by no means the most effective proponents of the Star Wars project. All they can contribute is words, while ideological industrialists have money. Not only can they finance research to document and spread the gospel—and conservative think tanks have been sprouting—they also have practical means to try to reshape the Congress. To help the Star Wars project gain approval General Graham of High Frontier organized the American Space Frontier Committee and by June 1984 was able to announce that its political action committee had raised $300,000 to support pro–space defense candidates and thus "send to the Congress men and women who understand that our country must build a defense against possible missile attack." The committee concentrated on defeating five Democratic congressmen who were contending that the Star Wars project would accelerate the arms race: George Brown and Mel Levine of California, Berkeley Bedell of Iowa, Nicholas Mavroules of Massachusetts, and James R. Jones of Oklahoma. It also opposed a Republican, Senator Charles Percy of Illinois. Its score card, however, was not impressive; only Senator Percy was defeated and there is no indication that Star Wars had any part in his defeat. We can expect the committee to be more active in 1986.

Perhaps the most effective support for Star Wars is now being generated not by ideology but by good free-enterprise greed. Firms in the hypertrophic defense industry, along with their thousands of technicians, are manifesting a deep patriotic enthusiasm for Star Wars. Since they are experienced in lobbying and wield heavy influence with members of Congress who have defense plants in their constituencies, they are creating formidable momentum for the project. Whether or not it would contribute to the security of the nation, it offers them security. Thus an investment analyst for the industry published a newsletter about the President's space program entitled "Money from Heaven," while another analyst wrote: "For the US aerospace industry the redirection of the strategic arms competition toward defense can hardly come soon enough."

Although basically supporting the program, the armed services are not all reacting in exactly the same way. The Air Force is the most enthusiastic, since air officers see space defense as opening a new fourth element in which wars can be waged—offering the prospect of a whole new service domain which the Air Force hopes to preempt. The sea belongs to the Navy, the land to the Army; and, the Air Force contends, it would be only natural for it to extend its dominion beyond the atmosphere into outer space.

In Navy circles one hears more muted enthusiasm for such a geopolitical concept. The Navy's reservations arise in considerable part because it has been counting on claiming a strategic mission the Air Force has so far monopolized. Since the Navy's Trident II submarines would be able to fire from precise positions thanks to the new NAVSTAR satellite navigation system, the reentry vehicle fired from the Trident II will have the "hard target kill" accuracy comparable to that of the MX—without the MX's vulnerability to a first strike. Thus in principle the Navy would favor an agreement with the Soviets to restrict the development of antisatellite weapons and thus safeguard its own navigation satellites—a position that, of course, the Air Force strenuously opposes. The cold war of interservice rivalries still persists on the home front.

Nevertheless, the Navy has also created a space command of its own, although a year later than the Air Force; and, however much the services disagree about their missions, the Star Wars project clearly promises expanded tables of organization with all kinds of new slots for ambitious officers. Still, in private talks, some military leaders in all services have expressed to me and others nervous concern not only that the President's program seems unrealistic and unattainable but also that the vast funds it would consume could drain resources from other more traditional programs.

Although some officials on the civilian side of the Pentagon no doubt secretly question either the feasibility or the political wisdom of the Strategic Defense Initiative, they carefully conceal their doubts. Already the President has created a new office under the secretary of defense to organize and run a program of research and development estimated to cost $26 billion over the next five years. The head of that office, Lieutenant General James A. Abramson, is already busy lobbying Congress for its approval.

4.

A major point so far largely overlooked in all this mindless hustle and bustle is that historical experience strongly tends to refute the assumptions of the President's proposal.

In the evolution of warfare, as such respected students of strategy as B. H. Liddell Hart and Major General J. F. C. Fuller repeatedly point out, the advantage shifts constantly back and forth between the offense and defense in a macabre rhythm. The all-conquering medieval knight weighted down by armor was, in due course, stopped in mid-gallop by massed archers and pikemen. The castle lost its defensive invulnerability when besiegers found that shot propelled by gunpowder could knock down its walls. The ironclad warship proved victim to the submarine and mine. The defensive advantage tragically shown by the machine gun in the trenches of Picardy was in time overcome by the tank and offensive aircraft.

The offense–defense pendulum process is succinctly described in the *Encyclopaedia Britannica*:

> Until the 19th century, offensive and defensive cycles were of long duration. Improvements in weapons have come so rapidly since the Napoleonic era that the swing from one to another is a matter of only a few years. Generals of all armies were confident at the outbreak of World War I that the offensive power of the arms of 1914 would prevail in a few months. The machine gun had the leading part in turning the conflict into a stalemate, however, and not until the last few months of the war did the tank provide the victors with an offensive weapon capable of breaking the deadlock. Even so, a school of military thought held after the war that the defensive remained powerful enough to curb an aggressor in the next conflict. The illusion was soon dispelled when the German armies of 1940 drove on to a succession of early victories.

The lesson from all this could hardly be clearer. Those who put their trust in the efficacy of defensive measures as a long-term solution to the current East-West competition are likely to make the same discovery as did the French general staff in 1940—that in today's world of fast-paced change, defensive measures have only a brief life span of effectiveness. Indeed many may never provide even momentary value.

To contend that American technology could swing the nuclear pendulum back toward the defense and keep it there is to believe in a magical force that can arrest all military motion. But not even lasers and computers are magical, and any Star Wars defense we might someday develop at exorbitant cost would be a quickly depreciating investment. The Soviets would never sit idly by watching us struggle to build a shield behind which—as they saw it—we might safely launch a first strike. They would do what other nations have done when presented with a comparable threat—commit whatever resources were required to develop defensive weapons of their own, as well as new devices to counter their enemy's defenses—no matter how bizarrely elaborate they might have to be.

At the same time they would drastically increase the quality and quantity of their offensive weapons so that, either by their mass use or by new technical countermeasures, they would be able to overwhelm our own defensive systems. Moreover, in the quite unlikely event that they should find themselves being outdistanced, one cannot completely reject the thought that they might strike preemptively, just as the Japanese chose to attack Pearl Harbor in 1941 because, by 1943, America would have completed its battleship program and thus gained decisive naval superiority.

The applicability to the Star Wars proposal of mankind's long experience should be obvious. Impelled by the vaulting momentum of modern science, the pendulum of advantage will—if we do not halt it by agreement—swing with increasing speed from offense to defense and back again, giving a relentless dynamic to the arms race. If, in today's fast-paced world, we yield to the credulous believers in a strategic nuclear defense, we are almost certain to discover, after wasting vast resources on an ephemeral project, that our country is in greater danger than ever.

The unique and invaluable achievement of the ABM treaty was to halt the pendulum swing, remove that competitive increment to momentum from the arms race, and thus restrict the arms rivalry to weapons for which control agreements were still feasible. It is the most important advance toward security that we have achieved from our negotiations with the Soviets. It would be tragic folly to discard it on the whim of a president who has repeatedly shown his ignorance of the most elementary facts on which our nuclear strategy is based. If we now, in a fatuous pursuit of false security through space defense, restart the pendulum, we shall very likely throw away our last chance to keep the weapons spiral from whirling without control onward and upward with accelerating speed.

Unhappily Americans today have a short attention span. Not only do we forget the lessons of two world wars but our government seems to have ignored even more recent experience that directly involved the nuclear defense issue. As early as the 1950s our leaders became concerned that the Soviets might be developing an effective ABM system to neutralize our offensive weapons. Just as the Pentagon today is, by conditioned reflex, exaggerating reports of Soviet progress toward missile defenses to bolster its own claim for new missions and resources, so officials thirty years ago were alarmed at overstated intelligence reports that Soviet installations with the quaint name of Galosh were being built to protect Moscow and that the Tallinn air defense system was really designed to knock down attacking missiles. How then did we react? Well, exactly as one may expect the Soviets to do if we proceed with the Star Wars project. Not only did we begin work on a defensive system of our own but we undertook to produce an offensive force that could overwhelm any possible Soviet defense. Our effort in that instance centered on the development of Multiple Independent Reentry Vehicles (MIRVs) that would enable each missile to carry a cluster of warheads.

The initial American flight test of MIRVs was held in August 1968 just as the superpowers were agreeing to enter the SALT I negotiations. In retrospect, it seems quite possible that, had President Nixon taken the initiative when he took office in January 1969, we might have reached an accord with the Soviets to halt MIRVing and restrict the building of more ICBM systems in a single package agreement. That would have sharply curtailed the momentum of the arms race, for with ABMs forbidden, there was no excuse for MIRVing. At the same time, if Soviet MIRVing could have been forestalled, we would not need an ABM system of our own to protect the US Minutemen forces.

But President Nixon, moved by the same interests and influences that are today impelling us toward Star Wars, rejected any such negotiations and proceeded with the MIRV program. His excuse was that we must go forward to build MIRVs in order to have a bargaining counter during a second phase of SALT talks. By that time, however, the Soviets, having felt compelled to invest major resources to catch up on MIRV technology, had lost interest in banning MIRVs.

That is a sad story, for it was our failure to ban MIRVing that strengthened our adversary's position at high cost to us, since the Soviets could hang three or four times as many MIRVs on a single huge SS-18 as we could hang on our smaller Minuteman. Thus they gained an enormous advantage by the operation. Indeed, it was this Soviet advantage that led to all the overheated rhetoric about the "window of vulnerability," which, as the Scowcroft Commission later determined, was simply a *trompe l'oeil* painting of a window by dexterous alarmists. Even so, the resulting excitement generated frantic pressure for the MX—that orphan missile, beloved by hard-liners and the weapons industry, for which no one can find a home.

5.

Today the administration's nuclear strategy is a mare's-nest of self-deception and contradictions. During past weeks the Star Wars proponents have been congratulating the President, saying that only his strategic defense initiative could have brought the Soviets back to the bargaining table. But even though one gives that assertion at least a Scots' verdict of "not proven," the achievement seems ephemeral. They were not reacting from weakness, as the administration spokesmen imply. Far from it. They simply saw the United States embarking on a foolish course that would be costly and dangerous and open the door for unlimited escalation. It was only natural that they should seek through diplomacy to forestall the creation of a new destructive competition in which they would feel compelled to engage—and vigorously so—should we refuse to give up the Star Wars project.

If we are prepared to offer nothing that could provide the basis for a possible deal, arranging for the representatives of two great nations to sit around a green baize table is not diplomacy but logistics. If it is true that the Soviets have agreed to talk only because they hope to forestall the Star Wars project, then nothing useful can be expected. The President has made it dogmatically clear that he will not bargain away his cherished vision; he will go forward with Star Wars no matter what happens or fails to happen at Geneva.

In the face of this adamantly expressed position it is absurd for administration spokesmen to imply that we might nevertheless persuade the Soviets to reduce their ICBM arsenal or at least restrict the addition of new systems. How could any belief be more fatuous—or more disingenuous? Even administration casuists should recognize that, facing the loudly trumpeted threat of an American ABM system, the Soviets must inevitably insist on keeping full freedom to build all the offensive missiles required to overwhelm that system.

Meanwhile the administration is trying to take the opponents of Star Wars off balance by asking in tones of injured innocence: Why all the excitement when the President is not now proposing to deploy or even test a missile defense system? All he is asking, they say, is that Congress appropriate $30 billion over the next five years to finance the research necessary to "provide the evidentiary basis for an informed discussion on whether and how to proceed in the system development." No doubt some have a taste for such clotted prose and indeed some members of Congress seem willing to be seduced by it; after all, it gives them a facile justification for going along with the White House. But it is clearly a trap all the same.

The point to be understood is that the President is not treating the Star Wars proposal as merely a somewhat expanded nuclear defense research program such as the United States and the Soviet Union have both been conducting for some years. Had the administration chosen to regard the project as that it could have increased the budget for such research from $1.4 billion to $3.7 billion for the next fiscal year just as it is contemplating under Star Wars. But instead the President has chosen to announce his initiative to the listening world in rhapsodic prose as a total change in policy. Moreover, that new policy, as Undersecretary of

Defense Ikle has announced, has now become "not an optional program" but "central" to our whole defense effort—whatever that may
mean. Moreover the administration is not just asking for an additional
$2.3 billion for the fiscal year but announcing a five-year program
estimated to cost $30 billion, which is hardly small change even for the
Pentagon.

How must all this look to the Soviets? They understand America well
enough to know that what is contemplated is not a mere increase in
appropriations for research but a critical change in United States policy,
setting in motion driving forces that will quickly acquire ever-increasing
momentum. Thus on February 19, the Defense Department announced
that in 1987, two years earlier than planned, it will use the space shuttle
to test "ways of tracking and targetting enemy missiles in space"—a
measure that may well violate the ABM treaty.

So, even if some Americans seem tempted to pass this program off as
merely prudent intensification of research, the Soviets are not that
gullible. They know full well that once we have spent such a vast sum
(together with additional billions for the normal overruns) any president
will be under almost irresistible pressure to continue the testing and
development of the system, no matter what $30 billion worth of
experimentation might indicate about possible success.

How will the Soviets react? They will immediately set about parallel
activities. They will do far more than simply augment the research
activities they are now undertaking. Indeed, if they did not take such
actions, they would be out of character, for the Soviet leaders are
anything but reckless.

Nor should anyone possibly expect the Russians to be put off by the
President's promise to consult with them before we test an ABM
weapon. Once we reach a point where testing is appropriate, we will
have made such great strides toward development that the Soviets—in
their view—will be lamentably far behind. So they must immediately
launch a similar program of their own.

That is not the only element of self-deception in the current proposal;
there is fraudulence both in its conception and promotion. In first
proposing the Star Wars project the President compared it by implication to the Manhattan Project, which brought about the first nuclear
bomb. But the Manhattan Project was vastly simpler; indeed in 1983 Dr.
Richard DeLauer, then the Pentagon's top scientist, testified that to
fulfill the objectives of the Star Wars project will require breakthroughs
in eight key technologies, each "equivalent to or greater than the
Manhattan Project." Nor is that the only critical point of difference.
America did not undertake the Manhattan Project at a time when the
other side was frantically seeking to develop countermeasures. During
the five years of research contemplated by the President's proposal, the

Soviets can be expected to provide at least partially effective answers to any ABM system we might devise.

The administration's scientists well know that it requires no great "breakthroughs" to contrive countermeasures but merely the application of existing technologies. Thus it is significant that our technicians are already vigorously working on countermeasures of our own. The Pentagon recently announced that it was expanding its countermeasures research at Norton Air Force Base in California, and in the next fiscal year will triple the funds appropriated for that work. The research will concentrate on the development of so-called "penetration aids" to help clear the way for our missiles against possible missile defenses by the Soviets. *The New York Times* reported on February 11, 1985:

> According to Air Force officials, once scientists and engineers have their hands on a weapon, it is relatively easy to design a countermeasure.
>
> "You can always beat the other guy's defenses if you know what he's got coming at you," said Major Skapin [of TRW, Inc., the principal civilian contractor for the program].
>
> "I don't think we've seen any defense yet that was effective enough that you couldn't develop an offense to counter it," said Bruce R. Abell, a spokesman for White House Science Adviser George A. Keyworth.

Just as we are stepping up our efforts to design countermeasures against nuclear defenses not yet installed, we can be certain the Soviets are doing the same thing. If we should mount space platforms from which to use defensive lasers or particle beams they would devise means to shoot them down; so we would have to equip those platforms with their own defenses, perhaps developing a protective fleet like the battle group around an aircraft carrier. Somehow it is all reminiscent of Dean Swift's version of an old comment on the human condition:

> . . . *a flea*
> *Hath smaller fleas that on him prey;*
> *And these have smaller fleas to bite 'em,*
> *And so proceed* ad infinitum.

What the President's defense initiative reflects is a fantasy that nuclear danger can be eliminated through some wonderful new invention—a purely mechanistic approach that denies the reality that the world will never be free from the nuclear threat until there is some reconciliation of interests and some agreement on coexistence between the nuclear powers. The naive faith that we can achieve security by some new system or gadget that blunts the edge of the Soviet sword runs counter to the advice of a widely experienced president—Dwight D. Eisenhower—who understood the nature of war. When, so he observed, we face crisis, as we inevitably shall, "there is a recurring temptation to feel that some spectacular and costly action could become the miraculous solution to all current difficulties"—an action such as "a huge increase in the new elements of our defense" or "a dramatic expansion in basic and applied research." But, he wisely continued, "in holding scientific research and discovery in respect, as we should, we must also be alert to the equal and opposite danger that public policy could itself become the captive of a scientific-technological elite."

As a military man of long experience, President Eisenhower was aware of the historic and ineluctable pendulum swing from offense to defense and back again, and he was sufficiently mature not to believe in the promise of a magic wand that would stop Soviet missiles in their tracks.

From all this it seems hard to reach any but a gloomy assessment of our current position. Unless Congress substantially reduces the requested appropriation for Star Wars defense and makes clear its disapproval of the President's drastic change in our nuclear policy, we shall be committed to a new stage of weapons competition that will further drain the resources of both the US and the USSR while at the same time creating new vested interests in continuing weapons development. Quite innocently we may thus give validity to the current faddish but foolish contention that arms control is no longer achievable for we shall have passed beyond the point where verification is possible.

Thus we may unwittingly confirm the President's assertion that his Star Wars proposal "holds the promise of changing the course of history." If Americans should buy that project we would not be purchasing security but nuclear escalation. We would restart the momentum of the offense-defense-offense pendulum, open the door for unlimited nuclear escalation, and compel the Soviets to compete even more fiercely in both defensive and offensive weapons. Yielding to pressure from the same elements now promoting it—ideology, wishful thinking, fear, and greed—we and the Soviets would almost inevitably try to put to offensive use the technology acquired in building space stations and exploiting the potential of lasers, particle beams, and other esoteric means of transferring energy. In addition, by building space-based defenses and thus foreshortening response times, we would be forced to entrust to computers rather than the human mind decisions that could threaten the survival of mankind.

The risks of this ill-conceived venture are thus enormous and they are increased by the possibility that the public will be so deceived by specious promises or confused by technological jargon that it will ignore the lessons of the past and acquiesce in a vision that seems to promise peace but will have the opposite result. Pursuing the President's Star Wars program will turn outer space into a new battlefield, increase the risks of catastrophic conflict, and enlarge man's ability to destroy civilization.

NOTES

1. See *The New York Times*, March 6, 1985.
2. See *The New York Times Magazine*, January 27, 1985.
3. See his speech of February 20, to the Philadelphia World Affairs Council.
4. See the *New York Post*, March 4, 1985.
5. See my article, "White House Roulette," in *The New York Review*, November 8, 1984.
6. See *Policy Review*, Winter 1985, pp. 37–38.
7. See *The New York Times*, January 24, 1985, p. 25.
8. See Hal Lindsey and C. C. Carlson, *The Late Great Planet Earth*, published by Zondervan in 1976, a book that has sold 18 million copies. See also *The Washington Post*, October 24, 1984.

26

The Return of Strategic Defense

LEON SLOSS

After many years of neglect, strategic defense is once again on the agenda for action and debate. The subject burst on the scene unexpectedly and dramatically with President Reagan's speech of March 23, 1983, which challenged the U.S. military, scientific and industrial communities to develop defenses against ballistic missiles with the ultimate goal of rendering the ballistic missile threat "impotent and obsolete."

The President's proposal was followed by a flurry of official and unofficial studies, articles, Congressional hearings, speeches, seminars and diplomatic exchanges which examined the technical, strategic, diplomatic and arms control issues related to ballistic missile defense. During the past year, claims and counterclaims have been made about the feasibility of defense, its impact on strategic stability, its role in strategy and its effect on arms control. The result has been a lively, if often confusing, controversy.

What follows is an effort to place the debate into a broader strategic perspective and to probe some of the policy issues raised by the Strategic Defense Initiative (SDI), as it is now called. The thesis that is reflected below may be summarized in four points:

1. The United States and its allies have undervalued strategic defense for the past two decades in developing both forces and plans; the Soviet Union has not. The prestigious *Times of London* has described this disparity succinctly as follows:

. . . Since the development of missiles, Western strategy has relied predominantly on a theory of deterrence which assumes that any attack can only be prevented by the threat of retaliation. The idea of partial defence—less than perfect, but surely useful—has been in eclipse. . . . At least the Soviet Union's attitude to defence has been consistent. It has never embraced the theory that one can ignore defence and rely solely on retaliation. . . . In fact, in spite of the 1972 [ABM] agreement, the Soviet Union has persisted with an active research and development programme into anti-missile defences.[1]

2. As a result of this neglect by the United States, a U.S.–Soviet strategic asymmetry has opened which transcends that shown when only offensive forces are compared, as has been the tendency in the West. The implications of this asymmetry have become more pronounced in connection with the shift by the United States away from the strategic doctrine of Assured Destruction toward a more demanding deterrent strategy that emphasizes countermilitary targeting and escalation control to counter various levels of potential aggression.

3. During the coming decade the United States will require some form of strategic defense in order to redress this imbalance and sustain an effective deterrent. On this point, the "Future Security Strategic Study" (or so-called Hoffman Report), which was commissioned in 1983 by the Department of Defense, concluded:

A satisfactory deterrent requires a combination of more discriminatory and effective offensive systems to respond to enemy attacks plus defensive systems to deny the achievement of enemy attack objectives. Such a deterrent can counter the erosion of confidence in our alliance guarantees caused by the adverse shifts in the military balances since the 1960s.[2]

4. Strategic defenses do not have to be perfect, or even near-perfect, to play a useful role in deterrence. To cite again from the "Future Security Strategy Study:" "Even a U.S. defense of limited capability can deny Soviet planners confidence in their ability to destroy a sufficient set of military targets to satisfy enemy objectives, thereby strengthening deterrence."[3]

A Strategic Assessment

Notwithstanding the diversity of the weapons systems that have been amassed in the nuclear arsenal of the United States—and the intricacy of the scenarios that have been invoked for their possible employment—those forces fulfill basically four roles:

1. *To deter aggression.* It is important to note that this role today extends beyond the deterrence of nuclear conflict itself to include a broad range of political and military threats from the potential adversary.

2. *To assure or reassure* those nations allied with the United States and under the umbrella of U.S. protective commitments. As Michael Howard has pointed out, the qualities of a nuclear posture required for reassurance may conflict with those required for deterrence.[4]

3. *To control escalation* if nuclear weapons ever are used. This calls for employment options and capabilities permitting limited and discriminate use of the weapons.

4. *To terminate conflict* on favorable terms. This concept is frequently stated, but not well understood.

Skepticism and controversy have fastened on the appropriateness of nuclear weapons and their effectiveness in all of these roles. Indeed, in recent years many have questioned whether nuclear weapons can be entrusted any mission whatsoever beyond deterring the opponent's use of such weapons. The fact remains that the United States and NATO have come to rely on nuclear weapons to a considerable extent for the coverage of all these roles. The reliance may well be excessive, but until a major effort is made to strengthen the Alliance's nonnuclear forces, it is likely to remain a fact of international life.

The past fifteen years have witnessed an evolution in U.S. nuclear doctrine—doctrine being defined as the body of goals and operational concepts set for nuclear forces by U.S. policymakers. Doctrine has been moving away from the *punitive* concept of Assured Destruction toward a more flexible and variegated concept which seeks the *denial* to the Soviets of confidence in the achievement of their political and military objectives by the use of force. As such, this doctrine requires more targeting options, more flexible procedures, more discriminate weapons and more endurance for both forces and command and control. The United States, under the past four administrations—Democratic and Republican—has sought to move doctrine in this direction because the West has been so heavily dependent on nuclear weapons to meet the range of objectives described above, and because Assured Destruction was simply not adequate as a doctrine for harnessing nuclear weapons to these varied roles. Indeed, the doctrine was threatening to become self-deterring, particularly in its applications to "extended deterrence" over third countries, thus adversely impacting on the dimension of assurance to our allies. The Soviets have attempted to exploit this situation by fomenting fears about the risks of nuclear war and doubt about U.S. nuclear assurances: this is a central objective of their "peace" offensive in Western Europe.

While U.S. doctrine has thus moved away from Assured Destruction, however, the United States has failed to acquire the full extent of capabilities needed to meet the rising demands inherent in that shift. Indeed, the gap between objectives and capabilities is substantial, and it does not appear to be narrowing. Several reasons account for the gap.

First, the Soviet Union has been laboring assiduously to block the United States from achieving the strategic objectives under the doctrine. Second, the doctrine is controversial: partly because it has sometimes been poorly articulated by spokesmen in the U.S. Government, it is often not well understood by the public and the Congress—and many of those who do basically comprehend it doubt its feasibility or fear its consequences. Third, the defense bureaucracy in Washington is not solidly behind the evolving doctrine, in large part because resources for the strategic forces compete with other defense programs.

Finally, a substantial number in the U.S. Congress are in revolt against the trend as a whole or oppose important aspects of it. There has been an effort, gaining support in the Congress, that would have the effect of driving strategy back to Assured Destruction by denying funds for programs necessary to implement the evolving U.S. doctrine. For example, over the past year members of Congress have mounted an attack on certain new weapons systems based on the misguided proposition that all counterforce weapons are "first-strike" weapons.

The fact is that, notwithstanding the reams of commentary on the subject, weapons systems are not generically first- or second-strike systems. Rather, doctrine—and in the final analysis the prevailing scenario of battle—will determine how weapons will be used. U.S. strategic nuclear doctrine has consistently emphasized retaliation, while Soviet strategic doctrine has just as consistently stressed preemption. To be sure, weapons that have a good counterforce capability *and that are vulnerable* will tend to be perceived as first-strike weapons, for this is the only mode in which they might be effectively used. Thus, critics of what they allege are first-strike capabilities, if they will be consistent in their fear, ought to show a good deal more concern for reducing the vulnerability of counterforce weapons rather than indiscriminately trying to block all such weapons programs. The attack on certain strategic programs also reflects a misplaced faith in what may be achieved by arms control, about which more will be said below.

Thus, the current strategic situation confronting the United States can be summarized as follows:

• The West has developed a strong dependence on nuclear weapons—some would say an overdependence. This is not desirable, but it is a fact. It has resulted from a failure of the NATO states and Japan to build and maintain adequate nonnuclear forces.

• The United States has evolved a *doctrine* (at least on paper) that is consistent with that dependence.

• Yet, we lack the strategic mix of offensive and defensive capabilities required fully to support the doctrine.

• Political support within the United States for the acquisition of the needed capabilities seems uncertain at best.

• Meanwhile, the Soviet Union has continued a concerted arms effort and a steady growth in military capabilities across-the-board, widening the strategic asymmetry described above.

This may seem an unduly gloomy assessment, but it is a realistic one. The United States has made progress in modernizing its strategic forces and will make greater strides in the years ahead if current programs are funded. Yet, even if those programs are carried through, they will not put us in a position fully to meet the goals of current U.S. doctrine, particularly as the Soviet Union will not be relaxing its drive to further its own strategic objectives and frustrate those of the United States. It is clear the Soviets also face problems, and they should not be minimized: indeed, we should take prudent advantage of them where possible. Yet, the United States must first and foremost tend to its own problems, which include prominently the vulnerability of U.S. strategic forces (and of their essential support-structure of command, control, communications and intelligence), a lack of flexibility and discrimination in weapons and plans for their use, and a serious lack of attention to the defense against attacking missiles and aircraft.

Broad Strategic Choices

Given the above assessment, what broad options are open to U.S. planners? Four are suggested here. The choices may not be mutually exclusive, but they denote at least a relative gravity of alternative U.S. policy investments.

1. *The United States can rely heavily on arms control.* No doubt, this is an approach that is tempting to the U.S. public and to many politicians. Even under optimistic expectations, however, it offers no solution to the fundamental strategic dilemmas described above. We have merely to look at the record. What it shows is that, while negotiated arms control may work at the margins to moderate competition in some areas, reliance on arms control as a central element in security policy is both illusory and foolhardy. As will be brought out below in connection with the 1972 ABM Treaty, the Soviets manifestly do not share our view of strategic stability and of the role of arms control agreements in bringing it about.

2. *The United States can reduce its commitments abroad* in order to lower demands on U.S. strategic forces in support of the "extended deterrent." As was demonstrated by the narrow defeat of Senator Sam Nunn's recent amendment in the U.S. Senate—which called for U.S. force withdrawals from Europe if the NATO allies failed to carry out their promised increases in defense—such commitment reductions could come about for other reasons. But to stage them on the explicit

premise of a dwindling strategic deterrent would surely be to sound the death knell for NATO as a military alliance and to chart the road to "Fortress America," thereby conceding to the Soviets their primary global objectives.

3. *The United States and its allies could increase and modernize non-nuclear forces*, thus lessening the reliance on the strategic deterrent. This option is highly desirable, but it is not likely to be implemented in adequate measure. Efforts to improve NATO's conventional forces have a long and not very encouraging history. The costs of meaningful modernization, while they certainly are not trivial, are affordable if the Alliance were to muster the will to press along this road. Yet, this will continues to be lacking in Europe as well as in Japan. Moreover, there is resistance in Europe to creating robust conventional capabilities precisely because of the fear of a "decoupling" of the defense of Western Europe from the U.S. strategic deterrent. Finally, NATO seemingly cannot agree on *how* to modernize. A variety of proposed solutions have been under consideration over the past several years. In particular, there is a great debate over the "deep-strike" concept and over the extent to which the Alliance should rely on technology as against operational reform. In sum, this is an appealing option, but unlikely to be realized—certainly not in the near-term.

4. *The United States can modernize the nuclear deterrent*. Such a modernization is required irrespective of possible progress under Option 3 above. The question concerns the direction of the modernization effort.

Strategic Modernization Options

There are three basic choices for modernizing U.S. strategic forces. In simplified form, they include: a continued emphasis on offense, a revolutionary shift to a defensive emphasis as suggested by President Reagan's "Star Wars" initiative, and a balanced mix of offensive and defensive forces.

Offense dominance represents the traditional U.S. approach to the design of its strategic nuclear posture and to the construct of the strategic deterrent. Yet, the approach has reached barren and increasingly dangerous ground. We are engaged in an arms race which the Soviets are winning because they are investing more resources and because their strategic posture and their procurement approach have been more balanced than ours. There are strong pressures in the United States for continuing the past emphasis on strategic offense: it represents an established path and one of least bureaucratic resistance. Yet, these are frail justifications for maintaining a course that bodes increasing jeopardy for the nation's fundamental security.

Defense dominance would veer to the opposite extreme. The President's speech on March 23, 1983, suggested a radical departure in strategy—

toward rendering nuclear weapons obsolete. On the whole, the U.S. Administration still sees this as a long-term goal, although some attention has been devoted lately to interim objectives and capabilities.

Most experts doubt that a perfect defense against ballistic missiles is technically feasible. Yet, no one today can confidently project the technical horizons of the coming decades—at least until far more research has been conducted. What does seem clear is that a U.S. strategic program heavily oriented to defense will be very costly— increasingly so if no constraints are imposed on Soviet offensive deployments. Moreover, there are serious potential instabilities in defense dominance, particularly if the defense itself is vulnerable. Rendering defenses less vulnerable—especially space-based defenses—may present one of the more challenging technical problems. In all, at best decades will be required to fulfill the promise of "Star Wars."

Therefore, even if the United States aims for a dominant defense in the long run, we are likely to witness an offense-defense mix for many years to come. Such a mix can strengthen deterrence and enhance stability. Defenses that are far less than perfect nevertheless can exercise important strategic roles:

• They augur to be reasonably effective against limited nuclear strikes, thus discouraging "cheap shots" by the Soviets or third parties. By permitting the United States the option of defending against, rather than retaliating for, such attacks, they would add a new element to crisis stability.

• They would increase the factors of uncertainty in the calculations of the would-be attacker, thus enhancing deterrence.

• They could strengthen deterrence in the theater and complement air defenses in protecting key facilities and forces abroad.

The idea of defense as a means of inhibiting a potential attacker's confidence in his plan of assault is fully consistent with current U.S. strategic doctrine, which is keyed precisely to this objective, but with offensive forces only. Looking farther ahead, defenses may be essential if deep cuts should eventually be negotiated in U.S. and Soviet offensive forces, for defense would provide a hedge against violations of negotiated ceilings.

Admittedly, the Soviets are not likely to remain inactive in the face of U.S. strategic defense programs. Thus, defenses may lead to new forms of arms competition, but it is not clear what form this competition will take or whether it will hold the dangerous implications of the current race.

The Strategic Defense Initiative

The Administration's Strategic Defense Initiative (SDI) denotes a technology development program; it does not incorporate a decision to deploy strategic defenses. The SDI emerged from six months of intensive study and discussion following the President's speech of March 23, 1983. Three major study efforts were involved: The Defense Technology Study (Fletcher Panel) focused on technology and concepts. The Future Security Strategy Study (Hoffman Study Group) examined the role of defenses in U.S. security policy. Also under the Future Security Strategy Study, an internal Defense Department effort (the Miller Study) centered on policy and strategic stability issues.

A major conclusion of the Defense Technology Study was that some new technologies look very promising in their potential application to missile defense, but need to be explored further. These include:

• Airborne optical sensors with high traffic-handling capability and reduced vulnerability to attack.
• High-acceleration, precision-guided, small interceptors which offer the potential of relatively inexpensive nonnuclear kill.
• Space-based sensors (possibly in deep space) with potentially very impressive traffic-handling capability, speed and discrimination.
• Space-based kinetic energy weapons, which could be available in less than a decade.
• Directed energy weapons, based in space or on the ground (interacting with mirrors in space). The earliest of these directed energy weapons systems are still well over a decade away.

The Study emphasized that considerable effort is needed to explore and test the potential of these technologies and to determine how they might be integrated into defense systems. The vulnerability of the space-based components of a BMD system was singled out as a particularly serious potential problem.

The concept of "layered" defense was examined by all three study groups. Each layer presents a different penetration problem for the offense, blunting some portion of the total attacking force. The principal layers considered were:

• A *boost-phase layer*, which would be primarily space-based and would seek to intercept attacking missiles during their boost-stage, before they can release their warheads and penetration aids.
• A *mid-course layer* featuring space-based sensors and ground-based nonnuclear interceptors.
• A *terminal defense* utilizing airborne optical sensors and ground-based nonnuclear interceptors.

Also under examination is the concept of a preferential defense, in which the defense can cover a wide area and the offensive planner would be uncertain as to precisely what targets would be defended and to what level. This, plus the synergy of several layers, would greatly complicate the attacker's problems in penetrating the defense. Particularly if the attacker is to have high confidence in destroying a larger number of dispersed targets (rather than merely a few cities) in order to achieve his objectives, even modest defenses, by denying that confidence, could exert a substantial deterrent effect.

The Issue of the ABM Treaty

The ABM Treaty of 1972, which sharply curtailed the deployment of anti-ballistic defenses by the two superpowers, is a salient example of the shortcomings of arms control. The Treaty was successfully negotiated because the United States had a program that the Soviets wanted to stop. In the early 1970s, Moscow reached the conclusion that U.S. anti-missile technology was substantially advanced beyond that of the Soviet Union. Thus, the Soviets sought to buy time to catch up. In order to halt the U.S. program, they were prepared to accept certain limits on their own ABM deployments. While this kind of Soviet incentive may improve the prospects of an arms control agreement, it also connotes that the Soviets are motivated primarily by direct considerations of self-interest, rather than by concepts of "stability." Moreover, there are not many situations today where the West is sufficiently ahead of the Soviet Union in military development in order to provide this incentive again.

The ABM Treaty also has illustrated the different behavior by the United States and the Soviet Union under arms control treaties. The Treaty did not prohibit research and development, and the Soviets have vigorously pressed their R & D in various dimensions of anti-missile technology ever since 1972. They have deployed an extensive radar network applicable to a nationwide ballistic missile defense. By contrast, in the United States even the modest requests by the U.S. Defense Department for funding anti-missile research and development have been consistently cut back by the Congress. The prevailing attitude in the Congress has been that, since the Treaty prohibits an ultimate ABM deployment, there is little merit to an energetic R & D effort. Leaving aside the issue of violations—and the U.S. Administration has given to the Congress evidence that the Soviets may have engaged in violations of the ABM Treaty—this history illuminates the inequitable consequences of arms agreements. While we cannot fault the Soviets for our own self-restraint, nevertheless the disparate U.S. and Soviet responses to negotiated arms limitations are a factor that we must constantly keep in mind in our overall arms control approach.

In any event, a consequence of the ABM Treaty is that the Soviets have come from well behind the United States in ABM technology to at least technological parity. Moreover, the ongoing Soviet program within the treaty limits alone has given them a "warm" production base for the potential deployment of a nationwide ABM system if the treaty were abrogated, breached or modified by agreement.

Meanwhile, the Treaty does not loom as an immediate obstacle to the SDI. The program is within the bounds of the ABM Treaty—at least until it were to move into a testing stage late in this decade. Yet, already the mere anticipation of that future contingency has made the SDI a burning issue among those who see the Treaty as the major historic accomplishment of arms control.

While, as has been noted, the Soviets have benefitted from the present treaty, it nevertheless imposes some constraint on their decisions concerning possible BMD deployments. Moscow would probably prefer to place the onus for any breaches of the treaty on the United States. Thus the Soviets are more likely to "creep out" from under the treaty than to "break out." The United States will need to weigh the benefits of ABM Treaty restraints against those of strategic ballistic missile defense at some point in the future. In the meantime, the possible (if not likely) abrogation by the Soviet Union of the Treaty is a contingency that the United States must constantly keep in mind in pursuing its own research and development effort.

The Road of Deterrent Redemption

The West has permitted its once vaunted nuclear deterrent to erode seriously. Thus far the consequences of that erosion have been visible primarily in the political arena. Public attitudes in the West have changed radically in the past decade, with the fear of nuclear war rising to the surface of political life. This shift in attitudes has been prompted by many factors, but it is at least to some extent—perhaps to a considerable one—a consequence of the shifted military balance in favor of the Soviet Union.

We need to strengthen the nuclear deterrent even as we strive to reduce the West's reliance on nuclear weapons through improvements in nonnuclear forces and through whatever can be accomplished in arms control. The way to bolster the nuclear component of deterrence is through a more balanced mix of offensive and defensive measures.

The SDI will permit the United States to explore, and eventually to demonstrate, promising technologies and concepts that could provide for an effective defense against nuclear attack in the future. Such a defense will not have to be perfect in order to muster a significant strategic role. Thus it is important to focus on intermediate options for the partial deployment of defenses, that, although limited in their coverage, could provide a relatively early means of enhancing deterrence.

The road pointed by the SDI faces many obstacles. The costs entailed by the program are bound to be substantial—at least in the longer run. Public and Congressional opposition in the United States already is evident, as is concern in allied countries. The Soviets have begun a propaganda offensive against the defense concept, and it can be expected to be intensified.

Nevertheless, a major stride has been taken merely in the act of placing strategic defense once again on the U.S. policy agenda. Some of the continuing questions on that agenda are:

- What purposes should defense serve?
- What kinds of defenses will this require?
- How rapidly will key technologies progress and be translated into systems?
- What should be the requisite mix of a new offense-defense balance?
- How will it be financed, and what will be the impact on other U.S. military programs?
- What will be the implications for strategic stability and arms control?
- What will be the Soviet reactions, and what will be the impact on our security if they continue to forge ahead in strategic defense?

The last question may be the most important of all in determining the scope and pace of U.S. strategic defense programs. James A. Thompson of the Rand Corporation, in recent testimony before the Defense Subcommittee of the House Appropriations Committee, concluded:

. . . Were we able to obtain a significant advantage over the USSR in strategic defenses, we could have a substantial measure of strategic superiority over them. This would be to our advantage. By the same token, however, should the Soviets obtain a significant advantage over us, the results could be strategically catastrophic for the United States.[5]

The SDI, therefore, represents not only the long-term promise of a revolutionary change in the role of nuclear weapons that was held out in the President's speech of March 1983: it could also usher in the opportunity for fashioning a more secure and stable U.S. deterrent far sooner. And it offers insurance against the prospect that Soviet advances in strategic defense could undermine the U.S. deterrent still further.

NOTES

1. Editorial, *Times of London*, June 13, 1984.

2. Fred S. Hoffman (Study Director), *Ballistic Missile Defenses and U.S. National Security*, Summary Report, prepared for the Future Security Strategy Study (FSSS), October 1983, p. 1.

3. Ibid., p. 2.

4. Michael Howard, "Reassurance and Deterrence: Western Defense in the 1980s," *Foreign Affairs*, Winter 1982/1983, pp. 300–324.

5. James A. Thompson, Statement before the Defense Appropriations Subcommittee of the House Appropriations Committee, May 9, 1984, in Rand Paper Series, P-6985, May 1984.

27

Reykjavik:
An Icelandic Saga

STANLEY HOFFMANN

The Geneva summit of November 1985, held after months of preparation, turned out to be an exercise in deliberate ambiguity.[1] The impro-
vised meeting of Reagan and Gorbachev in Reykjavik resulted in
unprecedented confusion. It took more than a week to dig out what
actually happened from under the public relations rubble accumulated
by American officials, who moved, with breathtaking speed and an eye
on the electorate, from unwarranted despair to unjustified optimism.

What happened in Iceland is a textbook case of careful planning on
one side while the other side was taken by surprise and lost both
initiative and perspective. The Geneva summit had reached a deadlock
over SDI. The Soviets had linked reductions on strategic nuclear
weapons to American willingness to curtail SDI. On these issues, no
progress was made in subsequent arms control negotiations. When
Gorbachev, in the middle of the crisis over the arrest of Nicholas
Daniloff, offered to meet the President in Iceland, the Americans
decided that he probably wanted to clinch an agreement on the
intermediate nuclear forces in Europe, a subject that the Soviets had
untied from SDI and over which much progress had been achieved in
negotiations in Geneva during 1986. A limited deal on reducing the
scope of nuclear tests also seemed possible. However, in Reykjavik
Gorbachev came back to what had been his strategy in Geneva: trading
reductions on offensive weapons for sharp limits on SDI. And he tied
both an agreement on intermediate forces and a deal on weapons testing
to this trade. But he made such a package far more attractive than he did
eleven months earlier, by offering more detailed and in some cases
bigger reductions than before.

The American team was taken by surprise because it had misinterpreted
Gorbachev's game. They thought he needed the guarantee of even a
limited success before agreeing to come to Washington. But to him
Reykjavik was simply Act II in a patient, long-term strategy aimed at
eroding SDI in exchange for deep reductions. His concern is with the
central front, so to speak, not with the sideshows. In Geneva, and in the
negotiations that followed, Soviet offers had failed to produce concessions from Reagan on SDI, yet Reagan's desire for an arms control
success, and his dream of moving toward a nonnuclear world, clearly

clashed with his drive for an uninhibited SDI. For Gorbachev, Reykjavik was a safe gamble. Aimed at smoking out Reagan, the Soviet plan would either lead to a breakthrough if Reagan finally accepted the deal, or make Reagan appear as an obstinate spoiler, and thus concentrate the world's attention on SDI if he didn't.

If this was a trap, as right-wing commentators put it, the best tactic for the American delegation would have been to refuse to fall into it and to move the meeting back to subjects of possible agreement, the only ones for which the Americans were prepared. A Soviet refusal would have put the onus for failure on Moscow. Instead, the meeting turned into an extravagant marathon in which Reagan's advisers went, in two days, much farther than during all the previous months, and the two chiefs found themselves lifted from the harsh realities and complexities of nuclear negotiations to competitive visions of utopia. The only concrete and definitive outcome such a magic carpet ride could have had would have been the sketch of a deal on offensive weapons and SDI. But that would have required, after Reykjavik, a far more detailed set of understandings than the two leaders could ever have drafted in two days.

The behavior of the American team, both at Reykjavik and after, vindicated Henry Kissinger's belief that affairs of state are too serious to be left to chiefs of government at summit meetings. On leaving Reykjavik, the American negotiators appeared, at first, deeply depressed, because they had hoped to come away from Iceland with some deals and had let themselves be tantalized by all the sweeping reductions the Soviets had dangled in front of them. They switched to equally excessive euphoria when, for reasons of image making and electoral politics, they chose to stress the magnitude of what had "almost" been accomplished, and exaggerated this quite a bit.

What was actually accomplished can be divided into two parts: the promise of a somewhat better nuclear world, and the delusion of a world beyond nuclear weapons. Concerning the former, it is now clear that what is within reach is (1) an agreement on intermediate nuclear forces, which would eliminate them in Europe and sharply reduce the number of Soviet SS-20s in Asia; (2) an agreement on reductions in strategic offensive weapons between 1986 and 1991, although the hyperbolic estimate of cuts amounting to 50 percent of such weapons ought to be resisted: the cuts in warheads and in launchers that were discussed do not amount to 50 percent, and some important issues, such as the scope of reductions affecting Soviet heavy land-based missiles—the missiles the US fears most—and sea-launched cruise missiles, were left vague; (3) an agreement on tests, short of a comprehensive ban.

This is not negligible. It is true that purely quantitative reductions do not remove the factors of instability and the incentives for preventive attack that the developments of the past fifteen years—including the multiplication of accurate, vulnerable, and unverifiable weapons, the flaws of command and control systems—have created. Nevertheless, reductions in weapons that cannot be used without disastrous consequence, and are in any case far too numerous to find "suitable" targets, are obviously desirable; and an agreement on reducing their numbers would also improve the political relations between the great powers.

However, even this road remains strewn with obstacles. The deal on intermediate forces discussed in Iceland goes beyond the mere reduction of SS-20s and American intermediate missiles to one hundred warheads on each side that had been envisaged before: it goes back to the famous "zero option" the Reagan administration had offered in 1981 in the firm belief that the Soviets would reject it. Those European leaders and NATO officials who had, at the time, argued for American deployment of intermediate missiles in Europe because their presence there would mean that Western Europe's security was clearly "coupled" to that of America, are beginning to complain that the removal of these weapons is a "decoupling" step, even if the SS-20s disappear and short-range weapons aimed at Western Europe are kept at current numbers. For Western Europe would still be exposed both to these weapons and to Soviet long-range strategic missiles, notwithstanding the presence of the NATO submarine fleet.

As for the complete package of agreements, it still depends on a resolution of the issue of SDI. Many observers have argued that a deal is possible, in the form of an interim agreement that would commit the US to the observance, for ten years, of the ABM treaty of 1972, i.e., to discarding the broad and self-serving interpretation of the treaty the Reagan administration developed in 1985. (Under this interpretation, ABM systems based on "other physical principles" than those that existed in 1972, for instance space-based lasers, are not prohibited by the treaty.) An interim agreement would also define with some precision such controversial terms as "components" of defensive systems (a term used in the ABM treaty) or "elements" of such systems (a term used in Gorbachev's draft proposals) or "laboratory research and testing." Such an interim agreement would also prevent the kinds of tests and deployments allowed by the ABM treaty—those of antitactical missile defenses and antisatellite weapons—from being used for the development of SDI.

Contrary to early reports, a compromise along these lines was not at all ruled out by Gorbachev's formula for an agreement on SDI at Reykjavik. Nor would such a compromise have obliged Reagan to give up either his dream of perfect defenses, or his more recent notion of defenses deployed as insurance against Soviet cheating, or accidents, or third nuclear powers. Few experts believe either that SDI could be deployed effectively during the next ten years, or that the kind of restrictions an interim agreement would entail would be fatal to research on SDI.

But Reagan may well fear that if such restrictions persist, SDI would never go beyond the research stage, given the extraordinary technological complexities of the program, its astronomical price tag, and the magnitude of the countermeasures Moscow might take. (Kissinger has written that even the very loose moratorium Reagan had offered to Moscow would lead to the abandonment of SDI.)[2] Moreover, Gorbachev also demanded that, at the end of the interim agreement, further moves, i.e., the possibility of SDI deployments, be subjected to "mutually acceptable" decisions: no unilateral pursuit of SDI would ultimately be possible. This is the opposite of Reagan's own proposal. Here we reach the issue of the world of the 1990s, and move from reality to utopia.

Both Reagan and Gorbachev have proposed drastic cuts in offensive nuclear weapons beyond 1991. Most experts agree that after a certain stage, when the numbers of offensive weapons on both sides have become low, each side is likely to worry increasingly about the vulnerability of the remaining ones, and about the decisive advantage the other side might gain from a major deception or technological breakthrough. Verification would become essential as cutbacks continue. Moreover, both sides, for different reasons, may fear that such reductions would severely impair their range of strategic choices. Soviet strategy has always envisaged a preemptive strike against the US, in order to limit damage to the USSR should war break out or appear inevitable. The US envisages attacks on Soviet military targets should Moscow's forces threaten to take over Western Europe.[3]

Whether each side, when confronted with such uncertainties, would want to proceed anyhow is far from obvious. But again, SDI complicates matters. Reagan wants it as a safeguard against Soviet deception or attacks. Gorbachev wants none of it. One of the main Soviet reasons for opposing SDI is the fear that a defensive shield would serve an offensive purpose as long as the US has any nuclear weapons—by allowing the US to believe that it could attack the Soviet Union without exposing itself to devastating retaliation. The problem with Reagan's position is that SDI, even unfettered from the constraints of the ABM treaty, may not be ready to play its role as an insurance policy by the early 1990s. It may well be hard, moreover, to convince Congress and the public that a program first presented as a response to Soviet heavy offensive missiles becomes even more necessary once these missiles are drastically cut back.

Let us assume, nevertheless, that dramatic cuts continue in the 1990s. Toward what end? At Reykjavik, as in the not so distant past—the Fifties and early Sixties, when both sides hurled plans of complete and general disarmament at each other—there was a remarkable difference between the two sides. The Soviet vision, first stated by Gorbachev last January, is that of a world without any superpower nuclear weapons or defensive systems at the end of ten years. Reagan proposed only the abolition of offensive ballistic missiles, also after ten years (although both Reagan and Donald Regan, after the meeting, talked about eliminating all nuclear weapons, and Gorbachev, in his speech of October 22, stated that Reagan had indeed, "albeit without special enthusiasm," consented to the elimination of all offensive nuclear arms[4]). Neither conception is acceptable to the other side. The Soviet design would either turn the other nuclear powers into superpowers, or depend on their being coerced into nuclear disarmament: an unlikely prospect. Moreover, even if this hurdle could be overcome, it would result in a world dominated no longer by the nuclear balance of terror, but by a conventional balance of power, which favors the USSR unless the US and its allies make a vast and costly effort at conventional rearmament, or unless both sides agree on large reductions in conventional forces: prospects that are hard to visualize, much less count on. Talks about such reductions in Europe have been going on fruitlessly for fifteen years.

As for the American scheme, it would remove from America's soil the threat of a Soviet ballistic missile attack, but preserve nuclear weapons on bombers and cruise missile systems in which the US has a major advantage. The US could still attack Soviet targets, for instance if a war breaks out in Europe or the Middle East. By consenting to such a scheme, Moscow would (1) wipe out its own current advantage (in numbers of ballistic missiles), (2) consolidate America's advantage, and (3) allow the US to deploy SDI, despite the disappearance of the only weapons (ballistic missiles) against which it is devised. Insofar as the other major Soviet reason for hostility to SDI is its general technological significance—i.e., the Soviet fear that it would widen the technological gap between Washington and Moscow and set back decisively the Soviet Union in its persistent quest for status and equality in world affairs—the American plan is clearly unacceptable.

The proponents of "disarmament" and those of "arms control," the radical champions of "abolition," and the moderate advocates of "amelioration" have been adversaries not only throughout the nuclear age but ever since the appearance of a world of sovereign states. Usually, statesmen have been either heady players of the game of power or, at best, moderates. Academics, theologians, philosophers have been prominent among the disarmers and abolitionists. When American and Soviet statesmen join their ranks, one must ask why. It may be for public relations reasons—joining the antinuclear bandwagon. Both Reagan's SDI (the perfect shield) and Gorbachev's proposal of last January,

Russia's clever move in this public chess game, try to exploit the longing for a saner world. It may be because a leap into a radically different world would actually benefit their own country's interests: This is most likely to be Gorbachev's other motive. It may also be because of a belief that all mankind would be better off. This seems to be George Shultz's reason for endorsing a world without nuclear ballistic missiles:

> If ever anything starts, thirty minutes later it's over with these awesome ballistic missiles. And there's nothing left of them and there's nothing left of us. . . .
>
> But if we can get rid of the threat of offensive ballistic missiles to us, which, remember, comes very fast—once they're shot off they can't be recalled—and they have a devastating impact. If we can get rid of that threat, which is the first time—the first time our land has been threatened, really, since the War of 1812, is by these ballistic missiles—we're better off.
>
> And no doubt, if you say, why then is the Soviet Union interested—the Soviet Union has shown over many wars that they are heroic in defending their homeland. Invading somebody else is another question, but they are heroic in defending their homeland.
>
> And so, they also must be concerned about the ballistic missiles that we have that can wipe that homeland out. So that's basically the essence of it.[5]

But quite apart from whether the West has the will and resources to match Soviet conventional forces, as Shultz argues, we have to think seriously about the more frequent objection to total nuclear disarmament, raised especially by many Western European officials (and by most Frenchmen). While a failure of nuclear deterrence could be fatal, "mutual assured destruction" (or rather deterrence) has proved to be workable: the superpowers have carefully avoided major military confrontations. However convincing the abstract arguments that the weapons are "unusable" because of the damage that would result from the other side's retaliation, uncertainty about their possible use acts as a deterrent. Historical experience shows, alas, that conventional deterrence has been far less successful: See even today the record of wars among nonnuclear powers. A "conventional" world would not live under the threat of total nuclear destruction, but conventional wars between the major powers might become far more likely again. Is that what we want?

Thus, after Reykjavik, we are faced with two major issues. In the months or years to come, Gorbachev will probably persist in his strategy of eroding SDI. He has warned that he counts on the "changeable internal political weather" in the US. In exchange for sticking to the concessions he made, he will keep insisting on a limitation of SDI. While even the reductions he offers do not fundamentally change our nuclear predicaments, they are important. At the same time, SDI, which has proved to be an excellent "bargaining chip," remains a source of confusion in the US. If one thinks of the maximalist claims made for it, it is a dangerous, unconvincing, and costly extravagance. In the more modest form of a protection for land-based missiles, or of "insurance" against the concealment of ballistic missiles, it is a program that begins to make sense only after reductions in offensive forces are agreed upon—yet its pursuit only makes such an agreement impossible. The two obstacles to a realistic reconsideration of SDI are the President's continuing dream of a perfect umbrella and the apocalyptic defense of SDI by hard-liners who are opposed to arms control and look toward the far-off day when SDI will confer on the US invincible power over the Soviet Union, notwithstanding all the evidence that this too is a fantasy.

The other issue is the shape of the world after a process curtailing the nuclear arms race has been carried out. Even though *The Wall Street Journal* tells us that MAD (mutual assured destruction) is dead,[6] it remains our condition until nuclear weapons have all been abolished—and even then the world will still live in their shadow, since they can be destroyed, but not de-discovered. Even if nobody cheats, they could, like the rats of Camus's *The Plague*, always return someday. Moreover, those who express the new, understandable, but somewhat facile revulsion against nuclear deterrence and cry for a world without nuclear weapons should start addressing some very tough questions, not only the Machiavellian one, of who would benefit most from a return to prenuclear politics, but also the ethical, or Kantian question: Do we want to make the world safe for the kinds of conventional wars that have devastated it twice during the first half of this century; or do we realize that the most fundamental issue in world politics is not the use or threat of nuclear force, but the use or threat of *force*, whether nuclear or not?

NOTES

1. See my analysis of Geneva and critique of SDI, "Fog Over the Summit," *The New York Review* (January 16).

2. *Newsweek* (October 13, 1986), p. 40.

3. Cf., Joseph S. Nye, Jr., "Farewell to Arms Control?" *Foreign Affairs* (Fall 1986), pp. 1–20.

4. *The New York Times* (October 23, 1986), p. A12.

5. From Shultz's interview on *The McNeil-Lehrer News Hour* (October 17, 1986).

6. Editorial, "Arms Control Unchained" (October 17, 1986), p. 28.

28

Nuclear Proliferation:
A Cause for Optimism?

D. W. HIESTER

INTRODUCTION

. . . The proliferation of nuclear weapons by any states that do not already possess them is an undesirable development for the global system that should be strenuously resisted. While an exposition of this argument is outside the scope of this article, it needs to be asserted clearly and not held to be a truism, since a number of analysts share the view that ". . . the measured spread of nuclear weapons is more to be welcomed than feared."[1] The contrary view, advocated here, is that the risks and uncertainties of further nuclear proliferation are such that they should neither be ignored nor viewed benignly.[2]

A second assumption is that the prospect of an international system with no further nuclear weapons proliferation is a realistic goal. What is striking in most of the writing on the subject is the tendency to assume that some proliferation is likely and unavoidable, no matter how undesirable. According to this view, concentration should be on elucidating policy choices aimed at limiting the rate and degree of proliferation that is bound to occur.[3]

The Current Situation

Several recent events have combined to change the air of pessimism pervading discussion of nuclear weapon issues. Most importantly, 'talks about talks' between the United States and the Soviet Union have led to a decision to begin a series of 'umbrella' negotiations in Geneva in March, the objectives of which ". . . will be to work out effective agreements aimed at preventing an arms race in space and terminating it on Earth, at limiting and reducing nuclear arms, and at strengthening strategic stability."[4] Whatever their outcome, the fact that the talks will have begun between the Superpowers with the ultimate aim of ". . . the complete elimination of nuclear arms everywhere," is bound to have a significant impact on international discussions of non-proliferation.

Leaving aside a discussion of either its merits or viability, the Strategic Defence Initiative (SDI) announced by President Reagan (which some have argued is the major factor which precipitated these new Soviet-American talks) has already started a long-term re-examination of the basic premise that the structure of nuclear deterrence between the NWS is stable. Whatever its outcome, this examination is bound to have a profound effect on the non-proliferation regime.

Finally, the recent agreement by the Soviet Union to allow international inspection of some of its nuclear power utilities for the first time, following similar moves by the United States, Britain and France, seemed to be timed with a view to influencing the September review conference.[5]

Definitions

Discussions of nuclear proliferation can be a definitional minefield.[6] The dictionary meaning of proliferate is to increase *rapidly* in numbers. However, in nuclear terms, the acquisition or explosion of even one nuclear device by a state which has not previously possessed any would be cited as a case of nuclear proliferation. *Vertical proliferation* is an increase, either quantitative or qualitative, in nuclear weapons by states already possessing them. *Horizontal proliferation* is an increase in the number of states possessing nuclear weapons. A *nuclear weapon* is held to be a nuclear explosive device coupled with a means of delivery.

It is with this definition that ambiguity begins to creep into the subject and it is precisely this ambiguity which certain states seek to exploit. Proliferation is said to require an overt act, an explosion. India exploded a nuclear device in 1974, but classified it as a Peaceful Nuclear Explosion (PNE) and declared its intention not to acquire nuclear weapons. Most observers would consider India to be a nuclear-weapons-capable state although not necessarily a NWS.

But the most important issue is that of *potential* nuclear weapons states, the growing number of states which are acquiring the means necessary for constructing a nuclear device but which leave their intentions undeclared, deliberately ambiguous, or openly declare their right and intention to acquire the technological capability without actually constructing a device. It is this category of states, most of whom have not signed the NPT, which causes the most concern in the short and medium term for the non-proliferation regime.

Attempts at Control

The nuclear era began in 1945 with the explosion on July 16, at Alamogordo, New Mexico, of the first nuclear device by the United States. There followed, on August 6th and August 9th, 1945, the attacks on Hiroshima and Nagasaki, the only time nuclear weapons have been used in warfare and the point at which the world became aware of their existence and their awful potential for destruction. Since then, there have been attempts to control, internationalise, or eliminate nuclear weapons. The first of these was the Baruch Plan which would have created an International Atomic Development Authority. The plan never got off the ground, mainly because the Soviet Union could hardly be expected to accept a US monopoly in this important area of knowledge, but it did leave behind a set of ideas which would be taken up again.

By 1953, the US nuclear monopoly had been broken, and in December of that year President Eisenhower proposed the 'Atoms for Peace' programme. The nuclear power industry was beginning to emerge as a spin-off from the research and development which had been carried out by the military sector. As this technology spread, there was an obvious desire on the part of the United States to benefit from its technological lead, but also to control the potentially dangerous aspects of the unrestricted world-wide growth of a nuclear power industry. It was foreseen that although in the case of the United States, the Soviet Union, and the United Kingdom, the nuclear power industry had been an outgrowth of military research and development, the reverse could occur and other states might seek to acquire civilian nuclear power technology as the starting point to a nuclear weapon programme.

As a result, the International Atomic Energy Agency (IAEA) was established in Vienna in 1957. The bargain offered was that states which accepted IAEA safeguards and inspection would receive assistance with their civil nuclear industries from the states already possessing the technology, the implication being that the participating states would not acquire nuclear weapons.

The next stage in the development of a nuclear non-proliferation regime required an evolution in the relations between the United States and the Soviet Union which would enable them to work together. These events will not be traced here but they resulted in the United States and the Soviet Union, together with the United Kingdom, sponsoring the NPT which was signed in 1968 and came into force on March 5th, 1970. By 1984, there were 123 NNWS participants in addition to the three sponsoring NWS.[7]

This act of co-operation between the US and the USSR, however dramatic in light of their past history, was based on mutual self-interest which was clear for all to see. More significant for the future of a successful non-proliferation regime, however, was the list of states which refused to join the NPT. This included two NWS, China and France. India refused to sign and exploded a device in 1974. Among the other non-signatories, it is the so-called 'threshold' states that are the major cause for concern. These include Israel, Pakistan, South Africa, Brazil, and Argentina. All are seen, for different reasons, to be potential proliferators, both in capability and motivation.

Interpretation

Many observers tend to view proliferation as widespread, continuing, and inevitable. Part of their conviction can be traced back to the 1974 Indian explosion. Until India became a nuclear state in 1974, there seemed to be a logical limit to the number of nuclear weapon states: first the two major victors of the Second World War, the new Superpowers, then Britain, and finally France and China. They were the five permanent members of the Security Council of the United Nations. For a decade this situation held, then came the Indian explosion. This event coincided with the 1974 oil crises and a perception of energy insecurity on the part of many states which led to an increased interest in nuclear power as an alternative source of energy.

A renewed concern about the dangers of nuclear proliferation followed these events. These fears were based on two related assumptions. The first was that there was an inextricable link between civil nuclear power technology, which was now becoming widespread, and the military uses of nuclear technology. States would simply move on a technological conveyor belt from one to the other. Much of this reasoning was based on the fact that although knowledge about nuclear bomb construction was widely available, the critical factor in becoming a NWS was access to weapons grade material. A nuclear power programme led to expertise in the creation and handling of nuclear fuels.

The second assumption was that if a state *could* acquire the bomb, it *would* acquire the bomb. The temptation provided by the capability would prove too great. Nuclear weapons proliferation was therefore inevitable and the concern became when, where, and how it would stop. The 'nth' country problem had been born.[8]

An entirely different interpretation can be put on the situation. What is striking is how slow and limited nuclear weapon proliferation has been given the dramatic impact nuclear weapons have had on the international system. We are living in the fifth decade of the nuclear era and yet there are only five known NWS. It is over ten years since India became the only other state known to have exploded a nuclear device.

The Nuclear States—1st Explosion

USA	1945
USSR	1949
UK	1952
FRANCE	1960
CHINA	1964
INDIA (PNE)	1974

There has not been a new entrant into the NWS 'club' in over twenty years and no new state has exploded a nuclear device in over ten years. Given the widespread dissemination of both knowledge and technology, this trend is both remarkable and reassuring.

Many commentators would argue that these observations miss the point entirely. Overt proliferation, explosion of a device, is no longer the issue. It is covert or latent proliferation, the acquisition of the potential to go nuclear in a short period of time, which many states are now actively pursuing, which is the problem. Moreover, they would argue that the twenty, or ten, year intervals have been just that, intervals, while states caught up with the technology, and that we now stand at the threshold of potentially rapid overt proliferation, with Pakistan at the head of the queue. Nuclear weapons confer power and prestige and the existing NWS presents an example that potential proliferators will inevitably emulate. The fact that India is often suggested as a sixth permanent member of the Security Council adds a certain strength to this reasoning. In addition, at least one state, Israel, is assumed to have already crossed the threshold without openly declaring or demonstrating its capability.

The important example to many potential proliferators, however, may not be the NWS, but the states that could go nuclear but do not, and yet still carry considerable power and/or prestige in the international system. Canada, Japan, the Federal Republic of Germany, Sweden—for different reasons none of these states has become a nuclear power although they have the capability. At present these states feel they are better off without the bomb than with it and it is this perception of their motivations which those concerned with non-proliferation should seek to perpetuate.

The above examples also lend weight to the proposition that nuclear weapons are not a technological inevitability once a nuclear programme has been embarked upon. The decision to become a NWS is about political choice, not technological innovation. A successful non-proliferation strategy will combine positive incentives to non-proliferation as well as disincentives to going nuclear.

Before looking at specific actions that might be taken to strengthen the non-proliferation regime, the cases of Pakistan and Israel need to be examined.

Pakistan

Consideration of Pakistan and its future actions is crucial to an understanding of the prospects for proliferation and the maintenance of the non-proliferation regime. Attempts by Pakistan, beginning in the early 1970s, to acquire both uranium enrichment and plutonium reprocessing facilities are widely known and have been extensively reported. Since the beginning of the 1980s, speculation has been rife that Pakistan was about to explode a nuclear device. Significantly, this has not yet occurred.

Throughout this period Pakistan has denied any intention to construct a nuclear bomb and has cited its widely acknowledged need for energy as the impetus to its peaceful nuclear programme. On the eve of Pakistan's recent elections, President Zia ul-Haq, while admitting success in uranium enrichment techniques, reiterated that it was being used for peaceful purposes and continued to deny that there was outside help from Libya or China.[9]

The reason for unease over Pakistan's nuclear intentions are obvious. India is Pakistan's major security concern. This has only been heightened by uncertainty over India's nuclear policy since 1974. Moreover, status and prestige are not irrelevant and the imputed desire to be the first state to acquire the 'Islamic Bomb,' aided and abetted by Libya, is said to be important.

The primary disincentive to Pakistan openly acquiring nuclear weapons is the nearly universal view that this will lead to greater insecurity for Pakistan. If Pakistan explodes a nuclear device, India will almost certainly start a nuclear weapons development programme of its own, precisely the outcome which Pakistan must want to avoid.

If Pakistan continues its assumed weapons research programme, the best that can be hoped for is that it never tests and never declares its possession of nuclear weapons, following the example of Israel. Should Pakistan explode a device, two outcomes are possible. One is that the view of the pessimists would be confirmed and more latent proliferators would follow Pakistan across the threshold to overt proliferation. Alternatively, the loss rather than the gain in security which Pakistan would suffer; the loss rather than the gain in prestige by becoming the proliferator in, and destabilizer of, the region; the loss in economic, technological, and military aid which would be sure to follow; and the inevitable international opprobrium which would fall upon Pakistan, all would combine to give pause to any state intending to follow it into the nuclear 'club.' Pakistan might in fact be the *last* nuclear state. For all these reasons, as each year passes without a Pakistani test explosion, the less likely it becomes, because the decision to do so becomes more difficult for its leaders.

Israel

It is generally accepted that Israel either has the bomb or is capable of assembling it so quickly that it makes no difference. It is also known that a number of other Middle Eastern states have nuclear programmes of varying degrees of sophistication. What does not necessarily follow from this is the commonly held view that nuclear proliferation in the region is inevitable.[10]

Israel falls into a category of international actors called 'pariah states.' A 'pariah state' is one whose legitimacy and/or continued right to exist as a distinct entity is called into question by a significant number of other actors in the system. The assumption is that such states will acquire nuclear weapons as a last resort to defend against a threat to their existence if they find themselves under attack from some, and abandoned by other, states in the system.[11] Israel is assumed to have the bomb as its ultimate deterrent to Arab attack and as an insurance policy against loss of US support.

But Israel has not tested, deployed, or declared that it has the bomb. Instead it pursues a policy of carefully orchestrated ambiguity. Officially, it declares it will not be the first or second state to introduce nuclear weapons into the region. Since both the United States and the Soviet Union are assumed to have already done so aboard their ships in the area, the declaration itself is intended to add official force to the policy of nuclear ambiguity.

Israel has strong incentives not to proliferate openly. This would undoubtedly lead to a number of Arab states eventually doing the same and to creation of the security threat Israeli policy seeks to avoid. Keeping the issue ambiguous actually creates incentives for the Arab states not to proliferate. Encouraging speculation about an Israeli bomb is a more effective deterrent than openly declaring that it exists. The restraints on Israel become reciprocal; "If you don't, we won't." This provides cause for reasonable optimism that nuclear weapon proliferation in the Middle East is at least not inevitable.

Some observers would argue that this is wishful thinking. The nuclear development programmes of many states in the region are well-known and documented. The question is not whether proliferation will occur but how, when, and at what pace and with what impact on the stability of the area. Shai Feldman, for instance, arguing that the dangers inherent in the transitional period from non-nuclear to nuclear status are great, proposes that an active policy of proliferation management should be pursued by the states themselves and outside powers, even if this actually encourages further proliferation.[12]

This seems to be dangerous advice based on an unnecessary acquiescence in a process that is far from inevitable. Admittedly, the states of the region pursue research and make huge investments which involve them in paying opportunity costs elsewhere. However, as has already been argued, the technology need not lead automatically to the bomb. The research has other applications. Moreover, acquiring the technical capability to go nuclear without developing it is the new option for many states both in and outside the region. This approach can preserve independence and feelings of national pride and sovereignty without running the risks inherent in pursuing development leading to open proliferation. It is this behaviour that is to be encouraged and managed, not a dangerous acquiescence in a non-inevitable process.

Specific Measures

The argument so far has concentrated on explaining why proliferation has been slow and limited and on proposing a speculative thesis that this situation could be maintained and that cause for optimism about containing nuclear proliferation is just as reasonable as the more pessimistic views that are prevalent in the literature. Is this, then, an argument for apathy based on a "satisfied view of the past"[13] projected into the future? No! As well as trying to create an atmosphere of optimism about preventing any further nuclear proliferation instead of acquiescing in a pessimistic prognosis, which could lead to a self-fulfilling outcome, there are some very important specific steps which can and should be taken. First and foremost, the NPT, whatever its faults and weaknesses, is still the most important bulwark against proliferation that exists, as much for non-members as for the signatories. Every effort must be made to maintain, then strengthen and broaden the scope of its coverage. It is essential that the NWS demonstrate in a tangible way their intention to keep their part of the NPT bargain and show some progress towards halting and then reversing vertical proliferation. If they do not, the widespread consensus on which the Treaty is based will dissolve, and with it any hope of bringing the states that remain outside the regime into the NPT.

One very specific step which the United States, the Soviet Union, and the United Kingdom could take would be to conclude a Comprehensive Test Ban Treaty (CTBT). The 1963 partial test ban treaty and subsequent agreements limited these states to underground nuclear test explosions of no more than 150 kilotons. A comprehensive ban would be on all testing by the signatories. This would serve two functions. It would limit the ability of the NWS to design new weapons and therefore put a strong restraint on vertical proliferation. This would be a powerful demonstration to the NNWS of the seriousness of purpose of the NWS, as well as being a further constraint on potential horizontal proliferation by creating a strong normative inhibition to any state exploding a nuclear device. In December, 1984, the UN General Assembly passed a resolution calling on the CTB committee of the Conference on Disarmament (CD) in Geneva to resume work. Significantly, no NWS voted against the resolution.[14]

A CTB is certainly not a panacea nor is it without significant technical and political difficulties.[15] Testing is important in ensuring the safety of nuclear stockpiles. Verification is a serious problem that has bedevilled the negotiations and should not be underestimated. However, existing and proposed seismic detection networks should be able to cope with all but the most sophisticated attempts at circumvention. Even if evasion were possible by the Superpowers, such evasion would be minimal and unlikely in itself to lead to developments which would undermine the central strategic balance between them. The benefits to both of a CTBT which strengthened the non-proliferation regime would be great. An early CTB might be most difficult for the United Kingdom, since it might present severe obstacles to its strategic modernization programme, but that, of course, is precisely the object of the exercise.

The balance of risks and benefits seems strongly to favour a CTB from the point of view of the NWS, and the barriers remain largely political, not technical. The incentives to political agreement on this issue are now very strong.

CONCLUSION

The striking thing about nuclear proliferation is that, while many see it as a widespread inevitability, it can still be said in 1985 that there has been little of it and its pace has been slow. Most states feel that they are better off without the bomb and it is this perception that should be encouraged and sustained. The basis of a non-proliferation strategy must be political, coupled with specific agreements and safeguard programmes. The NPT, IAEA, ideas drawn from the International Nuclear Fuel Cycle Evaluation (INFCE), a CTBT, bilateral safeguards in individual cases of technology transfer, all have a role to play. But the essential effort must be political, not technical, because choosing to go nuclear is a political, not a technical, decision. Attempts to control proliferation by technical fixes that are not universally accepted only mistake the cause and are therefore certain to be ineffective as well as practically unworkable; they may actually become a cause of proliferation if they reinforce feelings of discrimination on the part of potential proliferators who see the NWS as trying to protect their privileges and position in the international system.[16]

Hard choices will have to be made. If and when the 'pariah states' are 'redeemed' by the international system, their incentives to proliferate may be removed. Until that time, the Superpowers may have to extend security guarantees as a carrot to non-proliferation, and these may prove unpalatable to domestic and international public opinion. This opens up the so-called 'doves' dilemma,' where the supply of conventional arms, and the threat to halt their supply, are used to 'buy off' proliferation. Halting nuclear proliferation by boosting the conventional arms trade is seen as not only wrong but potentially self-defeating. Debates ensue as to whether provision of defensive conventional arms can stabilize a region while offensive arms do not.[17] Decisions in this area are never clear-cut or easy.

By far the greatest inhibition to proliferation is the perception on the part of potential proliferators that acquiring nuclear weapons will turn into a disaster for themselves, leading other states to acquire them in response, resulting in greater insecurity for the proliferators and instability for their region. The more states that participate in the non-proliferation regime, the greater the pressure on the states remaining outside not to proliferate and the greater the international odium that will fall on the first proliferator. The NWS and the non-nuclear advanced industrial states can employ carrots and sticks to encourage these perceptions.

The greatest contribution the NWS, especially the two Superpowers, can make is to begin to control vertical proliferation and move to reducing their arsenals. For their part, once the NWS take real and not just token steps in this direction, the NNWS must be willing to accept a double standard of nuclear 'haves' and 'have nots' if nuclear non-proliferation is the goal in a world where nuclear disarmament is not possible.

For those states that appear perilously close to proliferating, and for whom weapons acquisition *seems* almost inevitable, encouragement to follow the Israeli approach is still preferable to overt proliferation.[18] This is neither hypocritical nor foolish. The technical and military uncertainties for a state that has never tested its weapons are great, while the pressures against a political decision to explode a device and become an overt proliferator are enormous in the face of an international behavioural norm against such action.

George Quester has written,

> The most appropriate application of a realpolitik perspective to the nuclear proliferation question is thus certainly not to scoff at whether there is a problem or to hint that these weapons must spread by some sort of natural law, just as every other weapon has spread in the past. It is rather to note some high priority for the prevention of this spread, along with a frank realization that this will have to be achieved at a substantial cost elsewhere.[19]

Nuclear weapons are political weapons. They will not go away, but neither is their spread inevitable. Political leaders and analysts alike have a duty to concentrate the minds of decision-makers in potential nuclear states on the negative factors and not to create a self-fulfilling prophecy by virtually talking states into nuclear proliferation. In this vital area, atmosphere, tone, and perception count for a lot. Prestige, security, international approbation and free access to the peaceful uses of nuclear energy must be associated with the norm of abnegation of nuclear weapons.

NOTES

1. Kenneth N. Waltz, "The Spread of Nuclear Weapons: More May Be Better", *Adelphi Paper No. 171*, IISS, London, 1981, p. 30.

2. For discussions of this position see Ted Greenwood, "Discouraging Proliferation in the Next Decade and Beyond" in Ted Greenwood, *et al., Nuclear Proliferation*, McGraw-Hill, New York, 1977, pp. 27–30, and Joseph S. Nye, "Sustaining Non-Proliferation in the 1980s", *Survival*, Vol. XXIII, No. 3, May/June 1981, p. 104.

3. See footnote 2, Nye, pp. 104–105.

4. Joint Soviet-U.S. statement issued in Geneva on 8 January 1985.

5. *Financial Times*, 22 February 1985.

6. See Greenwood, "Discouraging Proliferation in the Next Decade and Beyond", *op. cit.*, pp. 30–36, and Nye, "Sustaining Non-Proliferation in the 1980s", *op. cit.*, pp. 104–105.

7. Chalmers Hardenbergh, "News of Negotiations," *ADIU Report*, Vol. 6 No. 6, November–December 1984, p. 13.

8. See criticism of this view by Richard K. Betts, "Paranoids, Pygmies, Pariahs and Nonproliferation", *Foreign Policy*, No. 26, Spring 1977, pp. 162–163.

9. *The Observer*, 24 February 1985.

10. For an exposition of this view see Shai Feldman, "A Nuclear Middle East", *Survival*, Vol. XXIII, No. 3, May/June 1981, pp. 107–115.

11. For a discussion of "pariah states" see Betts, "Paranoids, Pygmies, Pariahs and Nonproliferation", *op. cit.*, pp. 166–167, and Robert E. Harkavy, "Pariah states and nuclear proliferation", *International Organization*, Vol. 35, No. 1, Winter 1981, pp. 135–163.

12. Feldman, "A Nuclear Middle East," *op. cit.*, p. 115.

13. Nye, "Sustaining Non-Proliferation in the 1980s", *op. cit.*, p. 98.

14. Chalmers Hardenbergh, "News of Negotiations", *ADIU Report*, Vol. 7, No. 1, January–February 1985, p. 11.

15. For a discussion of these difficulties see Farooq Hussain, "The Impact of Weapons Test Restrictions", *Adelphi Paper No. 165*, IISS, London, 1981.

16. Nye, "Sustaining Non-Proliferation in the 1980s", *op. cit.*, p. 106.

17. For a review of these arguments see George H. Quester, "Nuclear proliferation: linkages and solutions", *International Organization*, Vol. 33, No. 4, Autumn, 1979, pp. 553–556.

18. Gerald Segal *et al., Nuclear War & Nuclear Peace*, Macmillan, London, 1983, pp. 31–32.

19. Quester, "Nuclear proliferation: linkages and solutions", *op. cit.*, p. 566.

PART THREE
The Crisis of Institutions

In Part Three we deal with a variety of institutions: international and domestic, political and economic. We also examine the roles of individuals in these organizations, as bureaucrats and as leaders.

Many of those concerned with ways to bring order to world politics have been intrigued with the possibility of world government—a global union in which a United States of the World would provide supervision and restraint to the management of relations among nations. Presumably, through an international parliament with binding powers on its members, conflict would be restricted. Others have viewed this solution as either unachievable, undesirable, or downright utopian; instead, they advocate the concept of collective security as embodied in both the charters of the League of Nations and the United Nations. Although the organizational differences between these two institutions are great, both were founded on the belief that international politics could be partially ordered by an agreement among states to deter and control their conflicts. The League of Nations ended in dismal failure, and many are disillusioned with the United Nations. The UN is seen by many as a tool of national interests (its organs a weapon in the hands of those who can obtain a majority in a given dispute) and a dangerous impediment to conflict reduction.

Christoph Mühlemann sets out to place the record of the United Nations in perspective. He cites its inability to prevent conflict worldwide and its bloated and politicized bureaucracy. He argues that the organization has no independent existence, but merely reflects its membership, their interests and objectives. Yet, Mühlemann points out, the United Nations serves an integral function covering a breadth of issues from conflict resolution to environmental protection.

In the early 1970's a new type of international organization emerged in international politics. The prime example of this type of organization is the Organization of Petroleum Exporting Countries (OPEC). OPEC is economically based: it was formed to facilitate the international sale of oil. This organization differed from those formed on a geographical base (the Organization of American States or the Organization of African Unity), an ideological base (NATO or the Warsaw pact), or an ethnic or cultural base (the Arab League). For a while OPEC seemed to be the wave of the future. A question widely asked was: could states attempt to create a cartel for other resources? OPEC became one of the most important international institutions in world politics—every decision on OPEC's pricing and production was carefully scrutinized by the international community.

Edward L. Morse points out that this apparent significance was based on a fundamental lack of understanding of cycles within the industry, which "has always been somewhat special and different from other commodity sectors". Although his article was updated for this volume, Morse wrote it, originally, before the Saudis fired their famous oil minister, Sheik Yamani in the fall of 1986, and attempted to raise prices and cut production in deference to the preferences of the Iranians. Whether or not a major fall in prices occurs, as Morse predicts, his analysis places developments in this crucial sector of international politics within a unique political perspective. In enables us to judge the future strength of OPEC.

Although the articles in the second section of Part Three focus primarily on the United States, they deal with problems of bureaucracy and authority that affect the actions of all governments and, hence, the degree of tranquility and stability in international relations.

We begin this section with an intriguing analysis by Geir Lundestad, who is attempting to discern whether the United States has behaved differently from other great powers. He analyzes the wide swings in American foreign policy, compares these swings to the record of other great powers, and then attempts to explain why fluctuations in the United States have been wider than elsewhere. Lundestad considers environmental, institutional, and cultural factors as the causes of these swings. In the results of his analysis, we can see that institutions function within a series of constraints whose origins may be found both within society and the broader international system. Therefore, the importance of institutions cannot be weighed adequately without viewing their role within a larger context.

The next article by Nicholas Wheeler and Phil Williams, however, addresses the American foreign policy-making machinery directly. Though Lundestad stresses cultural factors, these authors believe that American policy is in disarray largely because of "an increasingly fragmented political structure". Their analysis of the key institutions engaged in foreign policy formulation concludes with an evaluation of the relationship between these organizational units and the content of policy. Although they devote their final paragraphs to the challenges of Reagan's second term, their agenda will be applicable to his successors as well.

By contrast, Charles William Maynes argues that the causes of problems in American foreign policy are not restricted to personalities or bureaucratic organizations. He stresses instead that American policy makers have been weakened by the tools which have been placed at their disposal. The military instrument has been enhanced, but the political will to use it has declined. The size of the foreign assistance program has been reduced. Regional specialists in the State Department have less influence because foreign policy interest has diversified through American society. In order to compensate for these changes, Maynes argues that executive branch influence must be rebuilt, which can be accomplished by improving the quality of appointments, the flexibility of officials and the information at their disposal and the knowledge they possess.

These three critiques are reinforced by the 1986 revelations that the Reagan administration—led by its operatives at the National Security Council—had been selling arms to Iran secretly and diverting a sizeable portion of the profits to the *contras*. The resulting crisis raised an almost endless list of questions: What were the lessons for the conduct and organization of the National Security Council? Should NSC officials move from coordination to operations? What would the impact of secret dealings with Iran and the illegal diversion of funds be on the administration's credibility with its allies, the international effort to combat terrorism, relations with friendly Arab states, Washington's unique position as custodian of the Arab-Israeli peace process, and the future of the administration's Central American policy? Many students of foreign policy began to ask, how could yet another administration be engulfed in a debilitating controversy? Lundestad, Wheeler and Williams, and Maynes provide analyses of the American scene that may help guide students of foreign policy who are searching for answers to this disturbing question.

Any discussion of policy making would not be complete unless attention were drawn to the key leaders who are ultimately essential to understanding why foreign policy decisions are made in any country. A determined and vigorous leader at the pinnacle of a governmental hierarchy can greatly affect that government's policies as well as the international order.

In this edition we again chose not to include specific articles about great world leaders, having decided that in recent years no individual has dominated international politics in the manner of a Lenin or a Wilson.

*good for
saving face*

THE CRISIS OF INTERNATIONAL INSTITUTIONS

29

The UN: A Dream of Peace

*Editor
of
Swiss
paper*

☛CHRISTOPH MÜHLEMANN

In front of the UN's New York headquarters there stands a bronze sculpture which symbolizes the ideals of the world organization: a sword being beaten into a plowshare. Following the collapse of the League of Nations and the catastrophe of World War II, the founders of the United Nations—headed and sparked by America's President Franklin D. Roosevelt—drew up a charter in San Francisco in the year 1945. That document assigned to the new world body the task of maintaining international peace. In order to attain that supreme goal, the United Nations Organization was charged with preventing armed conflicts, mediating any hostilities which might break out and—here its aims went far beyond those of the erstwhile League of Nations—promoting higher living standards, full employment, and economic and social development for the peoples of the world. The sword was to be made superfluous for all time, and the plowshare would bring a life of human dignity for all mankind.

Anyone who looks and listens in the glass palace on the East River these days, more than 40 years later, soon realizes that the high-flying ideals of those San Francisco days may still be evoked now and again—as a magic formula from an irretrievably lost time, when American idealism was still capable of infusing new hope for an era of peace into a world battered by the destructiveness of war. But our hypothetical observer would also quickly notice that the principles of the UN Charter are now spewed out as if from a prayer-wheel; today's heralds of the UN's mission of peace seem like the priests of an oracle through which the gods may perhaps once have spoken, but in strange and almost incomprehensible terms which these days need much interpretation.

Hordes of wordsmiths and scholars strive for such clarification in the building on the East River, while the outside world continues swiftly to create new realities for which the old phrases are no longer adequate. But there is also talk inside the UN's glass palace about long-overdue changes, about a genuine confrontation with "the real world," about relinquishing old romantic notions, about the need for reforms. The mood in the UN's New York corridors these days might be circumscribed by the phrase: More will, less dogma. We are well into the era of secularization.

One of the most frequently heard criticisms levelled at the world organization is that it has failed most notably in carrying out its principal task, securing the peace, and therefore has become essentially unnecessary. It is estimated that, since the year of the UN's founding, some 20 million people have died in wars and violent conflicts. Why has the UN been unable to prevent these wars? This and similar questions arise again and again during talks inside the UN headquarters building about the meaning and purpose of the world organization. Within the now vast and tangled UN system there may still be some idealists who believe that, if it really wanted to, the United Nations could exert the power to prevent one of its member states from attacking another. But that is probably pure illusion. With World War II over, Roosevelt and Churchill considered the possibility of creating a kind of world police force—but it remained just an idea. As it was formed in 1945, the world organization has virtually no sovereignty of its own, much less the means to exert force. It has in no way limited the sovereignty of its members.

At the same time, unlike the League of Nations the UN is not totally powerless. It has an organ which, at least in theory, can act in a sovereign, independent manner: the Security Council. If agreement can be reached among its permanent members (the USA, USSR, Britain, France and the People's Republic of China) and at least four of its ten other rotating members, the Security Council can order the creation of UN troops and employ them to separate warring parties or to monitor an already achieved cease-fire. But the East-West conflict, which has dominated world politics since the UN was created, has blunted the organization's only effective peace-keeping instrument. The 1950 Security Council decision to send troops to Korea (mostly U.S. units, supplemented by smaller contingents from 15 other countries on the basis of bilateral agreements) came about essentially "by mistake," because the Soviet representative absented himself from the crucial meeting in protest. Ten years later UN peace-keeping forces were again employed, this time in the Congo, and largely to no effect. Since then some truce supervisory UN units have been sent out to various Middle Eastern locales. But the United Nations has never been able to prevent wars by military means, because preventive operations would logically violate the national sovereignty of member states.

In all honesty, the world body should not be blamed for its inability in this regard. As one long-time UN official provocatively but accurately expresses it, the organization was not created to be a "sovereign player" but merely a forum for talks and the exchange of information. Nevertheless, says this veteran, in some cases the "system" has managed to prevent the outbreak of hostilities, safeguard the peace or defuse existing crises. The forum of the UN, he points out, helps create "rhetorical fallback positions" and develop "rituals" which enable parties in conflict to avoid actual warfare without losing face.

One example cited by this UN official is that of Krushchev in 1962, who justified his backing down in the Cuban missile crisis by citing a UN appeal and claiming that the Soviet Union was thus showing its respect for the UN Charter and "international law." In a similar vein this gentleman recalls the Suez crisis of 1956 and the Lebanon conflict of 1982. But even he must admit that the "peace rituals" of the United Nations are used only by hostile parties who *want* a way out of a difficult situation. If such a will is lacking, the world organization is powerless; at most, by issuing a condemnation of an aggressor—as in the case of the USSR in Afghanistan—it can serve as "the conscience of the world."

Granted that this regrettable helplessness, this existence as "a mirror of the world as it really is" (to cite another source), is not the fault of the world body itself. Nevertheless it seems almost like mockery when a UN secretary general—not the present one—in extreme over-estimation of himself and his organization, writes that despite all its weaknesses the UN still offers the best "structure" for guaranteeing the survival of mankind. This is hollow rhetoric, and considering the state of the world today it can hardly serve as a justification for the UN's continued existence.

On the other hand, it is also exaggerated to simply write off the broadly ramified and often successful work of the UN system, or to ironically suggest that there is no point in improving the conditions of human existence without first insuring that there will continue to be any human existence to improve. Fundamentalists and cynics alike are poor counsellors, if the world organization is to find its way out of the crisis in which it unquestionably finds itself. Both, in the final analysis, base their evaluations on unrealistically high expectations.

The United Nations is certainly not, at any rate, as bad as many of its critics make it out to be. A whole range of special UN agencies and organizations has indeed helped to improve the living conditions of many people by, among other things, fighting against hunger and illiteracy. Poor countries without skilled specialists of their own are able to get expert assistance in technical, scientific and legal areas. In fact, taken as a whole the UN constitutes an enormous repository of human knowledge. It has done trail-blazing work in such fields as the codification of international law and the search for means with which to conduct the struggle against the international narcotics trade. Such examples of the organization's value are uncontested—but they seldom make headlines and thus seldom penetrate public awareness. For large segments of world opinion the United Nations is little more than a talkfest, a marketplace for the exchange of extreme, partisan, overblown rhetoric. It is indeed all of that. But the glass palace in New York is also a place of quiet encounters, of expert and objective talks, of laborious negotiations over some significant bones of contention.

Wild, undisciplined speeches give vent to frustrations and angers, perhaps at times compensating for a certain sense of powerlessness; and in the corridors of UN headquarters the representatives of mutually hostile nations manage some words of amicable dialogue. These things would seem to have little to do with the ideals of the Charter and the idealistic hopes of its authors. But neither the shouting nor the quiet exchange of ideas is pointless. When, in the tumult of a General Assembly session, the leaders of two nations can meet outside the limelight in a manner that would otherwise be impossible without one or the other of them losing face, their encounter may not prevent a war, but it could make the outbreak of one less likely.

The United Nations Organization is indeed no world government, no sovereign player on the world stage, and hence neither a bringer nor a disrupter of peace. It is nothing in itself, but only that which its members are willing and able to make of it.

At the end of 1983 the total UN system (headquarters and all special agencies and organizations) employed some 50,000 persons worldwide. The Secretariat alone had about 4,500 management-level people plus technical and administrative personnel totalling 11,500. Like the rest of the world organization, this "universal bureaucracy" has changed considerably since the founding of the UN more than 40 years ago. It is seldom mentioned in talk about the organization's success or failure, but in some respects the role of the UN bureaucracy is of far-reaching importance.

Toward the end of the UN jubilee year 1985 Maurice Bertrand, a leading member of the organization's internal Joint Inspection Unit who has since retired, authored a "memorandum on a reform of the United Nations." The document contains a long and, on the whole, devastating catalogue of shortcomings and weaknesses. It was written, says Bertrand, not in order to destroy the UN but to initiate structural reform.

A few of the approximately 200 paragraphs of this aide-memoire are concerned with personnel problems. The author notes that the professional qualifications of officials and experts in the UN system are totally inadequate, because there are no professional criteria for hiring such personnel nor any effective checks on their productivity. As a particularly crass external index for the mediocrity of much of the work accomplished, Bertrand cites the poor organization, linguistic clumsiness and analytical jumble of the vast flood of publications issued by the world organization.

Anyone who has ever tried to get a picture of the UN's complex work by studying UN-published texts knows exactly what Bertrand is criticizing. But in reading his courageous and important document, one cannot help recalling now and again that it is itself a product of the very system it is criticizing. Like some even more important evaluations he makes, Bertrand's criticisms of UN personnel remain rather superficial. He says nothing about the causes of the lamentable phenomena he names, although he naturally knows the reasons very well. In true UN fashion, any findings which might upset or incriminate members of the organization are simply not to be aired publicly. What is explicitly formulated in each case is the (generally minor) common denominator; the rest of the picture—and in many cases the heart of the matter—must be read between the lines, at best, or, like so many things in the UN system, remain insiders' knowledge.

Bertrand describes the external reality. Articles 100 and 101 of the UN Charter outline the concept of an independent world bureaucracy as envisioned by the founders, in these words:

> In the performance of their duties the Secretary-General and the staff shall not seek or receive instructions from any government or from any other authority external to the Organization. They shall refrain from any action which might reflect on their position as international officials responsible only to the Organization (Article 100, Para. 1).
>
> Each Member of the United Nations undertakes to respect the exclusively international character of the responsibilities of the Secretary-General and the staff and not to seek to influence them in the discharge of their responsibilities (Article 100, Para. 1).
>
> The paramount consideration in the employment of the staff and in the determination of the conditions of service shall be the necessity of securing the highest standards of efficiency, competence, and integrity. Due regard shall be paid to the importance of recruiting the staff on as wide a geographical basis as possible (Article 101, Para. 3).

In contrast to Bertrand, whose analysis more or less confines itself to complaints about the persistent violations of Article 101 of the Charter, a former UN personnel chief, James Jonah of Sierra Leone (who served as Assistant Secretary-General for Personnel until 1982), is far more explicit with his accusations in his book *Independence and Integrity*. At the beginning of the book he writes that, from the very outset, the Soviet Union and the other socialist countries rejected the concept of a career service in the UN Secretariat as stipulated in Article 100; what they wanted was more or less an intergovernmental Secretariat in which members of the various national bureaucracies would serve for a certain time and then return to their original posts back home. This has resulted in a situation in which UN officials from the East bloc, and later from Third World countries as well, are loyal not to the world organization but to their own home governments. It is evident that the demands of Article 101—efficiency, competence, and integrity—must remain partially or totally unfulfilled if the stipulations of Article 100 (the exclusively international character of the UN staff; responsible only to the Secretary-General and the Organization) are ignored. What happens then is that, instead of professional qualifications, political qualifications enter the picture. In this context it is interesting to note that, during the drafting of the UN Charter, the Soviet Union and the Ukraine attempted to torpedo Article 101 entirely, under the pretext that the document should not concern itself with such details.

The first attempt to create an independent, international bureaucracy was made by the League of Nations; thanks largely to the determination of its first secretary-general, Eric Drummond of Britain, the old League may have been more successful in this regard than its successor, the UN. But it should be kept in mind that, as a body essentially limited to Europe, the League of Nations had an easier time at least in agreeing on administrative guidelines and hiring officials who are committed to a shared professional ethos. Drummond's ideas were incorporated almost unaltered in the UN Charter, and in San Francisco the Americans succeeded in pushing through an additional reinforcement of the new organization's "internationalism." Paragraph 1 of Article 101 states: "The staff shall be appointed by the Secretary-General under regulations established by the General Assembly."

Thus the initial conditions for an international Secretariat, whose structural, intellectual and personal homogeneity would enable it to analyze and deal with global problems, were good when the UN was founded. But, as in the case of keeping the peace, so also in the realm of personnel, reality did not match the world body's ideals, at least not for long. The "Fall" came in 1953, and was brought about by a most unexpected party. It was the United States, whose political ideals had been the strongest molding influence on the UN Charter, which was the first to violate the independence of the United Nations bureaucracy. Imbued with the spirit of the McCarthy era and its vehement anti-communism, a Senate committee demanded the discharge of a number of UN officials of American origin who were accused of "communist tendencies." Secretary-General Trygve Lie put up opposition, but in vain. FBI officials out for interrogation forced their way into the "extraterritorial" premises of the UN Secretariat, and shortly before handing over his office to Dwight D. Eisenhower, Harry S. Truman issued a presidential order which would have made the UN Secretary-General dependent on "information" and "loyalty tests" from the U.S. government before hiring any Americans. There was little serious follow-up, however, and in 1965 President Johnson rescinded the ominous order.

In the meantime, however—while the case of Washington remained an isolated incident—it became evident that the Soviet Union was being far more thorough and consistent in imposing personnel limitations on the Secretary-General and seeing to it that they were adhered to. To sum it up, Soviet violations of Articles 100 and 101 of the UN Charter add up to a situation in which all UN officials with Soviet passports are proposed by Moscow, their UN service period is limited (with few exceptions) to five years, and they are charged with protecting Soviet interests within the United Nations.

A report issued by the U.S. Senate last May gives some idea of what Moscow considers to be its interests in the UN; they range from influencing daily agenda items and texts issued under the UN emblem, to a broad range of espionage activities (of the approximately 800 Soviet citizens who are hired by the world body as "international officials," about 25% are identified in this report as intelligence agents). The governments of the Soviet satellite states naturally use the same interpretation of the responsibilities of "their" UN personnel. In brief, the Kremlin uses the United Nations as an important and influential outpost for its own policies.

Compared to these machinations, the efforts of Third World countries to secure for themselves a kind of global "affirmative action" seem almost harmless. Their concern, in most cases, is to insure that an appropriate proportion of UN staff is made up of their people. While Moscow is concerned with the totalitarian control of the experts and administrators whom it sends to the UN, the employment demands of some African and Asian states inject a breath of tribal loyalty and paternalism into the UN Secretariat. If the Kremlin's political qualifications constitute a burden on the standards of the UN bureaucracy, how much more potent a cause of the failings enumerated by Maurice Bertrand must be the assignment of "sisters and cousins" (as one UN critic exaggeratedly puts it) by potentates of the southern hemisphere. Like the members of the East bloc, the countries of the Third World show little comprehension of the concept of an independent, international administration.

As in virtually all sectors of the UN system, changes in the Secretariat have gradually eroded the ideals of the organization's founders, ideals influenced primarily by Western values and experience. That is not a negative comment on the high idealism of San Francisco or on a world organization which cannot help changing along with the political world which it represents. The skepticism about the United Nations which is so widespread in the West is thoroughly justified—but it should not result in the proverbial tossing out of the baby with the bathwater. America and the other Western industrial nations should certainly not rest content with the truly desolate conditions which predominate in some sectors of the world body. As the USA has done in the case of UNESCO, they have the option of withdrawing or of threatening to withdraw; this should not be done out of resignation, however, but rather in an effort to encourage a process of rethinking (which, in fact, has already begun). An even better approach is to apply pressure from within for change and reform; given the current mood of frustration and self-criticism within the organization, the chances for improvement would seem to have risen once again.

In connection with the recognized need for reform of the system, high-ranking UN officials have suggested that nations which do not pursue any power interests of their own, but which are economically and politically independent and rich in intellectual resources, can play an important role in the United Nations. What is needed today are ideas and concepts, specialized knowledge and experience, not threats of brute force or exaggerated demands for outside aid and support. In this context the appointment of Jean-Pierre Hocké as UN High Commissioner for Refugees may be seen as a signal, a kind of cry from the darkness for competence and independence.

President Reagan, well known for his critical stance toward the UN, said not long ago that there is no point in demanding of the world body acts which it is incapable of performing; it is better to use it as a tool where it is capable of yielding results. The lesson to be learned from this dictum is that *Realpolitik* will not dispense with an organization simply because it has shortcomings—especially not when, like the UN, it is the only instrument available in a particular area of endeavor. There is no universal political body other than the United Nations, which is why it is "used" even by countries which do not think highly of its present state. In other words: There is no alternative to the United Nations today, and if some member-nations should hit on the idea of designing one and, whether for reasons of dissatisfaction or unfulfilled claims to power, try to actually start a "counter-UN," what would be lost—at the very least—would be the quality of universality.

There is no denying that a large part of the functional and coordination problems within the world organization stem precisely from the fact that virtually the entire world is represented in it. The most diverse political systems and views of law, diametrically opposed claims to power and territory, vie for expression and for recognition in the Secretariat, the General Assembly and the various special agencies. It is perfectly natural that this results in difficulties. But it is absurd to blame this on the UN or its staff, as is sometimes done. The problems of the balance of power, the unequal distribution of wealth, totally irreconcilable ideas about the value of human rights—these would exist in our world *whether or not* there is a United Nations Organization. The UN is simply the "place" where these divergent views and claims are put forward and discussed (amicably or aggressively), where solutions are at least sought—and the mere existence of a place where this multiplicity of opinions and concerns are brought together is a value in itself. Without the UN's "socializing effect," the anarchy in international affairs would be even greater than it is.

It may be force of circumstance, or perhaps in the course of its 40-year history the world organization has gradually generated a new consciousness. In any case, no country in the world today can avoid recognizing and acknowledging that there are questions—even vital, existential questions—which it cannot resolve by itself. Interdependence in economic, technological and social matters is a fact of contemporary history. But mutual dependence makes it mandatory that there be at least a minimum of rules and norms which are accepted all over the world. The United Nations is the place where that integrative work is done, whether in the realm of environmental protection or the narcotics trade, terrorism or space law.

One of the central tasks of the total UN system is the further development of international law. And even though there are seldom any spectacular breakthroughs, step after small step is taken in New York away from the international rule of might and toward the distant goal of an ideal condition, the universal rule of law. In terms of its Charter the UN is not suited to be a world government, but as a workshop in which to forge joint attempts at adjustment and conflict resolution its services should not be underestimated.

Created by the victors of World War II and their allies, the United Nations was given the paramount task of preventing future wars whenever possible. Many of its harshest critics today accuse it of having totally lost sight of the principle of maintaining the peace—or at least of being incapable of fulfilling its main mission. It is pointless to enumerate all the armed conflicts which have erupted since the UN's founding; those who believe the world organization essentially has failed will not be convinced otherwise by the observation that without the presence of the United Nations there might have been even more wars fought during these past decades. Such an assertion cannot be proven. What is certain is that the world—and with it the world organization—has been deeply changed by the ongoing East-West conflict, the rise of the Third World and its expression in what has come to be known as the North-South conflict. The search for world peace has become a more difficult and complex matter than the founders in San Francisco ever dreamed of. But the UN has not collapsed in the face of all that.

Considering what might have been the consequences of the decolonization of Africa and Asia—a main aspect of political history in recent decades—it might in fact be concluded that the world body has proven itself in a manner for which it was never created. It is without question one of the United Nations' historic achievements to have provided an incomparable, integrative forum for the large number of new nations which, though hardly well prepared for their independence, have burst onto the world stage since about 1955. Membership in the United Nations has provided a kind of confirmation and guarantee of their autonomy for the newly independent states; it is in the UN that they have gained their initial experience in diplomacy and negotiations; from the UN's broad range of expertise they have drawn proposals to help them resolve constitutional, administrative and technical problems; and finally, the General Assembly has provided them with a place where they can express their frustrations and ambitions. As a school for the Third World, the UN has gotten a bit out of hand in recent years, because the students have tried to take control of the classroom. In historical perspective, this had to be expected. However, thanks largely (but not exclusively) to the UN, the conflict-potential released by the process of decolonization has been contained, by and large. That, too, is an achievement in the service of world peace.

If the world body is so inept, so poor, it is difficult to explain why, with only a solitary exception, countries have not walked out. On careful evaluation, the advantages of membership obviously outweigh the disadvantages. Indonesia, which withdrew from the UN in 1965 over the West New Guinea conflict, meekly returned to the organization in September of the following year. Countries such as South Africa and Israel, which suffer the most from one-sided attacks on the part of the UN majority, nonetheless place great value on not being expelled.

The founding member which signed the Charter in 1945 with the greatest skepticism and the most reservations, the Soviet Union, discovered after a grumbling and minimalist beginning that the UN offers great potential for exerting one's influence. The United States, upon whose basic political and legal concepts the Charter was modelled, has lost much of its initial enthusiasm as the creation of a new kind of UN majority has come into vehement and sometimes malicious conflict with Washington's ideals and dominant position. Today, more than at any time in the past, the U.S. is toying with the idea of withdrawal. But it may be assumed—and Reagan's statement cited earlier points in that direction—that the leading Western power will not simply scuttle away, but will pick up the gauntlet that has been thrown down to it.

During the last General Assembly, when the United Nations celebrated its fortieth anniversary with some pomp and circumstance, its members were not even able to agree on a joint anniversary declaration. Despite months of intensive preparation, it proved impossible to reconcile the views of the democratic industrial nations and those of the developing countries. The result was an overwhelming sense of disappointment, ill-humor and self-criticism in the Secretariat and among the delegations, a mood which remains the basic tenor of all talks in the offices and corridors of the glass palace in New York.

The organization is too large, too complex, too powerless. Its activities have lost most of their transparency and are almost impossible to coordinate. Even the most modest attempts at reaching consensus come to grief over the incessant demands voiced by the "new majority" of Third World countries. These are the things one hears again and again in New York. At the same time precisely these self-critical remarks, and the increasing signs of a gradual change of attitude among some Third World delegations, give grounds for hope

Reforms are needed; rethinking is essential. But the UN has never stood still, and while its present condition is a desolate one there is probably a growing readiness to make constructive changes and to work in a more objective and problem-oriented manner in many areas. The UN's crisis could end in bitterness, but it could also be taken up as a challenge. The force of circumstance can impose discipline—but it takes time.

30

After the Fall:
The Politics of Oil

EDWARD L. MORSE

The most startling surprise in the international economy during the 1980s has been the fulfillment of prophecies made five years ago—often voiced, seldom believed—that oil prices would decline significantly from their peak price of over $40 a barrel in 1980–81. In fact, prices fell to less than $10 a barrel on the spot market in mid-1986 before they rebounded. The price increase in the winter of 1986–87 will likely prove to be short-lived. Oil prices will be volatile for at least three years.

There is almost universal agreement that, in the whole, lower oil prices are beneficial to the world economy. But very low prices will pose very big problems. A further dramatic decline in oil prices will have a revolutionary impact on world politics and the international economy of a magnitude tantamount to that of the oil price increases in 1973–74 and 1979–80.

An explanation of the events that are being triggered by an oil price collapse depends, first, on an understanding of the peculiar nature of the international oil trade, so unlike that of other commodities, and second, on a determination of exactly what happened this past winter. Then the conditions that allow a free-fall in oil prices can be defined. The consequences of such a price drop, including the implications for Western energy security, will become evident. And appropriate policy responses can be discussed.

Whatever emerges in the coming months, it is clear that the oil sector, with its fundamental effects on international economic and political affairs, will never again be anything like what it was.

II

The international petroleum industry has always been somewhat special and different from other commodity sectors. Given its pervasive influence on industrial growth, and the record of government and industry interventions over the decades, the oil sector has not generally functioned as a free transparent market in which price is determined by the interaction of many buyers and sellers. At most times in the past, rather, oil has been traded through a contrived mechanism to balance supply and demand. The market has also been a source of dynamic change since before the turn of the century, when oil was first produced in commercial quantities.

Throughout this period, beginning roughly in 1890, oil prices have experienced sharp cyclical change in a remarkably consistent pattern. The dollar price of oil in real terms has gone from trough to peak roughly every ten years, and then moved from peak to trough in the decade following. In the cycle that preceded the current phase, oil prices had reached a floor of less than $3 per barrel (in 1976 dollars) at the end of World War II, rising to a peak of about $4.25 in 1958. Throughout the 1960s, the real price of oil steadily declined, as low-cost Middle Eastern oil came on the market, and finally reached its trough at about $3.90 per barrel during 1969–70.

The last cycle was the most extraordinary, with the peak reached by oil prices in 1981—about $12.50, in real price terms—representing a 225-percent increase over the previous decade. If the pattern continues, we will be in for a long price decline that will probably reach bottom in the early 1990s, when price levels will hover at a level, expressed in 1986 dollars, of $8 to $10 per barrel.

The 20-year boom-and-bust pattern of the international oil market has shown another interesting pattern: each recent price trough has brought with it a reorganization of the petroleum industry, uniting governments and companies in actions to limit the damage of price declines and a contracting petroleum production cycle.

The first such extraordinary effort came with the price trough of 1932, when an oil glut developed in the United States. Oil companies and the governors of the various oil-producing states came together and agreed to impose production retraints. At various stages the Texas Railroad Commission and the U.S. federal government managed this "cartel." In the period after World War II, the "Seven Sisters" (the major international oil companies), which had discovered and developed new supplies outside of traditional sources, especially in the Middle East, worked together informally to expand and contract production when market balancing was required. In the late 1950s, another price trough resulted in the creation of the Organization of Petroleum Exporting Countries, which eventually developed strong mechanisms to control production levels and prices. OPEC had been formed in an effort to shift the burden of adjustment away from the oil producing members and back to the United States. Through the tumultuous 1970s, OPEC appeared to provide a successful mechanism for supporting prices via production restraints, but it was only in the early 1980s that the mechanism was actively tested. In early 1973 virtually no one imagined that an oil revolution was at hand, or that its impact would effect fundamental changes in the world's economy, the security of the West and the structure of the energy industry.

Today we can observe a similar set of revolutionary conditions, even though as recently as three years ago few foresaw that a price collapse would occur as rapidly as it has. This is because, until 1985, the gradually accelerating decline in oil prices was both masked and tempered by the appreciation of the U.S. dollar. Oil is priced in dollars, so Europe and Japan appeared to be paying more for their oil in 1985 than in 1981, and most OPEC countries' earnings were modestly improved. Now, as the dollar has depreciated relative to other currencies, the consuming countries have gained the benefits of lower oil prices, just as the exporters have suffered.

III

In the fall of 1985, oil prices began to firm up on the spot market as the winter heating season approached; then, in January and February 1986, they tumbled by more than $15 in just a few weeks. Why did the oil market, which had been weakening for four years, suddenly appear to collapse out of control?

The answer can be found in decisions taken in Saudi Arabia in the summer and fall of 1985. The Saudis decided to flood a weak market, with the intention of pushing prices down rapidly. They made certain their oil would be sold by changing the method by which it was priced. Traditionally the Saudis, like other OPEC producers and non-OPEC producers such as Mexico, Britain and Norway, had established official sales prices. The new approach—called netback pricing—assured refiners buying Saudi crudes of a profit on each barrel processed and sold as gasoline, diesel, fuel oil and other petroleum products. Through this new pricing scheme, Saudi oil was valued by the market price of the products into which it was refined (e.g., gasoline, heating oil), less the costs of refining and transportation. Saudi production increased from a low level of 2.5 million barrels or less a day to a new targeted daily level of 4.3 million barrels or more. Why did the Saudi government change its traditional, conservative approach to selling crude oil?

Let us look at the context of the past half-decade. The 1980s began with a nervous and tight oil market. The revolution in Iran and the curtailment of Iranian production in 1979–80 spurred an increase in the price of oil by more than two times, to $30 per barrel and above for oil sold under term contract and to more than $40 per barrel sold on a spot basis. These high prices, coming on top of the pricing revolution of 1973–74, ushered in a world recession. They also served to accelerate the search for oil outside OPEC, to encourage energy-saving investments, and to make virtually all competitive fuels (e.g., nuclear power, natural gas and coal) attractive alternatives to petroleum. Thus, demand for oil dropped, even as new oil supplies from non-OPEC sources were brought into production.

In order to protect the price of internationally traded oil, OPEC reached a series of internal agreements, first made in 1982–83 and updated several times thereafter, to restrict its members' production to 18 million barrels per day (in contrast to the OPEC peak production level of 31 million barrels per day, reached in 1981), and to allocate that production among its members by quota. Some ten million barrels a day of production capacity had to be left untapped, or shut in, in order to balance supply and demand at a price in the range of $25 to $28 per barrel. Saudi Arabia, with by far the largest reserves in OPEC (and the world), assumed the role of swing producer, adjusting its production level up and down to balance supply with demand and to protect the price. OPEC's bet was that a revival in world economic activity would soon commence, bringing with it higher demand for oil and more robust OPEC production.

The best was lost. Instead, OPEC saw its role in world oil trade diminish as new supplies outside OPEC came into the market. Through new investment, British and Norwegian production grew to new record levels in 1983, 1984 and 1985. India and Brazil, two of the largest developing countries, moved rapidly from being large importers toward achieving oil self-sufficiency. Other developing countries began to produce and export oil, and because of conservation, industrial restructuring and fuel switching in the industrial countries, oil demand never rebounded as the OPEC strategists had expected.

The members of OPEC, the Saudis and other Persian Gulf states in particular, saw their plight worsening. OPEC's share of free-world oil production shrank from a high of 55 percent in 1973 to 30 percent in 1985, and the cartel was unable to market production at its targeted volume. Despite a widespread view that the lower-producing OPEC countries were "cheating" by producing at levels higher than their quotas, the remarkable feature of the oil market during 1981–85 was that OPEC held together so well. It did so essentially because Saudi Arabia was willing to be the swing producer and adjust its production downward to balance the market. The result was low Saudi production and Saudi oil income of $28 billion in 1985 as opposed to its peak income of $113 billion in 1981.

OPEC came to understand that it could not go on playing the role of market balancer and price supporter alone. But despite several efforts to gain the support of Britain and Norway, the North Sea producers refused to limit their production until late in 1986, when Norway agreed to a modicum of cooperation. Instead, in order to protect their market shares, Norway and Britain abandoned administered pricing in 1984 and let the market determine the price for their crude. By last summer, the Saudis recognized that the only way they could be assured a minimally acceptable income was to reduce prices and increase production, punishing the North Sea producers with lower income in hopes of gaining their future cooperation.

What are the chances of success for this new Saudi gamble? Is there any way OPEC and non-OPEC producers can together or separately regain control over the oil market and assure a higher minimum price? Should the Saudis again fail in their tactics, what would be the consequences— for them, for OPEC, for other oil producers and for the world economy? The answers depend on certain fundamental changes that can now be discerned in the international oil industry.

IV

Successful oil market management depends on three basic conditions. The first is a limitation on the number of major participants in the market: the fewer the better. The second is the ability of the major players to take decisions to rationalize production, deciding where, for how long, and under what circumstances production is to be shut in. The third relates to the degree to which the petroleum industry is integrated, with networks of close ties between upstream activities (i.e., oil production) and downstream activities (oil refining and marketing). The more integrated the industry, the more amenable the market will be to constructive management.

Bearing this in mind, it can be seen that the revolution of the 1970s in the petroleum sector was manifold. It involved not only the quadrupling of oil prices and the emergence of a powerful OPEC cartel, but it also involved a wave of nationalizations in the developing countries, including Kuwait, Venezuela, Iraq, Peru and Saudi Arabia, of the oil-producing properties of the international oil companies. In the 1970s, nationalized firms accounted for nearly three-quarters of international production and included virtually all of the important oil exporters in the developing world.

Beyond the obvious transfer of equity interests, these nationalizations brought about fundamental and quite unintended changes in the structure of the oil market. They broke the linkages between the developing world's oil production and that of the industrialized countries, an essential connection if world production is to be rationalized. The nationalizations motivated the international oil companies to accelerate their search for oil in new frontier areas, including the North Sea and developing countries where governments permitted the companies to make reasonable profits. And finally, the nationalizations broke the tight coordination of production and refining, long considered a prerequisite to managing the petroleum economy by reducing price volatility.

The cumulative result of the developments of the 1970s is a paradoxical imbalance in the oil market, one that only invites pressures for substantially lower prices. For the past four years, supply and demand have been balanced only because the lowest-cost producers (the Middle East) have shut in their production. Meanwhile, the highest-cost producers have pumped oil at near maximum capacities and have had every incentive to expand production. This condition is exactly the opposite of what one would anticipate in a truly free market.

In a transparent and efficient marketplace, prices should decline toward the level of production expenses in the least-cost producing countries, and production capacity of higher-cost producers would be shut in until such time as demand warranted the production of higher-cost oil. In today's world, this would mean closing down production in the North Sea, Alaska and offshore North America, and the expanding of production in the Arabian peninsula. But the opposite has happened.

To further distort the classic model, new oil production is now anticipated from the North Sea, from new entrants to the ranks of oil producers and exporters such as Colombia and North Yemen, from steady increases in production elsewhere among importers in the developing world (Brazil and India), and from expected increases in

Iraqi and perhaps Iranian production—once they are no longer at war—due to the completion of new pipeline outlets.

Non-OPEC production rose by some 500,000 barrels a day in 1986, reaching nearly 28.8 million barrels, and by an additional similar amount in the following two or three years. With demand basically flat at 45.5 million barrels, even if prices fall, requirements for OPEC oil will average no more than 16.5 million barrels a day this year, some 700,000 barrels less than last year. This spring and summer, world oil demand is expected to drop to 44 million barrels a day; demand for OPEC oil should be no more than 15.6 million and perhaps as low as 14.5 million barrels—the lowest level since the oil price surge of 1973.

Furthermore, with the separation of production and refining operations, the volume of oil bought on the spot market rose in the late 1970s through the early 1980s from about five percent to perhaps 50 percent of all traded oil, creating enormous price volatility and, eventually, downward price pressure. Organized futures markets in petroleum products and crude oil came into existence in New York and London to compensate for the new volatility, providing opportunities not only for hedging, but also for speculation.

These structural circumstances bore down on the largest and most flexible of the producers, Saudi Arabia. By shutting in their production, Saudi Arabia and other OPEC countries have, in effect, subsidized the prices for the high-cost producers in the United States, Mexico and the North Sea countries. Saudi Arabia has now demonstrated its frustration at the heavy revenue burdens incurred by subsidizing oil production outside of OPEC. Its new policy of higher production was thus partially punitive in nature, aimed at forcing non-OPEC exporters and other producers to share in the burden of balancing the market.

These new efforts are accelerating another structural change in the petroleum market and the petroleum industry: OPEC has, at least for the time being, lost its role as a key player in the political economy of oil.

The members of OPEC are basically interested in maximizing the rents to be gained from oil exploitation. They also, as a group, have wanted to make certain that the burdens of any market adjustments, introduced to compensate for changing conditions of supply, demand and price, are pushed onto the oil-importing countries and the international oil companies. As of winter 1985–86, this approach had failed.

Despite this common purpose, the members of OPEC differ significantly one from another. Some (e.g., Saudi Arabia and the smaller producers around the Arabian peninsula) are high-reserve, low-population countries, the remaining members have low reserves and a high population. From another perspective, the relationships within OPEC are based on the fact that one producer, Saudi Arabia, is so much more significant than the others.

In this respect, the bargaining relationships within OPEC look strikingly like those within NATO. OPEC and NATO both are comprised of like-minded governments, targeting a common external "enemy," but also relating to one another through an array of asymmetrical relations: a large country at the "core" and many smaller and less influential countries around the "periphery." Within NATO it is the interest of the U.S. government to maximize its own freedom in dealing with the Soviet Union and to assure that its allies undertake policies that do not undermine its bilateral relations with the U.S.S.R. Similarly, it is in the interests of the smaller NATO countries to restrain the United States, to make its behavior more regular and predictable, and to maximize their own freedom of action to pursue individual foreign policies vis-à-vis the countries of the Eastern bloc.

OPEC, too, is comprised of a large country at the core of the organization (Saudi Arabia) and smaller countries along the periphery. It has been the Saudi intention for the past decade to maintain a moderate international petroleum sector, one in which the life of petroleum as an important commodity in international trade is stretched out as long as possible. This has meant that although the Saudis do not want to see the price of oil fall precipitously, they have also not been eager to see the price increase dramatically. It has been the Saudi objective to maximize its own freedom and to constrain that of its OPEC partners. Similarly, it has been the goal of virtually all of Saudi Arabia's partners in OPEC to enlarge their own freedom to produce and price oil and to keep Saudi behavior predictable and constrained. That tension between Saudi Arabia and the other OPEC producers resulted in the stalemate that the Saudi decision to regain its market share broke open.

Given their large external financial reserves, their links to banks in the industrialized countries and their military links to the United States, the Saudis are torn between the Western industrialized countries and their OPEC partners. From this perspective, it can be concluded that Saudi Arabia's recent behavior reflects an understanding that a fundamental structural shift is required in the way the international petroleum sector is governed. The older ties among OPEC countries may become less relevant than the process of establishing new alignments among oil producers and consumers.

The upshot of all these circumstances is clear. A radical restructuring of the oil industry and the oil market is about to take place. That restructuring will require new approaches to the sensible management of the petroleum economy. What is required is a simplification in the number of major participants in the market, a mechanism to organize production in correlation with demand, and a reintegration between upstream and downstream petroleum operations. This restructuring will not take place without an intervening step: namely a radical collapse in oil prices sometime during the next 18 months, perhaps as early as this summer. Oil prices in the range of $8 to $10 per barrel cannot be dismissed, despite OPEC's effort in the summer and winter of 1986 to curtail production further, and its interim success in boosting prices.

V

What will be the consequences of such a price collapse? If Saudi Arabia's gamble to push the costs of adjustment onto non-OPEC producers fails, as the preceding analysis of structural changes in the petroleum sector implies it might, there is no logical stopping place for the price of oil above $8–$10 per barrel. Oil industry analysts agree that production capacity will not be restrained *for reasons of cost* unless the price falls below $8 per barrel. Furthermore, at various points between $10 and $20 per barrel, new investments in energy conservation cease. New capital expenditures by oil companies are also reduced, eventually almost to the point of elimination.

Absent political intervention, and given the extraordinary overhang of supply, with OPEC's production capacity still some ten million barrels per day higher than current production levels, this situation can continue for a long time. With oil prices dropping toward $10 per barrel, it should take at least five years before lack of investment in new supplies and increases in demand triggered by low prices begin to push prices upward again—excluding, of course, the occurrence of a new supply disruption. Lack of new investment will result in dramatically decreasing production levels in certain parts of the world, probably most significantly in the United States. With oil priced at less than $16–$18 per barrel, new investments in the more costly techniques of secondary and tertiary recovery will cease. At less than $15 per barrel, stripper-well production, responsible for about one million barrels a day today, will be terminated. Overall, we can anticipate a decline in U.S. domestic production on the order of ten percent per annum.

In a relatively short period of time, therefore, Western economic security will begin to be threatened by a substantial decline in new energy investments. Given the steep rate of decline of some domestic reserves, the maintenance of American production at levels covering two-thirds of domestic consumption requires a constant effort to assure that new reserves are brought into commercial production. These reserves tend to be high cost and to require investments in secondary and tertiary recovery not needed elsewhere, particularly in the Middle East. Price uncertainty alone leads to the postponement of such investments. Very low prices preclude them.

The faster the decline to $10 a barrel and the longer it lasts, the more significant will be the implication for energy security and inflation in the 1990s. Without sustained efforts to seek out new sources of conventional oil supply, growing demand and diminishing surplus production capacity for petroleum could result in a price escalation in the 1990s not unlike that which the world experienced in the 1970s.

Beyond the economic effects are the political implications for Saudi Arabia and other Middle Eastern low-population oil producers. In the shorter term, a price decline will raise serious problems of political stability in all oil-exporting regimes. It would weaken the ability of the Saudi government to maintain the authority of the king vis-à-vis other members of the extended ruling family, given their sharp reductions in income. It would also affect their feelings toward the West in general, and the United States in particular, provoking a likely nationalistic response based on a belief that Western governments somehow engineered the price collapse in order to punish the Saudi regime (for reasons, for example, associated with America's ties to Israel). It would possibly further fuel Islamic fundamentalist nationalism in the Persian Gulf. In short, lower prices in a weakened Saudi regime could pose security dilemmas for America's strategic interests in the Arabian peninsula.

Over the longer run, especially if new exploration expenditures outside the Gulf are dramatically reduced, a price collapse would be a prelude to a reassertion of Saudi dominance in the international oil markets in the next decade, once the surplus production capacity of the world is drawn down. Such a development poses a dilemma for the West: this is true no matter whether one views the situation with the suspicion that heightened Middle Eastern control over the world's oil supplies will result in sharply higher prices and detrimental conditions for Western economic interests, or whether one believes that greater dependence on Saudi and Middle Eastern oil creates heightened vulnerabilities in fundamental Western economic and security interests. It is perhaps unwise to speculate on what type of Saudi regime will be in place in the 1990s when the United States and other Western countries will again be highly dependent on Middle Eastern supplies. It also matters less what the Saudis have been like in the past than what the implications are for Saudi behavior in the future. A new xenophobic Saudi leadership under circumstances of heightened Western dependence on Saudi oil might be dangerous indeed.

The concentration of extra production capacity that will be held by Middle Eastern countries in the 1990s could well make Western dependence much greater than it was in the 1970s. The "oil weapon" could return with a vengeance. In any event, the Saudi role as swing producer balancing the marketplace will be much more critical. Both the shorter- and longer-term consequences of a decline in oil prices therefore raise significant energy security questions.

Of special significance is the effect of lower prices on the oil exporting countries, especially those most heavily debt, such as Mexico and

Nigeria. Clearly, lower prices will result in lower revenues for virtually all of the oil exporting countries, whether they belong to OPEC or not (assuming OPEC production at its targeted level of 18 million barrels a day). *Petroleum Intelligence Weekly*, in its January 13, 1986, issue, calculated that $20 per barrel oil would result in total OPEC revenues of barely over $100 billion in comparison to total OPEC revenues last year of over $130 billion and, in 1980, of $280 billion. At $10 per barrel, revenues would drop to $50 billion, with demand levels still not increasing for a few years.

In such a scenario, the financial situation of virtually all indebted oil exporting countries would be jeopardized. Almost none would be able to service debt and also continue to import necessary consumer and capital goods. Political stability, already in question, would be in further danger, and bitterness among the OPEC countries toward one another and toward industrialized countries would be high.

A gentle decline in oil prices through December 1985 already brought nervousness to the international banking community and financial authorities in the United States and elsewhere before the latest price drop. A precipitous decline would create the fear of a tidal wave of bank failures, beginning with the regional banks of the southwestern United States and extending to the money-center banks as well, as the plight of debtors in the United States approaches in severity that of the developing countries.

The oil industry in the United States and elsewhere in the West will obviously be affected by a sharp drop in prices. So will the new crop of state-owned energy enterprises in the developing world. As oil prices fall toward $10 per barrel, the oil industry will bear an increasing share of the loss; governments will have to support a decreasing share because of the structure of most tax regimes. The oil companies' capital expenditures in new exploration investments will thus decline even more dramatically.

Each of the downward pricing spirals of the past century has resulted in a massive restructuring of the oil industry and in political efforts to put a floor under prices. The international petroleum industry has just adjusted to an extraordinary transformation during the last decade. Fifteen years ago, about 80 percent of the world's production of petroleum was dominated by the large international oil companies through their international activities. Now the oil industry has become both fragmented and decentralized.

The number of important producing companies, now including national oil companies as well as those owned by private shareholders, increased several fold. Today the national oil companies command an equal footing with the majors and independents as significant market participants. The international integration that once involved production abroad and refining in one's home country has been broken. And the number of parties participating in the international petroleum trade has increased from fewer than 20 to more than 100.

The future structure of the oil industry is by no means easy to foresee, but a radical rationalization seems inevitable. As a result of recent acquisitions and efforts to ward off corporate takeovers, the number of oil companies in the United States that have accumulated potentially dangerous levels of debt has increased. State-owned international oil companies, like Kuwait Petroleum Company and Petrobras of Brazil, which have engaged in wide-ranging international exploration, could well be giants among the survivors in the next decade. They will be joined by such companies as Petróleos de Venezuela as it proceeds to acquire substantially larger downstream assets in the consuming countries of Europe and North America.

The petroleum industry that will emerge from this shake-out will be rationalized along lines involving an amalgam of state-owned and private enterprises with multiple joint ventures between them.

A precipitous price collapse would, in short, carry with it revolutionary consequences that now can only be partially discerned. What can be done to guard against the most dangerous consequences of a price collapse?

VI

Various political actions have been proposed to prevent a free-fall in oil prices to the $10 level or below. Any of them, to be effective, would require increasingly unlikely and delicate coordination between OPEC and non-OPEC countries, between producing and consuming countries, between governments and multinational companies, or among the consuming countries on their own. Failing such an unlikely coordinated political intervention, we can anticipate a radical price drop soon; prices should then hover at extraordinarily low levels for at least a half-decade. Moreover, with ample supplies and a reluctance on the part of companies to hold inventories due to market uncertainty, the oil consuming world will experience price volatility over an annual cycle in response to higher winter heating season demand for crude oil and overall lower summer demand.

In recent months a number of experienced observers of the oil industry have reminded us of the error of considering the international petroleum market to be like other commodity markets. Melvin A. Conant and Paul Frankel, for example, have been arguing for more than a year for a substantive dialogue between OPEC and non-OPEC producers and between producers and consumers. Walter J. Levy has frequently warned that the West ought not to be lulled into a false sense of security by the oil glut that emerged after 1981. These warnings have been unheeded so far. The imminence of a price collapse reminds us that such pronouncements stem from long experience and observation of the petroleum sector and of the fragile underlying political base that has supported international oil prices over the past few years.

Analysis of the international petroleum economy and its momentous political implications is a relatively easy first step. It is quite another matter to lay out policy proposals for addressing the worst ramifications of a price collapse. If a destabilizing price collapse is to be prevented, a new regime for managing the petroleum sector is required, a regime to provide mechanisms of coordination among producing and importing countries, among consuming countries, between private companies and government companies, and between companies and governments. With all these interests at stake, no simplified solution could satisfy them all.

Yet simplified responses are what come out of politics. Thus, proposals for the immediate imposition of barriers to the import of petroleum and petroleum products into the United States are already receiving attention in the U.S. Congress. Import barriers would protect prices for U.S.-based producers and, therefore, would also protect bank loans to the oil industry. This solution has also become increasingly attractive in the United States in light of the budget deficit. Tariff barriers would raise government revenues and protect producer interests within the United States by providing a de facto floor price for petroleum production.

This policy approach had an intellectual force in the recent past, when the oil market was tight and when conservation and fuel-switching were to be encouraged. Under past conditions, an import fee would also have served to recapture some of the "rents" of oil production that OPEC countries were receiving. In today's climate, however, a unilateral import fee would create more problems than it would solve. A "go it alone" policy by the United States would actually have pernicious ramifications for virtually all the oil exporting countries of the world. It would also create significant trade frictions with our most important industrial trading partners.

In a slack market, with a supply overhang, oil would be competitively poised to enter the U.S. market at the domestic U.S. price minus the tariff barrier price. World oil prices would thereby tend to be depressed even further in any competitive effort by foreign producers to gain access to the U.S. market. In short, what might work satisfactorily in a tight marketplace would be counterproductive in a slack market. A tariff would defeat any interests the U.S. government might have in trying to assist other producing and exporting countries, such as Mexico and some of the OPEC countries. And it would completely ignore the effects that significantly lower prices would have on Britain, Norway and Canada.

It can be argued that there would be significant incentives to make an import tariff barrier multilateral by extending it well beyond the United States to include our industrial partners and Mexico as well. In all likelihood, a U.S. administration would probably seek to extend a tariff wall on a multilateral basis.

One system, in fact, is already in place through which the industrialized countries could collectively protect their gains in conservation, their future production base of petroleum and other conventional fuels, and their banking and trading system. It lies in the International Energy Agency (IEA), created in 1974 in the aftermath of the first oil shock, which includes nearly all of the 24 members of the Organization of Economic Cooperation and Development (OECD).

It should be recalled that the IEA, which is widely identified with its emergency oil-sharing arrangement, also has as a goal the promotion of petroleum resources within the IEA area. A mechanism instituted in 1974 to encourage "indigenous" IEA production was a floor under the price of oil; at that time the floor price was $7 a barrel. Political interests could now be refocused on a minimal floor price for oil on the order of $15 a barrel through the IEA mechanism.

In addition to protecting indigenous production and existing conservation gains, a tariff wall around the IEA to protect a minimum oil price would serve other interests as well. It would help resolve trade frictions among the industrialized countries with respect to petroleum products and petrochemicals, which are already heightened and which would be further exacerbated by a unilateral U.S. tariff. A multilateral oil tariff would serve financial interests by preventing panic and providing a rational basis for the settlement of at least a significant portion of oil-related debt. In all likelihood, it would be a condition of any U.S. administration's consent to such a scheme that it take in all of North America (including Mexico) and potentially much of the Western Hemisphere (i.e., Venezuela, Ecuador and possibly Colombia) within the tariff wall.

The IEA solution would have a more cosmopolitan impact if Mexico were to be protected by the tariff wall. Placing an effective floor under Mexican oil prices through Mexico's incorporation in the network would, first and foremost, be of importance to the United States for bilateral foreign policy reasons. Beyond that, it would be of interest to the banking community. Mexico, Brazil and Argentina together are the three largest debtor countries, responsible for nearly 30 percent of all outstanding developing-country debt. Argentina, being self-sufficient in oil, would have no need to require inclusion under the tariff wall's protection. Brazil, as a net oil importing country, would, on the whole, be better off with much lower oil prices so long as it was able to maintain adequate incentives for domestic exploration and production. Only

Mexico, among the large debtor countries, could gain substantially from inclusion in this system.

An expanded IEA tariff wall would clearly provide one of the few viable options for dealing with a price collapse, as it would help serve many highly politicized interests and take advantage of an institutional framework that already exists.

In the long run, however, a solution based on the IEA and its mechanisms would be inadequate to the tasks ahead. It would, by providing special preferential arrangements for North Sea, U.S. and Mexican oil, polarize relationships between the IEA countries and the rest of the world, in particular OPEC countries and other indebted developing countries. It would permanently solve neither the difficulties inherent in the petroleum sector, nor those in the financial and trade arenas.

An IEA solution would exclude OPEC from any role other than that of marginal supplier, or balancer, of the international petroleum market. And it would probably not serve the interests of many governments and companies whose relationships with producer governments and national oil companies have become far more complex than was the case in 1974. It is tempting, therefore, to look at an alternative approach, which has been proposed at various times during the past ten years or so: a global oil compact involving all of the major oil exporting and importing countries.

Even if a global compact among all parties concerned could be achieved in the current context or in the aftermath of a price collapse, there is a significant residue of mistrust concerning how long such an agreement could last. No one has forgotten how difficult it was for the Saudis in the late 1970s and early 1980s to induce discipline among OPEC countries to prevent prices from escalating so rapidly and to such high levels as to ensure OECD conservation, decreased demand, and the substitution of other forms of energy for oil. Nor have they forgotten how rapidly recent OPEC production and pricing agreements have disintegrated.

Western governments would understandably refuse to be involved in an agreement that would shore up OPEC countries today, since the OPEC countries would be expected to be the first to break such an agreement once the demand/supply balance tightened again. An even greater set of political forces is reluctant to engage in any market intervention, given the recollections of how market interventions have worked in the past: they have given rise to corruption, they have been unmanageable, and they have created distortions in the economy at least as onerous as the management of those interventions themselves.

None of these policy options augers well for OPEC. Nor is there necessarily a convincing case that OPEC would be able to "organize itself" to deal with the problem. The protectionist wall that will probably emerge around the IEA is also more likely to lead individual OPEC countries to try to make their own side deals with the industrialized governments in order to gain market share. Their distrust of one another, the history of failure of sustained concerted action in OPEC during the past four years, and the need of the most severely indebted OPEC countries to maximize their revenues by expanding production would, in all likelihood, keep OPEC fragmented. The prospects are therefore exceedingly low for OPEC members to act together. So, the possibility of OPEC reaching a marketing agreement with the industrial countries is also low.

VII

The main weakness in any possible market rationalization program that the consuming or producing countries, acting separately, might take relates to the structure of the international petroleum market. A coherent line of action requires strong linkages among the major oil producers in the world. It also requires integrated linkages between upstream production activities and downstream refining and marketing operations. Neither of these linkages is strong under present conditions.

An international oil market with slack demand, such as today's, could be regulated through coordinated action by producers to shut in production and withhold excess supplies from the marketplace. Similarly, the integrated linkages between production and refining could enable the major international companies to shift their profits between production and refining activities, depending on the state of the marketplace.

In today's world, how might such a rationalization of the petroleum market and industry develop? What actions along these lines can we anticipate from the Saudis and other participants in the world oil market?

Let us take another look at the two elements that form the necessary conditions for a new rationalization of the petroleum market: coordinated production and reintegration of upstream and downstream activities.

Coordination of production on a worldwide basis has proved to be the most elusive of goals for OPEC since 1982. OPEC could not manage this on its own, as the marginal or balancing supplier to the world market. It failed in efforts to co-opt the non-OPEC exporters. And it was unable to induce cooperation from international oil companies, with whom it had severed its ties through the nationalizations of the 1970s. But a basis might well exist to crystallize a new form of production rationalization, with or without the erection of a protective wall by the IEA countries. The Saudis are one key to this issue; the other key is the condition of the marketplace today and the plight of many of the large producing companies.

Given the extraordinary indebtedness of some major oil companies, one can imagine that a precipitous collapse of oil prices might create conditions conducive to a deal between some of these companies and some of the principal producing governments, especially Saudi Arabia. Once prices collapse, some of these companies will be desperate to find ways to sell or finance their debt, as a matter of corporate survival. One can imagine a process through which an entity of the Saudi government, or of the governments of other oil exporting countries, would offer to purchase the non-OPEC reserves of these companies. For the oil exporting country, a choice would then exist; it could shut down these newly acquired reserves in order to increase the market share from its own domestic production; or it could shut down production at home and produce from the newly acquired reserves within the protected barrier.

A related possibility would be to arrange a swap of assets between the exporting countries and the production companies. Here the same companies would gain equity access to lower-cost oil in the Middle East, while the exporting countries would gain downstream refining and marketing assets in exchange. For the companies to be induced by such a swap offer, a "kicker" would need to be offered, via lower taxes or lower costs, to provide them with higher cash flow to service their debt. So long as some reserves would be shut in, an asset swap would have the same effect as a sales/purchase arrangement between strong national oil companies and weak international oil producing companies.

If this type of arrangement were worked out on a sufficiently large scale, the objective of rationalizing production could be achieved on a global basis. Nor would such an arrangement have to be tremendously extensive. As long as two million to four million barrels of oil production were thus managed, a basis could be provided for putting a floor under oil prices through production controls, thereby benefiting most of the parties involved.

To a substantial degree the market is already creating incentives to tie together the interests of producers with those of refiners. Many of the OPEC countries have moved into downstream activities, either by building refineries in their own countries, as is the case with Saudi Arabia, or, as Kuwait and Venezuela have done, by purchasing downstream operations within the consuming marketplaces in Europe and the United States.

Crises create strange partnerships. The circumstances of a price collapse could well do this not only with respect to rationalizing production, but also with respect to reintegrating upstream and downstream operations. With an impending price collapse, the high-reserve, low-population oil exporting countries would almost certainly take further steps to integrate themselves into the consuming marketplace.

The national oil companies in the producing countries would thus be assured market access as the oil market becomes reintegrated. And the companies would gain new cash replenishment via partial sale of their downstream assets. And in a price collapse, downstream assets will have a much higher relative market value than will reserves.

The world has been abruptly reminded that the petroleum industry is cyclical and volatile. Its cycles are long term, but they involve enormous magnitudes of change in their impact on the petroleum industry itself, on oil end-users and on the macroeconomies of the world.

No commodity has been as politicized as oil. It is too fundamental to the operations of national economies for governments to allow free markets to operate without political guidance and administrative controls. Today's oil market is essentially out of control. The triumph by the marketplace over governmental intervention in the past half-decade has not brought with it the benefits of market transparency that market proponents once envisaged. It is beside the point that the reason these benefits have been so elusive is the record of politicization and interference by governments over past decades.

The question now is not whether a price collapse will create a new form of politically motivated intervention in the oil market by governments. The question, rather, is whether governments can take the necessary measures to reorient the petroleum sector in a manner compatible with all interests, guard their vested interests, and not create new impediments to market efficiency through which participants in the oil market will lose.

There are ways to build upon market tendencies to assure a rationalization of production and a reintegration of the marketplace, without which the benefits of an efficient marketplace will escape producers and consumers alike. There are ways to achieve success and avoid failure. But the question is whether governments will be able to analyze the problems at hand, in a sufficiently detached and rational manner, and thereby avoid major errors and guard their interests, as well as the interests of most producers and consumers in the world market today.

THE CRISIS OF NATIONAL INSTITUTIONS

31

Uniqueness and Pendulum Swings in US Foreign Policy

GEIR LUNDESTAD*

Is American foreign policy unique? Americans have tended to answer this question in the affirmative. This is true of both proponents and opponents of official policy, of whom the former have been by far the most numerous. They have generally seen America as special in its defense of general values and principles—democracy, the rights of neutral countries and the right to self-determination. We are all familiar with some of the images used to describe the special mission of the United States in the world: 'a city upon a hill', 'a chosen people', 'the Israel of our time', 'God's own country'. While other states had interests, the United States had responsibilities. Its prime mission was nothing less than to save the world.

On the political side an abundance of quotations can be used to illustrate this sense of uniqueness. Woodrow Wilson proclaimed that 'Whenever we use our power, we must use it with this conception always in mind—that we are using it for the benefit of the persons who are chiefly interested, and not for our own benefit.' John F. Kennedy

* The author is Professor of American Civilization at the University of Tromsø, Norway. He has been Chairman of the Council of the Norwegian Institute of International Affairs since 1977 and in 1983 was a visiting scholar at Harvard University. He is the author of several books on American foreign policy.

referred to '. . . our right to the moral leadership of this planet'.[1] Ronald Reagan has again and again reaffirmed the basic creed, the 'undeniable truth that America remains the greatest force for peace anywhere in the world today . . . the American dream lives—not only in the hearts and minds of our countrymen but in the hearts and minds of millions of the world's people in both free and oppressed societies who look to us for leadership. As long as that dream lives, as long as we continue to defend it, America has a future, and all mankind has reason to hope.'[2] Tension may easily develop between being unique on the one hand and defending universal values on the other. This tension is rarely explored.

For a long time the picture of America presented in American history textbooks did not differ very much from that of the politicians. The authoritative textbooks saw the United States as the young Siegfried, 'magically strong, and innocent of the burdens of history, yet at the same time an orphan, surrounded by potential enemies in an unrecognizable world.'[3] Although leading academic historians have usually been wary of such generalizations, numerous 'traditionalist' historians put the responsibility for the origins of the cold war squarely on the Soviet Union. It was, in the words of Arthur M. Schlesinger, Jr., long seen as '. . . the brave and essential response of free men to communist aggression'.[4]

Hardly anyone among the minority of the critics of American foreign policy has argued that the United States is the most evil country in the world. Instead critics have tended to agree that America had a service, even a mission, to perform. The problem was that America's true values had been corrupted by certain evil interests—flawed Presidents, the capitalistic system, 'merchants of death' or the military–industrial complex. In the 1972 presidential campaign George McGovern compared Richard Nixon to Hitler, but a more basic theme was his 'Come home, America'. The father of cold war revisionism, William Appleman Williams, called his seminal book *The tragedy of American diplomacy*.[5] The main tragedy, he wrote, was the way in which sincere idealism had been subverted by ulterior forces, in his opinion by the overvaluation of power and the greed of capitalism.

Most European observers have been rather sceptical about the American claim to uniqueness, particularly as it usually implied American superiority. To many Europeans, what was unique about America was its uncanny ability to make the most inspiring idealism coincide almost perfectly with rather ordinary national objectives. Or, as Winston Churchill put it in 1945 after listening to yet another American sermon on the evils of international power politics: 'Is having a Navy twice as strong as any other power "power politics"? Is having an overwhelming Air Force, with bases all over the world, "power politics"? Is having all the gold in the world buried in a cavern "power politics"? If not, what is "power politics"?'[6]

American leaders lectured the world on the dangers and immorality of spheres of influence, except of course the United States' sphere of influence in Latin America. Or they pressed for the internationalization of waterways, except for the Panama Canal. They argued for the principles of free trade, except in those few fields where the United States stood to lose from international competition. And, at the top of its hierarchy of values, the United States always stood for democracy, except when a popularly elected left-wing government could be seen working closely with the Soviet Union or when authoritarian law-and-order regimes were supported, for various reasons.

My introductory question about the uniqueness of America cannot be answered by logical exercise. We have to look at history. The surprising thing is how little has actually been done in the way of direct comparison between US policies and those of other great powers. Americans undoubtedly have perceived themselves as special. Most courses at American universities in US foreign relations are implicitly and often explicitly based on that premise. Has the United States really behaved very differently from other great powers?

Great Powers and Constant Objectives

In British foreign policy, it is generally alleged, balance-of-power considerations have been the guiding star. We are all familiar with Lord Palmerston's famous dictum, that Britain has 'no permanent friends . . . only permanent interests', and Churchill's description of Britain's alliance policy:

> For four hundred years the foreign policy of England has been to oppose the strongest, most aggressive, most dominating power on the Continent . . . it would have been easy and . . . tempting to join with the stronger and share the fruits of his conquest. However, we always took the harder course, joined with the less strong Powers, . . . and thus defeated and frustrated the continental military tyrant whoever he was . . .[7]

Britain thus tried to prevent Europe from falling under the domination of one country or one ruler, whether the Spain of Philip II, the France of Louis XIV and Napoleon, the Germany of William II and Hitler or the Soviet Union of Stalin and Khrushchev.

The French have always been preoccupied with the grandeur of their nation. Of more immediate concern, at least since 1870, has been the protection of their natural frontiers and, particularly in that context, the role of Germany. Only after the Second World War were French fears partially relieved. As the French writer François Mauriac put it: 'I love Germany so. Every day I thank God that there are two of them.'[8]

Russian, as well as Soviet, foreign policy appears to have been guided by that old axiom, 'That which stops growing begins to rot'. Force often provided the instrument and Pan-slavism and orthodoxy the rationaliations for Russia's expansion. The Soviet state has combined force with what its leaders call 'the laws of the class struggle' or what a Western observer has described as Soviet convictions 'both of the infallibility of the communist word and of the inevitability of a communist world.'[9]

What are the corresponding constant factors in American foreign policy, besides the sense of uniqueness? Isolationism was long seen as such a factor. Not any more. Instead in the 1960s and 1970s we heard much of American expansionism.

Certain constant objectives can be found in American foreign policy. Three in particular are often picked out: the physical survival of the United States, the perpetuation of the American way of life, and the promotion of the economic well-being of the American society.[10] At least since the Russian revolution of 1917, the containment of communism could be listed as a fourth objective.

These factors, however, are so general that with the possible exception of the term 'the American way of life' and its many ramifications, their various national counterparts could apply equally well to a great number of other states. Let me therefore introduce my favourite: the pendulum swings. Here is the argument: While there are of course elements of change in the foreign policies of all countries, the swings of the pendulum have been wider, not to say wilder, in the United States than in other great powers. Many states move from one position to a different one. In America the pendulum swings back and forth repeatedly.

Many observers have noted the swings of the American foreign policy pendulum. As early as 1951 the historian Dexter Perkins published his account of a 'cyclical theory of American foreign policy' where he distinguished between periods of peace, periods of rising nationalism that precede war, and periods of nationalism that follow war.[11] In 1952 Frank L. Klingberg divided the history of American foreign relations into periods of 'extroversion' and 'introversion', both of approximately 25 years' duration.[12]

Policy-makers have noticed the same swings. In their first meeting after Richard Nixon had been elected President in 1968, Henry Kissinger told the President-elect that 'the overriding problem was to free our foreign policy from its violent fluctuations between euphoria and panic, from the illusions that decisions depended largely on the idiosyncrasies of decision-makers.' Kissinger recommended a 'British' approach: 'Policy had to be related to some basic principles of national interest that transcended any particular Administration and would therefore be maintained as Presidents changed.'[13] In a recent issue of *Foreign Affairs*, Secretary of State George Shultz has stressed the same theme, although he felt that this was as much a problem for all democracies as specifically for an American one.[14]

So there is little really new in a theory of American foreign policy swings. What this article attempts to do is, first, to give specific examples of such swings; secondly, to provide some of the badly needed comparisons with policies of other great powers; and, thirdly, to review some of the explanations for why the swings on the American side are so much wider.

Some Basic Policy Swings

The basic swing on the American side in the last fifty years is the one from the isolationism of the 1930s—and the Neutrality Acts of 1935—37 represented the most extreme point of this isolationism—to America's very expansive role after the Second World War, a role which culminated in the dispatch of more than 500,000 men to that less than strategically vital area, Vietnam.

It has been argued, with considerable justice, that America's basic assumptions about the outside world changed far less than the dramatic shift in its outward appearance might indicate. The sense of being special, even morally superior, remained untouched. Under isolationism America had to be protected from the corrupting influences of the traditional great powers. After the Second World War most of these powers lay shattered. Now America was in a position of such strength that there was little chance of corruption by its evil surroundings. In fact, in many parts of the world the United States was invited by various local governments to play a larger role to forestall the spread of communism, to strengthen their national economies, to reduce colonial influence and to accomplish an assortment of other objectives.[15]

Although the 'involvement' pendulum has fluctuated considerably, internationalism and globalism have clearly maintained their position in American foreign policy since 1945. On this specific point, therefore, the swing on the American side is similar to some of the predominantly one-directional swings we have witnessed in the policies of other powers. The Soviet role in the world has also been growing. In the 1920s and 1930s Moscow partly isolated itself and partly was kept in isolation by others. In the 1940s this changed dramatically, but the Soviet Union still counted for little outside its border areas. Only in the 1950s and 1960s did it develop both the interest and the capabilities necessary to play a global role, similar to the one which the United States had already been performing for some time.

The importance of the old powers has declined. British foreign policy traditionally moved within three circles: the Atlantic, the Commonwealth, and Europe. The European dimension gradually became more and more important at the expense of the other two. Britain and France have both experienced sweeping changes in their colonial roles. Their empires are gone, and so are most other empires.

In West Germany the pendulum swung from Konrad Adenauer's staunch anti-communism to Willy Brandt's detente-oriented *Ostpolitik*. But, here again, the basic change was in one direction only. The Christian Democrats came to adhere to the basic course set by Brandt. In Britain, both Labour and the Conservatives moved closer to Europe. No party could reverse the colonial decline of the European powers.

In China, policy swung from the pro-Soviet line of the 1950s to the anti-Soviet attitude of the 1960s and 1970s, and from anti-Americanism to the opening to America in 1971–2. However, the repeated Chinese shifts between isolationism and involvement seem to approach the American swings which are the subject of this article.

Even movements from one position to another would normally be more dramatic on the American side. During the Second World War few nations pressed harder than the United States for the unconditional surrender of Germany and even for its de-industrialization in the form of the Morgenthau Plan. After the war, it took only a few years before the United States argued more strongly than anyone for the removal of most of the restrictions on West Germany's freedom of action, including the right to bear arms. Developments in Japan followed a rather similar pattern. Nowhere was the fascination with China and the support for Chiang Kai-shek greater than in the United States. After 'the loss of China', no European capital could measure up to Washington in its insistence on isolating the new rulers. Finally, in 1945 no people had higher hopes than the Americans for the United Nations. Again, disillusionment soon set in more severely here than in almost any other country.

The American Attitude to the Soviet Union and to Defence Spending

But the focus of this article is on recurrent change, swings back and forth, not simply from one position to another. It is here that the special nature of America's foreign policy is most pronounced. My examples and comparisons will come from two crucial fields, East–West relations and defence spending.

In Soviet–American relations since the Second World War at least four main periods, or swings of the pendulum, can be detected: the period during the war, the years from 1945/6 to 1963, from 1963 to the middle to late 1970s, and, finally the period since the late 1970s.[16]

American's conduct in the Second World War was characterized by faith in the possibility of cooperation with the Soviet Union. To give only a few, rather over-simplified, expressions of this: In March 1942 Franklin Roosevelt told Churchill, 'I know you will not mind my being brutally frank when I tell you that I think I can personally handle Stalin better than either your Foreign Office or my State Department. Stalin hates the guts of all your top people. He thinks he likes me better, and I hope he will continue to do so.'[17] In March 1943, *Life* published a special issue on the Soviet Union in which, among other things, Lenin was proclaimed 'perhaps the greatest man of modern times', the Russians 'one hell of a people . . . [who] to a remarkable degree . . . look like Americans, dress like Americans, and think like Americans', and the NKVD 'a national police similar to the FBI'.[18] As late as August 1945, 54 per cent of a sample of the public thought that the Soviet Union could be 'trusted to cooperate with us after the war is over'. That figure was only one per cent less than the wartime high immediately after the Yalta Conference. 30 per cent did not have such trust, while 16 per cent were undecided.[19]

Then in late 1945 the pendulum began to swing towards the other extreme. Soon 'Uncle Joe' Stalin was seen as another Hitler. As Truman later wrote about his own thinking after the North Korean attack on South Korea on 24 June 1950:

> In my generation this was not the first occasion when the strong had attacked the weak. I recalled some earlier instances: Manchuria, Ethiopia, Austria. I remember how each time that the democracies failed to act it had encouraged the aggressors to keep going ahead. Communism was acting in Korea just as Hitler, Mussolini and the Japanese had acted ten, fifteen and twenty years earlier.[20]

A student of Hollywood films has noted of this period: 'Gone are the brave Russian women fighters, the happy villagers, and the democratic allures of the rulers. In their place somber bureaucrats, counterparts of the Nazis, spread an atmosphere of oppression.'[21] The number of people who believed that the United States could cooperate with the Soviet Union fell rapidly. In 1957, only 3 per cent had a highly or even mildly favourable opinion of the Soviet Union, while 74 per cent expressed a highly unfavourable opinion.[22]

Then, after the Cuban missile crisis of 1962, the pendulum slowly began to swing the other way. Detente was arriving. Its climax was probably reached in 1972–3. At the signing of the SALT I agreement Richard Nixon waxed lyrical: 'The historians of some future age will write the year 1972 . . . that this was the year when America helped to lead the world up out of the lowlands of constant war and onto the high plateau of lasting peace.'[23]

Below the official level, detente and the Vietnam war caused Americans much soul-searching. To mention one example, revisionism flourished in historical writings on the origins of the cold war, and a rapidly growing group of American historians told a somewhat startled world that the United States, not the Soviet Union, as most of us in Western Europe had always believed, was to blame for the cold war. In 1972, 40 per cent of a sample expressed a favourable opinion of the Soviet Union, while 32 per cent had a very unfavourable and 22 per cent an unfavourable one. As late as 1967, only 19 per cent were favourable.[24]

In the late 1970s the pendulum started to swing the other way again. And it swung all the way to the other extreme. The swings did not get smaller, as many observers had argued they would. The new climate was clearly noticeable in the last years of the administration of President Carter, but the climax was reached with President Reagan. In June 1982 Reagan described to the British parliament '. . . the march of freedom and democracy which will leave Marxism–Leninism on the ash heap of history as it has left other tyrannies which stifle the freedom and muzzle the self-expression of the people.'[25] In short, the Soviet Union represented the 'focus of evil in the modern world . . . an evil empire'.

Again public confidence in the Soviet Union plummeted. After the Soviet invasion of Afghanistan, only 13 per cent of a sample had a favourable opinion of the Soviet Union; in September 1983, after the shooting down of the KAL airliner, only 9 per cent. This was the lowest level since the 1950s.[26]

There have been as many as six or seven different periods in the pattern of American defence spending since 1945, an observation which seems to indicate that levels of American defence spending do not depend exclusively or even primarily on perceptions of the Soviet Union. After the Second World War Truman thought $15bn. the absolute maximum figure that the United States could spend on defence, despite the fact that the 1945 defence budget had surpassed $80bn. With the Korean war, defence spending tripled in the course of three years, and in 1953 it came to $50bn. That constituted 13.8 per cent of the American GNP, the highest ever since the Second World War. (In 1945, 38.5 per cent of GNP had been allocated to defence.)[27]

Then Eisenhower brought 'fiscal responsibility' back again, and the 'new look' strategy was drawn up to reflect 'sound budgetary policies'. The result was that as late as 1960 the defence budget stood at only $46bn. (in current prices). John F. Kennedy proclaimed that 'we shall pay any price, bear any burden, meet any hardship, support any friend, oppose any foe, in order to assure the survival and success of liberty. This much we pledge—and more.'[28] Even if, as with so much American rhetoric, this remark was not to be interpreted literally, in the early 1960s defence expenditure again increased fairly rapidly. The war in southeast Asia soon made it rise even more steeply.

In the 1970s the defence budget declined. Although this was partly the result of reduced expenditure on the war in Vietnam, after inflation is taken into account it becomes clear that the budget had suffered a marked decline. When the 1978 defence budget passed the $100bn. mark the figure represented only 5 per cent of GNP, the lowest level since 1948.[29]

Finally, under the late Carter administration and even more under President Reagan, defence expenditure just could not be increased fast enough. President Reagan's total of $1,007,900m. over his first four years included the biggest build-up in peacetime in modern American history.[30] Reagan told the American Legion: 'Possibly some of you remember drilling with wooden guns and doing maneuvers with cardboard tanks. We must never repeat that experience.'[31]

It could be argued that since 1984 we have been witnessing the beginning of a new swing of the pendulum. In American–Soviet relations, the Reagan administration began to soften its rhetoric dramatically. Contacts were resumed, and in November 1985 President Reagan and the new Soviet leader, Mr Mikhail Gorbachev, met. The 1986 American defence budget amounted to $298.7bn. This latest increase, however, was due to inflation, since Congress now refused to agree to any real growth. In January 1981, 61 per cent of a sample of the American public had favoured increased defence spending. In February 1985 this figure was down to 16 per cent.[32] Only time will tell how lasting these changes will be, and how far back the pendulum will swing this time.

Britain, the Soviet Union and Defence Spending

If we compare American attitudes to the Soviet Union and defence spending with attitudes in Western Europe, and Britain in particular, pendulum swings appear here too but they seem to be on a smaller scale than in America. In 'soft' periods in the United Kingdom, British attitudes to the Soviet Union are generally 'harder' than in the United States, while in 'tough' periods they tend to be more conciliatory. This tendency is most noticeable at the top policy-making level, and is probably less pronounced in a comparison of public opinion in the two countries.

To simplify matters vastly: during the Second World War there was less faith in Britain than in America in the lasting nature of the common objectives of the Grand Alliance. As Churchill said in 1941 about his purpose in cooperating with the Soviet Union: 'I have only one purpose, the destruction of Hitler, and my life is much simplified thereby. If Hitler invaded Hell I would make at least a favourable reference to the Devil in the House of Commons.'[33] Balance-of-power considerations had brought Britain and the Soviet Union together. In the United States the balance of power was an evil concept. In Britain there was a less pronounced tendency to assume that the allies were becoming more and more alike as a result of sharing the same overriding objective in war. Most Cabinet members, both Conservative and Labour, the Foreign Office, the top military leaders and most of the establishment in general maintained an evident scepticism about Soviet intentions, although they—and Churchill himself—were influenced by the climate of wartime cooperation. At the level of public opinion, however, strong signs of a pro-Russian mood could be found.[34]

Between 1945 and early 1946, British–Soviet antagonism was more pronounced than the American–Soviet version. While during the first years after the war the British, like most West Europeans, were worried that the Americans might not show sufficient interest in containing the Soviet Union, they soon came to fear that they would do too much. In part this reflected European ambivalence toward the United States, an ambivalence most strongly expressed in non-European matters. But Europe's fears also illustrated the sweeping anti-communist mood in the United States. In December 1950 Attlee flew to Washington, to warn against American use of atomic weapons in Korea and to encourage the exploration of a settlement with the Soviet Union.[35] After Stalin's death in 1953 the British, again under Churchill's leadership, showed greater interest than the Americans in East–West summits and agreements. This shift towards dialogue continued under the Premiership of Anthony Eden and Harold Macmillan. It was undoubtedly stimulated in part by a lingering desire for Britain to play a world role and for a chance for the Prime Ministers to exercise their considerable diplomatic skills.[36] Again, at the level of public opinion the British change in attitude was probably similar to that in the United States, although direct comparisons are difficult. Any pro-Soviet mood gradually disappeared, and in the 1950s only 3 to 6 per cent approved and 70 to 80 per cent disapproved 'of the role the Soviet Union is now playing in world affairs'.[37]

This pattern was repeated in the period of detente and conservative reaction in the United States. Joseph Frankel has concluded that 'Whereas British governments used to lead during the previous attempts at an East–West detente, ever since 1968, they had begun to lag behind their partners.'[38] There were many reasons for this lag, which was apparent under both Wilson and Heath governments: a strong reaction against the Soviet invasion of Czechoslovakia in 1968, a certain distancing from the detente policies pursued by De Gaulle in France and Brandt in West Germany, a preoccupation with the 'east of Suez' debate, the expulsion of 105 Soviet representatives in 1971. Public opinion probably changed less in a pro-Soviet direction than it did in the United States. While in 1973–74 disapproval ratings of the Soviet Union had fallen to 39 per cent, approval had increased only to 17–18 per cent, with over 40 per cent answering 'don't know'.[39]

In the late 1960s and early 1970s the British, like most Europeans, probably expected less from detente than many Americans. Nor, for many different reasons, was there the same need in Britain to oversell detente in order to undermine opposition to agreement with the Soviet Union, as was the case in the United States.

The Europeans expected less and gained more: normalization of relations in Germany and Berlin, increased trade and human contacts across the East–West divide. The Americans expected more and gained less. For this and other reasons, events outside Europe—Soviet policies

Figure 1: NATO military expenditure, 1950–84[a]

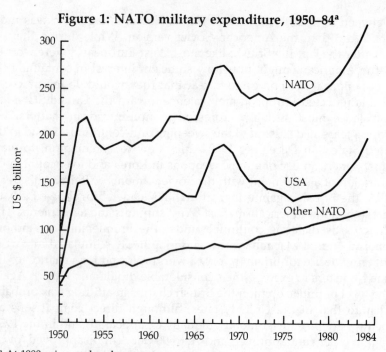

[a] At 1980 prices and exchange rates.
Source: This figure is gratefully reproduced by permission from *SIPRI yearbook 1985* (London: Taylor & Francis, 1985), p. 229.

in Angola, Ethiopia, and Afghanistan—brought about less of a detente backlash in Western Europe than in the United States. Even Prime Minister Margaret Thatcher, so close to President Reagan on many questions, wanted to maintain more open lines to the Soviet Union, as was illustrated in the gas pipeline dispute.

The smaller swings of the pendulum on the European side (plus Canada) with regard to defence expenditure are represented in Figure 1. The ups and downs on the American side are clearly visible. On the European side, the stability is quite remarkable: here there has been a fairly consistent, though small, increase in most years since 1950. (Roughly the same basic pattern is found if we look at individual countries in Western Europe.) To mention one example: while in the late 1970s the Americans came to feel rather strongly that they had to reverse an earlier decline, the Europeans pointed out that they had in fact been increasing their defence budgets all through the 1970s. But Figure 1 also illustrates the 'American' point, that the United States continues to out-spend the Europeans, despite the roughly equal size of America's economy and that of its European NATO partners.

Soviet Attitudes to the West and to Defence Spending

Winston Churchill described the Soviet Union as 'a riddle wrapped in a mystery inside an enigma'. In many ways it is of course true that Western knowledge about the Soviet Union is quite limited. In the analysis of political processes and the motivations behind actions, we in the West are generally dealing in varying degrees of ignorance.

Yet it can also be argued that Soviet actions are more predictable than American ones. To quote James Schlesinger: 'The passage of almost half a century has provided sufficient experience to make Soviet policy almost predictable. There is persistency, perhaps even consistency—and remarkably few sharp turns. Can the same be said of US attitudes and US policy? Hardly so.'[40]

Soviet attitudes to the United States appear to follow the same pattern and to have fluctuated less than American attitudes to the Soviet Union. The pattern probably also applies to Soviet defence spending. The Soviet foreign policy pendulum has certainly swung, but more narrowly than the American one.

During the Second World War and again in the period of detente in the late 1960s and early 1970s, euphoria about East–West cooperation was rather more controlled in Moscow than in Washington. Even in the struggle against Hitler's Germany the Western allies were kept at arm's length. The basic antagonism between capitalism and communism had not ceased to exist. The most significant lowering of the Soviet ideological guard was probably immediately after the invasion of Normandy in June 1944. For the first time, *Pravda* published figures on the massive aid the Soviet Union had been receiving from the West, primarily from the United States. Stalin even suggested that the Soviet Union, Britain and the United States should establish a joint staff to coordinate their operations. This new climate lasted only a few months. Soon Moscow reverted to the established line. The Red Army was the only decisive force in the war. Stalin was no longer interested in a joint military staff.[41]

A similar pattern was repeated in the 1970s, although Leonid Brezhnev certainly saw greater advantages in peaceful coexistence than Stalin. On 30 August 1973, in an editorial entitled 'Peaceful coexistence and the class war', *Pravda* praised East–West cooperation, but went on to state: 'The struggle between the proletariat and the bourgeoisie, between international socialism and imperialism, will continue until the complete and final victory of Communism throughout the world.'[42] At the 25th Party Congress in 1976, Brezhnev warned, 'Detente does not in the slightest way abolish and cannot abolish or change the laws of the class struggle. We do not conceal the fact that we see detente as a way to create more favourable conditions for peaceful socialist and communist construction.'[43]

Figure 2: Military spending, United States and Soviet Union, 1945–68[a]

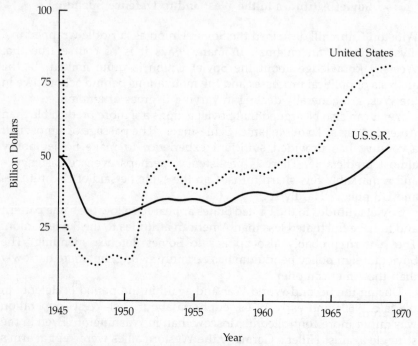

^a Soviet spending is nominal defence category, plus defence-related research and development. Figures are given in dollars, converted from roubles at ratios of domestic purchasing power rather than legal exchange rates.

Source: This figure is gratefully reproduced from George H. Quester, *Nuclear diplomacy: the first twenty-five years* (New York: Dunellen, 1970), p. 293.

Knowledge in the West about levels of Soviet defence spending is limited, and estimates on the subject are subject to a minefield of methodological problems. Still, to quote from a study by the Stockholm International Peace Research Institute, 'More trust can be placed in the trend than in the absolute level.'[44] Figure 2 illustrates the trend of the Soviet defence budget compared to that of the United States.

One fact seems to stand out from Figures 1 and 2, as well as from most other studies: the swings on the Soviet side are less violent. The decline in Soviet defence spending after the Second World War was much smaller than that on the American side. The wartime level had been lower, and Soviet spending remained higher in the immediate postwar period. In the late 1940s and early 1950s the Soviet defence budget did increase, but considerably less than in the United States. There was modest growth in the 1950s and somewhat quicker growth in the 1960s and into the 1970s. Although this development was neither sudden nor dramatic, a 3–4 per cent increase sustained over a long period will yield significant results. On the American side, defence spending fell in real terms in the 1970s after the build-up of the 1960s. Partly in order to compensate for this, in his first administration President Reagan increased real spending by an average of nearly 9 per cent, while the Central Intelligence Agency has estimated that Soviet defence expenditure, adjusted for inflation, has grown at about 2 per cent a year from 1976 to 1983.[45]

The American Swings Explained

How then do we explain these violent swings on the American side? Many different explanations have to be taken into account, of which each could justify a separate article, even a book.[46] I shall only offer some brief comments on what I consider the most important of all these factors.

First, countries have to change policies because the international environment changes. It would be a strange policy indeed which had remained unchanged in spite of the changes in the political and strategic map of the world since 1945. But why should this factor result in wider pendulum swings in America than in other countries? The United States has enjoyed greater freedom of action than most other countries. Its location in the Western hemisphere—plus the British navy—made it possible for the United States to choose isolationism. After the Second World War its new position as by far the world's strongest power formed the material background for the informal American empire.[47] The Europeans, on the other hand, simply had to involve themselves in each other's affairs. Isolationism was not a real option. After 1945, empire was not either.

The Soviet Union was the only country which resembled the United States in these respects. Its size, strength, and geographical location made it possible for Moscow to choose at least 'semi-isolation'. After the war the Red Army controlled most of Eastern Europe, and the Soviet Union was the second strongest power in the world. Its 'semi-isolation' came to an abrupt end. Again, the Soviet Union was dominated by an ideology with globalist aspirations, a source both of strength and of a sense of vulnerability. In the Soviet Union, as in the United States, there were fierce policy debates about the proper attitude to the outside world. To stretch the likeness a little further, the isolationists in the United States can in some ways be compared to the Slavophiles in Russia, and the internationalists to the Westernizers.[48]

Then, party politics have been mentioned as a factor explaining the American swings. Again, the definition of what constituted American national interests was undoubtedly influenced by the existence of and rivalry between the two parties with their different geographical, class and ethnic bases. But, once again, ideological differences between the major parties are rather smaller in the United States than in most other democracies.

Three slightly different institutional explanations would seem to be more important. First is the so-called presidential 'predecessor' argument. As John Gaddis has written, '. . . incoming administrations tend to define their geopolitical codes, not by an objective and dispassionate assessment of what is going on in the outside world, but by a determination not to repeat what they see as their immediate predecessor's errors.'[49] Every President has his own foreign policy. Regardless of what course Washington comes to pursue, the newest 'new' policy is always here to stay because, it will be argued, it is most directly in tune with the deepest desires of the American people. On the other hand, many of these 'predecessor' changes have been cosmetic, and have had more to do with presentation than substance.

The second explanation concerns the sharing of power. Arthur Schlesinger, Jr., has focused on one part of this: the ebbs and flows in the struggle for power between the President and Congress. Strong Presidents will, sooner or later, provoke a reaction from Congress, and congressional supremacy will, in turn, lead to a resurgence of presidential authority. The interventionism of Theodore Roosevelt and Woodrow Wilson stimulated the congressional isolationism of the 1920s and 1930s. Then, '. . . the memory of the deplorable congressional performance in foreign affairs . . . gave Americans in the postwar years an exalted conception of presidential power.' This led to Vietnam and, in turn, to the War Powers Act of 1973.[50]

Another aspect of power-sharing and of other constitutional arrangements is the fact that it is relatively easy to block legislation and appropriations. The result is that, in Joseph Nye's words, 'In order to shorten the lags in formulating consensus in our democracy, the political leadership must exaggerate the degree of external threat.'[51]

There is much to Schlesinger's point, but this article has dealt primarily with the many swings *within* presidential–congressional swings. Even in the period of executive leadership and relative bipartisanship, from the 1940s to the late 1960s, the swings of the policy pendulum were pronounced.

Nye's explanation, as a general element, probably lets the top political leadership off too lightly. Various administrations have undoubtedly, for tactical reasons, painted the international picture with a broader brush than was done in internal analyses. The public presentation of the Truman Doctrine in 1947, of the ideas behind National Security Document 68 in 1950, and of the prospects for detente in the early 1970s provide three examples among many.

On the other hand, the first two presentations in particular were not really that different from what policy-makers actually believed at the time. And there are examples of an administration swinging further out than public opinion (most recently, the policies of the Reagan administration). The public wanted both 'strength' and 'peace'. Only gradually did Reagan come to favour the latter.[52]

The third institutional factor concerns the politicized nature of large sections of the American executive branch, sections which would be staffed by permanent civil servants in most Western European countries. The stabilizing influence of the permanent career officials has been particularly strong in Britain (it was exaggerated only slightly in the popular 1980s TV series, *Yes, Minister*). Although the spoils system has been pushed back, many Europeans still find Harold Nicolson's comment that 'the American diplomatic service . . . [is] staffed by a constant succession of temporary amateurs . . ' not only witty but, frequently, all too true.[53]

An ambundance of examples of incompetence on the part of political leaders and their appointees has led many American foreign policy experts (and State Department career officials) to argue that the 'experts' should be given more power, than the influence of Congress should be reduced or even, as George Kennan has argued, that a parliamentary system should be introduced in America.[54] Most such proposals are politically unrealistic, to put it mildly. And it is necessary to remember that this is only one of a complex set of factors.

The Importance of American Cultural Factors

Frank Klingberg has related his extrovert–introvert cycles to swings in many other fields of human behaviour: the alternating strength of major political parties, war cycles, business fluctuations, even the rise and fall of civilizations. In Hegelian fashion he argued that 'the principle of rhythm' is perhaps a basic law in human society.[55]

Klingberg's pattern of extroversion–introversion generational swings, each about 25 years long, breaks down for the years after the Second World War. More specifically, the changes in American attitudes to the Soviet Union and to defence spending have been much shorter-lived than 25 years.

Although a general theory about rhythms can provide useful insights, I would play down the universality of the swings, seeing them instead as rather more typical of the United States. Then I would relate the rhythm theory to certain American cultural factors and argue that it is here we find perhaps the deepest explanation for the swings of American foreign policy.

American society, it can be argued, in many ways adheres to one overall ideology, and Americans are quite satisfied with the fundamental structure of their political system. But it is also possible to argue that the country is built on conflicting cultural sub-values. The exact mix between these values will vary from person to person, but to a larger extent than in most other countries, the basic conflict can probably be found within most US citizens. In some periods certain values will be emphasized, in other periods the opposite values will tend to dominate.

One such pair of cultural values is moralism v. pragmatism.[56] On the moralist side (again to simplify matters vastly), just as in 1862 the United States could not remain half free, half slave, so in 1917 and in 1941 Washington concluded that the world could not remain half free, half slave. After the Second World War the crusade against communism was based on a similar dichotomy.

On the pragmatic side, Americans used to feel (they are probably not so sure any more) that they were the world's leading 'how-to-do-it' people. If one approach does not work, you try something different. Since most Americans are not terribly patient—US athletes have traditionally been better sprinters than marathon runners—they will not wait long for the desired results. This impatience in itself provides an additional explanation for the swings. Aspiring politicians cater to this mood: 'If you elect me, the problem will go away'. This attitude has probably been even more pronounced in American–West European than American–Soviet relations, since the differences with Moscow are recognized as much deeper than any with the West Europeans.

A second pair of cultural values is optimism v. pessimism. As citizens of God's own country, most Americans take it for granted not only that the United States is the 'best' country in the world but also that it is bound to prevail in the long run. That old Army Corps of Engineers slogan, 'The difficult we do immediately; the impossible takes a little longer', has become part of the national creed. There is a solution to every problem. Europeans are less certain. America's foreign policy optimism has not been tempered by foreign occupation, nor even by invasions or defeats.

The conflict with the Soviet Union will be long and tough but, to quote George Kennan, a strong critic of the moralistic–legalistic tradition in American foreign policy:

> Surely, there was never a fairer test of national quality than this . . . the thoughtful observer of Russian–American relations will find no cause for complaint in the Kremlin's challenge to American society. He will rather experience a certain gratitude to a Providence which, by providing the American people with this implacable challenge, has made their entire security as a nation dependent on their pulling themselves together and accepting the responsibilities of moral and political leadership that history plainly intended them to bear.[57]

Caspar Weinberger even wrote about 'prevailing' in a nuclear war, and Reagan has assigned Marxism–Leninism to the ash heap of history.

At the same time, pessimism or, perhaps, rather a strong sense of vulnerability is often expressed. America is a fragile experiment and can be threatened so easily, either by infiltration from within (McCarthy's Communists in the State Department) or by attack from without—Pearl Harbor in 1941, or, according to the extreme version of Reagan's 'window of vulnerability' rhetoric, a Soviet first strike out of the blue. So, while the United States will win, threats are to be found everywhere.

Many other such pairs of values could be mentioned: power (in the sense of how many troops you have) v. ideas (often expressed in the form of a world community of interests); change (America as the world's most revolutionary country) v. stability (the United States as the prime defender of the *status quo*); good v. evil; war v. peace.[58]

The last two of these pairs would seem particularly important. There is a deep-rooted feeling in America (though not only there) that peace is the *normal* condition. Certainly wars and conflicts interrupt the normal, ideal state of affairs, but somehow the expectation remains that once the enemy is defeated—and its surrender should be unconditional—'normalcy' will be brought back. As Henry Kissinger has argued, 'Our deeper problem was conceptual. Because peace was believed to be "normal", many of our great international exertions were expected to bring about a final result, restoring normality by overcoming an intervening obstacle.'[59] The United States itself—and most democracies, for that matter—are considered almost constitutionally incapable of aggressive action. Thus in the postwar world only the Soviet Union stood between America and this world of 'sweet reason and peace'. Or, as Ronald Reagan phrased it in 1980 in a simplistic restatement of this belief: 'Let us not delude ourselves. The Soviet Union underlies all the unrest that is going on. If they weren't engaged in this game of dominoes, there would not be any hot spots in the world.'[60]

Either there is peace or there is war (or at least serious conflict). If the Soviet Union is an 'evil' power, then the United States has to respond accordingly. If the Soviet Union is a 'good' country, as was believed by so many during the Second World War and during the heyday of detente, then conflicts will disappear. The world is black or white, seldom grey. Americans apparently feel uncomfortable with the idea of cooperation in some fields and conflict in others. This underlying dichotomy of black-or-white would appear to be an important explanation for the violent shifts of mood in the United States.

CONCLUSION

It is implicitly assumed in some European quarters that its excessive foreign policy swings are the result of America's short history of close involvement in world affairs. The expectation is that with tradition will come wisdom. Perhaps the swings of the pendulum will lessen (though there have been few signs of this so far). Yet there are absolutely no grounds for arrogance on the part of Europe. As early as 1826, British Foreign Secretary George Canning declared with a flourish, 'I call in the New World to redress the balance of the old'. He was a bit premature. But the crucial role of the United States, or of the Soviet Union for that matter, in European politics since 1945 can only be understood in the light of the Europeans' self-inflicted destruction of their own European-dominated world system.

NOTES

1. For a recent treatment of the theme of American uniqueness see Loren Baritz, *Backfire: a history of how American culture led us into Vietnam and made us fight the way we did* (New York: William Morrow, 1985), pp 19–54.

2. Ronald Reagan in his speech to the American Legion, 22 Feb. 1983, as quoted in US Department of State, *Realism, strength, negotiation: key foreign policy statements of the Reagan administration* (Washington, D.C.: US Government Printing Office, May 1984), p. 6.

3. Frances FitzGerald, *America revised: what history textbooks have taught our children about their country, and how and why these textbooks have changed in different decades* (New York: Vintage, 1980), pp. 128–45. The quotation is from p. 137.

4. Arthur M. Schlesinger, Jr., 'The origins of the cold war,' *Foreign Affairs*, Fall 1967, Vol. 46, No. 1, p. 23.

5. William Appleman Williams, *The tragedy of American diplomacy* (New York: Delta, 1959; rev. and enlarged edn., 1962).

6. Quoted from Christopher Thorne, *Allies of a kind: the United States, Britain, and the war against Japan, 1941–1945* (Oxford: Oxford University Press, 1978), p. 515.

7. Winston S. Churchill, *The Second World War* (London: Cassell, 1948), Vol. 1, *The gathering storm*, p. 162.

8. Quoted from Richard J. Barnet, *The alliance: American–Europe–Japan: makers of the postwar world* (New York: Simon & Schuster, 1983), p. 248.

9. See, for instance, Adam B. Ulam, *Expansion and coexistence: Soviet foreign policy, 1917–1973* (New York: Praeger, 1974), pp. 3–30, esp. p. 12. For the Western observer, see Schlesinger, 'The origins of the cold war', p. 52.

10. These three factors have been taken from Seyom Brown, *The faces of power: constancy and change in United States foreign policy from Truman to Reagan* (New York: Columbia University Press, 1983), pp. 7–9.

11. Dexter Perkins, *The American approach to foreign policy* (New York: Atheneum, 1973), pp. 136–55. The book was originally published in 1951.

12. Frank L. Klingberg, 'The historical alternation of moods in American foreign policy', *World Politics*, Jan. 1952, Vol. 2, No. 1, pp. 239–73.

13. Henry F. Kissinger, *White House years* (Boston: Little, Brown, 1979), p. 12.

14. George P. Shultz, 'New realities and new ways of thinking', *Foreign Affairs*, Spr. 1985, Vol. 63, No. 4, pp. 705–21, particularly p. 706. See also James Schlesinger, 'The eagle and the bear', *Foreign Affairs*, Sum. 1985, Vol. 63, No. 5, pp. 937–61.

15. Geir Lundestad, 'Empire by invitation? The United States and Western Europe, 1945–1952', *Society for Historians of American Foreign Relations Newsletter*, Sept. 1984, Vol. 15, No. 3, pp. 1–21.

16. This brief survey of Soviet–American relations is based primarily on my *Øst, Vest, Nord, Sør: Hovedlinjer i internasjonal politikk 1945–1985* (Oslo: Universitetsforlaget, 1985). See also Joseph S. Nye, ed., *The making of America's Soviet policy* (New Haven: Yale University Press, 1984).

17. Warren F. Kimball, ed., *Churchill and Roosevelt: the complete correspondence*, Vol. 1, *Alliance emerging* (Princeton, NJ, Guildford: Princeton University Press, 1984), p. 421.

18. John Lewis Gaddis, *The United States and the origins of the cold war, 1941–1947* (New York: Columbia University Press, 1972), p. 38.

19. Hadley Cantril and Mildred Strunk, eds., *Public opinion 1935–1946* (Princeton NJ: Princeton University Press, 1951), pp. 370–1.

20. Harry S. Truman, *Years of trial and hope* (New York: Signet, 1965), pp. 378–9.

21. Quoted from Les K. Adler and Thomas G. Paterson, 'Red fascism: the merger of Nazi Germany and Soviet Russia in the American image of totalitarianism, 1930's–1950's', *American Historical Review*, Apr. 1970, Vol. 75, No. 2, p. 1054, note 50.

22. George H. Gallup, *The Gallup poll: public opinion 1935–1971* (New York: Random House, 1972), Vol. 2, *1949–1958*, p. 1464. See also p. 1266.

23. Gerard Smith, *Doubletalk: the story of the first Strategic arms Limitation Talks* (New York: Doubleday, 1980), p. 451.

24. George H. Gallup, *The Gallup poll: public opionion 1972–1977* (Wilmington: Scholarly Resources, 1978), Vol. 1, *1972–1975*, pp. 39, 129; Vol. 2, *1976–1977*, pp. 918–19.

25. US Department of State, *Realism, strength, negotiation*, p. 80.

26. William P. Bundy, 'A portentous year', *Foreign Affairs*, Suppl., 1983, Vol. 62, No. 3, p. 496, note 15.

27. A superior account of American defence policy since 1945 is found in John Lewis Gaddis, *Strategies of containment: a critical appraisal of postwar American national security policy* (Oxford: Oxford University Press, 1982). For the defence budget figures see p. 359.

28. *Public papers of the Presidents of the United States: John F. Kennedy, 1961* (Washington, D.C.: US Government Printing Office, 1962), p. 1.

29. Gaddis, *Strategies of containment*, p. 359. See also Samuel P. Huntington, 'The defense policy of the Reagan administration, 1981–1982', in Fred I. Greenstein, ed., *The Reagan presidency: an early assessment* (Baltimore: Johns Hopkins University Press, 1983), pp. 82–8.

30. Bill Keller, 'As military buildup eases, US evaluates spending', *International Herald Tribune*, 22 May 1985, p. 1.

31. US Department of State, *Realism, strength, negotiation*, p. 3.

32. *International Herald Tribune*, 22 May 1985, p. 5.

33. Churchill, *The Second World War*, Vol. 3, *The Grand Alliance*, p. 331.

34. For a brief analysis of the British public's attitude to the Soviet Union during the Second World War see Paul Addison, *The road to 1945* (London: Quartet, 1977), pp. 134–41. For the elite level see also D. Cameron Watt, 'Britain, the United States and the opening of the cold war', in Ritchie Ovendale, ed., *The foreign policy of the British Labour governments, 1945–1951* (Leicester: Leicester University Press, 1984), pp. 43–60.

35. See, for instance, Alan Bullock, *Ernest Bevin: Foreign Secretary, 1945–1951* (London: Heinemann, 1983), pp. 820–5.

36. For a summary of British policy towards the Soviet Union see Joseph Frankel, *British foreign policy 1945–1973* (London: Oxford University Press, 1975), pp. 193–203.

37. George H. Gallup, *The Gallup international public opinion polls: Great Britain 1937–1975* (New York: Random House, 1977), Vol. 1, *1937–1964*, pp. 241, 325.

38. Frankel, *British foreign policy 1945–1973*, p. 202. See also F. S. Northedge, *Descent from power: British foreign policy 1945–1973* (London: Allen & Unwin, 1974), pp. 265–70.

39. Gallup, *The Gallup international public opinion polls*, Vol. 2, *1965–1975*, pp. 1220–1321.

40. Schlesinger, 'The eagle and the bear', p. 952.

41. Vojtech Mastny, *Russia's road to the cold war: diplomacy, warfare, and the politics of communism, 1941–1945* (New York: Columbia University Press, 1979), pp. 162–5.

42. Adam B. Ulam, *Dangerous relations: the Soviet Union in world politics, 1970–1982* (Oxford: Oxford University Press, 1982), pp. 86–8.

43. Quoted from Robert H. Donaldson, 'Soviet policy in south Asia', in W. Raymond Duncan, *Soviet policy in the Third World* (New York: Pergamon, 1980), p. 234.

44. *SIPRI yearbook 1985* (London: Taylor & Francis, 1985), p. 251, note b.

45. *International Herald Tribune*, 22 May 1985, pp. 1, 5.

46. For a brief review of some such factors see Nye, *The making of America's Soviet policy*, pp. 4–8.

47. Lundestad, 'Empire by invitation?' pp. 1–3.

48. John Lukacs, *A new history of the cold war* (Garden City: Anchor, 1966), pp. 367–73.

49. John Gaddis, 'Strategies of containment', *The Society for Historians of American Foreign Relations Newsletter*, June 1980, Vol 11, No. 2, pp. 1–14. The quotation is from p. 11.

50. Arthur Schlesinger, Jr., 'Congress and the making of American foreign policy', *Foreign Affairs*, Fall 1972, Vol. 51, No. 1, pp. 78–113. The quotation is from p. 94. See also Arthur M. Schlesinger, Jr., *The imperial presidency* (Boston: Houghton Mifflin, 1973), esp. ch. 9.

51. Nye, *The making of America's Soviet policy*, pp. 6–7.

52. William Schneider, 'Public opinion', in Nye, *The making of America's Soviet policy*, pp. 11–35. See also Daniel Yankelovich and John Doble, 'The public mood: nuclear weapons and the USSR', *Foreign Affairs*, Fall 1984, Vol. 63, No. 1, pp. 33–46.

53. Sir Harold Nicolson, *Diplomacy* (Oxford: Oxford University Press, 1969), p. 120. See also Kenneth N. Waltz, *Foreign policy and democratic politics: the American and British experience* (Boston: Little, Brown, 1967), pp. 133–9.

54. Nye, *The making of America's Soviet policy*, pp. 329–54, esp. pp. 348–54; George F. Kennan, *American diplomacy, 1900–1950* (Chicago: Mentor, 1963), p. 82.

55. Klingberg, 'The historical alternation of moods in American foreign policy', pp. 260–8, particularly pp. 262–3.

56. John Spanier, *Games nations play: analyzing international politics* (New York: Praeger, 1972), pp. 325, 327–8.

57. George F. Kennan, 'The sources of Soviet conduct', *Foreign Affairs*, Sum. 1947, Vol. 29, No. 3, pp. 581–2.

58. For interesting comments on some of these pairs see Knud Krakau, 'American foreign relations: a national style?', *Diplomatic History*, Sum. 1984, Vol. 8, No. 3, pp. 253–72; Stanley Hoffmann, *Gulliver's troubles: or, the setting of American foreign policy* (New York: McGraw-Hill, 1968), part 2, esp. pp. 177–8.

59. Kissinger, *White House years*, p. 61.

60. Quoted from Robert Dallek, *Ronald Reagan: the politics of symbolism* (Cambridge, Mass.: Harvard University Press, 1984), p. 141.

32

United States Foreign Policy-Making: Chaos or Design?

NICHOLAS WHEELER and PHIL WILLIAMS

INTRODUCTION

De Tocqueville's assertion that the United States lacked most of the qualities necessary for the successful conduct of foreign policy is, arguably, more compelling in the 1980s than it has ever been. America's capacity to act as a twentieth century superpower is hindered by a political structure based on an eighteenth century constitution—a handicap which will become even more debilitating as the United States is confronted by the problems of the twenty-first century. Indeed, there already appears to be an inverse relationship between problems and performance: at the very time when the qualities of leadership and statesmanship are most in demand they are least in evidence. Far from eliciting a positive and imaginative response, the increasing complexities of foreign policy have generated a return to simple verities and outmoded beliefs. Problems which require long term strategies and solutions are met with short term palliatives which, ultimately, can only make the burden of adjustment that much greater. Indeed, United States policy-makers increasingly appear to be incapable of imposing clarity and consistency of purpose and continuity of design, let alone ensuring the efficient implementation of policy goals. Not only does this make it difficult for the United States to act as an effective leader of the Western Alliance but it also poses acute problems for the Soviet Union in trying to understand and assess its superpower adversary. United States policy-makers often complain that the Soviet political system is opaque and enigmatic. Yet the very openness and turbulence of the American system may be equally, if not more, disconcerting for Soviet observers and analysts. Conflicting signals and sharp discontinuities in both the substance and tone of policy are just two of the problems with which Soviet 'America watchers' have to contend. The task is difficult enough for European allies who share similar traditions and values with the United States. For the Soviet Union it may often prove impossible to understand a system which at times borders on the chaotic.

Although some of the reasons for the disarray in American foreign policy have to do with deeply embedded cultural traits, the main problems lie in an increasingly fragmented political structure. Whereas in the past the United States was able to compensate for these short-comings through the overwhelming economic and military power which gave it a dominant position in the international system, this is no longer the case. The Soviet challenge to American military supremacy has been accompanied by a challenge to America's economic preponderance from Western Europe and Japan. Furthermore, these developments have taken place against a background of increasing interdependence which, far from guaranteeing harmony, has added to the difficulties of managing both alliance and adversary relations.

In these circumstances the structural constraints on American foreign policy-making appear particularly damaging. The Presidency, which in the 1950s was regarded as the key to America's effectiveness in the superpower competition, is itself part of the problem: there are several features of the Presidency which suggest that it has become incapable of providing the managerial skills necessary to impose order on a disorderly process. Paradoxically, the difficulties have been exacerbated by a Congressional reassertion of rights and prerogatives, which has inhibited Presidential leadership without offering any substitute. The President's power to persuade has been undermined by the Congressional power to frustrate. Nor can the bureaucracy provide an alternative source of guidance or inspiration. The United States bureaucratic machine has become increasingly cumbersome, parochial and insensitive to the needs of both domestic and international constituencies. After elaborating upon these structural problems, this article considers some of the consequences not only for the policy-making process but also for the substance of the policies which emerge.

STRUCTURAL CONSTRAINTS

1. The Bureaucracy

Until the late 1940s the American foreign policy-making machine was relatively primitive and undeveloped. During the Second World War there had been a series of ad hoc arrangements such as the Navy-State-War Coordinating Committee. These were recognised as inadequate to the demands of Cold War, however, and in 1947 the apparatus for making national security policy was established with the creation of the National Security Council, the Central Intelligence Agency, and a unified Department of Defence. Although this process of enlargement and consolidation was a necessary response to novel and unprecedented demands, it has brought with it a new set of problems of its own. The bureaucracy is characterised by a number of features which detract from its ability to provide the independent advice and information needed by the chief executive:

—the primacy of organisational interests and perspectives over wider conceptions of national purpose;
—competition between different groups, agencies and departments for resources and influence;
—specialisation of roles and functions with the inevitable concomitants of tunnel vision and resistance to political direction and control;
—a pervasive conservatism based on the desire to protect organisational essences and maintain standard operational procedures.

In short, the American policy-making system is one characterised by multiple actors who are wedded to organisational routines and the protection of vested interests. One result of this is the prevalence of jurisdictional disputes and organisational conflicts which are complicated by the search for allies outside the executive branch. Congress, in particular, often becomes involved in these bureaucratic quarrels either as arbitrator or protagonist. While the role of arbitrator can be very constructive, Congressional intervention in executive branch disputes can also add to the complications. The role of Congress is both positive and negative.

2. Congress

Although the American system is often described as one of separated institutions sharing powers, it was the concentration of power in the Presidency which was the dominant theme in the 1950s and the first half of the 1960s. Congress did little more than rubber-stamp Presidential initiatives: in Korea and Vietnam the President appeared to be usurping the War Powers which constitutionally belonged to Congress; the power of the Senate to advise and consent to the ratification of treaties was also in jeopardy as Presidents made extensive use of executive agreements which did not require legislative approval. Indeed, there appeared to have been almost a structural transformation in American foreign policy as Presidents were allowed to proceed unhindered by Congressional criticism or opposition. Although this was partly a result of Presidential aggrandisement, it was also a consequence of Congressional deference, which encouraged what was almost an abdication of responsibility. In the early 1950s some of the most vigorous champions of Presidential power were to be found in the Senate. There were, of course, some critics of this trend towards a kind of 'Democratic Ceasarism', most notably Senators Robert Taft of Ohio and Kenneth Wherry of Nebraska. Their views, however, were rejected by a majority in the Congress in favour of that expressed by Senator Fulbright when he argued that the President had been hobbled by too niggardly a grant of power.[1] This approach was accompanied by the concentration of authority within both the House of Representatives and the Senate which enabled the President to ensure the success of most of his legislative proposals simply by consulting with a small number of key figures.

In the latter half of the 1960s, there was a profound change in these attitudes, which resulted in Congress attempting once again to assert its influence and fulfil the responsibilities given to it in the Constitution. Central to this resurgence—which stemmed in large part from the widespread disillusionment with the way in which both Johnson and Nixon wielded Presidential power—were efforts to legislate a new framework of laws whereby Congressional roles and participation in the making of foreign policy would be guaranteed. The War Powers Act and the Budget and Impoundment Control Act were perhaps the two most important manifestations of this attempt to 'co-determine' policy.[2]

If this new assertiveness made Congress less willing to accommodate Presidential preferences, it also became more difficult for the President to impose his policies and priorities. This was largely because the changes in attitude were accompanied by changes in the internal structure of Congress. The centralised leadership in both Houses gave way to a diffusion of power. The proliferation of subcommittees under-mined the authority of committee chairmen and the formal party leaders were unable to fill the breach. This made it all the more difficult for Presidents to build winning coalitions. If it was the case—as one commentator observed—that Congress consisted of 535 Secretaries of State, then the problems of consultation, coordination and consensus building became almost insuperable.[3] Furthermore, although the increased staff resources available both to individual members and to committees made Congress better informed and more creative, these improvements were to a large extent offset by what has been termed a 'new irresponsibility'.[4]

> The noisy position-taking and the frequent legislation did not mean that Congress was now ready to take on serious, continuing policy responsibility itself. Too often, rather than define issues and choices more clearly, legislators simply exploited them—while the media amplified their exaggerations. Rather than enforce an alternative policy when unwilling to follow the Presidential lead, Congress would simply increase the political cost of what the Executive Branch wanted to do.[5]

In other words, as Congress has once again become more important, it has also become less manageable.

This has been exacerbated by what a former Secretary for Health, Education and Welfare described as 'molecular government'.[6] Members of Congress have become more individualistic and less tied to party or the President; as a result they have also become more exposed to the activities of single issue pressure groups. Although the lobby has always worked extensively through the Congress, the changes of the 1970s encouraged the formation of close alliances between interest groups and their counterparts in Congress and in executive departments. The result has been that Congress has become, in Etzioni's term, 'semi-anarchic'.[7] Furthermore, these developments were in some ways symptomatic of broader trends in society, which have made it difficult to aggregate demands, achieve consensus, or build viable political coalitions. In the latter half of the 1970s and the early 1980s "there were growing divergences between different parts of the country: the interests of the sunbelt differed from those of the frostbelt; the interests of oil and gas-producing states were at odds with those of consumer states".[8] Such problems are neither novel nor unprecedented. In the past, however, they were contained or offset by the Presidency itself which was able to provide a unifying focus sufficiently powerful to overcome the tendencies towards fragmentation. In the late 1970s, they coincided with a period when the office of the Presidency itself began to exhibit severe difficulties.

3. The Presidency

From the 1930s to the 1950s, the Presidency appeared to be a considerable force for stability and continuity in American politics and society.

The record since the 1960s has been much more ambivalent. If Ronald Reagan serves out a full second term he will be the first President since Eisenhower to do so. Although fortuitous events obviously played a part in increasing Presidential turnover, it is only a little exaggeration to suggest that the election cycle has institutionalised an American version of what is generally thought of as a Soviet problem, i.e., succession crises. There are several dimensions of this.

The first is that increasingly the Presidency seems to be filled by candidates who are more adept at political campaigning than they are at policy-making. As the 1984 Presidential election campaign demonstrated, mastery of the media has become far more important than mastering the issues; image is more crucial than intellect.

The second is that there has been a trend away from the experienced Washington insider to the outsider. Closely related to this has been the rise of governors and the demise of Senators as Presidential candidates. Both Carter and Reagan were former governors, and both arrived in the White House on anti-Washington themes. Carter combined populism and moralism while Reagan promised to make America strong and to get government off the backs of the people. In both cases there has been an inevitable gap between promise and performance. Carter paid the price for this in 1980. Favourable economic trends enabled Reagan to avoid a similar fate in 1984, but the day of reckoning may simply have been postponed. The Republican Party in 1986 and 1988 will have to face the consequences of the promised performance gap especially if the budget deficit increases.

The third aspect of the institutionalised succession crises stems from this lack of an adequate apprenticeship system. Despite Roger Hilsman's claim that "the White House is no place for on the job training", there is no alternative. Yet this can be a highly painful process involving costly and sometimes irretrievable mistakes. However helpful the outgoing Presidential team attempts to be, it can still take a new President and his advisers 12 to 18 months to establish clear patterns, procedures and priorities. The difficulties are exacerbated by the turnover of personnel within the departments themselves. In this connection there has been "a deterioration of administrative competence, owing to the increasing number of political appointees in top management positions chosen for reasons (e.g., policy views, constituencies represented or political services rendered) other than the ability to manage".[9] Consequently, what James Sundquist has called the crisis of competence extends well beyond the Presidency itself;[10] and although it may be the greatest during the first year in the life of an Administration, it does not completely disappear thereafter.

The fourth difficulty caused by the Presidential election cycle—and compounded by the mid-term Congressional elections—is that there is little opportunity for reasoned statesmanship untarnished by calculations of personal or partisan advantage. As three seasoned analysts of American foreign policy have observed:

> Too often the motivating force for . . . Presidents in making key decisions during the past two decades has been either gaining short term political advantage—keeping political adversaries at bay, diverting attention from domestic problems, and scoring political points—or satisfying some set of values that bore little relation to reality but pleased political ideologues.[11]

It might be argued, of course, that there is nothing new in all this, that American foreign policy has always been dominated by considerations of political expediency, and that to expect anything else would be naive. Furthermore, the fragmentation of power and the diffusion of authority are more or less permanent features of American politics and society— and to suggest that the 1970s and 1980s are fundamentally different from earlier periods is to reveal a profound ignorance of American history.

Although these objections caution against over-exaggerating the novelty of the current difficulties, it can still be argued that the problems of the 1980s are of a qualitatively different order of severity from those which bedevilled the policy-makers of the 1950s and 1960s.[12] During this earlier period, the dominance of the Presidency and the docility of the Congress were buttressed by a high degree of bipartisanship or nonpartisanship on foreign policy, as well as by the judgement and expertise of the foreign policy establishment centred on the East Coast universities and law firms, and even more notably in the Council on Foreign Relations. These conditions no longer obtain. Vietnam eroded bipartisanship: liberal defections from the foreign policy consensus in the early 1970s were mirrored later in the decade by a conservative offensive against both the Carter Administration and prominent liberal Senators. At the same time, the parties themselves appeared to become much more rigid and ideological in their approach. There was far less tolerance in their respective parties for either conservative Democrats or liberal Republicans, thereby eroding—although not eliminating—the cross-party alignments which traditionally have facilitated centrist politics in the United States.[13] The consequences of the demise of the centre were heightened by the fact that this coincided, and in certain respects was closely bound up with, the decline of the 'establishment' and the emergence of what Gelb, Destler, and Lake describe as a 'professional elite' of full time foreign policy professionals.[14] Unlike the members of the establishment, who had other careers to pursue in law or business, the foreign policy professionals have a narrow focus. The distinction between members is whether they are in or out of power. If they are out of office their one aim is to get back in. This, of course, is related to the large influx of appointees associated with new Administrations. Inevitably the inflow is accompanied by an exodus, and the outgoing members of the elite, not unnaturally, are highly critical of the usurpers.

This tends to narrow the range of tolerance for Presidential policies and initiatives and gives the foreign policy debate a stridency that is unprecedented. The impact of this, and indeed all the other structural developments, must now be examined.

MAKING FOREIGN POLICY

Although political structures are not the only determinant of either the effectiveness or efficiency of foreign policy, they are obviously important. In the case of the United States, their impact has been highly detrimental to the conduct of foreign policy. The policy-making 'pathologies' extend from periodic intelligence failures through to incremental decision-making, poor coordination, and overselling of innovations as part of an attempt to establish what has been called 'policy legitimacy'.[15] The United States finds it difficult to cope with complexity and hard to accept mixed relationships, whether they be with allies who appear selective in their allegiance or adversaries who simultaneously engage in limited cooperation.

1. Intelligence Failures

The causes of intelligence failures, of course, go far wider than political structures and processes and include both cultural and psychological factors. Nevertheless, the organisational impediments to effective information processing are also very considerable. Specialisation and hierarchy are essential to the efficient functioning of bureaucracies, but also carry with them certain penalties. One of the problems with hierarchy, for example, is that it sometimes leads to a gap between the experts and the decision-makers; the larger and more layered the bureaucracy, the wider the gap. Perhaps even more damaging is the highly competitive nature of the American bureaucracy, the result of which is that information is regarded less in analytic terms than as a device for advancing organisational interests. As Alexander George has argued:

> Each organisational unit's participation in the identification and evaluation of policy options is shaped by its parochial interests and perspectives. Whether cynically or inadvertently, each unit tends to produce 'partisan analysis' of the issues and seeks to discredit by fair means or foul, the analysis produced by its rivals. As a result, the President may be misled or confused and may lack balanced, objective analysis of the options from which he must choose.[16]

During the Vietnam War, for example, information about the impact of military operations was distorted in order to protect or advance organisational goals. This was particularly so with the bombing campaign, where estimates of success were consistently exaggerated. The problems are not simply a result of the cynical manipulation of information, however. Intelligence and policy-making organisations have to work on the basis of relatively stable assumptions about the world. The difficulty is that these assumptions often become entrenched within the organisations, leading them to overlook signals which run counter to the conventional wisdom. A prime example of this can be seen in American estimates of the Shah's ability to maintain political control in Iran in the late 1970s. As one Congressional report concluded: very few analysts were "asking whether the Shah's autocracy would survive indefinitely; policy was premised on that assumption".[17] This tendency to rely on standard operational procedures and well-established beliefs has been strengthened by a vast increase in the workload facing officials. Marshall Shulman, who worked in both the Truman and Carter Administrations has suggested that there was a ten-fold increase in the work load between 1950 and 1980.[18] Such a development can hardly fail to have a numbing affect on the gathering and assessment of information.

It should not be assumed, of course, that these characteristics are unique to the United States. On the contrary, they are almost certainly typical of all large bureaucracies. Nevertheless, the political context within which the bureaucracy has to operate—especially the growing polarisation, the increased salience of ideology, and the dominance of the ideologues—has, at the very least, provided a permissive environment for these bureaucratic shortcomings. Furthermore, the reversion to militant anti-communism after the pragmatism of the early 1970s has added to the potential difficulties in dealing with both allies and adversaries. The rigid attitudes of the ideologues are almost invariably reinforced by their self-righteousness. The danger is that moves towards accommodation by the Soviet Union will be dismissed as insincere, when in fact they offer at least some potential for achieving a less hostile relationship. The intelligence failures which stem from institutionalised paranoia and a lack of empathy with an adversary are less dramatic than those which result from a lack of vigilance—but in the long term their effect might be even more insidious. Once the framework is established, there are all too few reappraisals. Policy tends to proceed along an established path—at least until one set of ideologues are replaced by another. The result is sterility, a sterility which is reinforced by an incremental approach to decision-making.

2. Incremental Decision-Making

Although incrementalism is sometimes applauded as an intellectual response to complexity and a way of coping with uncertainty, it also carries significant dangers. Indeed, it can all too easily degenerate into what George has described as 'sloppy, myopic incrementalism' in which there is no attempt to move beyond immediate problems and short term palliatives.[19] The strategy of muddling through is sometimes inappropriate, either because 'the mud is too thick' or because a change of direction is required.[20] Furthermore, incrementalism can often give the illusion that the policy-makers are maintaining their freedom of action, when in fact they are locking themselves in to a course of action which may prove extremely difficult to reverse. Involvement is much easier than extrication. The implication is that the much vaunted virtues of incrementalism—flexibility and freedom of manoeuvre—are often illusory. This is particularly so in relation to the commitment process: the crucial consideration about incremental commitments—as the United States discovered in Vietnam—is that they are still commitments. The key question, therefore, is not whether they grow by large leaps or small steps but whether the commitment is worth the sacrifices it may require.

These deficiencies in an incremental approach to decision-making are intensified to the extent that it is politically motivated. One of the benefits of incrementalism is that it sometimes facilitates consensus in a way that bolder initiatives do not. This is particularly necessary in the United States, where there are many actors in the process and where major departures often run into what Robert Lovett termed the 'foul-up factor' (any department or agency with any claim to jurisdiction over the policy area attempts to have some say in the decision). The difficulty, however, especially in view of the bureaucratic structure in the United States, is that incrementalism can very easily become stalemate. A policy designed to bring about marginal improvement is particularly vulnerable to those whose predominant concern is with maintaining the status quo. The Reagan Administration's arms control policy is a case in point. When there were some signs of flexibility and compromise on Intermediate Nuclear Forces, these were effectively vetoed by a few officials more concerned with ensuring deployment of the systems than with obtaining an arms control agreement.[21]

This is not to deny the existence of abrupt changes or sharp reversals in American foreign policy. The pressure of events or the change from one Administration to the next can bring major departures from incrementalism. Nevertheless, once the new framework is established it tends to be perpetuated until either the next foreign policy disaster or the accession of the next President. Furthermore, the framework itself is usually geared up to achieve short term benefits. In Reagan's first term, for example, attempts to establish a workable relationship with the Soviet Union were sacrificed in favour of anti-Soviet rhetoric and an emphasis on military strength, both of which were intended, in large part, to restore American feelings of self respect. Indeed, one of the problems with the Presidential election cycle and the four year term is that they encourage a short term perspective which reinforces the conservatism of the bureaucracy. Although concern with what Dean Acheson called the 'thundering present' is inherent in foreign policy, composed as it is of day to day issues and ad hoc responses, Presidents also focus on short term challenges for political reasons. If these problems are managed successfully, the electoral benefits may be considerable, if they are mismanaged, this can be politically disastrous for the incumbent. Even Presidents who are conscious of this trap may find it unavoidable. Jimmy Carter, for example, came to office committed to improving the international order, yet long term concerns were subordinated to more immediate management problems as the 1980 election approached. The hostage crisis gave this a particularly distinctive flavour in the election year itself, but the trend was evident even before the seizure of the American diplomats. The United States is not alone in its concern with the short term, but what makes American perspectives so disquieting is the importance of the United States in the world and the fact that an increasing number of issues, such as nuclear proliferation, poverty and instability in the Third World, and diminishing energy resources demand a long term perspective and require initiatives which do not have immediate electoral benefits. In other words, incrementalism may be indistinguishable from immobilism.

Some of the problems which cause this also make it extremely difficult for the United States to pursue policies which are consistent with each other. Indeed, United States foreign policy often appears to suffer from a lack of co-ordination.

3. Lack of Co-ordination

The United States policy-making process is characterised by the interplay of different groups, agencies, departments and individuals with differing interests and perspectives. The organisations involved are in some respects like feudal baronies whose main loyalties are to themselves rather than to the state; as quasi-independent organisations, they sometimes produce quasi-independent policies. As government has become disaggregated, so too has foreign policy. The implications of this are far-reaching. There may be times, for example, when actions will be taken without the approval of the President. On other occasions, high level decision-makers may find the different organisations ostensibly under their control working at cross-purposes. It is an exaggeration, but one with more than a grain of truth, to suggest that there may be no such thing as American foreign policy but only separate State Department or Defence Department or CIA foreign policies which, at best, will be unrelated and at worst inconsistent or incompatible.

Another characteristic of the multiple actors involved in the formulation and implementation of foreign policies is that some of them may actually have a veto power over certain decisions. This is generally implicit in the bureaucracy with its power of sitting still. It is probably most explicit in the Senate with its possession of what Woodrow Wilson once termed the 'treaty-marring powers'. Indeed, one third of the members of the Senate not only have the power to sabotage carefully calibrated agreements and to repudiate Presidential policies, but can do so in the name of constitutional responsibility. This was apparent in the Senate debate over SALT 2 in 1979.[22] Although, in the aftermath of Afghanistan, Carter deferred further consideration of the Treaty, it had already become apparent that if it did pass the Senate, it would be in such a heavily amended form that negotiations with the Soviet Union would have to be re-opened.

The existence of multiple groups with divergent opinions and policy preferences also complicates the public presentation of policies. Almost inevitably there is a temptation for the President and his leading advisers to attempt to manage different constituencies by orchestrating different words and deeds according to the particular audience to which they are appealing. There are two problems with this approach however. The first is that it does not always work. Jimmy Carter, for example, confronted a dilemma stemming from his campaign promises to cut the defence budget and his rapid realisation that such an option was fraught with dangers. His response was to cut back on Gerald Ford's projections for an increased defence budget while increasing military expenditures beyond those actually incurred by the Ford Administration. Carter subsequently emphasised the reduced projections to liberal audiences and the increased outlays to conservatives whose main concern was the Soviet threat. Almost inevitably the tactic failed: each group picked up the message intended for the other and Carter thereby succeeded in alienating both. The other problem with these contradictory signals, of course, was that they confused both allies and adversaries. Viewed from outside, what were domestic political manoeuvres appeared to be evidence of vacillation or indecision.

More worrying than tactical inconsistencies are the contradictions that sometimes appear between different officials. In the Carter Administration and during the first two years of the Reagan Administration there appeared to be a cacophony of voices offering divergent interpretations of American policy on a host of issues. With leading officials either unable or unwilling to agree among themselves, the responsibility for hammering out a common position falls even more obviously on the President aided by his National Security Adviser. Indeed, the National Security Council was set up in 1947 specially for the task of co-ordinating the diplomatic, military and economic dimensions of policy. Although it has not functioned as an advisory forum in the way originally intended, it has allowed the President to develop his own foreign policy staff— headed by the National Security Adviser. The role of the adviser was initially conceived as a neutral co-ordinator and manager—someone who would ensure that the foreign policy-making process was efficient—rather than as someone who would have a major impact on the substance of policies.[23] In the 1960s, however, this gradually changed and Walt Rostow, Johnson's Special Assistant on national security became a vigorous advocate rather than a detached manager. The role of the National Security Adviser was further enhanced by Henry Kissinger who eclipsed Secretary of State William Rogers and took on all his functions even before taking on the office of Secretary itself.

When Jimmy Carter appointed Zbigniew Brzezinski to the position of National Security Adviser, however, he made clear that he did not want another Kissinger. But although the President regarded Brzezinski as a 'policy thinker' whose role would be to generate new ideas and to manage the flow of information and advice to the President, problems arose because Brzezinski's thinking on crucial aspects of foreign policy was at odds with the approach favoured by Secretary of State Cyrus Vance. Although there were broad differences of philosophy between the two men, in practice the arguments revolved around American policy towards the Soviet Union. Had Carter given full support to either one of them, the political damage from what was a fundamental split in his foreign policy advisory team could probably have been contained. As it was, however, Carter appeared to oscillate between Brzezinski's hard-line approach and the more conciliatory stance advocated by Vance. The result was a period of considerable confusion at both the conceptual and the managerial levels. The position of National Security Adviser had become a liability rather than an asset. Although the position was initially intended to facilitate co-ordination, the emergence of the adviser as an additional policy-maker has added to the problems of co-ordination.

This was less of a problem in the first Reagan Administration, largely because of the people who filled the role. Any gains, however, were at least partially offset by the activism of Secretary of Defence Weinberger, who frequently seemed to encroach upon territory that was naturally the preserve of his counterpart at the State Department. Furthermore, the potential for conflict still exists should the National Security Adviser once again attempt to play an active role in determining policy rather than confining himself to managerial activities. The prospect for more effective co-ordination of policies, therefore, remains rather dismal. Given the need for consensus-building, even if a high degree of unity should exist between the President and his advisers, it is not clear that this can be translated into effective policy. Indeed this has typically led both to the overselling and the over-simplification of policies.

4. Oversell, Over-simplification and Oscillation

The fact that debate on foreign policy in Washington takes place before a variety of audiences means that "the alternatives must be very clear-cut and the arguments painted in colors that are both bold and bright".[24] Along with this goes a tendency to oversell the remedies to foreign policy problems. The danger with oversell is that it creates unrealistic expectations which, if they are subsequently disappointed, leads to a backlash against the policies. Presidential rhetoric, especially during election campaigns, has the same effect. Once again, this is something which existed prior to the 1970s. In the late 1940s, for example, the Truman Administration oversold the Marshall Plan and the North Atlantic Treaty in the sense that both were presented as sufficient to guarantee Western European security. When, in the aftermath of the outbreak of war in Korea, it was deemed necessary to send US troops to Europe, this appeared to contradict these earlier assurances, thereby generating vigorous protests from the Senate.[25] Nevertheless, the difficulties were exacerbated in the 1970s by the developments identified above. The impact of the Vietnam War, the rise of the professional elite, the politicisation of foreign policy and the demise of the centre made it much more difficult to build a stable and lasting coalition which would support President policies when they encountered unanticipated difficulties or failed to provide immediate and very visible payoffs. As one alternative proved unworkable internationally or was rejected domestically, the pendulum tended to swing in the opposite extreme. Nowhere was this more obvious than in superpower relations. Detente was oversold by the Nixon Administration as heralding an end to the era of confrontation and the beginning of the era of negotiation. This attempt to establish 'policy legitimacy' meant that any future Soviet actions which appeared inimical to the United States would be widely interpreted as a breach of faith. Unless detente did result in a fundamental change in the superpower relationship, however, this oversell could only provoke a reaction which would undermine the policy legitimacy it had been designed to establish. Indeed, this was in large part what happened. Agreements such as that on the Basic Principles of Relations between the superpowers were presented as a mutually accepted code of conduct constraining superpower rivalry in the Third World, rather than as a hastily drafted agreement containing inconsistencies and potential contradictions between Soviet and American interpretations. When the Soviet Union did not abide by American interpretations of the rules, therefore, the United States reacted not with an effort to reduce the ambiguities but with denunciation of Soviet conduct. The price of oversell was a widespread feeling that the United States had been duped.

However, the problem is not merely that policies have to be simplified in order to be sold. There are also serious difficulties in attempts to pursue complex strategies and policies. Kissinger's approach to detente is a case in point. Kissinger started from the premise that the superpower relationship was a mixed one containing elements of both conflict and cooperation. Furthermore, he devised a sophisticated approach to the Soviet Union designed to ensure that the cooperative elements prevailed and the Soviet Union engaged in self-restraint or even 'self containment.' This was to be achieved through a mixture of penalties and incentives. Kissinger hoped to entangle the Soviet Union in a web of interdependence thereby enabling the U.S. to offer benefits and inducements for 'good behaviour' and penalties for 'bad behaviour'. This strategy was undermined by domestic pressures, however, as the Jackson-Vanik Amendment to the trade bill made the granting to the Soviet Union of Most Favoured Nation status dependent on a liberalisation of Jewish emigration from the Soviet Union, while the Stevenson Amendment to the Export-Import Bank legislation restricted the amount of credit available to the Soviet Union. If Congress thereby took away one of the carrots, it also took away one of the sticks when it cut off covert aid to the anti-Soviet factions during the Angolan Civil War.

The implication of all this is alarming—not only do policies have to be simplified for public presentation, but only genuinely simple policies have much prospect of obtaining the necessary domestic support.

This conclusion is reinforced by the experience of the Carter Administration. Jimmy Carter's foreign policy recognised the need to deal with complexity. It attempted to get away from the obsessions with the Soviet Union and to treat problems in the Third World on their own merits rather than in the context of the superpower relationship. This approach was extremely difficult to sell to the American public and it is not coincidental that it was replaced in Carter's last year by a more traditional policy of containing the Soviet threat through military strength. This was taken even further in the first Reagan Administration as the President attempted to rebuild the foreign policy consensus of the 1950s with rhetoric that was reminiscent of the pronouncements of John Foster Dulles. Slogans became substitutes for strategies, while strength replaced subtlety in what Stanley Hoffmann has termed the 'new orthodoxy'.[26] Although there was a toning down of the hostile rhetoric during the Presidential election campaign of 1984, there were no serious discussions of how a more balanced relationship with the Soviet Union might be obtained or what it might look like.

What then are the prospects for the future? Will domestic political needs and the constraints of the American political system continue to militate against renewed attempts at superpower accommodation?

THE FUTURE

One of the more important tasks for Reagan's second term will be to obtain domestic acceptance for the idea of an 'adversary partnership' between the superpowers with all its ambiguities and apparent contradictions. This will not be easy. Reagan's appeal in 1980 was based upon the need to make America strong again. This imperative was underlined by analyses of Soviet behaviour which emphasised that Soviet strategic developments would encourage Soviet aggression. Not only did this help to justify and rationalise American strategic programmes but it also provided an air of certainty on issues which are inherently uncertain. The arguments that the Soviet strategic build up was about to provide a 'window of vulnerability' of American land-based missiles which in turn would create a 'window of opportunity' for Soviet adventurism were based on simplistic interpretations of the sources of Soviet conduct. They offered a 'reductionist' view of Soviet policy, which was deemed to be crucially dependent on the strategic balance and almost nothing else.[27] As one analyst observed:

> the period of peril theory is a self-contained system of thought. If its basic assumption of technological determinism and its projections of Soviet capabilities are accepted there is almost no way in which it can be invalidated. The argument therefore has a powerful persuasive appeal. Its ramifications can be derived in a seemingly logical way. No knowledge of Soviet history or of the complex structure of Soviet goals and motivations is required.[28]

It was largely because of their simplicity that such arguments appealed to a wide variety of groups and provided a basis on which Reagan was able to embark on a massive military programme and, during the first three years of his Administration, get most of what he wanted from Congress despite widespread concerns about the impact of defence spending on the overall budget deficit.

At the same time there has been growing concern about the Reagan Administration's lack of interest in arms control. Although this eased in early 1985 as a result of the resumption of arms control negotiations in Geneva, it may well increase if the talks fail to produce any agreement. This is all the more likely because of continuing fluctuations in the public mood. Concerns over the Soviet threat have become less salient than concerns over the danger of nuclear war. Indeed, one leading analyst of public attitudes has suggested that the traditional model of public opinion based on 'followership' has been "replaced by an unstable model of competing coalitions in which the noninternationalist mass public swings left or right unpredictably, in response to its current fears and concerns. Instead of a stable, two-track foreign policy, there is a situation of erratic alternation from one track to the other".[29] Yet this may offer some opportunities for Reagan's second term.

There seems to be a growing recognition in the public and in Congress that one dimensional policies towards the Soviet Union, whether they emphasise detente and cooperation or cold war and confrontation, are inadequate. The reaction against Reagan's policies of strength has been less intense than against Carter's policies of weakness. Nevertheless, having re-established American strength the President is in an advantageous position to re-establish genuine dialogue. This would, of course, require that President Reagan accept the need for a less simplistic approach to the Soviet Union, that he disregard the advice of the ideologues, and that he display a degree of empathy for Moscow that has hitherto been lacking. It is not clear that the Administration has either the will or the ability to transcend what is essentially an instinctive hostility to the Soviet Union. Indeed, the above analysis suggests that this is a daunting task. As well as appealing to the vested interests of certain groups, cold war policies have a simplicity that is helpful in establishing legitimacy and mobilising support. The challenge for Reagan's second term is to demonstrate that the United States is capable of developing and pursuing a sober, restrained foreign policy based on a mix of common and conflicting interests with Moscow. The structure of American policy-making, the changes in American politics in the 1960s and 1970s and the failure of past attempts to do this suggest that although the need may be great the expectations should be minimal. The only alternatives may, in fact, be chaos on the one side or a foreign policy design based on simplistic assumptions about the adversary on the other. If this is so then the future of American foreign policy will be even more turbulent than its recent past, and the United States will be both a formidable and an uncomfortable adversary and an equally uncomfortable ally.

NOTES

1. For the evolution of Fulbright's views see H. Johnson and B. M. Gwertzman. *Fulbright The Dissenter*, (London: Hutchinson, 1969).
2. See T. Franck and E. Weisband, *Foreign Policy By Congress*, (New York: Oxford University Press, 1979).
3. J. Sundquist, 'Congress and the President: Enemies or Partners' in L. C. Bodd and B. I. Oppenheimer (eds), *Congress Reconsidered*, (New York: Praeger, 1977).
4. I. M. Destler, L. H. Gelb and A. Lake, *Our Own Worst Enemy: The Unmaking of American Foreign Policy*, (New York: Simon & Schuster, 1983), p. 129.
5. *Ibid*, p. 143.
6. J. A. Califano Jnr., *Governing America*, (New York: Simon & Schuster, 1981), p. 451.
7. A. Etzioni, 'The Lack of Leadership: We found it in US', *National Journal*, 23 February, 1980, p. 335.
8. D. M. Hill and P. Williams, 'Conclusion: the legacy' in M. G. Abernathy, D. M. Hill and P. Williams (eds), *The Carter Years: The President and Policy Making*, (London: Frances Pinter, 1984), p. 213.
9. M. Nacht, 'American Security Interests Around the World' in J. F. Reichart and S. R. Sturm (eds), *American Defence Policy* (5th edition), (Baltimore: Johns Hopkins University Press, 1982), p. 257.
10. J. L. Sundquist, 'The Crisis of Competence in Our National Government', *Political Science Quarterly*, Vol. 95, No. 2, (Summer 1980), p. 190.
11. Destler, Gelb and Lake, *op. cit.*, p. 22.
12. The following argument rests heavily on Destler, Gelb and Lake, *op. cit.*
13. Destler, Gelb and Lake, *op. cit.*, p. 21.
14. *Ibid.*, p. 93.

15. The concept of policy legitimacy is developed in A. L. George, 'Domestic Constraints on Regime Changes in US Foreign Policy: The Need for Policy Legitimacy' in O. R. Holsti, R. M. Siverson, and A. L. George (eds), *Change in the International System*, (Boulder, Colorado: Westview Press, 1980).

16. A. L. George, *Presidential Decision Making: The Effective Use of Information and Advice*, (Boulder, Colorado: Westview Press, 1980), p. 112.

17. Quoted in M. Ledeen and W. Lewis, *Debacle: The American Failure in Iran*, (New York: Vintage Books, 1982), p. 125.

18. Quoted in Nacht, *op. cit.*

19. George, *Presidential Decision Making, op. cit.*, p. 41.

20. For a useful critique of incrementalism see Y. Dror, 'Muddling Through— Science or Inertia?', *Public Administration Review*, Vol. 24, (September 1974). pp. 153–7.

21. See S. Talbott, *Deadly Gambits: The Reagan Administration and the Stalemate in Nuclear Arms Control*, (New York: Knopf, 1984).

22. See P. Williams, 'The President, the Senate and SALT II', *Journal of Arms Control*, Vol. I, No. 1., (May 1980).

23. For the changing role of the National Security Advisers see I. M. Destler, *President, Bureaucrats and Foreign Policy*, (Princeton, NJ: Princeton University Press, 1972) and George, *op. cit.*, especially pp. 195–200.

24. R. Hilsman, *To Move a Nation*, (New York: Delta, 1967), p. 546.

25. For a fuller discussion see T. Lowi, 'Making Democracy Safe for the World' in J. Rosenau (ed.), *The Domestic Sources of Foreign Policy*, (New York: Free Press, 1967).

26. S. Hoffmann, *Dead Ends: American Foreign Policy in the New Cold War*, (Cambridge, Mass.: Ballinger, 1983), p. 121.

27. R. H. Johnson, 'Periods of Peril: The Window of Vulnerability and Other Myths', *Foreign Affairs*, (Spring 1983), p. 951.

28. *Ibid.*, p. 955.

29. W. Schneider, 'Public Opinion' in J. Nye (ed.), *The Making of America's Soviet Policy*, (New Haven and London: Yale University Press, 1984), p. 14.

33

Logic, Bribes, and Threats

CHARLES WILLIAM MAYNES

A characteristic of American foreign-policy critics is to seek the cause of national failure in personalities or in bureaucratic organization. Those critical of former Secretary of State Henry Kissinger's diplomatic performance criticize unscrupulous ambition or inveterate deviousness. Those displeased with Cyrus Vance's tenure at the State Department condemn a lawyer's mind or inadequate will. Alexander Haig, Jr.'s unhappy tenure as secretary of state is traced to the personality impact of a by-pass operation. Critics find all administrations to be badly organized: The National Security Council is either too strong or too weak; the White House plays either too important a role or no role at all.

There are at least two other causes of diplomatic failure: An administration's policy may be wrong or the country may not have the tools to carry it out. This last possibility has been inadequately explored. Are American's diplomatic tools as sturdy as they once were, and if not, what should the country do to restore their strength?

Hans Morgenthau, the great champion of the realist school of foreign policy, once maintained that a statesman has three tools in international affairs: logic, bribes, and threats. America has faced the world in recent years with a weakened hand in all three areas. Its foreign-policy failures, then, should perhaps be traced not so much to flawed personalities or to bad organization as to broken tools.

Of the three tools, threats have played the largest role in the foreign policies of most great powers, including the United States. Americans, however, do not like to believe this about their country. According to President Ronald Reagan, "America is the most peaceful, least warlike nation in modern history." But in truth, war has been central to America's growth and survival. The white settlers in North America built a nation through a series of wars with the Indians and America's neighbors that most historians now judge as either unjust or unfair. A chronology prepared in 1972 documented 199 military engagements that took place between 1798 and 1972 without a declaration of war. Most Americans are satisfied with the results, so there is little national inclination to reflect on the methods.

These realities provide some background for a startling quotation that Thomas Hughes, in his article "The Crack-Up: The Price of Collective Irresponsibility" in FOREIGN POLICY 40 (Fall 1980), uncovered several years ago. In 1904, Hugo Munsterberg, then a professor of psychology at Harvard University, had the following observations about American attitudes toward war and peace:

> In the attitude of the Americans toward foreign affairs, the love of peace and the delight in war combine to make a contrast which has rarely been seen. . . . This contradiction is the historical mark of the national American temperament. . . . The most characteristic feature is, that just those who show the love for war most energetically are none-the-less concerned and most earnestly so, for the advance of peace. President [Theodore] Roosevelt is the most striking example of the profound combination of those opposing tendencies in one human breast. . . . The Republic has in fact been the firmest partisan of peace, is now, and always will be so. While the riddle is— how can it be such a friend of peace when it was conceived in war, has settled its most serious problems by war, has gone to war again and again, has almost played with declarations of war, is at war today, and presumably will be at war many times again.

There is an answer to Munsterberg's riddle. For most Americans, foreign policy conjures up images of Europe. And there, until this century, America was at peace. It was nearer to home that the country was constantly at war. Most North Americans are scarcely aware of this chapter in their history. Most native and Latin Americans can never forget it.

Today, many influential figures express concern that, for a variety of reasons, the United States is no longer willing to use force to defend its interests. There appear to be two major groups participating in this movement. One comes from the traditional American Right, which appears to hope that an America that "stands tall" can restore again in the rest of the world that sense of deference that many conservatives believe the weak by nature owe the strong.

A new source of support for maintenance of the military instrument comes from some supporters of Israel, including some powerful sections of the American Jewish community. According to Hyman Bookbinder, director of the Washington office of the American Jewish Committee: "More and more Jews have come to recognize that we cannot show indifference to the whole question of defense of the West if we expect the defense of Israel to be supported by the United States. Traditionally, Jews have believed in spending more on social services and less on defense. But this attitude is changing." The *New Republic*, which follows these questions closely, has described American Jews as "exquisitely sensitive to the strength of the West."

But there is little utility in acquiring a military instrument if there is an absence of political will to use it. Many conservative commentators fear that as a result of America's involvement in the Vietnam War, it has lost that will. For that reason, many of the same figures and publications that press the hardest for increases in the American military budget also denounce the loudest the existence of the Vietnam syndrome that allegedly now makes the United States afraid to use force. During the June 1985 crisis involving the seizure by Shiite Moslem terrorists of a TWA airliner and its passengers, Haig worried about a "self-damaged sense of virility." Norman Podhoretz, editor of *Commentary* magazine, denounced the failure to follow the "tradition of manly honor."

During this escalating debate liberals have largely remained silent. One reason may be the new, promilitary position of some segments of the American Jewish community, always a critical element in the liberal coalition. Another, more important reason appears to be fear based on a sense, how well-founded is not clear, of domestic political reality. Liberals do not wish to appear too conciliatory in a world where no one can contend that all foreign governments harbor good intentions toward the United States. When liberals have spoken, it is therefore often in a "me-too" vein. Thus the new chairman of the House Armed Services Committee, Les Aspin (D.-Wisconsin), has urged that his party cease being the "Dr. No." of defense and find some programs that it can endorse. Representative Stephen Solarz (D.-New York) has proposed that liberals resist "Communist expansionism in the third world by providing arms and aid to non-Communist forces." These are two of the most thoughtful liberals in Congress, so their inability to come up with any other answer than "Liberals are tough, too," suggests that Reagan's opposition remains very much on the defensive when it comes to the issue of force.

An uneasy liberal toughness begs the question, however, of whether any amount of military strength can succeed in re-establishing force to its previous pre-eminent, and generally effective, role in American foreign policy. To answer the question it is necessary to examine more closely why force was indeed so effective in the past and appears so ineffective today.

The Decline of Force

Changes in three critical areas—technology, communications, and mores—explain the current inutility of force.

Sometimes a poet or a wag can capture in a sentence what others require a treatise or a tome to elucidate. The English author Hilaire Belloc did this, as he attempted in a single couplet to explain the dominance of the Europeans over the rest of the globe: " 'Whatever happens, we have got/ The Maxim Gun, and they have not.' " More specifically, the machine gun was the source of Western dominance. According to John Ellis in his *History of the Machine Gun*, the British, in their military campaigns in Africa, drew on African troops almost exclusively. The officers, however, were British: Their duty was to man the machine guns and at all costs to prevent their capture by any other forces.

With such advantages, British generals like Lord Kitchener could achieve astounding victories at virtually no cost. In conquering the Sudan, Kitchener's forces suffered 48 dead—of whom 3 were British officers and 25 were British enlisted men—and 434 wounded. At the same time, Kitchener's troops killed more than 11,000 dervish combatants. In 1905 the Germans faced a popular revolt among the Herreros in Namibia because of a decree that declared that from then on colored people had to consider white people superior beings and that in court one white person's testimony could be outweighed only by statements from seven colored witnesses. In the ensuing struggle, the Germans killed between 45,000 and 65,000 natives, leaving only 16,000 alive. These survivors were deported to other parts of the country. The resistance reportedly had only 2,500 rifles and was short of ammunition.

The United States faced a fierce resistance in the Philippines. Again, a decisive advantage in weaponry carried the day for the colonizer. Over a 13-month period the United States lost 245 men. The resistance lost 3,854.

It seems fair to conclude that never again will the West enjoy such an advantage in direct combat with troops from developing countries. For force to regain the role it once had, in other words, Western countries will be forced to resort to weapons of mass destruction or to accept significant casualties. That lesson seems clear in such recent North-South engagements as Vietnam and Afghanistan.

Western armies also enjoyed a major communications advantage in the past that no longer exists today. Before the arrival of the transistor radio, primitive peoples had no easy way to talk to one another over long distances. Western armies could follow a policy of divide and conquer that is now more difficult to implement. But there was another major advantage enjoyed by Western armies: They often could operate abroad on a scale little appreciated by the voters back home. Leon Wolff in *Little Brown Brother* (1960), his classic account of the American occupation of the Philippines, notes in this regard:

> That Spring, it was not publicly known that seventy thousand soldiers and sailors were being employed to crush the insurrection, nor that four hundred army posts had been set up throughout the islands to hold it in check. Severities committed by U.S. personnel seldom saw the light of day. Those that did were systematically denied or minimized.

The Pentagon's decision to bar the American press from covering the invasion of Grenada in October 1983 was an attempt to recreate in the Caribbean a military advantage the United States once enjoyed in the Philippines. The effort failed because of the vigorous reaction of the American press. But even if the press had been more compliant, the American military would not have received the benefit it expected because it was attributing to the power of the press alone a limitation on the use of force that is also explained by a change in popular mores. Thus many in the American military argue vehemently that press coverage of the war in Vietnam destroyed the legitimacy of the use of force as a tool of American foreign policy because it brought the ugliness and horror of war on to American television screens. The role of television in providing the general public with automatic knowledge of the carnage involved in any war now prevents any administration, according to this view, from rallying support for continuation of a war effort such as the one the United States conducted in Vietnam.

But one part of this argument does not fit the facts: It was not the television journalists who were the most effective in radically changing perceptions of the war effort but the print journalists. The journalist President John Kennedy tried to have thrown out of Vietnam was not a television anchor but David Halberstam of the *New York Times*. Other print journalists who had a major impact on popular attitudes were Seymour Hersh, with his exposure of the My Lai massacre, and

Harrison Salisbury, with his visit to Hanoi and his discovery that American bombing was not as precise as the Pentagon maintained.

What explains the impact of these print journalists, whose predecessors, after all, had been covering American victories and defeats since the founding of the Republic? The answer has to lie not in the print medium, which had always existed, but in a new ethical code that affected the readers who were receiving the message. And that code was not established during Vietnam and through television, but rather during World War II and with the Nuremberg War Crimes Tribunals. That war and those trials altered American attitudes about what was permissible in war.

In this regard, those who believe in the efficacy of force usually tend to pass over in silence the role that a lack of scruples traditionally has played in enhancing the impact of the military instrument. During the conquest of the Philippines, U.S. forces employed the so-called water cure to obtain information. This "cure" involved forcing 4 or 5 gallons of water down a captive's throat and then sitting on him to force it out. The process continued until the captive either talked or died. The American public was denied knowledge of such practices. But even if it had known, it might not have demanded an end to the use of torture because there was at the time a different moral code for fighting whites and nonwhites. And even in fighting whites, the metaphor was of sport. A future British field marshal, Garnet Wolseley, could write to his aunt in the middle of the last century, "Man shooting is the finest sport of all." Theodore Roosevelt could tell his sister of the excitement of shooting a Spanish officer during the Spanish-Americn War and seeing him double over "like a jack rabbit."

After World War II a new code prevailed. The media discovery that Vietcong prisoners were being put in so-called tiger cages acutely embarrassed Washington. Any hint that U.S.-supported rebels in Nicaragua may be employing torture or terror to gain some military end creates shock waves in Washington. In every case mere knowlege of the abuse influences policy. A picture is not necessary. True, a picture can have an even greater impact: Recall the sickened national reaction to the photograph of a South Vietnamese general shooting a helpless Vietcong captive in the head. But pictures are not critical, because the code is so strong. Mere knowledge that the United States may be violating the code is sufficient.

Administrations in Washington have attempted to confront the reality of this new code in two ways: Either they contend that military force can be used in conformity with terms of the new code because they have attained extraordinary precision in the use of force or they publicly pledge support for the code while accepting that they may have to violate it on a case-by-case basis through covert operations. Both approaches have severe limitations, but it is too difficult to prove the first or to hide the second.

The recent use of force in Lebanon demonstrated the limitations of the first approach. In fall 1983 the United States was eager to use military force for political ends in that country. In an effort to shore up the Lebanese government dominated by the Christian minority, the United States ordered the battleship *New Jersey* to fire into the hills surrounding Beirut. In response to public concern about innocent victims, U.S. officials replied that the *New Jersey's* guns were so accurate that firing them was "like tossing a Volkswagen onto a tennis court." There would be no unintended casualties. Then, nearly 2 years later, the U.S. Navy quietly announced that it was undertaking an extensive program to improve the accuracy of its recommissioned World War II battleships. It turned out that the *New Jersey* was using powder dating from the Korean War and that therefore its shells—each about the weight of a Volkswagen—tended to land wide of target. The next chapter in this saga came during the June 1985 hijacking of the TWA airliner. American passengers held hostage were forced by their captors to watch video-tapes of the damage to Lebanese villages caused by shells from the *New Jersey*.

An alternative to precision is to empty a target zone of innocent people. Central American armies have adopted the Vietnam War practice of declaring so-called free-fire zones, in which anyone left in the zone after a certain date is deemed to be a legitimate target. Whether barely literate peasants understand what is being proposed is an awkward question. What is indisputable is that this approach can work only for certain areas, not for a whole country.

Covert operations therefore became an attractive option because they seemed to offer an escape from the postwar standards. A secret report prepared as part of the 1954 Hoover Commission report on government organization was quite explicit on this point:

> It is now clear that we are facing an implacable enemy whose avowed objective is world domination by whatever means and at whatever cost. There are no rules in such a game. Hitherto acceptable norms of human conduct do not apply. If the U.S. is to survive, long-standing American concepts of "fair play" must be reconsidered. We must develop effective espionage and counterespionage services. We must learn to subvert, sabotage and destroy our enemies by more clever, more sophisticated and more effective methods than those used against us. It may become necessary that the American people will be made acquainted with, understand and support this fundamentally repugnant philosophy.

There are several major difficulties with covert operations. One is that they are hard to keep secret. When news of them becomes public, the American people are reluctant to support them, particularly if they reflect a "fundamentally repugnant philosophy." And there is a new problem: America's allies hold U.S. administrations to the same moral code as do the American people. Today, Western European popular attitudes about America are NATO's principal security problem. In April 1984, Jeane Kirkpatrick, then U.S. permanent representative to the United Nations, issued an eloquent warning to the West Europeans: If they continued to find some kind of moral equivalence between the United States and the USSR, then NATO would collapse by "mutual consent based on distrust on the European side and disgust on the American side." The intention of Kirkpatrick as an American official concerned about the future of the alliance was to warn the West European publics to watch their words. But West European officials also concerned about the alliance's future might in turn warn American administrations to watch their actions, particularly those that seem to establish in the minds of the West European publics any lasting suggestion of moral equivalence between the two superpowers.

From the foregoing it seems to follow that those who now are exuberantly pressing for a resharpening of the military instrument as a tool of U.S. foreign policy are not facing up to some important realities in terms of technical changes and popular attitudes. Force as an instrument of foreign policy is unlikely to regain in the future the role that it enjoyed in the past.

The Necessity for Bribes

Americans do not like to think of themselves as being in the business of bribery. Indeed, when it became known in the mid-1970s that many American businesses were resorting to payments under the table to gain foreign contracts, Congress quickly passed legislation to prohibit such behavior. Nevertheless, Morgenthau was right in identifying bribes as an important tool of foreign policy, although a more neutral term like "financial inducements" might gain a wider audience.

Such inducements are critical to the conduct of U.S. foreign policy. It is unlikely that any of the major diplomatic breakthroughs in the Middle East during the 1970s could have taken place without financial inducements. At the start of the decade Israel and Egypt received only an insignificant percentage of official American economic and military assistance—only 1 per cent. Fifteen years later, Israel and Egypt together are receiving 44 per cent of American military assistance and 55 per cent of its economic assistance.

It is common to criticize the share of the U.S. aid program absorbed by the Middle East, and indeed, that share is enormous. Nevertheless, the shift in aid priorities did yield important diplomatic benefits. From the standpoint of overall U.S. foreign policy, the key point now is the declining size of the American aid effort relative to that of other countries. In constant 1967 dollars U.S. official development assistance fell from roughly $3 billion in 1961 to $2.3 billion today, a drop of more than 20 per cent. During the 1970s U.S. administrations managed to sustain the actual flow of aid, after inflation was taken into account. Between 1970–1972 and 1980–1982 U.S. official development assistance in 1981 prices remained stable at approximately $7 billion in real terms. Given other pressures on the budget, that level might seem like an achievement, but the political impact of U.S. aid was bound to decline as other countries began major aid efforts of their own. During the 1970s, for example, official development assistance from the European Community rose from $8 billion to $12 billion and from Japan from $1.6 billion to $3.2 billion. During this period the Arab countries and members of the Warsaw Pact also became more serious aid competitors. The role of the Organization of Petroleum Exporting Countries (OPEC) is well known, but official development assistance from the Soviet-bloc countries rose 63 per cent btween 1975 and 1982.

Contributing to a reduction in American political influence through financial inducements was the privatization of financial flows that took place during the 1970s as the commercial banks became the principal source of funds for the developing countries. Bank money flowed without regard to any larger political design. As private capital flows began to substitute for official flows, what was once a tool of America's foreign-policy specialists—the flow of funds from rich to poor—became a problem.

These changes mean that increasingly America has to make its way in the world through the last tool Morgenthau mentioned—logic. Few would contend that in recent years American diplomacy has demonstrated special qualities of logical coherence or design. On the contrary, most critics contend that during the last decade American diplomacy has reached new heights of incoherence and unpredictability. Although the tendency is again to shift the blame on to specific individuals, there may be larger forces at work.

Indeed, for much of the postwar era secretaries of state and their colleagues benefited from a major advantage not available to administrations today: Most Americans regarded foreign affairs as an exotic area of expertise that only specialists could master. Then, foreign policy involved initiatives that the elite developed and that the public sometimes supported and sometimes opposed. Today the situation is often quite the reverse: Foreign policy may involve initiatives that the public develops and that the elite, in turn, sometimes supports and sometimes opposes. The country still has not adjusted to the transition.

In the past the elite encountered some popular resentment because of the privileges it enjoyed. But it also experienced popular respect because of the knowledge it was thought to possess. Now the elite retains the resentment but has lost the respect because more and more groups in

American society are able to contend that a number of their members are as knowledgeable as the elite.

Today the local rabbi or Roman Catholic priest may know as much about the Middle East or Central America as the regional specialists in the State Department. The tie between the Maryknoll religious order and key members of the Nicaraguan government is an example. Among the order's priests is Miguel d'Escoto Brockman, the foreign minister of Nicaragua, who was recently suspended from his priestly functions by the Vatican when he refused to relinquish his political office. The new superior general of the Maryknoll men's division still speaks regularly on the telephone with d'Escoto, whom he describes as neither a Marxist nor a Communist.

At various moments during the ongoing Polish crisis, policy disputes have broken out in Washington over which policy options are best designed to assist the survival of political attitudes represented by the banned Solidarity labor movement. Those inclined to disagree with the administration's recommendations have had an option not available to critics of earlier administrations: They can simply dial direct to prominent personalities in Poland and seek their opinion. The dial-direct telephone call has been a great leveler in the foreign-policy field, making an expert of anyone who possesses a full Rolodex.

Activism on an institutional level has paralleled this activism on an individual level. In the past 4 years the American Israel Public Affairs Committee has increased its membership from 8,000 to 50,000. The American-Arab Anti-Discrimination Committee increased its membership 20 per cent in 1984, to an overall total of 20,000. The Congressional Hispanic Caucus is taking a more active role on foreign-policy issues than it has in the past. Meanwhile, protests led by black Americans in front of the South African embassy in Washington have contributed to a total change in the direction of policymaking toward South Africa. In all previous administrations Africa policy flowed from the top down. Administration positions were at times considerably ahead of popular attitudes, and administration officials, particularly those in the State Department's Africa bureau, attempted to drum up support at the grassroots for a stronger Africa policy. Today, policy is being made from the bottom up, through such steps as motions in city councils to shift all city pension funds away from companies that invest in South Africa.

A sensitive question is, Why is America experiencing this great foreign-policy activism at the grassroots? Some suggest that various foreign-policy lobbies are placing private interests over those of the country. Senator Charles Mathias (R.-Maryland) expressed concern about the impact of ethnic foreign-policy lobbying in an article in the Summer 1981 issue of *Foreign Affairs* and was roundly denounced by a number of the lobbies in question for his treatment of the issue. Yet it is unquestionably true that some groups most active in foreign-policy lobbying have toward certain parts of the world an emotional attachment not necessarily shared with the same intensity by other Americans. Many Americans might join in or sympathize with the protests in front of the South African embassy on the grounds that it represents a government that is perpetuating racial injustice. But when Delegate Walter Fauntroy (D.-District of Columbia) explained his decision to join these protests with a reference to "Mother Africa," he raised a justification that for obvious reasons only a minority of Americans could ever share. The same point can be made about lobbying on the Middle East by Arab Americans or American Jews.

Yet there may be another explanation for grassroots activism besides the factor examined in the Mathias article. It may be that the impact of the foreign policy lobbies has grown not because they are suddenly so aggressive but because administrations are so weak. And the reason they are weak is that their knowledge monopoly has been broken. In short, an explanation may be that, relatively speaking, today the people know more and the elites know less than before.

Knowing more, of course, is not the same thing as knowing enough. But the issue of knowledge is central. Whatever the ultimate impact of his policies on the national interest—and the jury is still out—few would dispute that Kissinger was perhaps the most effective secretary of state since Dean Acheson. What explains this effectiveness? It may be that Kissinger temporarily re-established the knowledge monopoly within the State Department and the executive branch. Others outside the government might have had better sources of information than at any time in the postwar period, but no one claimed an equivalence in professional knowledge to the brilliant professor from Harvard University. A successor who tried could not repeat this performance because his skills were not comparable.

Foreign-Policy Adjustments

Can the tools of American foreign policy be resharpened? It is always easier to analyze than to prescribe, but a few guidelines for the future may be useful. Regarding threats, American foreign policy is simply going to have to adjust to the fact that force can never again play the role that it once did, primarily because developing countries are no longer the soft targets they once were, but also because the West can no longer be as ruthless in the use of force as it once was. The problem is less the Vietnam syndrome than a general consensus since World War II that "man shooting" is no longer the "finest sport of all."

But a reduced role is not the same thing as no role at all. In the nuclear field, a distinction exists between deterrence and coercion. Many doubt that nuclear weapons can ever be used as a diplomatic tool to compel another country to adopt a certain policy. The threat to use nuclear weapons for political purposes would be too incredible for the other country to believe the threat. Nevertheless, a country that possesses nuclear weapons can use them with great effect to deter other countries with nuclear weapons from employing such weapons in conflict.

In a somewhat similar way, conventional weapons are ceasing to have utility for the purposes of coercion but retain great value as a source of deterrence. The effort to use the guns of the *New Jersey* to compel the factions in Lebanon to accept a certain political order was a disaster, for the victims of the American bombardment could inflict high levels of damage on the United States. At the same time, knowledge that the United States, deeply angered by the seizure of some of its citizens as hostages, might retaliate savagely against targets in Lebanon, Syria, or Iran if more hostages were killed may have played a role in the final negotiated outcome.

The ability to undertake some kinds of covert actions may also be more useful as a means to deter rather than to compel. Preemptive covert actions that cross a certain moral threshold not only are wrong but also are unwise because of the risk of exposure and popular repudiation. Retaliatory action, however, may be necessary to deter unscrupulous powers from taking advantage of the United States.

From the perspective advanced, Secretary of Defense Caspar Weinberger is correct in asserting that force in terms of coercion should be used only when the country's most vital interests are at stake. Otherwise, whenever the casualty rates rise to a fairly high level—and they probably will in most engagements—an administration will find that it is unable to maintain political support for the effort. But Kissinger's veiled threat, so denounced at the time, to use force in the event that OPEC went so far as to threaten Western survival as opposed to Western pocketbooks was an appropriate form of deterrence. The oil flowed, even if at higher prices. The oiled rope around the West's neck was not tightened to force an unacceptable Middle East settlement.

If force can be used less often to compel, the United States probably will have to accept greater political diversity within its own sphere of influence. But even aggravating diversity is not the same thing as dangerous hostility. The United States needs a new doctrine in the Western Hemisphere to set limits to impermissible behavior on the part of rebellious states like Nicaragua. Mexico's foreign policy for most of the postwar era is suggestive of the diversity the United States might accept and the conformity it might seek under such a doctrine. For understandable historical reasons, Mexican foreign policy has often been rhetorically anti-American. And within the hemisphere, Mexico, particularly after its revolution, often refused to follow the U.S. lead on sensitive issues. One important postwar example was diplomatic recognition of communist Cuba. Mexico also took a number of steps in the interwar period, such as the expropriation of the U.S. oil industry, that exacerbated bilateral relations. In addition, Mexico was the only Latin American country to refuse to sign a military assistance agreement with the United States. It rejected the offer of Peace Corps volunteers. But for most of the postwar period Mexico also attempted to avoid conflict with the United States on major global issues. For example, it avoided membership on the United Nations Security Council, where it would be forced to take controversial stands on critical East-West issues. Mexican foreign policy clearly was formulated in Mexico City, not in some foreign capital.

Although Mexican foreign policy in recent years has aspired to a more global reach, its course for most of the postwar period may offer a guide for some of the smaller, Central American states that are going through a period of revolutionary turmoil. Nicaragua would have avoided much grief with the Carter and Reagan administrations if it had only followed the nonaligned position on such a totally nonhemispheric issue as the Soviet invasion of Afghanistan. But in turn, for smaller countries to know what the limits of U.S. tolerance might be, the United States has to spell them out. In short, Central America needs a new doctrine, which might be called Mexicanization, that would set those limits. Such a doctrine would have to go beyond the issue of Soviet bases—a casus belli for the United States—to some restraints on international behavior, but it would have to stop considerably short of the degree of political subservience that Washington has traditionally demanded in this hemisphere.

Regarding financial inducements, the United States certainly does not want to persuade other countries to relax their aid efforts simply so that the political impact of America's own effort may grow. But given declining aid levels in real terms since the 1960s and the enormous drain on resources of America's diplomatic effort in the Middle East, the United States does need a new source of income that might sustain political support. Every administration in recent years has had difficulty increasing the aid budget. It may be that the political task simply is too difficult. In that case, those concerned with this tool of foreign policy may want to try a different tack.

Perhaps because they believe that those who benefit also pay, Americans seem to support user taxes more than other taxes. Could there be a user tax to fund foreign aid? Certainly those who engage in international trade and finance benefit directly and disproportionately from the political purpose of aid—the maintenance of a stable, relatively benign, and predictable international order. Reflecting this benefit, the federal government might impose a development tax on the profits from international trade or financial transactions. Alternatively, the government might add a development tax to arms shipments, not with any expectations that such a tax would reduce such shipments but in the hope that a more reliable form of income generation could be developed.

Morgenthau's last category, logic, is the most difficult to change because the issues involve historical traditions and forms of governance. Because of international communications and a greater degree of sophistication among the American people, it seems fairly safe to predict that the executive branch will never regain its previous quasi monopoly on information, which was the key to its earlier, somewhat greater ability to prevail over opposition and to maintain foreign-policy coherence. Outside actors will maintain their new role in the policy process.

But if the executive branch can no longer regain its former preeminent position, there is no reason why it should not be able to gain a better position. Here the example of Acheson may be instructive. Acheson, because of his bearing, was often resented, but he also was usually respected. The reason may have been the unusual knowledge he brought to problems, which he gained not so much through brilliance as through leadership. Kissinger brought superior knowledge to problems because of the learning he so ably displayed. Acheson brought superior knowledge to problems because of the institution he so ably led.

A key to greater executive-branch influence, therefore, may be a rebuilding of the governmental foreign-policy institutions that recent presidents have done so much to tear down through poor appointments and campaign attacks on federal bureaucrats. If there is to be greater coherence in any administration's foreign policy, the representative of the administration must regularly be the best-informed person in the room. That has too rarely been the case since the arrival of the jet airplane, the dial telephone, and voluminous international reporting.

Tools alone do not make a foreign policy. They can be used wisely or foolishly. But without tools the most skillful negotiator may appear inept. Kissinger, featured as Superman on the cover of a national magazine because of his work in negotiating the disengagement agreements between Israel and Egypt, would have ended up a professional Clark Kent without his ability to draw lavishly from the American treasury. Even if opponents know that the use of force is problematical, they are more likely to negotiate fairly with the United States if they know it possesses a stout defense. And a clever voice is usually better than a loud voice.

In short, a better foreign policy requires better tools and a deeper understanding of their most appropriate use. And there is no better time to acquire both than now.

PART FOUR

The Problems of a Changing World Economy: Will the World as We Know it Survive?

It has become commonplace to evaluate the problems of the future. Discussions of the year 2000, "future shock", the energy crisis, the food crisis, the environmental crisis, and the population explosion have become widespread in the press and media. Many people view postindustrial society as a scientific utopia in which many of our pressing material problems will be solved. Others see the new society as plagued by the poisonous fruits of science and technology. Pessimism about the effects of scientific progress and economic growth has intensified among intellectual and professional elites. Indeed, to many observers such issues as the balance of power appear trivial at a time when our future existence seems imperiled by environmental conditions and careless application of new technologies rather than exclusively by an atomic Armageddon. In one year, 1986, these fears seemed to be confirmed by the explosion of the *Challenger* space shuttle in January and by the explosion at the Soviet nuclear power plant at Chernobyl in April.

The two articles which comprise this section have been selected because they persuasively address various aspects of changing conditions, with a special emphasis on economic factors. Peter F. Drucker provides a fascinating account of fundamental alterations which he believes have recently occurred in the world economy. He sees three major changes as permanent, not cyclical. They are (1) that the primary products economy has come "uncoupled" from the industrial economy, (2) that manufacturing production has become uncoupled from manufacturing employment and (3) that the "symbol" economy—capital movements, exchange rates and credit flows—has emerged as the driving force of the world economy, replacing the "real" economy—the flow of goods and services. His major conclusion is that "economic dynamics have decisively shifted from the national economy to the world economy."

We conclude this section and the volume with an intriguing article by Lester R. Brown which argues that expenditures on defense have become a source of weakness in the changing world economy. After detailing the huge increases in military expenditures worldwide and the intensified militarization of the Third World, Brown argues that the United States and the Soviet Union are suffering from their superpower burden in the military sphere. By comparison, Japan—with minimal military expenses—is at a net advantage vis-à-vis both superpowers. With huge debts and environmental deterioration a growing pressure on Third World economies, Brown believes that those countries which diminish their military expenses are more likely to make economic progress. He concludes with a message to the Soviets that unless they redefine national security in more economic terms their leadership in world affairs is likely to suffer.

The changing conditions these two authors identify must be included in any consideration of the course of future society. As these articles illustrate, some people speak optimistically about advances in science and industry and about progress in general, while others predict social and economic decline. Whether the issues are balance of power and nuclear proliferation or energy and food crisis, the problems of tomorrow are inextricably involved with justice and equality, scientific achievement, and political wisdom. The future, whether it brings a new age of rare achievement or a turbulent era of escalating crises, may make our thermonuclear era appear tranquil by comparison.

Edmund Burke once wrote, "society is indeed a contract . . . It is a partnership in all art; a partnership in every virtue, and in all perfection. As the ends of such a partnership cannot be obtained in many generations, it becomes a partnership not only between those who are living, but between those who are dead, and those who are to be born."

In a new society of pain or plenty, the links between generations may be broken as technology or turmoil makes it increasingly difficult for us to identify with the wars through which people have lived before us. Perhaps the greatest challenge of all in this future environment will be to maintain our links with tradition and preserve the best of human values as society continues to change. In the world arena a search for links to the past may become central to the quest for a form of order that will maintain what Burke called "the great primeval contract of eternal society."

<u>34</u>

The Changed World Economy

PETER F. DRUCKER

The talk today is of the "changing world economy." I wish to argue that the world economy is not "changing"; it has *already changed*—in its foundations and in its structure—and in all probability the change is irreversible.

Within the last decade or so, three fundamental changes have occurred in the very fabric of the world economy:

—The primary-products economy has come "uncoupled" from the industrial economy.

—In the industrial economy itself, production has come "uncoupled" from employment.

—Capital movements rather than trade (in both goods and services) have become the driving force of the world economy. The two have not quite come uncoupled, but the link has become loose, and worse, unpredictable.

These changes are permanent rather than cyclical. We may never understand what caused them—the causes of economic change are rarely simple. It may be a long time before economic theorists accept that there have been fundamental changes, and longer still before they adapt their theories to account for them. Above all, they will surely be most reluctant to accept that it is the world economy in control, rather than the macroeconomics of the nation-state on which most economic theory still exclusively focuses. Yet this is the clear lesson of the success stories of the last 20 years—of Japan and South Korea; of West Germany (actually a more impressive though far less flamboyant example than Japan); and of the one great success within the United States, the turnaround and rapid rise of an industrial New England, which only 20 years ago was widely considered moribund.

Practitioners, whether in government or in business, cannot wait until there is a new theory. They have to act. And their actions will be more likely to succeed the more they are based on the new realities of a changed world economy.

II

First, consider the primary-products economy. The collapse of non-oil commodity prices began in 1977 and has continued, interrupted only once (right after the 1979 petroleum panic), by a speculative burst that lasted less than six months; it was followed by the fastest drop in commodity prices ever registered. By early 1986 raw material prices were at their lowest levels in recorded history in relation to the prices of manufactured good and services—in general as low as at the depths of the Great Depression, and in some cases (e.g., lead and copper) lower than their 1932 levels.[1]

This collapse of prices and the slowdown of demand stand in startling contrast to what had been confidently predicted. Ten years ago the Club of Rome declared that desperate shortages for *all* raw materials were an absolute certainty by the year 1985. In 1980 the Carter Administration's *Global 2000 Report to the President: Entering the Twenty-First Century* concluded that world demand for food would increase steadily for at least 20 years; that worldwide food production would fall except in developed countries; and that real food prices would double. This forecast helps to explain why American farmers bought up all available farmland, thus loading on themselves the debt burden that now so threatens them.

Contrary to all these expectations, global agricultural output actually rose almost one-third between 1972 and 1985 to reach an all-time high. It rose the fastest in less-developed countries. Similarly, production of practically all forest products, metals and minerals has gone up between 20 and 35 percent in the last ten years—again with the greatest increases in less-developed countries. There is not the slightest reason to believe that the growth rates will slacken, despite the collapse of commodity prices. Indeed, as far as farm products are concerned, the biggest increase—at an almost exponential rate of growth—may still be ahead.[2]

Perhaps even more amazing than the contrast between such predictions and what has happened is that the collapse in the raw materials economy seems to have had almost no impact on the world industrial economy. If there is one thing considered "proven" beyond doubt in business cycle theory, it is that a sharp and prolonged drop in raw material prices inevitably, and within 18 to 30 months, brings on a worldwide depression in the industrial economy.[3] While the industrial economy of the world today is not "normal" by any definition of the term, it is surely not in a depression. Indeed, industrial production in the developed non-communist countries has continued to grow steadily, albeit at a somewhat slower rate in Western Europe.

Of course, a depression in the industrial economy may only have been postponed and may still be triggered by a banking crisis caused by massive defaults on the part of commodity-producing debtors, whether in the Third World or in Iowa. But for almost ten years the industrial world has run along as though there were no raw material crisis at all. The only explanation is that for the developed countries—excepting only the Soviet Union—the primary-products sector has become marginal where before it had always been central.

In the late 1920s, before the Great Depression, farmers still constituted nearly one-third of the U.S. population and farm income accounted for almost a quarter of the gross national product. Today they
account for less than five percent of population and even less of GNP.
Even adding the contribution that foreign raw material and farm
producers make to the American economy through their purchases of
American industrial goods, the total contribution of the raw material
and food producing economies of the world to the American GNP is, at
most, one-eighth. In most other developed countries, the share of the
raw materials sector is even lower. Only in the Soviet Union is the farm
still a major employer, with almost a quarter of the labor force working
on the land.

The raw material economy has thus come uncoupled from the
industrial economy. This is a major structural change in the world
economy, with tremendous implications for economic and social policy
as well as economic theory, in developed and developing countries
alike.

For example, if the ratio between the prices of manufactured goods
and the prices of non-oil primary products (that is, foods, forest
products, metals and minerals) had been the same in 1985 as it had been
in 1973, the 1985 U.S. trade deficit might have been a full one-third
less—$100 billion as against an actual $150 billion. Even the U.S. trade
deficit with Japan might have been almost one-third lower, some $35
billion as against $50 billion. American farm exports would have bought
almost twice as much. And industrial exports to a major U.S. customer,
Latin America, would have held; their near-collapse alone accounts for
a full one-sixth of the deterioration in U.S. foreign trade over the past
five years. If primary-product prices had not collapsed, America's
balance of payments might even have shown a substantial surplus.

Conversely, Japan's trade surplus with the world might have been a
full 20 percent lower. And Brazil in the last few years would have had an
export surplus almost 50 percent higher than its current level. Brazil
would then have had little difficulty meeting the interest on its foreign
debt and would not have had to endanger its economic growth by
drastically curtailing imports as it did. Altogether, if raw material prices
in relationship to manufactured goods prices had remained at the 1973
or even the 1979 level, there would be no crisis for most debtor
countries, especially in Latin America.[4]

III

What accounts for this change?

Demand for food has actually grown almost as fast as the Club of
Rome and the *Global 2000 Report* anticipated. But the supply has grown

much faster; it not only has kept pace with population growth, it has steadily outrun it. One cause of this, paradoxically, is surely the fear of worldwide food shortages, if not world famine, which resulted in tremendous efforts to increase food output. The United States led the parade with a farm policy of subsidizing increased food production. The European Economic Community followed suit, and even more success-fully. The greatest increases, both in absolute and in relative terms, however, have been in developing countries: in India, in post-Mao China and in the rice-growing countries of Southeast Asia.

And there is also the tremendous cut in waste. In the 1950s, up to 80 percent of the grain harvest of India fed rats and insects rather than human beings. Today in most parts of India the wastage is down to 20 percent. This is largely the result of unspectacular but effective "infra-structure innovations" such as small concrete storage bins, insecticides and three-wheeled motorized carts that take the harvest straight to a processing plant instead of letting it sit in the open for weeks.

It is not fanciful to expect that the true "revolution" on the farm is still ahead. Vast tracts of land that hitherto were practically barren are being made fertile, either through new methods of cultivation or through adding trace minerals to the soil. The sour clays of the Brazilian highlands or the aluminum-contaminated soils of neighboring Peru, for example, which never produced anything before, now produce substan-tial quantities of high-quality rice. Even greater advances have been registered in biotechnology, both in preventing diseases of plants and animals and in increasing yields.

In other words, just as the population growth of the world is slowing down quite dramatically in many regions, food production is likely to increase sharply.

Import markets for food have all but disappeared. As a result of its agricultural drive, Western Europe has become a substantial food exporter plagued increasingly by unsalable surpluses of all kinds of foods, from dairy products to wine, from wheat to beef. China, some observers predict, will have become a food exporter by the year 2000. India is about at that stage, especially with wheat and coarse grains. Of all major non-communist countries only Japan is still a substantial food importer, buying abroad about one-third of its food needs. Today most of this comes from the United States. Within five or ten years, however, South Korea, Thailand and Indonesia—low-cost producers that are fast increasing food output—are likely to try to become Japan's major suppliers.

The only remaining major food buyer on the world market may then be the Soviet Union—and its food needs are likely to grow.[5] However, the food surpluses in the world are so large—maybe five to eight times what the Soviet Union would ever need to buy—that its food needs are not by themselves enough to put upward pressure on world prices. On the contrary, the competition for access to the Soviet market among the surplus producers—the United States, Europe, Argentina, Australia, New Zealand (and probably India within a few years)—is already so intense as to depress world food prices.

For practically all non-farm commodities, whether forest products, minerals or metals, world demand is shrinking—in sharp contrast to what the Club of Rome so confidently predicted. Indeed, the amount of raw material needed for a given unit of economic output has been dropping for the entire century, except in wartime. A recent study by the International Monetary Fund calculates the decline as one and one-quarter percent a year (compounded) since 1900.[6] This would mean that the amount of industrial raw materials needed for one unit of industrial production is now no more than two-fifths of what it was in 1900. And the decline is accelerating. The Japanese experience is particularly striking. In 1984, for every unit of industrial production, Japan consumed only 60 percent of the raw materials consumed for the same volume of industrial production in 1973, 11 years earlier.

Why this decline in demand? It is not that industrial production is fading in importance as the service sector grows—a common myth for which there is not the slightest evidence. What is happening is much more significant. Industrial production is steadily switching away from heavily material-intensive products and processes. One of the reasons for this is the new high-technology industries. The raw materials in a semiconductor microchip account for one to three percent of total production cost; in an automobile their share is 40 percent, and in pots and pans 60 percent. But also in older industries the same scaling down of raw material needs goes on, and with respect to old products as well as new ones. Fifty to 100 pounds of fiberglass cable transmit as many telephone messages as does one ton of copper wire.

This steady drop in the raw material intensity of manufacturing processes and manufacturing products extends to energy as well, and especially to petroleum. To produce 100 pounds of fiberglass cable requires no more than five percent of the energy needed to produce one ton of copper wire. Similarly, plastics, which are increasingly replacing steel in automobile bodies, represent a raw material cost, including energy, of less than half that of steel.

Thus it is quite unlikely that raw material prices will ever rise substantially as compared to the prices of manufactured goods (or high-knowledge services such as information, education or health care) except in the event of a major prolonged war.

One implication of this sharp shift in the terms of trade of primary products concerns the developed countries, both major raw material exporters like the United States and major raw material importing countries such as Japan. For two centuries the United States has made maintenance of open markets for its farm products and raw materials central to its international trade policy. This is what it has always meant by an "open world economy" and by "free trade."

Does this still make sense, or does the United States instead have to accept that foreign markets for its foodstuffs and raw materials are in a long-term and irreversible decline? Conversely, does it still make sense for Japan to base its international economic policy on the need to earn enough foreign exchange to pay for imports of raw materials and foodstuffs? Since Japan opened to the outside world 120 years ago, preoccupation—amounting almost to a national obsession—with its dependence on raw material and food imports has been the driving force of Japan's policy, and not in economics alone. Now Japan might well start out with the assumption—a far more realistic one in today's world—that foodstuffs and raw materials are in permanent oversupply.

Taken to their logical conclusion, these developments might mean that some variant of the traditional Japanese policy—highly mercantilist with a strong de-emphasis on domestic consumption in favor of an equally strong emphasis on capital formation, and protection of infant industries—might suit the United States better than its own tradition. The Japanese might be better served by some variant of America's traditional policies, especially a shifting from favoring savings and capital formation to favoring consumption. Is such a radical break with more than a century of political convictions and commitments likely? From now on the fundamentals of economic policy are certain to come under increasing criticism in these two countries—and in all other developed countries as well.

These fundamentals will, moreover, come under the increasingly intense scrutiny of major Third World nations. For if primary products are becoming of marginal importance to the economies of the developed world, traditional development theories and policies are losing their foundations.[7] They are based on the assumption—historically a perfectly valid one—that developing countries pay for imports of capital goods by exporting primary materials—farm and forest products, minerals, metals. All development theories, however much they differ otherwise, further assume that raw material purchases by the industrially developed countries must rise at least as fast as industrial production in these countries. This in turn implies that, over any extended period of time, any raw material producer becomes a better credit risk and shows a more favorable balance of trade. These premises have become highly doubtful. On what foundation, then, can economic development be based, especially in countries that do not have a large enough population to develop an industrial economy based on the home market? As we shall presently see, these countries can no longer base their economic development on low labor costs.

IV

The second major change in the world economy is the uncoupling of manufacturing production from manufacturing employment. Increased manufacturing production in developed countries has actually come to mean *decreasing* blue-collar employment. As a consequence, labor costs are becoming less and less important as a "comparative cost" and as a factor in competition.

There is a great deal of talk these days about the "deindustrialization" of America. In fact, manufacturing production has risen steadily in absolute volume and has remained unchanged as a percentage of the total economy. Since the end of the Korean War, that is, for more than 30 years, it has held steady at 23–24 percent of America's total GNP. It has similarly remained at its traditional level in all of the other major industrial countries.

It is not even true that American industry is doing poorly as an exporter. To be sure, the United States is importing from both Japan and Germany many more manufactured goods than ever before. But it is also exporting more, despite the heavy disadvantages of an expensive dollar, increasing labor costs and the near-collapse of a major industrial market, Latin America. In 1984—the year the dollar soared—exports of American manufactured goods rose by 8.3 percent; and they went up again in 1985. The share of U.S.-manufactured exports in world exports was 17 percent in 1978. By 1985 it had risen to 20 percent—while West Germany accounted for 18 percent and Japan 16. The three countries together thus account for more than half of the total.

Thus it is not the American economy that is being "deindustrialized." It is the American labor force.

Between 1973 and 1985, manufacturing production (measured in constant dollars) in the United States rose by almost 40 percent. Yet manufacturing employment during that period went down steadily. There are now five million fewer people employed in blue-collar work in American manufacturing industry than there were in 1975.

Yet in the last 12 years total employment in the United States grew faster than at any time in the peacetime history of any country—from 82 to 110 million between 1973 and 1985—that is, by a full one-third. The entire growth, however, was in non-manufacturing, and especially in non-blue-collar jobs.

The trend itself is not new. In the 1920s one out of every three Americans in the labor force was a blue-collar worker in manufacturing. In the 1950s the figure was one in four. It now is down to one in every six—and dropping. While the trend has been running for a long time, it has lately accelerated to the point where—in peacetime at least—no increase in manufacturing production, no matter how large, is likely to reverse the long-term decline in the number of blue-collar jobs in manufacturing or in their proportion of the labor force.

This trend is the same in all developed countries, and is, indeed, even more pronounced in Japan. It is therefore highly probable that in 25 years developed countries such as the United States and Japan will employ no larger a proportion of the labor force in manufacturing than developed countries now employ in farming—at most, ten percent. Today the United States employs around 18 million people in blue-collar jobs in manufacturing industries. By 2010, the number is likely to be no more than 12 million. In some major industries the drop will be even sharper. It is quite unrealistic, for instance, to expect that the American automobile industry will employ more than one-third of its present blue-collar force 25 years hence, even though production might be 50 percent higher.

If a company, an industry or a country does not in the next quarter century sharply increase manufacturing production and at the same time sharply reduce the blue-collar work force, it cannot hope to remain competitive—or even to remain "developed." It would decline fairly fast. Britain has been in industrial decline for the last 25 years, largely because the number of blue-collar workers per unit of manufacturing production went down far more slowly than in all other non-communist developed countries. Even so, Britain has the highest unemployment rate among non-communist developed countries—more than 13 percent.

V

The British example indicates a new and critical economic equation: a country, an industry or a company that puts the preservation of blue-collar manufacturing jobs ahead of international competitiveness (which implies a steady shrinkage of such jobs) will soon have neither production nor jobs. The attempt to preserve such blue-collar jobs is actually a prescription for unemployment.

So far, this concept has achieved broad national acceptance only in Japan.[8] Indeed, Japanese planners, whether in government or private business, start out with the assumption of a doubling of production within 15 or 20 years based on a cut in blue-collar employment of 25 to 40 percent. A good many large American companies such as IBM, General Electric and the big automobile companies have similar forecasts. Implicit in this is the conclusion that a country will have less overall unemployment the faster it shrinks blue-collar employment in manufacturing.

This is not a conclusion that American politicians, labor leaders or indeed the general public can easily understand or accept. What confuses the issue even more is that the United States is experiencing several separate and different shifts in the manufacturing economy. One is the acceleration of the substitution of knowledge and capital for manual labor. Where we spoke of mechanization a few decades ago, we now speak of "robotization" or "automation." This is actually more a change in terminology than a change in reality. When Henry Ford introduced the assembly line in 1909, he cut the number of man-hours required to produce a motor car by some 80 percent in two or three years—far more than anyone expects to result from even the most complete robotization. But there is no doubt that we are facing a new, sharp acceleration in the replacement of manual workers by machines— that is, by the products of knowledge.

A second development—and in the long run this may be even more important—is the shift from industries that were primarily labor-intensive to industries that, from the beginning, are knowledge-intensive. The manufacturing costs of the semiconductor microchip are about 70 percent knowledge—that is, research, development and testing—and no more than 12 percent labor. Similarly with prescription drugs, labor represents no more than 15 percent, with knowledge representing almost 50 percent. By contrast, in the most fully robotized automobile plant labor would still account for 20 or 25 percent of the costs.

Another perplexing development in manufacturing is the reversal of the dynamics of size. Since the early years of this century, the trend in all developed countries has been toward ever larger manufacturing plants. The economies of scale greatly favored them. Perhaps equally important, what one might call the "economies of management" favored them. Until recently, modern management techniques seemed applicable only to fairly large units.

This has been reversed with a vengeance over the last 15 to 20 years. The entire shrinkage in manufacturing jobs in the United States has occurred in large companies, beginning with the giants in steel and automobiles. Small and especially medium-sized manufacturers have either held their own or actually added employees. In respect to market standing, exports and profitability too, smaller and middle-sized businesses have done remarkably better than big ones. The reversal of the dynamics of size is occurring in the other developed countries as well, even in Japan where bigger was always better and biggest meant best. The trend has reversed itself even in old industries. The most profitable automobile company these last years has not been one of the giants, but a medium-sized manufacturer in Germany—BMW. The only profitable steel companies, whether in the United States, Sweden or Japan, have been medium-sized makers of specialty products such as oil drilling pipe.

In part, especially in the United States, this is a result of a resurgence of entrepreneurship.[9] But perhaps equally important, we have learned in the last 30 years how to manage the small and medium-sized enterprise to the point where the advantages of smaller size, e.g., ease of communications and nearness to market and customer, increasingly outweigh what had been forbidding management limitations. Thus in the United States, but increasingly in the other leading manufacturing nations such as Japan and West Germany as well, the dynamism in the economy has shifted from the very big companies that dominated the world's industrial economy for 30 years after World War II to companies that, while much smaller, are professionally managed and largely publicly financed.

VI

Two distinct kinds of "manufacturing industry" are emerging. One is material-based, represented by the industries that provided economic growth in the first three-quarters of this century. The other is information- and knowledge-based: pharmaceuticals, telecommunications, analytical instruments and information processing such as computers. It is largely the information-based manufacturing industries that are growing.

These two groups differ not only in their economic characteristics but especially in their position in the international economy. The products of material-based industries have to be exported or imported as "products." They appear in the balance of trade. The products of information-based industries can be exported or imported both as "products" and as "services," which may not appear accurately in the overall trade balance.

An old example is the printed book. For one major scientific publishing company, "foreign earnings" account for two-thirds of total revenues. Yet the company exports few, if any, actual books—books are heavy. It sells "rights," and the "product" is produced abroad. Similarly, the most profitable computer "export sales" may actually show up in trade statistics as an "import." This is the fee some of the world's leading banks, multinationals and Japanese trading companies get for processing in their home office data arriving electronically from their branches and customers around the world.

In all developed countries, "knowledge" workers have already become the center of gravity of the labor force. Even in manufacturing they will outnumber blue-collar workers within ten years. Exporting knowledge so that it produces license income, service fees and royalties may actually create substantially more jobs than exporting goods.

This in turn requires—as official Washington seems to have realized—far greater emphasis in trade policy on "invisible trade" and on abolishing the barriers to the trade in services. Traditionally, economists have treated invisible trade as a step-child, if they noted it at all. Increasingly, it will become central. Within 20 years major developed countries may find that their income from invisible trade is larger than their income from exports.

Another implication of the "uncoupling" of manufacturing production from manufacturing employment is, however, that the choice between an industrial policy that favors industrial *production* and one that favors industrial *employment* is going to be a singularly contentious political issue for the rest of this century. Historically these have always been considered two sides of the same coin. From now on the two will increasingly pull in different directions; they are indeed already becoming alternatives, if not incompatible.

Benign neglect—the policy of the Reagan Administration these last few years—may be the best policy one can hope for, and the only one with a chance of success. It is probably not an accident that the United States has, after Japan, by far the lowest unemployment rate of any industrially developed country. Still, there is surely need also for systematic efforts to retrain and to place redundant blue-collar workers—something no one as yet knows how to do successfully.

Finally, low labor costs are likely to become less of an advantage in international trade simply because in the developed countries they are going to account for less of total costs. Moreover, the total costs of automated processes are lower than even those of traditional plants with low labor costs; this is mainly because automation eliminates the hidden but high costs of "not working," such as the expense of poor quality and rejects, and the costs of shutting down the machinery to change from one model of a product to another. Consider two automated American producers of televisions, Motorola and RCA. Both were almost driven out of the market by imports from countries with much lower labor costs. Both subsequently automated, with the result that these American-made products now successfully compete with foreign imports. Similarly, some highly automated textile mills in the Carolinas can underbid imports from countries with very low labor costs such as Thailand. On the other hand, although some American semiconductor companies have lower labor costs because thay do the labor-intensive work offshore, e.g., in West Africa, they are still the high-cost producers and easily underbid by the heavily automated Japanese.

The cost of capital will thus become increasingly important in international competition. And this is where, in the last ten years, the United States has become the highest-cost country—and Japan the lowest. A reversal of the U.S. policy of high interest rates and costly equity capital should thus be a priority for American decision-makers.

This demands that reduction of the government deficit, rather than high interest rates, becomes the first defense against inflation.

For developed countries, especially the United States, the steady downgrading of labor costs as a major competitive factor could be a positive development. For the Third World, especially rapidly industrializing countries such as Brazil, South Korea or Mexico, it is, however, bad news.

In the rapid industrialization of the nineteenth century, one country, Japan, developed by exporting raw materials, mainly silk and tea, at steadily rising prices. Another, Germany, developed by leap-frogging into the "high-tech" industries of its time, mainly electricity, chemicals and optics. A third, the United States, did both. Both routes are blocked for today's rapidly industrializing countries—the first because of the deterioration of the terms of trade for primary products, the second because it requires an infrastructure of knowledge and education far beyond the reach of a poor country (although South Korea is reaching for it). Competition based on lower labor costs seemed to be the only alternative; is this also going to be blocked?

VII

The third major change that has occurred in the world economy is the emergence of the "symbol" economy—capital movements, exchange rates and credit flows—as the flywheel of the world economy, in place of the "real" economy—the flow of goods and services. The two economies seem to be operating increasingly independently. This is both the most visible and the least understood of the changes.

World trade in goods is larger, much larger, than it has ever been before. And so is the "invisible trade," the trade in services. Together, the two amount to around $2.5 trillion to $3 trillion a year. But the London Eurodollar market, in which the world's financial institutions borrow from and lend to each other, turns over $300 billion each working day, or $75 trillion a year, a volume at least 25 times that of world trade.[10]

In addition, there are the foreign exchange transactions in the world's main money centers, in which one currency is traded against another. These run around $150 billion a day, or about $35 trillion a year—12 times the worldwide trade in goods and services.

Of course, many of these Eurodollars, yen and Swiss francs are just being moved from one pocket to another and may be counted more than once. A massive discrepancy still exists, and there is only one conclusion: capital movements unconnected to trade—and indeed largely independent of it—greatly exceed trade finance.

There is no one explanation for this explosion of international—or more accurately, transnational—money flows. The shift from fixed to floating exchange rates in 1971 may have given an initial impetus (though, ironically, it was meant to do the exact opposite) by inviting currency speculation. The surge in liquid funds flowing to petroleum producers after the two oil shocks of 1973 and 1979 was surely a major factor.

But there can be little doubt that the U.S. government deficit also plays a big role. The American budget has become a financial "black hole," sucking in liquid funds from all over the world, making the United States the world's major debtor country.[11] Indeed, it can be argued that it is the budget deficit that underlies the American trade and payments deficit. A trade and payments deficit is, in effect, a loan from the seller of goods and services to the buyer, that is, to the United States. Without it Washington could not finance its budget deficit, at least not without the risk of explosive inflation.

The way major countries have learned to use the international economy to avoid tackling disagreeable domestic problems is unprecedented: the United States has used high interest rates to attract foreign capital and avoid confronting its domestic deficit; the Japanese have pushed exports to maintain employment despite a sluggish domestic economy. This politicization of the international economy is surely also a factor in the extreme volatility and instability of capital flows and exchange rates.

Whichever of these causes is judged the most important, together they have produced a basic change: in the world economy of today, the "real" economy of goods and services and the "symbol" economy of money, credit and capital are no longer bound tightly to each other; they are, indeed, moving further and further apart.

Traditional international economic theory is still neoclassical, holding that trade in goods and services determines international capital flows and foreign exchange rates. Capital flows and foreign exchange rates since the first half of the 1970s have, however, moved quite independently of foreign trade, and indeed (e.g., in the rise of the dollar in 1984–85) have run counter to it.

But the world economy also does not fit the Keynesian model in which the "symbol" economy determines the "real" economy. The relationship between the turbulences in the world economy and the various domestic economies has become quite obscure. Despite its unprecedented trade deficit, the United States has had no deflation and has barely been able to keep inflation in check; it also has the lowest unemployment rate of any major industrial country except Japan, lower than that of West Germany, whose exports of manufactured goods and trade surpluses have been growing as fast as those of Japan. Conversely, despite the exponential growth of Japanese exports and an unprecedented Japanese trade surplus, the Japanese domestic economy is not booming but has remained remarkably sluggish and is not generating any new jobs.

Economists assume that the "real" economy and the "symbol" economy will come together again. They do disagree, however—and quite sharply—as to whether they will do so in a "soft landing" or in a head-on collision.

The "soft-landing" scenario—the Reagan Administration is committed to it, as are the governments of most of the other developed countries—expects the U.S. government deficit and the U.S. trade deficit to go down together until both attain surplus, or at least balance, sometime in the early 1990s. Presumably both capital flows and exchange rates will then stabilize, with production and employment high and inflation low in major developed countries.

In sharp contrast to this are the "hard-landing" scenarios.[12] With every deficit year the indebtedness of the U.S. government goes up, and with it the interest charges on the U.S. budget, which in turn raises the deficit even further. Sooner or later, the argument goes, foreign confidence in America and the American dollar will be undermined—some observers consider this practically imminent. Foreigners would stop lending money to the United States and, indeed, try to convert their dollars into other currencies. The resulting "flight from the dollar" would bring the dollar's exchange rates crashing down, and also create an extreme credit crunch, if not a "liquidity crisis" in the United States. The only question is whether the result for the United States would be a deflationary depression, a renewed outbreak of severe inflation or, the most dreaded affliction, "stagflation"—a deflationary, stagnant economy combined with an inflationary currency.

There is, however, a totally different "hard-landing" scenario, one in which Japan, not the United States, faces an economic crisis. For the first time in peacetime history the major debtor, the United States, owes its foreign debt in its own currency. To get out of this debt it does not need to repudiate it, declare a moratorium, or negotiate a "roll-over." All it has to do is devalue its currency and the foreign creditor has effectively been expropriated.

For "foreign creditor," read Japan. The Japanese by now hold about half of the dollars the United States owes to foreigners. In addition, practically all of their other claims on the outside world are in dollars, largely because the Japanese have resisted all attempts to make the yen an international trading currency lest the government lose control over it. Altogether, Japanese banks now hold more international assets than do the banks of any other country, including the United States. And practically all these assets are in U.S. dollars—$640 billion of them. A devaluation of the U.S. dollar thus would fall most heavily on the Japanese.

The repercussions for Japan extend deep into its trade and domestic economy. By far the largest part of Japan's exports goes to the United States. If there is a "hard landing," the United States might well turn protectionist almost overnight; it is unlikely that Americans would let in large volumes of imported goods were the unemployment rate to soar. But this would immediately cause severe unemployment in Tokyo and Nagoya and Hiroshima, and might indeed set off a true depression in Japan.

There is still another "hard-landing" scenario. In this version neither the United States, nor Japan, nor the industrial economies altogether, experience the "hard landing"; it would hit the already depressed producers of primary products.

Practically all primary materials are traded in dollars, and their prices might not go up at all should the dollar be devalued (they actually went down when the dollar plunged by 30 percent between summer 1985 and February 1986). Thus Japan may be practically unaffected by a dollar devaluation; Japan needs dollar balances only to pay for primary-product imports, as it buys little else on the outside and has no foreign debt. The United States, too, may not suffer, and may even benefit as its industrial exports become more competitive. But while the primary producers sell mainly in dollars, they have to pay in other developed nations' currencies for a large part of their industrial imports. The United States, after all, although the world's leading exporter of industrial goods, still accounts for only one-fifth of the total. And the dollar prices of the industrial goods furnished by others—the Germans, the Japanese, the French, the British, and so on—are likely to go up. This might bring about a further drop in the terms of trade for the already depressed primary producers. Some estimates of the possible deterioration go as high as ten percent, which would entail considerable hardship not only for metal mines in South America and Zimbabwe, but also for farmers in Canada, Kansas and Brazil.

One more possible scenario involves no "landings," either "soft" or "hard." What if the economists were wrong and both the American budget deficit and American trade deficit continue, albeit at lower levels than in recent years? This would happen if the outside world's willingness to put its money into the United States were based on other than purely economic considerations—on their own internal domestic politics, for example, or simply on the desire to escape risks at home that appear to be far worse than a U.S. devaluation.

This is the only scenario that is so far supported by hard facts rather than by theory. Indeed, it is already playing.

The U.S. government talked the dollar down by almost one-third (from a rate of 250 yen to 180 yen to the dollar) between summer 1985 and February 1986—one of the most massive devaluations ever of a major currency, though called a "readjustment." America's creditors unanimously supported this devaluation and indeed demanded it. More amazing still, they responded by increasing their loans to the United States, and substantially so. International bankers seem to agree that the United States is more creditworthy the more the lender stands to lose by lending to it!

A major reason for this Alice-in-Wonderland attitude is that the biggest U.S. creditors, the Japanese, clearly prefer even very heavy losses on their dollar holdings to domestic unemployment. And without exports to the United States, Japan might have unemployment close to that of Western Europe, nine to eleven percent, and concentrated in the most politically sensitive smokestack industries in which Japan is becoming increasingly vulnerable to competition from newcomers such as South Korea.

Similarly, economic conditions alone will not induce Hong Kong Chinese to withdraw the money they have transferred to American banks in anticipation of Hong Kong's reversion to Chinese sovereignty in 1997. These deposits amount to billions. The even larger amounts— at least several hundred billion—of "flight capital" from Latin America that have found refuge in the U.S. dollar will also not be lured away by purely economic incentives such as higher interest rates.

The sum needed from the outside to maintain both a huge U.S. budget deficit and a huge U.S. trade deficit would be far too big to make this the most probable scenario. But if political factors are in control, the "symbol" economy is indeed truly "uncoupled" from the "real" economy, at least in the international sphere. Whichever scenario proves right, none promises a return to any kind of "normalcy."

VIII

From now on exchange rates between major currencies will have to be treated in economic theory and business policy alike as a "comparative-advantage" factor, and a major one.

Economic theory teaches that the comparative-advantage factors of the "real" economy—comparative labor costs and labor productivity, raw material costs, energy costs, transportation costs and the like— determine exchange rates. Practically all businesses base their policies on this notion. Increasingly, however, it is exchange rates that decide how labor costs in country A compare to labor costs in country B. Exchange rates are thus a major "comparative cost" and one totally beyond business control. Any firm exposed to the international economy has to realize that it is in two businesses at the same time. It is both a maker of goods (or a supplier of services) and a "financial" business. It cannot disregard either.

Specifically, the business that sells abroad—whether as an exporter or through a subsidiary—will have to protect itself against three foreign exchange exposures: proceeds from sales, working capital devoted to manufacturing for overseas markets, and investments abroad. This will have to be done whether the business expects the value of its own currency to go up or down. Businesses that buy abroad will have to do likewise. Indeed, even purely domestic businesses that face foreign competition in their home market will have to learn to hedge against the currency in which their main competitors produce. If American businesses had been run this way during the years of the overvalued dollar, from 1982 through 1985, most of the losses in market standing abroad and in foreign earnings might have been prevented. They were management failures, not acts of God. Surely stockholders, but also the public in general, have every right to expect management to do better the next time around.

In respect to government policy there is one conclusion: don't be "clever." It is tempting to exploit the ambiguity, instability and uncertainty of the world economy to gain short-term advantages and to duck unpopular political decisions. But it does not work. Indeed, disaster is a more likely outcome than success, as all three of the attempts made so far amply indicate.

In the first attempt, the Carter Administration pushed down the U.S. dollar to artificial lows to stimulate the American economy through the promotion of exports. American exports did indeed go up—spectacularly so. But far from stimulating the domestic economy, this depressed it, resulting in simultaneous record unemployment and accelerated inflation—the worst of all possible outcomes.

President Reagan a few years later pushed up interest rates to stop inflation, and also pushed up the dollar. This did indeed stop inflation. It also triggered massive inflows of capital. But it so overvalued the dollar as to create a surge of foreign imports. As a result, the Reagan policy exposed the most vulnerable of the smokestack industries, such as steel and automobiles, to competition they could not possibly meet. It deprived them of the earnings they needed to modernize themselves. Also, the policy seriously damaged, perhaps irreversibly, the competitive position of American farm products in the world markets, and at the worst possible time. Worse still, his "cleverness" defeated Mr. Reagan's major purpose: the reduction of the U.S. government deficit. Because of the losses to foreign competition, domestic industry did not grow enough to produce higher tax revenues. Yet the easy and almost unlimited availability of foreign money enabled Congress (and the Administration) to postpone again and again action to cut the deficit.

In the third case the Japanese, too, may have been too clever in their attempt to exploit the disjunction between the international "symbol" and "real" economies. Exploiting an undervalued yen, the Japanese have been pushing exports—a policy quite reminiscent of America under the Carter Administration. But the Japanese policy similarly has failed to stimulate the domestic economy; it has been barely growing these last few years despite the export boom. As a result, the Japanese have become dangerously overdependent on one customer, the United States. This has forced them to invest huge sums in American dollars, even though every thoughtful Japanese (including, of course, individuals in the Japanese government and the Japanese central bank) has known all along that these investments would end up being severely devalued.

Surely these three lessons should have taught us that government economic policies will succeed to the extent to which they try to harmonize the needs of the two economies, rather than to the extent to which they try to exploit the disharmony between them. Or to repeat very old wisdom, "in finance don't be clever; be simple and conscientious." I am afraid this is advice that governments are not likely to heed soon.

IX

It is much too early to guess what the world economy of tomorrow will look like. Will major countries, for instance, succumb to traditional fears and retreat into protectionism? Or will they see a changed world economy as an opportunity?

Some parts of the main agenda, however, are fairly clear by now. Rapidly industrializing countries like Mexico or Brazil will need to formulate new development concepts and policies. They can no longer hope to finance their development by raw material exports, e.g., Mexican oil. It is also becoming unrealistic for them to believe that their low labor costs will enable them to export large quantities of finished goods to developed countries—something the Brazilians, for instance, still expect. They would do much better to go into "production sharing," that is, to use their labor advantage to become subcontractors to developed-country manufacturers for highly labor-intensive work that cannot be automated—some assembly operations, for instance, or parts and components needed only in relatively small quantities. Developed countries no longer have the labor to do such work, which even with the most thorough automation will still account for 15 to 20 percent of manufacturing work.

Such production sharing is, of course, how Singapore, Hong Kong and Taiwan bootstrapped their development. Yet in Latin America production sharing is still politically unacceptable and, indeed, anathema. Mexico, for instance, has been deeply committed since its beginnings as a modern nation in the early years of this century to making its economy less dependent on, and less integrated with, that of its big neighbor to the north. That this policy has been a total failure for 80 years has only strengthened its emotional and political appeal.

Even if production sharing is implemented to the fullest, it would not by itself provide enough income to fuel development, especially of countries so much larger than the Chinese "city-states." We thus need a new model and new policies.

Can we learn something from India? Everyone knows of India's problems—and they are legion. Few people seem to realize, however, that since independence India has done a better development job than almost any other Third World country: it has enjoyed the fastest increase in farm production and farm yields; a growth rate in manufacturing production equal to that of Brazil, and perhaps even of South Korea (India now has a bigger industrial economy than any but a handful of developed countries); the emergence of a large and highly entrepreneurial middle class; and, arguably, the greatest achievement in providing schooling and health care in the villages. Yet the Indians followed none of the established models. They did not, like Stalin, Mao and so many leaders of newly independent African nations, despoil the peasants to produce capital for industrial development. They did not export raw materials. And they did not export the products of cheap labor. Instead, since Nehru's death in 1964, India has followed a policy of strengthening agriculture and encouraging consumer goods production. India and its achievement are bound to get far more attention in the future.

The developed countries, too, need to think through their policies in respect to the Third World—and especially in respect to the "stars" of the Third World, the rapidly industrializing countries. There are some beginnings: the debt proposals recently put forward by Treasury Secretary James A. Baker, or the new lending criteria recently announced by the World Bank for loans to Third World countries, which will be made conditional on a country's overall development policies rather than on the soundness of individual projects. But these proposals are aimed more at correcting past mistakes than at developing new policies.

The other major agenda item is—inevitably—the international monetary system. Since the Bretton Woods Conference in 1944, the world monetary system has been based on the U.S. dollar as the reserve currency. This clearly does not work any more. The reserve-currency country must be willing to subordinate its domestic policies to the needs of the international economy, e.g., risk domestic unemployment to keep currency rates stable. And when it came to the crunch, the United States refused to do so—as Keynes, by the way, predicted 40 years ago.

The stability supposedly supplied by the reserve currency could be established today only if the major trading countries—at a minimum the

United States, West Germany and Japan—agreed to coordinate their economic, fiscal and monetary policies, if not to subordinate them to joint (and this would mean supranational) decision-making. Is such a development even conceivable, except perhaps in the event of world-wide financial collapse? The European experience with the far more modest European Currency Unit is not encouraging; so far, no European government has been willing to yield an inch for the sake of the ECU. But what else can be done? Have we come to the end of the 300-year-old attempt to regulate and stabilize money on which, after all, both the modern nation-state and the international system are largely based?

We are left with one conclusion: economic dynamics have decisively shifted from the national economy to the world economy.

Prevailing economic theory—whether Keynesian, monetarist or supply-side—considers the national economy, especially that of the large developed countries, to be autonomous and the unit of both economic analysis and economic policy. The international economy may be a restraint and a limitation, but it is not central, let alone determining. This "macroeconomic axiom" of the modern economist has become increasingly shaky. The two major subscribers to this axiom, Britain and the United States, have done least well economically in the last 30 years, and have also had the most economic instability.

West Germany and Japan never accepted the "macroeconomic axiom." Their universities teach it, of course, but their policymakers, both in government and in business, reject it. Instead, both countries all along have based their economic policies on the world economy, have systematically tried to anticipate its trends and exploit its changes as opportunities. Above all, both make the country's competitive position in the world economy the first priority in their policies—economic, fiscal, monetary, even social—to which domestic considerations are normally subordinated. And these two countries have done far better— economically and socially—than Britain and the United States these last 30 years. In fact, their focus on the world economy and the priority they give it may be the real "secret" of their success.

Similarly the "secret" of successful businesses in the developed world—the Japanese, the German carmakers like Mercedes and BMW, Asea and Erickson in Sweden, IBM and Citibank in the United States, but equally of a host of medium-sized specialists in manufacturing and in all kinds of services—has been that they base their plans and their policies on exploiting the world economy's changes as opportunities.

From now on any country—but also any business, especially a large one—that wants to prosper will have to accept that it is the world economy that leads and that domestic economic policies will succeed only if they strengthen, or at least do not impair, the country's international competitive position. This may be the most important—it surely is the most striking—feature of the changed world economy.

NOTES

1. When the price of petroleum dropped to $15 a barrel in February 1986, it was actually below its 1933 price (adjusted for the change in the purchasing power of the dollar). It was still, however, substantially higher than its all-time low in 1972–73, which in 1986 dollars amounted to $7–$8 a barrel.

2. On this see two quite different discussions by Dennis Avery, "U.S. Farm Dilemma: The Global Bad News Is Wrong," *Science*, Oct. 25, 1985; and Barbara Insel, "A World Awash in Grain," *Foreign Affairs*, Spring 1985.

3. The business cycle theory was developed just before World War I by the Russian mathematical economist, Nikolai Kondratieff, who made comprehensive studies of raw material price cycles and their impacts all the way back to 1797.

4. These conclusions are based on static analysis, which presumes that which products are bought and sold is not affected by changes in price. This is of course unrealistic, but the flaw should not materially affect the conclusions.

5. Although the African famine looms large in our consciousness, the total population of the affected areas is far too small to make any dent in world food surpluses.

6. David Sapsford, *Real Primary Commodity Prices: An Analysis of Long-Run Movements*, International Monetary Fund Internal Memorandum, May 17, 1985, (unpublished).

7. This was asserted as early as 1950 by the South American economist Raúl Prebisch in *The Economic Development of Latin America and its Principal Problems* (E/CN.12/89/REV.1), United Nations Economic Commission for Latin America. But then no one, including myself, believed him.

8. The Japanese government, for example, sponsors a finance company that makes long-term, low interest loans to small manufacturers to enable them to automate rapidly.

9. On this see my book: *Innovation and Entrepreneurship: Practice and Principles*, New York: Harper & Row, 1985.

10. A Eurodollar is a U.S. dollar held outside the United States.

11. This is cogently argued by Stephen Marris, for almost 30 years economic adviser to the Organization for Economic Cooperation and Development (OECD), in his *Deficits and the Dollar: The World Economy at Risk*, Washington: Institute of International Economics, December 1985.

12. Stephen Marris, *Deficits and the Dollar*, cited above, gives the clearest and most persuasive presentation of the hard-landing scenarios.

35

Redefining National Security

LESTER R. BROWN

Throughout most of the postwar period, an expanding economy permitted the world to have both more guns and more butter. For many countries, however, this age has come to an end. As pressures on natural systems and resources build, as the sustainable yield thresholds of local biological support systems are breached, and as oil reserves are depleted, governments can no longer both boost expenditures on armaments and deal effectively with the forces that are undermining their economies.

The choices are between continued militarization of the economy and restoration of its environmental support systems; between continued militarization and attempts to halt growth of the U.S. debt; between continued militarization and new initiatives to deal with the dark cloud of Third World debt that hangs over the world's economic future. The world does not have the financial resources and leadership time and attention to militarize and to deal with these new threats to security.

"National security" has become a commonplace expression, a concept regularly appealed to. It is used to justify the maintenance of armies, the development of new weapon systems, and the manufacture of armaments. A fourth of all the federal taxes in the United States and at least an equivalent amount in the Soviet Union are levied in its name.

Since World War II, the concept of national security has acquired an overwhelmingly military character, rooted in the assumption that the principal threat to security comes from other nations. Commonly veiled in secrecy, considerations of military threats have become so dominant that new threats to the security of nations—threats with which military forces cannot cope—are being ignored.

The new sources of danger arise from oil depletion, soil erosion, land degradation, shrinking forests, deteriorating grasslands, and climate alteration. These developments, affecting the natural resources and systems on which the economy depends, threaten not only national economic and political security, but the stability of the international economy itself.

Militarization of the World Economy

The notion that countries everywhere should be prepared to defend themselves at all times from any conceivable external treat is a relatively modern one. Prior to World War II, countries mobilized troops in times of war instead of relying on a large permanent military establishment. Since then, the military burden on the world economy has grown enormously. Global military expenditures in 1985 of $940 billion exceeded the income of the poorest half of humanity. Stated otherwise, they surpassed the combined gross national products of China, India, and African countries south of the Sahara. (See U.S. Arms Control and Disarmament Agency document in For Further Reading.)

Militarization can be measured nationally as the share of gross national product (GNP) devoted to the production of military goods and services, or as the military share of the federal budget. Globally, it can be judged by the military share of global product and the arms share of international trade. For international comparisons, the share of GNP used for military purposes is the best yardstick, since it can be applied to countries with widely differing economic systems. Militarization can also be gauged in terms of employment—the number of people serving in the armed forces, employed in weapons production, or involved in weapons research.

By all measures, the world economy has a decidedly more military cast today than it did a generation ago. Using 1984 dollars as the yardstick, world military expenditures totaled roughly $400 billion in 1960, some 4.7 percent of economic output. Expanding faster than the world economy since 1960, the growth in military spending has raised the military share of world economic activity to over 6 percent in 1985. During this quarter-century span, global military expenditures have increased every year, regardless of economic downturns, or of arms control treaties between the two superpowers.

Conflict Between the Superpowers

The principal force driving global militarization is the ideological conflict between the Soviet Union, with its socialist allies, and the United States, in alliance with the industrial democracies. In addition, alignment of the Third World states with the two military superpowers has made militarization a global phenomenon, independent of the level of economic development. The continued striving for an advantage has led to enormous growth in military expenditures in both camps. While the United States devoted some 7 percent of its GNP to defense in 1985, the Soviet Union, trying to maintain a competitive military establishment with a much smaller economy, allocated 14 percent.

Although the military efforts of the United States and the Soviet Union are aimed primarily at each other, the two countries have managed to avoid direct conflict. Not risking the engagement of each other's mutually destructive military capacity, the superpowers have waged their ideological conflict through proxies, including Korea, Vietnam, Afghanistan, and countries in East Africa and Central America. These campaigns have fueled Third World militarization, distorting priorities and postponing development. Mahbub ul Haq, chairman of Pakistan's planning commission, contends, "Developing countries can't afford the burden imposed on us by the tense geopolitical situation."

The Volatile Middle East

Another source of militarization has been the influx of oil wealth into the politically volatile Middle East. Traditional tensions between Arabs and Israelis have generated heavy armaments expenditures by Israel, Egypt, and Syria. More recently, conflicts among various Muslim sects have been a source of stress. Indeed, Muslim factionalism is a major factor in

Table 1
Military Expenditures as Share of GNP for Selected Countries, 1984

Country	Share (percentage)	Country	Share (percentage)
Industrial countries		India	3.5
Japan	1.0	Pakistan	5.4
Canada	2.1	China	8.0
West Germany	3.3		
United Kingdom	5.4	Africa	
United States	6.9	Nigeria	2.5
Soviet Union	14.0	South Africa	4.3
		Ethiopia	11.0
Middle East		Libya	17.5
Egypt	8.3		
Syria	13.0	Latin America	
Jordan	14.9	Mexico	0.6
Saudi Arabia	24.0	Brazil	0.7
Israel	29.0	Venezuela	1.3
		El Salvador	4.0
Asia		Chile	4.5
Sri Lanka	1.5	Nicaragua	10.2

Sources: U.S. Arms Control and Disarmament Agency, *World Military Expenditures and Arms Transfers, 1985* (Washington, D.C.: 1985); Stockholm International Peace Research Institute Yearbook, *World Armaments and Disarmament* (London: Taylor and Francis, 1985).

the costly conflict between Iraq and Iran that has already claimed several hundred thousand lives. Sadly, much of the region's windfall gains in oil income are being invested in militarization and in destruction of the region's petroleum infrastructure rather than in restoration of the region's degraded environmental support systems or in economic modernization.

Ideological conflicts worldwide, religious differences in the Middle East, and aggressive arms exporting have contributed to a rate of growth in Third World military expenditures that far exceeds that in the industrial world. Between 1960 and 1981, these outlays grew by some 7 percent per year, compared with 3.7 percent in the industrial world. In 1960, Third World military activities accounted for less than one-tenth of the global total; in 1981, they were more than one-fifth of a far larger total.

Military Share of GNP

The share of national product devoted to military purposes varies widely among countries. In the industrial world, the Soviet Union and the United States lead the list; their key allies in the Warsaw Pact and NATO, respectively, are not far behind (see Table 1). Japan, benefiting from U.S. defense of the region and a constitutional limit on its militarization, is spending just under 1 percent of its GNP for military purposes.

Within the Third World, military sectors are largest in the tension-ridden Middle East. Syria, Jordan, Saudi Arabia, and Israel spend between 13 and 29 percent of their economic resources to maintain large military establishments. Most disturbing, militarization is spreading rapidly in Africa, the region that can least afford it. The continent as a whole now spends $16 billion per year in this sector. In Latin America, military expenditures in Brazil and Mexico, the two most populous countries, are surprisingly low—averaging less than 1 percent of GNP. Central America, however, departs from the Latin norm, with El Salvador spending 4 percent and Nicaragua more than 10 percent of GNP for military purposes.

Commerce in Arms

Over the past quarter-century, the international commerce in arms has soared, largely because of the militarization of Third World economies that lack their own arms manufacturing capacity. Expenditures on arms imports have eclipsed those on other goods, including grain. For example, although world grain trade expanded at nearly 12 percent per year from 1970 to 1984, it was overtaken during the eighties by arms dealings, which grew at over 13 percent annually during the same period. As of 1984, world arms imports totaled $35 billion per year, compared with $33 billion worth of grain, putting guns ahead of bread in world commerce.

The United States and the Soviet Union dominate arms exports, together accounting for 53 percent of the world total in recent years. In 1984, U.S. arms exports totaled $7.7 billion, under 4 percent of the nation's total. Soviet arms exports of $9.4 billion accounted for nearly 12 percent of their exports, and earned enough foreign exchange to pay their grain import bill of $6 billion. The other ranking world exporters are U.S. allies France, the United Kingdom, West Germany, and Italy, which rank third through sixth as world arms suppliers.

Arms imports are much more widely dispersed among countries, though the Middle East accounts for over half the total. During the early eighties, seven of the ten leading Third World arms importers were in this region—Egypt, Syria, Iraq, Libya, Jordan, Saudi Arabia, and Israel. India, in fourth place, was the only country outside the region in the top.

Military Takeovers

In addition to its economic role, militarization has important political dimensions. As the military establishments gain strength in Third World countries, they often assume power by force. In some instances, military coups d'état are justified by the need to rescue a country from corruption or from economic deterioration as a result of inept leadership. More often, they reflect the ambition of military leaders who are ill equipped to lead, but who have acquired the weapons and the command of troops that allow them to assume leadership positions by force.

When governments are taken over by the military, they often shift priorities toward further militarization of the economy. During the decade since the military coup that overthrew Haile Selassie, for example, Ethiopia has assembled the largest army in sub-Saharan Africa, and now spends 42 percent of its budget for military purposes.

Weapons Research

Nowhere are the distorting efforts of militarization more evident than in its claims on the world's scientific personnel. Each year the world spends several times as much on research to increase the destructiveness of weapons as on attempts to raise the productivity of agriculture. Indeed, expenditures on weapons research, in which a half-million scientists are now employed, exceed the combined spending on developing new energy technologies, improving human health, raising agricultural productivity, and controlling pollution.

The military's dominance of the world's scientific research effort will certainly grow if the U.S. government proceeds with its proposed Strategic Defense Initiative. The largest research project ever launched, the so-called Star Wars project will further divert resources from humanity's most pressing needs. The effect of such distortions was noted by Colin Norman in a 1979 Worldwatch Paper: "The United States has the ability to survey virtually every square meter of the Soviet Union, yet the world's scientists have barely begun to survey the complex ecosystems of fast-disappearing tropical rain forests or the malignant spread of the world's deserts."

Costs to the Two Superpowers

The cost of the arms race to the superpowers goes beyond any mere fiscal reckoning. It is draining their treasuries, weakening their economies, and lowering their position in the international economic hierarchy. This long, drawn-out conflict is contributing to a realignment of the leading industrial countries, with Japan assuming a dominant position in the world economy. One of the keys to Japan's emergence as an economic superpower is its negligible level of military expenditures—less than 1 percent of GNP.

The doubling of the U.S. national debt, from $914 billion in 1980 to $1,841 billion in 1985, is due more to the growth in military expenditures than to any other factor. Between 1980 and 1985, U.S. military expenditures climbed from $134 billion to $244 billion (in current dollars). This increase of roughly $110 billion dwarfs growth in all other major economic sectors, including health, which increased $11 billion, and agriculture, which rose $15 billion.

Growing federal debt is also leading to record-high real interest rates (the rate of interest after subtracting for inflation) and an overvalued dollar that makes U.S. exports more costly, in turn weakening the country's competitive position.

Industry in the United States has been doubly handicapped by these soaring military expenditures. Averaging over $200 billion per year since 1981, U.S. military expenditures have totaled $1,000 billion during the first half of the eighties, siphoning capital away from investment in industrial plant and equipment and leaving the nation with outdated, inefficient industrial facilities.

The overvalued dollar and the lack of investment in new industrial capacity have dramatically altered the U.S. position in world trade. In 1980, the United States registered a trade deficit of $36 billion; it climbed to $70 billion in 1983, and to a staggering $150 billion in 1985. This ballooning U.S. trade deficit and the associated borrowing abroad to finance the federal debt have cost the country its position as the world's leading international investor. Almost overnight, the United States has become a debtor nation. This is a worrisome shift for the United States, as its international leadership role since World War II has derived in large part from its economic strength and prestige. The military expenditures that are weakening the United States economically are diminishing both its stature within the international community and its capacity to lead.

Costs to the Soviet Union

The Soviet Union, too, is paying a heavy price for its role in the arms race, retaining second-class economic status despite its wealth of natural resources. Military spending channels roughly one-seventh of the nation's resources to nonproductive uses. It also diverts leadership attention from the economic reforms required if the Soviet economy is to remain a world economic power.

From the early fifties through the late seventies, the Soviet economy grew at roughly 5 percent per year, a rate of expansion that brought progress on many fronts.

Now, Soviet industrial growth has slowed to a crawl. In agriculture, less grain is being produced now than in the late seventies. Production of livestock is expanding, but only with record feedgrain imports. Oil extraction peaked in 1983 and has fallen in each of the two years since. With the output of wheat and oil—the two principal commodities in the Soviet economy—either stagnating or declining, the economic prospect is less than bright. Falling production of oil, the source of over half the country's hard currency, will restrict the imports of essential products.

Environmental costs Land degradation is also weakening the economy. Extensive soil erosion, one source of declining land productivity, has long been a concern of Mikhail Gorbachev, predating his rise to leadership. But despite the concern of Gorbachev, other members of the Politburo, and Soviet soil scientists, little progress has been made in arresting this drain on Soviet agricultural productivity.

Growing water scarcity throughout the south central and southwestern parts of the country is another emerging constraint on Soviet economic activity, particularly agriculture. Although water is among the factors limiting crop production in these regions, the Soviets have made only minimal investments in water efficiency.

Similarly, the efficiency of energy and other resource use in the Soviet Union is among the lowest in the world. In contrast to the western industrial societies and China, which have reduced the oil intensity of their economies by roughly a fifth since the 1973 oil price boost, the Soviets have made little or no progress toward that end.

Technological backwardness One reason for the Soviet's inefficient use of resources is the lack of broadbased technological innovation. In key industries, such as oil extraction and the manufacture of motor vehicles and computers, the Soviet Union depends heavily on imported Western technology. Future gains in economic efficiency depend on the use of computers, but in this modernizing activity, the Soviets lag far behind, trailing even Third World countries such as Brazil and South Korea. In addition to production shortfalls, the shoddiness of Soviet consumer goods and farm equipment makes it virtually impossible for them to compete on the world market.

Ironically, the one sector in which the Soviet economy is competitive in world markets is weapons manufacture. By focusing on arms production to the exclusion of other sectors, the Soviet Union is able to maintain military production schedules and quality standards, but only by circumventing conventional management control mechanisms. To make sure that weapons manufacture proceeds on schedule, this sector can use its special status to reorder priorities in its favor and to commandeer industrial facilities or transport capacity. To maintain quality standards, for example, it can requisition the highest quality steels. Unfortunately, exercising this privileged status can disrupt the rest of the economy.

Japan as a World Leader

While the United States and the Soviet Union have been preoccupied with each other militarily, Japan has been moving to the fore econom-

ically. By some economic indicators, it now leads both military superpowers. In a world where the enormous investment in nuclear arsenals
has no practical use, the terms denoting leadership and dominance are
shifting in Japan's favor.

For many years, the Soviet Union has enjoyed its status as the world's
second-largest economy, the base from which it challenged the United
States' position of world leader. Japan's per capita income, which
surpassed that of the Soviet Union during the sixties, is now close to
double the Soviet's. If recent economic trends continue, Japan will
overtake the Soviet Union in total economic output before the century
ends, reducing it to third place. The combination of negligible defense
expenditures and high domestic savings has enabled the Japanese to
invest heavily in modernizing plant and equipment. This in turn
enhances the nation's competitive position, enabling it to run a large
foreign trade surplus, even though it imports virtually all its oil and
most of its raw materials.

As it narrows the output gap with the Soviet Union, Japan is
challenging U.S. dominance of world trade. In 1950, exports from the
United States exceeded those from Japan by more than 10 to 1. Over the
years, this gap slowly narrowed, until by 1970 it was little more than 2
to 1. As recently as 1980, it was still near this level, but the U.S.
advantage is disappearing during the eighties. By 1985, U.S. exports
were only 20 percent greater than those of Japan. The U.S. economy is
still twice as large as Japan's, and the country has a vastly superior
indigenous resource base of land, energy fuels, minerals, and forest
products. Nonetheless, the United States is in the process of abdicating
its role of world leadership. A country that is a net debtor, borrowing
heavily from the rest of the world, cannot effectively exercise economic
or political leadership.

New Threats to Security

The extensive deterioration of natural support systems and the declining
economic conditions evident in much of the Third World pose threats to
national and international security that now rival the traditional military
ones. Ecological stresses and resource scarcities eventually translate into
economic stresses with social and political dimensions: falling land productivity, falling per capita income, or rising external debt, to cite a few.

The first resource scarcity that dramatically affected the global economy was that of oil. The 1973 price hike sent shock waves throughout
the world, the reverberations of which are still being felt more than a
decade later. These and other consequences of oil reserve depletion
have dominated headlines over the past dozen years, but the depletion
of forests, grasslands and topsoil, and the alteration of the hydrological
cycle are of greater consequence over the long term.

Unfortunately for economic planners and policymakers, there has been little systematic gathering of data on the condition of these basic resources and support systems. But ecological deterioration adversely affects national economies, particularly in the Third World. The dramatic rise in external debt in recent years is perhaps the most visible manifestation of this ecological and economic deterioration, and the most worrisome new threat to security.

The Debt Threshold

There is a remarkable parallel between countries crossing the sustainable yield threshold of their biological support systems and those crossing the sustainable debt threshold. Once the demand on a biological system exceeds its sustainable yield, further growth in demand is satisfied by consuming the basic resource stock. In such a situation, the deterioration begins to feed on itself.

So it is with external debt: As it grows faster than the economy, eventually a point is reached where servicing the debt, even if limited to interest payments, becomes such a drain on the economy that output is actually reduced, as has occurred, for instance, in Brazil and Mexico. When governments can no longer pay all the interest, then the debt begins to expand, and the growth feeds on itself. Once countries cross these sustainable yield or debt-servicing thresholds, it is difficult for them to reverse the process.

In many Third World countries, the past three years have been a time of enforced austerity and sacrifice. Imports of consumer goods, including food, have been reduced; food subsidies have been eliminated; unemployment has risen. Belt-tightening has allowed Third World countries to maintain access to international credit and it has kept the lending banks solvent, but, because it has led to even greater debt, this approach has diminished the prospect of restoring a sustained improvement in living standards.

By the end of 1985, many Third World countries were delinquent in their debt payments and assessments of repayment prospects are grim. But they would be even grimmer if financial analysts understood what is happening to the environmental support systems underpinning most Third World economies. It is not a matter of an occasional country here or there experiencing deforestation, soil erosion, or land degradation. The great majority of Third World countries have crossed the sustainable yield thresholds of their basic biological support systems.

Countries Reducing Arms Outlays

A few governments have begun to redefine national security, putting more emphasis on economic progress and less on buying arms. At a time when global military expenditures are rising, some countries are actually cutting military outlays. A handful are reducing them sharply, not only as a share of GNP, but in absolute terms as well. Among these are China, Argentina, and Peru.

As recently as 1972, China was spending 14 percent of its GNP for military purposes, one of the highest levels in the world at the time. Beginning in 1975, however, China systematically began to reduce its military expenditures, and, except for 1979, it has reduced them in each of the last eight years. By 1985, military spending had fallen to 7.5 percent of its gross national product.

Indications are that this trend may continue throughout the eighties. In July 1985, Beijing announced a plan to invest $360 million over two years to retrain 1 million soldiers for return to civilian life. Such a move would cut the armed forces in China from 4.2 million in 1985 to 3.2 million in 1987, a drop of 24 percent. And worldwide, it would reduce the number of men and women under arms by some 4 percent.

In Argentina, the military government that was in office in the late seventies and early eighties increased military expenditures from the historical level of 1.5 percent of GNP to almost 4 percent. One of the first things that Raúl Alfonsín did as newly elected president in late 1983 was to announce a plan to lower this figure steadily. When he took office, there was broad public support for a reduction in arms expenditures, partly because of the ill-fated Falklands War, which undermined the military's credibility throughout Argentina. By 1984, arms outlays had been cut to half the peak level of 1980, earning Alfonsín a well-deserved reputation for reordering priorities, and shifting resources to social programs.

More recently, Peru has joined the ranks of those announcing plans to cut military expenditures. One of the first actions of President García on taking office in the summer of 1985 was a call to halt the regional arms race. García is convinced of the need to reduce the 5 percent of Peru's GNP allotted to the military, a sum that consumed one-fourth of the federal budget. As an indication of his sincerity, the president announced that he was canceling half of the order for 26 French Mirage fighter planes.

The overriding reason for cutting military expenditures in each of these three countries is economic. In effect, the three political leaders are defining security in much more economic terms. For the Chinese, the military sector was one place harboring the additional resources needed to achieve the desired gains in living standards. Once the goal of rapidly improving living standards was adopted, the reduction of resources devoted to the military was inevitable.

In Argentina, the economic incentive was burgeoning public debt, inflation, and a huge external debt that threatened to become unmanageable. One source of Argentina's external debt was the taste for modern arms exhibited by Alfonsín's predecessors. In Peru, the challenge was to arrest the decline in living standards. At the time García took office, payments on the international debt were $475 million in arrears, and the government was threatened with a complete cutoff of all new sources of investment capital. García found that internal economic decline was leading to social deterioration and political violence.

Encouragingly, the reductions in military expenditures undertaken in China, Peru, and Argentina were independent of any negotiated reductions in neighboring countries. China lowered its military outlays unilaterally, despite its 3,000-kilometer border with the Soviet Union, which has continued to increase its military might.

Over the next few years, as governments everywhere face difficulties in maintaining or improving living standards, others may also choose to reduce military expenditures. Quite apart from the positive momentum of the international peace movement in recent years, worsening economic conditions may become the key motivation for reversing the militarization of the past generation.

The Challenge

For many Third World countries, the threats to well-being and survival come not from other countries, but from each step that pushes them past the sustainable yield thresholds of their biological systems and the debt-servicing threshold of their economies. The estimated million lives lost to famine in Africa in 1984 and 1985 exceeds that in any conflict since World War II. How many more lives will be lost? No one knows, but the number of people at risk is growing as the disintegration of their life-support systems accelerates.

Reversing these trends requires a shift in development strategy, particularly where economic demands already exceed the sustainable yield of forests, grasslands, and soils. In these circumstances, continuing to rely primarily on narrow economic criteria—such as the time-honored rate of return on project investments—to shape development strategies can lead biological and economic systems to collapse. The only durable development strategy for many Third World countries is one that rests on environmental criteria, one that concentrates on restoring the economy's environmental support systems. Any other is destined to fail.

For national governments and international development agencies, the time has come to rethink development. Policies that once led to a sustained 5 percent global economic growth are no longer doing so. The rising economic tide that once pulled living standards up throughout the world is beginning to recede in many Third World countries. Understanding why this is so requires projections of both environmental and economic trends, and, more importantly, of their continuous and complex interaction. For example, food production forecasts are meaningful only if they allow for the effect of soil erosion on land productivity. The only agricultural projections that provide a solid base for policy are those that incorporate agronomic, ecological, and hydrological data as well as the more conventional economic and demographic information.

Once made, these projections could provide the rationale for launching massive tree-planting efforts, accelerating family planning programs, and making many of the other interventions so urgently needed. They are also the key to generating the support of the international community. Without some understanding of the consequences of continuing on the current path, governments will be reluctant to intervene to reverse ecological deterioration and associated economic decline. Unfortunately, the countries that are most affected by environmental deterioration are those least able to undertake these projections, suggesting an important new role for the World Bank and other development assistance groups.

Setting the Stage for Peace

National defense establishments are useless against these new threats to security. Neither bloated military budgets nor highly sophisticated weapons systems can halt deforestation or arrest the soil erosion now affecting so many Third World countries. Blocking external aggression may be relatively simple compared with stopping the deterioration of life-support systems.

The key to demilitarizing the world economy and shifting resources is a defusing of the arms race between the United States and the Soviet Union. Whether this can be achieved in the foreseeable future remains to be seen. But as the costs of maintaining the arms race multiply, both for the superpowers and for the world at large, the likelihood of reducing tensions may be improving.

In east Asia, traditional adversaries China and Japan appear to be in the process of establishing strong economic ties. In contrast to the United States, China appears to be abandoning military competition with the Soviet Union. With Japan showing little interest in becoming a military power, the stage is being set for peace in the region. Both countries have redefined security and reshaped their geopolitical strategies, accordingly setting aside any ideas of political domination in favor of pursuing mutually beneficial economic goals.

In Western Europe, France and Germany have battled each other periodically over the centuries, but armed conflict between these two countries now appears unlikely. It is difficult to imagine, in an economically integrated Europe, how either of these countries could possibly attack the other. Within North America, the United States, Canada, and Mexico have lived peacefully for generations. No armed forces face each other across national borders in this area. Although conflicts exist here, they center around isolated issues such as acid rain, illegal immigration, and trade restrictions, which do not appear likely to threaten their generally amiable relations.

If ideology gives way to pragmatism, as it is doing in China, then the conflicts and insecurities bred by the ideological distinctions between East and West can soften. Indeed, this ideological softening appears to be coloring China's foreign policy, improving its relations with other countries and contributing to its reduction of military expenditures.

If the Soviet Union adopts the reforms needed to get its economy moving ahead again, a similar ideological softening may result. Turning to the market to allocate resources and boost productivity could not only restructure the Soviet economy, but also reorient Soviet politics. Although pragmatism has typically taken a back seat to ideology in the Soviet Union, the leaders have demonstrated that they can be pragmatic when circumstances require, as when they import grain from the United States, their ideological rival.

For the world as a whole, the past generation has seen an overwhelming movement toward militarization. Apart from the heavy claim on public resources, the East-West conflict contributes to a psychological climate of suspicion and distrust that makes it next to impossible to address in a cooperative and international way the new threats to the security of nations. China and Argentina, which have already cut the military's share of their GNP in half, and Peru, which promises to do so, may provide the model for the future. If demilitarization could replace militarization, national governments would be free to reorder their priorities, and could return to paths of sustained progress.

Ironically, for the United States and the Soviet Union, maintaining a position of leadership may now depend on reducing military expenditures to strengthen their faltering economies. Acting thus in their own interests, they could set the stage for demilitarizing the world economy. Once it starts, demilitarization—like militarization—could feed on itself.

List of Contributors

Shaul Bakhash, Robinson Professor of History at George Mason University, is the author of *The Reign of the Ayatollahs: Iran and the Islamic Revolution.*

George W. Ball has held a number of high-ranking governmental positions, and is currently a lawyer in the counsel firm of Cleary, Gottlieb, Stein and Hamilton. He is the author of *The Discipline of Power* (1968, Atlantic, Little Brown), *Diplomacy for a Crowded World* (1976, Atlantic, Little Brown), *The Past Has Betrayed Another Pattern: Memoirs* (1982, W.W. Norton), and *Error and Betrayal in Lebanon* (1984).

Lester R. Brown is the Project Director of Worldwatch Institute. This article is abridged from Chapter 11 of *State of the World 1986: A Worldwatch Institute Report on Progress Toward a Sustainable Society* (New York: W.W. Norton & Co., 1986).

Ted Galen Carpenter is a foreign policy analyst at the CATO Institute, Washington, D.C.

Noam Chomsky is a professor of linguistics at MIT and the author of several books on contemporary politics, most recently, *Towards a New Cold War.*

Eliot A. Cohen teaches strategy at The Naval War College. Mr. Cohen is the author of *Citizens and Soldiers: The Dilemmas of Military Service* (Cornell). (The views he expresses in his article do not necessarily represent those of The Naval War College).

Cosmas Desmond was Director of the British Sector of Amnesty International, until in a blaze of publicity, he was dismissed—to be replaced by Jeremy Thorpe. His book *Persecution East and West* (1983) is based on this experience and on his years in South Africa, where he was involved in the struggle against apartheid.

Peter F. Drucker is Clarke Professor of Social Science and Management at the Claremont Graduate School, California.

Nick Eberstadt is a visiting fellow at the Harvard University Center for Population Studies and a visiting scholar at the American Enterprise Institute. He is the author of *Poverty in China* and the editor of *Fertility Decline in the Less Developed Countries.* This article is part of a larger work on American foreign aid policy.

Francis Fukuyama is a member of the political science department of the Rand Corporation and was formerly a member of the Policy Planning Staff of the State Department.

Richard N. Haass, formerly an official in the Departments of Defense and State, is a member of the faculty of Harvard University's John F. Kennedy School of Government.

Ivan L. Head is president of International Development Research in Ottawa, Canada.

D. W. Hiester is a lecturer in interdisciplinary studies in politics at the University of Kent. He teaches International Relations and European Studies in addition to the course "Nuclear War and Nuclear Peace." He has written on the European Community and East-West relations.

Stanley Hoffmann is the Douglas Dillon Professor of the Civilization of France and Chairman of the Center for European Studies at Harvard. He is the author of *Duties Beyond Borders* and *Dead Ends,* and co-editor of *The Mitterand Experiment.*

David Horowitz was the editor of *Ramparts* magazine and a founder of the Vietnam Solidarity Campaign. His early books include *Student* (1962) and *Empire and Revolution: A Radical Interpretation of Contemporary History* (1970). More recently he has been co-author (with Peter Collier) of *The Rockefellers: An American Dynasty* and *The Kennedys: An American Drama.* A somewhat different version of this article was read at Berkeley on April 4, 1986, at a conference entitled: "U.S./Nicaragua: Exploring the Possibilities for Peace."

Jerry F. Hough is J. B. Duke Professor of Political Science at Duke University, and a staff member of the Brookings Institution. He is the author of *The Struggle for the Third World: Soviet Debates and American Opinions,* published in 1986 by the Brookings Institution, Washington D.C.

Paul Johnson is the author of, most recently, *Modern Times: The World From the Twenties to the Eighties.* Formerly editor of the *New Statesman,* he now writes a regular column for the *Spectator* in London.

Charles Krauthammer is a senior editor of the *New Republic.*

Walter Laqueur is chairman of the research council of the Center for Strategic and International Studies, Georgetown University, author of

Guerrilla, first published in 1976, and *Terrorism*, 1977, and editor of the *Guerrilla Reader* and the *Terrorism Reader*.

Geir Lundestad is Professor of American Civilization at the University of Tromsø, Norway. He has been Chairman of the Council of the Norwegian Institute of International Affairs since 1977 and in 1983 was a visiting scholar at Harvard University. He is the author of several books on American foreign policy.

Vojtech Mastny is a professor of International Relations at Boston University and fellow of the Russian Research Center at Harvard University.

Senator Charles McC. Mathias, Jr. (R-Maryland), was a member of the Senate Foreign Relations Committee. He concluded 18 years of Senate service in January, 1987.

Charles William Maynes is the editor of *Foreign Policy* magazine.

Edward L. Morse is Managing Director of The Petroleum Finance Co., Ltd., Washington, D.C. He served as Deputy Assistant Secretary of State for Energy Policy from 1979 to 1981, and as Director of International Affairs for Phillips Petroleum Co. from 1981 to 1984.

Christoph Mühlemann is U.S. editor of the Swiss daily "Neue Zürcher Zeitung," where this article was first published.

Aryeh Neier is vice-chairman of the U.S. Helsinki Watch Committee and of the Fund for Free Expression and adjunct professor of law at New York University. He is the author of *Only Judgement, Dossier, Crime and Punishment, Defending My Enemy*, and of numerous articles.

Daniel Pipes is the Director of the Foreign Policy Research Institute in Philadelphia and is editor of *Orbis*.

Richard Pipes is Baird Professor of History at Harvard University and a prominent writer on the Soviet Union. He served as director of Harvard's Russian Research Center from 1968 to 1973 and held various committee positions in Washington, D.C. during the 1970's. He was also a member of the NSC staff during the first two years of the Reagan Administration.

Robert S. Ross is Assistant Director of the East Asian Institute and teaches Chinese politics and the international politics of East Asia at Columbia University.

K. P. Saksena is Professor of International Organization, School of International Studies, Jawaharlal Nehru University, New Delhi.

William C. Sherman was, until his retirement in 1986, Deputy Assistant Secretary for East Asian and Pacific Affairs. Ambassador Sherman has been a foreign service officer for more than thirty years and has served overseas in Japan and Italy.

Leon Sloss was Deputy Director of the Future Security Strategy Study, one of the study efforts commissioned by the U.S. Department of Defense in 1983 to probe the prospects and implications of anti-missile defense. Now President of Leon Sloss Associates, he also directed the study of U.S. nuclear targeting policy that led to Presidential Directive 59 in 1980, and has served in various high posts in the U.S. Government.

Xan Smiley lives in London and reports on Eastern Europe. Previously he was a correspondent in Africa for ten years during which time he wrote for *The New York Review of Books* and other publications. From 1977 to 1981 he edited *Africa Confidential,* a political newsletter.

Steven L. Spiegel is Professor of Political Science at UCLA. His most recent book is *The Other Arab-Israeli Conflict: Making America's Middle East Policy, from Truman to Reagan* (University of Chicago Press, 1985).

Seymour Weiss is a retired U.S. Ambassador who has also served as Director of the State Department's Bureau of Politico-Military Affairs. He is co-author (with John Lehman) of *Beyond the Salt II Failure.* This article is based on a paper originally presented at a Lehrman Institute Seminar.

Nicholas Wheeler is a tutor in the Department of International Politics, University College of Wales, Aberystwyth.

Phil Williams is a research fellow at the Royal Institute of International Affairs. He is the author of a Chatham House paper on *U.S. Troops in Europe* (London: Routledge and Kegan Paul, 1984) and *The Senate and U.S. Troops in Europe.*

Acknowledgments (continued)

"How Vulnerable is the West?" is a selection taken from "Survival Is Not Enough."
Copyright © 1984 by Richard Pipes. Reprinted by permission of Simon & Schuster, Inc.

"Do We Still Need Europe?" by Eliot A. Cohen. Eliot Cohen teaches strategy at the U.S.
Naval War College. The views presented in this article are the author's own, and do not
necessarily represent those of the Naval War College or any other government agency.
Reprinted from *Commentary*, January 1986, by permission; all rights reserved.

"The Evolution of the U.S.-Japan Alliance," by William C. Sherman. Reprinted by
permission from *SAIS Review*, Volume 5, No. 1, Winter/Spring 1985.

"International Bargaining and Domestic Politics: U.S.-China Relations Since 1972," by
Robert S. Ross. Reprinted by permission of Princeton University Press.

"Dateline Middle East: The Dangers of Disengagement," by Charles McC. Mathias, Jr.
Reprinted with permission from *Foreign Policy* 63 (Summer 1986). Copyright 1986 by the
Carnegie Endowment for International Peace.

"Paying Less Attention to the Middle East," by Richard N. Haass. Richard N. Haass,
formerly an official in the Departments of Defense and State, is a member of the faculty
of Harvard University's John F. Kennedy School of Government. Reprinted from
Comentary (Vol. 82, August 1986) by permission: all rights reserved.

"The Race For South Africa," by Paul Johnson. Reprinted from *Commentary*, September,
1985, by permission. All rights reserved.

"Sanctions and South Africa," by Cosmas Desmond. This article first appeared in *Third
World Quarterly*, January 1986 issue, Vol. 8 No. 1 and is copyright of the journal.

"The Present Danger," by Noam Chomsky. *Worldview*, February 1983. This article is an
excerpt from the original article, which appeared in *Beyond Survival*, edited by M. Albert
and D. Dellinger, South End Press, Boston. Copyright © 1982 by author. Reprinted with
permission.

"The Case Against Arms Control," by Seymour Weiss. Copyright © 1984 by author.
Reprinted from *Commentary*, November 1984, by permission; all rights reserved.

"The War for Star Wars," by George W. Ball. Reprinted with permission from *The New
York Review of Books*. Copyright © 1985 Nyrev, Inc.

"The Return of Strategic Defense," By Leon Sloss. Published originally in *Strategic Review*,
Summer 1984. Copyright © 1984 by United States Strategic Institute.

"Reykjavik: An Icelandic Saga," by Stanley Hoffman. Reprinted with permission from *The
New York Review of Books*. Copyright 1986 Nyrev, Inc.

"Nuclear Proliferation: A Cause for Optimism?" by D. W. Hiester. This Article first
appeared in *International Relations*, Volume VIII No. 3, May 1985. Copyright is held by
the David Davies Memorial Institute of International Studies, London.

"The U.N.: A Dream of Peace," by Christoph Mühlemann. The Author is U.S. Editor of
the Swiss Daily *Neue Zürcher Zeitung*, where the article was first published. Copyright ©
Swiss Review of World Affairs/Neue Zürcher Zeitung.

"After the Fall: The Politics of Oil," by Edward L. Morse. Reprinted by permission of
Foreign Affairs, (Spring 1986). Copyright, 1986 by the Council of Foreign Relations, Inc.

"Uniqueness and Pendulum Swings in U.S. Foreign Policy," by Geir Lundestad. Reprinted by permission from *International Affairs* (London, UK), Vol. 62 (3), published by
Butterworths. Copyright © 1986 *International Affairs*.

"United States Foreign Policy-Making: Chaos or Design?" by Nicholas Wheeler and Phil
Williams. This article first appeared in *International Relations*, Volume VIII No. 3, May
1985. Copyright is held by the David Davies Memorial Institute of International Studies,
London.

"Logic, Bribes, and Threats," by Charles William Maynes. Reprinted with permission
from *Foreign Policy* (#60 Fall 1985). Copyright 1985 by the Carnegie Endowment for
International Peace.

Acknowledgments (continued)

"The Changed World Economy," by Peter F. Drucker. Reprinted by permission of *Foreign Affairs*, (Spring 1986). Copyright, 1986, by the Council of Foreign Relations, Inc.

"Redefining National Security," by Lester R. Brown. Article reprinted from State of the World 1986, a Worldwatch Institute report on Progress Toward a Sustainable Society, edited by Lester R. Brown et al. By permission of Worldwatch Institute and W.W. Norton and Company, Inc. Copyright 1986, by Worldwatch Institute.